Heritage of Western Civilization

Heritage
of Western
Civilization

FOURTH EDITION
VOLUME I

Edited by

JOHN LOUIS BEATTY

OLIVER A. JOHNSON
University of California, Riverside

Prentice-Hall, Inc., Englewood Cliffs, New Jersey

Library of Congress Cataloging in Publication Data

BEATTY, JOHN LOUIS, ed. (date)
  Heritage of western civilization.

  Includes index.
  1. Civilization—History—Sources.   2. Literature—Collections.   I. Johnson, Oliver A., joint
author.   II. Title.
[CB5.B43 1977b]   909′.09′821   76-14894
ISBN 0-13-387209-2

Printed in the United States of America

10   9   8   7   6   5   4   3

Prentice-Hall International, Inc., *London*
Prentice-Hall of Australia Pty. Limited, *Sydney*
Prentice-Hall of Canada, Ltd., *Toronto*
Prentice-Hall of India Private Limited, *New Delhi*
Prentice-Hall of Japan, Inc., *Tokyo*
Prentice-Hall of Southeast Asia Pte. Ltd., *Singapore*

Contents

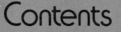

Preface to the Fourth Edition

It is with deep regret and a sense of personal loss that I report the death of my long-time friend and collaborator on *Heritage of Western Civilization,* John Louis Beatty, in March of 1975. At the time of his death, after a long illness brought on by complications resulting from wounds he suffered in combat in Germany during the Second World War, Beatty was engaged in planning this new edition of *Heritage.* As surviving editor I have completed the work that we began together. In acknowledgment of Beatty's contributions to *Heritage* over a period of more than fifteen years, I should like to dedicate the fourth edition to his memory.

In this new edition, certain selections that appeared in past editions have been deleted and a few others have been slightly shortened. These excisions have been made with careful consideration and with the aim of preserving, to the utmost extent possible, the basic integrity of the work. We have added several new selections: writings of Marcus Aurelius, Chateaubriand, Nietzsche, Kipling, and T. S. Eliot.

Oliver A. Johnson

Heritage of Western Civilization

King Hammurabi of Babylon receiving the laws from the sun god, Marduk. *(Culver Pictures, Inc.)*

The Ancient Near East

The source of Western civilization, the ancient Near East, lies in a relatively small area of land where three continents—Asia, Africa, and Europe—come together. Although our heritage is a long one, it is difficult to state with precision just when it began. Two quite different kinds of problems stand in the way of dating accurately the beginnings of our civilization. An obvious difficulty is that in the very early centuries people had not developed the art of writing so could not preserve a detailed or reliable account of their deeds. A more formidable obstacle lies in determining just what constitutes "civilization." Clearly we cannot decide when a civilization began until after we have determined what a civilization is. Historians, generally, have solved this problem by dating the birth of civilization from the time when people first began to live together in cities. Accepting this criterion, we can date the beginning of Western civilization in the fifth millennium B.C., when inhabitants of the ancient Near East began drifting down from the hills into the fertile river bottoms, abandoning their nomadic existence as herdsmen for a more settled life in towns.

Some historians, however, believe that civilization demands more than city life; in particular, they insist on the necessity of permanent, accurate records. This criterion implies the ability to write. Those who base civilization on the existence of written records have an additional point in their argument, for almost concurrent with the invention of writing at the end of the fourth millennium B.C. there occurred a second event of epochal significance. Usually called the "copper revolution," this development is important not only because it introduced a metal as the main constituent of arms and implements in place of stone, but also because it led to a vast expansion of commerce. Since few localities possessed copper deposits, it was necessary to transport the supplies long distances from their sources to their destinations. Extensive commerce required larger political units, more complex commercial organization, and better means of transportation and communication. All of these are basic ingredients of civilized life.

Whether we accept the notion that civilized life begins with life in the city or only with the development of a written language, we must recognize a fact often overlooked—that the temporal portion of Western history occupied by the civilizations of the ancient Near East is a large one indeed. If we take the year 500 B.C., when the first truly European civilization, classical Greece, entered its period of greatness, as a dividing line, we find that we have cut Western civilization almost exactly in half,

1

the last twenty-five hundred years belonging to the world of European and American history and the first twenty-five hundred years belonging to the history of the ancient Near East. And if we mark the beginning of civilization by the development of city life, we must tip the temporal balance in favor of the pre-Greek world.

Our knowledge of the ancient Near East comes from many sources. Important among these, of course, are written records. The Old Testament, for instance, is a treasure house of information about every facet of life in ancient times, revealing intimate details of the daily life not only of the tribes of Israel but also of their neighbors from Egypt to Mesopotamia. For those periods of history in which no written records exist, our most important sources of information are the findings of archeologists. Since the romantic discovery of the city of Troy a century ago by the German amateur, Heinrich Schliemann, archeologists have systematically dug up the sites where ancient people had built. They have been aided in their researches in various unexpected ways. For example, the most essential item in an ancient household, the clay pot, is almost indestructible. Although it may be broken and cast on a dump heap, the shards remain through the millennia waiting to be put together again. When the archeologist of the twentieth century has reassembled this humble object, he can learn much about its original owners from its composition, its shape, and its decoration. In addition, he can make shrewd deductions about the time it was originally molded from the relative depth of the layer in the dump from which he dug it up.

Again, the archeologist is greatly indebted in particular to the ancient Egyptians for their faith in immortality. Believing in a life after death much like that on earth, they filled the tombs of their deceased with everything necessary for a prosperous, happy existence. Preserved intact through the ages in the dry air of the Egyptian desert, ancient tombs like that of the pharaoh Tutenkhamon, who reigned in the fourteenth century B.C., have yielded dazzling treasures to the picks and shovels of modern diggers.

Because it spanned several millennia, the history of the ancient Near East is a complex affair. Nevertheless it is possible to distinguish four major Near Eastern centers of civilization: Mesopotamia, Egypt, Asia Minor and Syria, and the eastern Mediterranean Sea. Mesopotamia is generally conceded to have the oldest civilization. At a very early date people were attracted by the deep, rich soils created by the annual flooding of the two great rivers, the Tigris and Euphrates, as they flowed in a generally eastward direction to their ultimate destination in the Persian Gulf. The long history of Mesopotamia witnessed a succession of different groups of people gaining political domination over the land, only to be overcome and superseded by another group. A twofold reason lies behind this turbulent history. The land, because of its fertility, was extremely attractive and hence considered a worthy prize. In addition, it was very difficult to defend against invasion because it offered few natural barriers to deter attackers.

To reap maximum benefit from the fertile soil of the river valley, it was necessary to develop extensive systems of irrigation. Such an endeavor required large-scale cooperation, which in turn encouraged the development of legal relationships. The result was an early elaboration of a complex legal system, which was codified by the Babylonian king Hammurabi around 1700 B.C. and became one of the most important bequests of Mesopotamia to Western civilization.

Ancient Egypt, like Mesopotamia, was a civilization based on a river. To reach its mouth where it empties into the southeast corner of the Mediterranean Sea, the Nile meanders for nearly a thousand miles from its first cataract in upper Egypt. Most of the life of ancient Egypt was concentrated in a narrow strip of fertile land, ten to twenty miles wide, along the banks of the river. Egypt differed from Mesopotamia, however, in having a relatively tranquil history. Indeed, it was one of the most stable societies in the history of the world. The reason, again, was mainly geographical. Relatively isolated and protected from potential invaders by barriers of mountain and desert, the Egyptians were able to go about their affairs century after century unmolested by foreign intruders.

The third general area of the ancient Near East, Asia Minor and Syria, is more difficult to characterize briefly because its history was quite diverse. Including the Anatolian peninsula between the eastern Mediterranean and the Black seas as well as the narrow strip of land between the eastern end of the Mediterranean and the desert of Arabia, this land was the home of many very diverse groups of people. Because of their strategic location along the shores of the Mediterranean and astride the main overland routes connecting Egypt and Mesopotamia, the peoples of the area turned naturally to trade as a way of life. One group, the Phoenicians, took to the sea, sending their ships far and wide across the Mediterranean and even venturing beyond the Straits of Gibraltar into the Atlantic. Others turned to trade by land; a group known as Aramaeans dominated commerce in the Near East from their trading city of Damascus for centuries. Among the smallest, weakest, yet most influential of all Near Eastern peoples was a group of wandering tribes who presumably originated near the mouth of the Tigris and Euphrates and, after many vicissitudes, settled in the land of Canaan, on a thin coastal strip at the southeast corner of the Mediterranean. These were the Jewish people; their contribution to Western civilization requires no explanation.

The final important ancient Near Eastern civilization had its center in the islands of the eastern Mediterranean and the Aegean seas and along the coastal strips of the adjacent mainland, in Greece and Asia Minor. Of particular significance was the island of Crete, just off the southern tip of Greece. Here an advanced society developed, especially at the city of Cnossus, where an enormous and elaborate palace was built to house the royal family and their retainers. The Minoans, as the members of this civilization are generally called, naturally took to the sea and for centuries dominated the commerce of the Aegean area, from seaports on Crete, on other islands, and on the mainland. Although Minoan civilization declined after some unknown force attacked and destroyed the great palace at Cnossus around 1400 B.C., this city and the civilization it represented achieved a high level of wealth, splendor, and sophistication. In addition, it provided a link between the older civilizations in the ancient Near East and the first of European civilizations, classical Greece.

During the last thousand years of its period of greatness, civilization in the ancient Near East was characterized by the appearance of successive empires. Among the first of these was the Babylonian Empire of Hammurabi which took shape in Mesopotamia around 1700 B.C. There followed an Egyptian Empire and an Empire of the Hittites with its center in Anatolia. Overshadowing all of these in extent and influence were the last two imperial powers, first the Assyrians and then the Persians. Under their great leaders, Cyrus and Darius, the Persians gained control of all the ancient Near East from the Mediterranean shores in the West to the banks of the Indus River in India in the East. Around 500 B.C. they began to move across the Straits of the Dardanelles into Europe. Here they were met by the Greeks in a series of decisive encounters which were to shape the course of Western history to our own day.

The Code of Hammurabi

At the turn of the twentieth century a French archeological expedition unearthed one of the most magnificent finds of our times—a stele on which was inscribed the entire Code of Hammurabi. Found at Susa in Persia where it had been taken by an Elamite king as war booty in the twelfth century B.C., the stele is of stone, about eight feet tall, and contains approximately thirty-six hundred lines of writing. Although the stone has been damaged slightly, most of the writing, in cuneiform script, is legible. At the top of the stele is a well-executed carving showing Hammurabi receiving the laws from Marduk, the Sun God of Babylonia. After its discovery the stele was transported to Paris and placed in the Louvre.

Hammurabi, an Amonite, reigned as king of Babylonia for forty-three years, from 1728 to 1686 B.C. Although he was responsible for formulating and publishing the Code, he did not originate the laws that it contains. Rather the Code is a compilation and revision of older laws of Sumerian and Akkadian origin. These deal with almost every facet of life in the ancient Near East, including marriage and the family, the relationships among social classes, the regulations of land and business, labor relations, military service, religion, and crime. They are important not only for the light they shed on the society of that time but also for the influence they had on later Near Eastern law codes. In this regard it is instructive to compare the Code with the Mosaic law as it appears in the Old Testament. Both reveal, particularly in their sanction of the *lex talionis,* something of the cruelty and violence that was endemic throughout the ancient world.

For the selection that follows we have chosen the most important legal provisions of the Code, eliminating regulations of minor significance.

The Code of Hammurabi

1. If a seignior [1] accused another seignior and brought a charge of murder against him, but has not proved it, his accuser shall be put to death.

2. If a seignior brought a charge of sorcery against another seignior, but has not proved it, the one against whom the charge of sorcery was brought, upon going to the river,[2] shall throw himself into the river, and if the river has then overpowered him, his accuser shall take over his estate; if the river has shown that seignior to be innocent and he has accordingly come forth safe, the one who brought the charge of sorcery against him shall be put to death, while the one who threw himself into the river shall take over the estate of his accuser.

3. If a seignior came forward with false testimony in a case, and has not proved the word which he spoke, if that case was a case involving life, that seignior shall be put to death.

4. If he came forward with false testimony concerning grain or money, he shall bear the penalty of that case.

5. If a judge gave a judgment, rendered a decision, deposited a sealed document, but later has altered his judgment, they shall prove that that judge altered the judgment which he gave and he shall pay twelvefold the claim which holds in that case; furthermore, they shall expel him in the assembly from his seat of judgment and he shall never again sit with the judges in a case.

6. If a seignior stole the property of church or state, that seignior shall be put to death; also the one who received the stolen goods from his hand shall be put to death.

. . .

14. If a seignior has stolen the young son of another seignior, he shall be put to death.

15. If a seignior has helped either a male slave of the state or a female slave of the state or a male slave of a private citizen or a female slave of a private citizen to escape through the city-gate, he shall be put to death.

16. If a seignior has harbored in his house either a fugitive male or

---

[1] *awēlum* seems to be used in at least three senses: (1) sometimes to indicate a man of the higher class, a noble; (2) sometimes a free man of any class, high or low; and (3) occasionally a man of any class, from king to slave. I follow the ambiguity of the original and use the rather general term "seignior," as employed in Italian and Spanish, to indicate any free man of standing. [This and following notes are by the translator.]

[2] The river (the Euphrates) as judge in the case was regarded as god.

"The Code of Hammurabi," trans. Theophile J. Meek, in *The Ancient Near East: An Anthology of Texts and Pictures,* ed. J. B. Pritchard (Copyright © 1958 by Princeton University Press): selections from pp. 139, 141–45, 148–67. Reprinted by permission of Princeton University Press.

female slave belonging to the state or to a private citizen and has not brought him forth at the summons of the police, that householder shall be put to death.

· · ·

22. If a seignior committed robbery and has been caught, that seignior shall be put to death.

23. If the robber has not been caught, the robbed seignior shall set forth the particulars regarding his lost property in the presence of god, and the city and governor, in whose territory and district the robbery was committed, shall make good to him his lost property.

· · ·

25. If fire broke out in a seignior's house and a seignior, who went to extinguish it, cast his eye on the goods of the owner of the house and has appropriated the goods of the owner of the house, that seignior shall be thrown into that fire.

26. If either a private soldier or a commissary,[3] whose despatch on a campaign of the king was ordered, did not go or he hired a substitute and has sent him in his place, that soldier or commissary shall be put to death, while the one who was hired by him shall take over the estate.

27. In the case of either a private soldier or a commissary who was carried off while in the armed service of the king, if after his disappearance they gave his field and orchard to another and he has looked after his feudal obligations —if he has returned and reached his city, they shall restore his field and orchard to him and he shall himself look after his feudal obligations.

28. In the case of either a private soldier or a commissary, who was carried off while in the armed service of the king, if his son is able to look after the feudal obligations, the field and orchard shall be given to him and he shall look after the feudal obligations of his father.

29. If his son is so young that he is not able to look after the feudal obligations of his father, one-third of the field and orchard shall be given to his mother in order that his mother may rear him.

· · ·

34. If either a sergeant or a captain has appropriated the household goods of a soldier, has wronged a soldier, has let a soldier for hire, has abandoned a soldier to a superior in a lawsuit, has appropriated the grant which the king gave to a soldier, that sergeant or captain shall be put to death.

35. If a seignior has bought from the hand of a soldier the cattle or sheep which the king gave to the soldier, he shall forfeit his money.

36. In no case is the field, orchard, or house belonging to a soldier, a commissary, or a feudatory salable.

· · ·

42. If a seignior rented a field for cultivation, but has not produced grain in the field, they shall prove that he did no work on the field and he shall give grain to the owner of the field on the basis of those adjoining it.

· · ·

---

[3] The exact meaning of the two military terms used here, *redum* and *ba'irum,* is uncertain. The former means literally "follower" and is regularly used for the ordinary foot-soldier; the latter means literally "fisher, hunter," hence "commissary" here.

45. If a seignior let his field to a tenant and has already received the rent of his field, and later Adad has inundated the field or a flood has ravaged it, the loss shall be the tenant's.

46. If he has not received the rent of the field, whether he let the field for one-half or one-third the crop, the tenant and the owner of the field shall divide proportionately the grain which is produced in the field.

. . .

53. If a seignior was too lazy to make the dike of his field strong and did not make his dike strong and a break has opened up in his dike and he has accordingly let the water ravage the farmland, the seignior in whose dike the break was opened shall make good the grain that he let get destroyed.

54. If he is not able to make good the grain, they shall sell him and his goods, and the farmers whose grain the water carried off shall divide the proceeds.

. . .

98. If a seignior gave money to another seignior for a partnership, they shall divide equally in the presence of god the profit or loss which was incurred.

99. If a merchant lent money at interest to a trader for the purpose of trading and making purchases and sent him out on the road, the trader shall . . . on the road the money which was entrusted to him.

100. If he has realized a profit where he went, he shall write down the interest on the full amount of money that he borrowed and they shall count up the days against him and he shall repay his merchant.

101. If he has not realized a profit where he went, the trader shall repay to the merchant double the money that he borrowed.

102. If a merchant has lent money to a trader as a favor and he has experienced a loss where he went, he shall pay back the principal of the money to the merchant.

103. If, when he went on the road, an enemy has made him give up whatever he was carrying, the trader shall so affirm by god and then he shall go free.

. . .

106. If a trader borrowed money from a merchant and has then disputed the fact with his merchant, that merchant in the presence of god and witnesses shall prove that the trader borrowed the money and the trader shall pay to the merchant threefold the full amount of money that he borrowed.

107. When a merchant entrusted something to a trader and the trader has returned to his merchant whatever the merchant gave him, if the merchant has then disputed with him whatever the trader gave him, that trader shall prove it against the merchant in the presence of god and witnesses and the merchant shall pay to the trader sixfold whatever he received because he had a dispute with his trader.

108. If a woman wine seller, instead of receiving grain for the price of a drink, has received money by the large weight and so has made the value of the drink less than the value of the grain, they shall prove it against that wine seller and throw her into the water.

109. If outlaws have congregated in the establishment of a woman wine seller and she has not arrested those outlaws and did not take them

to the palace, that wine seller shall be put to death.

110. If a hierodule,[4] a nun, who is not living in a convent, has opened the door of a wineshop or has entered a wineshop for a drink, they shall burn that woman.

· · ·

120. If a seignior deposited his grain in another seignior's house for storage and a loss has then occurred at the granary or the owner of the house opened the storage-room and took grain or he has denied completely the receipt of the grain which was stored in his house, the owner of the grain shall set forth the particulars regarding his grain in the presence of god and the owner of the house shall give to the owner of the grain double the grain that he took.

· · ·

122. If a seignior wishes to give silver, gold, or any sort of thing to another seignior for safekeeping, he shall show to witnesses the full amount that he wishes to give, arrange the contracts, and then commit it to safekeeping.

123. If he gave it for safekeeping without witnesses and contracts and they have denied its receipt to him at the place where he made the deposit, that case is not subject to claim.

124. If a seignior gave silver, gold, or any sort of thing for safekeeping to another seignior in the presence of witnesses and he has denied the fact to him, they shall prove it against that seignior and he

shall pay double whatever he denied.

125. If a seignior deposited property of his for safekeeping and at the place where he made the deposit his property has disappeared along with the property of the owner of the house, either through breaking in or through scaling the wall, the owner of the house, who was so careless that he let whatever was given to him for safekeeping get lost, shall make it good and make restitution to the owner of the goods, while the owner of the house shall make a thorough search for his lost property and take it from its thief.

126. If the seignior's property was not lost, but he has declared, "My property is lost," thus deceiving his city council, his city council shall set forth the facts regarding him in the presence of god, that his property was not lost, and he shall give to his city council double whatever he laid claim to.

· · ·

128. If a seignior acquired a wife, but did not draw up the contracts for her, that woman is no wife.

129. If the wife of a seignior has been caught while lying with another man, they shall bind them and throw them into the water. If the husband of the woman wishes to spare his wife, then the king in turn may spare his subject.

130. If a seignior bound the betrothed wife of another seignior, who had had no intercourse with a male and was still living in her father's house, and he has lain in her bosom and they have caught him, that seignior shall be put to death, while that woman shall go free.

131. If a seignior's wife was ac-

---

[4] The exact meaning of the term used here, *nadītum*, is unknown, but it indicates some kind of religious functionary.

cused by her husband, but she was not caught while lying with another man, she shall make affirmation by god and return to her house.

132. If the finger was pointed at the wife of a seignior because of another man, but she has not been caught while lying with the other man, she shall throw herself into the river [5] for the sake of her husband.

. . .

138. If a seignior wishes to divorce his wife who did not bear him children, he shall give her money to the full amount of her marriage-price and he shall also make good to her the dowry which she brought from her father's house and then he may divorce her.

139. If there was no marriage-price, he shall give her one mina of silver as the divorce-settlement.

140. If he is a peasant, he shall give her one-third mina of silver.

141. If a seignior's wife, who was living in the house of the seignior, has made up her mind to leave in order that she may engage in business, thus neglecting her house and humiliating her husband, they shall prove it against her; and if her husband has then decided on her divorce, he may divorce her, with nothing to be given her as her divorce-settlement upon her departure. If her husband has not decided on her divorce, her husband may marry another woman, with the former woman living in the house of her husband like a maidservant.

142. If a woman so hated her husband that she has declared, "You may not have me," her record shall be investigated at her city council; and if she was careful and was not at fault, even though her husband has been going out and disparaging her greatly, that woman, without incurring any blame at all, may take her dowry and go off to her father's house.

143. If she was not careful, but was a gadabout, thus neglecting her house and humiliating her husband, they shall throw that woman into the water.

. . .

150. If a seignior, upon presenting a field, orchard, house, or goods to his wife, left a sealed document with her, her children may not enter a claim against her after the death of her husband, since the mother may give her inheritance to that son of hers whom she likes, but she may not give it to an outsider.

151. If a woman, who was living in a seignior's house, having made a contract with her husband that a creditor of her husband may not distrain her, has then had him deliver a written statement; if there was a debt against that seignior before he married that woman, his creditors may not distrain his wife; also, if there was a debt against that woman before she entered the seignior's house, her creditors may not distrain her husband.

152. If a debt has developed against them after that woman entered the seignior's house, both of them shall be answerable to the merchant.

153. If a seignior's wife has brought about the death of her husband because of another man, they shall impale that woman on stakes.

154. If a seignior has had intercourse with his daughter, they shall make that seignior leave the city.

---

[5] *I.e.,* submit to the water ordeal, with the river as divine judge.

155. If a seignior chose a bride for his son and his son had intercourse with her, but later he himself has lain in her bosom and they have caught him, they shall bind that seignior and throw him into the water.

156. If a seignior chose a bride for his son and his son did not have intercourse with her, but he himself has lain in her bosom, he shall pay to her one-half mina of silver and he shall also make good to her whatever she brought from her father's house in order that the man of her choice may marry her.

157. If a seignior has lain in the bosom of his mother after the death of his father, they shall burn both of them.

· · ·

159. If a seignior, who had the betrothal-gift brought to the house of his prospective father-in-law and paid the marriage-price, has then fallen in love with another woman and has said to his prospective father-in-law, "I will not marry your daughter," the father of the daughter shall keep whatever was brought to him.

160. If a seignior had the betrothal-gift brought to the house of the prospective father-in-law and paid the marriage-price, and the father of the daughter has then said, "I will not give my daughter to you," he shall pay back double the full amount that was brought to him.

· · ·

162. If, when a seignior acquired a wife, she bore him children and that woman has then gone to her fate, her father may not lay claim to her dowry, since her dowry belongs to her children.

163. If a seignior acquired a wife and that woman has gone to her fate without providing him with children, if his father-in-law has then returned to him the marriage-price which that seignior brought to the house of his father-in-law, her husband may not lay claim to the dowry of that woman, since her dowry belongs to her father's house.

· · ·

168. If a seignior, having made up his mind to disinherit his son, has said to the judges, "I wish to disinherit my son," the judges shall investigate his record, and if the son did not incur wrong grave enough to be disinherited, the father may not disinherit his son.

169. If he has incurred wrong against his father grave enough to be disinherited, they shall let him off the first time; if he has incurred grave wrong a second time, the father may disinherit his son.

170. When a seignior's first wife bore him children and his female slave also bore him children, if the father during his lifetime has ever said "My children!" to the children whom the slave bore him, thus having counted them with the children of the first wife, after the father has gone to his fate, the children of the first wife and the children of the slave shall share equally in the goods of the paternal estate, with the first-born, the son of the first wife, receiving a preferential share.

171. However, if the father during his lifetime has never said "My children!" to the children whom the slave bore him, after the father has gone to his fate, the children of the slave may not share in the goods of the paternal estate along with the children of the first wife; freedom for the slave and her children shall be effected, with the children of the

first wife having no claim at all against the children of the slave for service; the first wife shall take her dowry and the marriage-gift which her husband, upon giving it to her, wrote down on a tablet for her, and living in the home of her husband, she shall have the usufruct of it as long as she lives, without ever selling it, since her heritage belongs to her children.

· · ·

175. If either a palace or a private citizen's slave married the daughter of a seignior and she has borne children, the owner of the slave may not lay claim to the children of the seignior's daughter for service.

176. Furthermore, if a palace slave or a private citizen's slave married the daughter of a seignior and when he married her she entered the house of the palace slave or the private citizen's slave with the dowry from her father's house and after they were joined together they set up a household and so acquired goods, but later either the palace slave or the private citizen's slave has gone to his fate, the seignior's daughter shall take her dowry, but they shall divide into two parts whatever her husband and she acquired after they were joined together and the owner of the slave shall take one-half, with the seignior's daughter taking one-half for her children.

176a. If the seignior's daughter has no dowry, they shall divide into two parts whatever her husband and she acquired after they were joined together and the owner of the slave shall take one-half, with the seignior's daughter taking one-half for her children.

177. If a widow, whose children are minors, has made up her mind to enter the house of another, she may not enter without the consent of the judges; when she wishes to enter the house of another, the judges shall investigate the condition of her former husband's estate and they shall entrust her former husband's estate to her later husband and that woman and they shall have them deposit a tablet to the effect that they will look after the estate and also rear the young children, without ever selling the household goods, since the purchaser who purchases the household goods of a widow's children shall forfeit his money, with the goods reverting to their owner.

· · ·

181. If a father dedicated his daughter to deity as a hierodule, a sacred prostitute, or a devotee and did not present a dowry to her, after the father has gone to his fate, she shall receive as her share in the goods of the paternal estate her one-third patrimony, but she shall have only the usufruct of it as long as she lives, since her heritage belongs to her brothers.

· · ·

185. If a seignior adopted a boy in his own name and has reared him, that foster child may never be reclaimed.

186. If a seignior, upon adopting a boy, seeks out his father and mother when he had taken him, that foster child may return to his father's house.

· · ·

188. If a member of the artisan class took a son as a foster child and has taught him his handicraft, he may never be reclaimed.

189. If he has not taught him his handicraft, that foster child may return to his father's house.

. . .

195. If a son has struck his father, they shall cut off his hand.

196. If a seignior has destroyed the eye of a member of the aristocracy, they shall destroy his eye.

197. If he has broken another seignior's bone, they shall break his bone.

198. If he has destroyed the eye of a commoner or broken the bone of a commoner, he shall pay one mina of silver.

199. If he has destroyed the eye of a seignior's slave or broken the bone of a seignior's slave, he shall pay one-half his value.

200. If a seignior has knocked out a tooth of a seignior of his own rank, they shall knock out his tooth.

201. If he has knocked out a commoner's tooth, he shall pay one-third mina of silver.

. . .

209. If a seignior struck another seignior's daughter and has caused her to have a miscarriage, he shall pay ten shekels of silver for her fetus.

210. If that woman has died, they shall put his daughter to death.

. . .

215. If a physician performed a major operation on a seignior with a bronze lancet and has saved the seignior's life, or he opened up the eye-socket of a seignior with a bronze lancet and has saved the seignior's eye, he shall receive ten shekels of silver.

. . .

218. If a physician performed a major operation on a seignior with a bronze lancet and has caused the seignior's death, or he opened up the eye-socket of a seignior and has destroyed the seignior's eye, they shall cut off his hand.

. . .

224. If a veterinary surgeon performed a major operation on either an ox or an ass and has saved its life, the owner of the ox or ass shall give to the surgeon one-sixth shekel of silver as his fee.

225. If he performed a major operation on an ox or an ass and has caused its death, he shall give to the owner of the ox or ass one-fourth its value.

226. If a brander cut off the slave-mark of a slave not his own without the consent of the owner of the slave, they shall cut off the hand of that brander.

. . .

229. If a builder constructed a house for a seignior, but did not make his work strong, with the result that the house which he built collapsed and so has caused the death of the owner of the house, that builder shall be put to death.

230. If it has caused the death of a son of the owner of the house, they shall put the son of that builder to death.

231. If it has caused the death of a slave of the owner of the house, he shall give slave for slave to the owner of the house.

232. If it has destroyed goods, he shall make good whatever it destroyed; also, because he did not make the house strong which he built and it collapsed, he shall reconstruct the house which collapsed at his own expense.

. . .

236. If a seignior let his boat for hire to a boatman and the boatman was so careless that he has sunk or wrecked the boat, the boatman shall make good the boat to the owner of the boat.

237. When a seignior hired a boatman and a boat and loaded it with grain, wool, oil, dates, or any kind of freight, if that boatman was so careless that he has sunk the boat and lost what was in it as well, the boatman shall make good the boat which he sank and whatever he lost that was in it.

. . .

244. If a seignior hired an ox or an ass and a lion has killed it in the open, the loss shall be its owner's.

245. If a seignior hired an ox and has caused its death through carelessness or through beating, he shall make good ox for ox to the owner of the ox.

. . .

249. If a seignior hired an ox and god struck it and it has died, the seignior who hired the ox shall so affirm by god and then he shall go free.

250. If an ox, when it was walking along the street, gored a seignior to death, that case is not subject to claim.

251. If a seignior's ox was a gorer and his city council made it known to him that it was a gorer, but he did not pad its horns or tie up his ox, and that ox gored to death a member of the aristocracy, he shall give one-half mina of silver.

. . .

265. If a shepherd, to whom cattle or sheep were given to pasture, became unfaithful and hence has altered the cattlemark or has sold them, they shall prove it against him and he shall make good in cattle and sheep to their owner tenfold what he stole.

266. If a visitation of god has occurred in a sheepfold or a lion has made a kill, the shepherd shall prove himself innocent in the presence of god, but the owner of the sheepfold shall receive from him the animal stricken in the fold.

267. If the shepherd was careless and has let lameness develop in the fold, the shepherd shall make good in cattle and sheep the loss through the lameness which he let develop in the fold and give them to their owner.

. . .

278. If a segnior purchased a male or female slave and when his month was not yet complete, epilepsy attacked him, he shall return him to his seller and the purchaser shall get back the money which he paid out.

279. If a seignior purchased a male or female slave and he has then received a claim against him, his seller shall be responsible for the claim.

280. If a seignior has purchased in a foreign land the male or female slave of another seignior and when he has arrived home the owner of the male or female slave has identified either his male or his female slave, if that male and female slave are natives of the land, their freedom shall be effected without any money payment.

281. If they are natives of another land, the purchaser shall state in the presence of god what money he paid out and the owner of the

male or female slave shall give to the merchant the money he paid out and thus redeem his male or female slave.

282. If a male slave has said to his master, "You are not my master," his master shall prove him to be his slave and cut off his ear.

Egyptian Religious Hymns

The religion of ancient Egypt is an extremely complex subject. One authority, W. M. F. Petrie (writing in Hastings' *Encyclopedia of Religion and Ethics,* volume V), distinguishes six main historical strata of Egyptian theology: (1) pure animal worship, (2) animal-headed gods with human bodies, (3) human gods of the Osiris cycle, (4) cosmic gods of the Rā cycle, (5) abstract gods of principles, and (6) gods brought in from foreign sources. Such diversity, although it may suggest that the Egyptians were fickle and inconstant in their religious allegiances, is probably more truly understood as a natural development of religious consciousness taking place over a period of five thousand years, from prehistoric times to the beginning of the Christian era.

Long as Petrie's list of strata in Egyptian theology is, however, it still fails to include one important, and historically pervasive, facet of Egyptian religious worship. This aspect is *animism,* or the deification of forces of nature—a type of religion found in most, if not all, early civilizations. The selections that follow illustrate two forms of Egyptian animism: worship of the Nile and worship of the sun. Why the people of Egypt selected these two natural forces for deification is understandable. Each force formed a necessary condition for the sustenance of life in the valley, the Nile by its annual inundations of the land watering and nourishing the soil, and the sun by its warmth causing the crops to grow. Without the presence of both, the Nile valley would have been either a desert or a swamp in which Egyptian civilization as we know it would probably never have developed. The *Hymn to the Sun* has, in addition, another claim to our attention, for many scholars hold it to be the first clear statement of monotheism to appear in the West.

The two hymns presented here come from different epochs of Egyptian history. The exact date of the *Hymn to the Nile* is not known but scholars believe that it was composed for a festival held in Thebes celebrating the annual inundation of the land by the river. The *Hymn to the Sun,* dating from the Later Empire, was composed by King Ikhnaton, probably around 1370 B.C. Both hymns, unfortunately, have come down to us mutilated through the ravages of time. Parts that are missing from the original texts have either been reconstructed by the translators or are indicated by ellipses.

Hymn to the Nile

Praise to thee, O Nile, that issueth from the earth, and cometh to nourish Egypt. Of hidden nature, a darkness in the daytime. . . .

That watereth the meadows, he that Rē [1] hath created to nourish all cattle. That giveth drink to the desert places, which are far from water; it is his dew that falleth from heaven.

Beloved of Kēb,[2] director of the corn-god; that maketh to flourish every workshop of Ptah.[3]

Lord of fish, that maketh the water-fowl to go upstream. . . .

That maketh barley and createth wheat, so that he may cause the temples to keep festivals.

If he be sluggish,[4] the nostrils are stopped up,[5] and all men are impoverished; the victuals of the gods are diminished, and millions of men perish.

If he be niggardly the whole land is in terror and great and small lament. . . . Khnum [6] hath fash-

ioned him. When he riseth, the land is in exultation and every body is in joy. All jaws begin to laugh and every tooth is revealed.

He that bringeth victuals and is rich in food, that createth all that is good. The revered, sweet-smelling. . . . That createth herbage for the cattle, and giveth sacrifice to every god, be he in the underworld, in heaven, or upon earth. . . . That filleth the storehouses, and maketh wide the granaries, that giveth things to the poor.

He that maketh trees to grow according to every wish, and men have no lack thereof; the ship is built by his power, for there is no joinery with stones. . . .

. . . thy young folk and thy children shout for joy over thee, and men hail thee as king. Unchanging of laws, when he cometh forth in the presence of Upper and Lower Egypt. Men drink the water. . . .

He that was in sorrow is become glad, and every heart is joyful. Sobk, the child of Neith,[7] laugheth, and the divine Ennead, that is in thee, is glorious.

---

[1] The sun-god.

[2] The earth-god.

[3] Ptah, the craftsman, who fashions everything, could effect nothing without the Nile.

[4] On the occasion of a deficient inundation.

[5] Men no longer breathe and live.

[6] The ram-headed god, who fashions all that is.

---

[7] Sobk has the form of a crocodile and will originally have been a water-god, who rejoices in the inundation.

Adolph Erman, *The Literature of the Ancient Egyptians,* trans. A. M. Blackman (London: Methuen & Co., Ltd., 1927), pp. 146–49. Courtesy of Methuen & Co., Ltd.

Thou that vomitest forth, giving the fields to drink and making strong the people. He that maketh the one rich and loveth the other. He maketh no distinctions, and boundaries are not made for him.

Thou light, that cometh from the darkness! Thou fat for his cattle! He is a strong one, that createth. . . .

. . . one beholdeth the wealthy as him that is full of care, one beholdeth each one with his implements. . . . None, that (otherwise) goeth clad, is clad,[8] and the children of notables are unadorned. . . .

He that establisheth right, whom men love. . . . It would be but lies to compare thee with the sea, that bringeth no corn. . . . no bird descendeth in the desert. . . .

Men begin to play to thee on the harp, and men sing to thee with the hand.[9] Thy young folk and thy children shout for joy over thee, and deputations to thee are appointed.

He that cometh with splendid things and adorneth the earth! That causeth the ship to prosper before men; that quickeneth the hearts in them that are with child; that would fain have there be a multitude of all kinds of cattle.

When thou art risen in the city of the sovereign, then men are satisfied with a goodly list.[10] "I would like lotus flowers," saith the little one, "and all manner of things," saith the . . . commander, "and all manner of herbs," say the children. Eating bringeth forgetfulness of him.[11] Good things are scattered over the dwelling. . . .

When the Nile floodeth, offering is made to thee, cattle are slaughtered for thee, a great oblation is made for thee. Birds are fattened for thee, antelopes are hunted for thee in the desert. Good is recompensed unto thee.

Offering is also made to every other god, even as is done for the Nile, with incense, oxen, cattle, and birds (upon) the flame. The Nile hath made him his cave in Thebes, and his name shall be known no more in the underworld. . . .

All ye men, extol the Nine Gods, and stand in awe of the might which his son, the Lord of All, hath displayed, even he that maketh green the Two River-banks. Thou are verdant, O Nile, thou art verdant. He that maketh man to live on his cattle, and his cattle on the meadow! Thou art verdant, thou art verdant; O Nile, thou art verdant.

---

[8] For hard work, clothes are taken off.

[9] It is an old custom to beat time with the hand while singing.

[10] *I.e.,* a multitude of good things.

[11] The Nile.

Hymn to the Sun

Thy dawning is beautiful in the horizon
of heaven,
O living Aton,[1] Beginning of life!
When thou risest in the eastern horizon
of heaven,
Thou fillest every land with thy beauty;
For thou art beautiful, great, glittering,
high over the earth;
Thy rays, they encompass the lands,
even all thou hast made.
Thou art Rē, and thou hast carried
them all away captive;
Thou bindest them by thy love.
Though thou art afar, thy rays are on
earth;
Though thou art on high, thy
footprints are the day.

When thou settest in the western
horizon of heaven,
The world is in darkness like the dead.
They sleep in their chambers,
Their heads are wrapt up,
Their nostrils stopped, and none seeth
the other.
Stolen are all their things, that are
under their heads,
While they know it not.
Every lion cometh forth from his den,
All serpents, they sting.
Darkness reigns,
The world is in silence,
He that made them has gone to rest in
his horizon.

Bright is the earth,
When thou risest in the horizon,
When thou shinest as Aton by day.
The darkness is banished,

When thou sendest forth thy rays,
The Two Lands [2] are in daily festivity,
Awake and standing upon their feet,
For thou hast raised them up.
Their limbs bathed, they take their
clothing;
Their arms uplifted in adoration to thy
dawning.
Then in all the world, they do their
work.

All cattle rest upon their herbage,
All trees and plants flourish,
The birds flutter in their marshes.
Their wings uplifted in adoration to
thee.
All the sheep dance upon their feet,
All winged things fly,
They live when thou hast shone upon
them.

The barques sail up-stream and
down-stream alike.
Every highway is open because thou
hast dawned.
The fish in the river leap up before
thee,
And thy rays are in the midst of the
great sea.

Thou art he who createst the
man-child in woman,
Who makest seed in man,
Who giveth life to the son in the body
of his mother,
Who soothest him that he may not
weep,
A nurse even in the womb.
Who giveth breath to animate every
one that he maketh.

---

[1] [One of the names given to the sun-
god—*Ed.*]

[2] [Upper and Lower Egypt—*Ed.*]

Trans. James H. Breasted.

When he cometh forth from the body,
. . . on the day of his birth,
Thou openest his mouth in speech,
Thou suppliest his necessities.

When the chicklet crieth in the
    egg-shell,
Thou givest him breath therein, to
    preserve him alive.
When thou hast perfected him
That he may pierce the egg,
He cometh forth from the egg,
To chirp with all his might;
He runneth about upon his two feet,
When he hath come forth therefrom.
How manifold are all thy works!
They are hidden from before us,
O thou sole god, whose powers no
    other possesseth.
Thou didst create the earth according
    to thy desire.
While thou wast alone:
Men, all cattle large and small,
All that are upon the earth,
That go about upon their feet;
All that are on high,
That fly with their wings.
The countries of Syria and Nubia,
The land of Egypt;
Thou settest every man in his place,
Thou suppliest their necessities.
Every one has his possessions,
And his days are reckoned.
Their tongues are divers in speech,
Their forms likewise and their skins,
For thou divider, hast divided the
    peoples.

Thou makest the Nile in the Nether
    World,
Thou bringest it at thy desire, to
    preserve the people alive.
O lord of them all, when feebleness is
    in them,
O lord of every house, who risest for
    them,
O son of day, the fear of every distant
    land,
Thou makest also their life.
Thou hast set a Nile in heaven,
That it may fall for them,

Making floods upon the mountains,
    like the great sea;
And watering their fields among their
    towns.
How excellent are thy designs, O lord
    of eternity!
The Nile in heaven is for the strangers,
And for the cattle of every land, that
    go upon their feet;
But the Nile, it cometh from the
    Nether World for Egypt.

Thus thy rays nourish every garden,
When thou risest they live, and grow
    by thee.
Thou makest the seasons, in order to
    create all thy works:
Winter bringing them coolness,
And the heat of summer likewise.
Thou hast made the distant heaven to
    rise therein,
In order to behold all that thou didst
    make,
While thou wast alone,
Rising in thy form as living Aton,
Dawning, shining afar off and
    returning.
Thou makest the beauty of form,
    through thyself alone.
Cities, towns and settlements,
On highway or on river,
All eyes see thee before them,
For thou art Aton of the day over the
    earth.

Thou art in my heart,
There is no other that knoweth thee,
Save thy son Ikhnaton.
Thou hast made him wise in thy
    designs
And in thy might.
The world is in thy hand,
Even as thou hast made them.
When thou hast risen, they live;
When thou settest, they die.
For thou art duration, beyond thy
    mere limbs,
By thee man liveth,
And their eyes look upon thy beauty,
Until thou settest.
All labour is laid aside,

When thou settest in the west;
When thou risest, they are made to
  grow
. . . for the king.

Since thou didst establish the earth,
Thou hast raised them up for thy son,
Who came forth from thy limbs,
The king, living in truth,
The lord of the Two Lands

Nefer-khepru-Re, Wan-Re,
The son of Re, living in truth, lord of
  diadems,
Ikhnaton, whose life is long;
And for the great royal wife, his
  beloved,
Mistress of the Two Lands, Nefer
  nefru aton, Nofretete,
Living and flourishing for ever and
  ever.

The Old Testament

The Old Testament unquestionably ranks among the greatest creations of the mind of man. That it should have been produced at all is extraordinary; that it was the work of a weak, relatively insignificant nation which was regularly exploited and overrun by its more powerful neighbors is well-nigh incredible. Although we usually think of the Old Testament as a religious document, it is much more than that. In its pages are recorded, in infinite variety and rich detail, the full range of the historical experience of a remarkable people.

Because it is impossible to encompass the wealth of the Old Testament in a selection of a length appropriate for this book, we have chosen for illustration two of its main themes. These themes—the belief in one God (monotheism) and the concept of God as a moral being standing in definite moral relationships to man—are probably the most important contributions made by the ancient Jewish people to Western civilization. That the Old Testament books present views on these two subjects that are often inconsistent with each other should be neither surprising nor disconcerting, for these books reveal the gradually developing moral and religious consciousness of their authors. It is particularly instructive to compare one of the most mature expressions of moral consciousness in the ancient world as it appears in the selection from Ezekiel with the doctrine of "original sin" as it is first stated by St. Paul in his Epistle to the Romans and later developed by the Christian theologians St. Augustine and John Calvin. An interesting contrast, also, can be made between Hebraic and Greek religious attitudes as revealed in the Book of Job and in the myths of the Greek heroes. Whereas Job suffered in patience every plague from heaven, submitting his will to divine judgment, the mythical heroes of Greece were in constant rebellion against the decrees from Olympus.

The following selections have been taken from the King James Version of the Bible; however, their form has been altered slightly to make them more easily readable.

Genesis

In the beginning God created the heaven and the earth. And the earth was without form, and void; and darkness was upon the face of the deep. And the Spirit of God moved upon the face of the waters. And God said, "Let there be light": and there was light. And God saw the light, that it was good and God divided the light from the darkness. And God called the light Day, and the darkness he called Night. And the evening and the morning were the first day.

And God said, "Let there be a firmament in the midst of the waters, and let it divide the waters from the waters." And God made the firmament, and divided the waters which were under the firmament from the waters which were above the firmament: and it was so. And God called the firmament Heaven. And the evening and the morning were the second day.

And God said, "Let the waters under the heaven be gathered together unto one place, and let the dry land appear": and it was so. And God called the dry land Earth; and the gathering together of the waters called he Seas: and God saw that it was good. And God said, "Let the earth bring forth grass, the herb yielding seed, and the fruit tree yielding fruit after his kind, whose seed is in itself, upon the earth": and it was so. And the earth brought forth grass, and herb yielding seed after his kind, and the tree yielding fruit, whose seed was in itself, after his kind: and God saw that it was good. And the evening and the morning were the third day.

And God said, "Let there be lights in the firmament of the heaven to divide the day from the night; and let them be for signs, and for seasons, and for days, and years: and let them be for lights in the firmament of the heaven to give light upon the earth": and it was so. And God made two great lights; the greater light to rule the day, and the lesser light to rule the night: he made the stars also. And God set them in the firmament of the heaven to give light upon the earth. And to rule over the day and over the night, and to divide the light from the darkness: and God saw that it was good. And the evening and the morning were the fourth day.

And God said, "Let the waters bring forth abundantly the moving creature that hath life, and fowl that may fly above the earth in the open firmament of heaven." And God created great whales, and every living creature that moveth, which the waters brought forth abundantly, after their kind, and every winged fowl after his kind: and God saw that it was good. And God blessed them, saying, "Be fruitful, and multiply, and fill the water in the seas, and let fowl multiply in the earth." And the evening and the morning were the fifth day.

And God said, "Let the earth

Chapters 1, 2, 3.

bring forth the living creature after his kind, cattle, and creeping thing, and beast of the earth after his kind": and it was so. And God made the beast of the earth after his kind, and cattle after their kind, and every thing that creepeth upon the earth after his kind: and God saw that it was good.

And God said, "Let us make man in our image, after our likeness: and let them have dominion over the fish of the sea, and over the fowl of the air, and over the cattle, and over all the earth, and over every creeping thing that creepeth upon the earth." So God created man in his own image, in the image of God created he him: male and female created he them. And God blessed them, and God said unto them, "Be fruitful, and multiply, and replenish the earth, and subdue it: and have dominion over the fish of the sea, and over the fowl of the air, and over every living thing that moveth upon the earth."

And God said, "Behold, I have given you every herb bearing seed, which is upon the face of all the earth, and every tree, in the which is the fruit of a tree yielding seed; to you it shall be for meat. And to every beast of the earth, and to every fowl of the air, and to every thing that creepeth upon the earth, wherein there is life, I have given every green herb for meat": and it was so. And God saw every thing that he had made, and, behold, it was very good. And the evening and the morning were the sixth day.

Thus the heavens and the earth were finished, and all the host of them. And on the seventh day God ended his work which he had made; and he rested on the seventh day

from all his work which he had made. And God blessed the seventh day, and sanctified it: because that in it he had rested from all his work which God created and made.

These are the generations of the heavens and of the earth when they were created, in the day that the LORD God made the earth and the heavens. And every plant of the field before it was in the earth, and every herb of the field before it grew: for the LORD God had not caused it to rain upon the earth, and there was not a man to till the ground. But there went up a mist from the earth, and watered the whole face of the ground. And the LORD God formed man of the dust of the ground, and breathed into his nostrils the breath of life; and man became a living soul.

And the LORD God planted a garden eastward in Eden; and there he put the man whom he had formed. And out of the ground made the LORD God to grow every tree that is pleasant to the sight, and good for food; the tree of life also in the midst of the garden, and the tree of knowledge of good and evil. And a river went out of Eden to water a garden; and from thence it was parted, and became into four heads. The name of the first is Pison: that is it which compasseth the whole land of Havilah, where there is gold; and the gold of that land is good: there is bdellium and the onyx stone. And the name of the second river is Gihon: the same is it that compasseth the whole land of Ethiopia. And the name of the third river is Hiddekel: that is it which goeth toward the east of Assyria. And the fourth river is Euphrates. And the LORD God took the man, and put him into the garden of Eden to dress it and to keep it. And the LORD God commanded the man, saying, "Of every tree of the garden thou mayest freely eat: But of the tree of the knowledge of good and evil, thou shalt not eat of it: for in the day that thou eatest thereof thou shalt surely die."

And the LORD God said, "It is not good that the man should be alone; I will make an help meet for him." And out of the ground the LORD God formed every beast of the field, and every fowl of the air; and brought them unto Adam to see what he would call them: and whatsoever Adam called every living creature, that was the name thereof. And Adam gave names to all cattle, and to the fowl of the air, and to every beast of the field; but for Adam there was not found an help meet for him. And the LORD God caused a deep sleep to fall upon Adam, and he slept: and he took one of his ribs, and closed up the flesh instead thereof. And the rib, which the LORD God had taken from man, made he a woman, and brought her unto the man. And Adam said, "This is now bone of my bones, and flesh of my flesh: she shall be called Woman, because she was taken out of Man. Therefore shall a man leave his father and his mother, and shall cleave unto his wife: and they shall be one flesh." And they were both naked, the man and his wife, and were not ashamed.

Now the serpent was more subtil than any beast of the field which the LORD God had made. And he said unto the woman, "Yea, hath God said, 'Ye shall not eat of every tree of the garden'?" And the woman said unto the serpent, "We may eat of the fruit of the trees of the garden: But of the fruit of the tree which is in the midst of the garden God hath said, 'Ye shall not eat of it, neither shall ye touch it, lest ye die.' " And the serpent said unto the woman, "Ye shall not surely die: For God doth know that in the day ye eat thereof, then your eyes shall be opened, and ye shall be as gods, knowing good and evil." And when the woman saw that the tree was good for food, and that it was pleasant to the eyes, and a tree to be desired to make one wise, she took of the fruit thereof, and did eat, and gave also unto her husband with her and he did eat. And the eyes of them both were opened, and they knew that they were naked; and they sewed fig leaves together, and made themselves aprons.

And they heard the voice of the LORD God walking in the garden in the cool of the day: and Adam and his wife hid themselves from the presence of the LORD God amongst the trees of the garden. And the LORD God called unto Adam, and said unto him, "Where art thou?" And he said, "I heard thy voice in the garden, and I was afraid, because I was naked; and I hid myself." And he said, "Who told thee that thou wast naked? Hast thou eaten of the tree, whereof I commanded thee that thou shouldest not eat?" And the man said, "The woman whom thou gavest to be with me, she gave me of the tree, and I did eat." And the LORD God said unto the woman, "What is this that thou hast done?" And the woman said, "The serpent beguiled me, and I did eat." And the LORD God said unto the serpent, "Because thou hast done this, thou art cursed above all cattle, and above every beast of the field; upon thy belly shalt thou go, and dust shalt thou eat all the days of thy life: And I will put enmity between thee and the woman, and between thy seed and her seed; it shall bruise thy head, and thou shalt bruise his heel." Unto the woman he said, "I will greatly multiply thy sorrow and thy conception; in sorrow thou shalt bring forth children; and thy desire shall be to thy husband, and he shall rule over thee." And unto Adam he said, "Because thou hast hearkened unto the voice of thy wife, and hast eaten of the tree, of which I commanded thee, saying, 'Thou shalt not eat of it': cursed is the ground for thy sake; in sorrow shalt thou eat of it all the days of thy life; thorns also and thistles shall it bring forth to thee; and thou shalt eat the herb of the field; in the sweat of thy face shalt thou eat bread, till thou return unto the ground; for out of it wast thou taken: for dust thou art, and unto dust shalt thou return." And Adam called his wife's name Eve; because she was the mother of all living. Unto Adam also and to his wife did the LORD God make coats of skins, and clothed them.

And the LORD God said, "Behold, the man is become as one of us, to know good and evil: and now, lest he put forth his hand, and take also of the tree of life, and eat, and live for ever": Therefore the LORD God sent him forth from the garden of Eden, to till the ground from whence he was taken. So he drove out the man; and he placed at the east of the garden of Eden Cherubim and a flaming sword which turned every way, to keep the way of the tree of life.

Exodus

. . .

In the third month, when the children of Israel were gone forth out of the land of Egypt, the same day came they into the wilderness of Sinai. For they were departed from Rephidim, and were come to the desert of Sinai, and had pitched in the wilderness; and there Israel camped before the mount. And Moses went up unto God, and the LORD called unto him out of the mountain, saying, "Thus shalt thou say to the house of Jacob, and tell the children of Israel; 'Ye have seen what I did unto the Egyptians, and how I bare you on eagles' wings, and brought you unto myself. Now therefore, if ye will obey my voice indeed, and keep my covenant, then ye shall be a peculiar treasure unto me above all people: for all the earth is mine: And ye be unto me a kingdom of priests, and an holy nation.' These are the words which thou shalt speak unto the children of Israel."

And Moses came and called for

Chapters 19; 20:1–17; 21:1–25.

the elders of the people, and laid before their faces all these words which the LORD commanded him. And all the people answered together, and said, "All that the LORD hath spoken we will do." And Moses returned the words of the people unto the LORD. And the LORD said unto Moses, "Lo, I come unto thee in a thick cloud, that the people may hear when I speak with thee, and believe thee for ever." And Moses told the words of the people unto the LORD.

And the LORD said unto Moses, "Go unto the people, and sanctify them to day and to morrow, and let them wash their clothes. And be ready against the third day: for the third day the LORD will come down in the sight of all the people upon mount Sinai. And thou shalt set bounds unto the people round about, saying 'Take heed to yourselves, that ye go not up into the mount, or touch the border of it: whosoever toucheth the mount shall be surely put to death: There shall not an hand touch it, but he shall surely be stoned, or shot through; whether it be beast or man, it shall not live: when the trumpet soundeth long, they shall come up to the mount.' "

And Moses went down from the mount unto the people, and sanctified the people; and they washed their clothes. And he said unto the people, "Be ready against the third day: come not at your wives."

And it came to pass on the third day in the morning, that there were thunders and lightnings, and a thick cloud upon the mount, and the voice of the trumpet exceeding loud; so that all the people that was in the camp trembled. And Moses brought forth the people out of the camp to meet with God; and they stood at the nether part of the mount. And mount Sinai was altogether on a smoke, because the LORD descended upon it in fire: and the smoke thereof ascended as the smoke of a furnace, and the whole mount quaked greatly. And when the voice of the trumpet sounded long, and waxed louder and louder, Moses spake and God answered him by a voice. And the LORD came down upon the mount Sinai, on the top of the mount: and the LORD called Moses up to the top of the mount; and Moses went up. And the LORD said unto Moses, "Go down, charge the people, lest they break through unto the LORD to gaze, and many of them perish. Let the priests also, which come near to the LORD sanctify themselves, lest the LORD break forth upon them." And Moses said unto the LORD, "The people cannot come up to mount Sinai: for thou chargest us, saying, 'Set bounds about the mount, and sanctify it.' " And the LORD said unto him, "Away, get thee down, and thou shalt come up, thou, and Aaron with thee: but let not the priests and the people break through to come up unto the LORD, lest he break forth upon them." So Moses went down unto the people, and spake unto them.

And God spake all these words, saying, "I am the LORD thy God, which have brought thee out of the land of Egypt, out of the house of bondage. Thou shalt have no other gods before me. Thou shall not make unto thee any graven image, or any likeness of any thing that is in heaven above, or that is in the earth beneath, or that is in the water under the earth. Thou shalt not bow down thyself to them, nor serve them: for I the LORD thy God am a jealous God, visiting the iniquity of the fathers upon the children unto the third and fourth generation of them that hate me: And shewing mercy unto thousands of them that love me, and keep my commandments. Thou shalt not take the name of the LORD thy God in vain; for the LORD will not hold him guiltless that taketh his name in vain. Remember the sabbath day, to keep it holy. Six days shalt thou labour, and do all thy work: But the seventh day is the sabbath of the LORD thy God; in it thou shalt not do any work, thou, nor thy son, nor thy daughter, thy manservant, nor thy maidservant, nor thy cattle, nor the stranger that is within thy gates. For in six days the LORD made heaven and earth, the sea, and all that in them is, and rested the seventh day: wherefore the LORD blessed the sabbath day, and hallowed it. Honour thy father and thy mother: that thy days may be long upon the land which the LORD thy God giveth thee. Thou shalt not kill. Thou shalt not commit adultery. Thou shalt not steal. Thou shalt not bear false witness against thy neighbour. Thou shalt not covet thy neighbour's house, thou shalt not covet thy neighbour's wife, nor his manservant, nor his maidservant, nor his ox, nor his ass, nor any thing that is thy neighbour's.

· · ·

"Now these are the judgments which thou shalt set before them.

"If thou buy an Hebrew servant, six years he shall serve: and in the seventh he shall go out free for nothing. If he came in by himself, he shall go out by himself: if he were married, then his wife shall go out with him. If his master have given him a wife, and she have borne him sons or daughters; the wife and her children shall be her master's, and he shall go out by himself. And if the servant shall plainly say, 'I love my master, my wife, and my children; I will not go out free': Then his master shall bring him unto the judges; he shall also bring him to the door, or unto the door post; and his master shall bore his ear through with an awl; and he shall serve him for ever.

"And if a man sell his daughter to be a maidservant, she shall not go out as the menservants do. If she please not her master, who hath betrothed her to himself, then shall he let her be redeemed: to sell her unto a strange nation he shall have no power, seeing he hath dealt deceitfully with her. And if he have betrothed her unto his son, he shall deal with her after the manner of daughters. If he take him another wife; her food, her raiment, and her duty of marriage, shall he not diminish. And if he do not these three unto her, then shall she go out free without money.

"He that smiteth a man so that he die, shall be surely put to death. And if a man lie not in wait, but God deliver him into his hand; then I will appoint thee a place whither he shall flee. But if a man come presumptuously upon his neighbour to slay him with guile; thou shalt take him from mine altar, that he may die.

"And he that smiteth his father, or his mother, shall be surely put to death.

"And he that stealeth a man, and

selleth him, or if he be found in his hand, he shall surely be put to death.

"And he that curseth his father, or his mother, shall surely be put to death.

"And if men strive together, and one smite another with a stone, or with his fist, and he die not, but keepeth his bed: If he rise again, and walk abroad upon his staff, then shall he that smote him be quit: only he shall pay for the loss of his time, and shall cause him to be thoroughly healed.

"And if a man smite his servant, or his maid, with a rod, and he die under his hand; he shall be surely punished. Notwithstanding, if he continue a day or two, he shall not be punished: for he is his money.

"If men strive, and hurt a woman with child, so that her fruit depart from her, and yet no mischief follow: he shall be surely punished, according as the woman's husband will lay upon him; and he shall pay as the judges determine. And if any mischief follow, then thou shalt give life for life. Eye for eye, tooth for tooth, hand for hand, foot for foot. Burning for burning, wound for wound, stripe for stripe."

The First Book of the Kings

.   .   .

And it came to pass after many days, that the word of the LORD came to Elijah in the third year, saying, "Go, shew thyself unto Ahab; and I will send rain upon the earth." And Elijah went to shew himself unto Ahab. And there was a sore famine in Samaria. And Ahab called Obadiah, which was the governor of his house. (Now Obadiah feared the LORD greatly: For it was so, when Jezebel cut off the prophets of the LORD, that Obadiah took an hundred prophets, and hid them by fifty in a cave, and fed them with bread and water.) And Ahab said unto Obadiah, "Go into the land, unto all fountains of water, and unto all brooks: peradventure we may find grass to save the horses and mules alive, that we lose not all the beasts." So they divided the land between them to pass throughout it: Ahab went one way by himself, and Obadiah went another way by himself.

And as Obadiah was in the way, behold, Elijah met him: and he knew him, and fell on his face, and said, "Art thou that my lord Elijah?" And he answered him, "I am: go, tell thy lord, 'Behold, Elijah is here.'" And he said, "What have I sinned, that thou wouldest deliver thy servant into the hand of Ahab, to slay me? As the LORD thy God liveth, there is no nation or kingdom, whither my lord hath not sent to seek thee: and when they said, 'He is not there'; he took an oath of the kingdom and nation, that they found thee not. And now thou sayest, 'Go, tell thy lord, "Behold, Eli-

Chapter 18:1–45.

jah is here." ' And it shall come to pass, as soon as I am gone from thee, that the spirit of the LORD shall carry thee whither I know not; and so when I come and tell Ahab, and he cannot find thee, he shall slay me: but I thy servant fear the LORD from my youth. Was it not told my lord what I did when Jezebel slew the prophets of the LORD, how I hid an hundred men of the LORD's prophets by fifty in a cave, and fed them with bread and water? And now thou sayest, 'Go, tell thy lord, "Behold, Elijah is here" '; and he shall slay me."

And Elijah said, "As the LORD of hosts liveth, before whom I stand, I will surely shew myself unto him to day." So Obadiah went to meet Ahab, and told him: and Ahab went to meet Elijah.

And it came to pass, when Ahab saw Elijah, that Ahab said unto him, "Art thou he that troubleth Israel?" And he answered, "I have not troubled Israel; but thou, and thy father's house, in that ye have forsaken the commandments of the LORD, and thou hast followed Baalim. Now therefore send, and gather to me all Israel unto mount Carmel, and the prophets of Baal four hundred and fifty, and the prophets of the groves four hundred, which eat at Jezebel's table."

So Ahab sent unto all the children of Israel, and gathered the prophets together unto mount Carmel. And Elijah came unto all the people, and said, "How long halt ye between two opinions? If the LORD be God, follow him; but if Baal, then follow him." And the people answered him not a word. Then said Elijah unto the people, "I, even I only, remain a prophet of the LORD; but Baal's prophets are four hundred and fifty men. Let them therefore give us two bullocks; and let them choose one bullock for themselves, and cut it in pieces, and lay it on wood, and put no fire under: and I will dress the other bullock, and lay it on wood, and put no fire under: And call ye on the name of your gods, and I will call on the name of the LORD: and the God that answereth by fire, let him be God." And all the people answered and said, "It is well spoken."

And Elijah said unto the prophets of Baal, "Choose you one bullock for yourselves, and dress it first; for ye are many; and call on the name of your gods, but put no fire under." And they took the bullock which was given them, and they dressed it, and called on the name of Baal from morning even until noon, saying, "O Baal, hear us." But there was no voice, nor any that answered. And they leaped upon the altar which was made. And it came to pass at noon, that Elijah mocked them, and said, "Cry aloud: for he is a god; either he is talking, or he is pursuing, or he is in a journey, or peradventure he sleepeth, and must be awaked." And they cried aloud, and cut themselves after their manner with knives and lancets, till the blood gushed out upon them. And it came to pass, when midday was past, and they prophesied until the time of the offering of the evening sacrifice, that there was neither voice, nor any to answer, nor any that regarded.

And Elijah said unto all the people, "Come near unto me." And all the people came near unto him. And he repaired the altar of the LORD that was broken down. And Elijah took twelve stones, according to the number of the tribes of the sons of Jacob, unto whom the word of the LORD came, saying, "Israel shall be thy name": And with the stones he built an altar in the name of the LORD: and he made a trench about the altar, as great as would contain two measures of seed. And he put the wood in order, and cut the bullock in pieces, and laid him on the wood, and said, "Fill four barrels with water, and pour it on the burnt sacrifice, and on the wood." And he said, "Do it the second time." And they did it the second time. And he said, "Do it the third time." And they did it the third time. And the water ran round about the altar; and he filled the trench also with water. And it came to pass at the time of the offering of the evening sacrifice, that Elijah the prophet came near, and said, "LORD God of Abraham, Issac, and of Israel, let it be known this day that thou art God in Israel, and that I am thy servant, and that I have done all these things at thy word. Hear me, O LORD, hear me, that this people may know that thou art the LORD God, and that thou hast turned their heart back again."

Then the fire of the LORD fell, and consumed the burnt sacrifice, and the wood, and the stones, and the dust, and licked up the water that was in the trench. And when all the people saw it, they fell on their faces: and they said, "The LORD, he is the God; the LORD, he is the God." And Elijah said unto them, "Take the prophets of Baal; let not one of them escape." And they took them: and Elijah brought them down to the brook Kishon, and slew them there.

And Elijah said unto Ahab, "Get thee up, eat and drink; for there is a sound of abundance of rain." So Ahab went up to eat and to drink. And Elijah went up to the top of Carmel; and he cast himself down upon the earth, and put his face between his knees. And said to his servant, "Go up now, look toward the sea." And he went up and looked, and said, "There is nothing." And he said, "Go again seven more times." And it came to pass at the seventh time, that he said, "Behold there ariseth a little cloud, out of the sea, like a man's hand." And he said, "Go up, say unto Ahab, 'Prepare thy chariot, and get thee down, that the rain stop thee not.' " And it came to pass in the mean while, that the heaven was black with clouds and wind, and there was a great rain.

Isaiah

. . .

"Yet now hear, O Jacob my servant; and Israel, whom I have chosen: Thus saith the LORD that made thee, and formed thee from the womb, which will help thee; 'Fear not, O Jacob, my servant; and thou, Jesurun, whom I have chosen. For I will pour water upon him that is thirsty, and floods upon the dry ground: I will pour my spirit upon thy seed, and my blessing upon thine offspring: And they shall spring up as among the grass, as willows by the water courses. One shall say, "I am the LORD's"; and another shall call himself by the name of Jacob; and another shall subscribe with his hand unto the LORD, and surname himself by the name of Israel.' Thus saith the LORD the King of Israel, and his redeemer the LORD of hosts; 'I am the first, and I am the last; and beside me there is no God. And who, as I, shall call, and shall declare it, and set it in order for me, since I appointed the ancient people? And the things that are coming, and shall come, let them shew unto them. Fear ye not, neither be afraid: have not I told thee from that time, and have declared it? ye are even my witnesses. Is there a God beside me? Yea, there is no God; I know not any.

'They that make a graven image are all of them vanity; and their delectable things shall not profit; and they are their own witnesses; they see not, nor know; that they may be ashamed. Who hath formed a god, or molten a graven image that is profitable for nothing? Behold, all his fellows shall be ashamed: and the workmen, they are of men: let them all be gathered together, let them stand up; yet they shall fear, and they shall be ashamed together. The smith with the tongs both worketh in the coals, and fashioneth it with hammers, and worketh it with the strength of his arms: yea, he is hungry, and his strength faileth: he drinketh no water, and is faint. The carpenter stretcheth out his rule; he marketh it out with a line; he fitteth it with planes, and he marketh it out with the compass, and maketh it after the figure of a man, according to the beauty of a man; that it may remain in the house. He heweth him down cedars, and taketh the cypress and the oak, which he strengtheneth for himself among the trees of the forest: he planteth an ash, and the rain doth nourish it. Then shall it be for a man to burn: for he will take thereof, and warm himself; yea, he kindleth it and baketh bread; yea, he maketh a god, and worshippeth it; he make it a graven image, and falleth down thereto. He burneth part thereof in the fire; with part thereof he eateth flesh; he roasteth roast, and is satisfied: yea, he warmeth himself, and saith "Aha, I am

Chapters 44:1–19; 45:5–25.

warm, I have seen the fire." And the residue thereof he maketh a god, even his graven image: he falleth down unto it, and worshippeth it, and prayeth unto it, and saith, "Deliver me; for thou art my god." They have not known or understood: for he hath shut their eyes, that they cannot see; and their hearts, that they cannot understand. And none considereth in his heart, neither is there knowledge nor understanding to say, "I have burned part of it in the fire; yea, also I have baked bread upon the coals thereof; I have roasted flesh, and eaten it: and shall I make the residue thereof an abomination? shall I fall down to the stock of a tree?"

. . .

'I am the LORD, and there is none else, there is no God beside me: I girded thee, though thou hast not known me: That they may know from the rising of the sun, and from the west, that there is none beside me. I am the LORD, and there is none else. I form the light, and create darkness: I make peace, and create evil: I the LORD do all these things. Drop down, ye heavens, from above, and let the skies pour down righteousness: let the earth open, and let them bring forth salvation, and let righteousness spring up together: I the LORD have created it. Woe unto him that striveth with his Maker! Let the potsherd strive with the potsherds of the earth. Shall the clay say to him that fashioneth it, "What makest thou?" or thy work, "He hath no hands?" Woe unto him that saith unto his father, "What begettest thou?" or to the woman, "What hast thou brought forth?" '

"Thus saith the LORD, the Holy One of Israel, and his Maker, 'Ask me of things to come concerning my sons, and concerning the work of my hands command ye me. I have made the earth, and created man upon it: I, even my hands, have stretched out the heavens, and all their host have I commanded. I have raised him up in righteousness, and I will direct all his ways: he shall build my city, and he shall let go my captives, not for price nor reward,' saith the LORD of hosts.

"Thus saith the LORD, 'The labour of Egypt, and merchandise of Ethiopia and of the Sabeans, men of stature, shall come over unto thee, and they shall be thine: they shall come after thee; in chains they shall come over, and they shall fall down unto thee, they shall make supplication unto thee, saying, "Surely God is in thee; and there is none else, there is no God. Verily thou art a God that hidest thyself, O God of Israel, the Saviour." They shall be ashamed, and also confounded, all of them they shall go to confusion together that are makers of idols. But Israel shall be saved in the LORD with an everlasting salvation: ye shall not be ashamed nor confounded world without end.' For thus saith the LORD that created the heavens; God himself that formed the earth and made it; he hath established it, he created it not in vain, he formed it to be inhabited: 'I am the LORD: and there is none else. I have not spoken in secret, in a dark place of the earth: I said not unto the seed of Jacob, "Seek ye me in vain": I the LORD speak righteousness, I declare things that are right.

'Assemble yourselves and come; draw near together, ye that are escaped of the nations: they have no knowledge that set up the wood of their graven image, and pray unto a god that cannot save. Tell ye, and bring them near; yea, let them take counsel together; who hath declared this from ancient time? Who hath told it from that time? Have not I the LORD? And there is no God else beside me; a just God and a Saviour; there is none beside me. Look unto me, and be ye saved, all the ends of the earth: for I am God, and there is none else. I have sworn by myself, the word is gone out of my mouth in righteousness, and shall not return, that unto me every knee shall bow, every tongue shall swear. "Surely," shall one say, "in the LORD have I righteousness and strength": even to him shall men come; and all that are incensed against him shall be ashamed. In the LORD shall all the seed of Israel be justified, and shall glory.' "

Ezekiel

· · ·

The word of the LORD came unto me again, saying, "What mean ye, that ye use this proverb concerning the land of Israel, saying, 'The fathers have eaten sour grapes, and the children's teeth are set on edge'?"

"As I live," saith the LORD God, "ye shall not have occasion any more to use this proverb in Israel. Behold, all souls are mine; as the soul of the father, so also the soul of the son is mine: the soul that sinneth, it shall die. But if a man be just, and do that which is lawful and right, and hath not eaten upon the mountains, neither hath lifted up his eyes to the idols of the house of Israel, neither hath defiled his neighbour's wife, neither hath come near to a menstruous woman, and hath not oppressed any, but hath restored to the debtor his pledge, hath spoiled none by violence, hath given his bread to the hungry, and hath covered the naked with a garment; he that hath not given forth upon usury, neither hath taken any increase, that hath withdrawn his hand from iniquity, hath executed true judgment between man and man, hath walked in my statutes, and hath kept my judgments, to deal truly; he is just, he shall surely live," saith the LORD God.

"If he beget a son that is a robber, a shedder of blood, and that doeth the like to any one of these things, and that doeth not any of those duties, but even hath eaten upon the mountains, and defiled his neighbour's wife, hath oppressed the poor and needy, hath spoiled by violence, hath not restored the pledge, and hath lifted up his eyes to the idols, hath committed abomination, hath given forth upon usury,

Chapter 18.

and hath taken increase; shall he then live? He shall not live: he hath done all these abominations; he shall surely die; his blood shall be upon him.

"Now, lo, if he beget a son, that seeth all his father's sins which he hath done, and considereth, and doeth not such like, that hath not eaten upon the mountains, neither hath lifted up his eyes to the idols of the house of Israel, hath not defiled his neighbour's wife, neither hath oppressed any, hath not withholden the pledge, neither hath spoiled by violence, but hath given his bread to the hungry, and hath covered the naked with a garment, that hath taken off his hand from the poor, that hath not received usury nor increase, hath executed my judgments, hath walked in my statutes; he shall not die for the iniquity of his father, he shall surely live. As for his father, because he cruelly oppressed, spoiled his brother by violence, and did that which is not good among his people, lo, even he shall die in his iniquity.

"Yet say ye, 'Why? doth not the son bear the iniquity of the father?' When the son hath done that which is lawful and right, and hath kept all my statutes, and hath done them, he shall surely live. The soul that sinneth, it shall die. The son shall not bear the iniquity of the father, neither shall the father bear the iniquity of the son: the righteousness of the righteous shall be upon him, and the wickedness of the wicked shall be upon him. But if the wicked will turn from all his sins that he hath committed, and keep all my statutes, and do that which is lawful and right he shall surely live, he

shall not die. All his transgressions that he hath committed, they shall not be mentioned unto him: in his righteousness that he hath done he shall live.

"Have I any pleasure at all that the wicked should die?" saith the LORD God: "and not that he should return from his ways, and live? But when the righteous turneth away from his righteousness, and committeth iniquity, and doeth according to all the abominations that the wicked man doeth, shall he live? All his righteousness that he hath done shall not be mentioned: in his trespass that he hath trespassed, and in his sin that he hath sinned, in them shall he die.

"Yet ye say, 'The way of the LORD is not equal.' Hear now, O house of Israel; Is not my way equal? Are not your ways unequal? When a righteous man turneth away from his righteousness, and committeth iniquity, and dieth in them; for his iniquity that he hath done shall he die. Again, when the wicked man turneth away from his wickedness that he hath committed, and doeth that which is lawful and right, he shall save his soul alive. Because he considereth, and turneth away from all his transgressions that he hath committed, he shall surely live, he shall not die. Yet saith the house of Israel, 'The way of the Lord is not equal,' O house of Israel are not my ways equal? Are not your ways unequal? Therefore I will judge you, O house of Israel, every one according to his ways," saith the LORD God. "Repent, and turn yourselves from all your transgressions; so iniquity shall not be your ruin. Cast away from you all your transgressions; whereby ye have transgressed; and make you a new heart and a new spirit: for why will ye die, O house of Israel? For I have no pleasure in the death of him that dieth," saith the LORD God: "wherefore turn yourselves, and live ye."

The Book of Job

There was a man in the land of Uz, whose name was Job; and that man was perfect and upright, and one that feared God, and eschewed evil. And there were born unto him seven sons and three daughters. His substance also was seven thousand sheep, and three thousand camels, and five hundred yoke of oxen, and five hundred she asses, and a very great household; so that this man was the greatest of all the men of the east. And his sons went and feasted in their houses, every one his day; and sent and called for their three sisters to eat and to drink with them. And it was so, when the days of their feasting were gone about, that Job sent and sanctified them, and rose up early in the morning, and offered burnt offerings according to the number of them all: for Job said, "It may be that my sons have sinned, and cursed God in their hearts." Thus did Job continually.

Now there was a day when the sons of God came to present themselves before the LORD, and Satan came also among them. And the LORD said unto Satan, "Whence comest thou?" Then Satan answered the LORD, and said, "From going to and fro in the earth, and from walking up and down in it." And the LORD said unto Satan, "Hast thou considered my servant Job, that there is none like him in the earth, a perfect and an upright man, one that feareth God, and escheweth evil?" Then Satan answered the LORD, and said, "Doth Job fear God for nought? Hast not thou made an hedge about him, and about his house, and about all that he hath on every side? Thou hast blessed the work of his hands, and his substance is increased in the land. But put forth thine hand now, and touch all that he hath and he will curse thee to thy face." And the LORD said unto Satan, "Behold, all that he hath is in thy power; only upon himself put not forth thine hand." So Satan went forth from the presence of the LORD.

And there was a day when his sons and his daughters were eating and drinking wine in their eldest brother's house. And there came a messenger unto Job, and said, "The oxen are plowing, and the asses feeding beside them: And the Sabeans fell upon them, and took them away; yea, they have slain the servants with the edge of the sword; and I only am escaped alone to tell thee." While he was yet speaking, there came also another, and said, "The fire of God is fallen from

Chapters 1; 2:1–10; 10; 21:7–15; 23:2–12; 38; 40:1–14; 42:1–6, 10–17.

heaven, and hath burned up the sheep, and the servants, and consumed them; and I only escaped alone to tell thee." While he was yet speaking, there came also another, and said, "The Chaldeans made out three bands, and fell upon the camels, and have carried them away, yea, and slain the servants with the edge of the sword; and I only am escaped alone to tell thee." While he was yet speaking, there came also another, and said, "Thy sons and thy daughters were eating and drinking wine in their eldest brother's house: And, behold, there came a great wind from the wilderness, and smote the four corners of the house, and it fell upon the young men, and they are dead; and I only am escaped alone to tell thee." Then Job arose, and rent his mantle, and shaved his head, and fell down upon the ground, and worshipped. And said, "Naked came I out of my mother's womb, and naked shall I return thither: the LORD gave, and the LORD hath taken away; blessed be the name of the LORD." In all this Job sinned not, nor charged God foolishly.

Again there was a day when the sons of God came to present themselves before the LORD, and Satan came also among them to present himself before the LORD. And the LORD said unto Satan, "From whence comest thou?" And Satan answered the LORD, and said, "From going to and fro in the earth, and from walking up and down in it." And the LORD said unto Satan, "Hath thou considered my servant Job, that there is none like him in the earth, a perfect and an upright man, one that feareth God, and escheweth evil? And still he holdeth

fast his integrity, although thou movedst me against him, to destroy him without cause." And Satan answered the LORD, and said, "Skin for skin, yea, all that a man hath will he give for his life. But put forth thine hand now, and touch his bone and his flesh, and he will curse thee to thy face." And the LORD said unto Satan, "Behold, he is in thine hand; but save his life."

So went Satan forth from the presence of the LORD, and smote Job with sore boils from the sole of his foot unto his crown. And he took him a potsherd to scrape himself withal; and he sat down among the ashes.

Then said his wife unto him, "Dost thou still retain thine integrity? Curse God, and die." But he said unto her, "Thou speakest as one of the foolish women speaketh. What? shall we receive good at the hand of God, and shall we not receive evil?" In all this did not Job sin with his lips.

· · ·

[*And Job spake, and said,*] "My soul is weary of my life; I will leave my complaint upon myself; I will speak in the bitterness of my soul. I will say unto God, 'Do not condemn me; shew me wherefore thou contendest with me. Is it good unto thee that thou shouldest oppress, that thou shouldest despise the work of thine hands, and shine upon the counsel of the wicked? Hast thou eyes of flesh? or seest thou as man seeth? Are thy days as the days of man? Are thy years as man's days, that thou enquirest after mine iniquity, and searchest after my sin? Thou knowest that I am not wicked; and there is none that can deliver out of thine hand. Thine hands have made me and fashioned me together round about; yet thou dost destroy me. Remember, I beseech thee, that thou hast made me as the clay; and wilt thou bring me into dust again? Hast thou not poured me out as milk, and curdled me like cheese? Thou hast clothed me with skin and flesh, and hast fenced me with bones and sinews. Thou hast granted me life and favour, and thy visitation hath preserved my spirit. And these things hast thou hid in thine heart; I know that this is with thee.

'If I sin, then thou markest me, and thou wilt not acquit me from mine iniquity. If I be wicked, woe unto me; and if I be righteous, yet will I not lift up my head. I am full of confusion; therefore see thou mine affliction; for it increaseth. Thou huntest me as a fierce lion: and again thou shewest thyself marvellous upon me. Thou renewest thy witnesses against me, and increasest thine indignation upon me; changes and war are against me. Wherefore then hast thou brought me forth out of the womb? Oh that I had given up the ghost, and no eye had seen me! I should have been as though I had not been; I should have been carried from the womb to the grave. Are not my days few? Cease then, and let me alone, that I may take comfort a little, before I go whence I shall not return, even to the land of darkness and the shadow of death; a land of darkness, as darkness itself; and of the shadow of death, without any order, and where the light is as darkness.'

• • •

"Wherefore do the wicked live, become old, yea, are mighty in power? Their seed is established in their sight with them, and their offspring before their eyes. Their houses are safe from fear, neither is the rod of God upon them. Their bull gendereth, and faileth not; their cow calveth, and casteth not her calf. They send forth their little ones like a flock, and their children dance. They take the timbrel and harp, and rejoice at the sound of the organ. They spend their days in wealth, and in a moment go down to the grave. Therefore they say unto God, 'Depart from us; for we desire not the knowledge of thy ways. What is the Almighty, that we should serve him? And what profit should we have, if we pray unto him?'

• • •

"Even to day is my complaint bitter: my stroke is heavier than my groaning. Oh that I knew where I might find him! that I might come even to his seat! I would order my cause before him, and fill my mouth with arguments. I would know the words which he would answer me, and understand what he would say unto me. Will he plead against me with his great power? No; but he would put strength in me. There the righteous might dispute with him; so should I be delivered for ever from my judge. Behold, I go forward, but he is not there; and backward, but I cannot perceive him: On the left hand, where he doth work, but I cannot behold him: he hideth himself on the right hand, that I cannot see him. But he knoweth the way that I take: when he hath tried me, I shall come forth as gold. My foot hath held his steps, his way have I kept, and not declined. Neither have I gone back from the commandment of his lips; I have esteemed the words of his mouth more than my necessary food."

. . .

Then the LORD answered Job out of the whirlwind, and said, "Who is this that darkeneth counsel by words without knowledge? Gird up now thy loins like a man; for I will demand of thee, and answer thou me. Where wast thou when I laid the foundations of the earth? Declare, if thou hast understanding. Who hath laid the measures thereof, if thou knowest? Or who hath stretched the line upon it? Whereupon are the foundations thereof fastened? Or who laid the corner stone thereof; when the morning stars sang together, and all the sons of God shouted for joy? Or who shut up the sea with doors, when it brake forth, as if it had issued out of the womb? When I made the cloud the garment thereof, and thick darkness a swaddling band for it, and brake up for it my decreed place, and set bars and doors, and said, 'Hitherto shalt thou come, but no further: and here shall thy proud waves be stayed'? Hast thou commanded the morning since thy days; and caused the dayspring to know his place; that it might take hold of the ends of the earth, that the wicked might be shaken out of it? It is turned as clay to the seal; and they stand as a garment. And from the wicked their light is withholden, and the high arm shall be broken. Hast thou entered into the springs of the sea? Or hast thou walked in the search of the depth? Have the gates of death been opened unto thee? Or hast thou seen the

doors of the shadow of death? Hast thou perceived the breadth of the earth? Declare if thou knowest it all.

"Where is the way where light dwelleth? And as for darkness, where is the place thereof, that thou shouldest take it to the bound thereof, and that thou shouldest know the paths to the house thereof? Knowest thou it, because thou wast then born? Or because the number of thy days is great? Hast thou entered into the treasures of the snow? Or hast thou seen the treasures of the hail, which I have reserved against the time of trouble, against the day of battle and war? By what way is the light parted, which scattereth the east wind upon the earth? Who hath divided a watercourse for the overflowing of waters, or a way for the lightning or thunder; to cause it to rain on the earth, where no man is; on the Wilderness, wherein there is no man; to satisfy the desolate and waste ground; and to cause the bud of the tender herb to spring forth? Hath the rain a father? Or who hath begotten the drops of dew? Out of whose womb came the ice? And the hoary frost of heaven, who hath gendered it? The waters are hid as with a stone, and the face of the deep is frozen.

"Canst thou bind the sweet influences of Pleiades, or loose the bonds of Orion? Canst thou bring forth Massaroth in his season? Or canst thou guide Arcturus with his sons? Knowest thou the ordinances of heaven? Canst thou set the dominion thereof in the earth? Canst thou lift up thy voice to the clouds, that abundance of waters may cover thee? Canst thou send lightnings, that they may go, and say unto thee,

'Here we are'? Who hath put wisdom in the inward parts? Or who hath given understanding to the heart? Who can number the clouds in wisdom? Or who can stay the bottles of heaven, when the dust groweth into hardness, and the clods cleave fast together? Wilt thou hunt the prey for the lion? Or fill the appetite of the young lions, when they couch in their dens, and abide in the covert to lie in wait? Who provideth for the raven his food? When his young ones cry unto God, they wander for lack of meat."

· · ·

Moreover the LORD answered Job, and said, "Shall he that contendeth with the Almighty instruct him? He that reproveth God, let him answer it."

Then Job answered the LORD, and said, "Behold, I am vile; what shall I answer thee? I will lay mine hand upon my mouth. Once have I spoken; but I will not answer: yea, twice; but I will proceed no further."

Then answered the LORD unto Job out of the whirlwind, and said, "Gird up thy loins now like a man: I will demand of thee, and declare thou unto me. Wilt thou also disannul my judgment? Wilt thou condemn me, that thou mayest be righteous? Hast thou an arm like God? Or canst thou thunder with a voice like him? Deck thyself now with majesty and excellency; and array thyself with glory and beauty. Cast abroad the rage of thy wrath: and behold every one that is proud, and abase him. Look on every one that is proud, and bring him low; and tread down the wicked in their place. Hide them in the dust together; and bind their faces in secret. Then will

I also confess unto thee that thine own right hand can save thee."

· · ·

Then Job answered the LORD, and said, "I know that thou canst do every thing, and that no thought can be witholden from thee. Who is he that hideth counsel without knowledge? Therefore have I uttered that I understood not; things too wonderful for me, which I knew not. Hear, I beseech thee, and I will speak: I will demand of thee, and declare thou unto me. I have heard of thee by the hearing of the ear: but now mine eye seeth thee. Wherefore I abhor myself, and repent in dust and ashes."

· · ·

And the LORD turned the captivity of Job, when he prayed for his friends: also the LORD gave Job twice as much as he had before. Then came there unto him all his brethren, and all his sisters, and all they that had been of his acquaintance before, and did eat bread with him in his house: and they bemoaned him, and comforted him over all the evil that the LORD had brought upon him: every man also gave him a piece of money, and every one an earring of gold. So the LORD blessed the latter end of Job more than his beginning: for he had fourteen thousand sheep, and six thousand camels, and a thousand yoke of oxen, and a thousand she asses. He had also seven sons and three daughters. And he called the name of the first, Jemima; and the name of the second, Kezia; and the name of the third, Kerenhappuch. And in all the land were no women found so fair as the daughters of Job: and their father gave them inheritance among their brethren. After this lived Job an hundred and forty years, and saw his sons, and his son's sons, even four generations. So Job died, being old and full of days.

The death of Socrates. (*Culver Pictures, Inc.*)

Greece

The naval engagement fought between the Greeks and Persians off the island of Salamis in 480 B.C. must be ranked as one of the truly decisive battles of Western history. For at Salamis the Greeks, following up their victory at Marathon ten years earlier, succeeded in halting the imperial march of Xerxes to the west and hence in gaining a century and a half of security from foreign conquest. This relatively brief respite was brought to a close by the armies of Philip of Macedon and his son, Alexander the Great, in the latter part of the fourth century. But while it lasted, the Greeks perfected a civilization whose achievements still stand as objects of admiration and inspiration for the Western world.

The center of classical Greek civilization was the *polis,* or city-state. Ancient Greece was divided into hundreds of *poleis,* each a tiny unit politically independent and culturally unique. Athens, for example, one of the largest of the *poleis,* had a total population of just over 300 thousand and an area roughly equal that of Rhode Island. The forms of government varied widely from *polis* to *polis,* and even within the same *polis* at different times.

By far the most important form—at least as far as later Western history is concerned—was the Athenian democracy, particularly as it appeared in the Age of Pericles during the fifth century B.C. Although the Athenians shared with us the belief that democratic government means rule by the people, their democracy differed from ours in one important respect: Because of the very size and complexity of the nation in which we live, we must exercise our sovereignty through representatives, but in Athens the people could rule directly. Every adult male citizen was a member of the Assembly, the sole legislative body of the city-state. From the ranks of the Assembly a Council of Five Hundred was chosen annually to supervise the administrative affairs of the *polis.* From the Council, in turn, an executive committee of fifty was chosen to conduct the day-to-day business of administration for a term lasting one-tenth of a year. One member of this committee was then chosen as chairman for each twenty-four-hour period. Since all these selections were made by lot, any citizen of the *polis* might be called on to serve as the chief administrative officer of Athens for a day.

But for the average Greek the *polis* was more than just the political unit within which he happened to live. It was also the center of his social, intellectual, aesthetic, and religious life. Aristotle, in the beginning of his work on political theory, the *Politics,* takes a typically Greek attitude toward the *polis* in the statement which is usually translated, "Man is a political animal," but which in the original Greek reads, "Man is by nature an animal intended to live in a *polis*." Here Aristotle is implying that only within the *polis* can one live a truly human life. The philosopher Socrates expresses a similar feeling toward the *polis*. Though unjustly condemned to death by an Athenian court, he rejected a chance to escape from prison, insisting that, because he owed his very being to his *polis*, he must accept whatever Athens decreed for him, even execution.

Some scholars have been convinced that Athens in the fifth century B.C. represents the high point of Western civilization. In the words of the contemporary historian, H. D. F. Kitto, Athens "was clearly the most civilized society that has yet existed." Whether or not we accept this evaluation, it is true that today, over two thousand years later, the world still finds the accomplishments of the Athenians—in art and architecture, poetry, drama, history, political theory, science, mathematics, philosophy, and religion—a source of instruction and enjoyment.

One of the finest appreciations of Athens' achievements was made by a great Athenian leader—Pericles. The occasion was a funeral oration that he delivered in 431 B.C. just outside the city walls, to honor the Athenian soldiers who had fallen in the first year of the Peloponnesian War. For Pericles, the highest honor that could be paid to the dead was to say that they "were worthy of Athens." By Athens he referred not just to the city in which they had lived, but to the way of life that they, as Athenians, had shared. The Athenians, Pericles told his audience, are "lovers of the beautiful." The truth of Pericles' claim was self-evident; anyone listening to him could have verified it simply by turning his head and gazing back at the city itself. Had he done so he would have found the view dominated by the Acropolis, rising high above the plain and crowned with temples. In the center stood the Parthenon, completed less than a decade before Pericles delivered his oration. Dedicated to Athena, goddess of wisdom and protectress of Athens, the Parthenon embodied an ideal of beauty based on architectural symmetry or balance.

The ideal of balance so competely realized in the Parthenon was pursued in all forms of Greek art. And, outside the aesthetic realm, it was an ideal that pervaded Greek civilization. Just as the Greek experienced pleasure in a well-proportioned building, so he delighted in a well-balanced personality and tried in his life to follow the path of moderation. The life of moderation is summed up in Aristotle's famous doctrine of the Golden Mean, perhaps the most closely reasoned defense ever made of a civilization and its way of life. Behind the Greek ideal of moderation and balance stands the belief that the universe is a rational order, operating according to fixed laws. The orderliness of the universe, the Greeks argued, is good, hence order anywhere must be good, and disorder must be evil. When the Greeks translated this belief into aesthetic and moral terms, they found their ideal of beauty in the ordered symmetry of the Parthenon, and their conception of the good life in the moderation of the Golden Mean.

Because they were convinced that mankind is capable of reasoning, the Greeks concluded that we can comprehend the world in which we live. This faith—that people can understand the Universe—along with the conclusions the Greeks reached in their attempts to do so, is probably the greatest single contribution of the Greeks to Western civilization. The Greek faith in reason permeated their entire intellectual and cultural life. To take the most obvious example, it made possible their phenomenal achievements in science. Earlier civilizations in the ancient Near East had developed advanced technologies, but the Greeks were the first theoretical scientists in Western history. What set them apart from their predecessors was their ability to generalize, to see an object or event not simply in its individuality but as an instance of a universal rule or pattern. They were led to seek the general laws governing natural events—in other words, to become theoretical scientists—by their conviction that people can, by the use of their reasoning powers, discover the rational pattern of the Universe.

This tendency to generalize shows itself over and over again in Greek thought. Thucydides, in the introduction to his *History of the Peloponnesian War,* states that he is interested not just in recounting the events of the war but in revealing the general pattern of war. The Greek tragedians attempted to trace the patterns in which universal moral law revealed itself in people's lives. This emphasis on universal law in Greek tragedy led the twentieth-century philosopher A. N. Whitehead to conclude that the tragic poets must be considered the originators of scientific thought. Greek generalization reached its highest expression in Plato's Form of the Good, one of the most difficult concepts in Western thought. For Plato's belief that the Form of the Good is the heart of Reality is really a philosophical formulation of the Greek faith in the ultimate unity, rationality, and goodness of the Universe.

Yet the Greeks failed to generalize in one crucial area, that of practical politics, and it was this failure that led to their downfall. Loyalty to their own *polis* and jealousy of all the others prevented the Greeks from ever uniting to form a single nation. The unwillingness of the Greeks to cooperate in a common cause nearly led to disaster as early as the Persian Wars; for, as Herodotus makes clear, the Athenian naval commander at the battle of Salamis had to deceive his Peloponnesian allies to keep them from fleeing the enemy. The political disunity of the Greeks reached its climax a half century later, in the Peloponnesian War between Athens and Sparta. This war (431–404 B.C.) marked the turning point in the history of Greece. Though the Greeks produced much of value, particularly in science and philosophy, in later years, the great period of Greek civilization was ended by this long and costly struggle. The resources of the Greek *poleis,* of defeated Athens in particular, were dissipated, and in the fourth century the proud city-states fell easy prey to the invading Macedonians from the north. Thus ended one of the most brilliant episodes in the history of Western civilization.

Herodotus

History is the art of telling the most complicated and fascinating story ever related—the story of the human race and its past. Since history is essentially storytelling, the person who tells the story best, who is the ablest *raconteur,* is obviously the best historian. This does not mean that history is simply imaginative literature, however, for the records and the factual foundation of the past are the very warp and woof of the story. Thus, the storyteller must respect those qualities that are the essence of good historical writing: accuracy in assembling and presenting facts, right reason in analyzing the facts, and sobriety and judgment in interpreting the facts. But even the possession of these qualities will not insure that an author will write good history, for storytelling is above all else an act of communication, and an author who fails to communicate fails to tell the story. History is written to be read, and the best historian is the one who tells his tale with wit and imagination, using every literary device at his command to carry the reader along on the stream of his narrative.

The first historian to measure up to these demanding standards was Herodotus (484–c.424 B.C.), a citizen of the Greek city-state of Halicarnassus in Asia Minor. In the latter part of the fifth century B.C.

Herodotus undertook to record the history of the wars between the city-states of Greece and the great Persian Empire. His purpose, he tells us, was to preserve the memory of the great events that had occurred during the wars and of the heroic deeds that had been performed on both sides. He skillfully unfolded his tale in nine books, each named for one of the nine muses of Greek mythology. Herodotus was the first writer to go beyond the simple ticking-off of events in chronological sequence. He analyzed motives and searched for relationships between events, trying to generalize and to work out a broad pattern into which individual happenings could be fitted. For this reason he is often called "the father of history."

Occasionally, Herodotus is criticized for being naive or overcredulous, or even because he knew no language other than Greek. No matter how valid these criticisms may be, Herodotus did try to verify his accounts through logic and documentation, accepting or rejecting what was told him according to the lights of reason and credibility.

The following selections are from the first and eighth books of the *History of the Persian Wars.* The first is the general introduction from Book I, entitled "Clio" (after the muse of History); the second—

taken from Book VIII, entitled "Urania" (after the muse of Astronomy) —is a vivid account of the Battle of Salamis, fought between the Greek and Persian navies in 480 B.C.

The History of Herodotus

THE FIRST BOOK, ENTITLED "CLIO"

These are the researches of Herodotus of Halicarnassus, which he publishes, in the hope of thereby preserving from decay the remembrance of what men have done, and of preventing the great and wonderful actions of the Greeks and the Barbarians from losing their due meed of glory; and withal to put on record what were their grounds of feud.

. . .

THE EIGHTH BOOK, ENTITLED "URANIA"

[*The Greeks are facing a combined land–sea invasion by the Persians under Xerxes. The selection begins with a council of war attended by the naval leaders of the Greek* poleis *and their allies, who are attempting to decide how best to repel the invaders.*—Ed.]

When the captains from these various nations were come together at Salamis, a council of war was summoned and Eurybiades proposed that any one who liked to advise, should say which place seemed to him the fittest, amongst those still in the possession of the Greeks, to be the scene of a naval combat. Attica, he said, was not to be thought of now; but he desired their counsel as to the remainder. The speakers mostly advised, that the fleet should sail away to the Isthmus, and there give battle in defense of the Peloponnese; and they urged as a reason for this, that if they were worsted in a sea-fight at Salamis, they would be shut up in an island, where they could get no help; but if they were beaten near the Isthmus, they could escape to their homes.

As the captains from the Peloponnese were thus advising, there came an Athenian to the camp, who brought word that the Barbarians had entered Attica, and were ravaging and burning everything. For the division of the army under Xerxes was just arrived at Athens from its march through Boeotia, where it had burnt Thespiae and Plataea—both which cities were forsaken by their inhabitants, who had fled to the Peloponnese—and now it was laying waste all the possessions of the Athenians. Thespiae and Plataea had been burnt by the Persians, because they knew from the Thebans that neither of those cities had espoused their side.

Since the passage of the Hellespont and the commencement of the march upon Greece, a space of four months had gone by; one while the army made the crossing, and de-

The History of Herodotus, trans. G. Rawlinson (London, 1858).

layed about the region of the Hellespont; and three while they proceeded thence to Attica, which they entered in the archonship of Calliades. They found the city forsaken; a few people only remained in the temple, either keepers of the treasures, or men of the poorer sort. These persons having fortified the citadel with planks and boards, held out against the enemy. It was in some measure their poverty which had prevented them from seeking shelter in Salamis; but there was likewise another reason which in part induced them to remain. They imagined themselves to have discovered the true meaning of the oracle uttered by the Pythoness, which promised that "the wooden wall should never be taken"—the wooden wall, they thought, did not mean the ships, but the place where they had taken refuge.

The Persians encamped upon the hill over against the citadel, which is called Mars' hill by the Athenians, and began the seige of the place, attacking the Greeks with arrows whereto pieces of lighted tow were attached, which they shot at the barricade. And now those who were within the citadel found themselves in a most woeful case, for their wooden rampart betrayed them; still, however, they continued to resist. It was in vain that the Pisistratidae came to them and offered terms of surrender—they stoutly refused all parley, and among their other modes of defense, rolled down huge masses of stone upon the barbarians as they were mounting up to the gates: so that Xerxes was for a long time very greatly perplexed, and could not contrive any way to take them.

At last, however, in the midst of these many difficulties, the barbarians made discovery of an access. For verily the oracle had spoken truth; and it was fated that the whole mainland of Attica should fall beneath the sway of the Persians. Right in front of the citadel, but behind the gates and the common ascent—where no watch was kept, and no one would have thought it possible that any foot of man could climb—a few soldiers mounted from the sanctuary of Aglaurus, Cecrops' daughter, notwithstanding the steepness of the precipice. As soon as the Athenians saw them upon the summit, some threw themselves headlong from the wall, and so perished; while others fled for refuge to the inner part of the temple. The Persians rushed to the gates and opened them, after which they massacred the suppliants. When all were slain, they plundered the temple, and fired every part of the citadel.

∙ ∙ ∙

Meanwhile, at Salamis, the Greeks no sooner heard what had befallen the Athenian citadel, than they fell into such alarm that some of the captains did not even wait for the council to come to a vote, but embarked hastily on board their vessels, and hoisted sail as though they would take to flight immediately. The rest, who stayed at the council board, came to a vote that the fleet should give battle at the Isthmus. Night now drew on, and the captains, dispersing from the meeting, proceeded on board their respective ships.

Themistocles, as he entered his own vessel, was met by Mnesiphilus, an Athenian, who asked him what the council had resolved to do. On learning that the resolve was to stand away for the Isthmus, and there give battle on behalf of the Peloponnese, Mnesiphilus exclaimed:—

If these men shall sail away from Salamis, thou wilt have no fight at all for the one fatherland; for they will all scatter themselves to their own homes; and neither Eurybiades nor any one else will be able to hinder them, or to stop the breaking up of the armament. Thus will Greece be brought to ruin through evil counsels. But haste thee now; and, if there be any possible way, seek to unsettle these resolves—mayhap thou mightest persuade Eurybiades to change his mind, and continue here.

The suggestion greatly pleased Themistocles; and without answering a word, he went straight to the vessel of Eurybiades. Arrived there, he let him know that he wanted to speak with him on a matter touching the public service. So Eurybiades bade him come on board, and say whatever he wished. Then Themistocles, seating himself at his side, went over all the arguments which he had heard from Mnesiphilus, pretending as if they were his own, and added to them many new ones besides; until at last he persuaded Eurybiades, by his importunity, to quit his ship and again collect the captains to council.

As soon as they were come, and before Eurybiades had opened to them his purpose in assembling them together, Themistocles, as men are wont to do when they are very anxious, spoke much to divers of them; whereupon the Corinthian captain, Adeimantus, the son of Ocytus, observed—"Themistocles, at the games they who start too soon are scourged." "True," rejoined the other in his excuse, "but they who wait too late are not crowned."

Thus he gave the Corinthian at this time a mild answer; and towards Eurybiades himself he did not use any of those arguments which he had urged before, or say aught of the allies betaking themselves to flight if once they broke up from Salamis; it would have been ungraceful for him, when the confederates were present, to make accusation against any; but he had recourse to quite a new sort of reasoning, and addressed him as follows:—

With thee it rests, O! Eurybiades, to save Greece, if thou wilt only hearken unto me, and give the enemy battle here, rather than yield to the advice of those among us, who would have the fleet withdrawn to the Isthmus. Hear now, I beseech thee, and judge between the two courses. At the Isthmus thou wilt fight in an open sea, which is greatly to our disadvantage, since our ships are heavier and fewer in number than the enemy's; and further, thou wilt in any case lose Salamis, Megara, and Egina, even if all the rest goes well with us. The land and sea force of the Persians will advance together; and thy retreat will but draw them towards the Peloponnese, and so bring all Greece into peril. If, on the other hand, thou doest as I advise, these are the advantages which thou wilt so secure: in the first place, as we shall fight in a narrow sea with few ships against many, if the war follows the common course, we shall gain a great victory: for to fight in a narrow space is favorable to us—in an open sea, to them. Again, Salamis will in this case be preserved, where we have placed our wives and children. Nay, that very point by which ye set most store, is secured as much by the other: for whether we fight here or at the

Isthmus, we shall equally give battle in defence of the Peloponnese. Assuredly ye will not do wisely to draw the Persians upon that region. For if things turn out as I anticipate, and we beat them by sea, then we shall have kept your Isthmus free from the barbarians, and they will have advanced no further than Attica, but from thence have fled back in disorder; and we shall, moreover, have saved Megara, Egina, and Salamis itself, where an oracle has said that we are to overcome our enemies. When men counsel reasonably, reasonable success ensues; but when in their counsels they reject reason, God does not choose to follow the wanderings of human fancies.

When Themistocles had thus spoken, Adeimantus the Corinthian again attacked him, and bade him be silent, since he was a man without a city; at the same time, he called on Eurybiades not to put the question at the instance of one who had no country, and urged that Themistocles should show of what state he was envoy, before he gave his voice with the rest. This reproach he made, because the city of Athens had been taken, and was in the hands of the barbarians. Hereupon Themistocles spake many bitter things against Adeimantus and the Corinthians generally; and for proof that he had a country, reminded the captains, that with two hundred ships at his command all fully manned for battle, he had both city and territory as good as theirs; since there was no Grecian state which could resist his men if they were to make a descent.

After this declaration, he turned to Eurybiades, and addressing him with greater warmth and earnestness—"If thou wilt stay here," he said, "and behave like a brave man, all will be well—if not, thou will bring Greece to ruin. For the whole fortune of the war depends on our ships. Be thou persuaded by my words. If not, we will take our families on board, and go, just as we are, to Siris in Italy, which is ours from of old, and which the prophecies declare we are to colonise some day or other. You then, when you have lost allies like us, will hereafter call to mind what I have now said."

At these words of Themistocles, Eurybiades changed his determination; principally, as I believe, because he feared that if he withdrew the fleet to the Isthmus, the Athenians would sail away, and knew that without the Athenians, the rest of their ships could be no match for the fleet of the enemy. He therefore decided to remain, and give battle at Salamis.

And now, the different chiefs, notwithstanding their skirmish of words, on learning the decision of Eurybiades, at once made ready for the fight. Morning broke, and, just as the sun rose, the shock of an earthquake was felt both on shore and at sea; whereupon the Greeks resolved to approach the gods with prayer, and likewise to send and invite the Æacids to their aid. And this they did, with as much speed as they had resolved on it. Prayers were offered to all the gods; and Telamon and Ajax were invoked at once from Salamis, while a ship was sent to Egina to fetch Æacus himself, and the other Æacids.[1]

∙ ∙ ∙

The men belonging to the fleet of

---

[1] [Æacus was the mythical first king of Egina and father of Telamon and grandfather of Ajax; hence the term Æacids.—*Ed.*]

Xerxes, after they had seen the Spartan dead at Thermopylae, and crossed the channel from Trachis to Histiaea, waited there by the space of three days, and then sailing down through the Euripus, in three more came to Phalêrum. In my judgment, the Persian forces both by land and sea when they invaded Attica, were not less numerous than they had been on their arrival at Sêpias and Thermopylae. For against the Persian loss in the storm and at Thermopylae, and again in the sea-fights off Artemisium, I set the various nations which had since joined the king—as the Malians, the Dorians, the Locrians, and the Boeotians— each serving in full force in his army except the last, who did not number in their ranks either the Thespians or the Plataeans; and together with these, the Carystians, the Andrians, the Tenians, and the other people of the islands, who all fought on this side except the five states already mentioned. For as the Persians penetrated further into Greece, they were joined continually by fresh nations.

Reinforced by the contingents of all these various states, except Paros, the barbarians reached Athens. As for the Parians, they tarried at Cythnus, waiting to see how the war would go. The rest of the sea forces came safe to Phalêrum, where they were visited by Xerxes, who had conceived a desire to go aboard and learn the wishes of the fleet. So he came and sate in a seat of honour; and the sovereigns of the nations, and the captains of the ships, were sent for to appear before him, and as they arrived took their seats according to the rank assigned them by the king. In the first seat sate the king of Sidon; after him, the king of Tyre; then the rest in their order.

When the whole had taken their places, one after another, and were set down in orderly array, Xerxes, to try them, sent Mardonius and questioned each, whether a sea-fight should be risked or no.

Mardonius accordingly went round the entire assemblage, beginning with the Sidonian monarch, and asked this question; to which all gave the same answer, advising to engage the Greeks, except only Artemisia, who spake as follows:—

Say to the king, Mardonius, that these are my words to him: I was not the least brave of those who fought at Euboea, nor were my achievements there among the meanest; it is my right, therefore, O my lord, to tell thee plainly, what I think to be most for thy advantage now. This then is my advice. Spare thy ships, and do not risk a battle; for these people are as much superior to thy people in seamanship, as men to women. What so great need is there for thee to incur hazard at sea? Art thou not master of Athens, for which thou didst undertake thy expedition? Is not Greece subject to thee? Not a soul now resists thy advance. They who once resisted, were handled even as they deserved. Now learn how I expect that affairs will go with thy adversaries. If thou art not over-hasty to engage with them by sea, but wilt keep thy fleet near the land, then whether thou abidest as thou art, or marchest forward towards the Peloponnese, thou wilt easily accomplish all for which thou art come hither. The Greeks cannot hold out against thee very long; thou wilt soon part them asunder, and scatter them to their serveral homes. In the island where they lie, I hear they have no food in store; nor is it likely, if thy land force begins its march towards the Peloponnese, that they will remain quietly where they are—at least such as come from that region. Of a surety they *will not greatly trouble themselves to give battle on behalf of the Athenians. On the other hand, if thou art hasty to fight, I tremble lest the defeat of thy sea force bring harm likewise to thy land army. This, too, thou shouldst remember, O king; good masters are apt to have bad servants; and bad masters good ones. Now, as thou art the best of men, thy servants must needs be a sorry set. These Egyptians, Cyprians, Cilicians, and Pamphylians, who are counted in the number of thy subject-allies, of how little service are they to thee!*

As Artemisia spake, they who wished her well were greately troubled concerning her words, thinking that she would suffer some hurt at the king's hands, because she exhorted him not to risk a battle; they, on the other hand, who disliked and envied her, favoured as she was by the king above all the rest of the allies, rejoiced at her declaration, expecting that her life would be the forfeit. But Xerxes, when the words of the several speakers were reported to him, was pleased beyond all others with the reply of Artemisia; and whereas, even before this, he had always esteemed her much, he now praised her more than ever. Nevertheless, he gave orders that the advice of the greater number should be followed; for he thought that at Euboea the fleet had not done its best, because he himself was not there to see—whereas this time he resolved that he would be an eye-witness of the combat.

Orders were now given to stand out to sea; and the ships proceeded towards Salamis, and took up the stations to which they were directed, without let or hindrance from the enemy. The day, however, was too far spent for them to begin the battle, since night already approached: so they prepared to engage upon the morrow. The Greeks, meanwhile, were in great distress and alarm, more especially those of the Peloponnese; who were troubled that they had been kept at Salamis to fight on behalf of the Athenian territory; and feared that, if they should suffer defeat, they would be pent up and besieged in an island, while their own country was left unprotected.

. . .

At first they conversed together in low tones, each man with his fellow, secretly, and marvelled at the folly shown by Eurybiades; but presently the smothered feeling broke out, and another assembly was held; whereat the old subjects provoked much talk from the speakers, one side maintaining that it was best to sail to the Peloponnese and risk battle for that, instead of abiding at Salamis and fighting for a land already taken by the enemy; while the other, which consisted of the Athenians, Eginetans, and Megarians, was urgent to remain and have the battle fought where they were.

Then Themistocles, when he saw that the Peloponnesians would carry the vote against him, went out secretly from the council, and instructing a certain man what he should say, sent him on board a merchant ship to the fleet of the Medes. The man's name was Sicinnus; he was one of Themistocles' household slaves, and acted as tutor to his sons; in after times, when the Thespians were admitting persons to citizenship, Themistocles made him a Thespian, and a rich man to boot. The ship brought Sicinnus to the Persian fleet, and there he delivered his message to the leaders in these words:—

The Athenian commander has sent me to you privily, without the knowledge of the other Greeks. He is a wellwisher to the king's cause, and would rather success should attend on you than on his countrymen; wherefore he bids me tell you, that fear has seized the Greeks and they are meditating a hasty flight. Now then it is open to you to achieve the best work that ever ye wrought, if only ye will hinder their escaping. They no longer agree among themselves, so that they will not now make any resistance—nay, 'tis likely ye may see a fight already begun between such as favour and such as oppose your cause.

The Messenger, when he had thus expressed himself, departed and was seen no more.

Then the captains, believing all that the messenger had said, proceeded to land a large body of Persian troops on the islet of Psyttaleia, which lies between Salamis and the mainland; after which, about the hour of midnight, they advanced their western wing towards Salamis, so as to inclose the Greeks. At the same time the force stationed about Ceos and Cynosura moved forward, and filled the whole strait as far as Munychia with their ships. This advance was made to prevent the Greeks from escaping by flight, and to block them up in Salamis, where it was thought that vengeance might be taken upon them for the battles fought near Artemisium. The Persian troops were landed on the islet of Psyttaleia, because, as soon as the battle began, the men and wrecks were likely to be drifted thither, as the isle lay in the very path of the coming fight,—and they would thus be able to save their own men and destroy those of the enemy. All these movements were made in silence, that the Greeks might have no knowledge of them; and they occupied the whole night, so that the men had no time to get their sleep.

I cannot say that there is no truth in prophecies, or feel inclined to call in question those which speak with clearness, when I think of the following:—

When they shall bridge with their ships to the sacred strand of Diana, Girt with the golden falchion, and eke to marine Cynosura, Mad hope swelling their hearts at the downfall of beautiful Athens—Then shall godlike Right extinguish haughty Presumption, Insult's furious offspring, who thinketh to overthrow all things. Brass with brass shall mingle, and Mars with blood shall empurple Ocean's waves. Then—then shall the day of Grecia's freedom Come from Victory fair, and Saturn's son all-seeing.

When I look to this, and perceive how clearly Bacis spoke, I neither venture myself to say anything against prophecies, nor do I approve of others impugning them.

Meanwhile, among the captains at Salamis, the strife of words grew fierce. As yet they did not know that they were encompassed, but imagined that the barbarians remained in the same places where they had seen them the day before.

In the midst of their contention, Aristides, the son of Lysimachus, who had crossed from Egina, arrived in Salamis. He was an Athenian, and had been ostracised by the commonality, yet I believe, from what

I have heard concerning his character, that there was not in all Athens a man so worthy or so just as he. He now came to the council, and standing outside, called for Themistocles. Now Themistocles was not his friend, but his most determined enemy. However, under the pressure of the great dangers impending, Aristides forgot their feud, and called Themistocles out of the council, since he wished to confer with him. He had heard before his arrival of the impatience of the Peloponnesians to withdraw the fleet to the Isthmus. As soon therefore as Themistocles came forth, Aristides addressed him in these words:—

Our rivalry at all times, and especially at the present season, ought to be a struggle, which of us shall most advantage our country. Let me then say to thee, that so far as regards the departure of the Peloponnesians from this place, much talk and little will be found precisely alike. I have seen with my own eyes that which I now report; that, however much the Corinthians or Eurybiades himself may wish it, they cannot now retreat; for we are enclosed on every side by the enemy. Go in to them, and make this known.

"Thy advice is excellent," answered the other, "and thy tidings are also good. That which I earnestly desired to happen, thine eyes have beheld accomplished. Know that what the Medes have now done was at my instance; for it was necessary, as our men would not fight here at their own free will, to make them fight whether they would or no. But come now, as thou hast brought the good news, go in and tell it. For if I speak to them, they will think it a feigned tale, and will not believe

that the barbarians have inclosed us around. Therefore do thou go to them, and inform them how matters stand. If they believe thee, 'twill be for the best; but if otherwise, it will not harm. For it is impossible that they should now flee away, if we are indeed shut in on all sides, as thou sayest."

Then Aristides entered the assembly, and spoke to the captains: he had come, he told them, from Egina, and had but barely escaped the blockading vessels—the Greek fleet was entirely inclosed by the ships of Xerxes—and he advised them to get themselves in readiness to resist the foe. Having said so much, he withdrew. And now another contest arose, for the greater part of the captains would not believe the tidings.

But while they still doubted, a Tenian trireme, commanded by Paneatius the son of Sôsimenes, deserted from the Persians and joined the Greeks, bringing full intelligence. For this reason the Tenians were inscribed upon the tripod at Delphi among those who overthrew the barbarians. With this ship, which deserted to their side at Salamis, and the Lemnian vessel which came over before at Artemisium, the Greek fleet was brought to the full number of 380 ships; otherwise it fell short by two of that amount.

The Greeks now, not doubting what the Tenians told them, made ready for the coming fight. At dawn of day, all the men-at-arms were assembled together, and speeches were made to them, of which the best was that of Themistocles; who throughout contrasted what was noble with what was base, and bade them, in all that came within the range of man's nature and constitution, *always* to make choice of the nobler part. Having thus wound up his discourse, he told them to go at once on board their ships, which they accordingly did; and about this time the trireme, that had been sent to Egina for the Æacidae, returned; whereupon the Greeks put to sea with all their fleet.

The fleet had scarce left the land when they were attacked by the barbarians. At once most of the Greeks began to back water, and were about touching the shore, when Ameinias of Pallené, one of the Athenian captains, darted forth in front of the line, and charged a ship of the enemy. The two vessels became entangled, and could not separate, whereupon the rest of the fleet came up to help Ameinias, and engaged with the Persians. Such is the account which the Athenians give of the way in which the battle began; but the Eginetans maintain that the vessel which had been to Egina for the Æacidae, was the one that brought on the fight. It is also reported, that a phantom in the form of a woman appeared to the Greeks, and, in a voice that was heard from end to end of the fleet, cheered them on to the fight; first, however, rebuking them, and saying—"Strange men, how long are ye going to back water?"

Against the Athenians, who held the western extremity of the line towards Eleusis, were placed the Phoenicians; against the Lacedaemonians, whose station was eastward towards the Piraeus, the Ionians. Of these last a few only followed the advice of Themistocles, to fight backwardly; the greater number did far otherwise. I could mention here the names of many trierarchs who took vessels from the Greeks, but I shall pass over all excepting Theomêstor the son of Androdamas, and Phylacus the son of Histiaeus, both Samians. I show this preference to them, inasmuch as for this service Theomêstor was made tyrant of Samos by the Persians, while Phylacus was enrolled among the king's benefactors, and presented with a large estate in land. In the Persian tongue the king's benefactors are called Orosangs.

Far the greater number of the Persian ships engaged in this battle were disabled—either by the Athenians or by the Eginetans. For as the Greeks fought in order and kept their line, while the barbarians were in confusion and had no plan in anything that they did, the issue of the battle could scarce be other than it was. Yet the Persians fought far more bravely here than at Euboea, and indeed surpassed themselves; each did his utmost through fear of Xerxes, for each thought that the king's eye was upon himself.

What part the several nations, whether Greek or barbarian, took in the combat, I am not able to say for certain; Artemisia, however, I know, distinguished herself in such a way as raised her even higher than she stood before in the esteem of the king. For after confusion had spread throughout the whole of the king's fleet, and her ship was closely pursued by an Athenian trireme, she, having no way to fly, since in front of her were a number of friendly vessels, and she was nearest of all the Persians to the enemy, resolved on a measure which in fact proved her safety. Pressed by the Athenian pursuer, she bore straight against one of the ships of her own party, a Calyndian, which had Damasithymus, the Calyndian king, himself on board. I cannot say whether she had had any quarrel with the man while the fleet was at the Hellespont, or not—neither can I decide whether she of set purpose attacked his vessel, or whether it merely chanced that the Calyndian ship came in her way—but certain it is that she bore down upon his vessel and sank it, and that thereby she had the good fortune to procure herself a double advantage. For the commander of the Athenian trireme, when he saw her bear down on one of the enemy's fleet, thought immediately that her vessel was a Greek, or else had deserted from the Persians, and was now fighting on the Greek side; he therefore gave up the chase, and turned away to attack others.

Thus in the first place she saved her life by the action, and was enabled to get clear off from the battle; while further, it fell out that in the very act of doing the king an injury she raised herself to a greater height than ever in his esteem. For as Xerxes beheld the fight, he remarked (it is said) the destruction of the vessel, whereupon the bystanders observed to him—"Seest thou, master, how well Artemisia fights, and how she has just sunk a ship of the enmey?" Then Xerxes asked if it were really Artemisia's doing; and they answered, "Certainly; for they knew her ensign": while all made sure that the sunken vessel belonged to the opposite side. Everything, it is said, conspired to prosper the queen—it was especially fortunate for her, that not one of those on board the Calyndian ship survived to become her accuser. Xerxes, they say, in reply to the remarks made

to him, observed—"My men have behaved like women, and my women like men!"

There fell in this combat Ariabignes, one of the chief commanders of the fleet, who was son of Darius and brother of Xerxes, and with him perished a vast number of men of high repute, Persians, Medes, and allies. Of the Greeks there died only a few; for as they were able to swim, all those that were not slain outright by the enemy escaped from the sinking vessels and swam across to Salamis. But on the side of the barbarians more perished by drowning than in any other way, since they did not know how to swim. The great destruction took place when the ships which had been first engaged began to fly; for they who were stationed in the rear, anxious to display their valour before the eyes of the king, made every effort to force their way to the front, and thus became entangled with such of their own vessels as were retreating.

In this confusion the following event occurred: certain Phoenicians belonging to the ships which had thus perished made their appearance before the king, and laid the blame of their loss on the Ionians, declaring that they were traitors, and had willfully destroyed the vessels. But the upshot of this complaint was, that the Ionian captains escaped the death which threatened them, while their Phoenician accusers received death as their reward. For it happened that, exactly as they spoke, a Samothracian vessel bore down on an Athenian and sank it, but was attacked and crippled immediately by one of the Eginetan squadron. Now the Samothracians were expert with the javelin, and aimed their weapons so well, that they cleared the deck of the vessel which had disabled their own, after which they sprang on board, and took it. This saved the Ionians. Xerxes, when he saw the exploit, turned fiercely on the Phoenicians—(he was ready, in his extreme vexation, to find fault with any one)—and ordered their heads to be cut off, to prevent them, he said, from casting the blame of their own misconduct upon braver men. During the whole time of the battle Xerxes sate at the base of the hill called Ægaleôs, over against Salamis; and whenever he saw any of his own captains perform any worthy exploit he inquired concerning him; and the man's name was taken down by his scribes, together with the names of his father and his city. Ariarammes too, a Persian, who was a friend of the Ionians, and present at the time whereof I speak, had a share in bringing about the punishment of the Phoenicians.

When the rout of the barbarians began, and they sought to make their escape to Phalêrum, the Eginetans, awaiting them in the channel, performed exploits worthy to be recorded. Through the whole of the confused struggle the Athenians employed themselves in destroying such ships as either made resistance or fled to shore, while the Eginetans dealt with those which endeavoured to escape down the straits; so that the Persian vessels were no sooner clear of the Athenians than straightway they fell into the hands of the Eginetan squadron.

It chanced here that there was a meeting between the ship of Themistocles, which was hasting in pursuit of the enemy, and that of Polycritus, son of Crius the Egine-

tan, which had just charged a Sidonian trireme. The Sidonian vessel was the same that captured the Eginetan guardship off Sciathus, which had Pytheas, the son of Ischenous, on board—that Pytheas, I mean, who fell covered with wounds, and whom the Sidonians kept on board their ship, from admiration of his gallantry. This man afterwards returned in safety to Egina, for when the Sidonian vessel with its Persian crew fell into the hands of the Greeks, he was still found on board. Polycritus no sooner saw the Athenian trireme than knowing at once whose vessel it was, as he observed that it bore the ensign of the admiral, he shouted to Themistocles jeeringly, and asked him, in a tone of reproach, if the Eginetans did not show themselves rare friends to the Medes. At the same time, while he thus reproached Themistocles, Polycritus bore straight down on the Sidonian. Such of the barbarian vessels as escaped from the battle fled to Phalêrum, and there sheltered themselves under the protection of the land army.

The Greeks who gained the greatest glory of all in the seafight of Salamis were the Eginetans, and after them the Athenians. The individuals of most distinction were Polycritus the Eginetan, and two Athenians, Eumenes of Anayrus, and Aminias of Pallené; the latter of whom had pressed Artemisia so hard. And assuredly, as he had known that the vessel carried Artemisia on board, he would never have given over the chase till he had either succeeded in taking her, or else been taken himself. For the Athenian captains had received special orders touching the queen, and moreover a reward of ten thousand drachmas had been proclaimed for any one who should make her prisoner; since there was great indignation felt that a woman should appear in arms against Athens. However, as I said before, she escaped; and so did some others whose ships survived the engagement; and these were all now assembled at the port of Phalêrum.

The Athenians say that Adeimantus, the Corinthian commander, at the moment when the two fleets joined battle, was seized with fear, and being beyond measure alarmed, spread his sails, and hasted to fly away; on which the other Corinthians, seeing their leader's ship in full flight, sailed off likewise. They had reached in their flight that part of the coast of Salamis where stands the temple of Minerva Sciras, when they met a light bark, a very strange apparition: it was never discovered that any one had sent it to them, and till it appeared they were altogether ignorant how the battle was going. That there was something beyond nature in the matter they judged from this—that when the men in the bark drew near to their ships they addressed them, saying— "Adeimantus, while thou playest the traitor's part, by withdrawing all these ships, and flying away from the fight, the Greeks whom thou hast deserted are defeating their foes as completely as they ever wished in their prayers." Adeimantus, however, would not believe what the men said; whereupon they told him —"he might take them with him as hostages, and put them to death if he did not find the Greeks winning." Then Adeimantus put about, both he and those who were with him; and they rejoined the fleet when the victory was already gained. Such is the tale which the Athenians tell concerning them of Corinth; these latter however do not allow its truth. On the contrary, they declare that they were among those who distinguished themselves most in the fight. And the rest of Greece bears witness in their favour.

In the midst of the confusion Aristides, the son of Lysimachus, the Athenian, of whom I lately spoke as a man of the greatest excellence, performed the following service. He took a number of the Athenian heavy-armed troops, who had previously been stationed along the shore of Salamis, and landing with them on the islet of Psyttaleia, slew all the Persians by whom it was occupied.

As soon as the sea-fight was ended, the Greeks drew together to Salamis all the wrecks that were to be found in that quarter, and prepared themselves for another engagement, supposing that the king would renew the fight with the vessels still remained to him. Many of the wrecks had been carried away by a westerly wind to the coast of Attica, where they were thrown upon the strip of shore called Côlias. Thus not only were the prophecies of Bacis and Musaeus concerning this battle fulfilled completely, but likewise, by the place to which the wrecks were drifted, the prediction of Lysistratus, an Athenian soothsayer, uttered many years before these events, and quite forgotten at the time by all the Greeks, was fully accomplished. The words were:—

Then shall the sight of the oars fill Colian dames with amazement.

Sophocles

The life of Sophocles, the tragic poet, spanned the fifth century. Born in 496 B.C., he was just old enough to remember the battle of Marathon, and in 480 he led a chorus of Athenian youths in the ceremonial celebration of the naval victory at Salamis. He reached the height of his creative powers in the Age of Pericles. His *Antigone* was produced in 441, three years before the completion of the Parthenon, and his *King Oedipus* was produced around 430, the year before the death of Pericles. Sophocles died in 406 at the age of ninety, two years before the Athenian defeat in the Peloponnesian War.

To understand the tragic drama *Antigone,* we must realize that, according to Greek religion, the body of a deceased person had to be buried before the soul could enter Hades. Thus, Antigone had a sacred duty to bury her brother, a duty that she believed took precedence over all others, even obedience to the decrees of the state. The tragedy, therefore, can be interpreted as a clash between divine law, championed by Antigone, and human or political law, championed by Creon. Such an interpretation, however, does not exhaust the meaning of the play. Viewed as a dramatic portrayal of human character, the tragedy that destroys both Antigone and Creon becomes the inevitable result of a clash between two strong-willed individuals, each dedicated to an ideal in itself good, but neither willing to make any compromise between his ideal and that held by the other.

Antigone

CHARACTERS

ISMENE ⎫ *daughters of Oedipus*
ANTIGONE ⎭
CREON, *King of Thebes*
HAEMON, *son of* CREON
TEIRESIAS, *a blind prophet*
SENTRY

MESSENGER
EURYDICE, *wife of* CREON
CHORUS *of Theban elders*
King's attendants
Queen's attendants
BOY *leading* TEIRESIAS
SOLDIERS

Sophocles, "Antigone," in *The Theban Plays,* trans. E. F. Watling (Harmondsworth, Middlesex: Penguin Books, Ltd., 1947), pp. 126–62. Courtesy of Penguin Books, Ltd.

SCENE: Before the Palace at Thebes

Enter ISMENE from the central door of the Palace. ANTIGONE follows, anxious and urgent; she closes the door carefully, and comes to join her sister.

ANTIGONE: O sister! Ismene dear, dear sister Ismene!
You know how heavy the hand of God is upon us;
How we who are left must suffer for our father, Oedipus.
There is no pain, no sorrow, no suffering, no dishonour
We have not shared together, you and I.
And now there is something more. Have you heard this order,
This latest order that the King has proclaimed to the city?
Have you heard how our dearest are being treated like enemies?

ISMENE: I have heard nothing about any of those we love,
Neither good nor evil—not, I mean, since the death
Of our two brothers, both fallen in a day.
The Argive army, I hear, was withdrawn last night.
I know no more to make me sad or glad.

ANTIGONE: I thought you did not. That's why I brought you out here,
Where we shan't be heard, to tell you something alone.

ISMENE: What is it, Antigone? Black news, I can see already.

ANTIGONE: O Ismene, what do you think? Our two dear brothers . . .
Creon has given funeral honours to one,
And not to the other; nothing but shame and ignominy.
Eteocles has been buried, they tell me, in state,
With all honourable observances due to the dead.
But Polynices, just as unhappily fallen—the order

Says he is not to be buried, not to be mourned;
To be left unburied, unwept, a feast of flesh
For keen-eyed carrion birds. The noble Creon!
It is against you and me he has made this order.
Yes, against me. And soon he will be here himself
To make it plain to those that have not heard it,
And to enforce it. This is no idle threat;
The punishment for disobedience is death by stoning.
So now you know. And now is the time to show
Whether or not you are worthy of your high blood.

ISMENE: My poor Antigone, if this is really true,
What more can I do, or undo, to help you?

ANTIGONE: Will you help me? Will you do something with me? Will you?

ISMENE: Help you do what, Antigone? What do you mean?

ANTIGONE: Would you help me lift the body . . . you and me?

ISMENE: You cannot mean . . . to bury him? Against the order?

ANTIGONE: Is he not my brother, and yours, whether you like it
Or not? I shall never desert him, never.

ISMENE: How could you dare, when Creon has expressly forbidden it?

ANTIGONE: He has no right to keep me from my own.

ISMENE: O sister, sister, do you forget how our father
Perished in shame and misery, his awful sin
Self-proved, blinded by his own self-mutilation?
And then his mother, his wife—for she was both—
Destroyed herself in a noose of her own making.
And now our brothers, both in a

single day
Fallen in an awful exaction of death
for death,
Blood for blood, each slain by the
other's hand.
Now we two left; and what will be
the end of us,
If we transgress the law and defy
our king?
O think, Antigone; we are women;
it is not for us
To fight against men; our rulers are
stronger than we,
And we must obey in this, or in
worse than this.
May the dead forgive me, I can do
no other
But as I am commanded; to do
more is madness.

ANTIGONE: No; then I will not ask you
for your help.
Nor would I thank you for it, if
you gave it.
Go your own way; I will bury my
brother;
And if I die for it, what happiness!
Convicted of reverence—I shall be
content
To lie beside a brother whom I
love.
We have only a little time to please
the living,
But all eternity to love the dead.
There I shall lie for ever. Live, if
you will;
Live, and defy the holiest laws of
heaven.

ISMENE: I do not defy them; but I
cannot act
Against the State. I am not strong
enough.

ANTIGONE: Let that be your excuse,
then
I will go
And heap a mound of earth over
my brother.

ISMENE: I fear for you, Antigone; I
fear—

ANTIGONE: You need not fear for me.
Fear for yourself.

ISMENE: At least be secret. Do not
breathe a word.

I'll not betray your secret.

ANTIGONE: Publish it
To all the world! Else I shall hate
you more.

ISMENE: Your heart burns! Mine is
frozen at the thought.

ANTIGONE: I know my duty, where
true duty lies.

ISMENE: If you can do it; but you're
bound to fail.

ANTIGONE: When I have tried and
failed, I shall have failed.

ISMENE: No sense in starting on a
hopeless task.

ANTIGONE: Oh, I shall hate you if you
talk like that!
And he will hate you, rightly. Leave
me alone
With my own madness. There is no
punishment
Can rob me of my honourable
death.

ISMENE: Go then, if you are determined, to your folly.
But remember that those who love
you . . . love you still.

ISMENE *goes into the Palace.*

ANTIGONE *leaves the stage by a side
exit.*

Enter the CHORUS *of Theban elders.*

CHORUS: Hail the sun! the brightest of
all that ever
Dawned on the City of Seven
Gates, City of Thebes!
Hail the golden dawn over Dirce's
river
Rising to speed the flight of the
white invaders
Homeward in full retreat!
The army of Polynices was
gathered against us,
In angry dispute his voice was
lifted against us,
Like a ravening bird of prey he
swooped around us
With white wings flashing, with
flying plumes,
With armed hosts ranked in
thousands.
At the threshold of seven gates
in a circle of blood
His swords stood round us, his jaws

were opened against us;
But before he could taste our blood,
or consume us with fire,
He fled, fled with the roar of the
dragon behind him
And thunder of war in his
ears.
The Father of Heaven abhors
the proud tongue's boasting;
He marked the oncoming torrent,
the flashing stream
Of their golden harness, the clash
of their battle gear;
He heard the invader cry Victory
over our ramparts,
And smote him with fire to
the ground.
Down to the ground from the
crest of his hurricane on-
slaught
He swung, with the fiery brands of
his hate brought low:
Each and all to their doom of de-
struction appointed
By the god that fighteth for
us.
Seven invaders at seven gates,
seven defenders
Spoiled of their bronze for a tribute
to Zeus; save two
Luckless brothers in one fight
matched together
And in one death laid low.
Great is the victory, great be the
joy
In the city of Thebes, the city of
chariots.
Now is the time to fill the temples
With glad thanksgiving for war-
fare ended;
Shake the ground with the night-
long dances,
Bacchus afoot and delight abound-
ing.
But see, the King comes here,
Creon, the son of Menoeceus,
Whom the gods have appointed for
us
In our recent change of fortune.
What matter is it, I wonder,
That has led him to call us to-
gether

By his special proclamation?
The central door is opened, and
CREON *enters.*
CREON: My councillors: now that the
gods have brought our city
Safe through a storm of trouble to
tranquillity,
I have called you especially out of
all my people
To conference together, knowing
that you
Were loyal subjects when King
Laius reigned,
And when King Oedipus so wisely
ruled us,
And again, upon his death, faith-
fully served
His sons, till they in turn fell—
both slayers, both slain,
Both stained with brother-blood,
dead in a day—
And I, their next of kin, inherited
The throne and kingdom which I
now possess.
No other touchstone can test the
heart of a man,
The temper of his mind and spirit,
till he be tried
In the practice of authority and
rule.
For my part, I have always held
the view,
And hold it still, that a king whose
lips are sealed
By fear, unwilling to seek advice,
is damned.
And no less damned is he who puts
a friend
Above his country; I have no good
word for him.
As God above is my witness, who
sees all,
When I see any danger threatening
my people,
Whatever it may be, I shall declare
it.
No man who is his country's enemy
Shall call himself my friend. Of
this I am sure—
Our country is our life; only when
she
Rides safely, have we any friends

at all.

Such is my policy for our common weal.

    In pursuance of this, I have made a proclamation

Concerning the sons of Oedipus, as follows:

Eteocles, who fell fighting in defence of the city,

Fighting gallantly, is to be honoured with burial

And with all the rites due to the noble dead.

The other—you know whom I mean—his brother Polynices,

Who came back from exile intending to burn and destroy

His fatherland and the gods of his fatherland,

To drink the blood of his kin, to make them slaves—

He is to have no grave, no burial,

No mourning from anyone; it is forbidden.

He is to be left unburied, left to be eaten

By dogs and vultures, a horror for all to see.

I am determined that never, if I can help it,

Shall evil triumph over good. Alive

Or dead, the faithful servant of his country

Shall be rewarded.

CHORUS: Creon, son of Menoeceus,

You have given your judgment for the friend and for the enemy.

As for those that are dead, so for us who remain,

Your will is law.

CREON: See then that it be kept.

CHORUS: My lord, some younger would be fitter for that task.

CREON: Watchers are already set over the corpse.

CHORUS: What other duty then remains for us?

CREON: Not to connive at any disobedience.

CHORUS: If there were any so mad as to ask for death—

CREON: Ay, that is the penalty. There is always someone

Ready to be lured to ruin by hope of gain.

He turns to go. A SENTRY *enters from the side of the stage.*

CREON *pauses at the Palace door.*

SENTRY: My lord: if I am out of breath, it is not from haste.

I have not been running. On the contrary, many a time

I stopped to think and loitered on the way,

Saying to myself 'Why hurry to your doom,

Poor fool?' and then I said 'Hurry, you fool.

If Creon hears this from another man,

Your head's as good as off.' So here I am,

As quick as my unwilling haste could bring me;

In no great hurry, in fact. So now I am here . . .

But I'll tell my story . . . though it may be nothing after all.

And whatever I have to suffer, it can't be more

Than what God wills, so I cling to that for my comfort.

CREON: Good heavens, man, whatever is the matter?

SENTRY: To speak of myself first—I never did it, sir;

Nor saw who did; no one can punish me for that.

CREON: You tell your story with a deal of artful precaution.

It's evidently something strange.

SENTRY: It is.

So strange, it's very difficult to tell.

CREON: Well, out with it, and let's be done with you.

SENTRY: It's this, sir, The corpse . . . someone has just

Buried it and gone. Dry dust over the body

They scattered, in the manner of holy burial.

CREON: What! Who dared to do it?

SENTRY: I don't know, sir.

There was no sign of a pick, no

scratch of a shovel;
The ground was hard and dry—no
trace of a wheel;
Whoever it was has left no clues
behind him.
When the sentry on the first watch
showed it us,
We were amazed. The corpse was
covered from sight—
Not with a proper grave—just a
layer of earth—
As it might be, the act of some
pious passer-by.
There were no tracks of an animal
either, a dog
Or anything that might have come
and mauled the body.
Of course we all started pitching in
to each other,
Accusing each other, and might
have come to blows,
With no one to stop us; for anyone
might have done it,
But it couldn't be proved against
him, and all denied it.
We were all ready to take hot iron
in hand
And go through fire and swear by
God and heaven
We hadn't done it, nor knew of
anyone
That could have thought of doing
it, much less done it.
  Well, we could make nothing of
    it. Then one of our men
Said something that made all our
blood run cold—
Something we could neither refuse
to do, nor do,
But at our own risk. What he said
was 'This
Must be reported to the King; we
can't conceal it.'
So it was agreed. We drew lots for
it, and I,
Such is my luck, was chosen. So
here I am,
As much against my will as yours,
I'm sure;
A bringer of bad news expects no
welcome.

CHORUS: My lord, I fear—I feared it
from the first—
That this may prove to be an act of
the gods.
CREON: Enough of that! Or I shall lose
my patience.
Don't talk like an old fool, old
though you be.
Blasphemy, to say the gods could
give a thought
To carrion flesh! Held him in high
esteem,
I suppose, and buried him like a
benefactor—
A man who came to burn their
temples down,
Ransack their holy shrines, their
land, their laws?
Is that the sort of man you think
gods love?
Not they. No. There's a party of
malcontents
In the city, rebels against my word
and law,
Shakers of heads in secret, impa-
tient of rule;
They are the people, I see it well
enough,
Who have bribed their instruments
to do this thing.
Money! Money's the curse of man,
none greater.
That's what wrecks cities, banishes
men from home,
Tempts and deludes the most well-
meaning soul,
Pointing out the way to infamy and
shame.
Well, they shall pay for their suc-
cess.
(*To the* SENTRY)
See to it!
See to it, you! Upon my oath, I
swear,
As Zeus is my god above: either
you find
The perpetrator of this burial
And bring him here into my sight,
or death—
No, not your mere death shall pay
the reckoning,

But, for a living lesson against such infamy,
You shall be racked and tortured till you tell
The whole truth of this outrage; so you may learn
To seek your gain where gain is yours to get,
Not try to grasp it everywhere. In wickedness
You'll find more loss than profit.

SENTRY: May I say more?

CREON: No more; each word you say but stings me more.

SENTRY: Stings in your ears, sir, or in your deeper feelings?

CREON: Don't bandy words, fellow, about my feelings.

SENTRY: Though I offend your ears, sir, it is not I
But he that's guilty that offends your soul.

CREON: Oh, born to argue, were you?

SENTRY: Maybe so;
But still not guilty in this business.

CREON: Doubly so, if you have sold your soul for money.

SENTRY: To think that thinking men should think so wrongly!

CREON: Think what you will. But if you fail to find
The doer of this deed, you'll learn one thing:
Ill-gotten gain brings no one any good.

He goes into the Palace.

SENTRY: Well, heaven send they find him.
But whether or no,
They'll not find me again, that's sure. Once free,
Who never thought to see another day,
I'll thank my lucky stars, and keep away.

Exit.

CHORUS: Wonders are many on earth, and the greatest of these
Is man, who rides the ocean and takes his way
Through the deeps, through wind-swept valleys of perilous seas
That surge and sway.
He is master of ageless Earth, to his own will bending
The immortal mother of gods by the sweat of his brow,
As year succeeds to year, with toil unending
Of mule and plough.
He is lord of all things living; birds of the air,
Beasts of the field, all creatures of sea and land
He taketh, cunning to capture and ensnare
With sleight of hand;
Hunting the savage beast from the upland rocks,
Taming the mountain monarch in his lair,
Teaching the wild horse and the roaming ox
His yoke to bear.
The use of language, the wind-swift motion of brain
He learnt; found out the laws of living together
In cities, building him shelter against the rain
And wintry weather.
There is nothing beyond his power. His subtlety
Meeteth all chance, all danger conquereth.
For every ill he hath found its remedy,
Save only death.
O wondrous subtlety of man, that draws
To good or evil ways! Great honour is given
And power to him who upholdeth his country's laws.
And the justice of heaven.
But he that, too rashly daring, walks in sin
In solitary pride to his life's end,
At door of mine shall never enter in
To call me friend.

(Severally, seeing some persons approach from a distance)

O gods! A wonder to see!
Surely it cannot be—
It is no other—
Antigone!
Unhappy maid—
Unhappy Oedipus' daughter; it is
she they bring.
Can she have rashly disobeyed
The order of our King?

Enter the SENTRY, *bringing* ANTI-
GONE *guarded by two more soldiers.*

SENTRY: We've got her. Here's the
woman that did the deed.
We found her in the act of burying
him. Where's the King?

CHORUS: He is just coming out of the
palace now.

Enter CREON.

CREON: What's this? What am I just in
time to see?

SENTRY: My lord, an oath's a very
dangerous thing.
Second thoughts may prove us liars.
Not long since
I swore I wouldn't trust myself
again
To face your threats; you gave me
a drubbing the first time.
But there's no pleasure like an un-
expected pleasure,
Not by a long way. And so I've
come again,
Though against my solemn oath.
And I've brought this lady,
Who's been caught in the act of
setting that grave in order.
And no casting lots for it this time
—the prize is mine
And no one else's. So take her;
judge and convict her.
I'm free, I hope, and quit of the
horrible business.

CREON: How did you find her? Where
have you brought her from?

SENTRY: She was burying the man
with her own hands, and that's
the truth.

CREON: Are you in your senses? Do
you know what you are saying?

SENTRY: I saw her myself, burying the
body of the man

Whom you said not to bury. Don't
I speak plain?

CREON: How did she come to be seen
and taken in the act?

SENTRY: It was this way.
After I got back to the place,
With all your threats and curses
ringing in my ears,
We swept off all the earth that
covered the body,
And left it a sodden naked corpse
again;
Then sat up on the hill, on the
windward side,
Keeping clear of the stench of him,
as far as we could;
All of us keeping each other up to
the mark,
With pretty sharp speaking, not to
be caught napping this time.
So this went on some hours, till the
flaming sun
Was high in the top of the sky, and
the heat was blazing.
Suddenly a storm of dust, like a
plague from heaven,
Swept over the ground, stripping
the trees stark bare,
Filling the sky; you had to shut
your eyes
To stand against it. When at last it
stopped,
There was the girl, screaming like
an angry bird,
When it finds its nest left empty
and little ones gone.
Just like that she screamed, seeing
the body
Naked, crying and cursing the ones
that had done it.
Then she picks up the dry earth in
her hands,
And pouring out of a fine bronze
urn she's brought
She makes her offering three times
to the dead.
Soon as we saw it, down we came
and caught her.
She wasn't at all frightened. And
so we charged her
With what she'd done before, and

this. She admitted it,
I'm glad to say—though sorry too,
in a way.
It's good to save your own skin, but
a pity
To have to see another get into
trouble,
Whom you've no grudge against.
However, I can't say
I've ever valued anyone else's life
More than my own, and that's the
honest truth.

CREON (*to* ANTIGONE): Well, what do
you say—you, hiding your head
there:
Do you admit, or do you deny the
deed?

ANTIGONE: I do admit it. I do not deny
it.

CREON (*to the* SENTRY): You—you
may go. You are discharged
from blame.

Exit SENTRY.

Now tell me, in as few words as
you can,
Did you know the order forbidding
such an act?

ANTIGONE: I knew it, naturally. It was
plain enough.

CREON: And yet you dared to contra-
vene it?

ANTIGONE: Yes.
That order did not come from God.
Justice,
That dwells with the gods below,
knows no such law.
I did not think your edicts strong
enough
To overrule the unwritten unalter-
able laws
Of God and heaven, you being only
a man.
They are not of yesterday or to-day,
but everlasting,
Though where they came from,
none of us can tell.
Guilty of their transgression before
God
I cannot be, for any man on earth.
I knew that I should have to die,
of course,

With or without your order. If it be
soon,
So much the better. Living in daily
torment
As I do, who would not be glad to
die?
This punishment will not be any
pain.
Only if I had let my mother's son
Lie there unburied, then I could
not have borne it.
This I can bear. Does that seem
foolish to you?
Or is it you that are foolish to judge
me so?

CHORUS: She shows her father's stubborn spirit: foolish
Not to give way when everything's
against her.

CREON: Ah, but you'll see. The over-
obstinate spirit
Is soonest broken; as the strongest
iron will snap
If over-tempered in the fire to brit-
tleness.
A little halter is enough to break
The wildest horse. Proud thoughts
do not sit well
Upon subordinates. This girl's
proud spirit
Was first in evidence when she
broke the law;
And now, to add insult to her in-
jury,
She gloats over her deed. But, as I
live,
She shall not flout my orders with
impunity.
My sister's child—ay, were she
even nearer,
Nearest and dearest, she should not
escape
Full punishment—she, and her sis-
ter too,
Her partner, doubtless, in this bury-
ing.
Let her be fetched! She was in
the house just now;
I saw her, hardly in her right mind
either.
Often the thoughts of those who

plan dark deeds
Betray themselves before the deed is done.
The criminal who being caught still tries
To make a fair excuse, is damned indeed.
ANTIGONE: Now you have caught, will you do more than kill me?
CREON: No, nothing more; that is all I could wish.
ANTIGONE: Why then delay? There is nothing that you can say
That I should wish to hear, as nothing I say
Can weigh with you. I have given my brother burial.
What greater honour could I wish? All these
Would say that what I did was honourable,
But fear locks up their lips. To speak and act
Just as he likes is a king's prerogative.
CREON: You are wrong. None of my subjects thinks as you do.
ANTIGONE: Yes, sir, they do; but dare not tell you so.
CREON: And you are not only alone, but unashamed.
ANTIGONE: There is no shame in honouring my brother.
CREON: Was not his enemy, who died with him, your brother?
ANTIGONE: Yes, both were brothers, both of the same parents.
CREON: You honour one, and so insult the other.
ANTIGONE: He that is dead will not accuse me of that.
CREON: He will, if you honour him no more than the traitor.
ANTIGONE: It was not a slave, but his brother, that died with him.
CREON: Attacking his country, while the other defended it.
ANTIGONE: Even so, we have a duty to the dead.
CREON: Not to give equal honour to good and bad.
ANTIGONE: Who knows? In the country of the dead that may be the law.
CREON: An enemy can't be a friend, even when dead.
ANTIGONE: My way is to share my love, not share my hate.
CREON: Go then, and share your love among the dead.
We'll have no woman's law here, while I live.
Enter ISMENE *from the Palace.*
CHORUS: Here comes Ismene, weeping
In sisterly sorrow; a darkened brow,
Flushed face, and the fair cheek marred
With flooding rain.
CREON: You crawling viper! Lurking in my house
To suck my blood! Two traitors unbeknown
Plotting against my throne. Do you admit
To a share in this burying, or deny all knowledge?
ISMENE: I did it—yes—if she will let me say so.
I am as much to blame as she is.
ANTIGONE: No.
That is not just. You would not lend a hand
And I refused your help in what I did.
ISMENE: But I am not ashamed to stand beside you
Now in your hour of trial, Antigone.
ANTIGONE: Whose was the deed, Death and the dead are witness.
I love no friend whose love is only words.
ISMENE: O sister, sister, let me share your death,
Share in the tribute of honour to him that is dead.
ANTIGONE: You shall not die with me. You shall not claim
That which you would not touch. One death is enough.
ISMENE: How can I bear to live, if you must die?
ANTIGONE: Ask Creon. Is not he the one you care for?

ISMENE: You do yourself no good to taunt me so.

ANTIGONE: Indeed no: even my jests are bitter pains.

ISMENE: But how, O tell me, how can I still help you?

ANTIGONE: Help yourself. I shall not stand in your way.

ISMENE: For pity, Antigone—can I not die with you?

ANTIGONE: You chose; life was your choice, when mine was death.

ISMENE: Although I warned you that it would be so.

ANTIGONE: Your way seemed right to some, to others mine.

ISMENE: But now both in the wrong, and both condemned.

ANTIGONE: No, no. You live. My heart was long since dead,

So it was right for me to help the dead.

CREON: I do believe the creatures both are mad;

One lately crazed, the other from her birth.

ISMENE: Is it not likely, sir? The strongest mind

Cannot but break under misfortune's blows.

CREON: Yours did, when you threw in your lot with hers.

ISMENE: How could I wish to live without my sister?

CREON: You have no sister. Count her dead already.

ISMENE: You could not take her—kill your own son's bride?

CREON: Oh, there are other fields for him to plough.

ISMENE: No truer troth was ever made than theirs.

CREON: No son of mine shall wed so vile a creature.

ANTIGONE: O Haemon, can your father spite you so?

CREON: You and your paramour, I hate you both.

CHORUS: Sir, would you take her from your own son's arms?

CREON: Not I, but death shall take her.

CHORUS: Be it so.

Her death, it seems, is certain.

CREON: Certain it is.

No more delay. Take them, and keep them within—

The proper place for women. None so brave

As not to look for some way of escape

When they see life stand face to face with death.

The women are taken away.

CHORUS: Happy are they who know not the taste of evil.

From a house that heaven hath shaken

The curse departs not

But falls upon all of the blood,

Like the restless surge of the sea when the dark storm drives

The black sand hurled from the deeps

And the Thracian gales boom down

On the echoing shore.

In life and in death is the house of Labdacus stricken.

Generation to generation,

With no atonement,

It is scourged by the wrath of a god.

And now for the dead dust's sake is the light of promise,

The tree's last root, crushed out

By pride of heart and the sin

Of presumptuous tongue.

For what presumption of man can match thy power,

O Zeus, that art not subject to sleep or time

Or age, living for ever in bright Olympus?

To-morrow and for all time to come,

As in the past,

This law is immutable:

For mortals greatly to live is greatly to suffer.

Roving ambition helps many a man to good,

And many it falsely lures to light desires,

Till failure trips them unawares, and they fall

On the fire that consumes them.

Well was it said,
Evil seems good
To him who is doomed to suffer;
And short is the time before that
　suffering comes.
　　But here comes Haemon,
Your youngest son.
Does he come to speak his sorrow
For the doom of his promised
　bride,
The loss of his marriage hopes?
CREON: We shall know it soon, and
　need no prophet to tell us.
　　Enter HAEMON.
Son, you have heard, I think, our
　final judgment
On your late betrothed. No angry
　words, I hope?
Still friends, in spite of everything,
　my son?
HAEMON: I am your son, sir; by your
　wise decisions
My life is ruled, and them I shall
　always obey.
I cannot value any marriage-tie
Above your own good guidance.
CREON: Rightly said.
Your father's will should have your
　heart's first place.
Only for this do fathers pray for
　sons
Obedient, loyal, ready to strike
　down
Their fathers' foes, and love their
　fathers' friends.
To be the father of unprofitable
　sons
Is to be the father of sorrows, a
　laughingstock
To all one's enemies. Do not be
　fooled, my son,
By lust and the wiles of a woman.
　You'll have bought
Cold comfort if your wife's a
　worthless one.
No wound strikes deeper than love
　that is turned to hate.
This girl's an enemy; away with her,
And let her go and find a mate in
　Hades.
Once having caught her in a fla-
　grant act—

The one and only traitor in our
　State—
I cannot make myself a traitor too;
So she must die. Well may she pray
　to Zeus,
The God of Family Love. How, if
　I tolerate
A traitor at home, shall I rule
　those abroad?
He that is a righteous master of
　his house
Will be a righteous statesman. To
　transgress
Or twist the law to one's own plea-
　sure, presume
To order where one should obey,
　is sinful,
And I will have none of it.
He whom the State appoints must
　be obeyed
To the smallest matter, be it right
　—or wrong.
And he that rules his household,
　without a doubt,
Will make the wisest king, or, for
　that matter,
The staunchest subject. He will be
　the man
You can depend on in the storm of
　war,
The faithfullest comrade in the day
　of battle.
There is no more deadly peril than
　disobedience;
States are devoured by it, homes
　laid in ruins,
Armies defeated, victory turned to
　rout.
While simple obedience saves the
　lives of hundreds
Of honest folk. Therefore, I hold
　to the law,
And will never betray it—least of
　all for a woman.
Better be beaten, if need be, by a
　man,
Than let a woman get the better of
　us.
CHORUS: To me, as far as an old man
　can tell,
It seems your Majesty has spoken
　well.

HAEMON: Father, man's wisdom is the gift of heaven,
The greatest gift of all. I neither am
Nor wish to be clever enough to prove you wrong,
Though all men might not think the same as you do.
Nevertheless, I have to be your watchdog,
To know what others say and what they do,
And what they find to praise and what to blame.
Your frown is a sufficient silencer
Of any word that is not for your ears.
But I hear whispers spoken in the dark;
On every side I hear voices of pity
For this poor girl, doomed to the cruellest death,
And most unjust, that ever woman suffered
For an honourable action—burying a brother
Who was killed in a battle, rather than leave him naked
For dogs to maul and carrion birds to peck at.
Has she not rather earned a crown of gold?—
Such is the secret talk about the town.
Father, there is nothing I can prize above
Your happiness and well-being. What greater good
Can any son desire? Can any father
Desire more from his son? Therefore I say,
Let not your first thought be your only thought.
Think if there cannot be some other way.
Surely, to think your own the only wisdom,
And yours the only word, the only will,
Betrays a shallow spirit, an empty heart.
It is no weakness for the wisest man
To learn when he is wrong, know when to yield.
So, on the margin of a flooded river
Trees bending to the torrent live unbroken,
While those that strain against it are snapped off.
A sailor has to tack and slacken sheets
Before the gale, or find himself capsized.
So, father, pause, and put aside your anger.
I think, for what my young opinion's worth,
That, good as it is to have infallible wisdom,
Since this is rarely found, the next best thing
Is to be willing to listen to wise advice.

CHORUS: There is something to be said, my lord, for his point of view,
And for yours as well; there is much to be said on both sides.

CREON: Indeed! Am I to take lessons at my time of life
From a fellow of his age?

HAEMON: No lesson you need be ashamed of.
It isn't a question of age, but of right and wrong.

CREON: Would you call it right to admire an act of disobedience?

HAEMON: Not if the act were also dishonourable.

CREON: And was not this woman's action dishonourable?

HAEMON: The people of Thebes think not.

CREON: The people of Thebes!
Since when do I take my orders from the people of Thebes?

HAEMON: Isn't that rather a childish thing to say?

CREON: No, I am king, and responsible only to myself.

HAEMON: A one-man state? What sort of a state is that?

CREON: Why, does not every state belong to its ruler?

HAEMON: You'd be an excellent king —on a desert island.

CREON: Of course, if you're on the woman's side—

HAEMON: No, no—
Unless you're the woman. It's you I'm fighting for.

CREON: What, villain, when every word you speak is against me?

HAEMON: Only because I know you are wrong, wrong.

CREON: Wrong? To respect my own authority?

HAEMON: What sort of respect tramples on all that is holy?

CREON: Despicable coward! No more will than a woman!

HAEMON: I have nothing to be ashamed of.

CREON: Yet you plead her cause.

HAEMON: No, yours, and mine, and that of the gods of the dead.

CREON: You'll never marry her this side of death.

HAEMON: Then, if she dies, she does not die alone.

CREON: Is that a threat, you impudent—

HAEMON: Is it a threat
To try to argue against wrong-headedness?

CREON: You'll learn what wrong-headedness is, my friend, to your cost.

HAEMON: O father, I could call you mad, were you not my father.

CREON: Don't toady me, boy; keep that for your lady-love.

HAEMON: You mean to have the last word then?

CREON: I do.
And what is more, by all the gods in heaven,
I'll make you sorry for your impudence.
(Calling to those within)
Bring out that she-devil, and let her die
Now, with her bridegroom by to see it done!

HAEMON: That sight I'll never see. Nor from this hour
Shall you see me again. Let those that will

Be witness of your wickedness and folly.
Exit.

CHORUS: He is gone, my lord, in very passionate haste.
And who shall say what a young man's wrath may do?

CREON: Let him go! Let him do! Let him rage as never man raged,
He shall not save those women from their doom.

CHORUS: You mean, then, sire, to put them both to death?

CREON: No, not the one whose hand was innocent.

CHORUS: And to what death do you condemn the other?

CREON: I'll have her taken to a desert place
Where no man ever walked, and there walled up
Inside a cave, alive, with food enough
To acquit ourselves of the blood-guiltiness
That else would lie upon our commonwealth.
There she may pray to Death, the god she loves,
And ask release from death; or learn at last
What hope there is for those who worship death.
Exit.

CHORUS:
Where is the equal of Love?
Where is the battle he cannot win,
The power he cannot outmatch?
In the farthest corners of earth, in the midst of the sea,
He is there; he is here
In the bloom of a fair face
Lying in wait;
And the grip of his madness
Spares not god or man,
Marring the righteous man,
Driving his soul into mazes of sin
And strife, dividing a house.
For the light that burns in the eyes of a bride of desire
Is a fire that consumes.
At the side of the great gods

Aphrodite immortal
Works her will upon all.
The doors are opened and ANTI-
GONE *enters, guarded.*
But here is a sight beyond all bear-
ing,
At which my eyes cannot but weep;
Antigone forth faring
To her bridal-bower of endless
sleep.
ANTIGONE: You see me, countrymen,
on my last journey,
Taking my last leave of the light of
day;
Going to my rest, where death shall
take me
Alive across the silent river.
No wedding-day; no marriage-
music;
Death will be all my bridal dower.
CHORUS: But glory and praise go with
you, lady,
To your resting-place. You go with
your beauty
Unmarred by the hand of consum-
ing sickness,
Untouched by the sword, living and
free,
As none other that ever died before
you.
ANTIGONE: The daughter of Tantalus,
a Phrygian maid,
Was doomed to a piteous death on
the rock
Of Sipylus, which embraced and
imprisoned her,
Merciless as the ivy; rain and snow
Beat down upon her, mingled with
her tears,
As she wasted and died. Such was
her story,
And such is the sleep that I shall
go to.
CHORUS: She was a goddess of im-
mortal birth,
And we are mortals; the greater the
glory,
To share the fate of a god-born
maiden,
A living death, but a name undying.
ANTIGONE: Mockery, mockery! By the
gods of our fathers,

Must you make me a laughing-stock
while I yet live?
O lordly sons of my city! O Thebes!
Your valleys of rivers, your chariots
and horses!
No friend to weep at my banish-
ment
To a rock-hewn chamber of endless
durance,
In a strange cold tomb alone to
linger
Lost between life and death for
ever.
CHORUS: My child, you have gone
your way
To the outermost limit of daring
And have stumbled against Law
enthroned.
This is the expiation
You must make for the sin of your
father.
ANTIGONE: My father—the thought
that sears my soul—
The unending burden of the house
of Labdacus.
Monstrous marriage of mother and
son . . .
My father . . . my parents . . .
O hideous shame!
Whom now I follow, unwed, curse-
ridden,
Doomed to this death by the ill-
starred marriage
That marred my brother's life.
CHORUS: An act of homage is good in
itself, my daughter;
But authority cannot afford to con-
nive at disobedience.
You are the victim of your own
self-will.
ANTIGONE: And must go the way that
lies before me.
No funeral hymn; no marriage-
music;
No sun from this day forth, no
light,
No friend to weep at my departing.
Enter CREON.
CREON: Weeping and wailing at the
door of death!
There'd be no end of it, if it had
force

To buy death off. Away with her at
   once,
And close her up in her rock-
   vaulted tomb.
Leave her and let her die, if die she
   must,
Or live within her dungeon. Though
   on earth
Her life is ended from this day, her
   blood
Will not be on our hands.
ANTIGONE: So to my grave,
   My bridal-bower, my everlasting
      prison,
   I go, to join those many of my
      kinsmen
   Who dwell in the mansions of Per-
      sephone,
   Last and unhappiest, before my
      time.
   Yet I believe my father will be
      there
   To welcome me, my mother greet
      me gladly,
   And you, my brother, gladly see
      me come.
   Each one of you my hands have
      laid to rest,
   Pouring the due libations on your
      graves.
   It was by this service to your dear
      body, Polynices,
   I earned the punishment which now
      I suffer,
   Though all good people know it was
      for your honour.
      O but I would not have done the
         forbidden thing
   For any husband or for any son.
   For why? I could have had another
      husband
   And by him other sons, if one were
      lost;
   But, father and mother lost, where
      would I get
   Another brother? For thus prefer-
      ring you,
   My brother, Creon condemns me
      and hales me away,
   Never a bride, never a mother, un-
      friended,
   Condemned alive to solitary death.

What law of heaven have I trans-
   gressed? What god
Can save me now? What help or
   hope have I,
In whom devotion is deemed sacri-
   lege?
If this is God's will, I shall learn my
   lesson
In death; but if my enemies are
   wrong,
I wish them no worse punishment
   than mine.
CHORUS: Still the same tempest in the
   heart
   Torments her soul with angry gusts.
CREON: The more cause then have
   they that guard her
   To hasten their work; or they too
      suffer.
CHORUS: Alas, that word had the
   sound of death.
CREON: Indeed there is no more to
   hope for.
ANTIGONE: Gods of our fathers, my
   city, my home,
   Rulers of Thebes! Time stays no
      longer.
   Last daughter of your royal house
   Go I, his prisoner, because I hon-
      oured
   Those things to which honour truly
      belongs.
ANTIGONE *is led away.*
CHORUS: Such was the fate, my child,
   of Danae
   Locked in a brazen bower,
   A prison secret as a tomb,
   Where was no day.
   Daughter of kings, her royal womb
   Garnered the golden shower
   Of life from Zeus. So strong is
      Destiny,
   No wealth, no armoury, no tower,
   No ship that rides the angry sea
   Her mastering hand can stay.
      And Dryas' son, the proud
         Edonian king,
   Pined in a stony cell
   At Dionysus' bidding pent
   To cool his fire
   Till, all his full-blown passion spent,
   He came to know right well

What god his ribald tongue was
challenging
When he would break the fiery spell
Of the wild Maenads' revelling
And vex the Muses' choir.
It was upon the side
Of Bosporus, where the Black
Rocks stand
By Thracian Salmydessus over the
twin tide,
That Thracian Ares laughed to see
How Phineus' angry wife most
bloodily
Blinded his two sons' eyes that
mutely cried
For vengeance; crazed with jeal-
ousy
The woman smote them with the
weaving-needle in her hand.
Forlorn they wept away
Their sad step-childhood's misery
Predestined from their mother's ill-
starred marriage-day.
She was of old Erechtheid blood,
Cave-dwelling daughter of the
North-wind God;
On rocky steeps, as mountain pon-
ies play,
The wild winds nursed her maiden-
hood.
On her, my child, the grey Fates
laid hard hands, as upon thee.
Enter TEIRESIAS, *the blind prophet,
led by a boy.*
TEIRESIAS: Gentlemen of Thebes, we
greet you, my companion and I,
Who share one pair of eyes on our
journeys together—
For the blind man goes where his
leader tells him to.
CREON: You are welcome, father
Teiresias. What's your news?
TEIRESIAS: Ay, news you shall have;
and advice, if you can heed it.
CREON: There was never a time when
I failed to heed it, father.
TEIRESIAS: And thereby have so far
steered a steady course.
CREON: And gladly acknowledge the
debt we owe to you.
TEIRESIAS: Then mark me now; for
you stand on a razor's edge.

CREON: Indeed? Grave words from
your lips, good priest. Say on.
TEIRESIAS: I will; and show you all
that my skill reveals.
At my seat of divination, where I
sit
These many years to read the signs
of heaven,
An unfamiliar sound came to my
ears
Of birds in vicious combat, savage
cries
In strange outlandish language, and
the whirr
Of flapping wings; from which I
well could picture
The gruesome warfare of their
deadly talons.
Full of foreboding then I made the
test
Of sacrifice upon the altar fire.
There was no answering flame; only
rank juice
Oozed from the flesh and dripped
among the ashes,
Smouldering and sputtering; the
gall vanished in a puff,
And the fat ran down and left the
haunches bare.
Thus (through the eyes of my
young acolyte,
Who sees for me, that I may see for
others)
I read the signs of failure in my
quest.
And why? The blight upon us is
your doing.
The blood that stains altars and our
shrines,
The blood that dogs and vultures
have licked up,
It is none other than the blood of
Oedipus
Spilled from the veins of his ill-
fated son.
Our fires, our sacrifices, and our
prayers
The gods abominate. How should
the birds
Give any other than ill-omened
voices,
Gorged with the dregs of blood

that man has shed?
Mark this, my son: all men fall into
sin.
But sinning, he is not for ever lost
Hapless and helpless, who can
make amends
And has not set his face against
repentance.
Only a fool is governed by self-will.
Pay to the dead his due. Wound
not the fallen.
It is no glory to kill and kill again.
My words are for your good, as is
my will,
And should be acceptable, being for
your good.

CREON: You take me for your target,
reverend sir,
Like all the rest. I know your art
of old,
And how you make your commod-
ity
To trade and traffic in for your
advancement.
Trade as you will; but all the silver
of Sardis
And all the gold of India will not
buy
A tomb for yonder traitor. No. Let
the eagles
Carry his carcass up to the throne
of Zeus;
Even that would not be sacrilege
enough
To frighten me from my determina-
tion
Not to allow this burial. No man's
act
Has power enough to pollute the
goodness of God.
But great and terrible is the fall,
Teiresias,
Of mortal men who seek their own
advantage
By uttering evil in the guise of
good.

TEIRESIAS: Ah, is there any wisdom in
the world?

CREON: Why, what is the meaning of
that wide-flung taunt?

TEIRESIAS: What prize outweighs the
priceless worth of prudence?

CREON: Ay, what indeed? What mischief matches the lack of it?

TEIRESIAS: And there you speak of
your own symptom, sir.

CREON: I am loth to pick a quarrel
with you, priest.

TEIRESIAS: You do so, calling my divination false.

CREON: I say all prophets seek their
own advantage.

TEIRESIAS: All kings, say I, seek gain
unrighteously.

CREON: Do you forget to whom you
say it?

TEIRESIAS: No.
Our king and benefactor, by my
guidance.

CREON: Clever you may be, but not
therefore honest.

TEIRESIAS: Must I reveal my yet unspoken mind?

CREON: Reveal all; but expect no gain
from it.

TEIRESIAS: Does that still seem to you
my motive, then?

CREON: Nor is my will for sale, sir, in
your market.

TEIRESIAS: Then hear this. Ere the
chariot of the sun
Has rounded once or twice his
wheeling way,
You shall have given a son of your
own loins
To death, in payment for death—
two debts to pay:
One for the life that you have sent
to death,
The life you have abominably entombed;
One for the dead still lying above
ground
Unburied, unhonoured, unblest by
the gods below.
You cannot alter this. The gods
themselves
Cannot undo it. It follows of necessity
From what you have done. Even
now the avenging Furies,
The hunters of Hell that follow and
destroy,
Are lying in wait for you, and will

have their prey,
When the evil you have worked for
others falls on you.
Do I speak this for my gain? The
time shall come,
And soon, when your house will be
filled with the lamentation
Of men and women; and every
neighboring city
Will be goaded to fury against you,
for upon them
Too the pollution falls when the
dogs and vultures
Bring the defilement of blood to
their hearths and altars.
 I have done. You pricked me,
 and these shafts of wrath
Will find their mark in your heart.
You cannot escape
The sting of their sharpness.
Lead me home, my boy.
Let us leave him to vent his anger
on younger ears,
Or school his mind and tongue to
a milder mood
Than that which now possesses him.
Lead on.
Exit.

CHORUS: He has gone, my lord. He
has prophesied terrible things.
And for my part, I that was young
and now am old
Have never known his prophecies
proved false.

CREON: It is true enough; and my
heart is torn in two.
It is hard to give way, and hard to
stand and abide
The coming of the curse. Both ways
are hard.

CHORUS: If you would be advised, my
good lord Creon—

CREON: What must I do? Tell me, and
I will do it.

CHORUS: Release the woman from her
rocky prison.
Set up a tomb for him that lies
unburied.

CREON: Is it your wish that I consent
to this?

CHORUS: It is, and quickly. The gods
do not delay

The stroke of their swift vengeance
on the sinner.

CREON: It is hard, but I must do it.
Well I know
There is no armour against neces-
sity.

CHORUS: Go. Let your own hand do
it, and no other.

CREON: I will go this instant.
Slaves there! One and all.
Bring spades and mattocks out on
the hill!
My mind is made; 'twas I impris-
oned her,
And I will set her free. Now I be-
lieve
It is by the laws of heaven that man
must live.
Exit.

CHORUS:
O Thou whose name is many,
Son of the Thunderer, dear child
of his Cadmean bride,
Whose hand is mighty
In Italia,
In the hospitable valley
of Eleusis,
And in Thebes,
The mother-city of thy worshippers,
Where sweet Ismenus gently water-
eth
The soil whence sprang the harvest
of the dragon's teeth;
 Where torches on the crested
 mountains gleam,
And by Castalia's stream
The nymph-train in thy dance re-
joices,
When from the ivy-tangled glens
Of Nysa and from vine-clad plains
Thou comest to Thebes where the
immortal voices
Sing thy glad strains.
 Thebes, where thou lovest most
 to be,
With her, thy mother, the fire-
stricken one,
Sickens for need of thee.
Healer of all her ills;
Come swiftly o'er the high Parnas-
sian hills,
Come o'er the sighing sea.

The stars, whose breath is fire,
delight
To dance for thee; the echoing
night
Shall with thy praises ring.
Zeus-born, appear! With Thyiads
revelling
Come, bountiful
Iacchus, King!
Enter a MESSENGER, *from the side
of the stage.*

MESSENGER: Hear, men of Cadmus'
city, hear and attend,
Men of the house of Amphion,
people of Thebes!
What is the life of man? A thing
not fixed
For good or evil, fashioned for
praise or blame.
Chance raises a man to the heights,
chance casts him down,
And none can foretell what will be
from what is.
Creon was once an enviable man;
He saved his country from her
enemies,
Assumed the sovereign power, and
bore it well,
The honoured father of a royal
house.
Now all is lost; for life without
life's joys
Is living death; and such a life is
his.
Riches and rank and show of majesty
And state, where no joy is, are
empty, vain
And unsubstantial shadows, of no
weight
To be compared with happiness of
heart.

CHORUS: What is your news? Disaster
in the royal house?
MESSENGER: Death; and the guilt of it
on living heads.
CHORUS: Who dead? And by what
hand?
MESSENGER: Haemon is dead,
Slain by his own—
CHORUS: His father?
MESSENGER: His own hand.

His father's act it was that drove
him to it.
CHORUS: Then all has happened as the
prophet said.
MESSENGER: What's next to do, your
worships will decide.
The Palace door opens.
CHORUS: Here comes the Queen, Eury-
dice.
Poor soul,
It may be she has heard about her
son.
Enter EURYDICE, *attended by
women.*

EURYDICE: My friends, I heard something of what you were saying
As I came to the door. I was on my
way to prayer
At the temple of Pallas, and had
barely turned the latch
When I caught your talk of some
near calamity.
I was sick with fear and reeled in
the arms of my women.
But tell me what is the matter; what
have you heard?
I am not unacquainted with grief,
and I can bear it.

MESSENGER: Madam, it was I that saw
it, and will tell you all.
To try to make it any lighter now
Would be to prove myself a liar.
Truth
Is always best.
It was thus. I attended your hus-
band,
The King, to the edge of the field
where lay the body
Of Polynices, in pitiable state,
mauled by the dogs.
We prayed for him to the Goddess
of the Roads, and to Pluto,
That they might have mercy upon
him. We washed the remains
In holy water, and on a fire of
fresh-cut branches
We burned all that was left of him,
and raised
Over his ashes a mound of his na-
tive earth.
That done, we turned towards the
deep rock-chamber

Of the maid that was married with
death.
Before we reached it,
One that stood near the accursed
place had heard
Loud cries of anguish, and came to
tell King Creon.
As he approached, came strange
uncertain sounds
Of lamentation, and he cried aloud:
'Unhappy wretch! Is my foreboding true?
Is this the most sorrowful journey
that ever I went?
My son's voice greets me. Go, some
of you, quickly
Through the passage where the
stones are thrown apart,
Into the mouth of the cave, and see
if it be
My son, my own son Haemon that
I hear.
If not, I am the sport of gods.
We went
And looked, as bidden by our anxious master.
There in the furthest corner of the
cave
We saw her hanging by the neck.
The rope
Was of the woven linen of her
dress.
And, with his arms about her, there
stood he
Lamenting his lost bride, his luckless love,
His father's cruelty.
When Creon saw them,
Into the cave he went, moaning
piteously.
'O my unhappy boy,' he cried
again,
'What have you done? What madness brings you here
To your destruction? Come away,
my son,
My son, I do beseech you, come
away!'
His son looked at him with one
angry stare,
Spat in his face, and then without
a word

Drew sword and struck out. But his
father fled
Unscathed. Whereon the poor demented boy
Leaned on his sword and thrust it
deeply home
In his own side, and while his life
ebbed out
Embraced the maid in loose-enfolding arms,
His spurting blood staining her pale
cheeks red.
EURYDICE *goes quickly back into
the Palace.*
Two bodies lie together, wedded in
death,
Their bridal sleep a witness to the
world
How great calamity can come to
man
Through man's perversity.
CHORUS: But what is this?
The Queen has turned and gone
without a word.
MESSENGER: Yes. It is strange. The
best that I can hope
Is that she would not sorrow for
her son
Before us all, but vents her grief in
private
Among her women. She is too wise,
I think,
To take a false step rashly.
CHORUS: It may be.
Yet there is danger in unnatural
silence
No less than in excess of lamentation.
MESSENGER: I will go in and see,
whether in truth
There is some fatal purpose in her
grief.
Such silence, as you say, may well
be dangerous.
He goes in.
*Enter Attendants preceding the
King.*
CHORUS: The King comes here.
What the tongue scarce dares to tell
Must now be known
By the burden that proves too well
The guilt, no other man's

But his alone.

Enter CREON *with the body of* HAEMON.

CREON: The sin, the sin of the erring soul

Drives hard unto death.

Behold the slayer, the slain,

The father, the son.

O the curse of my stubborn will!

Son, newly cut off in the newness of youth,

Dead for my fault, not yours.

CHORUS: Alas, too late you have seen the truth.

CREON: I learn in sorrow. Upon my head

God has delivered this heavy punishment,

Has struck me down in the ways of wickedness,

And trod my gladness under foot.

Such is the bitter affliction of mortal man.

Enter the MESSENGER *from the Palace.*

MESSENGER: Sir, you have this and more than this to bear.

Within there's more to know, more to your pain.

CREON: What more? What pain can overtop this pain?

MESSENGER: She is dead—your wife, the mother of him that is dead—

The death-wound fresh in her heart. Alas, poor lady!

CREON: Insatiable Death, wilt thou destroy me yet?

What say you, teller of evil?

I am already dead,

And is there more?

Blood upon blood?

More death? My wife?

The central doors open, revealing the body of EURYDICE.

CHORUS: Look then, and see; nothing is hidden now.

CREON: O second horror!

What fate awaits me now?

My child here in my arms . . . and there, the other . . .

The son . . . the mother . . .

MESSENGER: There at the altar with the whetted knife

She stood, and as the darkness dimmed her eyes

Called on the dead, her elder son and this,

And with her dying breath cursed you, their slayer.

CREON: O horrible . . .

Is there no sword for me,

To end this misery?

MESSENGER: Indeed you bear the burden of two deaths.

It was her dying word.

CREON: And her last act?

MESSENGER: Hearing her son was dead, with her own hand

She drove the sharp sword home into her heart.

CREON: There is no man can bear this guilt but I.

It is true, I killed him.

Lead me away, away. I live no longer.

CHORUS: 'Twere best, if anything is best in evil times.

What's soonest done, is best, when all is ill.

CREON: Come, my last hour and fairest,

My only happiness . . . come soon.

Let me not see another day.

Away . . . away . . .

CHORUS: The future is not to be known; our present care

Is with the present; the rest is in other hands.

CREON: I ask no more than I have asked.

CHORUS: Ask nothing.

What is to be, no mortal can escape.

CREON: I am nothing. I have no life.

Lead me away . . .

That have killed unwittingly

My son, my wife.

I know not where I should turn,

Where look for help.

My hands have done amiss, my head is bowed

With fate too heavy for me.

Exit.

CHORUS: Of happiness the crown
   And chiefest part
   Is wisdom, and to hold
   The gods in awe.
   This is the law

That, seeing the stricken heart
Of pride brought down,
We learn when we are old.
EXEUNT

Thucydides

Thucydides (c.471–c.396 B.C.) was the greatest of classical historians, perhaps the greatest historian in Western civilization. Although not the equal of Herodotus as a relator of fascinating stories, he had a style of presentation that carries the reader along easily and gracefully. Thucydides' primary concern was to present the true history of the Peloponnesian War between Athens and Sparta, a war in which he himself was an active participant. As a general in the Athenian army he failed to prevent a Spartan force from capturing an important military stronghold, and was banished from Athens for twenty years. Much of this time he spent traveling in enemy territory and observing the course of the struggle.

In his search for truth, Thucydides imposed on himself certain critical techniques and methods. He ruthlessly discarded any story that could not be verified by documentary evidence or eyewitness accounts, or that failed to stand the test of a logical analysis. As a result, the *History of the Peloponnesian War* is an extraordinarily trustworthy source of knowledge about fifth-century Greece. There is one qualification, however: Thucydides often put speeches into the mouths of historical personages.

Thus, the Melian Dialogue and Pericles' Funeral Oration reproduced here appear as direct quotations, although they were actually written by Thucydides himself. Thucydides was careful to emphasize that this was simply a dramatic technique, however, and that he was trying only to convey the accurate meaning or general sense of what was said and not the full text of the speech as it was delivered.

Thucydides' contributions to the art of history include a meticulous use of source materials, an emphasis on rational and natural explanations of history and a denial of supernatural explanations, an understanding of military and naval strategy, and an awareness of the economic basis of military strength. Even his reason for writing the *History* is noteworthy. Herodotus had written, as he himself says, to preserve the memory of great events. But Thucydides wrote to instruct, to teach others the causes of events and the motivations behind men's actions, so that future generations might be able, by studying the record that he made available, to avoid the mistakes of the Greeks and the terrible consequences to which those mistakes had ultimately led.

History of the Peloponnesian War

BOOK I

1. Thucydides, an Athenian, wrote the history of the war in which the Peloponnesians and the Athenians fought against one another. He began to write when they first took up arms, believing that it would be great and memorable above any previous war.[1] For he argued that both states were then at the full height of their military power, and he saw the rest of the Hellenes either siding or intending to side with one or other of them. No movement ever stirred Hellas more deeply than this; it was shared by many of the Barbarians, and might be said even to affect the world at large.

22. As to the speeches which were made either before or during the war, it was hard for me, and for others who reported them to me, to recollect the exact words. I have therefore put into the mouth of each speaker the sentiments proper to the occasion, expressed as I thought he would be likely to express them, while at the same time I endeavored, as nearly as I could, to give the general purport of what was actually said. Of the events of the war I have not ventured to speak from any chance information, nor according to any notion of my own; I have described nothing but what I either saw myself, or learned from others of whom I made the most careful and particular inquiry. The task was a laborious one, because eye-witnesses of the same occurrences gave different accounts of them, as they remembered or were interested in the actions of one side or the other. And very likely the strictly historical character of my narrative may be disappointing to the ear. But if he who desires to have before his eyes a true picture of the events which have happened, and of the like events which may be expected to happen hereafter in the order of human things, shall pronounce what I have written to be useful, then I shall be satisfied. My history is an everlasting possession, not a prize composition which is heard and forgotten.

· · ·

BOOK II

· · ·

34. During the same winter,[2] in accordance with an old national custom, the funeral of those who first fell in this war was celebrated by the Athenians at the public charge. The ceremony is as follows: Three days before the celebration they erect a tent in which the bones of the dead are laid out, and every one brings to his own dead any offering which he pleases. At the

---

[1] [Thucydides is here referring to himself in the third person.—*Ed.*]

[2] [After the first year of the Peloponnesian War, 431 BC.—*Ed.*]

Thucydides, trans. B. Jowett, 2nd ed. (Oxford, 1900).

time of the funeral the bones are placed in chests of cypress wood, which are conveyed on hearses; there is one chest for each tribe. They also carry a single empty litter decked with a pall for all whose bodies are missing, and cannot be recovered after the battle. The procession is accompanied by any one who chooses, whether citizen or stranger, and the female relatives of the deceased are present at the place of interment and make lamentation. The public sepulchre is situated in the most beautiful spot outside the walls; there they always bury those who fall in war; only after the battle of Marathon the dead, in recognition of their pre-eminent valor, were interred on the field. When the remains have been laid in the earth, some man of known ability and high reputation, chosen by the city, delivers a suitable oration over them; after which the people depart. Such is the manner of interment; and the ceremony was repeated from time to time throughout the war. Over those who were the first buried Pericles was chosen to speak. At the fitting moment he advanced from the sepulchre to a lofty stage, which had been erected in order that he might be heard as far as possible by the multitude, and spoke as follows:—

Funeral speech

35. "Most of those who have spoken here before me have commended the law-giver who added this oration to our other funeral customs; it seemed to them a worthy thing that such an honor should be given at their burial to the dead who have fallen on the field of battle. But I should have preferred that, when men's deeds have been brave, they should be honored in deed only, and with such an honor as this public funeral, which you are now witnessing. Then the reputation of many would not have been imperilled on the eloquence or want of eloquence of one and their virtues believed or not as he spoke well or ill. For it is difficult to say neither too little nor too much; and even moderation is apt not to give the impression of truthfulness. The friend of the dead who knows the facts is likely to think that the words of the speaker fall short of his knowledge and of his wishes; another who is not so well informed, when he hears of anything which surpasses his own powers, will be envious and will suspect exaggeration. Mankind are tolerant of the praises of others so long as each hearer thinks that he can do as well or nearly as well himself, but, when the speaker rises above him, jealousy is aroused and he begins to be incredulous. However, since our ancestors have set the seal of their approval upon the practice, I must obey, and to the utmost of my power shall endeavor to satisfy the wishes and beliefs of all who hear me.

36. "I will speak first of our ancestors, for it is right and becoming that now, when we are lamenting the dead, a tribute should be paid to their memory. There has never been a time when they did not inhabit this land, which by their valor they have handed down from generation to generation, and we have received from them a free state. But if they were worthy of praise, still more were our fathers, who added to their inheritance, and after many

a struggle transmitted to us their sons this great empire. And we ourselves assembled here to-day, who are still most of us in the vigor of life, have chiefly done the work of improvement, and have richly endowed our city with all things, so that she is sufficient for herself both in peace and war. Of the military exploits by which our various possessions were acquired, or of the energy with which we or our fathers drove back the tide of war, Hellenic or Barbarian, I will not speak; for the tale would be long and is familiar to you. But before I praise the dead, I should like to point out by what principles of action we rose to power, and under what institutions and through what manner of life our empire became great. For I conceive that such thoughts are not unsuited to the occasion, and that this numerous assembly of citizens and strangers may profitably listen to them.

37. "Our form of government does not enter into rivalry with the institutions of others. We do not copy our neighbors, but are an example to them. It is true that we are called a democracy, for the administration is in the hands of the many and not of the few. But while the law secures equal justice to all alike in their private disputes, the claim of excellence is also recognized; and when a citizen is in any way distinguished, he is preferred to the public service, not as a matter of privilege, but as the reward of merit. Neither is poverty a bar, but a man may benefit his country whatever be the obscurity of his condition. There is no exclusiveness in our public life, and in our private intercourse we are not suspicious of one another, nor angry with our neighbor if he does what he likes; we do not put on sour looks at him which, though harmless, are not pleasant. While we are thus unconstrained in our private intercourse, a spirit of reverence pervades our public acts; we are prevented from doing wrong by respect for authority and for the laws, having an especial regard to those which are ordained for the protection of the injured as well as to those unwritten laws which bring upon the transgressor of them the reprobation of the general sentiment.

38. "And we have not forgotten to provide for our weary spirits many relaxations from toil; we have regular games and sacrifices throughout the year; at home the style of our life is refined; and the delight which we daily feel in all these things helps to banish melancholy. Because of the greatness of our city the fruits of the whole earth flow in upon us; so that we enjoy the goods of other countries as freely as of our own.

39. "Then, again, our military training is in many respects superior to that of our adversaries. Our city is thrown open to the world, and we never expel a foreigner or prevent him from seeing or learning anything of which the secret if revealed to an enemy might profit him. We rely not upon management or trickery, but upon our own hearts and hands. And in the matter of education, whereas they from early youth are always undergoing laborious exercises which are to make them brave, we live at ease, and yet are equally ready to face the perils which they face. And here is the proof. The Lacedaemonians come

into Attica not by themselves, but with their whole confederacy following; we go alone into a neighbor's country; and although our opponents are fighting for their homes and we on a foreign soil, we have seldom any difficulty in overcoming them. Our enemies have never yet felt our united strength; the care of a navy divides our attention, and on land we are obliged to send our own citizens everywhere. But they, if they meet and defeat a part of our army, are as proud as if they had routed us all, and when defeated they pretend to have been vanquished by us all.

40. "If then we prefer to meet danger with a light heart but without laborious training, and with a courage which is gained by habit and not enforced by law, are we not greatly the gainers? Since we do not anticipate the pain, although, when the hour comes, we can be as brave as those who never allow themselves to rest; and thus too our city is equally admirable in peace and in war. For we are lovers of the beautiful, yet simple in our tastes, and we cultivate the mind without a loss of manliness. Wealth we employ, not for talk and ostentation, but when there is a real use for it. To avow poverty with us is no disgrace: the true disgrace is in doing nothing to avoid it. An Athenian citizen does not neglect the state because he takes care of his own household; and even those of us who are engaged in business have a very fair idea of politics. We alone regard a man who takes no interest in public affairs, not as a harmless, but as a useless character; and if few of us are originators, we are all sound judges of a policy. The great imped-

iment to action is, in our opinion, not discussion, but the want of that knowledge which is gained by discussion preparatory to action. For we have a peculiar power of thinking before we act and of acting too, whereas other men are courageous from ignorance but hesitate upon reflection. And they are surely to be esteemed the bravest spirits who, having the clearest sense both of the pains and pleasures of life, do not on that account shrink from danger. In doing good, again, we are unlike others; we make our friends by conferring, not by receiving favors. Now, he who confers a favor is the firmer friend, because he would fain by kindness keep alive the memory of an obligation; but the recipient is colder in his feelings, because he knows that in requiting another's generosity he will not be winning gratitude, but only paying a debt. We alone do good to our neighbors not upon a calculation of interest, but in the confidence of freedom and in a frank and fearless spirit.

41. "To sum up: I say that Athens is the school of Hellas, and that the individual Athenian in his own person seems to have the power of adapting himself to the most varied forms of action with the utmost versatility and grace. This is no passing and idle word, but truth and fact; and the assertion is verified by the position to which these qualities have raised the state. For in the hour of trial Athens alone among her contemporaries is superior to the report of her. No enemy who comes against her is indignant at the reverses which he sustains at the hands of such a city; no subject complains that his masters are unworthy of him. And we shall as-

suredly not be without witnesses; there are mighty monuments of our power which will make us the wonder of this and of succeeding ages; we shall not need the praises of Homer or of any other panegyrist whose poetry may please for the moment, although his representation of the facts will not bear the light of day. For we have compelled every land and every sea to open a path for our valor, and have everywhere planted eternal memorials of our friendship and of our enmity. Such is the city for whose sake these men nobly fought and died; they could not bear the thought that she might be taken from them; and every one of us who survive should gladly toil on her behalf.

42. "I have dwelt upon the greatness of Athens because I want to show you that we are contending for a higher prize than those who enjoy none of these privileges, and to establish by manifest proof the merit of these men whom I am now commemorating. Their loftiest praise has been already spoken. For in magnifying the city I have magnified them, and men like them whose virtues made her glorious. And of how few Hellenes can it be said as of them, that their deeds when weighed in the balance have been found equal to their fame! Methinks that a death such as theirs has been gives the true measure of a man's worth; it may be the first revelation of his virtues, but is at any rate their final seal. For even those who come short in other ways may justly plead the valor with which they have fought for their country; they have blotted out the evil with the good, and have benefited the state more by their public services than they have injured her by their private actions. None of these men were enervated by wealth or hesitated to resign the pleasures of life; none of them put off the evil day in the hope, natural to poverty, that a man, though poor, may one day become rich. But, deeming that the punishment of their enemies was sweeter than any of these things, and that they could fall in no nobler cause, they determined at the hazard of their lives to be honorably avenged, and to leave the rest. They resigned to hope their unknown chance of happiness; but in the face of death they resolved to rely upon themselves alone. And when the moment came they were minded to resist and suffer, rather than to fly and save their lives; they ran away from the word of dishonor, but on the battle-field their feet stood fast, and in an instant, at the height of their fortune, they passed away from the scene, not of their fear, but of their glory.

43. "Such was the end of these men; they were worthy of Athens, and the living need not desire to have a more heroic spirit, although they may pray for a less fatal issue. The value of such a spirit is not to be expressed in words. Any one can discourse to you forever about the advantage of a brave defence which you know already. But instead of listening to him I would have you day by day fix your eyes upon the greatness of Athens, until you become filled with the love of her; and when you are impressed by the spectacle of her glory, reflect that this empire has been acquired by men who knew their duty and had the courage to do it, who in the hour of conflict had the fear of dishonor always

present to them, and who, if ever they failed in an enterprise, would not allow their virtues to be lost to their country, but freely gave their lives to her as the fairest offering which they could present at her feast. The sacrifice which they collectively made was individually repaid to them; for they received again each one for himself a praise which grows not old, and the noblest of all sepulchres—I speak not of that in which their remains are laid, but of that in which their glory survives, and is proclaimed always and on every fitting occasion both in word and deed. For the whole earth is the sepulchre of famous men; not only are they commemorated by columns and inscriptions in their own country, but in foreign lands there dwells also an unwritten memorial of them, graven not on stone but in the hearts of men. Make them your examples, and, esteeming courage to be freedom and freedom to be happiness, do not weigh too nicely the perils of war. The unfortunate who has no hope of a change for the better has less reason to throw away his life than the prosperous who, if he survives, is always liable to a change for the worse, and to whom any accidental fall makes the most serious difference. To a man of spirit, cowardice and disaster coming together are far more bitter than death, striking him unperceived at a time when he is full of courage and animated by the general hope.

44. "Wherefore I do not now commiserate the parents of the dead who stand here; I would rather comfort them. You know that your life has been passed amid manifold vicissitudes; and that they may be deemed fortunate who have gained most honor, whether an honorable death like theirs, or an honorable sorrow like yours, and whose days have been so ordered that the term of their happiness is likewise the term of their life. I know how hard it is to make you feel this, when the good fortune of others will too often remind you of the gladness which once lightened your hearts. And sorrow is felt at the want of those blessings, not which a man never knew, but which were a part of his life before they were taken from him. Some of you are of an age at which they may hope to have other children, and they ought to bear their sorrow better; not only will the children who may hereafter be born make them forget their own lost ones, but the city will be doubly a gainer. She will not be left desolate, and she will be safer. For a man's counsel cannot have equal weight or worth, when he alone has no children to risk in the general danger. To those of you who have passed their prime, I say; 'Congratulate yourselves that you have been happy during the greater part of your days; remember that your life of sorrow will not last long, and be comforted by the glory of those who are gone. For the love of honor alone is ever young, and not riches, as some say, but honor is the delight of men when they are old and useless.'

45. "To you who are the sons and brothers of the departed, I see that the struggle to emulate them will be an arduous one. For all men praise the dead, and, however preeminent your virtue may be, hardly will you be thought, I do not say to equal, but even to approach them. The living have their rivals

and detractors, but when a man is out of the way, the honor and good-will which he receives is unalloyed. And, if I am to speak of womanly virtues to those of you who will henceforth be widows, let me sum them up in one short admonition: To a woman not to show more weakness than is natural to her sex is a great glory, and not to be talked about for good or for evil among men.

46. "I have paid the required tribute, in obedience to the law, making use of such fitting words as I had. The tribute of deeds has been paid in part; for the dead have been honorably interred, and it remains only that their children should be maintained at the public charge until they are grown up; this is the solid prize with which, as with a garland, Athens crowns her sons living and dead, after a struggle like theirs. For where the rewards of virtue are greatest, there the noblest citizens are enlisted in the service of the state. And now, when you have duly lamented, every one his own dead, you may depart."

• • •

BOOK III

• • •

82. For not long afterwards [3] nearly the whole Hellenic world was in commotion; in every city the chiefs of the democracy and of the oligarchy were struggling, the one to bring in the Athenians, the other the Lacedaemonians. Now, in time of peace, men would have had no excuse for introducing either, and no desire to do so, but when they

were at war and both sides could easily obtain allies to the hurt of their enemies and the advantage of themselves, the dissatisfied party were only too ready to invoke foreign aid. And revolution brought upon the cities of Hellas many terrible calamities, such as have been and always will be while human nature remains the same, but which are more or less aggravated and differ in character with every new combination of circumstances. In peace and prosperity both states and individuals are actuated by high motives, because they do not fall under the dominion of imperious necessities; but war which takes away the comfortable provision of daily life is a hard master, and tends to assimilate men's characters to their conditions.

When troubles had once begun in the cities, those who followed carried the revolutionary spirit further and further, and determined to outdo the report of all who had preceded them by the ingenuity of their enterprises and the atrocity of their revenges. The meaning of words had no longer the same relation to things, but was changed by them as they thought proper. Reckless daring was held to be loyal courage; prudent delay was the excuse of a coward; moderation was the disguise of unmanly weakness; to know everything was to do nothing. Frantic energy was the true quality of man. A conspirator who wanted to be safe was a recreant in disguise. The lover of violence was always trusted, and his opponent suspected. He who succeeded in a plot was deemed knowing, but a still greater master in craft was he who detected one. On the other hand, he who

---

[3] [In 427 B.C., or four years after Pericles' Funeral Oration.—*Ed.*]

plotted from the first to have nothing to do with plots was a breaker up of parties and a poltroon who was afraid of the enemy. In a word, he who could outstrip another in a bad action was applauded, and so was he who encouraged to evil one who had no idea of it. The tie of party was stronger than the tie of blood, because a partisan was more ready to dare without asking why. (For party associations are not based upon any established law, nor do they seek the public good; they are formed in defiance of the laws and from self-interest.) The seal of good faith was not divine law, but fellowship in crime. If any enemy when he was in the ascendant offered fair words, the opposite party received them, not in a generous spirit, but by a jealous watchfulness of his actions. Revenge was dearer than self-preservation. Any agreements sworn to by either party, when they could do nothing else, were binding as long as both were powerless. But he who on a favorable opportunity first took courage and struck at his enemy when he saw him off his guard, had greater pleasure in a perfidious than he would have had in an open act of revenge; he congratulated himself that he had taken the safer course, and also that he had over-reached his enemy and gained the prize of superior ability. In general, the dishonest more easily gain credit for cleverness than the simple for goodness; men take a pride in the one, but are ashamed of the other.

The cause of all these evils was the love of power originating in avarice and ambition, and the party-spirit which is engendered by them when men were fairly embarked in a contest. For the leaders on either side used specious names, the one party professing to uphold the constitutional equality of the many, the other the wisdom of an aristocracy, while they made the public interests, to which in name they were devoted, in reality their prize. Striving in every way to overcome each other, they committed the most monstrous crimes; yet even these were surpassed by the magnitude of their revenges which they pursued to the very utmost, neither party observing any definite limits either of justice or public expediency, but both alike making the caprice of the moment their law. Either by the help of an unrighteous sentence, or grasping power with the strong hand, they were eager to satiate the impatience of party-spirit. Neither faction cared for religion; but any fair pretence which succeeded in effecting some odious purpose was greatly lauded. And the citizens who were of neither party fell a prey to both; either they were disliked because they held aloof, or men were jealous of their surviving.

83. Thus revolution gave birth to every form of wickedness in Hellas. The simplicity which is so large an element in a noble nature was laughed to scorn and disappeared. An attitude of perfidious antagonism everywhere prevailed; for there was no word binding enough, nor oath terrible enough to reconcile enemies. Each man was strong only in the conviction that nothing was secure; he must look to his own safety, and could not afford to trust others. Inferior intellects generally succeeded best. For, aware of their own deficiencies, and fearing the capacity of their opponents, for whom

they were no match in powers of speech, and whose subtle wits were likely to anticipate them in contriving evil, they struck boldly and at once. But the cleverer sort, presuming in their arrogance that they would be aware in time, and disdaining to act when they could think, were taken off their guard and easily destroyed.

· · ·

BOOK V

· · ·

84. In the ensuing summer, Alcibiades sailed to Argos with twenty ships, and seized any of the Argives who were still suspected to be of the Lacedaemonian faction, three hundred in number; and the Athenians deposited them in the subject islands near at hand. The Athenians next made an expedition against the island of Melos [4] with thirty ships of their own, six Chian, and two Lesbian, twelve hundred hoplites and three hundred archers besides twenty mounted archers of their own, and about fifteen hundred hoplites furnished by their allies in the islands. The Melians are colonists of the Lacedaemonians who would not submit to Athens like the other islanders. At first they were neutral and took no part. But when the Athenians tried to coerce them by ravaging their lands they were driven into open hostilities. The generals, Cleomedes the son of Lycomedes and Tisias the son of Tisimachus, encamped with the Athenian forces on the island. But before they did the country any harm they sent envoys to negotiate with the Melians. Instead of bringing these envoys before the people, the Meli-

ans desired them to explain their errand to the magistrates and to the chief men. They spoke as follows:—

85. "Since we are not allowed to speak to the people, lest, forsooth, they should be deceived by seductive and unanswerable arguments which they would hear set forth in a single uninterrupted oration (for we are perfectly aware that this is what you mean in bringing us before a select few), you who are sitting here may as well make assurance yet surer. Let us have no set speeches at all, but do you reply to each several statement of which you disapprove, and criticise it at once. Say first of all how you like this mode of proceeding."

86. The Melian representatives answered:—"The quiet interchange of explanations is a reasonable thing, and we do not object to that. But your warlike movements, which are present not only to our fears but to our eyes, seem to belie your words. We see that, although you may reason with us, you mean to be our judges; and that at the end of the discussion if the justice of our cause prevail and we therefore refuse to yield, we may expect war; if we are convinced by you, slavery."

87. ATHENIAN: Nay, but if you are only going to argue from fancies about the future, or if you meet us with any other purpose than that of looking your circumstances in the face and saving your city, we have done; but if this is your intention we will proceed.

88. MELIAN: It is an excusable and natural thing that men in our position should have much to say and should indulge in many fancies. But we admit that this conference has met to consider the question of

---

[4] [In 416 B.C.—*Ed.*]

our preservation; and therefore let the argument proceed in the manner which you propose.

89. ATHENIAN: Well, then, we Athenians will use no fine words; we will not go out of our way to prove at length that we have a right to rule, because we overthrew the Persians; or that we attack you now because we are suffering any injury at your hands. We should not convince you if we did; nor must you expect to convince us by arguing that, although a colony of the Lacedaemonians, you have taken no part in their expeditions, or that you have never done us any wrong. But you and we should say what we really think, and aim only at what is possible, for we both alike know that into the discussion of human affairs the question of justice only enters where the pressure of necessity is equal, and that the powerful exact what they can, and the weak grant what they must.

90. MELIAN: Well, then, since you set aside justice and invite us to speak of expediency, in our judgment it is certainly expedient that you should respect a principle which is for the common good; and that to every man when in peril a reasonable claim should be accounted a claim of right, and any plea which he is disposed to urge, even if failing of the point a little, should help his cause. Your interest in this principle is quite as great as ours, inasmuch as you, if you fall, will incur the heaviest vengeance, and will be the most terrible example to mankind.

91. ATHENIAN: The fall of our empire, if it should fall, is not an event to which we look forward with dismay; for ruling states such as Lacedaemon are not cruel to their vanquished enemies. And we are fighting not so much against the Lacedaemonians as against our own subjects who may some day rise up and overcome their former masters. But this is a danger which you may leave to us. And we will now endeavor to show that we have come in the interests of our empire, and that in what we are about to say we are only seeking the preservation of your city. For we want to make you ours with the least trouble to ourselves, and it is for the interests of us both that you should not be destroyed.

92. MELIAN: It may be your interest to be our masters, but how can it be ours to be your slaves?

93. ATHENIAN: To you the gain will be that by submission you will avert the worst; and we shall be all the richer for your preservation.

94. MELIAN: But must we be your enemies? Will you not receive us as friends if we are neutral and remain at peace with you?

95. ATHENIAN: No, your enmity is not half so mischievous to us as your friendship; for the one is in the eyes of our subjects an argument of our power, the other of our weakness.

96. MELIAN: But are your subjects really unable to distinguish between states in which you have no concern, and those which are chiefly your own colonies, and in some cases have revolted and been subdued by you?

97. ATHENIAN: Why, they do not doubt that both of them have a good deal to say for themselves on the score of justice, but they think that states like yours are left free because they are able to defend them-

selves, and that we do not attack them because we dare not. So that your subjection will give us an increase of security, as well as an extension of empire. For we are masters of the sea, and you who are islanders, and insignificant islanders too, must not be allowed to escape us.

98. MELIAN: But do you not recognise another danger? For once more, since you drive us from the plea of justice and press upon us your doctrine of expediency, we must show you what is for our interest, and, if it be for yours also, may hope to convince you:—Will you not be making enemies of all who are now neutrals? When they see how you are treating us they will expect you some day to turn against them; and if so, are you not strengthening the enemies whom you already have, and bringing upon you others who, if they could help, would never dream of being your enemies at all?

99. ATHENIAN: We do not consider our really dangerous enemies to be any of the peoples inhabiting the mainland who, secure in their freedom, may defer indefinitely any measures of precaution which they take against us, but islanders who, like you, happen to be under no control, and all who may be already irritated by the necessity of submission to our empire—these are our real enemies, for they are the most reckless and most likely to bring themselves as well as us into a danger which they cannot but foresee.

100. MELIAN: Surely then, if you and your subjects will brave all this risk, you to preserve your empire and they to be quit of it, how base and cowardly it would be in us, who

retain our freedom, not to do and suffer anything rather than be your slaves.

101. ATHENIAN: Not so, if you calmly reflect: for you are not fighting against equals to whom you cannot yield without disgrace, but you are taking counsel whether or not you shall resist an overwhelming force. The question is not one of honor but of prudence.

102. MELIAN: But we know that the fortune of war is sometimes impartial, and not always on the side of numbers. If we yield now all is over; but if we fight there is yet a hope that we may stand upright.

103. ATHENIAN: Hope is a good comforter in the hour of danger, and when men have something else to depend upon, although hurtful, she is not ruinous. But when her spendthrift nature has induced them to stake their all, they see her as she is in the moment of their fall, and not till then. While the knowledge of her might enable them to beware of her, she never fails. You are weak and a single turn of the scale might be your ruin. Do not you be thus deluded; avoid the error of which so many are guilty, who, although they might still be saved if they would take the natural means, when visible grounds of confidence forsake them, have recourse to the invisible to prophecies and oracles and the like, which ruin men by the hopes which they inspire in them.

104. MELIAN: We know only too well how hard the struggle must be against your power, and against fortune, if she does not mean to be impartial. Nevertheless we do not despair of fortune, for we hope to stand as high as you in the favor of heaven, because we are righteous,

and you against whom we contend are unrighteous; and we are satisfied that our deficiency in power will be compensated by the aid of our allies the Lacedaemonians; they cannot refuse to help us, if only because we are their kinsmen, and for the sake of their own honor. And therefore our confidence is not so utterly blind as you suppose.

105. ATHENIAN: As for the Gods, we expect to have quite as much of their favor as you: for we are not doing or claiming anything which goes beyond common opinion about divine or men's desires about human things. For of the Gods we believe, and of men we know, that by a law of their nature wherever they can rule they will. This law was not made by us, and we are not the first who have acted upon it; we did but inherit it, and shall bequeath it to all time, and we know that you and all mankind, if you were as strong as we are, would do as we do. So much for the Gods; we have told you why we expect to stand as high in their good opinion as you. And then as to the Lacedaemonians— when you imagine that out of very shame they will assist you, we admire the simplicity of your idea, but we do not envy you the folly of it. The Lacedaemonians are exceedingly virtuous among themselves, and according to their national standard of morality. But in respect of their dealings with others, although many things might be said, a word is enough to describe them—of all men whom we know they are the most notorious for identifying what is pleasant with what is honorable, and what is expedient with what is just. But how inconsistent is such a character with your present blind hope of deliverance!

106. MELIAN: That is the very reason why we trust them; they will look to their interest, and therefore will not be willing to betray the Melians, who are their own colonists, lest they should be distrusted by their friends in Hellas and play into the hands of their enemies.

107. ATHENIAN: But do you not see that the path of expediency is safe, whereas justice and honor involve danger in practice, and such dangers the Lacedaemonians seldom care to face?

108. MELIAN: On the other hand we think that whatever perils there may be, they will be ready to face them for our sakes, and will consider danger less dangerous where we are concerned. For if they need our aid we are close at hand, and they can better trust our loyal feeling because we are their kinsmen.

109. ATHENIAN: Yes, but what encourages men who are invited to join in a conflict is clearly not the good-will of those who summon them to their side, but a decided superiority in real power. To this no men look more keenly than the Lacedaemonians; so little confidence have they in their own resources that they only attack their neighbors when they have numerous allies, and therefore they are not likely to find their way by themselves to an island, when we are masters of the sea.

110. MELIAN: But they may send their allies: the Cretan sea is a large place; and the masters of the sea will have more difficulty in overtaking vessels which want to escape than the pursued in escaping. If the

attempt should fail, they may invade Attica itself, and find their way to allies of yours whom Brasidas did not reach; and then you will have to fight, not for the conquest of a land in which you have no concern, but nearer home, for the preservation of your confederacy and of your own territory.

111. ATHENIAN: Help may come from Lacedaemon to you as it has come to others, and should you ever have actual experience of it, then you will know that never once have the Athenians retired from a siege through fear of a foe elsewhere. You told us that the safety of your city would be your first care, but we remark that, in this long discussion, not a word has been uttered by you which would give a reasonable man expectation of deliverance. Your strongest grounds are hopes deferred, and what power you have is not to be compared with that which is already arrayed against you. Unless after we have withdrawn you mean to come, as even now you may, to a wiser conclusion, you are showing a great want of sense. For surely you cannot dream of flying to that false sense of honor which has been the ruin of so many when danger and dishonor were staring them in the face. Many men with their eyes still open to the consequences have found the word 'honor' too much for them, and have suffered a mere name to lure them on, until it has drawn down upon them real and irretrievable calamities; through their own folly they have incurred a worse dishonor than fortune would have inflicted upon them. If you are wise you will not run this risk; you ought to see that there can be no disgrace in yielding to a great city which invites you to become her ally on reasonable terms, keeping your own land, and merely paying tribute, and that you will certainly gain no honor if, having to choose between two alternatives, safety and war, you obstinately prefer the worse. To maintain our rights against equals, to be politic with superiors, and to be moderate towards inferiors is the path of safety. Reflect once more when we have withdrawn, and say to yourselves over and over again that you are deliberating about your one and only country, which may be saved or may be destroyed by a single decision.

112. The Athenians left the conference: the Melians, after consulting among themselves, resolved to persevere in their refusal, and made answer as follows:—"Men of Athens, our resolution is unchanged; and we will not in a moment surrender that liberty which our city, founded seven hundred years ago, still enjoys; we will trust to the good-fortune which by the favor of the Gods has hitherto preserved us, and for human help to the Lacedaemonians, and endeavor to save ourselves. We are ready however to be your friends, and the enemies neither of you nor of the Lacedaemonians, and we ask you to leave our country when you have made such a peace as may appear to be in the interest of both parties."

113. Such was the answer of the Melians; the Athenians, as they quitted the conference, spoke as follows:—"Well, we must say, judging from the decision at which you have arrived, that you are the only men who deem the future to be more cer-

tain than the present, and regard things unseen as already realized in your fond anticipation, and that the more you cast yourselves upon the Lacedaemonians and fortune, and hope, and trust them, the more complete will be your ruin."

114. The Athenian envoys returned to the army; and the generals, when they found that the Melians would not yield, immediately commenced hostilities. They surrounded the town of Melos with a wall, dividing the work among the several contingents. They then left troops of their own and of the allies to keep guard both by land and by sea, and retired with the greater part of their army; the remainder carried on the blockade.

.   .   .

116. . . . The place was now closely invested, and there was treachery among the citizens themselves. So the Melians were induced to surrender at discretion. The Athenians thereupon put to death all who were of military age, and made slaves of the women and children. They then colonised the island, sending thither five hundred settlers of their own.

The Last Days of Socrates

Although Socrates (c.470–399 B.C.) was an influential philosopher and teacher, he wrote nothing. Therefore, we must rely on secondary accounts for information about his life and beliefs. Such accounts, particularly the writings of his most famous disciple, Plato, make it possible to reconstruct the broad outlines of his career. Socrates was born in Athens, the son of a stonecutter. Instead of learning his father's trade, he began early in life to frequent the Athenian marketplace, where he listened to the intellectuals of the city argue questions of politics, art, morality, and philosophy.

Before long, he had acquired a reputation as a man of wisdom and had gathered about himself a group of young disciples, who were intrigued by the unusual manner in which he taught. Unlike the sophists ("wise men"), the professional teachers of the day who were willing to teach anyone anything for a suitable fee, Socrates professed to be completely ignorant. Instead of attempting to teach, he wandered about Athens seeking wisdom by asking questions of everyone he met, including the city's leading politicians, generals, artists, and philosophers. As might be expected, under Socrates' questioning many of the self-styled sages of Athens proved to be without wisdom. Although Socrates' unflinching quest for wisdom and truth won him many loyal followers, it inevitably aroused the enmity of those whose ignorance he unmasked. Through their influence in Athens, his enemies succeeded in having him brought to trial and condemned to death. But they were unable to silence him, for his words live on in the Dialogues of Plato.

Although he professed to have no wisdom of his own, Socrates did have a positive philosophy. The basic premise of his philosophy was the doctrine that *virtue is knowledge,* or that the good life is the life of wisdom. To gain knowledge and, hence, virtue, he believed, education is necessary. But knowledge is not something that can be poured into an individual from the outside. Rather, it is something that lies deep within each man and needs only to be drawn out. Socrates' method for bringing this inborn knowledge to the surface was to ask a series of questions, a technique that is known as the *dialectic method.*

The selections that follow are an account of the last days of Socrates written by Plato some time after the events described. Socrates had been haled into court by a group of accusers, a sort of "un-Athenian activities committee," who charged him with being an atheist and a corrupter of youth. In Plato's *Apology*, Socrates is represented as replying to the charges with a general defense of his way of life. In the *Crito*, Plato pictures Socrates waiting in prison for his execution and arguing with a friend (who has arranged for his escape) about whether he would be justified in running away, even though he has been unjustly convicted. The extract from the *Phaedo* records Socrates' death. These selections give us a fresh and living portrait of Socrates the man, a fairly comprehensive account of his philosophy, and a glimpse of the social and legal structure of the Athens of his day.

The Apology

SCENE: The Court of Justice

I cannot tell what impression my accusers have made upon you, Athenians: for my own part, I know that they nearly made me forget who I was, so plausible were they; and yet they have scarcely uttered one single word of truth. But of all their many falsehoods, the one which astonished me most, was when they said that I was a clever speaker, and that you must be careful not to let me mislead you. I thought that it was most impudent of them not to be ashamed to talk in that way; for as soon as I opened my mouth the lie will be exposed, and I shall prove that I am not a clever speaker in any way at all: unless, indeed, by a clever speaker they mean a man who speaks the truth. If that is their meaning, I agree with them that I am a much greater orator than they. My accusers, then I repeat, have said little or nothing that is true; but from me you shall hear the whole truth. Certainly you will not hear an elaborate speech, Athenians, drest up, like theirs, with words and phrases. I will say to you what I have to say, without preparation, and in the words which come first, for I believe that my cause is just; so let none of you expect anything else. Indeed, my friends, it would hardly be seemly for me, at my age, to come before you like a young man with his specious falsehoods. But there is one thing, Athenians, which I do most earnestly beg and entreat of you. Do not be surprised and do not interrupt, if in my defence I speak in the same way that I am accustomed to speak in the marketplace, at the tables of the money-changers, where many of you have heard me, and elsewhere. The truth is this. I am more than seventy years old, and this is the first time that I have ever come before a Court of Law; so your manner of speech here is quite strange to me. If I had been really a stranger, you would have forgiven me for speaking in the language and the fashion of my native country: and so now I ask you to grant me what I think I have a right to claim. Never mind

Trans. F. J. Church (1880).

the style of my speech—it may be better or it may be worse—give your whole attention to the question, Is what I say just, or is it not? That is what makes a good judge, as speaking the truth makes a good advocate.

I have to defend myself Athenians, first against the old false charges of my old accusers, and then against the later ones of my present accusers. For many men have been accusing me to you, and for very many years, who have not uttered a word of truth: and I fear them more than I fear Anytus and his companions, formidable as they are. But, my friends, those others are still more formidable; for they got hold of most of you when you were children, and they have been more persistent in accusing me with lies, and in trying to persuade you that there is one Socrates, a wise man, who speculates about the heavens, and who examines into all things that are beneath the earth, and who can "make the worse appear the better reason." These men, Athenians, who spread abroad this report, are the accusers whom I fear; for their hearers think that persons who pursue such inquiries never believe in the gods. And then they are many, and their attacks have been going on for a long time: and they spoke to you when you were at the age most readily to believe them: for you were all young, and many of you were children: and there was no one to answer them when they attacked me. And the most unreasonable thing of all is that commonly I do not even know their names: I cannot tell you who they are, except in the case of the comic poets. But all the rest who

have been trying to prejudice you against me, from motives of spite and jealousy, and sometimes, it may be, from conviction, are the enemies whom it is hardest to meet. For I cannot call any one of them forward in Court, to cross-examine him: I have, as it were, simply to fight with shadows in my defence, and to put questions which there is no one to answer. I ask you, therefore, to believe that, as I say, I have been attacked by two classes of accusers—first by Meletus and his friends, and then by those older ones of whom I have spoken. And, with your leave, I will defend myself first against my old enemies; for you heard their accusations first, and they were much more persistent than my present accusers are.

Well, I must make my defence, Athenians, and try in the short time allowed me to remove the prejudice which you have had against me for a long time. I hope that I may manage to do this, if it be good for you and for me, and that my defence may be successful; but I am quite aware of the nature of my task, and I know that it is a difficult one. Be the issue, however, as God wills, I must obey the law, and make my defence.

Let us begin again, then, and see what is the charge which has given rise to the prejudice against me, which was what Meletus relied on when he drew his indictment. What is the calumny which my enemies have been spreading about me? I must assume that they are formally accusing me, and read their indictment. It would run somewhat in this fashion: "Socrates is an evildoer, who meddles with inquiries into things beneath the earth, and in heaven, and who 'makes the worse appear the better reason,' and who teaches others these same things." That is what they say; and in the Comedy of Aristophanes you yourselves saw a man called Socrates swinging round in a basket, and saying that he walked the air, and talking a great deal of nonsense about matters of which I understand nothing, either more or less. I do not mean to disparage that kind of knowledge, if there is any man who possesses it. I trust Meletus may never be able to prosecute me for that. But, the truth is, Athenians, I have nothing to do with these matters, and almost all of you are yourselves my witnesses of this. I beg all of you who have heard me converse, and they are many, to inform your neighbors and tell them if any of you have ever heard me conversing about such matters, either more or less. That will show you that the other common stories about me are as false as this one.

But, the fact is, that not one of these stories is true; and if you have heard that I undertake to educate men, and exact money from them for so doing, that is not true either; though I think that it would be a fine thing to be able to educate men, as Gorgias of Leontini, and Prodicus of Ceos, and Hippias of Elis do. For each of them, my friends, can go into any city, and persuade the young men to leave the society of their fellow-citizens, with any of whom they might associate for nothing, and to be only too glad to be allowed to pay money for the privilege of associating with themselves. And I believe that there is another wise man from Paros residing in Athens at this moment. I happened to meet Callias, the son of Hipponicus, a man who has spent more money on the Sophists than every one else put together. So I said to him—he has two sons—"Callias, if your two sons had been foals or calves, we could have hired a trainer for them who would have made them perfect in the excellence which belongs to their nature. He would have been either a groom or a farmer. But whom do you intend to take to train them, seeing that they are men? Who understands the excellence which belongs to men and to citizens? I suppose that you must have thought of this, because of your sons. Is there such a person," said I, "or not?" "Certainly there is," he replied. "Who is he," said I, "and where does he come from, and what is his fee?" "His name is Evenus, Socrates," he replied. "He comes from Paros, and his fee is five minae." Then I thought that Evenus was a fortunate person if he really understood this art and could teach so cleverly. If I had possessed knowledge of that kind, I should have given myself airs and prided myself on it. But, Athenians, the truth is that I do not possess it.

Perhaps some of you may reply: "But, Socrates, what is this pursuit of yours? Whence come these calumnies against you? You must have been engaged in some pursuit out of the common. All these stories and reports of you would never have gone about, if you had not been in some way different from other men. So tell us what your pursuits are, that we may not give our verdict in the dark." I think that that is a fair question, and I will try to explain to you what it is that has raised these calumnies against me, and given me this name. Listen, then: some of you perhaps will think that I am jesting, but I assure you that I will tell you the whole truth. I have gained this name, Athenians, simply by reason of a certain wisdom. But by what kind of wisdom? It is by just that wisdom which is, I believe, possible to men. In that, it may be, I am really wise. But the men of whom I was speaking just now must be wise in a wisdom which is greater than human wisdom, or in some way which I cannot describe, for certainly I know nothing of it myself, and if any man says that I do, he lies and wants to slander me. Do not interrupt me, Athenians, even if you think that I am speaking arrogantly. What I am going to say is not my own: I will tell you who says it, and he is worthy of your credit. I will bring the god of Delphi to be the witness of the fact of my wisdom and of its nature. You remember Chaerephon. From youth upwards he was my comrade; and he went into exile with the people,[1] and with the people he returned. And you remember, too, Chaerephon's character; how vehement he was in carrying through whatever he took in hand. Once he went to Delphi and ventured to put this question to the oracle,—I entreat you again, my friends, not to cry out,—he asked if there was any man who was wiser than I: and the priestess answered that there was no man. Chaerephon himself is dead, but his brother here will confirm what I say.

Now see why I tell you this. I

am going to explain to you the origin of my unpopularity. When I heard of the oracle I began to reflect: What can God mean by this dark saying? I know very well that I am not wise, even in the smallest degree. Then what can he mean by saying that I am the wisest of men? It cannot be that he is speaking falsely, for he is a god and cannot lie. And for a long time I was at a loss to understand his meaning: then, very reluctantly, I turned to seek for it in this manner. I went to a man who was reputed to be wise, thinking that there, if anywhere, I should prove the answer wrong, and meaning to point out to the oracle its mistake, and to say, "You said that I was the wisest of men, but this man is wiser than I am." So I examined the man —I need not tell you his name, he was a politician—but this was the result, Athenians. When I conversed with him I came to see that, though a great many persons, and most of all he himself, thought that he was wise, yet he was not wise. And then I tried to prove to him that he was not wise, though he fancied that he was: and by so doing I made him, and many of the bystanders, my enemies. So when I went away, I thought to myself, "I am wiser than this man: neither of us probably knows anything that is really good, but he thinks that he has knowledge, when he has not, while I, having no knowledge, do not think that I have. I seem, at any rate, to be a little wiser than he is on this point: I do not think that I know what I do not know." Next I went to another man who was reputed to be still wiser than the last, with exactly the same result. And there again I

---

[1] [At the time of the oligarchy of the Thirty, 404 B.C.—*Trans.*]

made him, and many other men, my enemies.

Then I went on to one man after another, seeing that I was making enemies every day, which caused me much unhappiness and anxiety: still I thought that I must set God's command above everything. So I had to go to every man who seemed to possess any knowledge, and search for the meaning of the oracle: and, Athenians, I must tell you the truth; verily, by the dog of Egypt, this was the result of the search which I made at God's bidding. I found that the men, whose reputation for wisdom stood highest, were nearly the most lacking in it; while others, who were looked down on as common people, were much better fitted to learn. Now, I must describe to you the wanderings which I undertook, like a series of Heraclean labours, to make full proof of the oracle. After the politicians, I went to the poets, tragic, dithyrambic, and others, thinking that there I should find myself manifestly more ignorant than they. So I took up the poems on which I thought that they had spent most pains, and asked them what they meant, hoping at the same time to learn something from them. I am ashamed to tell you the truth, my friends, but I must say it. Almost any one of the bystanders could have talked about the works of these poets better than the poets themselves. So I soon found that it is not by wisdom that the poets create their works, but by a certain natural power and by inspiration, like soothsayers and prophets, who say many fine things, but who understand nothing of what they say. The poets seemed to me to be in a similar case. And at the same time I perceived that, because of their poetry, they thought that they were the wisest of men in other matters too, which they were not. So I went away again, thinking that I had the same advantage over the poets that I had over the politicians.

Finally, I went to the artizans, for I knew very well that I possessed no knowledge at all, worth speaking of, and I was sure that I should find that they knew many fine things. And in that I was not mistaken. They knew what I did not know, and so far they were wiser than I. But, Athenians, it seemed to me that the skilled artizans made the same mistake as the poets. Each of them believed himself to be extremely wise in matters of the greatest importance, because he was skilful in his own art: and this mistake of theirs threw their real wisdom into the shade. So I asked myself, on behalf of the oracle, whether I would choose to remain as I was, without either their wisdom or their ignorance, or to possess both, as they did. And I made answer to myself and to the oracle that it was better for me to remain as I was.

By reason of this examination, Athenians, I have made many enemies of a very fierce and bitter kind, who have spread abroad a great number of calumnies about me, and people say that I am "a wise man." For the bystanders always think that I am wise myself in any matter wherein I convict another man of ignorance. But, my friends, I believe that only God is really wise: and that by this oracle he meant that men's wisdom is worth little or nothing. I do not think that he meant that Socrates was wise. He only made use of my name, and took me as an example, as though he would say to men, "He among you is the wisest, who, like Socrates, knows that in very truth his wisdom is worth nothing at all." And therefore I still go about testing and examining every man whom I think wise, whether he be a citizen or a stranger, as God has commanded me; and whenever I find that he is not wise, I point out to him on the part of God that he is not wise. And I am so busy in this pursuit that I have never had leisure to take any part worth mentioning in public matters, or to look after my private affairs. I am in very great poverty by reason of my service to God.

And besides this, the young men who follow me about, who are the sons of wealthy persons and have a great deal of spare time, take a natural pleasure in hearing men cross-examined: and they often imitate me among themselves: then they try their hands at cross-examining other people. And, I imagine, they find a great abundance of men who think that they know a great deal, when in fact they know little or nothing. And then the persons who are cross-examined get angry with me instead of with themselves, and say that Socrates is an abominable fellow who corrupts young men. And when they are asked, "Why, what does he do? what does he teach?" they do not know what to say; but, not to seem at a loss, they repeat the stock charges against all philosophers, and allege that he investigates things in the air and under the earth, and that he teaches people to disbelieve in the gods, and "to make the worse appear the better reason." For, I

fancy, they would not like to confess the truth, which is that they are shown up as ignorant pretenders to knowledge that they do not possess. And so they have been filling your ears with their bitter calumnies for a long time, for they are zealous and numerous and bitter against me; and they are well disciplined and plausible in speech. On these grounds Meletus and Anytus and Lycon have attacked me. Meletus is indignant with me on the part of the poets, and Anytus on the part of the artizans and politicians, and Lycon on the part of the orators. And so, as I said at the beginning, I shall be surprised if I am able, in the short time allowed me for my defence, to remove from your minds this prejudice which has grown so strong. What I have told you, Athenians, is the truth: I neither conceal, nor do I suppress anything, small or great. And yet I know that it is just this plainness of speech which makes me enemies. But that is only a proof that my words are true, and that the prejudice against me, and the causes of it, are what I have said. And whether you look for them now or hereafter, you will find that they are so.

[*Socrates then cross-examines and discredits his chief accuser.—* Ed.]

• • •

Perhaps some one will say: "Are you not ashamed, Socrates, of following pursuits which are very likely now to cause your death?" I should answer him with justice, and say: My friend, if you think that a man of any worth at all ought to reckon the chances of life and death when he acts, or that he ought to think of anything but whether he is acting rightly or wrongly, and as a good or a bad man would act, you are grievously mistaken. According to you, the demigods who died at Troy would be men of no great worth, and among them the son of Thetis, who thought nothing of danger when the alternative was disgrace. For when his mother, a goddess, addressed him, as he was burning to slay Hector, I suppose in this fashion, "My son, if thou avengest the death of thy comrade Patroclus, and slayest Hector, thou wilt die thyself, for 'fate awaits thee straightway after Hector's death'"; he heard what she said, but he scorned danger and death; he feared much more to live a coward, and not to avenge his friend. "Let me punish the evil-doer and straightway die," he said, "that I may not remain here by the beaked ships, a scorn of men, encumbering the earth." Do you suppose that he thought of danger or of death? For this, Athenians, I believe to be the truth. Wherever a man's post is, whether he has chosen it of his own will, or whether he has been placed at it by his commander, there it is his duty to remain and face the danger, without thinking of death, or of any other thing, except dishonour.

When the generals whom you chose to command me, Athenians, placed me at my post at Potidaea, and at Amphipolis, and at Delium, I remained where they placed me, and ran the risk of death, like other men: and it would be very strange conduct on my part if I were to desert my post now from fear of death or of any other thing, when God has commanded me, as I am persuaded that he has done, to spend my life in searching for wisdom, and in examining myself and others. That would indeed be a very strange thing: and then certainly I might with justice be brought to trial for not believing in the gods: for I should be disobeying the oracle, and fearing death, and thinking myself wise, when I was not wise. For to fear death, my friends, is only to think ourselves wise, without being wise: for it is to think that we know what we do not know. For anything that men can tell, death may be the greatest good that can happen to them: but they fear it as if they knew quite well that it was the greatest of evils. And what is this but that shameful ignorance of thinking that we know what we do not know? In this manner too, my friends, perhaps I am different from the mass of mankind: and if I were to claim to be at all wiser than others, it would be because I do not think that I have any clear knowledge about the other world, when, in fact, I have none. But I do know very well that it is evil and base to do wrong, and to disobey my superior, whether he be man or god. And I will never do what I know to be evil, and shrink in fear from what, for all that I can tell, may be a good. And so, even if you acquit me now, and do not listen to Anytus' argument that, if I am to be acquitted, I ought never to have been brought to trial at all; and that, as it is, you are bound to put me to death, because, as he said, if I escape, all your children will forthwith be utterly corrupted by practising what Socrates teaches; if you were therefore to say to me, "Socrates, this time we will not listen to Anytus: we will let you go; but on this condition, that you cease from carrying on this search of yours, and from philosophy; if you are found following those pursuits again, you shall die": I say, if you offered to let me go on these terms, I should reply:—"Athenians, I hold you in the highest regard and love; but I will obey God rather than you: and as long as I have breath and strength I will not cease from philosophy, and from exhorting you, and declaring the truth to everyone of you whom I meet, saying, as I am wont, 'My excellent friend, you are a citizen of Athens, a city which is very great and very famous for wisdom and power of mind; are you not ashamed of caring so much for the making of money, and for reputation, and for honour? Will you not think or care about wisdom, and truth, and the perfection of your soul?' " And if he disputes my words, and says that he does care about these things, I shall not forthwith release him and go away: I shall question him and cross-examine him and test him: and if I think that he has not virtue, though he says that he has, I shall reproach him for setting the lower value on the most important things, and a higher value on those that are of less account. This I shall do to every one whom I meet, young or old, citizen or stranger: but more especially to the citizens, for they are more nearly akin to me. For, know well, God has commanded me to do so. And I think that no better piece of fortune has ever befallen you in Athens than my service to God. For I spend my whole life in going about and persuading you all to give your first and chiefest care to the perfection of your souls, and not till you have done that to think

of your bodies, or your wealth; and telling you that virtue does not come from wealth, but that wealth, and every other good thing which men have, whether in public, or in private, comes from virtue. If then I corrupt the youth by this teaching, the mischief is great: but if any man says that I teach anything else, he speaks falsely. And therefore, Athenians, I say, either listen to Anytus, or do not listen to him: either acquit me, or do not acquit me: but be sure that I shall not alter my way of life; no, not if I have to die for it many times.

Do not interrupt me, Athenians. Remember the request which I made to you, and listen to my words. I think that it will profit you to hear them. I am going to say something more to you, at which you may be inclined to cry out: but do not do that. Be sure that if you put me to death, who am what I have told you that I am, you will do yourselves more harm than me. Meletus and Anytus can do me no harm: that is impossible: for I am sure that God will not allow a good man to be injured by a bad one. They may indeed kill me, or drive me into exile, or deprive me of my civil rights; and perhaps Meletus and others think those things great evils. But I do not think so: I think that it is a much greater evil to do what he is doing now, and to try to put a man to death unjustly. And now, Athenians, I am not arguing in my own defence at all, as you might expect me to do: I am trying to persuade you not to sin against God, by condemning me, and rejecting his gift to you. For if you put me to death, you will not easily find another man to fill my place.

God has sent me to attack the city, as if it were a great and noble horse, to use a quaint simile, which was rather sluggish from its size, and which needed to be aroused by a gadfly: and I think that I am the gadfly that God has sent to the city to attack it; for I never cease from settling upon you, as it were, at every point, and rousing, and exhorting, and reproaching each man of you all day long. You will not easily find any one else, my friends, to fill my place: and if you take my advice, you will spare my life. You are vexed, as drowsy persons are, when they are awakened, and of course, if you listen to Anytus, you could easily kill me with a single blow, and then sleep on undisturbed for the rest of your lives, unless God were to care for you enough to send another man to arouse you. And you may easily see that it is God who has given me to your city: a mere human impulse would never have led me to neglect all my own interests, or to endure seeing my private affairs neglected now for so many years, while it made me busy myself unceasingly in your interests, and go to each man of you by himself, like a father, or an elder brother, trying to persuade him to care for virtue. There would have been a reason for it, if I had gained any advantage by this conduct, or if I had been paid for my exhortations; but you see yourselves that my accusers, though they accuse me of everything else without blushing, have not had the effrontery to say that I ever either exacted or demanded payment. They could bring no evidence of that. And I think that I have sufficient evidence of

the truth of what I say in my poverty.

Perhaps it may seem strange to you that, though I am so busy in going about in private with my counsel, yet I do not venture to come forward in the assembly, and take part in the public councils. You have often heard me speak of my reason for this, and in many places: it is that I have a certain divine sign from God, which is the divinity that Meletus has caricatured in his indictment. I have had it from childhood: it is a kind of voice, which whenever I hear it, always turns me back from something which I was going to do, but never urges me to act. It is this which forbids me to take part in politics. And I think that it does well to forbid me. For, Athenians, it is quite certain that if I had attempted to take part in politics, I should have perished at once and long ago, without doing any good either to you or to myself. And do not be vexed with me for telling the truth. There is no man who will preserve his life for long, either in Athens or elsewhere, if he firmly opposes the wishes of the people, and tries to prevent the commission of much injustice and illegality in the State. He who would really fight for justice, must do so as a private man, not in public, if he means to preserve his life, even for a short time.

I will prove to you that this is so by very strong evidence, not by mere words, but by what you value highly, actions. Listen then to what has happened to me, that you may know that there is no man who could make me consent to do wrong from the fear of death; but that I would perish at once rather than give way. What I am going to tell you may be a commonplace in the Courts of Law; nevertheless it is true. The only office that I ever held in the State, Athenians, was that of Senator. When you wished to try the ten generals, who did not rescue their men after the battle of Arginusae, in a body, which was illegal, as you all came to think afterwards, the tribe Antiochis, to which I belong, held the presidency. On that occasion I alone of all the presidents opposed your illegal action, and gave my vote against you. The speakers were ready to suspend me and arrest me; and you were clamouring against me, and crying out to me to submit. But I thought that I ought to face the danger out in the cause of law and justice, rather than join with you in your unjust proposal, from fear of imprisonment or death. That was before the destruction of the democracy. When the oligarchy came, the Thirty sent for me, with four others, to the Council-Chamber and ordered us to bring over Leon the Salaminian from Salamis, that they might put him to death. They were in the habit of frequently giving similar orders to many others, wishing to implicate as many men as possible in their crimes. But then I again proved, not by mere words, but by my actions, that, if I may use a vulgar expression, I do not care a straw for death; but that I do care very much indeed about not doing anything against the laws of God or man. That government with all its power did not terrify me into doing anything wrong, but when we left the Council-Chamber, the other four went over to Salamis, and brought Leon across to Athens; and I went away home: and if the rule of the Thirty had not been destroyed soon aftrewards, I should very likely have been put to death for what I did then. Many of you will be my witnesses in this matter.

Now do you think that I should have remained alive all these years, if I had taken part in public affairs, and had always maintained the cause of justice like an honest man, and had held it a paramount duty, as it is, to do so? Certainly not, Athenians, nor any other man either. But throughout my whole life, both in private, and in public, whenever I have had to take part in public affairs, you will find that I have never yielded a single point in a question of right and wrong to any man; no, not to those whom my enemies falsely assert to have been my pupils. But I was never any man's teacher. I have never withheld myself from any one, young or old, who was anxious to hear me converse while I was about my mission; neither do I converse for payment, and refuse to converse without payment: I am ready to ask questions of rich and poor alike, and if any man wishes to answer me, and then listen to what I have to say, he may. And I cannot justly be charged with causing these men to turn out good or bad citizens: for I never either taught, or professed to teach any of them any knowledge whatever. And if any man asserts that he ever learnt or heard any thing from me in private, which every one else did not hear as well as he, be sure that he does not speak the truth.

Why is it, then, that people delight in spending so much time in my company? You have heard why, Athenians. I told you the whole truth when I said that they delight in hearing me examine persons who think that they are wise when they are not wise. It is certainly very amusing to listen to that. And, I say, God has commanded me to examine men in oracles, and in dreams, and in every way in which the divine will was ever declared to man. This is the truth, Athenians, and if it were not the truth, it would be easily refuted. For if it were really the case that I have already corrupted some of the young men, and I am now corrupting others, surely some of them, finding as they grew older that I had given them evil counsel in their youth, would have come forward to-day to accuse me and take their revenge. Or if they were unwilling to do so themselves, surely their kinsmen, their fathers, or brothers, or other relatives, would, if I had done them any harm, have remembered it, and taken their revenge. Certainly I see many of them in Court. Here is Crito, of my own deme and of my own age, the father of Critobulus; here is Lysanias of Sphettus, the father of Aeschinus: here is also Antiphon of Cephisus, the father of Epigenes. Then here are others, whose brothers have spent their time in my company; Nicostratus, the son of Theozotides, and brother of Theodotus—and Theodotus is dead, so he at least cannot entreat his brother to be silent: here is Paralus, the son of Demodocus, and the brother of Theages: here is Adeimantus, the son of Ariston, whose brother is Plato here: and Aeantodorus, whose brother is Aris-

todorus. And I can name many others to you, some of whom Meletus ought to have called as witnesses in the course of his own speech: but if he forgot to call them then, let him call them now—I will stand aside while he does so—and tell us if he has any such evidence. No, on the contrary, my friends, you will find all these men ready to support me, the corrupter, the injurer of their kindred, as Meletus and Anytus call me. Those of them who have been already corrupted might perhaps have some reason for supporting me: but what reason can their relatives, who are grown up, and who are uncorrupted, have, except the reason of truth and justice, that they know very well that Meletus is a liar, and that I am speaking the truth?

Well, my friends, this, together it may be with other things of the same nature, is pretty much what I have to say in my defence. There may be some one among you who will be vexed when he remembers how, even in a less important trial than this, he prayed and entreated the judges to acquit him with many tears, and brought forward his children and many of his friends and relatives in Court, in order to appeal to your feelings; and then finds that I shall do none of these things, though I am in what he would think the supreme danger. Perhaps he will harden himself against me when he notices this: it may make him angry, and he may give his vote in anger. If it is so with any of you—I do not suppose that it is, but in case it should be so—I think that I should answer him reasonably if I said: "My friend, I have kinsmen too, for, in the words of Homer, 'I am not born of sticks and stones,' but of woman"; and so, Athenians, I have kinsmen, and I have three sons, one of them a lad, and the other two still children. Yet I will not bring any of them forward before you, and implore you to acquit me. And why will I do none of these things? It is not from arrogance, Athenians, nor because I hold you cheap: whether or not I can face death bravely is another question: but for my own credit, and for your credit, and for the credit of our city, I do not think it well, at my age, and with my name, to do anything of that kind. Rightly or wrongly, men have made up their minds that in some way Socrates is different from the mass of mankind. And it will be a shameful thing if those of you who are thought to excell in wisdom, or in bravery, or in any other virtue, are going to act in this fashion. I have often seen men with a reputation behaving in a strange way at their trial, as if they thought it a terrible fate to be killed, and as though they expected to live for ever, if you did not put them to death. Such men seem to me to bring discredit on the city: for any stranger would suppose that the best and most eminent Athenians, who are selected by their fellow-citizens to hold office, and for other honours, are no better than women. Those of you, Athenians, who have any reputation at all, ought not to do these things: and you ought not to allow us to do them: you should show that you will be much more merciless to men who make the city ridiculous by these pitiful pieces of acting, than to men who remain quiet.

But apart from the question of credit, my friends, I do not think that it is right to entreat the judge to acquit us, or to escape condemnation in that way. It is our duty to convince his mind by reason. He does not sit to give away justice to his friends, but to pronounce judgment: and he has sworn not to favour any man whom he would like to favour, but to decide questions according to law. And therefore we ought not to teach you to forswear yourselves; and you ought not to allow yourselves to be taught, for then neither you nor we would be acting righteously. Therefore, Athenians, do not require me to do these things, for I believe them to be neither good nor just nor holy; and, more especially do not ask me to do them today, when Meletus is prosecuting me for impiety. For were I to be successful, and to prevail on you by my prayers to break your oaths, I should be clearly teaching you to believe that there are no gods; and I should be simply accusing myself by my defence of not believing in them. But, Athenians, that is very far from the truth. I do believe in the gods as no one of my accusers believes in them: and to you and to God I commit my cause to be decided as is best for you and for me.

[*He is found guilty by 281 votes to 220, and in a second vote is condemned to death*—Ed.]

• • •

You have not gained very much time, Athenians, and, as the price of it, you will have an evil name from all who wish to revile the city, and they will cast in your teeth that you put Socrates, a wise man, to death. For they will certainly call me wise, whether I am wise or not, when they want to reproach you. If you would have waited for a little while, your wishes would have been fulfilled in the course of nature; for you see that I am an old man, far advanced in years, and near to death. I am speaking not to all of you, only to those who have voted for my death. And now I am speaking to them still. Perhaps, my friends, you think that I have been defeated because I was wanting in the arguments by which I could have persuaded you to acquit me, if, that is, I had thought it right to do or to say anything to escape punishment. It is not so. I have been defeated because I was wanting, not in arguments, but in overboldness and effrontery: because I would not plead before you as you would have liked to hear me plead, or appeal to you with weeping and wailing, or say and do many other things, which I maintain are unworthy of me, but which you have been accustomed to from other men. But when I was defending myself, I thought that I ought not to do anything unmanly because of the danger which I ran, and I have not changed my mind now. I would very much rather defend myself as I did, and die, than as you would have had me do, and live. Both in a law suit, and in war, there are some things which neither I nor any other man may do in order to escape from death. In battle a man often sees that he may at least escape from death by throwing down his arms and falling on his knees before the pursuer to beg for his life. And there are many other ways of avoiding death in every danger, if a man will not scruple to say and to do anything. But, my friends, I think that

it is a much harder thing to escape from wickedness than from death; for wickedness is swifter than death. And now I, who am old and slow, have been overtaken by the slower pursuer: and my accusers, who are clever and swift, have been overtaken by the swifter pursuer, which is wickedness. And now I shall go hence, sentenced by you to death; and they will go hence, sentenced by truth to receive the penalty of wickedness and evil. And I abide by this award as well as they. Perhaps it was right for these things to be so: and I think that they are fairly measured.

And now I wish to prophesy to you, Athenians who have condemned me. For I am going to die, and that is the time when men have most prophetic power. And I prophesy to you who have sentenced me to death, that a far severer punishment than you have inflicted on me, will surely overtake you as I am dead. You have done this thing, thinking that you will be relieved from having to give an account of your lives. But I say that the result will be very different from that. There will be more men who will call you to account, whom I have held back, and whom you did not see. And they will be harder masters to you than I have been, for they will be younger, and you will be more angry with them. For if you think that you will restrain men from reproaching you for your evil lives by putting them to death, you are very much mistaken. That way of escape is hardly possible, and it is not a good one. It is much better, and much easier, not to silence reproaches, but to make yourselves as perfect as you can. This is my parting prophecy to you who have condemned me.

With you who have acquitted me I should like to converse touching this thing that has come to pass, while the authorities are busy, and before I go to the place where I have to die. So, I pray you, remain with me until I go hence: there is no reason why we should not converse with each other while it is possible. I wish to explain to you, as my friends, the meaning of what has befallen me. A wonderful thing has happened to me, judges—for you I am right in calling judges. The prophetic sign, which I am wont to receive from the divine voice, has been constantly with me all through my life till now, opposing me in quite small matters if I were not going to act rightly. And now you yourselves see what has happened to me; a thing which might be thought, and which is sometimes actually reckoned, the supreme evil. But the sign of God did not withstand me when I was leaving my house in the morning, nor when I was coming up hither to the Court, nor at any point in my speech, when I was going to say anything: though at other times it has often stopped me in the very act of speaking. But now, in this matter, it has never once withstood me, either in my words or my actions. I will tell you what I believe to be the reason of that. This thing that has come upon me must be a good: and those of us who think that death is an evil must needs be mistaken. I have a clear proof that that is so; for my accustomed sign would certainly have opposed me, if I had not been going to fare well.

And if we reflect in another way we shall see that we may well hope that death is a good. For the state of death is one of two things: either the dead man wholly ceases to be, and loses all sensation; or, according to the common belief, it is a change and a migration of the soul unto another place. And if death is the absence of all sensation, and like the sleep of one whose slumbers are unbroken by any dreams, it will be a wonderful gain. For if a man had to select that night in which he slept so soundly that he did not even see any dreams, and had to compare with it all the other nights and days of his life, and then had to say how many days and nights in his life he had spent better and more pleasantly than this night, I think that a private person, nay, even the great King himself, would find them easy to count, compared with the others. If that is the nature of death, I for one count it a gain. For then it appears that eternity is nothing more than a single night. But if death is a journey to another place, and the common belief be true, that there are all who have died, what good could be greater than this, my judges? Would a journey not be worth taking, at the end of which, in the other world, we should be released from the self-styled judges who are here, and should find the true judges, who are said to sit in judgment below, such as Minos, and Rhadamanthus, and Aeacus, and Triptolemus, and the other demigods who were just in their lives? Or what would you not give to converse with Orpheus and Musaeus and Hesiod and Homer? I am willing to die many times, if this be true. And for my own part I should have a wonderful interest in meeting there Palamedes, and Ajax the son of Telamon, and the other men of old who have died through an unjust judgment, and in comparing my experiences with theirs. That I think would be no small pleasure. And, above all, I could spend my time in examining those who are there, as I examine men here, and in finding out which of them is wise, and which of them thinks himself wise, when he is not wise. What would we not give, my judges, to be able to examine the leader of the great expedition against Troy, or Odysseus, or Sisyphus, or countless other men and women whom we could name? It would be an infinite happiness to converse with them, and to live with them, and to examine them. Assuredly there they do not put men to death for doing that. For besides the other ways in which they are happier than we are, they are immortal, at least if the common belief be true.

And you too, judges, must face death with a good courage, and believe this as a truth, that no evil can happen to a good man, either in life, or after death. His fortunes are not neglected by the gods; and what has come to me to-day has not come by chance. I am persuaded that it was better for me to die now, and to be released from trouble: and that was the reason why the sign never turned me back. And so I am hardly angry with my accusers, or with those who have condemned me to die. Yet it was not with this mind that they accused me and condemned me, but meaning to do me an injury. So far I may find fault with them.

Yet I have one request to make of them. When my sons grow up, visit them with punishment, my friends, and vex them in the same way that I have vexed you, if they seem to you to care for riches, or for any other thing, before virtue: and if they think that they are something, when they are nothing at all, reproach them, as I have reproached you, for not caring for what they should, and for thinking that they are great men when in fact they are worthless. And if you will do this, I myself and my sons will have received our deserts at your hands.

But now the time has come, and we must go hence; I to die, and you to live. Whether life or death is better is known to God, and to God only.

Crito

SCENE: The Prison of Socrates

SOCRATES: Why have you come at this hour, Crito? Is it not still early?

CRITO: Yes, very early.

SOCRATES: About what time is it?

CRITO: It is just day-break.

SOCRATES: I wonder that the jailor was willing to let you in.

CRITO: He knows me now, Socrates, I come here so often; and

Trans. F. J. Church (1880).

besides, I have done him a service.

SOCRATES: Have you been here long?

CRITO: Yes; some time.

SOCRATES: Then why did you sit down without speaking? why did you not wake me at once?

CRITO: Indeed, Socrates, I wish that I myself were not so sleepless and sorrowful. But I have been wondering to see how sweetly you sleep. And I purposely did not wake you, for I was anxious not to disturb your repose. Often before, all through your life, I have thought that your temper was a happy one; and I think so more than ever now, when I see how easily and calmly you bear the calamity that has come to you.

SOCRATES: Nay Crito, it would be absurd if at my age I were angry at having to die.

CRITO: Other men as old are overtaken by similar calamities, Socrates; but their age does not save them from being angry with their fate.

SOCRATES: That is so: but tell me, why are you here so early?

CRITO: I am the bearer of bitter news, Socrates: not bitter, it seems, to you; but to me, and to all your friends, both bitter and grievous: and to none of them, I think, is it more grievous than to me.

SOCRATES: What is it? Has the ship come from Delos, at the arrival of which I am to die?

CRITO: No, it has not actually arrived: but I think that it will be here to-day, from the news which certain persons have brought from Sunium, who left it there. It is clear from their news that it will be here to-day; and then, Socrates, to-morrow your life will have to end.

SOCRATES: Well, Crito, may it end fortunately. Be it so, if so the gods will. But I do not think that the ship will be here to-day.

CRITO: Why do you suppose not?

SOCRATES: I will tell you. I am to die on the day after the ship arrives, am I not?

CRITO: That is what the authorities say.

SOCRATES: Then I do not think that it will come to-day, but to-morrow. I judge from a certain dream which I saw a little while ago in the night: so it seems to be fortunate that you did not wake me.

CRITO: And what was this dream?

SOCRATES: A fair and comely woman, clad in white garments, seemed to come to me, and call me and say, "O Socrates—
The third day hence shalt thou
    fair Phthia reach."

CRITO: What a strange dream, Socrates!

SOCRATES: But its meaning is clear; at least to me, Crito.

CRITO: Yes, too clear, it seems. But, O my good Socrates, I beseech you for the last time to listen to me and save yourself. For to me your death will be more than a single disaster: not only shall I lose a friend the like of whom I shall never find again, but many persons, who do not know you and me well, will think that I might have saved you if I had been willing to spend money, but that I neglected to do so. And what character could be more disgraceful than the character of caring more for money than for one's friends? The world will never believe that we were anxious to save you, but that you yourself refused to escape.

SOCRATES: But, my excellent Crito, why should we care so much about the opinion of the world? The best men, of whose opinion it is worth our while to think, will believe that we acted as we really did.

CRITO: But you see, Socrates, that it is necessary to care about the opinion of the world too. This very thing that has happened to you proves that the multitude can do a man not the least, but almost the greatest harm, if he be falsely accused to them.

SOCRATES: I wish that the multitude were able to do a man the greatest harm, Crito, for then they would be able to do him the greatest good too. That would have been well. But, as it is, they can do neither. They cannot make a man either wise or foolish: they act wholly at random.

CRITO: Well, be it so. But tell me this, Socrates. You surely are not anxious about me and your other friends, and afraid lest, if you escape, the informers should say that we stole you away, and get us into trouble, and involve us in a great deal of expense, or perhaps in the loss of all our property, and, it may be, bring some other punishment upon us besides? If you have any fear of that kind, dismiss it. For of course we are bound to run those risks, and still greater risks than those if necessary, in saving you. So do not, I beseech you, refuse to listen to me.

SOCRATES: I am anxious about that, Crito, and about much besides.

CRITO: Then have no fear on that score. There are men who, for no very large sum, are ready to bring you out of prison into safety. And then, you know, these informers are cheaply bought, and there would be no need to spend much upon them. My fortune is at your service, and I think that it is sufficient: and if you have any feeling about making use of my money, there are strangers in Athens, whom you know, ready to use theirs; and one of them, Simmias of Thebes, has actually brought enough for this very purpose. And Cebes and many others are ready too. And therefore, I repeat, do not shrink from saving yourself on that ground. And do not let what you said in the Court, that if you went into exile you would not know what to do with yourself, stand in your way; for there are many places for you to go to, where you will be welcomed. If you choose to go to Thessaly, I have friends there who will make much of you, and shelter you from any annoyance from the people of Thessaly.

And besides, Socrates, I think that you will be doing what is wrong, if you abandon your life when you might preserve it. You are simply playing the game of your enemies; it is exactly the game of those who wanted to destroy you. And what is more, to me you seem to be abandoning your children too: you will leave them to take their chance in life, as far as you are concerned, when you might bring them up and educate them. Most likely their fate will be the usual fate of children who are left orphans. But you ought not to beget children unless you mean to take the trouble of bringing them up and educating them. It seems to me that you are choosing the easy way, and not the way of a good and brave man, as you ought, when you have been talking all your life long of the value that you set upon virtue. For my part, I feel ashamed both for you, and for us who are your friends. Men will think that the whole of this thing which has happened to you—your appearance in court to take your trial, when you need not have appeared at all; the very way in which the trial was conducted; and then lastly this, for the crowning absurdity of the whole affair, is due to our cowardice. It will look as if we had shirked the danger out of miserable cowardice; for we did not save you, and you did not save yourself, when it was quite possible to do so, if we had been good for anything at all. Take care, Socrates, lest these things be not evil only, but also dishonourable to you and to us. Consider then; or rather the time for consideration is past; we must resolve; and there is only one plan possible. Everything must be done to-night. If we delay any longer, we are lost. O Socrates, I implore you not to refuse to listen to me.

SOCRATES: My dear Crito, if your anxiety to save me be right, it is most valuable: but if it be not right, its greatness makes it all the more dangerous. We must consider then whether we are to do as you say, or not; for I am still what I always have been, a man who will listen to no voice but the voice of the reasoning which on consideration I find to be truest. I cannot cast aside my former arguments because this misfortune has come to me. They seem to me to be as true as ever they were, and I hold exactly the same ones in honour and esteem as I used to: and if we have no better reasoning to substitute for them, I certainly shall not agree to your proposal, not even though the power of the multitude should scare us with fresh terrors, as children are scared with hobgoblins, and inflict upon us new fines, and imprisonments, and deaths. How then shall

we most fitly examine the question? Shall we go back first to what you say about the opinions of men, and ask if we used to be right in thinking that we ought to pay attention to some opinions, and not to others? Used we to be right in saying so before I was condemned to die, and has it now become apparent that we were talking at random, and arguing for the sake of argument, and that it was really nothing but play and nonsense? I am anxious, Crito, to examine our former reasoning with your help, and to see whether my present position will appear to me to have affected its truth in any way, or not; and whether we are to set it aside, or to yield assent to it. Those of us who thought at all seriously, used always to say, I think, exactly what I said just now, namely, that we ought to esteem some of the opinions which men form highly, and not others. Tell me, Crito, if you please, do you not think that they were right? For you, humanly speaking, will not have to die to-morrow, and your judgment will not be biased by that circumstance. Consider then: do you not think it reasonable to say that we should not esteem all the opinions of men, but only some, nor the opinions of all men, but only of some men? What do you think? Is not this true?

CRITO: It is.

SOCRATES: And we should esteem the good opinions, and not the worthless ones?

CRITO: Yes.

SOCRATES: But the good opinions are those of the wise, and the worthless ones those of the foolish?

CRITO: Of course.

SOCRATES: And what used we to say about this? Does a man who is in training, and who is in earnest about it, attend to the praise and blame and opinion of all men, or of the one man only who is a doctor or a trainer?

CRITO: He attends only to the opinion of the one man.

SOCRATES: Then he ought to fear the blame and welcome the praise of this one man, not of the many?

CRITO: Clearly.

SOCRATES: Then he must act and exercise, and eat and drink in whatever way the one man who is his master, and who understands the matter, bids him; not as others bid him?

CRITO: That is so.

SOCRATES: Good. But if he disobeys this one man, and disregards his opinion and his praise, and esteems instead what the many, who understand nothing of the matter, say, will he not suffer for it?

CRITO: Of course he will.

SOCRATES: And how will he suffer? In what direction, and in what part of himself?

CRITO: Of course in his body. That is disabled.

SOCRATES: You are right. And, Crito, to be brief, is it not the same, in everything? And, therefore, in questions of right and wrong, and of the base and the honourable, and of good and evil, which we are now considering, ought we to follow the opinion of the many and fear that, or the opinion of the one man who understands these matters (if we can find him), and feel more shame and fear before him than before all other men? For if we do not follow him, we shall cripple and maim that part of us which, we used to say, is improved by right and disabled by wrong. Or is this not so?

CRITO: No, Socrates, I agree with you.

SOCRATES: Now, if, by listening to the opinions of those who do not understand, we disable that part of us which is improved by health and crippled by disease, is our life worth living, when it is crippled? It is the body, is it not?

CRITO: Yes.

SOCRATES: Is life worth living with the body crippled and in a bad state?

CRITO: No, certainly not.

SOCRATES: Then is life worth living when that part of us which is maimed by wrong and benefited by right is crippled? Or do we consider that part of us, whatever it is, which has to do with right and wrong to be of less consequence than our body?

CRITO: No, certainly not.

SOCRATES: But more valuable?

CRITO: Yes, much more so.

SOCRATES: Then, my excellent friend, we must not think so much of what the many will say of us; we must think of what the one man, who understands right and wrong, and of what Truth herself will say of us. And so you are mistaken to begin with, when you invite us to regard the opinion of the multitude concerning the right and the honourable and the good, and their opposites. But, it may be said, the multitude can put us to death?

CRITO: Yes, that is evident. That may be said, Socrates.

SOCRATES: True. But, my excellent friend, to me it appears that the conclusion which we have just reached, is the same as our conclusion of former times. Now consider whether we still hold to the belief, that we should set the highest value, not on living, but on living well?

CRITO: Yes, we do.

SOCRATES: And living well and honourably and rightly mean the same thing: do we hold to that or not?

CRITO: We do.

SOCRATES: Then, starting from these premises, we have to consider whether it is right or not right for me to try to escape from prison, without the consent of the Athenians. If we find that it is right, we will try: if not, we will let it alone. I am afraid that considerations of expense, and of reputation, and of bringing up my children, of which you talk, Crito, are only the reflections of our friends, the many, who lightly put men to death, and who would, if they could, as lightly bring them to life again, without a thought. But reason, which is our guide, shows us that we can have nothing to consider but the question which I asked just now: namely, shall we be doing right if we give money and thanks to the men who are to aid me in escaping, and if we ourselves take our respective parts in my escape? Or shall we in truth be doing wrong, if we do all this? And if we find that we should be doing wrong, then we must not take any account either of death, or of any other evil that may be the consequence of remaining quietly here, but only of doing wrong.

CRITO: I think that you are right, Socrates. But what are we to do?

SOCRATES: Let us consider that together, my good sir, and if you can contradict anything that I say, do so, and I will be convinced: but if you cannot, do not go on repeating to me any longer, my dear friend, that I should escape without the consent of the Athenians. I am very anxious to act with your approval: I do not want you to think me mistaken. But now tell me if you agree with the doctrine from which I start, and try to answer my questions as you think best.

CRITO: I will try.

SOCRATES: Ought we never to do wrong intentionally at all; or may we do wrong in some ways, and not in others? Or, as we have often agreed in former times, is it never either good or honourable to do wrong? Have all our former conclusions been forgotten in these few days? Old men as we were, Crito, did we not see, in days gone by, when we were gravely conversing with each other, that we were no better than children? Or is not what we used to say most assuredly the truth, whether the world agrees with us or not? Is not wrong-doing an evil and a shame to the wrong-doer in every case, whether we incur a heavier or a lighter punishment than death as the consequence of doing right? Do we believe that?

CRITO: We do.

SOCRATES: Then we ought never to do wrong at all?

CRITO: Certainly not.

SOCRATES: Neither, if we ought never to do wrong at all, ought we to repay wrong with wrong, as the world thinks we may?

CRITO: Clearly not.

SOCRATES: Well then, Crito, ought we to do evil to any one?

CRITO: Certainly I think not, Socrates.

SOCRATES: And is it right to repay evil with evil, as the world thinks, or not right?

CRITO: Certainly it is not right.

SOCRATES: For there is no difference, is there, between doing evil to a man, and wronging him?

CRITO: True.

SOCRATES: Then we ought not to repay wrong with wrong or do harm to any man, no matter what we may have suffered from him. And in conceding this, Crito, be careful that you do not concede more than you mean. For I know that only a few men hold, or ever will hold this opinion. And so those who hold it, and those who do not, have no common ground of argument; they can of necessity only look with contempt on each other's belief. Do you therefore consider very carefully whether you agree with me and share my opinion. Are we to start in our inquiry from the doctrine that it is never right either to do wrong, or to repay wrong with wrong, or to avenge ourselves on any man who harms us, by harming him in return? Or do you disagree with me and dissent from my principle? I myself have believed in it for a long time, and I believe in it still. But if you differ in any way, explain to me how. If you still hold to our former opinion, listen to my next point.

CRITO: Yes, I hold to it, and I agree with you. Go on.

SOCRATES: Then, my next point, or rather my next question, is this: Ought a man to perform his just agreements, or may he shuffle out of them?

CRITO: He ought to perform them.

SOCRATES: Then consider. If I escape without the State's consent, shall I be injuring those whom I ought least to injure, or not? Shall I be abiding by my just agreements or not?

CRITO: I cannot answer your question, Socrates. I do not understand it.

SOCRATES: Consider it in this way. Suppose the laws and the commonwealth were to come and appear to me as I was preparing to run away (if that is the right phrase to describe my escape) and were to ask, "Tell us, Socrates, what have you in your mind to do? What do you mean by trying to escape, but to destroy us, the laws, and the whole city, so far as in you lies? Do you think that a state can exist and not be overthrown, in which the decisions of law are of no force, and are disregarded and set at nought by private individuals?" How shall we answer questions like that, Crito? Much might be said, especially by an orator, in defence of the law which makes judicial decisions supreme. Shall I reply, "But the state has injured me: it has decided my cause wrongly." Shall we say that?

CRITO: Certainly we will, Socrates.

SOCRATES: And suppose the laws were to reply, "Was that our agreement? or was it that you would submit to whatever judgments the state should pronounce?" And if we were to wonder at their words, perhaps they would say, "Socrates, wonder not at our words, but answer us; you yourself are accustomed to ask questions and to answer them. What complaint have you against us and the city, that you are trying to destroy us? Are we not, first, your parents? Through us your father took your mother and begat you. Tell us, have you any fault to find with those of us that are the laws of marriage?" "I have none," I should reply. "Or have you any fault to find with those of us that regulate the nurture and education of the child, which you, like others, received? Did not we do well in bidding your father educate you in music and gymnastic?" "You did," I should say. "Well then, since you were brought into the world and nurtured and educated by us, how, in the first place, can you deny that you are our child and our slave, as your fathers were before you? And if this be so, do you think that your rights are on a level with ours? Do you think that you have a right to retaliate upon us if we should try to do anything to you? You had not the same rights that your father had, or that your master would have had, if you had been a slave. You had no right to retaliate upon them if they ill-treated you, or to answer them if they reviled you, or to strike them back if they struck you, or to repay them evil with evil in any way. And do you think that you may retaliate on your country and its laws? If we try to destroy you, because we think it right, will you in return do all that you can to destroy us, the laws, and your country, and say that in so doing you are doing right, you, the man, who in truth thinks so much of virtue? Or are you too wise to see that your country is worthier, and more august, and more sacred, and holier, and held in higher honour both by the gods and by all men of understanding, than your father and your mother and all your other ancestors; and that it is your bounden duty to reverence it, and to submit to it, and to approach it more humbly than you would approach your father, when it is angry with you; and either to do whatever it bids you to do or to persuade it to excuse you; and to obey in silence if it

orders you to endure stripes or imprisonment, or if it send you to battle to be wounded or to die? That is what is your duty. You must not give way, nor retreat, nor desert your post. In war, and in the court of justice, and everywhere, you must do whatever your city and your country bid you do, or you must convince them that their commands are unjust. But it is against the law of God to use violence to your father or to your mother; and much more so is it against the law of God to use violence to your country." What answer shall we make, Crito? Shall we say that the laws speak truly, or not?

CRITO: I think that they do.

SOCRATES: "Then consider, Socrates," perhaps they would say, "if we are right in saying that by attempting to escape you are attempting to injure us. We brought you into the world, we nurtured you, we educated you, we gave you and every other citizen a share of all the good things we could. Yet we proclaim that if any man of the Athenians is dissatisfied with us, he may take his goods and go away whithersoever he pleases: we give that permission to every man who chooses to avail himself of it, so soon as he has reached man's estate, and sees us, the laws, and the administration of our city. No one of us stands in his way or forbids him to take his goods and go wherever he likes, whether it be to an Athenian colony, or to any foreign country, if he is dissatisfied with us and with the city. But we say that every man of you who remains here, seeing how we administer justice, and how we govern the city in other matters, has agreed, by the very fact of remaining here, to do whatsoever we bid him. And, we say, he who disobeys us, does a threefold wrong: he disobeys us who are his parents, and he disobeys us who fostered him, and he disobeys us after he has agreed to obey us, without persuading us that we are wrong. Yet we did not bid him sternly to do whatever we told him. We offered him an alternative; we gave him his choice, either to obey us, or to convince us that we were wrong: but he does neither.

"These are the charges, Socrates, to which we say that you will expose yourself, if you do what you intend; and that not less, but more than other Athenians." And if I were to ask, "And why?" they might retort with justice that I have bound myself by the agreement with them more than other Athenians. They would say, "Socrates, we have very strong evidence that you were satisfied with us and with the city. You would not have been content to stay at home in it more than other Athenians, unless you had been satisfied with it more than they. You never went away from Athens to the festivals, save once to the Isthmian games, nor elsewhere except on military service; you never made other journeys like other men; you had no desire to see other cities or other laws; you were contented with us and our city. So strongly did you prefer us, and agree to be governed by us: and what is more, you begat children in this city, you found it so pleasant. And besides, if you had wished, you might at your trial have offered to go into exile. At that time you could have done with the State's consent, what you are trying now to do without it. But then you

gloried in being willing to die. You said that you preferred death to exile. And now you are not ashamed of those words: you do not respect us the laws, for you are trying to destroy us: and you are acting just as a miserable slave would act, trying to run away, and breaking the covenant and agreement which you made to submit to our government. First, therefore, answer this question. Are we right, or are we wrong, in saying that you have agreed not in mere words, but in reality to live under our government?" What are we to say, Crito? Must we not admit that it is true?

CRITO: We must, Socrates.

SOCRATES: Then they would say, "Are you not breaking your covenants and agreements with us? And you were not led to make them by force or by fraud: you had not to make up your mind in a hurry. You had seventy years in which you might have gone away, if you had been dissatisfied with us, or if the agreement had seemed to you unjust. But you preferred neither Lacedaemon nor Crete, though you are fond of saying that they are well governed, nor any other state, either of the Hellenes, or the Barbarians. You went away from Athens less than the lame and the blind and the cripple. Clearly you, far more than other Athenians, were satisfied with the city, and also with us who are its laws: for who would be satisfied with a city which had no laws? And now will not you abide by your agreement? If you take our advice, you will, Socrates: then you will not make yourself ridiculous by going away from Athens.

"For consider: what good will you do yourself or your friends by thus transgressing, and breaking your agreement? It is tolerably certain that they, on their part, will at least run the risk of exile, and of losing their civil rights, or of forfeiting their property. For yourself, you might go to one of the neighbouring cities, to Thebes or to Megara for instance—for both of them are well governed—but, Socrates, you will come as an enemy to these commonwealths; and all who care for their city will look askance at you, and think that you are a subverter of law. And you will confirm the judges in their opinion, and make it seem that their verdict was a just one. For a man who is a subverter of law, may well be supposed to be a corrupter of the young and thoughtless. Then will you avoid well-governed states and civilised men? Will life be worth having, if you do? Or will you consort with such men, and converse without shame—about what, Socrates? About the things which you talk of here? Will you tell them that virtue, and justice, and institutions, and law are the most precious things that men can have? And do you not think that that will be a shameful thing in Socrates? You ought to think so. But you will leave these places; you will go to the friends of Crito in Thessaly: for there there is most disorder and licence: and very likely they will be delighted to hear of the ludicrous way in which you escaped from prison, dressed up in peasant's clothes, or in some other disguise which people put on when they are running away, and with your appearance altered. But will no one say how you, an old man, with probably only a few more years to live, clung so greedily to life that

you dared to transgress the highest laws? Perhaps not, if you do not displease them. But if you do, Socrates, you will hear much that will make you blush. You will pass your life as the flatterer and the slave of all men; and what will you be doing but feasting in Thessaly? It will be as if you had made a journey to Thessaly for an entertainment. And where will be all our old sayings about justice and virtue then? But you wish to live for the sake of your children? You want to bring them up and educate them? What? will you take them with you to Thessaly, and bring them up and educate them there? Will you make them strangers to their own country, that you may bestow this benefit on them too? Or supposing that you leave them in Athens, will they be brought up and educated better if you are alive, though you are not with them? Yes; your friends will take care of them. Will your friends take care of them if you make a journey to Thessaly, and not if you make a journey to Hades? You ought not to think that, at least if those who call themselves your friends are good for anything at all.

"No, Socrates, be advised by us who have fostered you. Think neither of children, nor of life, nor of any other thing before justice, that when you come to the other world you may be able to make your defence before the rulers who sit in judgment there. It is clear that neither you nor any of your friends will be happier, or juster, or holier in this life, if you do this thing, nor will you be happier after you are dead. Now you will go away wronged, not by us, the laws, but by men. But if you repay evil with evil, and wrong with wrong in this shameful way, and break your agreements and covenants with us, and injure those whom you should least injure, yourself, and your friends, and your country, and us, and so escape, then we shall be angry with you while you live, and when you die our brethren, the laws in Hades, will not receive you kindly; for they will know that on earth you did all that you could to destroy us. Listen then to us, and let not Crito persuade you to do as he says."

Know well, my dear friend Crito, that this is what I seem to hear, as the worshippers of Cybele seem, in their frenzy, to hear the music of flutes: and the sound of these words rings loudly in my ears, and drowns all other words. And I feel sure that if you try to change my mind you will speak in vain; nevertheless, if you think that you will succeed, say on.

CRITO: I can say no more, Socrates.

SOCRATES: Then let it be, Crito: and let us do as I say, seeing that God so directs us.

Phaedo

SCENE: The Prison of Socrates

. . .

When he had finished speaking Crito said, "Be it so, Socrates. But have you any commands for your friends or for me about your children, or about other things? How shall we serve you best?"

"Simply by doing what I always tell you, Crito. Take care of your own selves, and you will serve me and mine and yourselves in all that you do, even though you make no promises now. But if you are careless of your own selves, and will not follow the path of life which we have pointed out in our discussions both today and at other times, all your promises now, however profuse and earnest they are, will be of no avail."

"We will do our best," said Crito. "But how shall we bury you?"

"As you please," he answered;

"only you must catch me first, and not let me escape you." And then he looked at us with a smile and said, "My friends, I cannot convince Crito that I am the Socrates who has been conversing with you, and arranging his arguments in order. He thinks that I am the body which he will presently see a corpse, and he asks how he is to bury me. All the arguments which I have used to prove that I shall not remain with you after I have drunk the poison, but that I shall go away to the happiness of the blessed, with which I tried to comfort you and myself, have been thrown away on him. Do you therefore be my sureties to him, as he was my surety at the trial, but in a different way. He was surety for me then that I would remain; but you must be my sureties to him that I shall go away when I am dead, and not remain with you: then he will

Trans. F. J. Church (1880).

feel my death less; and when he sees my body being burnt or buried, he will not be grieved because he thinks that I am suffering dreadful things: and at my funeral he will not say that it is Socrates whom he is laying out, or bearing to the grave, or burying." "For, dear Crito," he continued, "you must know that to use words wrongly is not only a fault in itself; it also creates evil in the soul. You must be of good cheer, and say that you are burying my body: and you must bury it as you please, and as you think right."

With these words he rose and went into another room to bathe himself: Crito went with him and told us to wait. So we waited, talking of the argument, and discussing it, and then again dwelling on the greatness of the calamity which had fallen upon us: it seemed as if we were going to lose a father, and to be orphans for the rest of our life. When he had bathed, and his children had been brought to him,—he had two sons quite little, and one grown up,—and the women of his family were come, he spoke with them in Crito's presence, and gave them his last commands; then he sent the women and children away, and returned to us. By that time it was near the hour of sunset, for he had been a long while within. When he came back to us from the bath he sat down, but not much was said after that. Presently the servant of the Eleven came and stood before him and said, "I know that I shall not find you unreasonable like other men, Socrates. They are angry with me and curse me when I bid them drink the poison because the authorities make me do it. But I have found you all along the noblest and

gentlest and best man that has ever come here; and now I am sure that you will not be angry with me, but with those who you know are to blame. And so farewell, and try to bear what must be as lightly as you can; you know why I have come." With that he turned away weeping, and went out.

Socrates looked up at him, and replied, "Farewell: I will do as you say." Then he turned to us and said, "How courteous the man is! And the whole time that I have been here, he has constantly come in to see me, and sometimes he has talked to me, and has been the best of men; and now, how generously he weeps for me! Come, Crito, let us obey him: let the poison be brought if it is ready; and if it is not ready, let it be prepared."

Crito replied, "Nay, Socrates, I think that the sun is still upon the hills; it has not set. Besides, I know that other men take the poison quite late, and eat and drink heartily, and even enjoy the company of their chosen friends, after the announcement has been made. So do not hurry; there is still time."

Socrates replied, "And those whom you speak of, Crito, naturally do so; for they think that they will be gainers by so doing. And I naturally shall not do so; for I think that I should gain nothing by drinking the poison a little later, but my own contempt for so greedily saving up a life which is already spent. So do not refuse to do as I say."

Then Crito made a sign to his slave who was standing by; and the slave went out, and after some delay returned with the man who was to give the poison, carrying it prepared in a cup. When Socrates saw him, he asked, "You understand these things, my good sir, what have I to do?"

"You have only to drink this," he replied, "and to walk about until your legs feel heavy, and then lie down; and it will act of itself." With that he handed the cup to Socrates, who took it quite cheerfully, without trembling, and without any change of colour or of feature, and looked up at the man with that fixed glance of his, and asked, "What say you to making a libation from this draught? May I, or not?" "We only prepare so much as we think sufficient, Socrates," he answered. "I understand," said Socrates. "But I suppose that I may, and must, pray to the gods that my journey hence may be prosperous: that is my prayer; be it so." With these words he put the cup to his lips and drank the poison quite calmly and cheerfully. Till then most of us had been able to control our grief fairly well; but when we saw him drinking, and then the poison finished, we could do so no longer: my tears came fast in spite of myself, and I covered my face and wept for myself: it was not for him, but at my own misfortune in losing such a friend. Even before that Crito had been unable to restrain his tears, and had gone away; and Apollodorus, who had never once ceased weeping the whole time, burst into a loud cry, and made us one and all break down by his sobbing and grief, except only Socrates himself. "What are you doing, my friends?" he exclaimed. "I sent away the women chiefly in order that they might not offend in this way; for I have heard that a man should die in silence. So calm yourselves and bear up." When we heard that we were ashamed, and we ceased from weeping. But he walked about, until he said that his legs were getting heavy, and then he lay down on his back, as he was told. And the man who gave the poison began to examine his feet and legs, from time to time: then he pressed his foot hard, and asked if there was any feeling in it; and Socrates said, "No": and then his legs, and so higher and higher, and showed us that he was cold and stiff. And Socrates felt himself, and said that when it came to his heart, he should be gone. He was already growing cold about the groin, when he uncovered his face, which had been covered, and spoke for the last time. "Crito," he said, "I owe a cock to Asclepius; do not forget to pay it." "It shall be done," replied Crito. "Is there anything else that you wish?" He made no answer to this question; but after a short interval there was a movement, and the man uncovered him, and his eyes were fixed. Then Crito closed his mouth and his eyes.

Such was the end of our friend, a man, I think, who was the wisest and justest, and the best man that I have ever known.

Plato

Among the host of handsome and brilliant young men who dogged the footsteps of Socrates about Athens, one youth stood out from the rest, both physically and intellectually. His real name was Aristocles, but he soon acquired the nickname Plato ("the broad-shouldered one"). The son of a wealthy and noble family—on his mother's side he was descended from the great law-giver, Solon—Plato (427–347 B.C.) was preparing for a career in politics when the trial and execution of Socrates changed the course of his life. He abandoned his political career and turned to philosophy, opening a school on the outskirts of Athens dedicated to the Socratic search for wisdom. Plato's school, known as the Academy, was the first university in the history of the West. It continued in operation for over nine hundred years, from 387 B.C. until it was closed by an edict of the Roman Emperor Justinian in A.D. 529.

Unlike Socrates, Plato was a writer as well as a teacher. His writings are in the form of dialogues, with Socrates as the principal speaker. In the selection that follows, the "Allegory of the Cave" (perhaps the most famous passage in all his works), Plato describes symbolically the predicament in which man finds himself and proposes a way of salvation. In addition, the Allegory presents, in brief form, most of Plato's major philosophical theories: his belief that the world revealed by our senses is not the real world but only a poor copy of it, and that the real world can be apprehended only intellectually; his idea that knowledge cannot be transferred from teacher to student, but rather that education consists of directing the student's mind toward what is real and important and allowing him to apprehend it for himself; his faith that the universe ultimately is good; his conviction that enlightened men have an obligation to the rest of society, and that a good society must be one in which truly wise men are the rulers. Woven into these themes is a defense of the life of Socrates and a condemnation of Athenian society for having executed him.

The Allegory is from Book VII of Plato's best-known work, *The Republic,* which represents a conversation between Socrates and some friends on the nature of justice, and which includes Plato's plan for an ideal state ruled by philosophers.

The Republic

[THE ALLEGORY OF THE CAVE]

Next, said I [Socrates], here is a parable to illustrate the degrees in which our nature may be enlightened or unenlightened. Imagine the condition of men living in a sort of cavernous chamber underground, with an entrance open to the light and a long passage all down the cave. Here they have been from childhood, chained by the leg and also by the neck, so that they cannot move and can see only what is in front of them, because the chains will not let them turn their heads. At some distance higher up is the light of a fire burning behind them; and between the prisoners and the fire is a track with a parapet built along it, like the screen at a puppet-show, which hides the performers while they show their puppets over the top.

I see, said he.

Now behind this parapet imagine persons carrying along various artificial objects, including figures of men and animals in wood or stone or other materials, which project above the parapet. Naturally, some of these persons will be talking, others silent.[1]

It is a strange picture, he said, and a strange sort of prisoners.

Like ourselves, I replied; for in the first place prisoners so confined would have seen nothing of themselves or of one another, except the shadows thrown by the fire-light on the wall of the Cave facing them, would they?

Not if all their lives they had been prevented from moving their heads.

And they would have seen as little of the objects carried past.

Of course.

Now, if they could talk to one another, would they not suppose that their words referred only to those passing shadows which they saw?

Necessarily.

And suppose their prison had an echo from the wall facing them? When one of the people crossing behind them spoke, they could only suppose that the sound came from the shadow passing before their eyes.

---

[1] [A modern Plato would compare his Cave to an underground cinema, where the audience watch the play of shadows thrown by the film passing before a light at their backs. The film itself is only an image of "real" things and events in the world outside the cinema. For the film Plato has to substitute the clumsier apparatus of a procession of artificial objects carried on their heads by persons who are merely part of the machinery, providing for the movement of the objects and the sounds whose echo the prisoners hear. The parapet prevents these persons' shadows from being cast on the wall of the Cave.—*Trans.*]

The Republic of Plato, trans. F. H. Cornford (Oxford: The Clarendon Press, 1941). Reprinted by permission of the Oxford University Press, Oxford.

No doubt.

In every way, then, such prisoners would recognize as reality nothing but the shadows of those artificial objects.

Inevitably.

Now consider what would happen if their release from the chains and the healing of their unwisdom should come about in this way. Suppose one of them set free and forced suddenly to stand up, turn his head, and walk with eyes lifted to the light; all these movements would be painful, and he would be too dazzled to make out the objects whose shadows he had been used to see. What do you think he would say, if someone told him that what he had formerly seen was meaningless illusion, but now, being somewhat nearer to reality and turned towards more real objects, he was getting a truer view? Suppose further that he were shown the various objects being carried by and were made to say, in reply to questions, what each of them was. Would he not be perplexed and believe the objects now shown him to be not so real as what he formerly saw?

Yes, not nearly so real.

And if he were forced to look at the firelight itself, would not his eyes ache, so that he would try to escape and turn back to the things which he could see distinctly, convinced that they really were clearer than these other objects now being shown to him?

Yes.

And suppose someone were to drag him away forcibly up the steep and rugged ascent and not let him go until he had hauled him out into the sunlight, would he not suffer pain and vexation at such treatment, and, when he had come out into the light, find his eyes so full of its radiance that he could not see a single one of the things that he was now told were real?

Certainly he would not see them all at once.

He would need, then, to grow accustomed before he could see things in that upper world. At first it would be easiest to make out shadows, and then the images of men and things reflected in water, and later on the things themselves. After that, it would be easier to watch the heavenly bodies and the sky itself by night, looking at the light of the moon and stars rather than the Sun and the Sun's light in the daytime.

Yes, surely.

Last of all, he would be able to look at the Sun and contemplate its nature, not as it appears when reflected in water or any alien medium, but as it is in itself in its own domain.

No doubt.

And now he would begin to draw the conclusion that it is the Sun that produces the seasons and the course of the year and controls everything in the visible world, and moreover is in a way the cause of all that he and his companions used to see.

Clearly he would come at last to that conclusion.

Then if he called to mind his fellow prisoners and what passed for wisdom in his former dwelling-place, he would surely think himself happy in the change and be sorry for them. They may have had a practice of honouring and commending one another, with prizes for the man who had the keenest eye for the passing shadows and the best memory for the order in which they followed or accompanied one another, so that he could make a good guess as to which was going to come next. Would our released prisoner be likely to covet those prizes or to envy the men exalted to honour and power in the Cave? Would he not feel like Homer's Achilles, that he would far sooner "be on earth as a hired servant in the house of a landless man" or endure anything rather than go back to his old beliefs and live in the old way?

Yes, he would prefer any fate to such a life.

Now imagine what would happen if he went down again to take his former seat in the Cave. Coming suddenly out of the sunlight, his eyes would be filled with darkness. He might be required once more to deliver his opinion on those shadows, in competition with the prisoners who had never been released, while his eyesight was still dim and unsteady; and it might take some time to become used to the darkness. They would laugh at him and say that he had gone up only to come back with his sight ruined; it was worth no one's while even to attempt the ascent. If they could lay hands on the man who was trying to set them free and lead them up, they would kill him.[2]

Yes, they would.

Every feature in this parable, my dear Glaucon, is meant to fit our earlier analysis. The prison dwelling corresponds to the region revealed to us through the sense of sight, and the fire-light within it to the power

of the Sun. The ascent to see the things in the upper world you may take as standing for the upward journey of the soul into the region of the intelligible; then you will be in possession of what I surmise, since that is what you wish to be told. Heaven knows whether it is true; but this, at any rate, is how it appears to me. In the world of knowledge, the last thing to be perceived and only with great difficulty is the essential Form of Goodness. Once it is perceived, the conclusion must follow that, for all things, this is the cause of whatever is right and good; in the visible world it gives birth to light and to the lord of light, while it is itself sovereign in the intelligible world and the parent of intelligence and truth. Without having had a vision of this Form no one can act with wisdom, either in his own life or in matters of state.

So far as I can understand, I share your belief.

Then you may also agree that it is no wonder if those who have reached this height are reluctant to manage the affairs of men. Their souls long to spend all their time in that upper world—naturally enough, if here once more our parable holds true. Nor, again, is it at all strange that one who comes from the contemplation of divine things to the miseries of human life should appear awkward and ridiculous when, with eyes still dazed and not yet accustomed to the darkness, he is compelled, in a law-court or elsewhere, to dispute about the shadows of justice or the images that cast those shadows, and to wrangle over the notions of what is right in the minds of men who have never beheld Justice itself.

---

[2] [An allusion to the fate of Socrates. —*Trans.*]

It is not at all strange.

No; a sensible man will remember that the eyes may be confused in two ways—by a change from light to darkness or from darkness to light; and he will recognize that the same thing happens to the soul. When he sees it troubled and unable to discern anything clearly, instead of laughing thoughtlessly, he will ask whether, coming from a brighter existence, its unaccustomed vision is obscured by the darkness, in which case he will think its condition enviable and its life a happy one; or whether, emerging from the depths of ignorance, it is dazzled by excess of light. If so, he will rather feel sorry for it; or, if he were inclined to laugh, that would be less ridiculous than to laugh at the soul which has come down from the light.

That is a fair statement.

If this is true, then, we must conclude that education is not what it is said to be by some, who profess to put knowledge into a soul which does not possess it, as if they could put sight into blind eyes. On the contrary, our own account signifies that the soul of every man does possess the power of learning the truth and the organ to see with; and that, just as one might have to turn the whole body round in order that the eye should see light instead of darkness, so that entire soul must be turned away from this changing world, until its eye can bear to contemplate reality and that supreme splendour which we have called the Good. Hence there may well be an art whose aim would be to effect this very thing, the conversion of the soul, in the readiest way; not to put the power of sight into the soul's eye, which already has it, but to ensure that, instead of looking in the wrong direction, it is turned the way it ought to be.

Yes, it may well be so.

It looks, then, as though wisdom were different from those ordinary virtues, as they are called, which are not far removed from bodily qualities, in that they can be produced by habituation and exercise in a soul which has not possessed them from the first. Wisdom, it seems, is certainly the virtue of some diviner faculty, which never loses its power, though its use for good or harm depends on the direction towards which it is turned. You must have noticed in dishonest men with a reputation for sagacity the shrewd glance of a narrow intelligence piercing the objects to which it is directed. There is nothing wrong with their power of vision, but it has been forced into the service of evil, so that the keener its sight, the more harm it works.

Quite true.

And yet if the growth of a nature like this had been pruned from earliest childhood, cleared of those clinging overgrowths which come of gluttony and all luxurious pleasure and, like leaden weights charged with affinity to this mortal world, hang upon the soul, bending its vision downwards; if, freed from these, the soul were turned round towards true reality, then this same power in these very men would see the truth as keenly as the objects it is turned to now.

Yes, very likely.

Is it not also likely, or indeed certain after what has been said, that a state can never be properly governed either by the uneducated who know nothing of truth or by men who are allowed to spend all their days in the pursuit of culture? The ignorant have no single mark before their eyes at which they must aim in all the conduct of their own lives and of affairs of state; and the others will not engage in action if they can help it, dreaming that, while still alive, they have been translated to the Islands of the Blest.

Quite true.

It is for us, then, as founders of a commonwealth, to bring compulsion to bear on the noblest natures. They must be made to climb the ascent to the vision of Goodness, which we called the highest object of knowledge; and, when they have looked upon it long enough, they must not be allowed, as they now are, to remain on the heights, refusing to come down again to the prisoners or to take any part in their labours and rewards, however much or little these may be worth.

Shall we not be doing them an injustice, if we force on them a worse life than they might have?

You have forgotten again, my friend, that the law is not concerned to make any one class specially happy, but to ensure the welfare of the commonwealth as a whole. By persuasion or constraint it will unite the citizens in harmony, making them share whatever benefits each class can contribute to the common good; and its purpose in forming men of that spirit was not that each should be left to go his own way, but that they should be instrumental in binding the community into one.

True, I had forgotten.

You will see, then, Glaucon, that there will be no real injustice in compelling our philosophers to watch over and care for the other citizens. We can fairly tell them that their compeers in other states may quite reasonably refuse to collaborate: there they have sprung up, like a self-sown plant, in despite of their country's institutions; no one has fostered their growth, and they cannot be expected to show gratitude for a care they have never received. "But," we shall say, "it is not so with you. We have brought you into existence for your country's sake as well as for your own, to be like leaders and kingbees in a hive; you have been better and more thoroughly educated than those others and hence you are more capable of playing your part both as men of thought and as men of action. You must go down, then, each in his turn, to live with the rest and let your eyes grow accustomed to the darkness. You will then see a thousand times better than those who live there always; you will recognize every image for what it is and know what it represents, because you have seen justice, beauty, and goodness in their reality; and so you and we shall find life in our commonwealth no mere dream, as it is in most existing states, where men live fighting one another about shadows and quarrelling for power, as if that were a great prize; whereas in truth government can be at its best and free from dissension only where the destined rulers are least desirous of holding office."

Quite true.

Then will our pupils refuse to listen and to take their turns at sharing in the work of the community, though they may live together for most of their time in a purer air?

No; it is a fair demand, and they are fair-minded men. No doubt, unlike any ruler of the present day, they will think of holding power as an unavoidable necessity.

Yes, my friend; for the truth is that you can have a well-governed society only if you can discover for your future rulers a better way of life than being in office; then only will power be in the hands of men who are rich, not in gold, but in the wealth that brings happiness, a good and wise life. All goes wrong when, starved for lack of anything good in their own lives, men turn to public affairs hoping to snatch from thence the happiness they hunger for. They set about fighting for power, and this internecine conflict ruins them and their country. The life of true philosophy is the only one that looks down upon offices of state; and access to power must be confined to men who are not in love with it; otherwise rivals will start fighting. So whom else can you compel to undertake the guardianship of the commonwealth, if not those who, besides understanding best the principles of government, enjoy a nobler life than the politician's and look for rewards of a different kind?

There is indeed no other choice.

Aristotle

Aristotle (384–322 B.C.) was a native of Macedonia. At the age of eighteen he journeyed to Athens and enrolled as a student in the Academy, where he remained for twenty years until the death of Plato. He then moved to Asia Minor to become political advisor to the ruler of a small kingdom. While there he married the king's niece. It is said that he spent his honeymoon gathering seashells for use in scientific studies. From Asia Minor he was called back to his native Macedonia to serve as tutor to Alexander (later "the Great"), who was then a boy of twelve. When Alexander set out to conquer the world, Aristotle returned to Athens and established a school of his own, the Lyceum, as a rival to the Academy. For the next eleven years he divided his time among teaching, public lecturing, and writing. His philosophical system is known as the *peripatetic* (or "walking") philosophy, a title derived from his habit of pacing back and forth as he lectured. At the death of Alexander in 323, Aristotle, because of his former association with the conqueror, found himself unpopular in Athens. Fearing the anger of the mob and remembering the fate of Socrates, he fled the city, not wishing, as he put it, "to give the Athenians a second chance of sinning against philosophy." He died in exile the following year.

Aristotle was a remarkably productive writer. His extant works include major treatises on physics, astronomy, zoology, biology, botany, psychology, logic, ethics, metaphysics, political theory, constitutional history, rhetoric, and the theory of art. His influence on the intellectual history of the West has been at least equal to that of Plato. Wherever his works have been studied, there has been intellectual ferment, activity, and development. Partly as a result of Aristotle's influence, the Moslems of the Near East enjoyed an intellectual golden age while Europe was still deep in the Dark Ages. The rediscovery of Aristotle by Europeans, through their contact with the Moslems, contributed directly to the cultural awakening in Europe that culminated in the high Middle Ages of the thirteenth century. Since the rise of modern science, the philosophy of Aristotle has come under increasingly sharp attack; nevertheless many of his main concepts and theories remain alive and vigorous in our own century.

The following selection is from one of Aristotle's major works, *The Politics.* His views, in *The Politics,* on the social nature of man, the purpose of government, and the most desirable kind of society, have formed the basis, along with Plato's *Republic,* for almost all subsequent political theory in the West.

The Politics

BOOK I

Observation shows us, first, that every polis (or state) is a species of association, and, secondly, that all associations are instituted for the purpose of attaining some good— for all men do all their acts with a view to achieving something which is, in their view, a good. We may therefore hold on the basis of what we actually observe that all associations aim at some good; and we may also hold that the particular association which is the most sovereign of all, and includes all the rest, will pursue this aim most, and will thus be directed to the most sovereign of all goods. This most sovereign and inclusive association is the polis, as it is called, or the political association.

It is a mistake to believe that the "statesman" is the same as the monarch of a kingdom, or the manager of a household, or the master of a number of slaves. Those who hold this view consider that each of these persons differs from the others not with a difference of kind, but merely with a difference of degree, and according to the number, or the paucity, of the persons with whom he deals. On this view a man who is concerned with few persons is a master: one who is concerned with more is the manager of a household: one who is concerned with

still more is a "statesman," or a monarch. This view abolishes any real differences between a large household and a small polis; and it also reduces the difference between the "statesman" and the monarch to the one fact that the latter has an uncontrolled and sole authority, while the former exercises his authority in conformity with the rules imposed by the art of statesmanship and as one who rules and is ruled in turn. But this is a view which cannot be accepted as correct. There is an *essential* difference between these persons, and between the associations with which they are concerned.

Our point will be made clear if we proceed to consider the matter according to our normal method of analysis. Just as, in all other fields, a compound should be analyzed until we reach its simple and un-compounded elements (or, in other words, the smallest atoms of the whole which it constitutes), so we must also consider analytically the elements of which a polis is composed. We shall then gain a better insight into the difference from one another of the persons and associations just mentioned; and we shall also be in a position to discover whether it is possible to attain a systematic view of the general issues involved.

If, accordingly, we begin at the

The Politics of Aristotle, trans. E. Barker (Oxford: The Clarendon Press, 1947), pp. 1–7, 110–25, 129–34, 180–83. Reprinted by permission of the Oxford University Press, Oxford.

beginning, and consider things in the process of their growth, we shall best be able, in this as in other fields, to attain scientific conclusions by the method we employ. First of all, there must necessarily be a union or pairing of those who cannot exist without one another. Male and female must unite for the reproduction of the species—not from deliberate intention, but from the natural impulse, which exists in animals generally as it also exists in plants, to leave behind them something of the same nature as themselves. Next, there must necessarily be a union of the naturally ruling element with the element which is naturally ruled, for the preservation of both. The element which is able, by virtue of its intelligence, to exercise forethought, is naturally a ruling and master element; the element which is able, by virtue of its bodily power, to do what the other element plans, is a ruled element, which is naturally in a state of slavery; and master and slave have accordingly as they thus complete one another a common interest. The female and the slave, we may pause to note, are naturally distinguished from one another. Nature makes nothing in a spirit of stint, as smiths do when they make the Delphic knife to serve a number of purposes: she makes each separate thing for a separate end; and she does so because each instrument has the finest finish when it serves a single purpose and not a variety of purposes. Among the barbarians, however, contrary to the order of nature the female and the slave occupy the same position—the reason being that no naturally ruling element exists among them, and conjugal union thus comes to be a union of a female who is a slave with a male who is also a slave. This is why our poets have said,

Meet it is that barbarous peoples
    should be governed by the Greeks

—the assumption being that barbarian and slave are by nature one and the same.

The first result of these two elementary associations of male and female, and of master and slave is the household or family. Hesiod spoke truly in the verse,

First house, and wife, and ox to draw
    the plough,

for oxen serve the poor in lieu of household slaves. The first form of association naturally instituted for the satisfaction of daily recurrent needs is thus the family; and the members of the family are accordingly termed by Charondas "associates of the breadchest," as they are also termed by Epimenides the Cretan "associates of the manger." The next form of association—which is also the *first* to be formed from more households than one, and for the satisfaction of something more than daily recurrent needs—is the village. The most natural form of the village appears to be that of a colony or offshoot from a family; and some have thus called the members of the village by the name of "sucklings of the same milk," or, again, of "sons and the sons of sons." This, it may be noted, is the reason why each Greek polis was originally ruled—as the peoples of the barbarian world still are—by kings. They were formed of persons who were already monarchically governed, *i.e.* they were formed from households and villages, and households are always monarchically governed by the eldest of the kin, just as villages, when they are off-shoots from the household, are similarly governed in virtue of the kinship between their members. This primitive kinship is what Homer describes, in speaking of the Cyclopes:

> Each of them ruleth
> Over his children and wives,

a passage which shows that they lived in scattered groups, as indeed men generally did in ancient times. The fact that men generally were governed by kings in ancient times, and that some still continue to be governed in that way, is the reason that leads us all to assert that the gods are also governed by a king. We make the lives of the gods in the likeness of our own—as we also make their shapes.

When we come to the final and perfect association, formed from a number of villages, we have already reached the polis—an association which may be said to have reached the height of full self-sufficiency; or rather to speak more exactly we may say that while it *grows* for the sake of mere life and is so far, and at that stage, still short of full self-sufficiency, it *exists* when once it is fully grown for the sake of a good life and is therefore fully self-sufficient.

Because it is the completion of associations existing by nature, every polis exists by nature, having itself the same quality as the earlier associations from which it grew. It is the end or consummation to which those associations move, and

the "nature" of things consists in their end or consummation; for what each thing is when its growth is completed we call the nature of that thing, whether it be a man or a horse or a family. Again, and this is a second reason for regarding the state as natural, the end, or final cause, is the best. Now self-sufficiency which is the object of the state to bring about is the end, and so the best; and on this it follows that the state brings about the best, and is therefore natural, since nature always aims at bringing about the best.

From these considerations it is evident that the polis belongs to the class of things that exist by nature, and that man is by nature an animal intended to live in a polis. He who is without a polis, by reason of his own nature and not of some accident, is either a poor sort of being, or a being higher than man: he is like the man of whom Homer wrote in denunciation:

"Clanless and lawless and heartless is he."

The man who is such by nature, *i.e.* unable to join in the society of a polis, at once plunges into a passion for war; he is in the position of a solitary advanced piece in a game of draughts.

The reason why man is a being meant for political association, in a higher degree than bees or other gregarious animals can ever associate, is evident. Nature, according to our theory, makes nothing in vain; and man alone of the animals is furnished with the faculty of language. The mere making of sounds serves to indicate pleasure and pain, and is thus a faculty that belongs to animals in general: their nature enables them to attain the point at which they have perceptions of pleasure and pain, and can signify those perceptions to one another. But language serves to declare what is advantageous and what is the reverse, and it therefore serves to declare what is just and what is unjust. It is the peculiarity of man, in comparison with the rest of the animal world, that he alone possesses a perception of good and evil, of the just and the unjust, and of other similar qualities; and it is association in a common perception of these things which makes a family and a polis.

We may now proceed to add that though the individual and the family are prior in the order of time the polis is prior in the order of nature to the family and the individual. The reason for this is that the whole is necessarily prior in nature to the part. If the whole body be destroyed, there will not be a foot or a hand, except in that ambiguous sense in which one uses the same word to indicate a different thing, as when one speaks of a "hand" made of stone; for a hand, when destroyed by the destruction of the whole body, will be no better than a stone "hand." All things derive their essential character from their function and their capacity; and it follows that if they are no longer fit to discharge their function, we ought not to say that they are still the same things, but only that, by an ambiguity, they still have the same names.

We thus see that the polis exists by nature and that it is prior to the individual. The proof of both propositions is the fact that the polis is a whole, and that individuals are simply its parts. Not being self-sufficient when they are isolated, all individuals are so many parts all equally depending on the whole which alone can bring about self-sufficiency. The man who is isolated —who is unable to share in the benefits of political association, or has no need to share because he is already self-sufficient—is no part of the polis, and must therefore be either a beast or a god. Man is thus intended by nature to be a part of a political whole, and there is therefore an immanent impulse in all men towards an association of this order. But the man who first *constructed* such an association was none the less the greatest of benefactors. Man, when perfected, is the best of animals; but if he be isolated from law and justice he is the worst of all. Injustice is all the graver when it is armed injustice; and man is furnished from birth with arms such as, for instance, language which are intended to serve the purposes of moral prudence and virtue, but which may be used in preference for opposite ends. That is why, if he be without virtue, he is a most unholy and savage being, and worse than all others in the indulgence of lust and gluttony. Justice which is his salvation belongs to the polis; for justice, which is the determination of what is just, is an ordering of the political association.

. . .

BOOK III

. . .

We have next to consider the subject of constitutions. Is there a single type, or are there a number of types? If there are a number of types, what are these types; how many of them are there; and how do they differ? A constitution (or polity) may be defined as "the organization of a polis, in respect of its offices generally, but especially in respect of that particular office which is sovereign in all issues." The civic body is everywhere the sovereign of the state; in fact the civic body is the polity (or constitution) itself. In democratic states, for example, the people is sovereign: in oligarchies, on the other hand, the few have that position; and this difference of the sovereign bodies is the reason why we say that the two types of constitution differ—as we may equally apply the same reasoning to other types besides these.

It is thus evident that there are a number of types of constitution, but before we discuss their nature we must first ascertain two things— the nature of the end for which the state exists, and the various kinds of authority to which men and their associations are subject. So far as the first of these things is concerned, it has already been stated, in our first book (where we were concerned with the management of the household and the control of slaves), that "man is an animal impelled by his nature to live in a polis." A *natural impulse* is thus one reason why men desire to live a social life even when they stand in no need of mutual succour; but they are also drawn together by a *common interest,* in proportion as each attains a share in good life through the union of all in a form of political association. The good life is the chief end, both for the community as a whole and for each of us individually. But men also come together, and form and maintain political associations, merely for the

sake of life, for perhaps there is some element of the good even in the simple act of living, so long as the evils of existence do not preponderate too heavily. It is an evident fact that most men cling hard enough to life to be willing to endure a good deal of suffering, which implies that life has in it a sort of healthy happiness and a natural quality of pleasure.

So far of the end for which the state exists. As regards the second question, it is easy enough to distinguish the various kinds of rule or authority of which men commonly speak; and indeed we have often had occasion to define them ourselves in works intended for the general public. The rule of a master is one kind; and here, though there is really a common interest which unites the natural master and the natural slave, the fact remains that the rule is primarily exercised with a view to the master's interest, and only incidentally with a view to that of the slave, who must be preserved in existence if the rule itself is to remain. Rule over wife and children, and over the household generally, is a second kind of rule, which we have called by the name of household management. Here the rule is either exercised in the interest of the ruled or for the attainment of some advantage common to both ruler and ruled. Essentially it is exercised in the interest of the ruled, as is also plainly the case with other arts besides that of ruling, such as medicine and gymnastics—though an art may incidentally be exercised for the benefit of its practitioner, and there is nothing to prevent (say) a trainer from becoming occasionally a member of the class he instructs,

in the same sort of way as a steersman is always one of the crew. Thus
a trainer or steersman primarily
considers the good of those who are
subject to his authority; but when
he becomes one of them personally,
he incidentally shares in the benefit
of that good—the steersman thus
being also a member of the crew,
and the trainer (though still a
trainer) becoming also a member of
the class which he instructs.

This principle also applies to a
third kind of rule—that exercised
by the holders of political office.
When the constitution of a state is
constructed on the principle that its
members are equals and peers, the
citizens think it proper that they
should hold office by turns which
implies that the office of ruler is primarily intended for the benefit of
the ruled and is therefore a duty to
be undertaken by each in turn,
though incidentally the ruler shares
in the general benefit by virtue of
being himself a member of the citizen body. At any rate this is the
natural system, and the system
which used to be followed in the
days when men believed that they
ought to serve by turns, and each
assumed that others would take over
the duty of considering his benefit,
just as he had himself, during his
term of office, considered the interest of others. Today the case is
altered. Moved by the profits to be
derived from office and the handling
of public property, men want to
hold office continuously. It is as if
the holders of office were sick men,
who got the benefit of permanent
health by being permanently in office: at any rate their ardour for
office is just what it would be if that

were the case. The conclusion which
follows is clear. Those constitutions
which consider the common interest
are *right* constitutions, judged by
the standard of absolute justice.
Those constitutions which consider
only the personal interest of the
rulers are all *wrong* constitutions,
or *perversions* of the right forms.
Such perverted forms are despotic
whereas the polis is an association
of freemen.

Now that these matters have
been determined, the next subject
for consideration is the number and
nature of the different constitutions.
We may first examine the class of
right constitutions and consider its
different species; the different perversions will at once be apparent
when the right constitutions have
been determined. The term "constitution" signifies the same thing as
the term "civic body." The civic
body in every polis is the sovereign;
and the sovereign must necessarily
be either One, or Few, or Many. On
this basis we may say that when the
One, or the Few, or the Many, rule
with a view to the common interest,
the constitutions under which they
do so must necessarily be right constitutions. On the other hand the
constitutions directed to the personal interest of the One, or the
Few, or the Masses, must necessarily be perversions. They deviate
from the true standard by not regarding the interest of all, and are
thus involved in a dilemma: either
the name of citizen cannot be given
to persons who share in the constitution but whose interests are not
regarded, or, if the name is to be
given, they must have their share
of the benefits. Among forms of

government by a single person Kingship, in the general use of language, denotes the species which looks to the common interest. Among forms of government by a few persons (but more than one) Aristocracy denotes the species which similarly looks to that interest—that name being given to this species either because the best are the rulers, or because its object is what is best for the state and its members. Finally, when the masses govern the state with a view to the common interest, the name used for this species is the generic name common to all constitutions (or polities)—the name of "Polity." There is a good reason for the usage which gives to this form the generic name, and not a special name which connotes, as the name "Aristocracy" does, a special excellence. It is possible for one man, or a few, to be of outstanding excellence; but when it comes to a large number, we can hardly expect a fine edge of all the varieties of excellence. What we can expect particularly is the military kind of excellence, which is the kind that shows itself in a mass. This is the reason why the defence forces are the most sovereign body under this constitution, and those who possess arms are the persons who enjoy constitutional rights.

These are the three subdivisions of the class of right constitutions. Three perversions correspond to them. Tyranny is the perversion of Kingship; Oligarchy of Aristocracy; and Democracy of Polity. Tyranny is a government by a single person directed to the interest of that person; Oligarchy is directed to the interest of the well-to-do; Democracy is directed to the interest of the poorer classes. None of the three is directed to the advantage of the whole body of citizens.

We must treat at somewhat greater length of the nature of each of these last constitutions. There are certain difficulties involved; and when one is pursuing a philosophical method of inquiry in any branch of study, and not merely looking to practical considerations, the proper course is to set out the truth about every particular with no neglect or omission. Tyranny, as has just been said, is single-person government of the political association on the lines of despotism, *i.e.* treating the citizens as a master treats slaves: oligarchy exists where those who have property are the sovereign authority of the constitution; and conversely democracy exists where the sovereign authority is composed of the poorer classes, and not of the owners of property. The first difficulty which arises concerns the definition just given of democracy and oligarchy. We have defined democracy as the sovereignty of numbers; but we can conceive a case in which the majority who hold the sovereignty in a state are the well-to-do. Similarly oligarchy is generally stated to be the sovereignty of a small number; but it might conceivably happen that the poorer classes were fewer in number than the well-to-do, and yet—in virtue of superior vigour—were the sovereign authority of the constitution. In neither case could the definition previously given of these constitutions be regarded as true. We might attempt to overcome the difficulty by combining both of the factors—wealth with paucity of numbers, and poverty with mass. On this basis oligarchy might be defined as the constitution under which the rich, being also few in number, hold the offices of the state; and similarly democracy might be defined as the constitution under which the poor, being also many in number, are in control. But this involves us in another difficulty. If our new definition is exhaustive, and there are no forms of oligarchy and democracy other than those enumerated in that definition, what names are we to give to the constitutions just suggested as conceivable—those where the wealthy form a majority and the poor a minority, and where the wealthy majority in the one case, and the poor minority in the other, are the sovereign authority of the constitution? The course of the argument thus appears to show that the factor of number—the small number of the sovereign body in oligarchies, or the large number in democracies—is an accidental attribute, due to the simple fact that the wealthy are generally few and the poor are generally numerous. Therefore the causes originally mentioned, *i.e.* small and large numbers, are not in fact the real causes of the difference between oligarchies and democracies. The real ground of the difference between oligarchy and democracy is poverty and riches. It is inevitable that any constitution should be an oligarchy if the rulers under it are rulers in virtue of riches, whether they are few or many; and it is equally inevitable that a constitution under which the poor rule should be a democracy.

It happens, however, as we have just remarked, and this is why number becomes an accidental attribute of both of these constitutions, that the rich are few and the poor are numerous. It is only a few who have riches, but all alike share in free status; and these are the real grounds on which the two parties, the oligarchical and the democratic, dispute the control of the constitution.

We must next ascertain, now that we have discovered the social ground on which they rest, what are the distinctive principles attributed by their advocates to oligarchy and democracy, and what are the oligarchical and the democratic conceptions of justice. Both oligarchs and democrats have a hold on a sort of conception of justice; but they both fail to carry it far enough, and neither of them expresses the true conception of justice in the whole of its range. In democracies, for example, justice is considered to mean equality in the distribution of office. It does mean equality—but equality for those who are equal, and not for all. In oligarchies, again, inequality in the distribution of office is considered to be just; and indeed it is— but only for those who are unequal, and not for all. The advocates of oligarchy and democracy both refuse to consider this factor—who are the persons to whom their principles properly apply—and they both make erroneous judgments. The reason is that they are judging *in their own case;* and most men, as a rule, are bad judges where their own interests are involved. Justice is relative to persons; and a just distribution is one in which the relative values of the things given correspond to those of the persons receiving—a point which has already been made in the *Ethics*. It follows that a just distribution of offices among a number of different persons will involve a consideration of the personal values, or merits, of each of those persons. But the advocates of oligarchy and democracy, while they agree about what constitutes equality in the *thing,* disagree about what constitutes it in *persons*. The main reason for this is the reason just stated—they are judging, and judging erroneously, in their own case; but there is also another reason— they are misled by the fact that they are professing a sort of conception of justice, and professing it up to a point, into thinking that they profess one which is absolute and complete. The oligarchs think that superiority on one point—in their case wealth—means superiority on all: the democrats believe that equality in one respect—for instance, that of free birth—means equality all round.

Both sides, however, fail to mention the really cardinal factor, *i.e.* the nature of the end for which the state exists. If property were the end for which men came together and formed an association, men's share in the offices and honours of the state would be proportionate to their share of property; and in that case the argument of the oligarchical side —that it is not just for a man who has contributed one pound to share equally in a sum of a hundred pounds (or, for that matter, in the interest accruing upon that sum) with the man who has contributed all the rest—would appear to be a strong argument. But the end of the state is not mere life; it is, rather, a good quality of life. If mere life were the end, there might be a state

of slaves, or even a state of animals; but in the world as we know it any such state is impossible, because slaves and animals do not share in true felicity and free choice, *i.e.* the attributes of a good quality of life. Similarly, it is not the end of the state to provide an alliance for mutual defence against all injury, or to ease exchange and promote economic intercourse. If that had been the end, the Etruscans and the Carthaginians, who are united by such bonds, would be in the position of belonging to a single state; and the same would be true of all peoples who have commercial treaties with one another. It is true that such peoples have agreements about imports and exports; treaties to ensure just conduct in the course of trade; and written terms of alliance for mutual defence. On the other hand they have no common offices of state to deal with these matters: each, on the contrary, has its own offices, confined to itself. Neither of the parties concerns itself to ensure a proper quality of character among the members of the other; neither of them seeks to ensure that all who are included in the scope of the treaties shall be free from injustice and from any form of vice; and neither of them goes beyond the aim of preventing its own members from committing injustice in the course of trade against the members of the other. But it is the cardinal issue of goodness or badness in the life of the polis which always engages the attention of any state that concerns itself to secure a system of good laws well obeyed. The conclusion which clearly follows is that any polis which is truly so called, and is not merely one in name, must devote itself to the end of encouraging goodness. Otherwise, a political association sinks into a mere alliance, which only differs in space, *i.e.* in the contiguity of its members, from other forms of alliance where the members live at a distance from one another. Otherwise, too, law becomes a mere covenant—or (in the phrase of the Sophist Lycophron) "a guarantor of men's rights against one another"—instead of being, as it should be, a rule of life such as will make the members of a polis good and just.

That this is the case, *i.e.* that a polis is truly a polis only when it makes the encouragement of goodness its end, may be readily proved. If two different sites could be united in one, so that the polis of Megara and that of Corinth were embraced by a single wall, that would not make a single polis. If the citizens of two cities intermarried with one another, that would not make a single polis—even though intermarriage is one of the forms of social life which are characteristic of a polis. Nor would it make a polis if a number of persons—living at a distance from one another, but not at so great a distance but that they could still associate—had a common system of laws to prevent their injuring one another in the course of exchange. We can imagine, for instance, one being a carpenter, another a farmer, a third a shoemaker, and others producing other goods; and we can imagine a total number of as many as 10,000. But if these people were associated in nothing further than matters such as exchange and alliance, they would still have failed to reach the stage of a polis. Why should this be the case?

It cannot be ascribed to any lack of contiguity in such an association. The members of a group so constituted might come together on a single site; but if that were all—if each still treated his private house as if it were a state, and all of them still confined their mutual assistance to action against aggressors (as if it were only a question of a defensive alliance)—if, in a word, the spirit of their intercourse were still the same after their coming together as it had been when they were living apart—their association, even on its new basis, could not be deemed by any accurate thinker to be a polis. It is clear, therefore, that a polis is not an association for residence on a common site, or for the sake of preventing mutual injustice and easing exchange. These are indeed conditions which must be present before a polis can exist; but the presence of all these conditions is not enough, in itself, to constitute a polis. What constitutes a polis is an association of households and clans in a good life, for the sake of attaining a perfect and self-sufficing existence. This consummation, however, will not be reached unless the members inhabit one and the self-same place and practise intermarriage. It was for this reason, *i.e.* to provide these necessary conditions, that the various institutions of a common social life—marriage-connexions, kin-groups, religious gatherings, and social pastimes generally—arose in cities. But these institutions are the business of friendship and not the purpose of the polis. It is friendship and not a polis which consists in the pursuit of a common social life. The end and purpose of a polis is the good life, and the institutions of social life are means to that end. A polis is constituted by the association of families and villages in a perfect and self-sufficing existence; and such an existence, on our definition, consists in a life of true felicity and goodness.

It is therefore for the sake of good actions, and not for the sake of social life, that political associations must be considered to exist. This conclusion enables us to attain a proper conception of justice. Those who contribute most to an association of this character, *i.e.* who contribute most to good action, have a greater share in the polis and should therefore, in justice, receive a larger recognition from it than those who are equal to them (or even greater) in free birth and descent, but unequal in civic excellence, or than those who surpass them in wealth but are surpassed by them in excellence. From what has been said it is plain that both sides to the dispute about constitutions, *i.e.* both the democratic and the oligarchical side, profess only a partial conception of justice.

A difficulty arises when we turn to consider what body of persons should be sovereign in the polis. We can imagine five alternatives: the people at large; the wealthy; the better sort of men; the one man who is best of all; the tyrant. But all these alternatives appear to involve unpleasant results: indeed, how can it be otherwise? Take, for example, the first alternative. What if the poor, on the ground of their being a majority, proceed to divide among themselves the possessions of the wealthy—will not this be unjust? "No, by heaven" (a democrat may reply); "it has been justly decreed

so by the sovereign." "But if this is not the extreme of injustice" (we may reply in turn), "what *is?*" Whenever a majority of any sort, irrespective of wealth or poverty, divides among its members the possessions of a minority, that majority is obviously ruining the state. But goodness can never ruin anything that has goodness, nor can justice, in its nature, be ruinous to a state. It is therefore clear that a law of this kind, *i.e.* a law of spoliation passed by a majority of any sort, cannot possibly be just. To treat such a law as just is really to justify tyranny. The tyrant's acts too, on the principle alleged by the democrats that any decree of the sovereign is just, must necessarily be just; for he too uses coercion by virtue of superior power in just the same sort of way as the people coerce the wealthy. We may now take the alternative that the wealthy are sovereign. Is it just that a minority composed of the wealthy should rule? If they too behave like the others—if they plunder and confiscate the property of the people—can their action be called just? If it can, the action of the people, in the converse case, must equally be termed just. It is clear that all these acts of oppression, whether by the people, the tyrant, or the wealthy are mean and unjust. But what of the next alternative? Should the better sort of men have authority and be sovereign in all matters? In that case, the rest of the citizens will necessarily be debarred from honours, since they will not enjoy the honour of holding civic office. We speak of offices as honours; and when a single set of persons hold office permanently, the rest of the community must necessarily be debarred from all honours. We come to a last alternative. Is it better than any of the other alternatives that the one best man should rule? This is still more oligarchical than the rule of the wealthy few or the few of the better sort because the number of those debarred from honours is even greater. It may perhaps be urged that there is still another alternative; that it is a poor sort of policy to vest sovereignty in any person or body of persons, subject as persons are to the passions that beset men's souls; and that it is better to vest it in law. But this does not solve the difficulty. The law itself may incline either towards oligarchy or towards democracy; and what difference will the sovereignty of law then make in the problems which have just been raised? The consequences already stated will follow just the same.

The other alternatives may be reserved for a later inquiry; but the first of the alternatives suggested— that the people at large should be sovereign rather than the few best —would appear to be defensible, and while it presents some difficulty it perhaps also contains some truth. There is this to be said for the Many. Each of them by himself may not be of a good quality; but when they all come together it is possible that they may surpass—collectively and as a body, although not individually —the quality of the few best. Feasts to which many contribute may excel those provided at one man's expense. In the same way, when there are many who contribute to the process of deliberation, each can bring his share of goodness and moral prudence; and when all meet together the people may thus become something in the nature of a single person, who—as he has many feet, many hands, and many senses —may also have many qualities of character and intelligence. This is the reason why the Many are also better judges than the few of music and the writing of poets: some appreciate one part, some another, and all together appreciate all. We may note that this combination of qualities, which gives the Many their merit, can also be traced in cases of *individual* merit. The thing which makes a good man differ from a unit in the crowd—as it is also the thing which is generally said to make a beautiful person differ from one who is not beautiful, or an artistic representation differ from ordinary reality—is that elements which are elsewhere scattered and separate are here combined in a unity. It is this unity which counts; for if you take the elements separately, you may say of an artistic representation that it is surpassed by the eye of this person or by some other feature of that.

It is not clear, however, that this combination of qualities, which we have made the ground of distinction between the many and the few best, is true of all popular bodies and all large masses of men. Perhaps it may be said, "By heaven, it is clear that there are some bodies of which it cannot possibly be true; for if you included them, you would, by the same token, be found to include a herd of beasts. That would be absurd; and yet what difference is there between these bodies and a herd of beasts?" All the same, and in spite of this objection, there is nothing to prevent the view we have stated from being true of *some* popular bodies.

It would thus seem possible to solve, by the considerations we have advanced, both the problem raised in the previous chapter "What body of *persons* should be sovereign?" and the further problem which follows upon it, "What are the *matters* over which freemen, or the general body of citizens—men of the sort who neither have wealth nor can make any claim on the ground of goodness—should properly exercise sovereignty?" It may be argued, from one point of view, that it is dangerous for men of this sort to share in the highest offices, as injustice may lead them into wrongdoing, and thoughtlessness into error. But it may also be argued, from another point of view, that there is serious risk in not letting them have *some* share in the enjoyment of power; for a state with a body of disfranchised citizens who are numerous and poor must necessarily be a state which is full of enemies. The alternative left is to let them share in the deliberative and judicial functions; and we thus find Solon, and some of the other legislators, giving the people the two general functions of electing the magistrates to office and of calling them to account at the end of their tenure of office, but *not* the right of holding office themselves in their individual capacity. There is wisdom in such a policy. When they all meet together, the people display a good enough gift of perception, and combined with the better class they are of service to the state (just as impure food, when it is mixed

with pure, makes the whole concoction more nutritious than a small amount of the pure would be); but each of them is imperfect in the judgments he forms by himself. . . .

In all arts and sciences the end in view is some good. In the most sovereign of all the arts and sciences —and this is the art and science of politics—the end in view is the greatest good and the good which is most pursued. The good in the sphere of politics is justice; and justice consists in what tends to promote the common interest. General opinion makes it consist in some sort of equality. Up to a point this general opinion agrees with the philosophical inquiries which contain our conclusions on ethics. In other words, it holds that justice involves two factors—things, and the persons to whom things are assigned —and it considers that persons who are equal should have assigned to them equal things. But here there arises a question which must not be overlooked. Equals and unequals— yes; but equals and unequals *in what?* This is a question which raises difficulties, and involves us in philosophical speculation on politics. It is possible to argue that offices and honours ought to be distributed unequally, *i.e.* that superior amounts should be assigned to superior persons, on the basis of superiority *in any respect whatsoever*—even though there were similarity, and no shadow of any difference, in every other respect; and it may be urged, in favour of this argument, that where people differ from one another there must be a difference in what is just and proportionate to their merits. If this argument were accepted, the mere fact of a better complexion, or greater height, or any other such advantage, would establish a claim for a greater share of political rights to be given to its possessor. But is not the argument obviously wrong? To be clear that it is, we have only to study the analogy of the other arts and sciences. If you were dealing with a number of flute-players who were equal in their art, you would not assign them flutes on the principle that the better born should have a greater amount. Nobody will play the better for being better born; and it is to those who are better at the job that the better supply of tools should be given. If our point is not yet plain, it can be made so if we push it still further. Let us suppose a man who is superior to others in flute-playing, but far inferior in birth and beauty. Birth and beauty may be greater goods than ability to play the flute, and those who possess them may, upon balance, surpass the flute-player more in these qualities than he surpasses them in his flute-playing; but the fact remains that *he* is the man who ought to get the better supply of flutes. If it is to be recognized in connexion with a given function, superiority in quality such as birth —or for that matter wealth—ought to contribute something to the performance of that function; and here these qualities contribute nothing to such performance.

There is a further objection. If we accept this argument that offices and honours should be assigned on the basis of excellence in *any* respect, every quality will have to be commensurable with every other. You will begin by reckoning a given degree of (say) height as superior to a given degree of some other quality, and you will thus be driven to pit height in general against (say) wealth and birth in general. But on this basis—*i.e.* that, *in a given case,* A is counted as excelling in height to a greater degree than B does in goodness, and that, *in general,* height is counted as excelling to a greater degree than goodness does— qualities are made commensurable. We are involved in mere arithmetic; for if amount X of some quality is "better" than amount Y of some other, some amount which is other than X must clearly be equal to it, *i.e.* must be *equally* good. This is impossible because things that differ in quality cannot be treated in terms of quantity, or regarded as commensurable. It is therefore clear that in matters political just as in matters belonging to other arts and sciences there is no good reason for basing a claim to the exercise of authority on any and every kind of superiority. Some may be swift and others slow; but this is no reason why one should have more political rights, and the others less. It is in athletic contests that the superiority of the swift receives its reward. Claims to political rights must be based on the ground of contribution to the elements which constitute the being of the state. There is thus good ground for the claims to honour and office which are made by persons of good descent, free birth, or wealth. Those who hold office must necessarily be free men and taxpayers: a state could not be composed entirely of men without means, any more than it could be composed entirely of slaves. But we must add that if wealth and free birth are necessary elements, the temper of justice and a martial habit are also necessary. These too are elements which must be present if men are to live together in a state. The one difference is that the first two elements are necessary to the simple existence of a state, and the last two for its good life.

If we are thinking in terms of contribution to the state's existence, all of the elements mentioned, or at any rate several of them, may properly claim to be recognized in the award of honours and office; but if we are thinking in terms of contribution to its good life, then culture and goodness, as we have noted already, may be regarded as having the justest claim. On the other hand —and following our principle that it is not right for men who are equal in one respect, and only in one, to have an equal share of all things as the democrats claim, or for men who are superior in one respect to have a superior share of everything as the oligarchs claim—we are bound to consider all constitutions which recognize such claims as perverted forms. We have noted already that there is a certain sense in which all the contributors of the different elements are justified in the claims they advance, though none of them is absolutely justified. (a) The rich are so far justified that they have a larger share of the land, which is a matter of public interest: they are also, as a rule, more reliable in matters of contract. (b) The free and the nobly born who both contribute the element of birth may claim recognition together as being closely connected. The better-born are citizens to a greater extent

than the low-born; and good birth has always honour in its own country. In addition and apart from any honour paid them the descendants of better men are likely to be intrinsically better; good birth means goodness of the whole stock. (c) Similarly we may also allow that goodness of character has a just claim; for in our view the virtue of justice, which is necessarily accompanied by all the other virtues and which may thus be identified with *general* virtue or goodness is a virtue which acts in social relations and is therefore one of the elements essential to the existence of political society. (d) But there is a further claim that may also be urged. Besides the claim of individuals, based on their having the particular attribute of wealth or birth or goodness, there is the claim of the people at large, based on its having, collectively, still more of all these attributes. The many may urge their claims against the few: taken together and compared with the few they are stronger, richer, and better.

Let us suppose these rival claimants—for example, the good, the wealthy and well-born, and some sort of general body of citizens—all living together in a single state. Will they fall to disputing which of them is to govern, or will they agree? This issue is not a matter of dispute in any of the constitutions mentioned in our previous classification. These constitutions differ in virtue of different groups being sovereign: one of them is distinguished by sovereignty being vested in the wealthy; another by its being vested in the good; and so with each of the rest. But the question we are discussing is different. It is a question of determining who is to govern when the claims of different groups are simultaneously present. Suppose, for example, that the good are exceedingly few in number: how are we to settle their claim? Must we only have regard to the fact that they are few for the function they have to discharge; and must we therefore inquire whether they will be able to manage a state, or numerous enough to compose one? Here there arises a difficulty which applies not only to the good, but to all the different claimants for political office and honour. It may equally be held that there is no justice in the claim of a few to rule on the ground of their greater wealth, or on that of their better birth; and there is an obvious reason for holding this view. If there is any *one* man who in turn is richer than all the rest, this one man must rule over all on the very same ground of justice which the few rich plead for *their* right to rule; and similarly any one man who is preeminent in point of good birth must carry the say over those who claim on the ground of birth. In aristocracies, too, the same logic may be applied in the matter of merit or goodness. If some one man be a better man than all the other good men who belong to the civic body, this one man should be sovereign on the very same ground of justice which the other men plead in defence of *their* right to govern. Even the claims of the Many may be challenged by this line of argument. If the reason why they should be sovereign is their being stronger than the Few, we are logically driven to conclude that where one man is stronger than all the rest—or a group of more

than one, but fewer than the Many, is stronger—that one man or group must be sovereign instead of the Many.

All these considerations would seem to prove that none of the principles, wealth, birth, goodness, and the strength of numbers, in virtue of which men claim to rule and to have all others subject to their rule, is a proper principle. Take, for example, those who claim to be sovereign over the citizen body on the ground of goodness; or take, again, those who base their claim on the ground of wealth. The claims of both may be justly challenged by the masses; for there is nothing whatever to prevent the Many—collectively if not individually—from being better, or richer, than the Few. This last reflection enables us to take another step, and to meet a difficulty which is sometimes raised and discussed. The difficulty is this. Suppose that the Many are actually better, taken as a whole, than the Few: what, in that case, is the proper policy for a lawgiver who wishes to enact right laws to the best of his power? Should he direct his legislation to the benefit of the better sort, or should he direct it to that of the majority? We may reply that the benefit of neither ought to be considered exclusively; that what is "right" should be understood as what is "equally right"; and what is "equally right" is what is for the benefit of the whole state and for the common good of its citizens. Citizens, in the common sense of that term, are *all* who share in the civic life of ruling and being ruled in turn. In the particular sense of the term, they vary from constitution to constitution; and under an ideal constitution they must be those who are able and willing to rule and be ruled with a view to attaining a way of life according to goodness.

· · ·

BOOK IV

· · ·

We have now to consider what is the best constitution and the best way of life for the *majority* of states and men. In doing so we shall not employ, for the purpose of measuring "the best," a standard of excellence above the reach of ordinary men, or a standard of education requiring exceptional endowments and equipment, or the standard of a constitution which attains an ideal height. We shall only be concerned with the sort of life which most men are able to share and the sort of constitution which it is possible for most states to enjoy. The "aristocracies," so called, of which we have just been treating, will not serve us for this purpose: they either lie, at one extreme, beyond the reach of most states, or they approach, at the other, so closely to the constitution called "polity" that they need not be considered separately and must be treated as identical with it. The issues we have just raised can all be decided in the light of one body of fundamental principles. If we adopt as true the statements made in the *Ethics*—(1) that a truly happy life is a life of goodness lived in freedom from impediments, and (2) that goodness consists in a mean—it follows that the best way of life for the *majority* of men is one which consists in a mean, and a mean of the kind attainable by every individual. Further, the same criteria which determine whether the citizen-body, *i.e.* all its

members, considered as *individuals,* have a good or bad way of life must also apply to the constitution; for a constitution is the way of life of a citizen-body. In all states there may be distinguished three parts, or classes, of the citizen-body—the very rich; the very poor; and the middle class which forms the mean. Now it is admitted, as a general principle, that moderation and the mean are always best. We may therefore conclude that in the ownership of all gifts of fortune a middle condition will be the best. Men who are in this condition are the most ready to listen to reason. Those who belong to either extreme—the over-handsome, the over-strong, the over-noble, the over-wealthy; or at the opposite end the over-poor, the over-weak, the utterly ignoble—find it hard to follow the lead of reason. Men in the first class tend more to violence and serious crime: men in the second tend too much to roguery and petty offences; and most wrong-doing arises either from violence or roguery. It is a further merit of the middle class that its members suffer least from ambition, which both in the military and the civil sphere is dangerous to states. It must also be added that those who enjoy too many advantages—strength, wealth, connexions, and so forth—are both unwilling to obey and ignorant how to obey. This is a defect which appears in them from the first, during childhood and in home-life: nurtured in luxury, they never acquire a habit of discipline, even in the matter of lessons. But there are also defects in those who suffer from the opposite extreme of a lack of advantages: they are far too mean and poor-spirited. We have thus, on the one hand, people who are ignorant how to rule and only know how to obey, as if they were so many slaves, and, on the other hand, people who are ignorant how to obey any sort of authority and only know how to rule as if they were masters of slaves. The result is a state, not of freemen, but only of slaves and masters: a state of envy on the one side and on the other contempt. Nothing could be further removed from the spirit of friendship or the temper of a political community. Community depends on friendship; and when there is enmity instead of friendship, men will not even share the same path. A state aims at being, as far as it can be, a society composed of equals and peers who, as such, can be friends and associates; and the middle class, more than any other, has this sort of composition. It follows that a state which is based on the middle class is bound to be the best constituted in respect of the elements, *i.e.* equals and peers, of which, in our view, a state is naturally composed. The middle classes besides contributing, in this way, to the security of the state enjoy a greater security themselves than any other class. They do not, like the poor, covet the goods of others; nor do others covet their possessions, as the poor covet those of the rich. Neither plotting against others, nor plotted against themselves, they live in freedom from danger; and we may well approve the prayer of Phocylides

Many things are best for the middling:
Fain would I be of the state's middle
    class.

It is clear from our argument,

first, that the best form of political society is one where power is vested in the middle class, and, secondly, that good government is attainable in those states where there is a large middle class—large enough, if possible, to be stronger than both of the other classes, but at any rate large enough to be stronger than either of them singly; for in that case its addition to either will suffice to turn the scale, and will prevent either of the opposing extremes from becoming dominant. It is therefore the greatest of blessings for a state that its members should possess a moderate and adequate property. Where some have great possessions, and others have nothing at all, the result is either an extreme democracy or an unmixed oligarchy; or it may even be—indirectly, and as a reaction against both of these extremes—a tyranny. Tyranny is a form of government which may grow out of the headiest type of democracy, or out of oligarchy; but it is much less likely to grow out of constitutions of the middle order, or those which approximate to them, *e.g.* moderate oligarchies. We shall explain the reason later when we come to treat of revolutions and constitutional change.

Meanwhile, it is clear that the middle type of constitution is best for the *majority* of states. It is the one type free from faction; where the middle class is large, there is least likelihood of faction and dissension among the citizens. Large states are generally more free from faction just because they have a large middle class. In small states, on the other hand, it is easy for the whole population to be divided into only two classes; nothing is left in the middle, and all—or almost all—are either poor or rich. The reason why democracies are generally more secure and more permanent than oligarchies is the character of their middle class, which is more numerous, and is allowed a larger share in the government, than it is in oligarchies. Where democracies have no middle class, and the poor are greatly superior in number, trouble ensues, and they are speedily ruined. It must also be considered a proof of its value that the best legislators have come from the middle class. Solon was one, as his own poems prove: Lycurgus was another (and not, as is sometimes said, a member of the royal family); and the same is true of Charondas and most of the other legislators. . . .

Plutarch

Little is known of the life of Plutarch; there are many legends but few verifiable facts. He was a Greek, born in Boeotia around A.D. 40, and educated in Athens. He spent much of his life in the service of his native city-state, although he seems to have found time for considerable travel, including several brief visits to Rome, where he devoted himself to study. He died, highly honored, in Boeotia around A.D. 120.

It is difficult to consider Plutarch as anything other than a moralist. Although his fame rests firmly on the merits of his major work, *The Parallel Lives,* he was neither a great biographer nor a good historian. In his biographies he does not attempt to provide complete accounts of the lives of his subjects; rather, he carefully selects details and anecdotes to point up the good or bad qualities in the character and the actions of the person. As history, *The Parallel Lives* gives only imperfect accounts of an age, with no attempt to recount events systematically.

Even the organization of the book reveals the moralist at work. The lives are arranged in pairs, with the biography of a prominent Greek followed by the biography of a distinguished Roman. Frequently a pair of parallel lives is accompanied by a chapter in which the two are compared. It is in these comparisons that Plutarch reveals his penchant for drawing moral conclusions.

The following selection is from the life of Alexander. In *The Parallel Lives* this brief biography is followed, for obvious reasons, by the life of Julius Caesar. This particular translation was made in the seventeenth century by the English poet John Dryden.

Alexander

It being my purpose to write the lives of Alexander the king, and of Caesar, by whom Pompey was destroyed, the multitude of their great actions affords so large a field that I were to blame if I should not by way of apology forewarn my reader that I have chosen rather to epitomize the most celebrated parts of their story, than to insist at large on every particular circumstance of it. It must be borne in mind that

Plutarch's Lives, trans. John Dryden (Boston, 1859).

my design is not to write histories, but lives. And the most glorious exploits do not always furnish us with the clearest discoveries of virtue or vice in men; sometimes a matter of less moment, an expression or a jest, informs us better of their characters and inclinations, than the most famous sieges, the greatest armaments, or the bloodiest battles whatsoever. Therefore as portrait-painters are more exact in the lines and features of the face, in which the character is seen, than in the other parts of the body, so I must be allowed to give my more particular attention to the marks and indications of the souls of men, and while I endeavor by these to portray their lives, may be free to leave more weighty matters and great battles to be treated of by others.

· · ·

Alexander was born the sixth of Hecatombaeon, which month the Macedonians call Lous, the same day that the temple of Diana at Ephesus was burnt; which Hegesias of Magnesia makes the occasion of a conceit, frigid enough to have stopped the conflagration. The temple, he says, took fire and was burnt while its mistress was absent, assisting at the birth of Alexander. And all the Eastern soothsayers who happened to be then at Ephesus, looking upon the ruin of this temple to be the forerunner of some other calamity, ran about the town, beating their faces, and crying, that this day had brought forth something that would prove fatal and destructive to all Asia.

Just after Philip had taken Potidaea, he received these three messages at one time, that Parmenio had overthrown the Illyrians in a great battle, that his race-horse had won the course at the Olympic games, and that his wife had given birth to Alexander; with which being naturally well pleased, as an addition to his satisfaction, he was assured by the diviners that a son, whose birth was accompanied with three successes, could not fail of being invincible.

The statues that gave the best representation of Alexander's person, were those of Lysippus (by whom alone he would suffer his image to be made), those peculiarities which many of his successors afterwards and his friends used to affect to imitate, the inclination of his head a little on one side towards his left shoulder, and his melting eye, having been expressed by this artist with great exactness. But Apelles, who drew him with thunderbolts in his hand, made his complexion browner and darker than it was naturally; for he was fair and of a light color, passing into ruddiness in his face and upon his breast. Aristoxenus in his Memoirs tells us that a most agreeable odor exhaled from his skin, and that his breath and body all over was so fragrant as to perfume the clothes which he wore next him; the cause of which might probably be the hot and adust temperament of his body. For sweet smells, Theophrastus conceives, are produced by the concoction of moist humours by heat, which is the reason that those parts of the world which are driest and most burnt up, afford spices of the best kind, and in the greatest quantity; for the heat of the sun exhausts all the superfluous moisture which lies in the surface of bodies, ready to generate putrefaction. And this hot constitution, it may be, rendered Alexander so addicted to drinking, and so choleric. His temperance, as to the pleasures of the body, was apparent in him in his very childhood, as he was with much difficulty incited to them, and always used them with great moderation; though in other things he was extremely eager and vehement, and in his love of glory, and the pursuit of it, he showed a solidity of high spirit and magnanimity far above his age. For he neither sought nor valued it upon every occasion, as his father Philip did (who affected to show his eloquence almost to a degree of pedantry, and took care to have the victories of his racing chariots at the Olympic games engraven on his coin), but when he was asked by some about him, whether he would run a race in the Olympic games, as he was very swift-footed, he answered, he would, if he might have kings to run with him. Indeed, he seems in general to have looked with indifference, if not with dislike, upon the professed athletes. He often appointed prizes, for which not only tragedians and musicians, pipers and harpers, but rhapsodists also, strove to outvie one another; and delighted in all manner of hunting and cudgel-playing, but never gave any encouragement to contests either of boxing or of the pancratium.

While he was yet very young, he entertained the ambassadors from the king of Persia, in the absence of his father, and entering much into conversation with them, gained so much upon them by his affability, and the questions he asked them, which were far from being childish or trifling (for he inquired of them the length of the ways, the nature

of the road into inner Asia, the character of their king, how he carried himself to his enemies, and what forces he was able to bring into the field), that they were struck with admiration of him, and looked upon the ability so much famed of Philip, to be nothing in comparison with the forwardness and high purpose that appeared thus early in his son. Whenever he heard Philip had taken any town of importance, or won any signal victory, instead of rejoicing at it altogether, he would tell his companions that his father would anticipate every thing, and leave him and them no opportunities of performing great and illustrious actions. For being more bent upon action and glory than either upon pleasure or riches, he esteemed all that he should receive from his father as a diminution and prevention of his own future achievements; and would have chosen rather to succeed to a kingdom involved in troubles and wars, which would have afforded him frequent exercise of his courage, and a large field of honor, than to one already flourishing and settled, where his inheritance would be an inactive life, and the mere enjoyment of wealth and luxury.

The care of his education, as it might be presumed, was committed to a great many attendants, preceptors, and teachers, over the whole of whom Leonidas, a near kinsman of Olympias, a man of an austere temper, presided, who did not indeed himself decline the name of what in reality is a noble and honorable office, but in general his dignity, and his near relationship, obtained him from other people the title of Alexander's foster father and governor. But he who took upon him the actual place and style of his pedagogue, was Lysimachus the Acarnanian, who, though he had nothing specially to recommend him, but his lucky fancy of calling himself Phoenix, Alexander Achilles, and Philip Peleus, was therefore well enough esteemed, and ranged in the next degree after Leonidas.

Philonicus the Thessalian brought the horse Bucephalas to Philip, offering to sell him for thirteen talents; but when they went into the field to try him, they found him so very vicious and unmanageable, that he reared up when they endeavored to mount him, and would not so much as endure the voice of any of Philip's attendants. Upon which, as they were leading him away as wholly useless and untractable, Alexander, who stood by, said, "What an excellent horse do they lose, for want of address and boldness to manage him!" Philip at first took no notice of what he said; but when he heard him repeat the same thing several times, and saw that he was much vexed to see the horse sent away, "Do you reproach," said he to him, "those who are older than yourself, as if you knew more, and were better able to manage him than they?" "I could manage this horse," replied he, "better than others do." "And if you do not," said Philip, "what will you forfeit for your rashness?" "I will pay," answered Alexander, "the whole price of the horse." At this the whole company fell a laughing; and as soon as the wager was settled amongst them, he immediately ran to the horse, and taking hold of the bridle, turned him directly towards the sun, having, it seems, observed that he was disturbed at and afraid of the motion of his own shadow; then letting him go forward a little, still keeping the reins in his hand, and stroking him gently when he found him begin to grow eager and fiery, he let fall his upper garment softly, and with one nimble leap securely mounted him, and when he was seated, by little and little drew in the bridle, and curbed him without either striking or spurring him. Presently, when he found him free from all rebelliousness, and only impatient for the course, he let him go at full speed, inciting him now with a commanding voice, and urging him also with his heel. Philip and his friends looked on at first in silence and anxiety for the result, till seeing him turn at the end of his career, and come back rejoicing and triumphing for what he had performed, they all burst out into acclamations of applause; and his father, shedding tears, it is said, for joy, kissed him as he came down from his horse, and in his transport, said, "O my son, look thee out a kingdom equal to and worthy of thyself, for Macedonia is too little for thee."

After this, considering him to be of a temper easy to be led to his duty by reason, but by no means to be compelled, he always endeavored to persuade rather than to command or force him to any thing; and now looking upon the instruction and tuition of his youth to be of greater difficulty and importance, than to be wholly trusted to the ordinary masters in music and poetry, and the common school subjects, and to require, as Sophocles says,

The bridle and the rudder too,

he sent for Aristotle, the most learned and most celebrated philosopher of his time, and rewarded him with a munificence proportionable to and becoming the care he took to instruct his son. For he repeopled his native city Stagira, which he had caused to be demolished a little before, and restored all the citizens who were in exile or slavery, to their habitations. As a place for the pursuit of their studies and exercises, he assigned the temple of the Nymphs, near Mieza, where, to this very day, they show you Aristotle's stone seats, and the shady walks which he was wont to frequent. It would appear that Alexander received from him not only his doctrines of Morals, and of Politics, but also something of those more abstruse and profound theories which these philosophers, by the very names they gave them, professed to reserve for oral communication to the initiated, and did not allow many to become acquainted with. For when he was in Asia, and heard Aristotle had published some treatises of that kind, he wrote to him, using very plain language to him in behalf of philosophy, the following letter:

Alexander to Aristotle greeting. You have not done well to publish your books of oral doctrine; for what is there now that we excel others in, if those things which we have been particularly instructed in be laid open to all? For my part, I assure you, I had rather excel others in the knowledge of what is excellent, than in the extent of my power and dominion. Farewell.

And Aristotle, soothing this passion for preeminence, speaks, in his excuse for himself, of these doctrines, as in fact both published and not published; as indeed, to say the truth, his books on metaphysics are written in a style which makes them useless for ordinary teaching, and instructive only, in the way of memoranda, for those who have been already conversant in that sort of learning.

Doubtless also it was to Aristotle, that he owed the inclination he had, not to the theory only, but likewise to the practice of the art of medicine. For when any of his friends were sick, he would often prescribe them their course of diet, and medicines proper to their disease, as we may find in his epistles. He was naturally a great lover of all kinds of learning and reading; and Onesicritus informs us, that he constantly laid Homer's *Iliad,* according to the copy corrected by Aristotle, called the casket copy, with his dagger under his pillow, declaring that he esteemed it a perfect portable treasure of all military virtue and knowledge. When he was in the upper Asia, being destitute of other books, he ordered Harpalus to send him some; who furnished him with Philistus's History, a great many of the plays of Euripides, Sophocles, and Aeschylus, and some dithyrambic odes, composed by Telestes and Philoxenus. For awhile he loved and cherished Aristotle no less, as he was wont to say himself, than if he had been his father, giving this reason for it, that as he had received life from the one, so the other had taught him to live well. But afterwards, upon some mistrust of him, yet not so great as to make him do him any hurt, his familiarity and friendly kindness to him abated so much of its former force and affectionateness, as to make it evident he was alienated from him. However, his violent thirst after and passion for learning, which were once implanted, still grew up with him, and never decayed; as appears by his veneration of Anaxarchus, by the present of fifty talents which he sent to Xeonocrates, and his particular care and esteem of Dandamis and Calanus.

. . .

Soon after, the Grecians, being assembled at the Isthmus, declared their resolution of joining with Alexander in the war against the Persians, and proclaimed him their general. While he stayed here, many public ministers and philosophers came from all parts to visit him, and congratulated him on his election, but contrary to his expectation, Diogenes of Sinope,[1] who then was living at Corinth, thought so little of him, that instead of coming to compliment him, he never so much as stirred out of the suburb called the Cranium, where Alexander found him lying alone in the sun. When he saw so much company near him, he raised himself a little, and vouchsafed to look upon Alexander; and when he kindly asked him whether he wanted any thing, "Yes," said he, "I would have you stand from between me and the sun." Alexander was so struck at this answer, and surprised at the greatness of the man, who had taken so little notice of him, that as he went away, he told his followers who were laughing at the moroseness of the philosopher, that if he were

not Alexander, he would choose to be Diogenes.

Then he went to Delphi, to consult Apollo concerning the success of the war he had undertaken, and happening to come on one of the forbidden days, when it was esteemed improper to give any answers from the oracle, he sent messengers to desire the priestess to do her office; and when she refused, on the plea of a law to the contrary, he went up himself, and began to draw her by force into the temple, until tired and overcome with his importunity, "My son," said she, "thou art invincible." Alexander taking hold of what she spoke, declared he had received such an answer as he wished for, and that it was needless to consult the god any further. Among other prodigies that attended the departure of his army, the image of Orpheus at Libethra, made of cypresswood, was seen to sweat in great abundance, to the discouragement of many. But Aristander told him, that far from presaging any ill to him, it signified he should perform acts so important and glorious as would make the poets and musicians of future ages labor and sweat to describe and celebrate them.

His army, by their computation who make the smallest amount, consisted of thirty thousand foot, and four thousand horse; and those who make the most of it, speak but of forty-three thousand foot, and three thousand horse. Aristobulus says, he had not a fund of above seventy talents for their pay, nor had he more than thirty days' provision, if we may believe Duris; Onesicritus tells us, he was two hundred talents in debt. However narrow and dis-

---

[1] [A famous Greek philosopher, who lived in a tub and went about carrying a lighted lantern "in search of an honest man."—*Ed.*]

proportionable the beginnings of so vast an undertaking might seem to be, yet he would not embark his army until he had informed himself particularly what means his friends had to enable them to follow him, and supplied what they wanted, by giving good farms to some, a village to one, and the revenue of some hamlet or harbor town to another. So that at last he had portioned out or engaged almost all the royal property; which giving Perdiccas an occasion to ask him what he would leave himself, he replied, his hopes. "Your soldiers," replied Perdiccas, "will be your partners in those," and refused to accept of the estate he had assigned him. Some others of his friends did the like, but to those who willingly received, or desired assistance of him, he liberally granted it, as far as his patrimony in Macedonia would reach, the most part of which was spent in these donations.

With such vigorous resolutions, and his mind thus disposed, he passed the Hellespont, and at Troy sacrificed to Minerva, and honored the memory of the heroes who were buried there, with solemn libations; especially Achilles, whose gravestone he anointed, and with his friends, as the ancient custom is, ran naked about his sepulchre, and crowned it with garlands, declaring how happy he esteemed him, in having while he lived so faithful a friend, and when he was dead, so famous a poet to proclaim his actions. While he was viewing the rest of the antiquities and curiosities of the place, being told he might see Paris's harp, if he pleased, he said, he thought it not worth looking on, but he should be glad to see that of Achilles, to which he used to sing the glories and great actions of brave men.

In the mean time Darius's captains having collected large forces, were encamped on the further bank of the river Granicus, and it was necessary to fight, as it were, in the gate of Asia for an entrance into it. The depth of the river, with the unevenness and difficult ascent of the opposite bank, which was to be gained by main force, was apprehended by most, and some pronounced it an improper time to engage, because it was unusual for the kings of Macedonia to march with their forces in the month called Daesius. But Alexander broke through these scruples, telling them they should call it a second Artemisium. And when Parmenio advised him not to attempt any thing that day, because it was late, he told him that he should disgrace the Hellespont, should he fear the Granicus. And so without more saying, he immediately took the river with thirteen troops of horse, and advanced against whole showers of darts thrown from the steep opposite side, which was covered with armed multitudes of the enemy's horse and foot, notwithstanding the disadvantage of the ground and the rapidity of the stream; so that the action seemed to have more of frenzy and desperation in it, than of prudent conduct. However, he persisted obstinately to gain the passage, and at last with much ado making his way up the banks, which were extremely muddy and slippery, he had instantly to join in a mere confused hand-to-hand combat with the enemy, before he could draw up his men, who were still passing over, into any order. For the enemy pressed upon him with loud and warlike outcries; and charging horse against horse, with their lances, after they had broken and spent these, they fell to it with their swords. And Alexander, being easily known by his buckler, and a large plume of white feathers on each side of his helmet, was attacked on all sides, yet escaped wounding, though his cuirass was pierced by a javelin in one of the joinings. And Rhoesaces and Spithridates, two Persian commanders, falling upon him at once, he avoided one of them, and struck at Rhoesaces, who had a good cuirass on, with such force, that his spear breaking in his hand, he was glad to betake himself to his dagger. While they were thus engaged, Spithridates came up on one side of him, and raising himself upon his horse, gave him such a blow with his battle-axe on the helmet, that he cut off the crest of it, with one of his plumes, and the helmet was only just so far strong enough to save him, that the edge of the weapon touched the hair of his head. But as he was about to repeat his stroke, Clitus, called the black Clitus, prevented him, by running him through the body with his spear. At the same time Alexander despatched Rhoesaces with his sword. While the horse were thus dangerously engaged, the Macedonian phalanx passed the river, and the foot on each side advanced to fight. But the enemy hardly sustained the first onset, soon gave ground and fled, all but the mercenary Greeks, who, making a stand upon a rising ground, desired quarter, which Alexander, guided rather by passion than judgment, refused to grant, and charging them

himself first, had his horse (not Bucephalas, but another) killed under him. And this obstinacy of his to cut off these experienced desperate men, cost him the lives of more of his own soldiers than all the battle before, besides those who were wounded. The Persians lost in this battle twenty thousand foot, and two thousand five hundred horse. On Alexander's side, Aristobulus says there were not wanting above four and thirty, of whom nine were foot-soldiers; and in memory of them he caused so many statues of brass, of Lysippus's making, to be erected. And that the Grecians might participate the honor of his victory, he sent a portion of the spoils home to them, particularly to the Athenians three hundred bucklers, and upon all the rest he ordered this inscription to be set: "Alexander the son of Philip, and the Grecians, except the Lacedaemonians, won these from the barbarians who inhabit Asia." All the plate and purple garments, and other things of the same kind that he took from the Persians, except a very small quantity which he reserved for himself, he sent as a present to his mother.

This battle presently made a great change of affairs to Alexander's advantage. For Sardis itself, the chief seat of the barbarian's power in the maritime provinces, and many other considerable places were surrendered to him; only Halicarnassus and Miletus stood out, which he took by force, together with the territory about them. After which he was a little unsettled in his opinion how to proceed. Sometimes he thought it best to find out Darius as soon as he could, and put all to the hazard of a battle; another while he looked upon it as a more prudent course to make an entire reduction of the seacoast, and not to seek the enemy till he had first exercised his power here and made himself secure of the resources of these provinces. While he was thus deliberating what to do, it happened that a spring of water near the city of Xanthus in Lycia, of its own accord swelled over its banks, and threw up a copper plate upon the margin, in which was engraven in ancient characters, that the time would come, when the Persian empire should be destroyed by the Grecians. Encouraged by this accident, he proceeded to reduce the maritime parts of Cilicia and Phoenicia, and passed his army along the seacoasts of Pamphylia with such expedition that many historians have described and extolled it with that height of admiration, as if it were no less than a miracle, and an extraordinary effect of divine favor, that the waves which usually come rolling in violently from the main, and hardly ever leave so much as a narrow beach under the steep, broken cliffs at any time uncovered, should on a sudden retire to afford him passage. Menander, in one of his comedies, alludes to this marvel when he says:

Was Alexander ever favored more?
Each man I wish for meets me at my
   door,
And should I ask for passage through
   the sea,
The sea I doubt not would retire for
   me.

But Alexander himself in his epistles mentions nothing unusual in this at all, but says he went from Phaselis, and passed through what they call the Ladders. At Phaselis he stayed some time, and finding the statue of Theodectes, who was a native of this town and was now dead, erected in the marketplace, after he had supped, having drunk pretty plentifully, he went and danced about it, and crowned it with garlands, honoring not ungracefully in his sport, the memory of a philosopher whose conversation he had formerly enjoyed, when he was Aristotle's scholar.

• • •

Darius was by this time upon his march from Susa, very confident, not only in the number of his men, which amounted to six hundred thousand, but likewise in a dream, which the Persian soothsayers interpreted rather in flattery to him, than according to the natural probability. He dreamed that he saw the Macedonian phalanx all on fire, and Alexander waiting on him, clad in the same dress which he himself had been used to wear when he was courier to the late king; after which, going into the temple of Belus, he vanished out of his sight. The dream would appear to have supernaturally signified to him the illustrious actions the Macedonians were to perform, and that as he from a courier's place had risen to the throne, so Alexander should come to be master of Asia, and not long surviving his conquests, conclude his life with glory. Darius's confidence increased the more, because Alexander spent so much time in Cilicia, which he imputed to his cowardice. But it was sickness that detained him there, which some say he contracted from his fatigues, others from bathing in the river Cydnus, whose waters were exceedingly cold. However it happened, none of his physicians would venture to give him any remedies, they thought his case so desperate, and were so afraid of the suspicions and ill-will of the Macedonians if they should fail in the cure; till Philip, the Acarnanian, seeing how critical his case was, but relying on his own well-known friendship for him, resolved to try the last efforts of his art, and rather hazard his own credit and life, than suffer him to perish for want of physic, which he confidently administered to him, encouraging him to take it boldly, if he desired a speedy recovery, in order to prosecute the war. At this very time, Parmenio wrote to Alexander from the camp, bidding him have a care of Philip, as one who was bribed by Darius to kill him, with great sums of money, and a promise of his daughter in marriage. When he had perused the letter, he put it under his pillow, without showing it so much as to any of his most intimate friends, and when Philip came in with the potion, he took it with great cheerfulness and assurance, giving him meantime the letter to read. This was a spectacle well worth being present at, to see Alexander take the draught, and Philip read the letter at the same time, and then turn and look upon one another, but with different sentiments; for Alexander's looks were cheerful and open, to show his kindness to and confidence in his physician, while the other was full of surprise and alarm at the accusation, appealing to the gods to witness his innocence, sometimes lifting up his hands to heaven, and then throwing himself down by the bedside, and beseech-ing Alexander to lay aside all fear, and follow his directions without apprehension. For the medicine at first worked so strongly as to drive, so to say, the vital forces into the interior; he lost his speech, and falling into a swoon, had scarce any sense or pulse left. However, in no long time, by Philip's means, his health and strength returned, and he showed himself in public to the Macedonians, who were in continual fear and dejection until they saw him abroad again.

· · ·

In his diet, also, he was most temperate, as appears, omitting many other circumstances, by what he said to Ada, whom he adopted, with the title of mother, and afterwards created queen of Garia. For when she out of kindness sent him every day many curious dishes, and sweetmeats, and would have furnished him with some cooks and pastry-men, who were thought to have great skill, he told her he wanted none of them, his preceptor, Leonidas, having already given him the best, which were a night march to prepare for breakfast, and a moderate breakfast to create an appetite for supper. Leonidas also, he added, used to open and search the furniture of his chamber, and his wardrobe, to see if his mother had left him any thing that was delicate or superfluous. He was much less addicted to wine than was generally believed; that which gave people occasion to think so of him was, that when he had nothing else to do, he loved to sit long and talk, rather than drink, and over every cup hold a long conversation. For when his affairs called upon him, he would not be detained, as other generals often were, either by wine, or sleep, nuptial solemnities, spectacles, or any other diversion whatsoever; a convincing argument of which is, that in the short time he lived, he accomplished so many and so great actions. When he was free from employment, after he was up, and had sacrificed to the gods, he used to sit down to breakfast, and then spend the rest of the day in hunting, or writing memoirs, giving decisions on some military questions, or reading. In marches that required no great haste, he would practise shooting as he went along, or to mount a chariot, and alight from it in full speed. Sometimes, for sport's sake, as his journals tell us, he would hunt foxes and go fowling. When he came in for the evening, after he had bathed and was anointed, he would call for his bakers and chief cooks, to know if they had his dinner ready. He never cared to dine till it was pretty late and beginning to be dark, and was wonderfully circumspect at meals that every one who sat with him should be served alike and with proper attention; and his love of talking, as was said before, made him delight to sit long at his wine. And then, though otherwise no prince's conversation was ever so agreeable, he would fall into a temper of ostentation and soldierly boasting, which gave his flatterers a great advantage to ride him, and made his better friends very uneasy. For though they thought it too base to strive who should flatter him most, yet they found it hazardous not to do it; so that between the shame and the danger, they were in a great strait how to behave themselves. After such an entertainment, he was wont to bathe, and then per-

haps he would sleep till noon, and sometimes all day long. He was so very temperate in his eating, that when any rare fish or fruits were sent him, he would distribute them among his friends, and often reserve nothing for himself. His table, however, was always magnificent, the expense of it still increasing with his good fortune, till it amounted to ten thousand drachmas a day, to which sum he limited it, and beyond this he would suffer none to lay out in any entertainment where he himself was the guest.

· · ·

After he had reduced all Asia on this side of the Euphrates, he advanced towards Darius, who was coming down against him with a million of men. In his march, a very ridiculous passage happened. The servants who followed the camp, for sport's sake divided themselves into two parties, and named the commander of one of them Alexander, and of the other Darius. At first they only. pelted one another with clods of earth, but presently took to their fists, and at last, heated with the contention, they fought in good earnest with stones and clubs, so that they had much ado to part them; till Alexander, upon hearing of it, ordered the two captains to decide the quarrel by single combat, and armed him who bore his name himself, while Philotas did the same to him who represented Darius. The whole army were spectators of this encounter, willing from the event of it to derive an omen of their own future success. After they had fought stoutly a pretty long while, at last he who was called Alexander had the better, and for a reward of his prowess, had twelve villages given him, with leave to wear the Persian dress. So we are told by Eratosthenes.

But the great battle of all that was fought with Darius, was not, as most writers tell us, at Arbela, but at Gaugamela. . . . The oldest of his commanders, and chiefly Parmenio, when they beheld all the plain between Niphates and the Gordyaean mountains shining with the lights and fires which were made by the barbarians, and heard the uncertain and confused sound of voices out of their camp, like the distant roaring of a vast ocean, were so amazed at the thoughts of such a multitude, that after some conference among themselves, they concluded it an enterprise too difficult and hazardous for them to engage so numerous an enemy in the day, and therefore meeting the king as he came from sacrificing, besought him to attack Darius by night, that the darkness might conceal the danger of the ensuing battle. To this he gave them the celebrated answer, "I will not steal a victory," which though some at the time thought a boyish and inconsiderate speech, as if he played with danger, others, however, regarded as an evidence that he confided in his present condition, and acted on a true judgment of the future, not wishing to leave Darius, in case he were worsted, the pretext of trying his fortune again, which he might suppose himself to have, if he could impute his overthrow to the disadvantage of the night, as he did before to the mountains, the narrow passages, and the sea. For while he had such numerous forces and large dominions still remaining, it was not any want of men or arms that could

induce him to give up the war, but only the loss of all courage and hope upon the conviction of an undeniable and manifest defeat.

After they were gone from him with this answer, he laid himself down in his tent and slept the rest of the night more soundly than was usual with him, to the astonishment of the commanders, who came to him early in the morning, and were fain themselves to give order that the soldiers should breakfast. But at last, time not giving them leave to wait any longer, Parmenio went to his bedside, and called him twice or thrice by his name, till he waked him, and then asked him how it was possible, when he was to fight the most important battle of all, he could sleep as soundly as if he were already victorious. "And are we not so, indeed," replied Alexander smiling, "since we are at last relieved from the trouble of wandering in pursuit of Darius through a wide and wasted country, hoping in vain that he would fight us?" And not only before the battle, but in the height of the danger, he showed himself great, and manifested the self-possession of a just foresight and confidence. For the battle for some time fluctuated and was dubious. The left wing, where Parmenio commanded, was so impetuously charged by the Bactrian horse that it was disordered and forced to give ground, at the same time that Mazaeus had sent a detachment round about to fall upon those who guarded the baggage, which so disturbed Parmenio, that he sent messengers to acquaint Alexander that the camp and baggage would be all lost unless he immediately relieved the rear by a considerable reinforcement drawn out of the front. This message being brought him just as he was giving the signal to those about him for the onset, he bade them tell Parmenio that he must have surely lost the use of his reason, and had forgotten, in his alarm, that soldiers, if victorious, become masters of their enemies' baggage; and if defeated, instead of taking care of their wealth or their slaves, have nothing more to do but to fight gallantly and die with honor. When he had said this, he put on his helmet, having the rest of his arms on before he came out of his tent, which were a coat of the Sicilian make, girt close about him, and over that a breast-piece of thickly quilted linen, which was taken among other booty at the battle of Issus. The helmet, which was made by Theophilus, though of iron, was so well wrought and polished, that it was as bright as the most refined silver. To this was fitted a gorget of the same metal, set with precious stones. His sword, which was the weapon he most used in fight, was given him by the king of the Citieans, and was of an admirable temper and lightness. The belt which he also wore in all engagements, was of much richer workmanship than the rest of his armor. It was a work of the ancient Helicon, and had been presented to him by the Rhodians, as a mark of their respect to him. So long as he was engaged in drawing up his men, or riding about to give orders or directions, or to view them, he spared Bucephalas, who was now growing old, and made use of another horse; but when he was actually to fight, he sent for him again, and as soon as he was mounted, commenced the attack.

He made the longest address that day to the Thessalians and other Greeks, who answered him with loud shouts, desiring him to lead them on against the barbarians, upon which he shifted his javelin into his left hand, and with his right lifted up towards heaven, besought the gods, as Callisthenes tells us, that if he was of a truth the son of Jupiter, they would be pleased to assist and strengthen the Grecians. At the same time the augur Aristander, who had a white mantle about him, and a crown of gold on his head, rode by and showed them an eagle that soared just over Alexander, and directed his flight towards the enemy; which so animated the beholders, that after mutual encouragements and exhortations, the horses charged at full speed, and were followed in a mass by the whole phalanx of the foot. But before they could well come to blows with the first ranks, the barbarians shrunk back, and were hotly pursued by Alexander, who drove those that fled before him into the middle of the battle, where Darius himself was in person, whom he saw from a distance over the foremost ranks, conspicuous in the midst of his life-guard, a tall and fine-looking man, drawn in a lofty chariot, defended by an abundance of the best horse, who stood close in order about it, ready to receive the enemy. But Alexander's approach was so terrible, forcing those who gave back upon those who yet maintained their ground, that he beat down and dispersed them almost all. Only a few of the bravest and valiantest opposed the pursuit, who were slain in their king's presence, falling in heaps upon one another, and in the very pangs of death striving to catch hold of the horses. Darius now seeing all was lost, that those who were placed in front to defend him were broken and beat back upon him, that he could not turn or disengage his chariot without great difficulty, the wheels being clogged and entangled among the dead bodies, which lay in such heaps as not only stopped, but almost covered the horses, and made them rear and grow so unruly, that the frighted charioteer could govern them no longer, in this extremity was glad to quit his chariot and his arms, and mounting, it is said, upon a mare that had been taken from her foal, betook himself to flight. But he had not escaped so either, if Parmenio had not sent fresh messengers to Alexander, to desire him to return and assist him against a considerable body of the enemy which yet stood together, and would not give ground. For, indeed, Parmenio is on all hands accused of having been sluggish and unserviceable in this battle, whether age had impaired his courage, or that, as Callisthenes says, he secretly disliked and envied Alexander's growing greatness. Alexander, though he was not a little vexed to be so recalled and hindered from pursuing his victory, yet concealed the true reason from his men, and causing a retreat to be sounded, as if it were too late to continue the execution any longer, marched back towards the place of danger, and by the way met with the news of the enemy's total overthrow and flight.

This battle being thus over, seemed to put a period to the Persian empire, and Alexander, who was now proclaimed king of Asia, returned thanks to the gods in magnificent sacrifices, and rewarded his friends and followers with great sums of money, and palaces, and governments of provinces. And eager to gain honor with the Grecians, he wrote to them that he would have all tyrannies abolished, that they might live free according to their own laws, and specially to the Plataeans, that their city should be rebuilt, because their ancestors had permitted their countrymen of old to make their territory the seat of the war, when they fought with the barbarians for their common liberty. He sent also part of the spoils into Italy, to the Crotoniats, to honor the zeal and courage of their citizen Phayllus, the wrestler, who, in the Median war, when the other Grecian colonies in Italy disowned Greece, that he might have a share in the danger, joined the fleet at Salamis, with a vessel set forth at his own charge. So affectionate was Alexander to all kind of virtue, and so desirous to preserve the memory of laudable actions.

• • •

At the taking of Susa, Alexander found in the palace forty thousand talents in money already coined, besides an unspeakable quantity of other furniture and treasure; amongst which was five thousand talents' worth of Hermionian purple, that had been laid up there an hundred and ninety years, and yet kept its color as fresh and lively as at first. The reason of which, they say, is that in dyeing the purple they made use of honey, and of white oil in the white tincture, both which after the like space of time preserve the clearness and brightness of their lustre. Dinon also relates that the Persian kings had water fetched from the Nile and the Danube, which they laid up in their treasuries as a sort of testimony of the greatness of their power and universal empire.

The entrance into Persia was through a most difficult country, and was guarded by the noblest of the Persians, Darius himself having escaped further. Alexander, however, chanced to find a guide in exact correspondence with what the Pythia had foretold when he was a child, that a lycus should conduct him into Persia. For by such an one, whose father was a Lycian, and his mother a Persian, and who spoke both languages, he was now led into the country, by a way something about, yet without fetching any considerable compass. Here a great many of the prisoners were put to the sword, of which himself gives this account, that he commanded them to be killed in the belief that it would be for his advantage. Nor was the money found here less, he says, than at Susa, besides other movables and treasure, as much as ten thousand pair of mules and five thousand camels could well carry away. Amongst other things he happened to observe a large statue of Xerxes thrown carelessly down to the ground in the confusion made by the multitude of soldiers pressing into the palace. He stood still, and accosting it as if it had been alive, "Shall we," said he, " neglectfully pass thee by, now thou art prostrate on the ground, because thou once invadedst Greece, or shall we erect thee again in consideration of the greatness of thy mind and thy other virtues?" But at last, after he had paused some time, and silently considered with himself, he went on without taking any further notice of it. In this place he took up his winter quarters, and stayed four months to refresh his soldiers. It is related that the first time he sat on the royal throne of Persia, under the canopy of gold, Demaratus, the Corinthian, who was much attached to him and had been one of his father's friends, wept, in an old man's manner, and deplored the misfortune of those Greeks whom death had deprived of the satisfaction of seeing Alexander seated on the throne of Darius.

From hence designing to march against Darius, before he set out, he diverted himself with his officers at an entertainment of drinking and other pastimes, and indulged so far as to let every one's mistress sit by and drink with them. The most celebrated of them was Thais, an Athenian, mistress of Ptolemy, who was afterwards king of Egypt. She, partly as a sort of well-turned compliment to Alexander, partly out of sport, as the drinking went on, at last was carried so far as to utter a saying, not misbecoming her native country's character, though somewhat too lofty for her own condition. She said it was indeed some recompense for the toils she had undergone in following the camp all over Asia, that she was that day treated in, and could insult over, the stately palace of the Persian monarchs. But, she added, it would please her much better, if while the king looked on, she might in sport, with her own hands, set fire to the court of that Xerxes who reduced the city of Athens to ashes, that it might be recorded to posterity, that the women who followed Alexander had taken a severer revenge on the Persians for the sufferings and affronts of Greece, than all the famed commanders had been able to do by sea or land. What she said was received with such universal liking and murmurs of applause, and so seconded by the encouragement and eagerness of the company, that the king himself, persuaded to be of the party, started from his seat, and with a chaplet of flowers on his head, and a lighted torch in his hand, led them the way, while they went after him in a riotous manner, dancing and making loud cries about the place; which when the rest of the Macedonians perceived, they also in great delight ran thither with torches; for they hoped the burning and destruction of the royal palace was an argument that he looked homeward, and had no design to reside among the barbarians. Thus some writers give their account of this action, while others say it was done deliberately; however, all agree that he soon repented of it, and gave order to put out the fire.

· · ·

When he came into Persia, he distributed money among the women, as their own kings had been wont to do, who as often as they came thither, gave every one of them a piece of gold; on account of which custom, some of them, it is said, had come but seldom, and Ochus was so sordidly covetous, that to avoid this expense, he never visited his native country once in all his reign. Then finding Cyrus's sepul-chre opened and rifled, he put Polymachus, who did it, to death, though he was a man of some distinction, a born Macedonian of Pella. And after he had read the inscription, he caused it to be cut again below the old one in Greek characters; the words being these: "O man, whosoever thou art, and from whencesoever thou comest (for I know thou wilt come), I am Cyrus, the founder of the Persian empire; do not grudge me this little earth which covers my body." The reading of this sensibly touched Alexander, filling him with the thought of the uncertainty and mutability of human affairs. . . .

At Susa, he married Darius' daughter Statira, and celebrated also the nuptials of his friends, bestowing the noblest of the Persian ladies upon the worthiest of them, at the same time making it an entertainment in honor of the other Macedonians whose marriages had already taken place. At this magnificent festival, it is reported, there were no less than nine thousand guests, to each of whom he gave a golden cup for the libations. Not to mention other instances of his wonderful magnificence, he paid the debts of his army, which amounted to nine thousand eight hundred and seventy talents. But Antigenes, who had lost one of his eyes, though he owed nothing, got his name set down in the list of those who were in debt, and bringing one who pretended to be his creditor, and to have supplied him from the bank, received the money. But when the cheat was found out, the king was so incensed at it, that he banished him from court, and took away his command, though he was an excellent soldier, and a man of great courage. For when he was but a youth, and served under Philip at the siege of Perinthus, where he was wounded in the eye by an arrow shot out of an engine, he would neither let the arrow be taken out, nor be persuaded to quit the field, till he had bravely repulsed the enemy and forced them to retire into the town. Accordingly he was not able to support such a disgrace with any patience, and it was plain that grief and despair would have made him kill himself, but that the king fearing it, not only pardoned him, but let him also enjoy the benefit of his deceit.

The thirty thousand boys whom he left behind him to be taught and disciplined, were so improved at his return, both in strength and beauty, and performed their exercises with such dexterity and wonderful agility, that he was extremely pleased with them, which grieved the Macedonians, and made them fear he would have the less value for them. And when he proceeded to send down the infirm and maimed soldiers to the sea, they said they were unjustly and infamously dealt with, after they were worn out in his service upon all occasions, now to be turned away with disgrace and sent home into their country among their friends and relations, in a worse condition than when they came out; therefore they desired him to dismiss them one and all, and to account his Macedonians useless, now he was so well furnished with a set of advancing boys, with whom, if he pleased, he might go on and conquer the world. These speeches so incensed Alexander, that after he had given them a great deal of reproachful language in his passion, he drove them away, and committed the watch to Persians, out of whom he chose his guards and attendants. When the Macedonians saw him escorted by these men, and themselves excluded and shamefully disgraced, their high spirits fell, and conferring with one another, they found that jealousy and rage had almost distracted them. But at last coming to themselves again, they went without their arms, with only their undergarments on, crying and weeping, to offer themselves at his tent, and desired him to deal with them as their baseness and ingratitude deserved. However, this would not prevail; for though his anger was already somewhat mollified, yet he would not admit them into his presence, nor would they stir from thence, but continued two days and nights before his tent, bewailing themselves, and imploring him as their lord to have compassion on them. But the third day he came out to them, and seeing them very humble and penitent, he wept himself a great while, and after a gentle reproof spoke kindly to them, and dismissed those who were unserviceable with magnificent rewards, and with this recommendation to Antipater, that when they came home, at all public shows and in the theatres, they should sit on the best and foremost seats, crowned with chaplets of flowers. He ordered, also, that the children of those who had lost their lives in his service, should have their fathers' pay continued to them.

· · ·

As he was upon his way to Babylon, Nearchus, who had sailed back out of the ocean up the mouth of the river Euphrates, came to tell him he had met with some Chaldaean diviners, who had warned him against Alexander's going thither. Alexander, however, took no thought of it, and went on, and when he came near the walls of the place, he saw a great many crows fighting with one another, some of whom fell down just by him. After this, being privately informed that Apollodorus, the governor of Babylon, had sacrificed, to know what would become of him, he sent for Pythagoras, the soothsayer, and on his admitting the thing, asked him, in what condition he found the victim; and when he told him the liver was defective in its lobe, "A great presage indeed!" said Alexander. However, he offered Pythagoras no injury, but was sorry that he had neglected Nearchus's advice, and stayed for the most part outside the town, removing his tent from place to place, and sailing up and down the Euphrates. Besides this, he was disturbed by many other prodigies. A tame ass fell upon the biggest and handsomest lion that he kept, and killed him by a kick. And one day after he had undressed himself to be anointed, and was playing at ball, just as they were going to bring his clothes again, the young men who played with him perceived a man clad in the king's robes, with a diadem upon his head, sitting silently upon his throne. They asked him who he was, to which he gave no answer a good while, till at last coming to himself, he told them his name was Dionysius, that he was of Messenia, that for some crime of which he was accused, he was brought thither from the sea-side, and had been kept long in prison, that Serapis appeared to him, had freed him from his chains, conducted him to that place, and commanded him to put on the king's robe and diadem, and to sit where they found him, and to say nothing. Alexander, when he heard this, by the direction of his soothsayers, put the fellow to death, but he lost his spirits, and grew diffident of the protection and assistance of the gods, and suspicious of his friends. His greatest apprehension was of Antipater and his sons, one of whom, Iolaus, was his chief cupbearer; and Cassander, who had lately arrived, and had been bred up in Greek manners, the first time he saw some of the barbarians adore the king, could not forbear laughing at it aloud, which so incensed Alexander, that he took him by the hair with both hands, and dashed his head against the wall. Another time, Cassander would have said something in defence of Antipater to those who accused him, but Alexander interrupting him, said, "What is it you say? Do you think people, if they had received no injury, would come such a journey only to calumniate your father?" To which when Cassander replied, that their coming so far from the evidence was a great proof of the falseness of their charges, Alexander smiled, and said those were some of Aristotle's sophisms, which would serve equally on both sides; and added, that both he and his father should be severely punished, if they were found guilty of the least injustice towards those who complained. All which made such a deep impression of terror in Cassander's mind, that long after, when he was king of Macedonia, and master of Greece, as he was walking up and down at Delphi, and looking at the statues, at the sight of that of Alexander he was suddenly struck with alarm, and shook all over, his eyes rolled, his head grew dizzy, and it was long before he recovered himself.

When once Alexander had given way to fears of supernatural influence, his mind grew so disturbed and so easily alarmed, that if the least unusual or extraordinary thing happened, he thought it a prodigy or a presage, and his court was thronged with diviners and priests whose business was to sacrifice and purify and foretell the future. So miserable a thing is incredulity and contempt of divine power on the one hand, and so miserable, also, superstition on the other, which like water, where the level has been lowered, flowing in and never stopping, fills the mind with slavish fears and follies, as now in Alexander's case. But upon some answers which were brought him from the oracle concerning Hephaestion, he laid aside his sorrow, and fell again to sacrificing and drinking, and having given Nearchus a splendid entertainment, after he had bathed, as was his custom, just as he was going to bed, at Medius's request he went to supper with him. Here he drank all the next day, and was attacked with a fever, which seized him, not as some write, after he had drunk of the bowl of Hercules; nor was he taken with any sudden pain in his back, as if he had been struck with a lance, for these are the inventions of some authors who thought it their duty to make the last scene of so great an action as tragical and moving as

they could. Aristobulus tells us, that in the rage of his fever and a violent thirst, he took a draught of wine, upon which he fell into delirium, and died on the thirtieth day of the month Daesius.

But the journals give the following record. On the eighteenth of the month, he slept in the bathing-room on account of his fever. The next day he bathed and removed into his chamber, and spent his time in playing at dice with Medius. In the evening he bathed and sacrificed, and ate freely, and had the fever on him through the night. On the twentieth, after the usual sacrifices and bathing, he lay in the bathing-room and heard Nearchus's narrative of his voyage, and the observations he had made in the great sea. The twenty-first he passed in the same manner, his fever still increasing, and suffered much during the night. The next day the fever was very violent, and he had himself removed and his bed set by the great bath, and discoursed with his principal officers about finding fit men to fill up the vacant places in the army. On the twenty-fourth he was much worse, and was carried out of his bed to assist at the sacrifices, and gave order that the general officers should wait within the court, while the inferior officers kept watch without doors. On the twenty-fifth he was removed to his palace on the other side of the river, where he slept a little, but his fever did not abate, and when the generals came into his chamber, he was speechless, and continued so the following day. The Macedonians, therefore, supposing he was dead, came with great clamors to the gates, and menaced his friends so that they were forced to admit them, and let them pass through unarmed along by his bedside. The same day Python and Seleucus were despatched to the temple of Serapis to inquire if they should bring Alexander thither, and were answered by the god, that they should not remove him. On the twenty-eighth, in the evening, he died. This account is most of it word for word as it is written in the diary.

A conjectural restoration of Imperial Rome. (*Culver Pictures, Inc.*)

Rome

One historian of classical civilization has stated flatly, "Far and away the most important and frequent events in ancient history are wars."[1] As we have seen, two of the great classical historians chose war as their theme—Herodotus with his description of the conflict between the Greeks and the Persians, and Thucydides with his analysis of the struggle of Greek against Greek in the Peloponnesian War. The inter-Greek wars were ended only by conquest from the north and the beginnings of the spectacular military career of Alexander the Great of Macedonia. While all these wars were occupying the attention of the eastern Mediterranean world, to the west another mighty military machine was being forged, a machine that was to sweep out from its homeland to conquer the civilized world. By 338 B.C., two years before the accession of Alexander, the first major step on the long road to empire had been taken by a city-state on the Tiber River known as Rome. Rome had conquered her Latin neighbors and incorporated them into the Roman state.

In the succeeding three hundred years, Rome enjoyed the most sustained series of military triumphs the world had ever seen. By 265 B.C., she had extended her rule over most of the Italian peninsula; by about 200 B.C., she had brought most of Spain, the rest of Italy, and Sicily, Corsica, and Sardinia under her dominion; during the next hundred years she conquered southern Gaul, the rest of Spain, parts of North Africa, Macedonia, Greece, and about half of Asia Minor; and by the time of the birth of Jesus, the rest of Asia Minor, Syria, Egypt, most of North Africa, and all of Gaul had been added to the Roman tribute lists. Of course, these remarkable conquests were not carried out without occasional reverses and defeats. Hannibal's invasion and occupation of the Italian peninsula from 218 B.C. to 203 B.C. was the most serious reversal. But, though Hannibal's success pointed to certain Roman weaknesses, it revealed the sources of Roman strength as well.

The long road to empire was engineered and paved by the Roman army. Seldom has there been a finer military machine than the one developed by the Republic of Rome. Quite early, Rome transformed her armed forces from an ill-trained mob into a professional, highly trained, rigorously disciplined body of citizen-soldiers who could be used at great distances from Rome and who served for long periods of time. The weapons of the Roman soldier were superior to those of his oppo-

---

[1] Michael Grant, *Ancient History* (London: Methuen & Co., Ltd., 1952), p. 128.

nents, particularly after the adoption of a short cut-and-thrust sword which made him especially effective in close combat. The fundamental unit of the Roman army was the legion, an adaptation of the successful Macedonian phalanx. In its final form, the legion was composed of three thousand heavily armed infantrymen, all so dedicated to the honor and reputation of the legion that the defeat of the legion or the loss of its eagles constituted an unthinkable disgrace. Reinforcing their devotion to the legion was a deep-seated loyalty to Rome.

Somehow the Romans managed to instill this devotion to Rome even into the peoples they conquered, and Roman citizenship became highly prized and eagerly sought. The leaders of the Roman Republic wisely offered the allies and former enemies of Rome a limited citizenship, with the possibility of full citizenship later on. Thus, all shared the hope of being able to say *"Civis Romanus sum"*—I am a Roman citizen. What a powerful phrase! The man who could say that was protected by the fear of Roman law and of Roman justice; he shared in the glory that was Rome and the triumphs that were Roman; he contributed to the governance of the worldwide empire, for he could vote in its elections, serve in its courts, and act as an official in its administration.

If military success was a glory of the Roman Republic, it was also a curse. The creation of a world empire led to the creation of an imperial organization—an organization that the republican city-state of Rome was incapable of maintaining without undergoing violent internal change. The peasant-soldiers began to grumble over being kept away from the land year after year; the military leaders became too accustomed to commanding obedience; the mother-city became too used to triumph and success. All contributed to the final disappearance of the Republic. The citizen's loyalty to his legion and to the Republic was transformed into loyalty to his commander, and the legions became private armies. Plutarch may have admired his Caesar, but only because Caesar sought to restore political order to the chaos that had developed in the last century of the Roman Republic. The disappearance of the small land-owner, the development of a wealthy class, corruption in government administration, and the evolution of a complex bureaucracy to administer the empire were all factors in the disintegration of the old system and the emergence of the Roman Empire.

The concept of empire—and of emperor—took several generations to emerge fully. But it was clearly present when Augustus took the title *princeps* (first citizen), even though he continued the fiction of republican rule after his triumph over both the Senate and the assassins of Julius Caesar. Happily for Rome, Augustus and his successor, Tiberius, were talented and powerful enough to resolve the civil difficulties and to stabilize the administration so that Rome was able to withstand the abuse and corruption of the regimes that followed. Not even madness, frivolity, and palace intrigue could disturb the quiet workings of the Empire—the civil administration functioned smoothly, the army maintained the peace, commerce was active, and industry continued prosperous. The *Pax Romana* lasted two hundred years, during which time the civilized world enjoyed a new freedom from the perennial warfare of the ancient world.

During these centuries of peace Roman civilization achieved the heights of its glory. Its accomplishments in architecture have rarely been matched. Recognizing the arch (which the Greeks had not appreciated) as a thing of beauty as well as utility, the Romans were able to bridge wide rivers, to supply the vast city of Rome with water from far-off hills and mountains, and to erect the Colosseum, which seated nearly fifty thousand spectators at the gladiatorial games and contests. The realistic portrait sculpture of the Romans has never been equaled. Perhaps this excellence was a reflection of the practical, hard, peasant virtues of the Roman citizen. But the greatest triumphs of Roman civilization lay not in art, architecture, literature, or speculative thought, but in the realm of the practical and the everyday. Law, military order, and civil administration were the accomplishments that were most truly Roman. And these three most clearly reveal the Roman genius—the desire for order and efficiency and the ability to attain them. This desire, together with the Roman dedication to duty, right, state, and honor, is manifest in the works of Cicero and the teachings of Marcus Aurelius.

The Roman world made its greatest contribution to Western civilization almost inadvertently, when an obscure province under Roman rule produced the man Jesus. Although his life and teachings have inspired millions in succeeding ages, Jesus himself would undoubtedly have questioned the organization that grew up to spread his beliefs. The first two centuries after Christ were a time of peace and tranquillity, but also a time in which the common man felt lost and devoid of spiritual comfort. The Christian faith proffered security and balm for the difficulties of this world and salvation in the next. And as the faith spread, the Roman genius for order and efficiency again manifested itself; for the growing Church, with its increasingly complex activities, modeled its organization on that of the civil administration. Bishops established cathedrals in provincial urban centers, and local churches were set up in the smaller cities and towns. The capstone to this structure was natural, obvious, and logical: the bishop of Rome was to head the Church just as the emperor led the Empire.

But Rome could not solve the problems of world dominion. The Empire had stabilized the regime created by the Republic, but it had been unable to develop a solution to the basic problems raised by empire. How could a state maintain a great army without being dominated by it? Or, a different problem, how could a city-state maintain a very large army of citizen-soldiers without extending citizenship to them? And if citizenship were extended, how could it instill in these citizens the same dedication and devotion found in the native Roman? Whatever the problems were and whatever solutions to them hindsight might offer, one thing at least remains: the history and glory of Rome lasted over eight hundred years, a long time indeed in the recorded history of civilization.

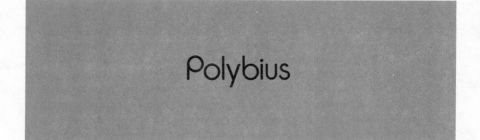

Polybius

Any eyewitness account of an event has intrinsic value. When the witness is a person of intellectual and emotional detachment, his account is likely to be much more rewarding. Substance is added to the narrative, too, when the observer is a man with analytical powers of the first order. Such a person was the Greek historian Polybius, who continued the great tradition of Herodotus and Thucydides.

Polybius (c.205–c.123 B.C.) was brilliantly equipped to write the history of his time, for he had had a literary education and was widely experienced in affairs of state. He had served both as a *hipparch* (cavalry commander) in the armed forces of his native city-state of Megalopolis and as a diplomat charged with the delicate task of reconciling his fellow Greeks to their somewhat anomalous relationship to the rapidly expanding Roman Republic. When the Romans carried Polybius off to Italy (167 B.C.) as one of a thousand Greek hostages, he took advantage of the opportunity and launched into the writing of his *Histories.* Through the intervention of a friend, he was able to spend most of his sixteen years of exile in Rome, where he could examine original documents and observe the workings of the Roman government at first hand. His circle of friends included many of the most powerful men of the time. In 150 B.C. he was permitted to return to Greece, where he bent all his efforts toward creating an atmosphere of understanding between the Greeks and the Romans. Polybius died at the age of eighty-two, after falling from a horse.

The following selection reflects his experiences in Rome and the observations he made while he was there. Taken from Book VI of the *Histories,* it is, as Polybius says, "a disquisition on the Roman constitution."

The Histories

BOOK VI

Preface

1. I am aware that some will be at a loss to account for my interrupting the course of my narrative for the sake of entering upon the following disquisition on the Roman constitution. But I think that I have already in many passages made it

The Histories of Polybius, trans. Evelyn S. Shuckburgh (London, 1889), I.

fully evident that this particular branch of my work was one of the necessities imposed on me by the nature of my original design; and I pointed this out with special clearness in the preface which explained the scope of my history. I there stated that the feature of my work which was at once the best in itself, and the most instructive to the students of it, was that it would enable them to know and fully realise in what manner, and under what kind of constitution, it came about that nearly the whole world fell under the power of Rome in somewhat less than fifty-three years—an event certainly without precedent. This being my settled purpose, I could see no more fitting period than the present for making a pause, and examining the truth of the remarks about to be made on this constitution. In private life if you wish to satisfy yourself as to the badness or goodness of particular persons, you would not, if you wish to get a genuine test, examine their conduct at a time of uneventful repose, but in the hour of brilliant success or conspicuous reverse. For the true test of a perfect man is the power of bearing with spirit and dignity violent changes of fortune. An examination of a constitution should be conducted in the same way: and therefore being unable to find in our day a more rapid or more signal change than that which has happened to Rome, I reserved my disquisition on its constitution for this place. . . .

What is really educational and beneficial to students of history is the clear view of the causes of events, and the consequent power of choosing the better policy in a particular case. Now in every practical undertaking by a state we must regard as the most powerful agent for success or failure the form of its constitution; for from this as from a fountainhead all conceptions and plans of action not only proceed, but attain their consummation. . . .

• • •

3. Of the Greek republics, which have again and again risen to greatness and fallen into insignificance, it is not difficult to speak, whether we recount their past history or venture an opinion on their future. For to report what is already known is an easy task, nor is it hard to guess what is to come from our knowledge of what has been. But in regard to the Romans it is neither an easy matter to describe their present state, owing to the complexity of their constitution; nor to speak with confidence of their future, from our inadequate acquaintance with their peculiar institutions in the past whether affecting their public or their private life. It will require then no ordinary attention and study to get a clear and comprehensive conception of the distinctive features of this constitution.

Now, it is undoubtedly the case that most of those who profess to give us authoritative instruction on this subject distinguish three kinds of constitutions, which they designate *kingship, aristocracy, democracy.* But in my opinion the question may be fairly put to them, whether they name these as being the *only* ones, or as the best. In either case I think they are wrong. For it is plain that we must regard as the *best* constitution that which partakes of all these three elements. And this is no mere assertion, but has been proved by the example of Lycurgus, who was the first to construct a constitution—that of Sparta—on this principle. Nor can we admit that these are the only forms: for we have had before now examples of absolute and tyrannical forms of government, which, while differing as widely as possible from kingship, yet appear to have some points of resemblance to it; on which account all absolute rulers falsely assume and use, as far as they can, the title of king. Again there have been many instances of oligarchical governments having in appearance some analogy to aristocracies, which are, if I may say so, as different from them as it is possible to be. The same also holds good about democracy.

• • •

11. . . . I will now endeavour to describe [the constitution] of Rome at the period of their disastrous defeat at Cannae.

I am fully conscious that to those who actually live under this constitution I shall appear to give an inadequate account of it by the omission of certain details. Knowing accurately every portion of it from personal experience, and from having been bred up in its customs and laws from childhood, they will not be struck so much by the accuracy of the description, as annoyed by its omissions; nor will they believe that the historian has purposely omitted unimportant distinctions, but will attribute his silence upon the origin of existing institutions or other important facts to ignorance. What is told they depreciate as insignificant or beside the purpose; what is omitted they desiderate as vital to the question: their object being to appear to know more than the writers. But a good critic should not judge a writer by what he leaves unsaid, but from what he says: if he detects mis-statement in the latter, he may then feel certain that ignorance accounts for the former; but if what he says is accurate, his omissions ought to be attributed to deliberate judgment and not to ignorance. So much for those whose criticisms are prompted by personal ambition rather than by justice.

Another requisite for obtaining a judicious approval for an historical disquisition, is that it should be germane to the matter in hand; if this is not observed, though its style may be excellent and its matter irreproachable, it will seem out of place, and disgust rather than please. . . .

As for the Roman constitution, it had three elements, each of them possessing sovereign powers: and their respective share of power in the whole state had been regulated with such a scrupulous regard to equality and equilibrium, that no one could say for certain, not even a native, whether the constitution as a whole were an aristocracy or democracy or despotism. And no wonder: for if we confine our observation to the power of the Consuls we should be inclined to regard it as despotic; if on that of the Senate, as aristocratic; and if finally one looks at the power possessed by the people it would seem a clear case of democracy. What the exact powers of these several parts were, and still, with slight modifications, are, I will now state.

12. The Consuls, before leading out the legions, remain in Rome and are supreme masters of the administration. All other magistrates, except the Tribunes, are under them and take their orders. They intro-

duce foreign ambassadors to the Senate; bring matters requiring deliberation before it; and see to the execution of its decrees. If, again, there are any matters of state which require the authorisation of the people, it is their business to see to them, to summon the popular meetings, to bring the proposals before them, and to carry out the decrees of the majority. In the preparations for war, also, and in a word in the entire administration of a campaign, they have all but absolute power. It is competent to them to impose on the allies such levies as they think good, to appoint the Military Tribunes, to make up the roll for soldiers and select those that are suitable. Besides they have absolute power of inflicting punishment on all who are under their command while on active service: and they have authority to expend as much of the public money as they choose, being accompanied by a quaestor who is entirely at their orders. A survey of these powers would in fact justify our describing the constitution as despotic,—a clear case of royal government. Nor will it affect the truth of my description, if any of the institutions I have described are changed in our time, or in that of our posterity: and the same remarks apply to what follows.

13. The Senate has first of all the control of the treasury, and regulates the receipts and disbursements alike. For the Quaestors cannot issue any public money for the various departments of the state without a decree of the Senate, except for the service of the Consuls. The Senate controls also what is by far the largest and most important expendi-
ture, that, namely, which is made by the censors every lustrum for the repair or construction of public buildings; this money cannot be obtained by the censors except by the grant of the Senate. Similarly all crimes committed in Italy requiring a public investigation, such as treason, conspiracy, poisoning, or wilful murder, are in the hands of the Senate. Besides, if any individual or state among the Italian allies requires a controversy to be settled, a penalty to be assessed, help or protection to be afforded,—all this is the province of the Senate. Or again, outside Italy, if it is necessary to send an embassy to reconcile warring communities, or to remind them of their duty, or sometimes to impose requisitions upon them, or to receive their submission, or finally to proclaim war against them,—this too is the business of the Senate. In like manner the reception to be given foreign ambassadors in Rome, and the answers to be returned to them, are decided by the Senate. With such business the people have nothing to do. Consequently, if one were staying at Rome when the Consuls were not in town, one would imagine the constitution to be a complete aristocracy: and this has been the idea entertained by many Greeks, and by many kings as well, from the fact that nearly all the business they had to do with Rome was settled by the Senate.

14. After this one would naturally be inclined to ask what part is left for the people in the constitution, when the Senate has these various functions, especially the control of the receipts and expenditure of the exchequer; and when the Consuls, again, have absolute power

over the details of military preparation, and an absolute authority in the field? There is, however, a part left the people, and it is a most important one. For the people is the sole fountain of honour and of punishment; and it is by these two things and these alone that dynasties and constitutions and, in a word, human society are held together: for where the distinction between them is not sharply drawn both in theory and practice, there no undertaking can be properly administered,—as indeed we might expect when good and bad are held in exactly the same honour. The people then is the only court to decide matters of life and death; and even in cases where the penalty is money, if the sum to be assessed is sufficiently serious, and especially when the accused have held the higher magistracies. And in regard to this arrangement there is one point deserving especial commendation and record. Men who are on trial for their lives at Rome, while sentence is in process of being voted,—if even only one of the tribes whose votes are needed to ratify the sentence has not voted,— have the privilege at Rome of openly departing and condemning themselves to a voluntary exile. Such men are safe at Naples or Praeneste or at Tibur, and at other towns with which this arrangement has been duly ratified on oath.

Again, it is the people who bestow offices on the deserving, which are the most honourable rewards of virtue. It has also the absolute power of passing or repealing laws; and, most important of all, it is the people who deliberate on the question of peace or war. And when provisional terms are made for alliance, suspension of hostilities, or treaties, it is the people who ratify them or the reverse.

These considerations again would lead one to say that the chief power in the state was the people's, and that the constitution was a democracy.

15. Such, then, is the distribution of power between the several parts of the state. I must now show how each of these several parts can, when they choose, oppose or support each other.

The Consul, then, when he has started on an expedition with the powers I have described, is to all appearance absolute in the administration of the business in hand; still he has need of the support both of people and Senate, and, without them, is quite unable to bring the matter to a successful conclusion. For it is plain that he must have supplies sent to his legions from time to time; but without a decree of the Senate they can be supplied neither with corn, nor clothes, nor pay, so that all the plans of a commander must be futile, if the Senate is resolved either to shrink from danger or hamper his plans. And again, whether a Consul shall bring any undertaking to a conclusion or no depends entirely on the Senate: for it has absolute authority at the end of a year to send another Consul to supersede him, or to continue the existing one in his command. Again, even to the successes of the generals, the Senate has the power to add distinction and glory, and on the other hand to obscure their merits and lower their credit. For these high achievements are brought in tangible form before the eyes of the citizens by what are called "triumphs." But in these triumphs the commanders cannot celebrate with proper pomp, or in some cases celebrate at all, unless the Senate concurs and grants the necessary money. As for the people, the Consuls are pre-eminently obliged to court their favour, however distant from home may be the field of their operations; for it is the people, as I have said before, that ratifies, or refuses to ratify, terms of peace and treaties; but most of all because when laying down their office they have to give an account of their administration before it. Therefore in no case is it safe for the Consuls to neglect either the Senate or the goodwill of the people.

16. As for the Senate, which possesses the immense power I have described, in the first place it is obliged in public affairs to take the multitude into account, and respect the wishes of the people; and it cannot put into execution the penalty for offences against the republic, which are punishable with death, unless the people first ratifies its decrees. Similarly even in matters which directly affect the senators,— for instance, in the case of a law depriving senators of certain dignities and offices, or even actually cutting down their property,—even in such cases the people has the sole power of passing or rejecting the law. But most important of all is the fact that, if the Tribunes interpose their veto, the Senate not only is unable to pass a decree, but cannot even hold a meeting at all, whether formal or informal. Now, the Tribunes are always bound to carry out the decree of the people, and above all things to have regard to their wishes: therefore, for all these reasons the Senate stands in awe of the multitude, and cannot neglect the feelings of the people.

17. In like manner the people on its part is far from being independent of the Senate, and is bound to take its wishes into account both collectively and individually. For contracts, too numerous to count, are given out by the censors in all parts of Italy, for the repairs or construction of public buildings; there is also the collection of revenue from many rivers, harbours, gardens, mines, and land—every thing, in a word, that comes under the control of the Roman government: and in all these the people at large are engaged; so that there is scarcely a man, so to speak, who is not interested either as a contractor or as being employed in the works. For some purchase the contracts from the censors for themselves; and others go partners with them; while others again go security for these contractors, or actually pledge their property to the treasury for them. Now over all these transactions the Senate has absolute control. It can grant an extension of time; and in case of unforeseen accident can relieve the contractors from a portion of their obligation, or release them from it altogether, if they are absolutely unable to fill it. And there are many details in which the Senate can inflict great hardships, or, on the other hand, grant great indulgences to the contractors: for in every case the appeal is to it. But the most important point of all is that the judges are taken from its members in the majority trials, whether public or private, in which the charges are heavy. Consequently, all citizens are much at its

mercy; and being alarmed at the uncertainty as to when they may need its aid, are cautious about resisting or actively opposing its will. And for a similar reason men do not rashly resist the wishes of the Consuls, because one and all may become subject to their absolute authority on a campaign.

18. The result of this power of the several estates for mutual help or harm is a union sufficiently firm for all emergencies, and a constitution than which it is impossible to find a better. For whenever any danger from without compels them to unite and work together, the strength which is developed by the State is so extraordinary, that everything required is unfailingly carried out by the eager rivalry shown by all classes to devote their whole minds to the need of the hour, and to secure that any determination come to should not fail for want of promptitude; while each individual works, privately and publicly alike, for the accomplishment of the business in hand. Accordingly, the peculiar constitution of the State makes it irresistible, and certain of obtaining whatever it determines to attempt. Nay, even when these external alarms are past, and the people are enjoying their good fortune and the fruits of their victories, and, as usually happens, growing corrupted by flattery and idleness, show a tendency to violence and arrogance,— it is in these circumstances, more than ever, that the constitution is seen to possess within itself the power of correcting abuses. For when any one of the three classes becomes puffed up, and manifests an inclination to be contentious and unduly encroaching, the mutual interdependency of all the three, and the possibility of the pretentions of any one being checked and thwarted by the others, must plainly check this tendency: and so the proper equilibrium is maintained by the impulsiveness of the one part being checked by its fear of the other.

· · ·

The Roman republic compared with others

43. Nearly all historians have recorded as constitutions of eminent excellence those of Lacedaemonia, Crete, Mantinea, and Carthage. Some have also mentioned those of Athens and Thebes. The former I may allow to pass; but I am convinced that little need be said of the Athenian and Theban constitutions: their growth was abnormal, the period of their zenith brief, and the changes they experienced unusually violent. Their glory was a sudden and fortuitous flash, so to speak; and while they still thought themselves prosperous, and likely to remain so, they found themselves involved in circumstances completely the reverse. The Thebans got their reputation for valour among the Greeks, by taking advantage of the senseless policy of the Lacedaemonians, and the hatred of the allies toward them, owing to the valour of one, or at most two, men who were wise enough to appreciate the situation. Since fortune quickly made it evident that it was not the peculiarity of their constitution, but the valour of their leaders, which gave the Thebans their success. For the great power of Thebes notoriously took its rise, attained its zenith, and fell to the ground with the lives

of Epaminondas and Pelopidas. We must therefore conclude that it was not its constitution, but its men, that caused the high fortune which it then enjoyed.

44. A somewhat similar remark applies to the Athenian constitution also. For though it perhaps had more frequent interludes of excellence, yet its highest perfection was attained during the brilliant career of Themistocles; and having reached that point it quickly declined, owing to its essential instability. For the Athenian demus is always in the position of a ship without a commander. In such a ship, if fear of the enemy, or the occurrence of a storm induce the crew to be of one mind and to obey the helmsman, everything goes well; but if they recover from this fear, and begin to treat their officers with contempt, and to quarrel with each other because they are no longer all of one mind,—one party wishing to continue the voyage, and the other urging the steersman to bring the ship to anchor; some letting out the sheets, and others hauling them in, and ordering the sails to be furled,—their discord and quarrels make a sorry show to lookers-on; and the position of affairs is full of risk to those on board engaged in the same voyage: and the result has often been that, after escaping the dangers of the wildest seas, and the most violent storms, they wreck their ship in harbour and close to shore. And this is what has often happened to the Athenian constitution. For, after repelling, on various occasions, the greatest and most formidable dangers by the valour of its people and their leaders, there have been times when, in periods of secure tranquillity, it has

gratuitously and recklessly encountered disaster. Therefore I need say no more about either it, or the Theban constitution: in both of which a mob manages everything on its own unfettered impulse—a mob in the one city distinguished for headlong outburst of fiery temper, in the other trained in long habits of violence and ferocity.

45. Passing to the Cretan polity there are two points which deserve our consideration. The first is how such writers as Ephorus, Xenophon, Callisthenes and Plato—who are the most learned of the ancients—could assert that it was like that of Sparta; and secondly how they came to assert that it was at all admirable. I can agree with neither assertion; and I will explain why I say so. And first as to its dissimilarity with the Spartan constitution. The peculiar merit of the latter is said to be its land laws, by which no one possesses more than another, but all citizens have an equal share in the public land. The next distinctive feature regards the possession of money: for as it is utterly discredited among them, the jealous competition which arises from inequality of wealth is entirely removed from the city. A third peculiarity of the Lacedaemonian polity is that, of the officials by whose hands and with whose advice the whole government is conducted, the kings hold an hereditary office, while the members of the Gerusia are elected for life.

46. Among the Cretans the exact reverse of all these arrangements obtains. The laws allow them to possess as much land as they can get with no limitation whatever. Money is so highly valued among them, that its possession is not only

thought to be necessary but in the highest degree creditable. And in fact greed and avarice are so native to the soil in Crete, that they are the only people in the world among whom no stigma attaches to any sort of gain whatever. Again all their offices are annual and on a democratical footing. I have therefore often felt at a loss to account for these writers speaking of the two constitutions, which are radically different, as though they were closely united and allied. But, besides overlooking these important differences, these writers have gone out of their way to comment at length on the legislation of Lycurgus: "He was the only important legislator," they say, "who saw the important points. For there being two things on which the safety of a commonwealth depends,—courage in the face of the enemy and concord at home,—by abolishing covetousness, he with it removed all motive for civil broil and contest: whence it has been brought about that the Lacedaemonians are the best governed and most united people in Greece." Yet while giving utterance to these sentiments, and though they see that, in contrast to this, the Cretans by their ingrained avarice are engaged in countless public and private seditions, murders and civil wars, they yet regard these facts as not affecting their contention, but are bold enough to speak of the two constitutions as alike. Ephorus, indeed, putting aside names, employs expressions so precisely the same, when discoursing on the two constitutions, that, unless one noticed the proper names, there would be no means whatever of distinguishing which of the two he was describing.

47. In what the difference between them consists I have already stated. I will now address myself to showing that the Cretan constitution deserves neither praise nor imitation.

In my mind, then, there are two things fundamental to every state, in virtue of which its powers and constitution become desirable or objectionable. These are customs and laws. Of these the desirable are those which make men's private lives holy and pure, and the public character of the state civilised and just. The objectionable are those whose effect is the reverse. As, then, when we see good customs and good laws prevailing among certain people, we confidently assume that in consequence of them, the men and their civil constitution will be good also, so when we see private life full of covetousness, and public policy of injustice, plainly we have reason for asserting their laws, particular customs, and general constitution to be bad. Now, with few exceptions, you could find no habits prevailing in private life more steeped in treachery than those in Crete, and no public policy more inequitable. Holding, then, the Cretan constitution to be neither like the Spartan, nor worthy of choice or imitation, I reject it from the comparison which I have instituted.

Nor again would it be fair to introduce the Republic of Plato, which is also spoken of in high terms by some philosophers. For just as we refuse admission to the athletic contests to those actors or athletes who have not acquired a recognised position or trained for them, so we ought not to admit this Platonic constitution to the contest for the prize of merit unless it can first point to some genuine and practical achievement. Up to this time the notion of bringing it into comparison with the constitutions of Sparta, Rome, and Carthage would be like putting up a statue to compare with living and breathing men. Even if such a statue were faultless in point of art, the comparison of the lifeless with the living would naturally leave an impression of imperfection and incongruity upon the minds of the spectators.

48. I shall therefore omit these, and proceed with my description of the Laconian constitution. Now it seems to me that for securing unity among the citizens, for safeguarding the Laconian territory, and preserving the liberty of Sparta inviolate, the legislation and provisions of Lycurgus were so excellent, that I am forced to regard his wisdom as something superhuman. For the equality of landed possessions, the simplicity in their food, and the practice of taking it in common, which he established, were well calculated to secure morality in private life and to prevent civil broils in the State; as also their training in the endurance of labours and dangers to make men brave and noble minded: but when both these virtues, courage and high morality, are combined in one soul or in one state, vice will not readily spring from such a soil, nor will such men easily be overcome by their enemies. By constructing his constitution therefore in this spirit, and of these elements, he secured two blessings to the Spartans—safety for their territory, and a lasting freedom for themselves after he was gone. He appears however to have made no one provision whatever, particular or general, for the acquisition of the territory of their neighbours; or for the assertion of their supremacy; or, in a word, for any policy of aggrandisement at all. What he had still to do was to impose such a necessity, or create such a spirit among the citizens, that, as he had succeeded in making their individual lives independent and simple, the public character of the state should also become independent and moral. But the actual fact is, that, though he made them the most disinterested and soberminded men in the world, as far as their own ways of life and their national institutions were concerned, he left them in regard to the rest of Greece ambitious, eager for supremacy, and encroaching in the highest degree.

49. For in the first place is it not notorious that they were the first Greeks to cast a covetous eye upon the territory of their neighbours, and that accordingly they waged a war of subjugation on the Messenians? In the next place is it not related in all histories that in their dogged obstinacy they bound themselves with an oath never to desist from the siege of Messene until they had taken it? And lastly it is known to all that in their efforts for supremacy in Greece they submitted to do the bidding of those whom they had once conquered in war. For when the Persians invaded Greece, they conquered them, as champions of the liberty of the Greeks; yet when the invaders had retired and fled, they betrayed the cities of Greece into their hands by the peace of Antalcidas, for the sake of getting money to secure their supremacy over the Greeks. It was then

that the defect in their constitution was rendered apparent. For as long as their ambition was confined to governing their immediate neighbours, or even the Peloponnesians only, they were content with the resources and supplies provided by Laconia itself, having all material of war ready to hand, and being able without much expenditure of time to return home or convey provisions with them. But directly they took in hand to despatch naval expeditions, or to go on campaigns by land outside the Peloponnese, it was evident that neither their iron currency, nor their use of crops for payment in kind, would be able to supply them with what they lacked if they abided by the legislation of Lycurgus; for such undertakings required money universally current, and goods from foreign countries. Thus they were compelled to wait humbly at Persian doors, impose tribute on the islanders, and exact contribution from all the Greeks: knowing that, if they abided by the laws of Lycurgus, it was impossible to advance any claims upon any outside power at all, much less upon the supremacy in Greece.

50. My object, then, in this digression is to make it manifest by actual fact that, for guarding their own country with absolute safety, and for preserving their own freedom, the legislation of Lycurgus was entirely sufficient; and for those who are content with these objects we must concede that there neither exists, nor ever has existed, a constitution and civil order preferable to that of Sparta. But if any one is seeking aggrandisement, and believes that to be a leader and ruler and despot of numerous subjects, and to have all looking and turning to him, is a finer thing than that,— in this point of view we must acknowledge that the Spartan constitution is deficient, and that of Rome superior and better constituted for obtaining power. And this has been proved by actual facts. For when the Lacedaemonians strove to possess themselves of the supremacy in Greece, it was not long before they brought their own freedom itself into danger. Whereas the Romans, after obtaining supreme power of the Italians themselves, soon brought the whole world under their rule,— in which achievement the abundance and availability of their supplies largely contributed to their success.

51. Now the Carthaginian constitution seems to me originally to have been well contrived in these most distinctively important particulars. For they had kings, and the Gerusia had the powers of an aristocracy, and the multitude were supreme in such things as affected them; and on the whole the adjustment of its several parts was very like that of Rome and Sparta. But about the period of its entering on the Hannibalian war the political state of Carthage was on the decline, that of Rome improving. For whereas there is in every body, or polity, or business a natural stage of growth, zenith, and decay; and whereas everything in them is best at the zenith; we may thereby judge of the difference between these two constitutions as they existed at that period. For exactly so far as the strength and prosperity of Carthage preceded that of Rome in point of time, by so much was Carthage then past its prime, while Rome was exactly at its zenith, as far as its

political constitution was concerned. In Carthage therefore the influence of the people in the policy of the state had already risen to be supreme, while at Rome the Senate was at the height of its power: and so, as in the one measures were deliberated upon by the many, in the other by the best men, the policy of the Romans in all public undertakings proved the stronger; on which account, though they met with capital disasters, by force of prudent counsels they finally conquered the Carthaginians in the war.

52. If we look however at separate details, for instance at the provisions for carrying on a war, we shall find that whereas for a naval expedition the Carthaginians are the better trained and prepared,—as it is only natural with a people with whom it has been hereditary for many generations to practise this craft, and to follow the seaman's trade above all nations in the world, —yet, in regard to military service on land, the Romans train themselves to a much higher pitch than the Carthaginians. The former bestow their whole attention upon this department: whereas the Carthaginians wholly neglect their infantry, though they do take some slight interest in the cavalry. The reason of this is that they employ foreign mercenaries, the Romans native and citizen levies. It is in this point that the latter polity is preferable to the former. They have their hopes of freedom ever resting on the courage of mercenary troops: the Romans on the valour of their own citizens and the aid of their allies. The result is that even if the Romans have suffered a defeat at first, they renew the war with undiminished forces, which the Carthaginians cannot do. For, as the Romans are fighting for country and children, it is impossible for them to relax the fury of their struggle; but they persist with obstinate resolution until they have overcome their enemies. What has happened in regard to their navy is an instance in point. In skill the Romans are much behind the Carthaginians, as I have already said; yet the upshot of the whole naval war has been a decided triumph for the Romans, owing to the valour of their men. For although nautical science contributes largely to success in sea-fights, still it is the courage of the marines that turns the scale most decisively in favour of victory. The fact is that Italians as a nation are by nature superior to Phoenicians and Libyans both in physical strength and courage; but still their habits also do much to inspire the youth with enthusiasm for such exploits. One example will be sufficient of the pains taken by the Roman state to turn out men ready to endure anything to win a reputation in their country for valour.

53. Whenever one of their illustrious men dies, in the course of his funeral, the body with all its paraphernalia is carried into the forum to the Rostra, as a raised platform there is called, and sometimes is propped upright upon it so as to be conspicuous, or, more rarely, is laid upon it. Then with all the people standing round, his son, if he has left one of full age and he is there, or, failing him, one of his relations, mounts the Rostra and delivers a speech concerning the virtues of the deceased, and the successful exploits performed by him in his lifetime. By these means the people are reminded

of what has been done, and made to see it with their own eyes,—not only such as were engaged in the actual transactions but those also who were not;—and their sympathies are so deeply moved, that the loss appears not to be confined to the actual mourners, but to be a public one affecting the whole people. After the burial and all the usual ceremonies have been performed, they place the likeness of the deceased in the most conspicuous spot in his house, surmounted by a wooden canopy or shrine. This likeness consists of a mask made to represent the deceased with extraordinary fidelity both in shape and colour. These likenesses they display at public sacrifices adorned with much care. And when any illustrious member of the family dies, they carry these masks to the funeral, putting them on men whom they thought as like the originals as possible in height and other personal peculiarities. And these substitutes assume clothes according to the rank of the person represented: if he was a consul or praetor, a toga with purple stripes; if a censor, whole purple; if he had also celebrated a triumph or performed any exploit of that kind, a toga embroidered with gold. These representatives also ride themselves in chariots, while the fasces and axes, and all the other customary insignia of the particular offices, lead the way, according to the dignity of the rank in the state enjoyed by the deceased in his lifetime; and on arriving at the Rostra they all take their seats on ivory chairs in their order. There could not easily be a more inspiring spectacle than this for a young man of noble ambitions and virtuous aspirations. For can we conceive any one to be unmoved at the sight of all the likenesses collected together of the men who have earned glory, all as it were living and breathing? Or what could be a more glorious spectacle?

54. Besides, the speaker over the body about to be buried, after having finished the panegyric of this particular person, starts upon the others whose representatives are present, beginning with the most ancient, and recounts the successes and achievements of each. By this means the glorious memory of brave men is continually renewed; the fame of those who have performed any noble deed is never allowed to die; and the renown of those who have done good service to their country becomes a matter of common knowledge to the multitude, and part of the heritage of posterity. But the chief benefit of the ceremony is that it inspires young men to shrink from no exertion for the general welfare, in the hope of obtaining the glory which awaits the brave. And what I say is confirmed by this fact. Many Romans have volunteered to decide a whole battle by single combat; not a few have deliberately accepted certain death, some in time of war to secure the safety of the rest, some in time of peace to preserve the safety of the commonwealth. There have also been instances of men in office putting their own sons to death, in defiance of every custom and law, because they rated the interests of their country higher than those of natural ties even with their nearest and dearest. There are many stories of this kind, related of many men in Roman history; but one will be enough for our present purpose;

and I will give the name as an instance to prove the truth of my words.

55. The story goes that Horatius Cocles, while fighting with two enemies at the head of the bridge over the Tiber, which is the entrance to the city on the north, seeing a large body of men advancing to support his enemies, and fearing that they would force their way into the city, turned round, and shouted to those behind him to hasten back to the other side and break down the bridge. They obeyed him: and whilst they were breaking the bridge, he remained at his post receiving numerous wounds, and checked the progress of the enemy: his opponents being panic stricken, not so much by his strength as by the audacity with which he held his ground. When the bridge had been broken down, the attack of the enemy was stopped; and Cocles then threw himself into the river with his armour on and deliberately sacrificed his life, because he valued the safety of his country and his own future reputation more highly than his present life, and the years of existence that remained to him. Such is the enthusiasm and emulation for noble deeds that are engendered among the Romans by their customs.

56. Again the Roman customs and principles regarding money transactions are better than those of the Carthaginians. In the view of the latter nothing is disgraceful that makes for gain; with the former nothing is more disgraceful than to receive bribes and to make profit by improper means. For they regard wealth obtained from unlawful transactions to be as much a subject of reproach, as a fair profit from the most unquestioned source is of commendation. A proof of the fact is this. The Carthaginians obtain office by open bribery, but among the Romans the penalty for it is death. With such a radical difference, therefore, between the rewards offered to virtue among the two people, it is natural that the ways adopted for obtaining them should be different also.

But the most important difference for the better which the Roman commonwealth appears to me to display is in their religious beliefs. For I conceive that what in other nations is looked upon as a reproach, I mean a scrupulous fear of the gods, is the very thing which keeps the Roman Commonwealth together. To such an extraordinary height is this carried among them, both in private and public business, that nothing could exceed it. Many people might think this unaccountable; but in my opinion their object is to use it as a check upon the common people. If it were possible to form a state wholly of philosophers, such a custom would perhaps be unnecessary. But seeing that every multitude is fickle, and full of lawless desires, unreasoning anger, and violent passion, the only resource is to keep them in check by mysterious terrors and scenic effects of this sort. Wherefore, to my mind, the ancients were not acting without purpose or at random, when they brought in among the vulgar those opinions about the gods, and the belief in the punishments in Hades: much rather do I think that men nowadays are acting rashly and foolishly in rejecting them. This is the reason why, apart from anything else, Greek statesmen, if entrusted with a single talent, though protected by ten checking-clerks, as many seals, and twice as many witnesses, yet cannot be induced to keep faith: whereas among the Romans, in their magistracies and embassies, men have the handling of a great amount of money, and yet from pure respect to their oath keep their faith intact. And, again, in other nations it is a rare thing to find a man who keeps his hands out of the public purse, and is entirely pure in such matters: but among the Romans it is a rare thing to detect a man in the act of committing such a crime. . . .

Recapitulation and conclusion

57. That to all things, then, which exist there is ordained decay and change I think requires no further arguments to show: for the inexorable course of nature is sufficient to convince us of it.

But in all polities we observe two sources of decay existing from natural causes, the one external, the other internal and self-produced. The external admits of no certain or fixed definition, but the internal follows a definite order. What kind of polity, then, comes naturally first, and what second, I have already stated in such a way, that those who are capable of taking in the whole drift of my argument can henceforth draw their own conclusions as to the future of the Roman polity. For it is quite clear, in my opinion. When a commonwealth, after warding off many great dangers, has arrived at a high pitch of prosperity and undisputed power, it is evident that, by the lengthened continuance of great wealth within it, the manner of life of its citizens will become more extravagant; and that the rivalry for office, and in other spheres of activity, will become fiercer than it ought to be. And as this state of things goes on more and more, the desire of office and the shame of losing reputation, as well as the ostentation and extravagance of living, will prove the beginning of a deterioration. And of this change the people will be credited with being the authors, when they become convinced that they are being cheated by some from avarice, and are puffed up with flattery by others from love of office. For when that comes about, in their passionate resentment and acting under the dictates of anger, they will refuse to obey any longer, or to be content with having equal powers with their leaders, but will demand to have all or far the greatest themselves. And when that comes to pass the constitution will receive a new name, which sounds better than any other in the world, liberty or democracy; but, in fact, it will become that worst of all governments, mob-rule.

Cicero

The philosophy of Stoicism, although it had been originated by Greeks, was carried to its full development by Romans. Indeed, it might well be called the "official" philosophy of classical Rome, for it numbered among its outstanding spokesmen such political leaders as the emperor Marcus Aurelius and the statesmen Seneca and Cicero. One might wonder that such men, engaged in practical politics, should find time for philosophizing; nevertheless, they must be credited with two contributions, both of great historical significance, to Stoic political and moral theory. The first of these is the doctrine of Natural Law: the theory that Nature (or the Universe), because it is the embodiment of an indwelling Reason, is governed by rational Laws and that people, being partakers of this universal Reason, are capable of discovering these Laws of Nature and ought, as rational beings, to live in accord with them. This doctrine, since its formulation by the Roman Stoics, has persisted as the dominant tradition in Western political theory, underlying the social structure of the Middle Ages and receiving its classic modern affirmation in the preamble to the American Declaration of Independence.

The second Roman contribution to Stoicism is the notion of "cosmopolitanism." The Law of Nature, being universal, stands above the edicts of any nation; hence, individuals, whatever their nationality or status, are bound equally by this Law. As a rational being, everyone is "a citizen of the whole universe, considered as a single Commonwealth." Here the Roman philosophers made a complete break in theory from the political provincialism embodied in the traditional distinction between "Greek" and "barbarian," a break paralleling that in practice which the Roman Empire made from the political isolationism of the Greek city-state.

Cicero was one of the last political leaders of the Roman Republic, holding numerous offices in the government, including that of consul in 63 B.C. He was proscribed and executed in 43 B.C. by the Second Triumvirate. His dialogue *The Laws* is modeled after one of the same name written by Plato, whom he admired greatly. The three persons of the dialogue represent Cicero and his brothers, Marcus of course being Cicero himself. The selection included here is from Books I and II.

The Laws

MARCUS: The whole subject of universal law and jurisprudence must be comprehended in this discussion, in order that this which we call civil law, may be confined in some one small and narrow space of nature. For we shall have to explain the true nature of moral justice, which must be traced back from the nature of man. And laws will have to be considered by which all political states should be governed. And last of all, shall we have to speak of those laws and customs of nations which are framed for the use and convenience of particular countries (in which even our own people will not be omitted), which are known by the title of civil laws.

QUINTUS: You take a noble view of the subject, my brother, and go to the fountainhead, in order to throw light on the subject of our consideration; and those who treat civil law in any other manner, are not so much pointing out the paths of justice as those of litigation.

MARCUS: That is not quite the case, my Quintus. It is not so much the science of law that produces litigation, as the ignorance of it. But more of this by-and-by. At present let us examine the first principles of Right.

Now, many learned men have maintained that it springs from law. I hardly know if their opinion be not correct, at least according to their own definition; for "law," say they, "is the highest reason implanted in nature, which prescribes those things which ought to be done, and forbids the contrary." And when this same reason is confirmed and established in men's minds, it is then law.

They therefore conceive that prudence is a law, whose operation is to urge us to good actions, and restrain us from evil ones. And they think, too, that the Greek name for law, which is derived from the word, to distribute, implies the very nature of the thing, that is, to give every man his due. The Latin name, *lex,* conveys the idea of selections, *a legendo.* According to the Greeks, therefore, the name of law implies an equitable distribution: according to the Romans, an equitable selection. And, indeed, both characteristics belong peculiarly to law.

And if this be a correct statement, which it seems to me for the most part to be, then the origin of right is to be sought in the law. For this is the true energy of nature, this is the very soul and reason of a wise man, and the test of virtue and vice. But since all this discussion of ours relates to a subject, the terms of which are of frequent occurrence in the popular language of the citizens, we shall be sometimes obliged to use the same terms as the vulgar, and to call that law, which in its written enactments sanctions what it thinks fit by special commands or prohibitions.

Let us begin, then, to establish

Trans. C. D. Yonge (London, 1853).

the principles of justice on that supreme law, which has existed from all ages before any legislative enactments were drawn up in writing, or any political governments constituted.

QUINTUS: That will be more convenient, and more sensible with reference to the subject of the discussion which we have determined on.

MARCUS: Shall we, then, seek for the origin of justice at its fountainhead? when we have discovered which, we shall be in no doubt to what these questions which we are examining ought to be referred.

QUINTUS: Such is the course I would advise.

ATTICUS: I also subscribe to your brother's opinion.

MARCUS: Since, then, we wish to maintain and preserve the constitution of that republic which Scipio, in those six books which I have written under that title, has proved to be the best, and since all our laws are to be accommodated to the kind of political government there described, we must also treat of the general principles of morals and manners, and not limit ourselves on all occasions to written laws; but I purpose to trace back the origin of right from nature itself, who will be our best guide in conducting the whole discussion.

ATTICUS: You will do right, and when she is our guide it is absolutely impossible for us to err.

MARCUS: Do you then grant, my Atticus (for I know my brother's opinion already), that the entire universe is regulated by the power of the immortal Gods, that by their nature, reason, energy, mind, divinity, or some other word of clearer signification, if there be such, all things are governed and directed? for if you will not grant me this, that is what I must begin by establishing.

ATTICUS: I grant you all you can desire. But owing to this singing of birds and babbling of waters, I fear my fellow-learners can scarcely hear me.

MARCUS: You are quite right to be on your guard; for even the best men occasionally fall into a passion, and they will be very indignant if they hear you denying the first article of this notable book, entitled "The Chief Doctrines of Epicurus," in which he says "that God takes care of nothing, neither of himself nor of any other being!"

ATTICUS: Pray proceed, for I am waiting to know what advantage you mean to take of the concession I have made you.

MARCUS: I will not detain you long. This is the bearing which they have on our subject. This animal—prescient, sagacious, complex, acute, full of memory, reason, and counsel, which we call man—has been generated by the supreme God in a most transcendent condition. For he is the only creature among all the races and descriptions of animated beings who is endued with superior reason and thought, in which the rest are deficient. And what is there, I do not say in man alone, but in all heaven and earth, more divine than reason, which, when it becomes right and perfect, is justly termed wisdom?

There exists, therefore, since nothing is better than reason, and since this is the common property of God and man, a certain aboriginal rational intercourse between divine and human natures. But where reason is common, there right reason must also be common to the same parties; and since this right reason is what we call law, God and men must be considered as associated by law. Again, there must also be a communion of right where there is communion of law. And those who have law and right thus in common, must be considered members of the same commonwealth.

And if they are obedient to the same rule and the same authority, they are even much more so to this one celestial regency, this divine mind and omnipotent deity. So that the entire universe may be looked upon as forming one vast commonwealth of gods and men. And, as in earthly states certain ranks are distinguished with reference to the relationships of families, according to a certain principle which will be discussed in its proper place, that principle, in the nature of things, is far more magnificent and splendid by which men are connected with the Gods, as belonging to their kindred and nation.

For when we are reasoning on universal nature, we are accustomed to argue (and indeed the truth is just as it is stated in that argument) that in the long course of ages, and the uninterrupted succession of celestial revolutions, there arrived a certain ripe time for the sowing of the human race; and when it was sown and scattered over the earth, it was animated by the divine gift of souls. And as men retained from their terrestrial origin those other particulars by which they cohere together, which are frail and perishable, their immortal spirits were ingenerated by the Deity. From which circumstance it may be truly said,

that we possess a certain consanguinity, and kindred, and fellowship with the heavenly powers. And among all the varieties of animals, there is not one except man which retains any idea of the Divinity. And among men themselves, there is no nation so savage and ferocious as not to admit the necessity of believing in a God, however ignorant they may be what sort of God they ought to believe in. From whence we conclude that every man must recognise a Deity, who has any recollection and knowledge of his own origin.

Now, the law of virtue is the same in God and man, and in no other disposition besides them. This virtue is nothing else than a nature perfect in itself, and wrought up to the most consummate excellence. There exists, therefore, a similitude between God and man. And as this is the case, what connection can there be which concerns us more nearly, and is more certain?

Since, then, the Deity has been pleased to create and adorn man to be the chief and president of all terrestrial creatures, so it is evident, without further argument, that human nature has also made very great advances by its own intrinsic energy; that nature, which without any other instruction than her own, has developed the first rude principles of the understanding, and strengthened and perfected reason to all the appliances of science and art.

ATTICUS: Oh ye immortal Gods! to what a distance back are you tracing the principles of justice! However, you are discoursing in such a style that I will not show any impatience to hear what I expect you to say on the Civil Law. But I will listen patiently, even if you spend the whole day in this kind of discourse; for assuredly these, which perhaps you are embracing in your argument for the sake of others, are grander topics than even the subject itself for which they prepare the way.

MARCUS: You may well describe these topics as grand, which we are now briefly discussing. But of all the questions which are ever the subject of discussion among learned men, there is none which it is more important thoroughly to understand than this, that man is born for justice, and that law and equity have not been established by opinion, but by nature. This truth will become still more apparent if we investigate the nature of human association and society.

For there is no one thing so like or so equal to another, as in every instance man is to man. And if the corruption of customs, and the variation of opinions, did not induce an imbecility of minds, and turn them aside from the course of nature, no one would more nearly resemble than all men would resemble all men. Therefore, whatever definition we give of man, will be applicable to the whole human race. And this is a good argument that there is no dissimilarity of kind among men; because if this were the case, one definition could not include all men.

In fact, reason, which alone gives us so many advantages over beasts, by means of which we conjecture, argue, refute, discourse, and accomplish and conclude our designs, is assuredly common to all men; for the faculty of acquiring knowledge is similar in all human minds, though the knowledge itself may be endlessly diversified. By the same senses we all perceive the same objects, and those things which move the senses at all, do move in the same way the senses of all men. And those first rude elements of intelligence which, as I before observed, are the earliest developments of thought, are similarly impressed upon all men; and that faculty of speech which is the interpreter of the mind, agrees in the ideas which it conveys, though it may differ in the words by which it expresses them. And therefore there exists not a man in any nation, who, if he adopts nature for his guide, may not arrive at virtue.

Nor is this resemblance which all men bear to each other remarkable in those things only which are in accordance with right reason, but also in errors. For all men alike are captivated by pleasure, which, although it is a temptation to what is disgraceful, nevertheless bears some resemblance to natural good; for, as by its delicacy and sweetness it is delightful, it is through a mistake of the intellect adopted as something salutary.

And by error scarcely less universal, we shun death as if it were a dissolution of nature, and cling to life because it keeps us in that existence in which we were born. Thus, likewise, we consider pain as one of the greatest evils, not only on account of its present asperity, but also because it seems the precursor of mortality. Again, on account of the apparent resemblance between renown with honour, those men appear to us happy who are honoured, and miserable who happen to be inglorious. In like manner our minds are all similarly susceptible of inquietudes, joys, desires, and fears; nor if different men have different opinions, does it follow that those who deify dogs and cats, do not labour under superstition equally with other nations, though they may differ from them in the forms of its manifestation.

Again, what nation is there which has not a regard for kindness, benignity, gratitude, and mindfulness of benefits? What nation is there in which arrogance, malice, cruelty, and unthankfulness, are not reprobated and detested? And while this uniformity of opinions proves that the whole race of mankind is united together, the last point is that a system of living properly makes men better. If what I have said meets your approbation, I will proceed; or if any doubts occur to you, we had better clear them up first.

ATTICUS: There is nothing which strikes us, if I may reply for both of us.

MARCUS: It follows, then, that nature made us just that we might share our goods with each other, and supply each other's wants. You observe in this discussion, whenever I speak of nature, I mean nature in its genuine purity, but that there is, in fact, such corruption engendered by evil customs, that the sparks, as it were, of virtue which have been given by nature are extinguished, and that antagonist vices arise around it and become strengthened.

But if, as nature prompts them to, men would with deliberate judgment, in the words of the poet, "being men, think nothing that concerns mankind indifferent to them," then would justice be cultivated equally by all. For to those to whom nature has given reason, she has also given right reason, and therefore also law, which is nothing else than right reason enjoining what is good, and forbidding what is evil. And if nature has given us law, she hath also given us right. But she has bestowed reason on all, therefore right has been bestowed on all. And therefore did Socrates deservedly execrate the man who first drew a distinction between utility and nature, for he used to complain that this error was the source of all human vices, to which this sentence of Pythagoras refers—"The things belonging to friends are common"— and that other, "Friendly equality." From whence it appears, that when a wise man has displayed this benevolence which is so extensively and widely diffused towards one who is endowed with equal virtue, then that phenomenon takes place which is altogether incredible to some people, but which is a necessary consequence, that he loves himself not more dearly than he loves his friend. For how can a difference of interests arise where all interests are similar? If there could be ever so minute a difference of interests, then there would be an end of even the nature of friendship, the real meaning of which is such, that there is no friendship at all the moment that a person prefers anything happening to himself rather than to his friend.

Now, these preliminary remarks have been put forward as a preparation for the rest of our discourse and argument, in order that you may more easily understand that nature herself is the foundation of justice.

And when I have explained this a little more at large, then I will proceed to the consideration of that civil law from which all these arguments of mine are derived.

QUINTUS: Then you have not much to add, my brother, for the arguments you have already used have sufficiently proved to Atticus, or at all events to me, that nature is the fountain of justice.

ATTICUS: How could I maintain any other opinion, since you have now established these points—first, that we have been provided as we are and adorned by the gifts of the Gods; secondly, that all mankind have but one similar and common principle of living together; and, lastly, that all men are bound together by a certain natural indulgence and affection, as well as social rights? And as we have, rightly as I think, admitted the truth of these principles, how can we, with any consistency, separate from nature that law and justice which are her moral developments?

MARCUS: You are quite right, and that is the proper view of the case. But in conformity with the method of philosophers, (I do not mean the older sages of philosophy, but those modern ones, who have erected a magazine, as it were, of wisdom), those questions which were formerly discussed loosely and unconstrainedly, are now examined with strictness and distinctness. Nor will these men allow that we have done justice to the subject which we have now before us, unless we demonstrate in a distinct discussion that right is a part of nature.

ATTICUS: You seem to have renounced your liberty in debate, my Cicero; or are you become a man who, in discussion, rather follows the authority of others, than develops his individual sentiments?

MARCUS: Not always, Atticus. But you see what the line of this present conversation is, and how the main object of this whole discussion is to strengthen the foundation of commonwealths, to establish their forces, and to benefit their population.

I am, therefore, particularly anxious to avoid arguments which have not been thoroughly examined and carefully considered. Not that I expect to demonstrate my doctrine to the satisfaction of all men, for that is impossible; but I hope to do so to that of those who think that all just and honourable things deserve to be cultivated even for their own sake, and that nothing whatever can be properly called a good which is not intrinsically praiseworthy, or at least that there can exist no great good whatever which is truly laudable on its own account. . . . But were it the fear of punishment, and not the nature of the thing itself, that ought to restrain mankind from wickedness, what I would ask, could give villains the least uneasiness, abstracting from all fears of this kind? And yet none of them was ever so audaciously impudent, but what he either denied that the action in question had been committed by him, or pretended some cause or other for his just indignation, or sought a defence of his deed in some right of nature. And if the wicked dare to appeal to this principle, with what respect ought not good men to treat them?

But if either direct punishment,

or the fear of it, be what deters men from a vicious and criminal course of life, and not the turpitude of the thing itself, then none can be guilty of injustice, and the greatest offenders ought rather to be called imprudent than wicked.

On the other hand, those among us who are determined to the practice of goodness, not by its own intrinsic excellence, but for the sake of some private advantage, are cunning rather than good men. For what will not that man do in the dark who fears nothing but a witness and a judge? Should he meet a solitary individual in a desert place, whom he can rob of a large sum of money, and altogether unable to defend himself from being robbed, how will he behave? In such a case our man, who is just and honourable from principle and the nature of the thing itself, will converse with the stranger, assist him, and show him the way. But he who does nothing for the sake of another, and measures everything by the advantage it brings to himself, it is obvious, I suppose, how such a one will act: and should he deny that he would kill the man, or rob him of his treasure, his reason for this cannot be that he apprehends there is any moral turpitude in such actions, but only because he is afraid of a discovery, that is to say, that bad consequences will thence ensue—a sentiment this at which not only learned men but even clowns must blush.

It is therefore an absurd extravagance in some philosophers to assert, that all things are necessarily just which are established by the civil laws and the institutions of nations. Are then the laws of tyrants just, simply because they are laws? Suppose the thirty tyrants of Athens had imposed certain laws on the Athenians? or, suppose again that these Athenians were delighted with these tyrannical laws, would these laws on that account have been considered just? For my own part, I do not think such laws deserve any greater estimation than that passed during our own interregnum, which ordained that the dictator should be empowered to put to death with impunity whatever citizens he pleased, without hearing them in their own defence.

For there is but one essential justice which cements society, and one law which establishes this justice. This law is right reason, which is the true rule of all commandments and prohibitions. Whoever neglects this law, whether written or unwritten, is necessarily unjust and wicked.

But if justice consists in submission to written laws and national customs, and if, as the same school affirms, everything must be measured by utility alone, he who thinks that such conduct will be advantageous to him will neglect the laws, and break them if it is in his power. And the consequence is, that real justice has really no existence if it have not one by nature, and if that which is established as such on account of utility is overturned by some other utility.

But if nature does not ratify law, then all the virtues may lose their sway. For what becomes of generosity, patriotism, or friendship? Where will the desire of benefitting our neighbours, or the gratitude that acknowledges kindness, be able to exist at all? For all these virtues proceed from our natural inclination to love mankind. And this is the true basis of justice, and without this not only the mutual charities of men, but the religious services of the Gods, would be at an end; for these are preserved, as I imagine, rather by the natural sympathy which subsists between divine and human beings, than by mere fear and timidity.

But if the will of the people, the decrees of the senate, the adjudications of magistrates, were sufficient to establish rights, then it might become right to rob, right to commit adultery, right to substitute forged wills, if such conduct were sanctioned by the votes or decrees of the multitude. But if the opinions and suffrages of foolish men had sufficient weight to out-balance the nature of things, then why should they not determine among them, that what is essentially bad and pernicious should henceforth pass for good and beneficial? Or why, since law can make right out of injustice, should it not also be able to change evil into good?

But we have no other rule by which we may be capable of distinguishing between a good or a bad law than that of nature. Nor is it only right and wrong which are discriminated by nature, but generally all that is honourable is by this means distinguished from all that is shameful; for common sense has impressed in our minds the first principles of things, and has given us a general acquaintance with them; by which we connect with virtue every honourable quality, and with vice all that is disgraceful.

But to think that these differences exist only in opinion, and not in nature, is the part of an idiot. For even the virtue of a tree or a horse, in which expression there is an abuse of terms, does not exist in our opinion only, but in nature; and if that is the case, then what is honourable and disgraceful must also be discriminated by nature.

For if opinion could determine respecting the character of universal virtue, it might also decide respecting particular or partial virtues. But who will dare to determine that a man is prudent and cautious, not from his general conduct, but from some external appearances? For virtue evidently consists in perfect reason, and this certainly resides in nature. Therefore so does all honour and honesty in the same way.

For as what is true and false, creditable and discreditable, is judged of rather by their essential qualities than their external relations, so the consistent and perpetual course of life, which is virtue, and the inconsistency of life, which is vice, are judged of according to their own nature—and that inconstancy must necessarily be vicious.

We form an estimate of the opinions of youths, but not by their opinions. Those virtues and vices which reside in their moral natures must not be measured by opinions. And so of all moral qualities, we must discriminate between honourable and dishonourable by reference to the essential nature of the things themselves.

The good we commend, must needs contain in itself something commendable; for as I before stated, goodness is not a mode of opinion, but of nature. For if it were otherwise, opinion alone might constitute virtue and happiness, which is the most absurd of suppositions. And since we judge of good and evil by their nature, and since good and evil are the first principles of nature, certainly we should judge in the same manner of all honourable and all shameful things, referring them all to the law of nature.

But we are often too much disturbed by the dissensions of men and the variation of opinions. And because the same thing does not happen with reference to our senses, we look upon them as certain by nature. Those objects indeed, which sometimes present to us one appearance, sometimes another, and which do not always appear to the same people in the same way, we term fictions of the senses; but it is far otherwise. For neither parent, nor nurse, nor master, nor poet, nor drama, deceive our senses; nor do popular prejudices seduce them from the truth. But all kinds of snares are laid for the mind, either by those errors which I have just enumerated, which, taking possession of the young and uneducated, imbue them deeply, and bend them any way they please; or by that pleasure which is the imitator of goodness, being thoroughly and closely implicated with all our senses —the prolific mother of all evils. For she so corrupts us by her blandishments, that we no longer perceive some things which are essentially excellent because they have none of this deliciousness and pruriency.

It follows that I may now sum up the whole of this argument by asserting, as is plain to every one from these positions which have been already laid down, that all right and all that is honourable is to be sought for its own sake. In truth, all virtuous men love justice and equity for

what they are in themselves; nor is it like a good man to make a mistake, and love that which does not deserve their affection. Right, therefore, is desirable and deserving to be cultivated for its own sake; and if this be true of right, it must be true also of justice. What then shall we say of liberality? Is it exercised gratuitously, or does it covet some reward and recompense? If a man does good without expecting any recompense for his kindness, then it is gratuitous: if he does expect compensation, it is a mere matter of traffic. Nor is there any doubt that he who truly deserves the reputation of a generous and kind-hearted man, is thinking of his duty, not of his interest. In the same way the virtue of justice demands neither emolument nor salary, and therefore we desire it for its own sake. And the case of all the moral virtues is the same, and so is the opinion of them.

Besides this, if we weigh virtue by the mere utility and profit that attend it, and not by its own merit, the one virtue which results from such an estimate will be in fact a species of vice. For the more a man refers all his actions especially to his own advantage, the further he recedes from probity; so that they who measure virtue by profit, acknowledge no other virtue than this, which is a kind of vice. For who can be called benevolent, if no one ever acts kindly for the sake of another? And where are we to find a grateful person, if those who are disposed to be so can find no benefactor to whom they can show gratitude? What will become of sacred friendship, if we are not to love our friend for his own sake with all our heart and soul, as people say? if we are even to desert and discard him, as soon as we despair of deriving any further assistance or advantage from him. What can be imagined more inhuman than this conduct? But if friendship ought rather to be cultivated on its own account, so also for the same reason are society, equality, and justice desirable for their own sakes. If this be not so, then there can be no such thing as justice at all; for the most unjust thing of all is to seek a reward for one's just conduct.

What then shall we say of temperance, sobriety, continence, modesty, bashfulness, and chastity? Is it the fear of infamy, or the dread of judgments and penalties, which prevent men from being intemperate and dissolute? Do men then live in innocence and moderation, only to be well spoken of, and to acquire a certain fair reputation? Modest men blush even to speak of indelicacy. And I am greatly ashamed of those philosophers, who assert that there are no vices to be avoided but those which the laws have branded with infamy. For what shall I say? Can we call those persons truly chaste, who abstain from adultery merely for the fear of public exposure, and that disgrace which is only one of its many evil consequences? For what can be either praised or blamed with reason, if you depart from that great law and rule of nature, which makes the difference between right and wrong? Shall corporal defects, if they are remarkable, shock our sensibilities, and shall those of the soul make no impression on us?—of the soul, I say, whose turpitude is so evidently proved by its vices. For what is

there more hideous than avarice, more brutal than lust, more contemptible than cowardice, more base than stupidity and folly? Well, then, are we to call those persons unhappy, who are conspicuous for one or more of these, on account of some injuries, or disgraces, or sufferings to which they are exposed, or on account of the moral baseness of their sins? And we may apply the same test in the opposite way to those who are distinguished for their virtue.

Lastly, if virtue be sought for on account of some other things, it necessarily follows that there is something better than virtue. Is it money, then? is it fame, or beauty, or health? all of which appear of little value to us when we possess them; nor can it be by any possibility certainly known how long they will last. Or is it (what it is shameful even to utter) that basest of all, pleasure? Surely not; for it is in the contempt and disdain of pleasure that virtue is most conspicuous. . . . But the real state of the case is, that since law ought to be both a correctress of vice and a recommender of virtue, the principles on which we direct our conduct ought to be drawn from her. And, thus it comes to pass wisdom is the mother of all the virtuous arts, from the love of which the Greeks have composed the word Philosophy; and which is beyond all contradiction the richest, the brightest, and the most excellent of the gifts which the Gods have bestowed on the life of mankind. For wisdom alone has taught us, among other things, the most difficult of all lessons, namely, *to know ourselves,* a precept so forcible and so comprehensive, that it has been attributed not to a man, but to the God of Delphi himself.

For he who knows himself must in the first place be conscious that he is inspired by a divine principle. And he will look upon his rational part as a resemblance to some divinity consecrated within him, and will always be careful that his sentiments as well as his external behavior be worthy of so inestimable a gift of God. And after he has thoroughly examined himself and tested himself in every way, he will become aware what signal advantages he has received from nature at his entrance into life, and with what infinite means and appliances he is furnished for the attainment and acquisition of wisdom, since in the very beginning of all things, he has, as it were, the intelligible principles of things delineated, as it were, on his mind and soul, by the enlightening assistance of which, and the guidance of wisdom, he sees that he shall become a good and consequently a happy man.

For what can be described or conceived more truly happy than the state of that man, whose mind having attained to an exact knowledge and perception of virtue, has entirely discarded all obedience to and indulgence of the body, and has trampled on voluptuousness as a thing unbecoming the dignity of his nature, and has raised himself above all fear of death or pain; who maintains a benevolent intercourse with his friends, and has learnt to look upon all who are united to him by nature as his kindred; who has learnt to preserve piety and reverence towards the Gods and pure religion; and who has sharpened and improved the perceptions of his mind, as well as of his eyesight, to choose the good and reject the evil, which virtue from its foreseeing things is called Prudence?

When this man shall have surveyed the heavens, the earth, and the seas, and studied the nature of all things, and informed himself from whence they have been generated, to what state they will return, and of the time and manner of their dissolution, and has learnt to distinguish what parts of them are mortal and perishable, and what divine and eternal—when he shall have almost attained to a knowledge of that Being who superintends and governs these things, and shall look on himself as not confined within the walls of one city, or as the member of any particular community, but as a citizen of the whole universe, considered as a single Commonwealth: amid such a grand magnificence of things as this, and such a prospect and knowledge of nature, what a knowledge of himself, O ye immortal Gods, will a man arrive at! That is the warning of the Pythian Apollo. And how insignificant will he then esteem, how thoroughly will he condemn and despise, those things which by vulgar minds are held in the highest admiration!

And all these acquirements he will secure and guard as by a sort of fence, by the knowledge how to distinguish truth from falsehood, and by a certain science and art of reasoning which teaches him to know what consequences follow from premises, and what proposition is contrary to another. And when such a person feels that nature has designed him for civil society, he will not rest contented with these subtle disquisitions alone, but will put in practice that more comprehensive and continuous eloquence by which he may be able to govern nations, to establish laws, to punish malefactors, to defend the honest part of mankind, and publish the praises of great men: by which also he may fitly put forth precepts of safety, and panegyrics of virtue, in a way suited to persuade his countrymen: by which also he may be able to rouse them to the practice of virtue, and turn them from wickedness, to comfort the afflicted, and, in fine, to immortalize the wise consultations and noble actions of the brave and wise, and to punish the shame and infamy of wicked men by handing them down in undying records. And of all these important things which are perceived to be in man by those who wish to attain a knowledge of themselves, the parent and nurse is wisdom.

ATTICUS: You have given us a very dignified and just eulogium on her. But on what do you mean your remarks to bear?

MARCUS: In the first place, my Atticus, I mean them to bear on those jurisprudential topics which we shall hereafter discuss, which are well nigh as important as the preceding. For these moral principles we have already developed, would not be so grand and so interesting, if the sources from which they arise were not also full of sublimity and beauty. And for the rest, I prosecute this inquiry with pleasure, and I trust with justice; for I cannot with any conscience pass over in silence that study to which I am devoted, and which has made me all that I am.

ATTICUS: You speak truly, and as that study deserves; and it was, as you say, proper to do so in this discussion.

MARCUS: Let us, then, once more examine, before we come to the consideration of particular laws, what is the power and nature of law in general; lest, when we come to refer everything to it, we occasionally make mistakes from the employment of incorrect language, and show ourselves ignorant of the force of those terms which we ought to employ in the definition of laws.

QUINTUS: This is a very necessary caution, and the proper method of seeking truth.

MARCUS: This, then, as it appears to me, has been the decision of the wisest philosophers,—that law was neither a thing contrived by the genius of man, nor established by any decree of the people, but a certain eternal principle, which governs the entire universe, wisely commanding what is right and prohibiting what is wrong. Therefore they called that aboriginal and supreme law the mind of God, enjoining or forbidding each separate thing in accordance with reason. On which account it is, that this law, which the Gods have bestowed on the human race, is so justly applauded. For it is the reason and mind of a wise Being equally able to urge us to good and to deter us from evil.

QUINTUS: You have, on more than one occasion, already touched on this topic. But before you come to treat of the laws of nations, I wish you would endeavour to explain the force and power of this divine and celestial law, lest the torrent of custom should overwhelm our understanding, and betray us into the vulgar method of expression.

MARCUS: From our childhood we have learned, my Quintus, to call such phrases as this, "that a man appeals to justice, and goes to law," and many similar expressions, law; but, nevertheless, we should understand that these, and other similar commandments and prohibitions, have sufficient power to lead us on to virtuous actions and to call us away from vicious ones. Which power is not only far more ancient than any existence of states and peoples, but is coeval with God himself, who beholds and governs both heaven and earth. For it is impossible that the divine mind can exist in a state devoid of reason; and divine reason must necessarily be possessed of a power to determine what is virtuous and what is vicious. Nor, because it was nowhere written, that one man should maintain the pass of a bridge against the enemy's whole army, and that he should order the bridge behind him to be cut down, are we therefore to imagine that the valiant Cocles did not perform this great exploit agreeably to the laws of nature and the dictates of true bravery. Again, though in the reign of Tarquin there was no written law concerning adultery, it does not therefore follow that Sextus Tarquinius did not offend against the eternal law when he committed a rape of Lucretia, daughter of Tricipitinus. For even then he had the light of reason deduced from the nature of things, that incites to good actions and dissuades from evil ones; and which does not begin for the first time to be a law when it is drawn up in writing, but from the first moment that it exists. And this existence of moral obligation is co-eternal with

that of the divine mind. Therefore, the true and supreme law, whose commands and prohibitions are equally authoritative, is the right reason of the Sovereign Jupiter.

QUINTUS: I grant you, my brother, that whatever is just is also at all times the true law; nor can this true law either be originated or abrogated by the written forms in which decrees are drawn up.

MARCUS: Therefore, as that Divine Mind, or reason, is the supreme law, so it exists in the mind of the sage, so far as it can be perfected in man. But with respect to civil laws, which are drawn up in various forms, and framed to meet the occasional requirements of the people, the name of law belongs to them not so much by right as by the favour of the people. For men prove by some such arguments as the following, that every law which deserves the name of a law, ought to be morally good and laudable. It is clear, say they, that laws were originally made for the security of the people, for the preservation of states, for the peace and happiness of society; and that they who first framed enactments of that kind, persuaded the people that they would write and publish such laws only as should conduce to the general morality and happiness, if they would receive and obey them. And then such regulations, being thus settled and sanctioned, they justly entitled *Laws*. From which we may reasonably conclude, that those who made unjustifiable and pernicious enactments for the people, acted in a manner contrary to their own promises and professions, and established anything rather than laws, properly so called, since it is evident that the very signification of the word *law,* comprehends the whole essence and energy of justice and equity.

I would, therefore, interrogate you on this point, my Quintus, as those philosophers are in the habit of doing. If a state wants something for the want of which it is reckoned no state at all, must not that something be something good?

QUINTUS: A very great good.

MARCUS: And if a state has no law, is it not for that reason to be reckoned no state at all?

QUINTUS: We must needs say so.

MARCUS: We must therefore reckon law among the very best things.

QUINTUS: I entirely agree with you.

MARCUS: If, then, in the majority of nations, many pernicious and mischievous enactments are made, which have no more right to the name of law than the mutual engagements of robbers, are we bound to call them laws? For as we cannot call the recipes of ignorant and unskilful empirics, who give poisons instead of medicines, the prescriptions of a physician, so likewise we cannot call that the true law of a people, of whatever kind it may be, if it enjoins what is injurious, let the people receive it as they will. For law is the just distinction between right and wrong, made conformable to that most ancient nature of all, the original and principal regulator of all things, by which the laws of men should be measured, whether they punish the guilty or protect and preserve the innocent.

QUINTUS: I quite understand you, and think that no law but that of justice should either be proclaimed as one or enforced as one. . . .

MARCUS: Let this, therefore, be a fundamental principle in all societies, that the Gods are the supreme lords and governors of all things,—that all events are directed by their influence, and wisdom, and Divine power; that they deserve very well of the race of mankind; and that they likewise know what sort of person every one really is; that they observe his actions, whether good or bad; that they take notice with what feelings and with what piety he attends to his religious duties, and that they are sure to make a difference between the good and the wicked.

For when once our minds are confirmed in these views, it will not be difficult to inspire them with true and useful sentiments. For what can be more true than that no man should be so madly presumptuous as to believe that he has either reason or intelligence, while he does not believe that the heaven and the world possesses them likewise, or to think that those things which he can scarcely comprehend by the greatest possible exertion of his intellect, are put in motion without the agency of reason?

In truth, we can scarcely reckon him a man, whom neither the regular courses of the stars, nor the alternations of day and night, nor the temperature of the seasons, nor the productions that nature displays for his use and enjoyment, urge to gratitude towards heaven.

And as those beings which are furnished with reason are incomparably superior to those which want it, and as we cannot say, without impiety, that anything is superior to the universal Nature, we must therefore confess that divine reason is contained within her. And who will dispute the utility of these sentiments, when he reflects how many cases of the greatest importance are decided by oaths; how much the sacred rites performed in making treaties tend to assure peace and tranquillity; and what numbers of people the fear of divine punishment has reclaimed from a vicious course of life, and how sacred the social rights must be in a society where a firm persuasion obtains the immediate intervention of the immortal gods, both as witnesses and judges of our actions? Such is the "preamble of the law," to use the expression of Plato.

Suetonius

It is very doubtful that anyone, anywhere, at any time has ever claimed Suetonius' *Lives of the Caesars* to be a dispassionate, objective account of the careers of the men he chose to examine. As a matter of fact, this effective Roman polemicist was a very able practical psychologist, using a rather subtle literary trick to destroy those about whom he wrote. One clear example of this trickery (among others) can be identified in his allusions to the relationship between Julius Caesar and the king of Bithynia.

But this type of device should not obscure the real debt historians of Imperial Rome owe to this remarkable biographer. His work remains one of the major sources of information about his subjects, and his wealth of anecdotal detail has provided later writers with material obtainable nowhere else. Also, Suetonius' style or pattern of treatment was taken as the best possible by nearly all biographers from his time to the Renaissance. This pattern was rigid almost to the point of being tedious—first an account of the subject's family and lineage, next an account of his birth and education, then a strict chronological recital of his career, followed by a physical description and a character analysis, and lastly, the story of his death. Naturally, the character analysis section offered considerable scope for the moral commentary and platitudinous sermonizing in which Suetonius seems to have delighted. To appreciate the influence of Suetonius on later biographers it is necessary only to compare the following selection with Einhard's *Life of the Emperor Charles* (see pp. 289–308).

Suetonius (Caius Suetonius Tranquillus) was born in the last third of the first century and died about the middle of the second century after Christ. One of the few firm facts known about his life is that he was for a time private secretary to the Emperor Hadrian. As such he may have had access to official documents and records, but whether he took advantage of this opportunity is open to question. However, his influence cannot be denied. As a literary model and as an important source of information he takes his place with Plutarch (a contemporary) as a major figure in the historiography of the classical world. The selection that follows is from his biography of Julius Caesar.

The Lives of the Caesars

BOOK I

The deified Julius

. . .

Caesar's very first enactment after becoming consul [in 59 B.C.] was, that the proceedings both of the senate and of the people should day by day be compiled and published. He also revived a by-gone custom, that during the months when he did not have the fasces an orderly should walk before him, while the lictors followed him. He brought forward an agrarian law too, and when his colleague announced adverse omens, he resorted to arms and drove him from the Forum; and when next day Bibulus made complaint in the senate and no one could be found who ventured to make a motion, or even to express an opinion about so high-handed a proceeding (although decrees had often been passed touching less serious breaches of the peace), Caesar's conduct drove him to such a pitch of desperation, that from that time until the end of his term he did not leave his house, but merely issued proclamations announcing adverse omens.

From that time on Caesar managed all the affairs of state alone and after his own pleasure; so that sundry witty fellows, pretending by way of jest to sign and seal testamentary documents, wrote, "Done in the consulship of Julius and Caesar," instead of "Bibulus and Caesar," writing down the same man twice, by name and by surname. Presently too the following verses were on everyone's lips:—

In Caesar's year, not Bibulus', an act
    took place of late;
For naught do I remember done in
    Bibulus' consulate.

The plain called Stellas, which had been devoted to public uses by the men of by-gone days, and the Campanian territory, which had been reserved to pay revenues for the aid of the government, he divided without casting lots among twenty thousand citizens who had three or more children each. When the publicans asked for relief, he freed them from a third part of their obligation, and openly warned them in contracting for taxes in the future not to bid too recklessly. He freely granted everything else that anyone took into his head to ask, either without opposition or by intimidating anyone who tried to object. Marcus Cato, who tried to delay proceedings, was dragged from the House by a lictor at Caesar's command and taken off to prison. When Lucius Lucullus was somewhat too outspoken in his opposition, he filled him with such fear of malicious prosecution, that Lucullus actually fell on his knees before him. Because Cicero, while pleading in court, deplored the state of the times, Caesar transferred the orator's enemy Publius Clodius that

Suetonius: The Lives of the Caesars, trans. J. C. Rolfe.

very same day from the patricians to the plebeians, a thing for which Clodius had for a long time been vainly striving; and that too at the ninth hour. Finally, taking action against all the opposition in a body, he bribed an informer to declare that he had been egged on by certain men to murder Pompey, and to come out upon the rostra and name the guilty parties according to a prearranged plot. But when the informer had named one or two to no purpose and not without suspicion of double-dealing, Caesar, hopeless of the success of his overhasty attempt, is supposed to have had him taken off by poison.

At about the same time he took to wife Calpurnia, daughter of Lucius Piso, who was to succeed him in the consulship, and affianced his own daughter Julia to Gnaeus Pompeius, breaking a previous engagement with Servilius Caepio, although the latter had shortly before rendered him conspicuous service in his contest with Bibulus. And after this new alliance he began to call upon Pompey first to give his opinion in the senate, although it had been his habit to begin with Crassus, and it was the rule for the consul in calling for opinions to continue throughout the year the order which he had established on the Kalends of January.

Backed therefore by his father-in-law and son-in-law, out of all the numerous provinces he made the Gauls his choice, as the most likely to enrich him and furnish suitable material for triumphs. At first, it is true, by the bill of Vatinius he received only Cisalpine Gaul with the addition of Illyricum; but presently he was assigned Gallia Comata as

well by the senate, since the members feared that even if they should refuse it, the people would give him this also. Transported with joy at this success, he could not keep from boasting a few days later before a crowded house, that having gained his heart's desire to the grief and lamentation of his opponents, he would therefore from that time mount on their heads; and when someone insultingly remarked that that would be no easy matter for any woman, he replied in the same vein that Semiramis too had been queen in Syria and the Amazons in days of old had held sway over a great part of Asia.

When at the close of his consulship the praetors Gaius Memmius and Lucius Domitius moved an inquiry into his conduct the previous year, Caesar laid the matter before the senate; and when they failed to take it up, and three days had been wasted in fruitless wrangling, went off to his province. Whereupon his quaestor was at once arraigned on several counts, as a preliminary to his own impeachment. Presently he himself too was prosecuted by Lucius Antistius, tribune of the commons, and it was only by appealing to the whole college that he contrived not to be brought to trial, on the ground that he was absent on public service. Then to secure himself for the future, he took great pains always to put the magistrates for the year under personal obligation, and not to aid any candidates or suffer any to be elected, save as guaranteed to defend him in his absence. And he did not hesitate in some cases to exact an oath to keep this pledge or even a written contract.

When however Lucius Domitius, candidate for the consulship, openly threatened to effect as consul what he had been unable to do as praetor, and to take his armies from him, Caesar compelled Pompeius and Crassus to come to Luca, a city in his province, where he prevailed on them to stand for a second consulship, to defeat Domitius; and he also succeeded through their influence in having his term as governor of Gaul made five years longer. Encouraged by this, he added to the legions which he had received from the state others at his own cost, one actually composed of men of Transalpine Gaul and bearing a Gallic name too (for it was called Alauda), which he trained in the Roman tactics and equipped with Roman arms; and later on he gave every man of it citizenship. After that he did not let slip any pretext for war, however unjust and dangerous it might be, picking quarrels as well with allied as with hostile and barbarous nations; so that once the senate decreed that a commission be sent to inquire into the condition of the Gallic provinces, and some even recommended that Caesar be handed over to the enemy. But as his enterprises prospered, thanksgivings were appointed in his honour oftener and for longer periods than for anyone before his time.

During the nine years of his command this is in substance what he did. All that part of Gaul which is bounded by the Pyrenees, the Alps and the Cevennes, and by the Rhine and Rhone rivers, a circuit of some thirty-two hundred miles, with the exception of some allied states which had rendered him good service, he reduced to the form of a province; and imposed upon it a yearly tribute of forty million sesterces. He was the first Roman to build a bridge and attack the Germans beyond the Rhine, and he inflicted heavy losses upon them. He invaded the Britons too, a people unknown before, vanquished them, and exacted moneys and hostages. Amid all these successes he met with adverse fortune but three times in all: in Britain, where his fleet narrowly escaped destruction in a violent storm; in Gaul, when one of his legions was routed at Gergovia; and on the borders of Germany, when his lieutenants Titurius and Aurunculeius were ambushed and slain.

Within this same space of time he lost first his mother, then his daughter, and soon afterwards his grandchild. Meanwhile, as the community was aghast at the murder of Publius Clodius, the senate had voted that only one consul should be chosen, and expressly named Gnaeus Pompeius. When the tribunes planned to make him Pompey's colleague, Caesar urged them rather to propose to the people that he be permitted to stand for a second consulship without coming to Rome, when the term of his governorship drew near its end, to prevent his being forced for the sake of the office to leave his province prematurely and without finishing the war. On the granting of this, aiming still higher and flushed with hope, he neglected nothing in the way of lavish expenditure or of favours to anyone, either in his public capacity or privately. He began a forum with the proceeds of his spoils, the ground for which cost more than a hundred million sesterces. He announced a combat of gladiators and a feast for the people in memory of his daughter, a thing quite without precedent. To raise the expectation of these events to the highest possible pitch, he had the material for the banquet prepared in part by his own household, although he had let contracts to the markets as well. He gave orders too that whenever famous gladiators fought without winning the favour of the people, they should be rescued by force and kept for him. He had the novices trained, not in a gladiatorial school by professionals, but in private houses by Roman knights and even by senators who were skilled in arms, earnestly beseeching them, as is shown by his own letters, to give the recruits individual attention and personally direct their exercises. He doubled the pay of the legions for all time. Whenever grain was plentiful, he distributed it to them without stint or measure, and now and then gave each man a slave from among the captives.

Moreover, to retain his relationship and friendship with Pompey, Caesar offered him his sister's granddaughter Octavia in marriage, although she was already the wife of Gaius Marcellus, and asked for the hand of Pompey's daughter, who was promised to Faustus Sulla. When he had put all Pompey's friends under obligation, as well as the great part of the senate, through loans made without interest or at a low rate, he lavished gifts on men of all other classes, both those whom he invited to accept his bounty and those who applied to him unasked, including even freedmen and slaves who were special favourites of their masters or patrons. In short, he was the sole and ever ready help of all who were in legal difficulties or in debt and of young spendthrifts, excepting only those whose burden of guilt or of poverty was so heavy, or who were so given up to riotous living, that even he could not save them; and to these he declared in the plainest terms that what they needed was a civil war.

He took no less pains to win the devotion of princes and provinces all over the world, offering prisoners to some by the thousand as a gift, and sending auxiliary troops to the aid of others whenever they wished, and as often as they wished, without the sanction of the senate or people, besides adorning the principal cities of Asia and Greece with magnificent public works, as well as those of Italy and the provinces of Gaul and Spain. At last, when all were thunderstruck at his actions and wondered what their purpose could be, the consul Marcus Claudius Marcellus, after first making proclamation that he purposed to bring before the senate a matter of the highest public moment, proposed that a successor to Caesar be appointed before the end of his term, on the ground that the war was ended, peace was established, and the victorious army ought to be disbanded; also that no account be taken of Caesar at the elections, unless he were present, since Pompey's subsequent action had not annulled the decree of the people. And it was true that when Pompey proposed a bill touching the privileges of officials, in the clause where he debarred absentees from candidacy for office he forgot to make a special exception in Caesar's case, and did not correct the oversight until the law had been inscribed on a tablet of bronze and deposited in the treasury. Not content with depriving Caesar of his provinces and his privilege, Marcellus also moved that the colonists whom Caesar had settled in Novum Comum by the bill of Vatinius should lose their citizenship, on the ground that it had been given from political motives and was not authorized by the law.

Greatly troubled by these measures, and thinking, as they say he was often heard to remark, that now that he was the leading man of the state, it was harder to push him down from the first place to the second than it would be from the second to the lowest, Caesar stoutly resisted Marcellus, partly through vetoes of the tribunes and partly through the other consul, Servius Sulpicius. When next year Gaius Marcellus, who had succeeded his cousin Marcus as consul, tried the same thing, Caesar by a heavy bribe secured the support of the other consul, Aemilius Paulus, and of Gaius Curio, the most reckless of the tribunes. But seeing that everything was being pushed most persistently, and that even the consuls-elect were among the opposition, he sent a written appeal to the senate, not to take from him the privilege which the people had granted, or else to compel the others in command of armies to resign also; feeling sure, it was thought, that he could more readily muster his veterans as soon as he wished, than Pompey his newly levied troops. He further proposed a compromise to his opponents, that after giving up eight legions and Transalpine Gaul, he be allowed to keep two legions and Cisalpine Gaul, or at least one

legion and Illyricum, until he was elected consul.

But when the senate declined to interfere, and his opponents declared that they would accept no compromise in a matter affecting the public welfare, he crossed to Hither Gaul, and after holding all the assizes, halted at Ravenna, intending to resort to war if the senate took any drastic action against the tribunes of the commons who interposed vetoes in his behalf. Now this was his excuse for the civil war, but it is believed that he had other motives. Gnaeus Pompeius used to declare that since Caesar's own means were not sufficient to complete the works which he had planned, nor to do all that he had led the people to expect on his return, he desired a state of general unrest and turmoil. Others say that he dreaded the necessity of rendering an account for what he had done in his first consulship contrary to the auspices and the laws, and regardless of vetoes; for Marcus Cato often declared, and took oath too, that he would impeach Caesar the moment he had disbanded his army. It was openly said too that if he was out of office on his return, he would be obliged, like Milo, to make his defence in a court hedged about by armed men. The latter opinion is the more credible one in view of the assertion of Asinius Pollio, that when Caesar at the battle of Pharsalus saw his enemies slain or in flight, he said, word for word: "They would have it so. Even I, Gaius Caesar, after so many great deeds, should have been found guilty, if I had not turned to my army for help." Some think that habit had given him a love of power, and that weighing the strength of his adversaries against his own, he grasped the opportunity of usurping the despotism which had been his heart's desire from early youth. Cicero too was seemingly of this opinion, when he wrote in the third book of his *De Officiis* that Caesar ever had upon his lips these lines of Euripides, of which Cicero himself adds a version:—

If wrong may e'er be right, for a
  throne's sake
Were wrong most right:—be God in
  all else feared.

Accordingly, when word came that the veto of the tribunes had been set aside and they themselves had left the city, he at once sent on a few cohorts with all secrecy, and then, to disarm suspicion, concealed his purpose by appearing at a public show, inspecting the plans of a gladiatorial school which he intended building, and joining as usual in a banquet with a large company. It was not until after sunset that he set out very privily with a small company, taking the mules from a bakeshop hard by and harnessing them to a carriage; and when his lights went out and he lost his way, he was astray for some time, but at last found a guide at dawn and got back to the road on foot by narrow bypaths. Then, overtaking his cohorts at the river Rubicon, which was the boundary of his province, he paused for a while, and realising what a step he was taking, he turned to those about him and said: "Even yet we may draw back; but once cross yon little bridge, and the whole issue is with the sword."

As he stood in doubt, this sign was given him. On a sudden there appeared hard by a being of wondrous stature and beauty, who sat and played upon a reed; and when not only the shepherds flocked to hear him, but many of the soldiers left their posts, and among them some of the trumpeters, the apparition snatched a trumpet from one of them, rushed to the river, and sounding the war-note with mighty blast, strode to the opposite bank. Then Caesar cried: "Take we the course which the signs of the gods and the false dealing of our foes point out. The die is cast," said he.

Accordingly, crossing with his army, and welcoming the tribunes of the commons, who had come to him after being driven from Rome, he harangued the soldiers with tears, and rending his robe from his breast besought their faithful service. It is even thought that he promised every man a knight's estate, but that came of a misunderstanding; for since he often pointed to the finger of his left hand as he addressed them and urged them on, declaring that to satisfy all those who helped him to defend his honour he would gladly tear his very ring from his hand, those on the edge of the assembly, who could see him better than they could hear his words, assumed that he said what his gesture seemed to mean; and so the report went about that he had promised them the right of the ring and four hundred thousand sesterces as well.

The sum total of his movements after that is, in their order, as follows: He overran Umbria, Picenum, and Etruria, took prisoner Lucius Domitius, who had been irregularly named his successor, and was holding Corfinium with a garrison, let him go free, and then proceeded along the Adriatic to Brundisium, where Pompey and the consuls had taken refuge, intending to cross the sea as soon as might be. After vainly trying by every kind of hindrance to prevent their sailing, he marched off to Rome, and after calling the senate together to discuss public business, went to attack Pompey's strongest forces, which were in Spain under command of three of his lieutenants—Marcus Petreius, Lucius Afranius, and Marcus Varro —saying to his friends before he left, "I go to meet an army without a leader, and I shall return to meet a leader without an army." And in fact, though his advance was delayed by the siege of Massilia, which had shut its gates against him, and by extreme scarcity of supplies, he nevertheless quickly gained a complete victory.

Returning thence to Rome, he crossed into Macedonia, and after blockading Pompey for almost four months behind mighty ramparts, finally routed him in the battle at Pharsalus, followed him in his flight to Alexandria, and when he learned that his rival had been slain, made war on King Ptolemy, whom he perceived to be plotting against his own safety as well; a war in truth of great difficulty, convenient neither in time nor place, but carried on during the winter season, within the walls of a well-provisioned and crafty foeman, while Caesar himself was without supplies of any kind and ill-prepared. Victor in spite of all, he turned over the rule of Egypt to Cleopatra and her younger brother, fearing that if he made a province of it, it might one day under a headstrong governor be a source of revolution. From Alexandria he crossed to Syria, and from there went to Pontus, spurred on by the news that Pharnaces, son of Mithridates the Great, had taken advantage of the situation to make war, and was already flushed with numerous successes; but Caesar vanquished him in a single battle within five days after his arrival and four hours after getting sight of him, often remarking on Pompey's good luck in gaining his principal fame as a general by victories over such feeble foemen. Then he overcame Scipio and Juba, who were patching up the remnants of their party in Africa, and the sons of Pompey in Spain.

In all the civil wars he suffered not a single disaster except through his lieutenants, of whom Gaius Curio perished in Africa, Gaius Antonius fell into the hands of the enemy in Illyricum, Publius Dolabella lost a fleet also off Illyricum, and Gnaeus Domitius Calvinus an army in Pontus. Personally he always fought with the utmost success, and the issue was never even in doubt save twice: once at Dyrrachium, where he was put to flight, and said of Pompey, who failed to follow up his success, that he did not know how to use a victory; again in Spain, in the final struggle, when, believing the battle lost, he actually thought of suicide.

Having ended the wars, he celebrated five triumphs, four in a single month, but at intervals of a few days, after vanquishing Scipio; and another on defeating Pompey's sons. The first and most splendid was the Gallic triumph, the next the Alexandrian, then the Pontic, after that the African, and finally the Spanish, each differing from the rest in its equipment and display of spoils. As he rode through the Velabrum on the day of his Gallic triumph, the axle of his chariot broke, and he was all but thrown out; and he mounted the Capitol by torchlight, with forty elephants bearing lamps on his right and his left. In his Pontic triumph he displayed among the show-pieces of the procession an inscription of but three words, "I came, I saw, I conquered," not indicating the events of the war, as the others did, but the speed with which it was finished.

To each and every foot-soldier of his veteran legions he gave twenty-four thousand sesterces by way of booty, over and above the two thousand apiece which he had paid them at the beginning of the civil strife. He also assigned them lands, but not side by side, to avoid dispossessing any of the former owners. To every man of the people, besides ten pecks of grain and the same number of pounds of oil, he distributed the three hundred sesterces which he had promised at first, and one hundred apiece to boot because of the delay. He also remitted a year's rent in Rome to tenants who paid two thousand sesterces or less, and in Italy up to five hundred sesterces. He added a banquet and a dole of meat, and after his Spanish victory two dinners; for deeming that the former of these had not been served with a liberality creditable to his generosity, he gave another five days later on a most lavish scale.

He gave entertainments of divers kinds: a combat of gladiators and also stage-plays in every ward all over the city, performed too by actors of all languages, as well as races in the circus, athletic contests, and a sham sea-fight. In the gladiatorial contest in the Forum Furius Leptinus, a man of praetorian stock, and Quintus Calpenus, a former senator and pleader at the bar, fought to a finish. A Pyrrhic dance was performed by the sons of the princes of Asia and Bithynia. During the plays Decimus Laberius, a Roman Knight, acted a farce of his own composition, and having been presented with five hundred thousand sesterces and a gold ring, passed from the stage through the orchestra and took his place in the fourteen rows. For the races the circus was lengthened at either end and a broad canal was dug all about it; then young men of the highest rank drove four-horse and two-horse chariots and rode pairs of horses, vaulting from one to the other. The game called Troy was performed by two troops, of younger and of older boys. Combats with wild beasts were presented on five successive days, and last of all there was a battle between two opposing armies, in which five hundred foot-soldiers, twenty elephants, and thirty horsemen engaged on each side. To make room for this, the goals were taken down and in their place two camps were pitched over against each other. The athletic competitions lasted for three days in a temporary stadium built for the purpose in the region of the Campus Martius. For the naval battle a pool was dug in the lesser Codeta and there was a contest of ships of two, three, and four banks of oars, belonging to the Tyrian and Egyptian fleets, manned by a large force of fighting men. Such a throng flocked to all these shows from every quarter, that many strangers had to lodge in tents pitched in the streets or along the roads, and the press was often such that many were crushed to death, including two senators.

Then turning his attention to the reorganisation of the state, he reformed the calendar, which the negligence of the pontiffs had long since so disordered, through their privilege of adding months or days at pleasure, that the harvest festivals did not come in summer nor those of the vintage in the autumn; and he adjusted the year to the sun's course by making it consist of three hundred and sixty-five days, abolishing the intercalary month, and adding one day every fourth year. Furthermore, that the correct reckoning of seasons might begin with the next Kalends of January, he inserted two other months between those of November and December; hence the year in which these arrangements were made was one of fifteen months, including the intercalary month, which belonged to that year according to the former custom.

He filled the vacancies in the senate, enrolled additional patricians, and increased the number of praetors, aediles, and quaestors, as well as of the minor officials; he reinstated those who had been degraded by official action of the censors or found guilty of bribery by verdict of the jurors. He shared the elections with the people on this basis: that except in the case of the consulship, half of the magistrates should be appointed by the people's choice, while the rest should be those whom he had personally nominated. And these he announced in brief notes like the following, circulated in each tribe: "Caesar the Dictator to this or that tribe. I commend to you so and so, to hold their

positions by your votes." He admitted to office even the sons of those who had been proscribed. He limited the right of serving as jurors to two classes, the equestrian and senatorial orders, disqualifying the third class, the tribunes of the treasury.

He made the enumeration of the people neither in the usual manner nor place, but from street to street aided by the owners of blocks of houses, and reduced the number of those who received grain at public expense from three hundred and twenty thousand to one hundred and fifty thousand. And to prevent the calling of additional meetings at any future time for purposes of enrollment, he provided that the places of such as died should be filled each year by the praetors from those who were not on the list.

Moreover, to keep up the population of the city, depleted as it was by the assignment of eighty thousand citizens to colonies across the sea, he made a law that no citizen older then twenty or younger than forty, who was not detained by service in the army, should be absent from Italy for more than three successive years; that no senator's son should go abroad except as the companion of a magistrate or on his staff; and that those who made a business of grazing should have among their herdsmen at least one-third who were men of free birth. He conferred citizenship on all who practised medicine at Rome, and on all teachers of the liberal arts, to make them more desirous of livng in the city and to induce others to resort to it.

As to debts, he disappointed those who looked for their cancellation, which was often agitated, but finally decreed that the debtors should satisfy their creditors according to a valuation of their possessions at the price which they had paid for them before the civil war, deducting from the principal whatever interest had been paid in cash or pledged through bankers; an arrangement which wiped out about a fourth part of their indebtedness. He dissolved all guilds, except those of ancient foundation. He increased the penalties for crimes; and inasmuch as the rich involved themselves in guilt with less hesitation because they merely suffered exile, without any loss of property, he punished murderers of freemen by the confiscation of all their goods, as Cicero writes, and others by the loss of one-half.

He administered justice with the utmost conscientiousness and strictness. Those convicted of extortion he even dismissed from the senatorial order. He annulled the marriage of an ex-praetor, who had married a woman the very day after her divorce, although there was no suspicion of adultery. He imposed duties on foreign wares. He denied the use of litters and the wearing of scarlet robes or pearls to all except to those of a designated position and age, and on set days. In particular he enforced the law against extravagance, setting watchmen in various parts of the market, to seize and bring to him dainties which were exposed for sale in violation of the law; and sometimes he sent his lictors and soldiers to take from a dining-room any articles which had escaped the vigilance of his watchmen, even after they had been served.

In particular, for the adornment and convenience of the city, also for the protection and extension of the Empire, he formed more projects and more extensive ones every day: first of all, to rear a temple to Mars, greater than any in existence, filling up and levelling the pool in which he had exhibited the sea-fight, and to build a theatre of vast size, sloping down from the Tarpeian rock; to reduce the civil code to fixed limits, and of the vast and prolix mass of statutes to include only the best and most essential in a limited number of volumes; to open to the public the greatest possible libraries of Greek and Latin books, assigning to Marcus Varro the charge of procuring and classifying them; to drain the Pomptine marshes; to let out the water from Lake Fucinus; to make a highway from the Adriatic across the summit of the Apennines as far as the Tiber; to cut a canal through the Isthmus; to check the Dacians, who had poured into Pontus and Thrace; then to make war on the Parthians by way of Lesser Armenia, but not to risk a battle with them until he had first tested their mettle.

All these enterprises and plans were cut short by his death. But before I speak of that, it will not be amiss to describe briefly his personal appearance, his dress, his mode of life, and his character, as well as his conduct in civil and military life.

He is said to have been tall of stature, with a fair complexion, shapely limbs, a somewhat full face, and keen black eyes; sound of health, except that towards the end he was subject to sudden fainting fits and to nightmare as well. He was twice attacked by the falling sickness during his campaigns. He was somewhat overnice in the care of his person, being not only carefully trimmed and shaved, but even having superfluous hair plucked out, as some have charged; while his baldness was a disfigurement which troubled him greatly, since he found that it was often the subject of the gibes of his detractors. Because of it he used to comb forward his scanty locks from the crown of his head, and of all the honours voted him by the senate people there was none which he received or made use of more gladly than the privilege of wearing a laurel wreath at all times. They say, too, that he was remarkable in his dress; that he wore a senator's tunic with fringed sleeves reaching to the wrist, and always had a girdle over it, though rather a loose one; and this, they say, was the occasion of Sulla's *mot,* when he often warned the nobles to keep an eye on the ill-girt boy.

He lived at first in the Subura in a modest house, but after he became pontifex maximus, in the official residence of the Sacred Way. Many have written that he was very fond of elegance and luxury; that having laid the foundations of a country-house on his estate at Nemi and finished it at great cost, he tore it all down because it did not suit him in every particular, although at the time he was still poor and heavily in debt; and that he carried tessellated and mosaic floors about with him on his campaigns.

They say that he was led to invade Britain by the hope of getting pearls, and that in comparing their size he sometimes weighed them with his own hand; that he was always a most enthusiastic collector of gems, carvings, statues, and pic-

tures by early artists; also of slaves of exceptional figure and training at enormous prices, of which he himself was so ashamed that he forbade their entry in his accounts.

It is further reported that in the provinces he gave banquets constantly in two dining-halls, in one of which his officers or Greek companions, in the other Roman civilians and the more distinguished of the provincials reclined at table. He was so punctilious and strict in the management of his household, in small matters as well as in those of greater importance, that he put his baker in irons for serving him with one kind of bread and his guests with another; and he inflicted capital punishment on a favourite freedman for adultery with the wife of a Roman knight, although no complaint was made against him.

There was no stain on his reputation for chastity except his intimacy with King Nicomedes, but that was a deep and lasting reproach, which laid him open to insults from every quarter. I say nothing of the notorious lines of Licinius Calvus:

Whate'er Bithynia had, and Caesar's paramour.

I pass over, too, the invectives of Dolabella and the elder Curio, in which Dolabella calls him "the queen's rival, the inner partner of the royal couch," and Curio, "the brothel of Nicomedes and the stew of Bithynia." I take no account of the edicts of Bibulus, in which he posted his colleague as "the queen of Bithynia," saying that "of yore he was enamoured of a king, but now of a king's estate." At this same time, so Marcus Brutus declares, one Octavius, a man whose disordered mind made him somewhat free with his tongue, after saluting Pompey as "king" in a crowded assembly, greeted Caesar as "queen." But Gaius Memmius makes the direct charge that he acted as cup-bearer to Nicomedes with the rest of his wantons at a large dinner-party, and that among the guests were some merchants from Rome, whose names Memmius gives. Cicero, indeed, is not content with having written in sundry letters that Caesar was led by the king's attendants to the royal apartments, that he lay on a golden couch arrayed in purple, and that the virginity of this son of Venus was lost in Bithynia; but when Caesar was once addressing the senate in defence of Nysa, daughter of Nicomedes, and was enumerating his obligations to the king, Cicero cried: "No more of that, pray, for it is well known what he gave you, and what you gave him in turn." Finally, in his Gallic triumph his soldiers, among the bantering songs which are usually sung by those who follow the chariot, shouted these lines, which became a by-word:—

All the Gauls did Caesar vanquish,
  Nicomedes vanquished him:
Lo! now Caesar rides in triumph,
  victor over all the Gauls,
Nicomedes does not triumph, who
  subdued the conqueror.

That he was unbridled and extravagant in his intrigues is the general opinion, and that he seduced many illustrious women, among them Postumia, wife of Servius Sulpicius, Lollia, wife of Aulus Gabinius, Tertulla, wife of Marcus Crassus, and even Gnaeus Pompey's wife, Mucia. At all events there is no doubt that Pompey was taken to task by the elder and that younger Curio, as well as by many others, because through a desire for power he had afterwards married the daughter of a man on whose account he divorced a wife who had borne him three children, and whom he had often referred to with a groan as an Aegisthus. But beyond all others Caesar loved Servilla, the mother of Marcus Brutus, for whom in his first consulship he bought a pearl costing six million sesterces. During the civil war, too, besides other presents, he knocked down some fine estates to her in a public auction at a nominal price, and when some expressed their surprise at the low figure, Cicero wittily remarked: "It's a better bargain than you think, for there is a third off." And in fact it was thought that Servilla was prostituting her own daughter Tertia to Caesar.

That he did not refrain from intrigues in the provinces is shown in particular by this couplet, which was also shouted by the soldiers in his Gallic triumph:—

Men of Rome, keep close your
  consorts, here's a bald adulterer.
Gold in Gaul you spent in dalliance,
  which you borrowed here in Rome.

He had love affairs with queens too, including Eunoe the Moor, wife of Bogudes, on whom, as well as on her husband, he bestowed many splendid presents, as Naso writes; but above all with Cleopatra, with whom he often feasted until daybreak, and he would have gone through Egypt with her in her state-barge almost to Aethiopia, had not his soldiers refused to follow him. Finally he called her to Rome and did not let her leave until he had ladened her with high honours and rich gifts, and he allowed her to give his name to the child which she bore. In fact, according to certain Greek writers, this child was very like Caesar in looks and carriage. Mark Anthony declared to the senate that Caesar had really acknowledged the boy, and that Gaius Matius, Gaius Oppius, and other friends of Caesar knew this. Of these Gaius Oppius, as if admitting that the situation required apology and defence, published a book, to prove that the child whom Cleopatra fathered on Caesar was not his. Helvius Cinna, tribune of the commons, admitted to several that he had a bill drawn up in due form, which Caesar had ordered him to propose to the people in his absence, making it lawful for Caesar to marry what wives he wished, and as many as he wished, "for the purpose of begetting children." But to remove all doubt that he had an evil reputation for shameless vice and for adultery, I have only to add that the elder Curio in one of his speeches calls him "every woman's man and every man's woman."

That he drank very little wine not even his enemies denied. There is a saying of Marcus Cato that Caesar was the only man who undertook to overthrow the state when sober. Even in the matter of food Gaius Oppius tells us that he was so indifferent, that once when his host served stale oil instead of fresh, and the other guests would have none of it, Caesar partook even more plentifully than usual, not to seem to charge his host with carelessness or lack of manners.

Neither when in command of armies nor as a magistrate at Rome did he show a scrupulous integrity; for as certain men have declared in their memoirs, when he was proconsul in Spain, he not only begged money from the allies, to help pay his debts, but also attacked and sacked some towns of the Lusitanians although they did not refuse his terms and opened their gates to him on his arrival. In Gaul he pillaged shrines and temples of the gods filled with offerings, and oftener sacked towns for the sake of plunder than for any fault. In consequence he had more gold than he knew what to do with, and offered it for sale throughout Italy and the provinces at the rate of three thousand sesterces the pound. In his first consulship he stole three thousand pounds of gold from the Capitol, replacing it with the same weight of gilded bronze. He made alliances and thrones a matter of barter, for he extorted from Ptolemy alone in his own name and that of Pompey nearly six thousand talents, while later on he met the heavy expenses of the civil wars and of his triumphs and entertainments by the most barefaced pillage and sacrilege.

In eloquence and in the art of war he either equalled or surpassed the fame of their most eminent representatives. After his accusation of Dolabella, he was without question numbered with the leading advocates. At all events when Cicero reviews the orators in his *Brutus,* he says that he does not see to whom Caesar ought to yield the palm, declaring that his style is elegant as well as transparent, even grand and in a sense noble. Again in a letter to Cornelius Nepos he writes thus of Caesar: "Come now, what orator would you rank above him of those who have devoted themselves to nothing else? Who has cleverer or more frequent epigrams? Who is either more picturesque or more choice in diction?" He appears, at least in his youth, to have imitated the manner of Caesar Strabo, from whose speech entitled "For the Sardinians" he actually transferred some passages word for word to a trial address of his own. He is said to have delivered himself in a high-pitched voice with impassioned action and gestures, which were not without grace. He left several speeches, including some which are attributed to him on insufficient evidence. Augustus had good reason to think that the speech "For Quintus Metellus" was rather taken down by shorthand writers who could not keep pace with his delivery, than published by Caesar himself; for in some copies I find that even the title is not "For Metellus," but, "Which He Wrote for Metellus," although the discourse purports to be from Caesar's lips, defending Metellus and himself against the charges of their common detractors. Augustus also questions the authenticity of the address "To His Soldiers in Spain," although there are two sections of it, one purporting to have been spoken at the first battle, the other at the second, when Asinius Pollio writes that because of the sudden onslaught of the enemy he actually did not have time to make an harangue.

He left memoirs too of his deeds in the Gallic war and in the civil strife with Pompey; for the author of the Alexandrian, African, and Spanish Wars is unknown; some think it was Oppius, others Hirtius, who also supplied the final book of the Gallic War, which Caesar left unwritten. With regard to Caesar's memoirs Cicero, also in the *Brutus* speaks in the following terms: "He wrote memoirs which deserve the highest praise; they are naked in their simplicity, straightforward yet graceful, stripped of all rhetorical adornment, as of a garment; but while his purpose was to supply material to others, on which those who wished to write history might draw, he haply gratified silly folk, who will try to use the curling-irons on his narrative, but he has kept men of any sense from touching the subject." Of these same memoirs Hirtius uses this emphatic language: "They are so highly rated in the judgment of all men, that he seems to have deprived writers of an opportunity, rather than given them one; yet our admiration for this feat is greater than that of others; for they know how well and faultlessly he wrote, while we know besides how easily and rapidly he finished his task." Asinius Pollio thinks that they were put together somewhat carelessly and without strict regard for truth; since in many cases Caesar was too ready to believe the accounts which others gave of their actions, and gave a perverted account of his own, either designedly or perhaps from forgetfulness; and he thinks that he intended to rewrite and revise them. He left besides a work in two volumes "On Analogy," the same number of "Speeches Criticising Cato," in addition to a poem, entitled "The Journey." He wrote the first of these works while crossing the Alps and returning to his army from Hither Gaul, where he had held the assizes; the second about the time of the battle of Munda, and the third in the course of a twenty-four days' journey from Rome to Farther Spain. Some letters of his to the senate are also preserved, and he seems to have been the first to reduce such documents to pages and the form of a notebook, whereas previously consuls and generals sent their reports written right across the sheet. There are also letters of his to Cicero, as well as to his intimates on private affairs, and in the latter, if he had anything confidential to say, he wrote it in cipher, that is, by so changing the order of the letters of the alphabet, that not a word could be made out. If anyone wishes to decipher these, and get at their meaning, he must substitute the fourth letter of the alphabet, namely D, for A, and so with the others. We also have mention of certain writings of his boyhood and early youth, such as the "Praises of Hercules," a tragedy "Oedipus," and a "Collection of Apophthegms"; but Augustus forbade the publication of all these minor works in a very brief and frank letter sent to Pompeius Macer, whom he had selected to set his libraries in order.

He was highly skilled in arms and horsemanship, and of incredible powers of endurance. On the march he headed his army, sometimes on horseback, but oftener on foot, bareheaded both in the heat of the sun and in the rain. He covered great distances with incredible speed, making a hundred miles a day in a hired carriage and with little bag-

gage, swimming the rivers which barred his path or crossing them on inflated skins, and very often arriving before the messengers sent to announce his coming.

In the conduct of his campaigns it is a question whether he was more cautious or more daring, for he never led his army where ambuscades were possible without carefully reconnoitering the country, and he did not cross to Britain without making personal inquiries about the harbours, the course, and the approach to the island. But on the other hand, when news came that his camp in Germany was beleaguered, he made his way to his men through the enemies' pickets, disguised as a Gaul. He crossed from Brundisium to Dyrrachium in winter time, running the blockade of the enemy's fleets; and when the troops which he had ordered to follow him delayed to do so, and he had sent to fetch them many times in vain, at last in secret and alone he boarded a small boat at night with his head muffled up; and he did not reveal who he was, or suffer the helmsman to give way to the gale blowing in their teeth, until he was all but overwhelmed by the waves.

No regard for religion ever turned him from any undertaking, or even delayed him. Though the victim escaped as he was offering sacrifice, he did not put off his expedition against Scipio and Juba. Even when he had a fall as he disembarked, he gave the omen a favourable turn by crying: "I hold thee fast, Africa." Furthermore, to make the prophecies ridiculous which declared that the stock of the Scipios was fated to be fortunate and invincible in that province, he kept with him in camp a contemptible fellow belonging to the Cornelian family, to whom the nickname Salvito had been given as a reproach for his manner of life.

He joined battle, not only after planning his movements in advance but on a sudden opportunity, often immediately at the end of a march, and sometimes in the foulest weather, when one would least expect him to make a move. It was not until his later years that he became slower to engage, through a conviction that the oftener he had been victor, the less he ought to tempt fate, and that he could not possibly gain as much by success as he might lose by a defeat. He never put his enemy to flight without also driving him from his camp, thus giving him no respite in his panic. When the issue was doubtful, he used to send away the horses, and his own among the first, to impose upon his troops the greater necessity of standing their ground by taking away that aid to flight.

He rode a remarkable horse, too, with feet that were almost human; for its hoofs were cloven in such a way as to look like toes. This horse was foaled on his own place, and since the soothsayers had declared that it foretold the rule of the world for its master, he reared it with the greatest care, and was the first to mount it, for it would endure no other rider. Afterwards, too, he dedicated a statue of it before the temple of Venus Genetrix. . . .

Marcus Aurelius

No visitor to Rome who is interested in history and art should miss the magnificent bronze statue of Marcus Aurelius seated on a horse and gazing out over the city from the Capitoline hill. Although portrayed in the full majesty of a Roman emperor, the figure nevertheless conveys a feeling of understanding and compassion for the human condition. For Marcus, besides being emperor of Rome, was also a Stoic philosopher (see p. 191). About the statue Nathaniel Hawthorne has written (in *The Marble Faun*): "It is the most majestic representation of the kingly character that ever the world has seen." One account of the reason for its preservation is that during the Middle Ages it was believed to be a statue of the emperor Constantine (who had become a Christian), and therefore was not destroyed.

The nephew and adopted son of the emperor Antoninus Pius, Marcus (121–180) ascended to the purple on the death of Antoninus in the year 161. He is often referred to as the last of the "good emperors." Unfortunately, much of his reign was spent far from Rome on military campaigns along the borders of the empire in the Danube valley. During his campaigning on the frontier Marcus wrote his *Meditations.* Unlike Cicero, who embodied his Stoic philosophy in writings concerned with statecraft and law, Marcus turned his attention to the universal but personal problems of human life and fate. The *Meditations,* in which most of the major themes of Stoicism are affirmed, were probably not meant for publication but were rather simply a written soliloquy that Marcus held with himself, summing up his thoughts of each day. In reading the selection, do not forget that the author of these meditations was the emperor of Rome, the most powerful political figure in the Western world.

Meditations

BOOK II

1. Begin the morning by saying to yourself, "I shall meet with the busybody, the ungrateful, arrogant, deceitful, envious, unsocial." All of these things happen to them by reason of their ignorance of what is

Marcus Aurelius Antoninus, *Meditations,* trans. George Long. Minor changes have been made in the spelling and punctuation of the translation.

good and evil. But I who have seen the nature of the good that it is beautiful, and of the bad that it is ugly, and the nature of him who does wrong, that it is akin to me, not only of the same blood or seed, but that it participates in the same intelligence and the same portion of the divinity, I can neither be injured by any of them, for no one can fix on me what is ugly, nor can I be angry with my kinsman, nor hate him. For we are made for cooperation, like feet, like hands, like eyelids, like the rows of the upper and lower teeth. To act against one another then is contrary to nature; and it is acting against one another to be vexed and to turn away.

2. Whatever this is that I am, it is a little flesh and breath, and the ruling part. Throw away your books; no longer distract yourself; it is not allowed. But as if you were now dying, despise the flesh; it is blood and bones and a network, a contexture of nerves, veins, and arteries. See the breath also, what kind of a thing it is, air, and not always the same, but every moment sent out and again sucked in. The third then is the ruling part. Consider thus: You are an old man; no longer let this be a slave, no longer be pulled by the strings like a puppet to unsocial movements, no longer be either dissatisfied with your present lot, or shrink from the future.

3. All that is from the gods is full of providence. That which is from fortune is not separated from nature or without an interweaving and involution with the things which are ordered by providence. From thence all things flow; and there is besides necessity, and that which is for the advantage of the whole universe, of which you are a part. But that is good for every part of nature which the nature of the whole brings, and what serves to maintain this nature. Now the universe is preserved, as by the changes of the elements so by the changes of things compounded of the elements. Let these principles be enough for you, let them always be fixed opinions. But cast away the thirst after books, that you may not die murmuring, but cheerfully, truly, and from your heart thankful to the gods.

4. Remember how long you have been putting off these things, and how often you have received an opportunity from the gods, and yet do not use it. You must now at last perceive of what universe you are a part, and of what administrator of the universe your existence is an efflux, and that a limit of time is fixed for you, which if you do not use for clearing away the clouds from your mind, it will go and you will go, and it will never return.

5. Every moment think steadily as a Roman and a man to do what you have in hand with perfect and simple dignity, and feeling of affection, and freedom, and justice; and to give yourself relief from all other thoughts. And you will give yourself relief, if you do every act of your life as if it were the last, laying aside all carelessness and passionate aversion from the commands of reason, and all hypocrisy, and self-love, and discontent with the portion which has been given to you. You see how few the things are, the which if a man lays hold of, he is able to live a life which flows in quiet, and is like the existence of the gods; for the gods on their part will require

nothing more from him who observes these things.

. . .

7. Do the things external which fall upon you distract you? Give yourself time to learn something new and good, and cease to be whirled around. But then you must also avoid being carried about the other way. For those too are triflers who have wearied themselves in life by their activity, and yet have no object to which to direct every movements of their own minds must thoughts.

8. Though not observing what is in the mind of another a man has seldom been seen to be unhappy; but those who do not observe the movements of their own minds must of necessity be unhappy.

9. This you must always bear in mind, what is the nature of the whole, and what is my nature, and how this is related to that, and what kind of a part it is of what kind of a whole; and that there is no one who hinders you from always doing and saying the things which are according to the nature of that of which you are a part.

. . .

11. Since it is possible that you may depart from life this very moment, regulate every act and thought accordingly. But to go away from among men, if there are gods, is not a thing to be afraid of, for the gods will not involve you in evil; but if indeed they do not exist, or if they have no concern about human affairs, what is it to me to live in a universe devoid of gods or devoid of providence? But in truth they do exist, and they do care for human things, and they have put all the means in man's power to enable

him not to fall into real evils. And as to the rest, if there was anything evil, they would have provided for this also, that it should be altogether in a man's power not to fall into it. Now that which does not make a man worse, how can it make a man's life worse? But neither through ignorance, nor having the knowledge, but not the power to guard against or correct these things, is it possible that the nature of the universe has overlooked them; nor is it possible that it has made so great a mistake, either through want of power or want of skill, that good and evil should happen indiscriminately to the good and the bad. But death certainly, and life, honor and dishonor, pain and pleasure, all these things equally happen to good men and bad, being things which make us neither better nor worse. Therefore they are neither good nor evil.

12. How quickly all things disappear, in the universe the bodies themselves, but in time the remembrance of them; what is the nature of all sensible things, and particularly those which attract with the bait of pleasure, or terrify by pain, or are noised abroad by vapory fame; how worthless and contemptible, and sordid, and perishable, and dead they are—all this it is the part of the intellectual faculty to observe. To observe too who these are whose opinions and voices give reputation; what death is, and the fact that, if a man looks at it in itself, and by the abstractive power of reflection resolves into their parts all the things which present themselves to the imagination in it, he will then consider it to be nothing else than an operation of nature; and if anyone is afraid of an operation of na-

ture, he is a child. This, however, is not only an operation of nature, but it is also a thing which conduces to the purposes of nature. To observe too how man comes near to the deity, and by what part of him, and when this part of man is so disposed.

• • •

14. Though you should be going to live three thousand years, and as many times ten thousand years, still remember that no man loses any other life than this which he now lives, nor lives any other than this which he now loses. The longest and shortest are thus brought to the same. For the present is the same to all, though that which perishes is not the same; and so that which is lost appears to be a mere moment. For a man cannot lose either the past or the future; for what a man has not, how can anyone take this from him? These two things then you must bear in mind; the one, that all things from eternity are of like forms and come round in a circle, and that it makes no difference whether a man shall see the same things during a hundred years or two hundred, or an infinite time; and the second, that the longest liver and he who will die soonest lose just the same. For the present is the only thing of which a man can be deprived, if it is true that this is the only thing which he has, and that a man cannot lose a thing if he has it not.

• • •

16. The soul of man does violence to itself, first of all, when it becomes an abscess and, as it were, a tumor on the universe, so far as it can. For to be vexed at anything which happens is a separation of ourselves from nature, in some part

of which the natures of all other things are contained. In the next place, the soul does violence to itself when it turns away from any man, or even moves towards him with the intention of injuring, such as are the souls of those who are angry. In the third place, the soul does violence to itself when it is over-powered by pleasure or by pain. Fourthly, when it plays a part, and does or says anything insincerely and untruly. Fifthly, when it allows any act of its own and any movement to be without an aim, and does anything thoughtlessly and without considering what it is, it being right that even the smallest things be done with reference to an end; and the end of rational animals is to follow the reason and the law of the most ancient city and polity.

17. Of human life the time is a point, and the substance is in a flux, and the perception dull, and the composition of the whole body subject to putrefaction, and the soul a whirl, and fortune hard to divine, and fame a thing devoid of judgment. And, to say all in a word, everything which belongs to the body is a stream, and what belongs to the soul is a dream and vapor, and life is a warfare and a stranger's sojourn, and after-fame is oblivion. What then is that which is able to conduct a man? One thing and only one—philosophy. But this consists in keeping the spirit within a man free from violence and unharmed, superior to pains and pleasures, doing nothing without a purpose, nor yet falsely and with hypocrisy, not feeling the need of another man's doing or not doing anything; and besides, accepting all that happens and all that is allotted, as com-

ing from thence, wherever it is, from whence he himself came; and, finally, waiting for death with a cheerful mind, as being nothing else than a dissolution of the elements of which every living being is compounded. But if there is no harm to the elements themselves in each continually changing into another, why should a man have any apprehension about the change and dissolution of all the elements? For it is according to nature, and nothing is evil which is according to nature.

BOOK IV

3. Men seek retreats for themselves, houses in the country, seashores, and mountains; and you too are wont to desire such things very much. But this is altogether a mark of the most common sort of men, for it is in your power whenever you shall choose to retire into yourself. For nowhere either with more quiet or more freedom from trouble does a man retire than into his own soul, particularly when he has within him such thoughts that by looking into them he is immediately in perfect tranquillity; and I affirm that tranquillity is nothing else than the good ordering of the mind. Constantly then give to yourself this retreat, and renew yourself; and let your principles be brief and fundamental, which, as soon as you shall recur to them, will be sufficient to cleanse the soul completely, and to send you back free from all discontent with the things to which you return. For with what are you discontented? With the badness of men? Recall to your mind this conclusion, that rational animals exist for one an-

other, and that to endure is a part of justice, and that men do wrong involuntarily; and consider how many already, after mutual enmity, suspicion, hatred, and fighting, have been stretched dead, reduced to ashes; and be quiet at last. But perhaps you are dissatisfied with that which is assigned to you out of the universe. Recall to your recollection this alternative; either there is providence or atoms; or remember the arguments by which it has been proved that the world is a kind of political community. But perhaps corporeal things will fasten upon you. Consider then further that the mind mingles not with the breath, whether moving quietly or violently, when it has once drawn itself apart and discovered its own power, and think also of all that you have heard and assented to about pain and pleasure. But perhaps the desire of the thing called fame will torment you. See how soon everything is forgotten, and look at the chaos of infinite time on each side of the present, and the emptiness of applause, and the changeableness and want of judgment in those who pretend to give praise, and the narrowness of the space within which it is circumscribed. For the whole earth is a point, and how small a nook in it is this your dwelling, and how few are there in it, and what kind of people are they who will praise you.

This then remains: Remember to retire into this little territory of your own, and above all do not distract or strain yourself, but be free and look at things as a man, as a human being, as a citizen, as a mortal. But among the things readiest to your hand to which you shall turn, let there be these, which are two. One is that things do not touch the soul, for they are external and remain immovable; but our perturbations come only from the opinion which is within. The other is that all these things, which you see, change immediately and will no longer be; and constantly bear in mind how many of these changes you have already witnessed. The universe is transformation; life is opinion.

4. If our intellectual part is common to us, the reason also, in respect of which we are rational beings is common to us. If this is so, common also is the reason which commands us what to do and what not to do; if this is so, there is a common law also; if this is so, we are fellow-citizens; if this is so, we are members of some political community; if this is so, the world is in a manner a state. For of what other common political community will any one say that the whole human race are members? And from thence, from the common political community comes also our very intellectual faculty and reasoning faculty and our capacity for law; or whence do they come? For as my earthly part is a portion given to me from certain earth, and that which is watery from another element, and that which is hot and fiery from some peculiar source (for nothing comes out of that which is nothing, as nothing also returns to non-existence), so also the intellectual part comes from some source.

• • •

19. He who has a vehement desire for posthumous fame does not consider that everyone of those who remember him will himself also die very soon; then again also they who have succeeded them, until the whole remembrance shall have been extinguished as it is transmitted through men who foolishly admire and perish. But suppose that those who will remember are even immortal, and that the remembrance will be immortal, what then is this to you? And I say not what is it to the dead, but what is it to the living? What is praise, except indeed so far as it has a certain utility?

• • •

32. Consider, for example, the times of Vespasian. You will see all these things, people marrying, bringing up children, sick, dying, warring, feasting, trafficking, cultivating the ground, flattering, obstinately arrogant, suspecting, plotting, wishing for some to die, grumbling about the present, loving, heaping up treasure, desiring consulship, kingly power. Well then, that life of these people no longer exists at all. Again, remove to the times of Trajan. Again, all is the same. Their life too is gone. In like manner view also the other epochs of time and of whole nations, and see how many after great efforts soon fell and were resolved into the elements. But chiefly you should think of those whom you have yourself known distracting themselves about idle things, neglecting to do what was in accordance with their proper constitution, and to hold firmly to this and to be content with it. And herein it is necessary to remember that the attention given to everything has its proper value and proportion. For thus you will not be dissatisfied, if you apply yourself to smaller matters no further than is fit.

• • •

43. Time is like a river made up of the events which happen, and a violent stream; for as soon as a thing has been seen, it is carried away and another comes in its place, and this will be carried away too.

44. Everything which happens is as familiar and well known as the rose in spring and the fruit in summer; for such is disease, and death, and calumny, and treachery, and whatever else delights fools or vexes them.

• • •

48. Think continually how many physicians are dead after contracting their eyebrows over the sick; and how many astrologers after predicting with great pretensions the death of others; and how many philosophers after endless discourses on death or immortality; how many heroes after killing thousands; and how many tyrants who have used their power over men's lives with terrible insolence as if they were immortal; and how many cities are entirely dead, so to speak, Helice and Pompeii and Herculaneum, and others innumerable. Add to the reckoning all whom you have known, one after another. One man after burying another has been laid out dead, and another buries him; and all this in a short time. To conclude, always observe how ephemeral and worthless human things are, and what was yesterday a little mucus tomorrow will be a mummy or ashes. Pass then through this little space of time conformably to nature, and end your journey in content, just as an olive falls off when it is ripe, blessing nature who produced it, and thanking the tree on which it grew.

BOOK VI

13. When we have meat before us and such eatables, we receive the impression that this is the dead body of a fish, and this is the dead body of a bird or of a pig; and again, that this Falernian is only a little grape juice, and this purple robe some sheep's wool dyed with the blood of a shellfish. Such then are these impressions, and they reach the things themselves and penetrate them, and so we see what kind of things they are. Just in the same way ought we to act all through life, and where there are things which appear most worthy of our approbation we ought to lay them bare and look at their worthlessness and strip them of all the words by which they are exalted. For outward show is a wonderful perverter of the reason and when you are most sure that you are employed about things worth your pains, it is then that it cheats you most.

• • •

16. Neither is transpiration, as in plants, a thing to be valued, nor respiration, as in domesticated animals and wild beasts, nor the receiving of impressions by the appearances of things, nor being moved by desires as puppets by strings, nor assembling in herds, nor being nourished by food; for this is just like the act of separating and parting with the useless part of our food. What then is worth being valued? To be received with clapping of hands? No. Neither must we value the clapping of tongues, for the praise which comes from the many is a clapping of tongues. Sup-

pose then that you have given up this worthless thing called fame, what remains that is worth valuing? This, in my opinion—to move yourself and restrain yourself in conformity to your proper constitution, to which end both all employments and arts lead. For every art aims at this, that the thing which has been made should be adapted to the work for which it has been made; and both the vine-planter who looks after the vine, and the horse-breaker, and he who trains the dog, seek this end. But the education and the teaching of youth aim at something. In this then is the value of the education and the teaching. And if this is well, you will not seek anything else. Will you not cease to value many other things too? Then you will be neither free, nor sufficient for your own happiness, nor without passion. For of necessity you must be envious, jealous, and suspicious of those who can take away those things, and plot against those who have that which you value. Of necessity a man must be altogether in a state of perturbation who wants any of these things; and besides, he must often find fault with the gods. But to reverence and honor your own mind will make you content with yourself, and in harmony with society, and in agreement with the gods, that is, praising all that they give and have ordered.

• • •

30. Take care that you are not made into a Caesar, that you are not dyed with this dye; for such things happen. Keep yourself then simple, good, pure, serious, free from affectation, a friend of justice, a worshipper of the gods, kind, affectionate, strenuous in all proper acts. Strive to continue to be such as philosophy wished to make you. Reverence the gods, and help men. Life is short. There is only one fruit of this life, a pious disposition and social acts. Do everything as a disciple of Antoninus [uncle of Marcus Aurelius and Roman emperor, 138–161]. Remember his constancy in every act which was conformable to reason, and his evenness in all things, and his piety, and the serenity of his countenance, and his sweetness, and his disregard of empty fame, and his efforts to understand things; and how he would never let anything pass without having first most carefully examined it and clearly understood it; and how he bore with those who blamed him unjustly without blaming them in return; how he did nothing in a hurry; and how he listened not to calumnies, and how exact an examiner of manners and actions he was; and not given to reproach people, nor timid, nor suspicious, nor a sophist; and with how little he was satisfied, such as lodging, bed, dress, food, servants; and how laborious and patient; and how he was able on account of his sparing diet to hold out to the evening, not even requiring to relieve himself by any evacuations except at the usual hour; and his firmness and uniformity in his friendship; and how he tolerated freedom of speech in those who opposed his opinions; and the pleasure that he had when any man showed him anything better; and how religious he was without superstition. Imitate all this that you may have as good a conscience, when your last hour comes, as he had.

• • •

44. If the gods have determined about me and about the things which must happen to me, they have determined well, for it is not easy even to imagine a duty without forethought; and as to doing me harm, why should they have any desire towards that? For what advantage would result to them from this or to the whole, which is the special object of their providence? But if they have not determined about me individually, they have certainly determined about the whole at least, and the things which happen by way of sequence in this general arrangement I ought to accept with pleasure and to be content with them. But if they determine about nothing—which it is wicked to believe, or if we do believe it, let us neither sacrifice nor pray nor swear by them nor do anything else which we do as if the gods were present and lived with us—but if however the gods determine about none of the things which concern us, I am able to determine about myself, and I can inquire about that which is useful; and that is useful to every man which is conformable to his own constitution and nature. But my nature is rational and social, and my city and country, so far as I am Antoninus, is Rome, but so far as I am a man, it is the world. The things then which are useful to these cities are alone useful to me.

The New Testament

In the province of Judaea, tucked away in a far corner of the Roman Empire, was born midway through the reign of Augustus a man whose influence on world history was far to surpass that of the *princeps*—Jesus of Nazareth. We have chosen from the New Testament selections illustrating the teachings of Jesus and the early history and theological doctrines of his followers. From the Gospel of St. Matthew comes the Sermon on the Mount, the most complete and one of the most beautiful statements of the religious views of Jesus. The Acts is a historical book detailing the activities of the founders of the Christian church in the years immediately following the crucifixion of Christ, as seen through the eyes of the early church fathers several years later. Of crucial importance to Western history is the transformation of Christianity from the exclusive possession of an obscure Jewish sect into a message of salvation open to Gentiles as well as to Jews. This was the first step on Christianity's long road to religious domination of the Western world. The selection from Romans contains a statement of Christian doctrine by the Apostle Paul, one of the most influential of all Christian theologians. It was Paul who began the task of developing the teachings of Jesus into an organized and consistent body of theological doctrine.

The cornerstone of Paul's doctrine is the theory of original sin, with its related concepts of predestination, election, and grace. Originated by Paul, elaborated by St. Augustine in the fifth century, and reiterated by the Protestant reformer John Calvin in the sixteenth century, the doctrine of original sin is of fundamental importance in the history of Christian theology. Although of lesser significance, the notion of justification by faith, also included in the selection from Romans, has had a long history. It is associated particularly with the Protestant theology of Martin Luther. The New Testament selections have been taken from the King James Version of the Bible, with slight alterations in form.

St. Matthew

And seeing the multitudes, he went up into a mountain: And when he was set, his disciples came unto him: And he opened his mouth, and taught them, saying, "Blessed are the poor in spirit: for theirs is the kingdom of heaven. Blessed are they that mourn: for they shall be comforted. Blessed are the meek: for they shall inherit the earth. Blessed are they which do hunger and thirst after righteousness: for they shall be filled. Blessed are the merciful: for they shall obtain mercy. Blessed are the pure in heart: for they shall see God. Blessed are the peacemakers: for they shall be called the children of God. Blessed are they which are persecuted for righteousness' sake: for theirs is the kingdom of heaven. Blessed are ye, when men shall revile you, and persecute you, and shall say all manner of evil against you falsely, for my sake. Rejoice, and be exceeding glad: for great is your reward in heaven: for so persecuted they the prophets which were before you.

"Ye are the salt of the earth: but if the salt have lost his savour, wherewith shall it be salted? It is thenceforth good for nothing, but to be cast out, and to be trodden under foot of men. Ye are the light of the world. A city that is set on a hill cannot be hid. Neither do men light a candle, and put it under a bushel, but on a candlestick; and it giveth light unto all that are in the house. Let your light so shine before men, that they may see your good works, and glorify your Father which is in heaven.

"Think not that I am come to destroy the law, or the prophets: I am not come to destroy, but to fulfil. For verily I say unto you, till heaven and earth pass, one jot or one tittle shall in no wise pass from the law, till all be fulfilled. Whosoever therefore shall break one of these least commandments, and shall teach men so, he shall be called the least in the kingdom of heaven: but whosoever shall do and teach them, the same shall be called great in the kingdom of heaven. For I say unto you, that except your righteousness shall exceed the righteousness of the scribes and Pharisees, ye shall in no case enter into the kingdom of heaven.

"Ye have heard that it was said by them of old time, Thou shalt not kill; and whosoever shall kill shall be in danger of the judgment. But I say unto you, That whosoever is angry with his brother without a cause shall be in danger of the judgment: and whosoever shall say to his brother, 'Ra-ca,' shall be in danger of the council: but whosoever shall say, 'Thou fool,' shall be in danger of hell fire. Therefore if thou bring thy gift to the altar, and there rememberest that thy brother hath ought against thee; leave there thy gift before the altar, and go thy way; first be reconciled to thy brother, and then come and offer

Chapters 5, 6, 7.

thy gift. Agree with thine adversary quickly, whiles thou art in the way with him; lest at any time the adversary deliver thee to the judge, and the judge deliver thee to the officer, and thou be cast into prison. Verily I say unto thee, Thou shalt by no means come out thence, till thou hast paid the uttermost farthing.

"Ye have heard that it was said by them of old time, Thou shalt not commit adultery. But I say unto you, That whosoever looketh on a woman to lust after her hath committed adultery with her already in his heart. And if thy right eye offend thee, pluck it out, and cast it from thee: for it is profitable for thee that one of thy members should perish, and not that thy whole body should be cast into hell. And if thy right hand offend thee, cut it off, and cast it from thee: for it is profitable for thee that one of thy members should perish, and not that thy whole body should be cast into hell. It hath been said, Whoever shall put away his wife, let him give her a writing of divorcement. But I saw unto you, That whosoever shall put away his wife, saving for the cause of fornication, causeth her to commit adultery: and whosoever shall marry her that is divorced committeth adultery.

"Again, ye have heard that it hath been said by them of old time, Thou shalt not forswear thyself, but shalt perform unto the Lord thine oaths. But I say unto you, Swear not at all; neither by heaven; for it is God's throne: nor by the earth; for it is his footstool: neither by Jerusalem; for it is the city of the great King. Neither shalt thou swear by thy head, because thou canst not make one hair white or black. But let your communication be, Yea, yea; Nay, nay: for whatsoever is more than these cometh of evil.

"Ye have heard that it hath been said, An eye for an eye, and a tooth for a tooth. But I say unto you, That ye resist not evil: but whosoever shall smite thee on thy right cheek, turn to him the other also. And if any man will sue thee at the law, and take away thy coat, let him have thy cloke also. And whosoever shall compel thee to go a mile, go with him twain. Give to him that asketh thee, and from him that would borrow of thee turn not thou away.

"Ye have heard that it hath been said, Thou shalt love thy neighbor, and hate thine enemy. But I say unto you, Love your enemies, bless them that curse you, do good to them that hate you, and pray for them which despitefully use you, and persecute you; that ye may be the children of your Father which is in heaven: for he maketh his sun to rise on the evil and on the good, and sendeth rain on the just and on the unjust. For if ye love them which love you, what reward have ye? Do not even the publicans the same? And if ye salute your brethren only, what do ye more than others? Do not even the publicans so? Be ye therefore perfect, even as your Father which is in heaven is perfect.

"Take heed that ye do not your alms before men, to be seen of them: otherwise ye have no reward of your Father which is in heaven. Therefore when thou doest thine alms; do not sound a trumpet before thee, as the hypocrites do in the synagogues and in the streets, that they may have glory of men. Verily I say unto you, they have their reward. But when thou doest alms, let not thy left hand know what thy right hand doeth: that thine alms may be in secret: and thy Father which seeth in secret himself shall reward thee openly.

"And when thou prayest, thou shalt not be as the hypocrites are: for they love to pray standing in the synagogues and in the corners of the streets, that they may be seen of men. Verily I say unto you, They have their reward. But thou, when thou prayest, enter into thy closet, and when thou hast shut thy door, pray to thy Father which is in secret: and thy Father which seeth in secret shall reward thee openly. But when ye pray, use not vain repetitions, as the heathen do: for they think that they shall be heard for their much speaking. Be not ye therefore like unto them: for your father knoweth what things ye have need of, before ye ask him. After this manner therefore pray ye: Our Father which art in heaven, hallowed be thy name. Thy kingdom come. Thy will be done in earth, as it is in heaven. Give us this day our daily bread. And forgive us our debts, as we forgive our debtors. And lead us not into temptation, but deliver us from evil: For thine is the kingdom, and the power, and the glory, for ever. A-men.

"For if ye forgive men their trespasses, your heavenly Father will also forgive you: But if ye forgive not men their trespasses, neither will your father forgive your trespasses.

"Moreover when ye fast, be not, as the hypocrites, of a sad countenance: for they disfigure their faces, that they may appear unto men to fast. Verily I say unto you, They have their reward. But thou, when thou fastest, anoint thine head, and wash thy face; that thou appear not unto men to fast, but unto thy Father which is in secret: and thy Father, which seeth in secret, shall reward thee openly.

"Lay not up for yourselves, treasures upon earth, where moth and rust doth corrupt, and where thieves break through and steal. But lay up for yourselves treasures in heaven, where neither moth nor rust doth corrupt, and where thieves do not break through nor steal: For where your treasure is, there will your heart be also. The light of the body is the eye: if therefore thine eye be single thy whole body shall be full of light. But if thine eye be evil, thy whole body shall be full of darkness. If therefore the light that is in thee be darkness, how great is that darkness!

"No man can serve two masters: for either he will hate the one, and love the other; or else he will hold to the one, and despise the other. Ye cannot serve God and mammon. Therefore I say unto you, Take no thought for your life, what ye shall eat, or what ye shall drink; nor yet for your body, what ye shall put on. Is not the life more than meat, and the body than raiment? Behold the fowls of the air: for they sow not, neither do they reap, nor gather into barns; yet your heavenly Father feedeth them. Are ye not much better than they? Which of you by taking thought can add one cubit unto his stature? And why take ye thought for raiment? Consider the lilies of the field, how they grow; they toil not, neither do they spin: And yet I say unto you, That even Solomon in all his glory was not arrayed like one of these. Wherefore, if God so clothe the grass of the field, which today is, and tomorrow is cast into the oven, shall he not much more clothe you, O ye of little faith? Therefore take no thought, saying, What shall we eat? or, What shall we drink? or, Wherewithal shall we be clothed? (For after all these things do the Gentiles seek:) for your heavenly Father knoweth that ye have need of all these things. But seek ye first the kingdom of God, and his righteousness; and all these things shall be added unto you. Take therefore no thought for the morrow: for the morrow shall take thought for the things of itself. Sufficient unto the day is the evil thereof.

"Judge not, that ye be not judged. For with what judgment ye judge, ye shall be judged: and with what measure ye mete, it shall be measured to you again. And why beholdest thou the mote that is in thy brother's eye, but considerest not the beam that is in thine own eye? Or how wilt thou say to thy brother, Let me pull out the mote out of thine eye; and, behold, a beam is in thine own eye? Thou hypocrite, first cast out the beam out of thine own eye; and then shalt thou see clearly to cast out the mote out of thy brother's eye.

"Give not that which is holy unto the dogs, neither cast ye your pearls before swine, lest they trample them under their feet, and turn again and rend you.

"Ask, and it shall be given you; seek, and ye shall find; knock, and it shall be opened unto you: For every one that asketh receiveth; and he that seeketh findeth; and to him that knocketh it shall be opened. Or what man is there of you, whom if his son ask bread, will he give him a stone? Or if he ask a fish, will he give him a serpent? If ye then, being evil, know how to give good gifts unto your children, how much more shall your Father which is in heaven give good things to them that ask him? Therefore all things whatsoever ye would that men should do to you, do ye even so to them: for this is the law and the prophets.

"Enter ye in at the strait gate: for wide is the gate, and broad is the way, that leadeth to destruction, and many there be which go in thereat: Because strait is the gate, and narrow is the way, which leadeth unto life, and few there be that find it.

"Beware of false prophets, which come to you in sheep's clothing, but inwardly they are ravening wolves. Ye shall know them by their fruits. Do men gather grapes of thorns, or figs of thistles? Even so every good tree bringeth forth good fruit; but a corrupt tree bringeth forth evil fruit. A good tree cannot bring forth evil fruit, neither can a corrupt tree bring forth good fruit. Every tree that bringeth not forth good fruit is hewn down, and cast into the fire. Wherefore by their fruits ye shall know them.

"Not every one that saith unto me, Lord, Lord, shall enter into the kingdom of heaven; but he that doeth the will of my Father which is in heaven. Many will say to me in that day, Lord, Lord, have we not prophesied in thy name? And in thy name have cast out devils? And in thy name done many wonderful works? And then will I profess unto them, I never knew you; depart from me, ye that work iniquity.

"Therefore whosoever heareth these sayings of mine, and doeth them I will liken him unto a wise man, which built his house upon a rock: And the rain descended, and the floods came, and the winds blew, and beat upon that house and it fell not: for it was founded upon a rock. And every one that heareth these sayings of mine, and doeth them not, shall be likened unto a foolish man, which built his house upon the sand: And the rain descended, and the floods came, and the winds blew, and beat upon that house; and it fell: and great was the fall of it." And it came to pass, when Jesus had ended these sayings, the people were astonished at his doctrine: For he taught them as one having authority, and not as the scribes.

The Acts of the Apostles

The former treatise have I made, O Theophilus, of all that Jesus began both to do and teach, until the day in which he was taken up, after that he through the Holy Ghost had given commandments unto the apostles whom he had chosen. To whom also he shewed himself alive after his passion by many infallible proofs, being seen of them forty days, and speaking of the things pertaining to the kingdom of God: And, being assembled together with them, commanded them that they should not depart from Jerusalem, but wait for the promise of the Father, which, saith he, ye have heard of me. For John truly baptized with water; but ye shall be baptized with the Holy Ghost not many days hence.

When they therefore were come together, they asked of him, saying, "Lord, wilt thou at this time restore again the kingdom to Israel?" And he said unto them, "It is not for you to know the times or the seasons, which the Father hath put in his own power. But ye shall receive power, after that the Holy Ghost is come upon you: and ye shall be witnesses unto me both in Jerusalem, and in all Judaea, and in Samaria, and unto the uttermost part of the earth." And when he had spoken these things, while they beheld, he was taken up; and a cloud received him out of their sight. And while they looked stedfastly toward heaven as he went up, behold, two men stood by them in white apparel; which also said, "Ye men of Galilee, why stand ye gazing up into heaven? This same Jesus, which is taken up from you into heaven, shall so come in like manner as ye have seen him go unto heaven." Then returned they unto Jerusalem from the mount called Olivet, which is from Jerusalem a sabbath day's journey.

And when the day of Pentecost was fully come, they were all with one accord in one place. And suddenly there came a sound from heaven as of a rushing mighty wind, and it filled all the house where they were sitting. And there appeared

Chapters 1:1–12; 2:1–41; 6:7–15; 7:1–2, 51–60; 8:1–3; 9:1–22; 10.

unto them cloven tongues like as of fire, and it sat upon each of them. And they were all filled with the Holy Ghost, and began to speak with other tongues, as the Spirit gave them utterance. And there were dwelling at Jerusalem Jews, devout men, out of every nation under heaven. Now when this was noised abroad, the multitude came together, and were confounded, because that every man heard them speak in his own language. And they were all amazed and marvelled, saying one to another, "Behold, are not all these which speak Galilaeans? And how hear we every man in our own tongue, wherein we were born? Parthians, and Medes, and Elamites, and the dwellers in Mesopotamia, and in Judaea, and Cappadocia, in Pontus, and Asia. Phrygia, and Pamphylia, in Egypt, and in the parts of Libya about Cyrene, and strangers of Rome, Jews and proselytes, Cretes and Arabians, we do hear them speak in our tongues the wonderful works of God." And they were all amazed, and were in doubt, saying one to another, "What meaneth this?" Others mocking said, "These men are full of new wine."

But Peter, standing up with the eleven, lifted up his voice, and said unto them, "Ye men of Judaea, and all ye that dwell at Jerusalem, be this known unto you, and hearken to my words: For these are not drunken, as ye suppose, seeing it is but the third hour of the day. But this is that which was spoken by the prophet Joel; 'And it shall come to pass in the last days,' saith God, 'I will pour out of my Spirit upon all flesh: and your sons and your daughters shall prophesy, and your young men shall see visions, and your old men shall dream dreams:

And on my servants and on my handmaidens I will pour out in those days of my Spirit; and they shall prophesy. And I will shew wonders in heaven above, and signs in the earth beneath; blood, and fire, and vapour of smoke: The sun shall be turned into darkness, and the moon into blood, before the great and notable day of the Lord come. And it shall come to pass, that whosoever shall call on the name of the Lord shall be saved.' Ye men of Israel, hear these words; Jesus of Nazareth, a man approved of God among you by miracles and wonders and signs, which God did by him in the midst of you, as ye yourselves also know: Him, being delivered by the determinate counsel and foreknowledge of God, ye have taken, and by wicked hands have crucified and slain: Whom God hath raised up, having loosed the pains of death: because it was not possible that he should be holden of it. For David speaketh concerning him, 'I foresaw the Lord always before my face, for he is on my right hand, that I should not be moved. Therefore did my heart rejoice, and my tongue was glad; moreover also my flesh shall rest in hope: Because thou wilt not leave my soul in hell, neither wilt thou suffer thine Holy One to see corruption. Thou hast made known to me the ways of life; thou shalt make me full of joy with thy countenance.' Men and brethren, let me freely speak unto you of the patriarch David, that he is both dead and buried, and his sepulchre is with us unto this day. Therefore being a prophet, and knowing that God had sworn with an oath to him, that of the fruit of his loins, according to the flesh, he would raise up Christ to sit on his throne; he seeing this before spake of the resurrection of Christ, that his soul was not left in hell neither his flesh did see corruption. Thus Jesus hath God raised up, whereof we all are witnesses. Therefore being by the right hand of God exalted, and having received of the Father the promise of the Holy Ghost, he hath shed forth this, which ye now see and hear. For David is not ascended into the heavens: but he saith himself, 'The LORD said unto my Lord, "Sit thou on my right hand, until I make thy foes thy footstool." ' Therefore let all the houses of Israel know assuredly, that God hath made that same Jesus, whom ye have crucified, both Lord and Christ."

Now when they heard this, they were pricked in their heart, and said unto Peter and to the rest of the apostles, "Men and brethren, what shall we do?" Then Peter said unto them, "Repent, and be baptized every one of you in the name of Jesus Christ for the remission of sins, and ye shall receive the gift of the Holy Ghost. For the promise is unto you, and to your children, and to all that are afar off, even as many as the Lord our God shall call." And with many other words did he testify and exhort, saying, "Save yourselves from this untoward generation."

Then they that gladly received his word were baptized; and the same day there were added unto them about three thousand souls.

· · ·

And the word of God increased; and the number of the disciples multiplied in Jerusalem greatly; and a great company of the priests were obedient to the faith. And Stephen, full of faith and power, did great wonders and miracles among the people.

Then there arose certain of the synagogue, which is called the synagogue of the Libertines, and Cyrenians, and Alexandrians, and of them of Cilicia and of Asia, disputing with Stephen. And they were not able to resist the wisdom and the spirit by which he spake. Then they suborned men, which said, "We have heard him speak blasphemous words against Moses, and against God." And they stirred up the people, and the elders, and the scribes, and came upon him, and caught him, and brought him to the council, and set up false witnesses, which said, "This man ceaseth not to speak blasphemous words against this holy place, and the law: For we have heard him say that this Jesus of Nazareth shall destroy this place, and shall change the customs which Moses delivered us." And all that sat in the council, looking stedfastly on him, saw his face as it had been the face of an angel.

Then said the high priest, "Are these things so?" And he said, "Men, brethren, and fathers, hearken: [*After defending himself by an appeal to the Old Testament, Stephen concludes*] Ye stiffnecked and uncircumcised in heart and ears, ye do always resist the Holy Ghost: as your fathers did, so do ye. Which of the prophets have not your fathers persecuted? And they have slain them which shewed before of the coming of the Just One; of whom ye have been now the betrayers and murderers: who have received the law by the disposition of angels, and have not kept it."

When they heard these things, they were cut to the heart, and they gnashed on him with their teeth. But he, being full of the Holy Ghost, looked up stedfastly into heaven, and saw the glory of God, and Jesus standing on the right hand of God, and said, "Behold, I see the heavens opened, and the Son of man standing on the right hand of God." Then they cried out with a loud voice, and stopped their ears, and ran upon him with one accord, and cast him out of the city, and stoned him: and the witnesses laid down their clothes at a young man's feet, whose name was Saul. And they stoned Stephen, calling upon God, and saying, "Lord Jesus, receive my spirit." And he kneeled down, and cried with a loud voice, "Lord, lay not this sin to their charge." And when he had said this, he fell asleep.

And Saul was consenting unto his death. And at that time there was a great persecution against the church which was at Jerusalem; and they were all scattered abroad throughout the regions of Judaea and Samaria, except the apostles. And devout men carried Stephen to his burial, and made great lamentation over him. As for Saul, he made havoc of the church, entering into every house, and haling men and women committed them to prison.

. . .

And Saul, yet breathing out threatenings and slaughter against the disciples of the Lord, went unto the high priest, and desired of him letters to Damascus to the synagogues, that if he found any of this way, whether they were men or women, he might bring them bound unto Jerusalem. And as he journeyed, he came near Damascus: and suddenly there shined round about him a light from heaven. And

he fell to the earth, and heard a voice saying unto him, "Saul, Saul, why persecutest thou me?" And he said, "Who art thou, Lord?" And the Lord said, "I am Jesus whom thou persecutest: it is hard for thee to kick against the pricks." And he trembling and astonished said, "Lord, what wilt thou have me to do?" And the Lord said unto him, "Arise, and go into the city, and it shall be told thee what thou must do." And the men which journeyed with him stood speechless, hearing a voice, but seeing no man. And Saul arose from the earth; and when his eyes were opened he saw no man: but they led him by the hand, and brought him into Damascus. And he was three days without sight, and neither did eat nor drink.

And there was a certain disciple at Damascus, named Ananias; and to him said the Lord in a vision, "Ananias." And he said, "Behold, I am here, Lord." And the Lord said unto him, "Arise, and go into the street which is called Straight, and enquire in the house of Judas for one called Saul, of Tarsus: for, behold, he prayeth, and hath seen in a vision, a man named Ananias coming in, and putting his hand on him, that he might receive his sight." Then Ananias answered, "Lord, I have heard by many of this man, how much evil he hath done to thy saints at Jerusalem: And here he hath authority from the chief priests to bind all that call on thy name." But the Lord said unto him, "Go thy way: for he is a chosen vessel unto me, to bear my name before the Gentiles, and kings, and the children of Israel: For I will shew him how great things he must suffer for my name's sake." And Ananias went his way and entered into the house; and putting his hands on him said, "Brother Saul, the Lord, even Jesus, that appeared unto thee in the way as thou camest, hath sent me, that thou mightest receive thy sight, and be filled with the Holy Ghost." And immediately there fell from his eyes as it had been scales: and he received sight forthwith, and arose, and was baptized. And when he had received meat, he was strengthened.

Then was Saul certain days with the disciples which were at Damascus. And straightway he preached Christ in the synagogues, that he is the Son of God. But all that heard him were amazed, and said; "Is not this he that destroyed them which called on this name in Jerusalem, and came hither for that intent, that he might bring them bound unto the chief priests?" But Saul increased the more in strength, and confounded the Jews which dwelt at Damascus, proving that this is very Christ.

· · ·

There was a certain man in Caesarea called Cornelius, a centurion of the band called the Italian band. A devout man, and one that feared God with all his house, which gave much alms to the people, and prayed to God always. He saw in a vision evidently about the ninth hour of the day an angel of God coming in to him, and saying unto him, "Cornelius." And when he looked on him, he was afraid, and said, "What is it, Lord?" And he said unto him, "Thy prayers and thine alms are come up for a memorial before God. And now send men to Joppa, and call for one Simon, whose surname is Peter: He lodgeth with one Simon a tanner,

whose house is by the sea side: he shall tell thee what thou oughtest to do." And when the angel which spake unto Cornelius was departed, he called two of his household servants, and a devout soldier of them that waited on him continually; and when he had declared all these things unto them, he sent them to Joppa.

On the morrow, as they went on their journey, and drew nigh into the city, Peter went up upon the housetop to pray about the sixth hour. And he became very hungry, and would have eaten: but while they made ready, he fell into a trance, and saw heaven opened, and a certain vessel descending unto him, as it had been a great sheet knit at the four corners, and let down to the earth: wherein were all manner of four-footed beasts of the earth, and wild beasts, and creeping things, and fowls of the air. And there came a voice to him, "Rise, Peter; kill, and eat." But Peter said, "Not so, Lord; for I have never eaten any thing that is common or unclean." And the voice spake unto him again the second time, "What God hath cleansed, that call not thou common." This was done thrice: and the vessel was received up again into heaven. Now while Peter doubted in himself what this vision which he had seen should mean, behold, the men which were sent from Cornelius had made enquiry for Simon's house, and stood before the gate, and called, and asked whether Simon, which was surnamed Peter, were lodged there.

While Peter thought on the vision, the Spirit said unto him, "Behold, three men seek thee. Arise therefore, and get thee down, and go with them, doubting nothing:

for I have sent them." Then Peter went down to the men which were sent unto him from Cornelius; and said, "Behold, I am he whom ye seek: what is the cause wherefore ye are come?" And they said, "Cornelius the centurion, a just man, and one that feareth God, and of good report among all the nation of the Jews, was warned from God by an holy angel to send for thee into his house, and to hear words of thee." Then called he them in, and lodged them. And on the morrow Peter went away with them, and certain brethren from Joppa accompanied him. And the morrow after they entered into Caesarea. And Cornelius waited for them, and had called together his kinsmen and near friends. And as Peter was coming in, Cornelius met him, and fell down at his feet, and worshipped him. But Peter took him up, saying, "Stand up; I myself also am a man." And as he talked with him, he went in, and found many that were come together. And he said unto them, "Ye know how that it is an unlawful thing for a man that is a Jew to keep company, or come unto one of another nation; but God hath shewed me that I should not call any man common or unclean. Therefore came I unto you without gainsaying, as soon as I was sent for: I ask therefore for what intent ye have sent for me?" And Cornelius said, "Four days ago I was fasting until this hour; and at the ninth hour I prayed in my house, and, behold, a man stood before me in bright clothing. And said, 'Cornelius, thy prayer is heard, and thine alms are had in remembrance in the sight of God. Send therefore to Joppa, and call hither Simon, whose surname is Peter; he is lodged in the house of

one Simon a tanner by the sea side: who, when he cometh, shall speak unto thee.' Immediately therefore I sent to thee; and thou hast well done that thou art come. Now therefore are we all here present before God, to hear all things that are commanded thee of God."

Then Peter opened his mouth, and said, "Of a truth I perceive that God is no respecter of persons: But in every nation he that feareth him, and worketh righteousness, is accepted with him. The word which God sent unto the children of Israel, preaching peace by Jesus Christ (He is Lord of all:) That word, I say, ye know, which was published throughout all Judaea, and began from Galilee, after the baptism which John preached; how God anointed Jesus of Nazareth with the Holy Ghost and with power: who went about doing good, and healing all that were oppressed of the devil; for God was with him. And we are witnesses of all things which he did both in the land of the Jews, and in Jerusalem; whom they slew and hanged on a tree: Him God raised up the third day, and shewed him openly; not to all the people, but unto witnesses chosen before of God, even to us, who did eat and drink with him after he rose from the dead. And he commanded us to preach unto the people, and to testify that it is he which was ordained of God to be the Judge of quick and dead. To him give all the prophets witness, that through his name whosoever believeth in him shall receive remission of sins."

While Peter yet spake these words, the Holy Ghost fell on all them which heard the word. And they of the circumcision which believed were astonished, as many as came with Peter, because that on the Gentiles also was poured out the gift of the Holy Ghost. For they heard them speak with tongues, and magnify God. Then answered Peter, "Can any man forbid water, that these should not be baptized, which have received the Holy Ghost as well as we?" And he commanded them to be baptized in the name of the Lord.

The Epistle of Paul the Apostle to the Romans

• • •

As it is written, There is none righteous, no, not one: There is none that understandeth, there is none that seeketh after God. They are all gone out of the way, they are together become unprofitable; there is none that doeth good, no, not one. Their throat is an open sepulchre; with their tongues they have used deceit; the poison of asps is under their lips: Whose mouth is full of cursing and bitterness: Their feet are swift to shed blood: Destruction and misery are in their ways: And the way of peace have they not known: There is no fear of God before their eyes.

Now we know that what things soever the law saith, it saith to them who are under the law: that every mouth may be stopped, and all the world may become guilty before God. Therefore by the deeds of the law there shall no flesh be justified in his sight: for by the law is the knowledge of sin. But now the righteousness of God without the law is manifested, being witnessed by the law and the prophets; even the righteousness of God which is by faith of Jesus Christ unto all and upon all them that believe: for there is no difference. For all have sinned, and come short of the glory of God; being justified freely by his grace through the redemption that is in Christ Jesus: Whom God hath set forth to be a propitiation through faith in his blood, to declare his righteousness for the remission of sins that are past, through the forbearance of God; to declare, I say, at this time his righteousness: that he might be just, and the justifier of him which believeth in Jesus. Where is boasting then? It is excluded. By what law? or works? Nay: but by the law of faith. Therefore we conclude that a man is justified by faith without the deeds of the law. Is he the God of the Jews only? Is he not also of the Gentiles? Yes, of the Gentiles also: Seeing it is one God, which shall justify the circumcision by faith, and uncircumcision through faith. Do we then make void the law through faith? God forbid: yea, we establish the law.

• • •

Therefore being justified by faith, we have peace with God through our Lord Jesus Christ: By whom also we have access by faith into this grace wherein we stand, and rejoice in hope of the glory of God.

Chapters 3:10–31; 5:6; 9:8–21.

And not only so, but we glory in tribulations also: knowing that tribulation worketh patience; and patience, experience; and experience, hope: And hope maketh not ashamed; because the love of God is shed abroad in our hearts by the Holy Ghost which is given unto us. For when we were yet without strength, in due time Christ died for the ungodly. For scarcely for a righteous man will one die: yet peradventure for a good man some would even dare to die. But God commandeth his love toward us, in that, while we were yet sinners, Christ died for us. Much more then, being now justified by his blood, we shall be saved from wrath through him. For if, when we were enemies, we were reconciled to God by the death of his Son, much more, being reconciled, we shall be saved by his life. And not only so, but we also joy in God through our Lord Jesus Christ, by whom we have now received the atonement.

Wherefore, as by one man sin entered into the world, and death by sin; and so death passed upon all men, for that all have sinned. (For until the law sin was in the world: but sin is not imputed when there is no law. Nevertheless death reigned from Adam to Moses, even over them that had not sinned after the similitude of Adam's transgression, who is the figure of him that was to come. But not as the offence, so also is the free gift. For if through the offence of one many be dead, much more the grace of God, and the gift by grace, which is by one man, Jesus Christ, hath abounded unto many. And not as it was by one that sinned, so is the gift: for the judgment was by one to condemnation, but the free gift is of many offences unto justification. For if by one man's offence death reigned by one; much more they which receive abundance of grace and of the gift of righteousness shall reign in life by one, Jesus Christ.) Therefore as by the offence of one judgment came upon all men to condemnation; even so, by the righteousness of one the free gift came upon all men unto justification of life. For as by one man's disobedience many were made sinners, so by the obedience of one shall many be made righteous. Moreover the law entered, that the offence might abound. But where sin abounded, grace did much more abound: That as sin hath reigned unto death, even so might grace reign through righteousness unto eternal life by Jesus Christ our Lord.

What shall we say then? Shall we continue in sin, that grace may abound? God forbid. How shall we, that are dead to sin, live any longer therein? Know ye not, that so many of us as were baptized into Jesus Christ were baptized into his death? Therefore we are buried with him by baptism into death: that like as Christ was raised up from the dead by the glory of the Father, even so we also should walk in newness of life. For if we have been planted together in the likeness of his death, we shall be also in the likeness of his resurrection: Knowing this, that our old man is crucified with him, that the body of sin might be destroyed, that henceforth we should not serve sin. For he that is dead is freed from sin. Now if we be dead with Christ, we believe that we shall also live with him: Knowing that Christ being raised from the dead dieth no more; death hath no more dominion over him.

For in that he died, he died unto sin once: but in that he liveth, he liveth unto God. Likewise reckon ye also yourselves to be dead indeed unto sin, but alive unto God through Jesus Christ our Lord.

Let not sin therefore reign in your mortal body, that ye should obey it in the lusts thereof. Neither yield ye your members as instruments of unrighteousness unto sin: but yield yourselves unto God, as those that are alive from the dead, and your members as instruments of righteousness unto God. For sin shall not have dominion over you: for ye are not under the law, but under grace. What then? Shall we sin, because we are not under the law, but under grace? God forbid. Know ye not, that to whom ye yield yourselves servants to obey, his servants ye are to whom ye obey; whether of sin unto death, or of obedience unto righteousness? But God be thanked, that ye were the servants of sin, but ye have obeyed from the heart that form of doctrine which was delivered you. Being then made free from sin, ye became the servants of righteousness.

I speak after the manner of men because of the infirmity of your flesh: for as ye have yielded your members servants to uncleanness and to iniquity unto iniquity; even so now yield your members servants to righteousness unto holiness. For when ye were the servant of sin, ye were free from righteousness. What fruit had ye then in those things whereof ye are now ashamed? For the end of those things is death. But now being made free from sin, and become servants of God, ye have your fruit unto holiness, and the end everlasting life. For the wages of sin is death; but the gift of God is eternal life through Jesus Christ our Lord.

· · ·

They which are the children of the flesh, these are not the children of God: but the children of the promise are counted for the seed. For this is the word of promise. At this time will I come, and Sarah shall have a son. And not only this; but when Rebecca also had conceived by one, even by our father Isaac; (for the children being not yet born, neither having done any good or evil, that the purpose of God according to election might stand, not of works, but of him that calleth): it was said unto her, The elder shall serve the younger. As it is written, Jacob have I loved, but Esau have I hated. What shall we say then? Is there unrighteousness with God? God forbid. For he saith to Moses, I will have mercy on whom I will have mercy, and I will have compassion on whom I will have compassion. So then it is not of him that willeth, nor of him that runneth, but of God that sheweth mercy. For the scripture saith unto Pharaoh, Even for this same purpose have I raised thee up, that I might shew my power in thee, and that my name might be declared throughout all the earth. Therefore hath he mercy on whom he will have mercy, and whom he will he hardeneth. Thou wilt say then unto me, Why doth ye yet find fault? For who hath resisted his will? Nay but, O man, who art thou that repliest against God? Shall the thing formed say to him that formed it, Why hast thou made me thus? Hath not the potter power over the clay, of the same lump to make one vessel unto honour, and another unto dishonour?

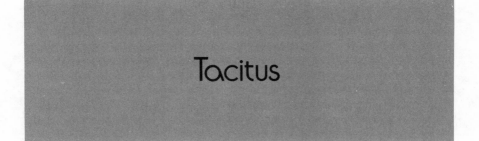

Tacitus

Probably the best way to introduce the following treatise is simply to acknowledge it to be what it really is—a sermon written for the edification of the Roman reading public. Tacitus described the customs and manners of the tribes of Germany, not to show the threat these people formed to the security and stability of the Roman Empire, but rather to contrast their barbarian freedom and simple lives with the decadence and servility of the upper classes of first century A.D. Rome. Tacitus longed to see the virtues of the old Republican society reestablished so that Rome itself could escape the creeping decline he thought he sensed in the imperial system.

Tacitus' reasons for writing the sermon on Germany may be found in his biography. He was born into a prominent Roman family, probably of senatorial rank, around the year A.D. 55. Much of his life was spent in public service under the emperors Vespasian, Titus, and Domitian. The "reign of terror" which took place in the last three years of Domitian's reign profoundly moved Tacitus. Domitian was frightened of conspiracies against his life, so he instituted an almost systematic plan aimed at the extermination of all those who had plotted against him. Then this plan was extended to include all who might someday plot against him. Tacitus, who sat in the senate which condemned to death many of the finest Romans of the time, felt himself and his colleagues degraded by their servility and acquiescence to these judicial murders. His work on Germany was a product of these circumstances.

Tacitus died about A.D. 120, after a long and distinguished career in both the literary world and the world of affairs.

A Treatise on the Situation, Manners, and Inhabitants of Germany

Germany is separated from Gaul, Rhaetia, and Pannonia, by the rivers Rhine and Danube; from Sarmatia and Dacia, by mountains and mutual dread. The rest is surrounded by an ocean, embracing broad promontories and vast insular tracts, in which our military expedi-

The Oxford translation, revised (London, 1854).

tions have lately discovered various nations and kingdoms. The Rhine, issuing from the inaccessible and precipitous summit of the Rhaetic Alps, bends gently to the west, and falls into the Northern Ocean. The Danube, poured from the easy and gently-raised ridge of Mount Abnoba, visits several nations in its course, till at length it bursts out by six channels into the Pontic sea: a seventh is lost in marshes.

The people of Germany appear to me indigenous, and free from intermixture with foreigners, either as settlers or casual visitants. For the emigrants of former ages performed their expeditions not by land, but by water; and that immense, and, if I may so call it, hostile ocean, is rarely navigated by ships from our world. Then, besides the dangers of a boisterous and unknown sea, who would relinquish Asia, Africa, or Italy, for Germany, a land rude in its surface, rigorous in its climate, cheerless to every beholder and cultivator, except a native? In their ancient songs, which are their only records or annals, they celebrate the god Tuisto, sprung from the earth, and his son Mannus, as the fathers and founders of their race. To Mannus they ascribe three sons, from whose names the people bordering on the ocean are called Ingaevones; those inhabiting the central parts, Herminones; the rest, Istaevones. Some, however, assuming the licence of antiquity, affirm that there were more descendants of the god, from whom more appellations were derived; as those of the Marsi, Gambrivii, Suevi, and Vandali; and that these are the genuine and original names. That of Germany, on the other hand, they assert to be a modern addition; for that the people who first crossed the Rhine, and expelled the Gauls, and are now called Tungri, were then named Germans; which appellation of a particular tribe, not of a whole people, gradually prevailed; so that the title of Germans, first assumed by the victors in order to excite terror, was afterwards adopted by the nation in general. They have likewise the tradition of a Hercules of their country, whose praises they sing before those of all other heroes as they advance to battle.

A peculiar kind of verses is also current among them, by the recitation of which, termed "barding," they stimulate their courage; while the sound itself serves as an augury of the event of the impending combat. For, according to the nature of the cry proceeding from the line, terror is inspired or felt: nor does it seem so much an articulate song, as the wild chorus of valour. A harsh, piercing note, and a broken roar, are the favourite tones; which they render more full and sonorous by applying their mouths to their shields. Some conjecture that Ulysses, in the course of his long and fabulous wanderings, was driven into the ocean, and landed in Germany, and that Asciburgium, a place situated on the Rhine, and at this day inhabited, was founded by him, and named 'Aoki vpylov. They pretend that an altar was formerly discovered here, consecrated to Ulysses, with the name of his father Laertes subjoined; and that certain monuments and tombs, inscribed with Greek characters, are still extant upon the confines of Germany and Rhaetia. These allegations I shall neither attempt to confirm nor to refute: let every one believe concerning them as he is disposed.

I concur in opinion with those who deem the Germans never to have intermarried with other nations; but to be a race, pure, unmixed, and stamped with a distinct character. Hence a family likeness pervades the whole, though their numbers are so great: eyes stern and blue; ruddy hair, large bodies, powerful in sudden exertions, but impatient of toil and labour, least of all capable of sustaining thirst and heat. Cold and hunger they are accustomed by their climate and soil to endure.

The land, though varied to a considerable extent in its aspect, is yet universally shagged with forests, or deformed by marshes: moister on the side of Gaul, more bleak on the side of Noricum and Pannonia. It is productive of grain, but unkindly to fruit-trees. It abounds in flocks and herds, but in general of a small breed. Even the beeve kind are destitute of their usual stateliness and dignity of head: they are, however, numerous, and form the most esteemed, and, indeed, the only species of wealth. Silver and gold the gods, I know not whether in their favour or anger, have denied to this country. Not that I would assert that no veins of these metals are generated in Germany; for who has made the search? The possession of them is not coveted by these people as it is by us. Vessels of silver are indeed to be seen among them, which have been presented to their ambassadors and chiefs; but they are held in no higher estimation than earthenware. The borderers, however, set a value on gold and silver for the purposes of commerce, and have learned to distinguish several kinds of our coin, some of which they prefer to others: the remoter inhabitants continue the more simple and ancient usage of bartering commodities. The money preferred by the Germans is the old and well-known species, such as the Serrati and Bigati. They are also better pleased with silver than gold; not on account of any fondness for that metal, but because the smaller money is more convenient in their common and petty merchandise.

Even iron is not plentiful among them; as may be inferred from the nature of their weapons. Swords or broad lances are seldom used; but they generally carry a spear (called in their language framea), which has an iron blade, short and narrow, but so sharp and manageable, that, as occasion requires, they employ it either in close or distant fighting. This spear and a shield are all the armour of the cavalry. The foot have, besides, missile weapons, several to each man, which they hurl to an immense distance. They are either naked, or lightly covered with a small mantle; and have no pride in equipage: their shields only are ornamented with the choicest colours. Few are provided with a coat of mail; and scarcely here and there one with a casque or helmet. Their horses are neither remarkable for beauty nor swiftness, nor are they taught the various evolutions practiced with us. The cavalry either bear down straightforwards, or wheel once to the right, in so compact a body that none is left behind the rest. Their principal strength, on the whole, consists in their infantry, hence in an engagement these are intermixed with the cavalry; so well accordant with the nature of equestrian combats is the agility of those foot soldiers, whom they select from the whole body of their youth, and place in the front of the line. Their number, too, is determined; a hundred from each canton: and they are distinguished at home by a name expressive of this circumstance; so that what at first was only an appellation of number, becomes thenceforth a title of honour. Their line of battle is disposed in wedges. To give ground, provided they rally again, is considered rather as a prudent stratagem, than cowardice. They carry off their slain even while the battle remains undecided. The greatest disgrace that can befall them is to have abandoned their shields. A person branded with this ignominy is not permitted to join in their religious rites, or enter their assemblies, so that many, after escaping from battle, have put an end to their infamy by the halter.

In the election of kings they have regard to birth; in that of generals, to valour. Their kings have not an absolute or unlimited power; and their generals command less through the force of authority, than of example. If they are daring, adventurous, and conspicuous in action, they procure obedience from the admiration they inspire. None, however, but the priests are permitted to judge offenders to inflict bonds or stripes; so that chastisement appears not as an act of military discipline, but as the instigation of the god whom they suppose present with warriors. They also carry with them to battle certain images and standards taken from the sacred groves. It is a principal incentive to their courage, that their squadrons and battalions are not formed by men fortuitously collected, but by the assemblages of families and clans. Their pledges also are near at hand; they have within hearing the yells of their women, and the cries of their children. These, too, are revered witnesses of each man's conduct, these his most liberal applauders. To their mothers and their wives they bring their wounds for relief, nor do these dread to count or to search out the gashes. The women also administer food and encouragement to those who are fighting.

Tradition relates, that armies beginning to give way have been rallied by the females, through the earnestness of their supplications, the interposition of their bodies, and the pictures they have drawn of impending slavery, a calamity which these people bear with more impatience for their women than themselves; so that those states who have been obliged to give among their hostages the daughters of noble families, are the most effectually bound to fidelity. They even suppose somewhat of sanctity and prescience to be inherent in the female sex; and therefore neither despise their counsels, nor disregard their responses. We have beheld, in the reign of Vespasian, Veleda, long reverenced by many as a deity. Aurima, moreover, and several others, were formerly held in equal veneration, but not with a servile flattery, nor as though they made them goddesses.

Of the gods, Mercury is the principal object of their adoration; whom, on certain days, they think it lawful to propitiate even with human victims. To Hercules and Mars they offer the animals usually allotted for sacrifice. Some of the Suevi also perform sacred rites to Isis. What was the cause and origin of this foreign worship, I have not been able to discover; further than that her being represented with the symbol of a galley, seems to indicate an imported religion. They conceive it unworthy the grandeur of celestial beings to confine their deities within walls, or to represent them under a human similitude: woods and groves are their temples; and they affix names of divinity to that secret power, which they behold with the eye of adoration alone.

No people are more addicted to divination by omens and lots. The latter is performed in the following simple manner. They cut a twig from a fruit-tree, and divide it into small pieces, which, distinguished by certain marks, are thrown promiscuously upon a white garment. Then, the priest of the canton, if the occasion be public; if private, the master of the family; after an invocation of the gods, with his eyes lifted up to heaven, thrice takes out each piece, and, as they come up, interprets their signification according to the marks fixed upon them. If the result proves unfavourable, there is no more consultation on the same affair that day; if propitious, a confirmation by omens is still required. In common with other nations, the Germans are acquainted with the practice of auguring from the notes and flight of birds; but it is peculiar to them to derive admonitions and presages from horses also. Certain of these animals, milk-white, and untouched by earthly labour, are pastured at the public expense in the sacred woods and groves. These, yoked to a consecrated chariot, are accompanied by the priest, and king, or chief person of the community, who attentively observe their manner of neighing and snorting; and no kind of augury is more credited, not only among the populace, but among the nobles and priests. For the latter consider themselves as the ministers of the gods, and the horses, as privy to the divine will. Another kind of divination, by which they explore the event of momentous wars, is to oblige a prisoner, taken by any means whatsoever from the nation with whom they are at variance, to fight with a picked man of their own, each with his own country's arms; and, according as the victory falls, they presage success to the one or to the other party.

On affairs of smaller moment, the chiefs consult; on those of greater importance, the whole community; yet with this circumstance, that which is referred to the decision of the people, is first maturely discussed by the chiefs. They assemble, unless upon some sudden emergency, on stated days, either at the new or full moon, which they account the most auspicious season for beginning any enterprise. Nor do they, in their computation of time, reckon, like us, by the number of days, but of nights. In this way they arrange their business; in this way they fix their appointments; so that, with them, the night seems to lead the day. An inconvenience produced by their liberty is, that they do not all assemble at a stated time, as if it were in obedience to a command; but two or three days are lost in the delays of convening. When they all think fit, they sit down armed. Silence is proclaimed by the priests, who have on this occasion a coercive power. Then the king, or chief, and such others as are conspicuous for age, birth, military renown, or eloquence, are heard; and gain attention rather from their ability to persuade, than their authority to command. If a proposal displeases, the assembly rejects it by an inarticulate murmur; if it proves agreeable, they clash their javelins, for the most honourable expression of assent among them is the sound of arms.

Before this council, it is likewise allowed to exhibit accusations, and to prosecute capital offences. Punishments are varied according to the nature of the crime. Traitors and deserters are hung upon trees: cowards, dastards, and those guilty of unnatural practices, are suffocated in mud under a hurdle. This difference of punishment has in view the principle, that villainy should be exposed while it is punished, but turpitude concealed. The penalties annexed to slighter offences are also proportioned to the delinquency. The convicts are fined in horses and cattle: part of the mulct goes to the king or state; part to the injured person, or his relations. In the same assemblies chiefs are also elected, to administer justice through the cantons and districts. A hundred companions, chosen from the people, attend upon each of them, to assist them as well with their advice as their authority.

The Germans transact no business, public or private, without being armed; but it is not customary for any person to assume arms till the state has approved his ability to use them. Then, in the midst of the assembly, either one of the chiefs, or the father, or a relation, equips the youth with a shield and javelin. These are to them the manly gown; this is the first honour conferred on youth: before this they are considered as part of a household, afterwards, of the state. The dignity of chieftain is bestowed even on mere lads, whose descent is eminently illustrious, or whose fathers have performed signal services to the public; they are associated, however, with those of mature strength, who have already been declared capable of service; nor do they blush to be seen in the rank of companions. For the state of companionship itself has its several degrees, determined by the judgment of him whom they follow; and there is a great emulation among the companions, which shall possess the highest place in the favour of their chief; and among the chiefs, which shall excel in the number and valour of his companions. It is their dignity, their strength, to be always surrounded with a large body of select youth, an ornament in peace, a bulwark in war. And not in his own country alone, but among the neighbouring states, the fame and glory of each chief consists in being distinguished for the number and bravery of his companions. Such chiefs are courted by embassies; distinguished by presents; and often by their reputation alone decide a war.

In the field of battle, it is disgraceful for the chief to be surpassed in valour; it is disgraceful for the companions not to equal their chief; but it is reproach and infamy during a whole succeeding life to retreat from the field surviving him. To aid, to protect him; to place their own gallant actions to the account of his glory, is their first and most sacred engagement. The chiefs fight for victory; the companions for their chief. If their native country be long sunk in peace and inaction, many of the young nobles repair to some other state then engaged in war. For, besides that repose is unwelcome to their race, and toils and perils afford them a better opportunity of distinguishing themselves; they are unable, without war and violence, to maintain a large train of followers. The companion requires from the liberality of his chief, the warlike steed, the bloody and conquering spear: and in place of pay, he expects to be supplied with a table, homely indeed, but plentiful. The funds for this munificence must be found in war and rapine; nor are they so easily persuaded to cultivate the earth, and await the produce of the seasons, as to challenge the foe, and expose themselves to wounds, nay, they even think it base and spiritless to earn by sweat what they might purchase with blood.

During the intervals of war, they pass their time less in hunting than in a sluggish repose, divided between sleep and the table. All the bravest of the warriors, committing the care of the house, the family affairs, and the lands, to the women, old men, and weaker part of the domestics, stupify themselves in inaction: so wonderful is the contrast presented by nature, that the same persons love indolence, and hate tranquillity! It is customary for the several states to present, by voluntary and individual contributions, cattle or grain to their chiefs, which are accepted as honorary gifts, while they serve as necessary supplies. They are peculiarly pleased with presents from neighbouring nations, offered not only by individuals, but by the community at large; such as fine horses, heavy armour, rich housings, and gold chains. We have now taught them also to accept of money.

It is well known that none of the German nations inhabit cities, or even admit of contiguous settlements. They dwell scattered and separate, as a spring, a meadow, or a grove may chance to invite them. Their villages are laid out, not like ours in rows of adjoining buildings, but every one surrounds his house with a vacant space, either by way of security against fire, or through ignorance of the art of building. For, indeed, they are unacquainted with the use of mortar and tiles; and for every purpose employ rude unshapen timber, fashioned with no regard to pleasing the eye. They bestow more than ordinary pains on coating certain parts of their buildings with a kind of earth, so pure and shining that it gives the appearance of painting. They also dig subterraneous caves, and cover them over with a great quantity of dung. These they use as winter-retreats, and granaries; for they preserve a moderate temperature; and upon an invasion, when the open country is plundered, these recesses remain unviolated, either because the enemy is ignorant of them, or because he will not trouble himself with the search.

The clothing common to all is a sagum fastened by a clasp, or, in want of that, a thorn. With no other covering, they pass whole days on the hearth, before the fire. The more wealthy are distinguished by a vest, not flowing loose, like those of the Sarmatians and Parthians, but girt close, and exhibiting the shape of every limb. They also wear the skins of beasts, which the people near the borders are less curious in selecting or preparing than the more remote inhabitants, who cannot by commerce procure other clothing. These make choice of particular skins, which they variegate with spots, and strips of the furs of marine animals, the produce of the exterior ocean, and seas to us unknown. The dress of the women does not differ from that of the men; except that they more frequently wear linen, which they stain with purple, and do not lengthen their upper garment into sleeves, but leave exposed the whole arm, and part of the breast.

The matrimonial bond is, nevertheless, strict and severe among them; nor is there anything in their manners more commendable than this. Almost singly among the barbarians, they content themselves with one wife; a very few of them excepted, who, not through incontinence, but because their alliance is solicited on account of their rank, practice polygamy. The wife does not bring a dowry to her husband, but receives one from him. The parents and relations assemble, and pass their approbation on the presents—presents not adapted to please a female taste, or decorate the bride; but oxen, a caparisoned steed, a shield, spear, and sword. By virtue of these, the wife is espoused, and she in turn makes a present of some arms to her husband. This they consider as the firmest bond of union; these, the sacred mysteries, the conjugal deities. That the woman may not think herself excused from exertions or fortitude, or exempt from the casualties of war, she is admonished by the very ceremonial of her marriage, that she comes to her husband as a partner in toils and dangers; to suffer and to dare equally with him, in peace and in war: this is indicated by the yoked oxen, the harnessed steed, the offered arms. Thus she is to live; thus to die. She receives what she is to return inviolate and honoured to her children; what her daughters-in-law are to receive, and again transmit to her grandchildren.

They live, therefore, fenced around with chastity; corrupted by no seductive spectacles, no convivial incitements. Men and women are alike unacquainted with clandestine correspondence. Adultery is extremely rare among so numerous a people. Its punishment is instant, and at the pleasure of the husband. He cuts off the hair of the offender, strips her, and in presence of her relations expels her from his house, and pursues her with stripes through the whole village. Nor is any indulgence shown to a prostitute. Neither beauty, youth, nor riches can procure her a husband; for none there looks on vice with a smile, or calls mutual seduction the way of the world. Still more exemplary is the practice of those states in which none but virgins marry, and the expectations and wishes of a wife are at once brought to a period. Thus, they take one husband as one body and one life; that no thought, no desire, may extend beyond him; and he may be loved not only as their husband, but as their marriage. To limit the increase of children, or put to death any of the later progeny, is accounted infamous: and good habits have there more influence than good laws elsewhere.

In every house the children grow up, thinly and meanly clad, to that bulk of body and limb which we behold with wonder. Every mother suckles her own children, and does not deliver them into the hands of servants and nurses. No indulgence distinguishes the young master from the slave. They lie together amidst the same cattle, upon the same ground, till age separates, and valour marks out, the freeborn. The youths partake late of the pleasures of love, and hence pass the age of puberty unexhausted: nor are the virgins hurried into marriage; the same maturity, the same full growth, is required: the sexes unite equally matched, and robust: and the children inherit the vigour of their parents. Children are regarded with equal affection by their maternal uncles as by their fathers: some even consider this as the more sacred bond of consanguinity, and prefer it in the requisition of hostages, as if it held the mind by a firmer tie, and the family by a more extensive obligation. A person's own children, however, are his heirs and successors; and no wills are made. If there be no children, the next in order of inheritance are brothers, paternal and maternal uncles. The more numerous are a man's relations and kinsmen, the more comfortable is his old age; nor is it here any advantage to be childless.

It is an indispensable duty to adopt the enmities of a father or relation, as well as their friendships: these, however, are not irreconcilable or perpetual. Even homicide is atoned by a certain fine in cattle and sheep; and the whole family accepts the satisfaction, to the advantage of the public weal, since quarrels are most dangerous in a free state. No people are more addicted to social entertainments, or more liberal in the exercise of hospitality. To refuse any person whatever admittance under their roof, is accounted flagitious. Every one according to his ability feasts his guest: when his provisions are exhausted, he who was late the host, is now the guide and companion to another hospitable board. They enter the next house uninvited, and are received with equal cordiality. No one makes a distinction with respect to the rights of hospitality, between a stranger and an acquaintance. The departing guest is presented with whatever he may ask for; and with the same freedom a boon is desired in return. They are pleased with presents; but think an obligation incurred either when they give or receive.

[Their manner of living with their guests is easy and affable.] As soon as they arise from sleep, which they generally protract till late in the day, they bathe, usually in warm water, as cold weather chiefly prevails there. After bathing they take their meal, each on a distinct seat, and at a separate table. Then they proceed, armed, to business; and not less frequently to convivial parties, in which it is no disgrace to pass days and nights, without intermission, in drinking. The frequent quarrels that rise amongst them, when intoxicated, seldom terminate in abusive language, but more frequently in blood. In their feasts, they generally deliberate on the reconcilement of enemies, on family alliances, on the appointment of chiefs, and finally on peace and war; conceiving that at no time the soul is more opened to sincerity, or warmed to heroism. These people, naturally void of artifice or disguise, disclose the most secret emotions of their hearts in the freedom of festivity. The minds of all being thus displayed without reserve, the subjects of their deliberation are again canvassed the next day; and each time has its advantages. They consult when unable to dissemble; they determine when not liable to mistake.

Their drink is a liquor prepared from barley or wheat brought by fermentation to a certain resemblance of wine. Those who border on the Rhine also purchase wine. Their food is simple, wild fruits, fresh venison, or coagulated milk. They satisfy hunger without seeking the elegances and delicacies of the table. Their thirst for liquor is not quenched with equal moderation. If their propensity to drunkenness be gratified to the extent of their wishes, intemperance proves as effectual in subduing them as the force of arms.

They have only one kind of public spectacle, which is exhibited in every company. Young men, who make it their diversion, dance naked amidst drawn swords and presented spears. Practice has conferred skill at this exercise, and skill has given grace; but they do not exhibit for hire or gain: the only reward of this pastime, though a hazardous one, is the pleasure of the spectators. What is extraordinary, they play at dice, when sober, as a serious business: and that with such a desperate venture of gain or loss, that, when everything else is gone, they set their liberties and persons on the last throw. The loser goes into voluntary servitude; and, though the youngest and strongest, patiently suffers himself to be bound and sold. Such is their obstinacy in a bad practice—they themselves call it honour. The slaves thus acquired are exchanged away in commerce, that the winner may get rid of the scandal of his victory.

The rest of their slaves have not, like ours, particular employments in the family allotted them. Each is the master of a habitation and household of his own. The lord requires from him a certain quantity of grain, cattle, or cloth, as from a tenant, and so far only the subjection of the slave extends. His domestic offices are performed by his own wife and children. It is usual to scourge a slave, or punish him with chains or hard labour. They are sometimes killed by their masters; not through severity of chastisement, but in the heat of passion, like an enemy; with the difference, that it is done with impunity. Freedmen are little superior to slaves; seldom filling any important office in the family; never in the state, except in those tribes which are under regal government. There, they rise above the free-born, and even the nobles: in the rest, the subordinate condition of the freedmen is a proof of freedom.

Lending money upon interest, and increasing it by usury, is unknown amongst them: and this ignorance more effectually prevents the practice than a prohibition would do. The lands are occupied by townships, in allotments proportional to the number of cultivators; and are afterwards parcelled out among the individuals of the district, in shares according to the rank and condition of each person. The wide extent of plain facilitates this partition. The arable lands are annually changed, and a part left fallow; nor do they attempt to make the most of the fertility and plenty of the soil, by their own industry in planting orchards, inclosing meadows, and watering gardens. Corn is the only product required from the earth: hence their year is not divided into so many seasons as ours; for, while they know and distinguish by name Winter, Spring, and Summer, they are unacquainted equally with the appellation and bounty of Autumn.

Their funerals are without parade. The only circumstance to which they attend, is to burn the bodies of eminent persons with some particular kinds of wood. Neither vestments nor perfumes are heaped upon the pile: the arms of the deceased, and sometimes his horse, are given to the flames; the tomb is a mound of turf. They condemn the elaborate and costly honours of monumental structures, as mere burthens to the dead. They soon dismiss tears and lamentations; slowly, sorrow and regret. They think it the women's part to bewail their friends, the men's to remember them.

· · ·

Medieval life in town and country. (*Culver Pictures, Inc.*)

The Middle Ages

When we look back from the twentieth century to the Middle Ages, we are confronted with countless difficulties and contradictions. At times the medieval period seems to have been an age of unrelieved violence and warfare, of treachery, intrigue, and bloodshed. At other times the thousand years from 400 to 1400 seem to have been an "Age of Faith"—an age in which Western man sought to relate human life on earth both to God and to man's eternal destiny. A third impression is that the Middle Ages was a time when society sought stability and security above all else.

It is difficult to reconcile these three impressions, and perhaps it is futile to try. In a sense, they are all valid; the Middle Ages was bloody, *and* religious, *and* stable. To try to resolve all this diversity into a perfectly understandable whole would be to fall under the criticism of the historian who claimed that "history is a chaos upon which historians impose a pattern."

Yet we can attempt to understand the principles and ideals that were accepted and professed by medieval society. For one segment of the population (roughly one-sixth) the world centered around military life—a life dedicated to concepts of honor, justice, bravery, strength, skill, and loyalty. For another segment (roughly one-tenth) the world centered around a concern for the souls of men. To the friars, the priests, and the clerics, this life was transient and unreal, and only the life hereafter had any real meaning. For the rest of the people who lived during the Middle Ages (certainly the vast majority of the population) life was simply a matter of accepting the four seasons, hard work, the need to cultivate the soil, the dictates of the Church, and the demands of the military caste.

Ideally, every element of the social order had its clearly defined function, which suggests that the Middle Ages at least tried to maintain a stability in which every man could lead his life in peace, although perhaps not in plenty. But since stability is a difficult ideal to realize, let alone to maintain, the corollary was control over all elements that might tend to disturb the established way of life. The Church tried (though not very successfully) to eliminate the constant fighting of the feudal class by decreeing the Truce and Peace of God which forbade warfare at certain times. The feudal structure itself was designed to define the rank and station of all its members. A knight swore oaths of allegiance and fidelity to a lord and "became his man"; he was obliged to support his lord against enemies, to protect the lord's family, and to serve at the lord's court. In return, the lord granted lands to his vassal and guaranteed him military protection and knightly station. The lands granted were called the "fief" or "feodum" (whence feudalism), and they were actually worked by serfs. The fief was composed of one or more estates called "manors"; there, too, a mutual contractual obligation existed between the lord of the manor and the serf. In return for military protection the serf accepted the jurisdiction of the lord's court, contracted to work a fixed number of days for the lord, and agreed to pay fixed rents to the lord, of the type listed in the *Surveys of Certain Manors Belonging to the Abbey of Peterborough.* Legally the serf could not leave the manor without the consent of the lord, but also (and most importantly) the serf could not be put off the land, nor could the fixed rents be raised. In short, the serf was guaranteed his living, however poor it might have been.

In the later Middle Ages, after the revival of trade and of town life, the desire to guarantee a livelihood to everyone was reflected in the gild organization, and in the many regulations that were imposed on the manufacture and distribution of goods. By agreement within the gild, techniques were prescribed, monopoly was forbidden both in buying and selling, prices were fixed, and all gildsmen shared the market; no one was permitted to "get ahead" of his fellow gildsmen. The very concept of the "just price" was an attempt to show that too high a price cheated the buyer and too low a price cheated the seller. In either case, one was deprived of his goods and his well-being.

But stability remained mostly an ideal that was striven for, rather than an actuality that was attained. The failure of the Middle Ages to achieve real stability sprang from the inevitable conflict between medieval political theory and practice on the one hand and medieval theological outlook and organization on the other. Christianity could not be reconciled with militarism; the two were completely antithetical, despite efforts to develop the notion of the "Christian knight" and the "soldiers of God." An even more important source of conflict between the feudal structure and the Catholic hierarchy, however, was the inescapable logic of the situation itself. In a deeply religious age—in any age, for that matter—men are moved to demonstrate their faith and to glorify their God by building beautiful churches or by giving gifts to support the faith. In the Middle Ages, most bequests took the form of land given over to the maintenance of church officials and functionaries or to provide the necessities of monasteries and nunneries.

This practice created two major difficulties that made conflict between the Church and the feudal system inevitable. First, the land had originally been granted (but not given outright) to a vassal by his liege lord in exchange for military service; if the land was then bequeathed by the vassal to the Church, who was to provide military service to the liege lord? Could a priest or a bishop hire someone to perform the feudal obligations and still remain a Christian? The second major difficulty arose from the vassal's obligation to swear oaths of allegiance, fidelity, and homage to his liege in order to be "invested" with his fief. Here feudalism ran directly afoul of the Church. A bishop, for instance, had already sworn fidelity to the pope at Rome and could not very well serve two masters, his feudal lord and his ecclesiastical superior.

Out of these difficulties the whole investiture controversy arose, a controversy that developed into a struggle for supreme political power between the feudal monarchs and the popes. The monarchs were victorious, although the question has never been clearly resolved for the hierarchy of the Catholic Church. In the late Middle Ages the Church mobilized all its arsenal of spiritual weapons in an attempt to win the controversy— papal letters, encyclicals, bulls, interdict, and excommunication. All was to no avail, however. And the use of these spiritual weapons to gain political ends itself tended to discredit them and to deprive the Church of its moral authority. So in a real sense the Church itself helped to prepare the way for the secular attitudes that were to characterize the Renaissance.

St. Augustine

For three hundred years after the death of Christ, the Christian churches were engaged in a continuing struggle. Confronted by scores of pagan cults in the Mediterranean world and by the persecution of the Roman government, the new religion was unable to establish its supremacy until the fourth century. Early in that century, under the emperors Galerius and Constantine (himself a convert), Christianity was recognized and tolerated; later in the century, under Theodosius, it was proclaimed as the official religion of the Roman Empire.

But the problems of the churches were far from over, for a host of controversies now arose within the ranks of the Christians themselves. The most critical controversy was over questions of doctrine. Innumerable sects, each preaching its special version of Christian doctrine and combating the views of the others, were scattered throughout the empire. Clearly, if Christianity was to survive, some order had to be brought out of such theological chaos. Into this scene of confusion stepped Augustine (354–430). Highly intelligent, firmly devoted to his conception of the truth, and possessed of unusual administrative ability, Augustine was admirably fitted for the task first of developing a theological doctrine for the Christian religion and then of making that doctrine prevail.

After having been attracted as a youth to various pagan cults, Augustine was converted to Christianity in 386 through the influence of Ambrose, Bishop of Milan. Following his conversion, Augustine devoted most of the rest of his life to formulating and disseminating what he believed to be the true Christian doctrine. The main features of this doctrine are given in the following selection, taken from *The Enchiridion* ("Manual"). The central concept, as with St. Paul, is original sin, but with Augustine the theory becomes systematically articulated. Once he had worked out his doctrine completely, Augustine was in a good position to brand opposing theories as heresies. And he devoted much of his time, thought, and energy, especially in later life, to doctrinal controversies in an effort to purge Christian theology of all heretical elements. He was singularly successful in this endeavor, and orthodox Christianity (even with the later additions made by Thomas Aquinas and others) has remained basically Augustinian.

The Enchiridion

• • •

God's judgments upon fallen men and angels. The death of the body is man's peculiar punishment.

. . . Now the evils I have mentioned are common to all who for their wickedness have been justly condemned by God, whether they be men or angels. But there is one form of punishment peculiar to man —the death of the body. God had threatened him with this punishment of death if he should sin, leaving him indeed to the freedom of his own will, but yet commanding his obedience under pain of death; and He placed him amid the happiness of Eden, as it were in a protected nook of life, with the intention that, if he preserved his righteousness, he should thence ascend to a better place.

Through Adam's sin his whole posterity were corrupted, and were born under the penalty of death, which he had incurred.

Thence, after his sin, he was driven into exile, and by his sin the whole race of which he was the root was corrupted in him, and thereby subjected to the penalty of death. And so it happens that all descended from him, and from the woman who had led him into sin, and was condemned at the same time with him,—being the offspring of carnal lust on which the same punishment of disobedience was visited,—were tainted with the original sin, and were by it drawn through divers errors and sufferings into that last and endless punishment which they suffer in common with the fallen angels, their corrupters and masters, and the partakers of their doom. And thus "by one man sin entered into the world, and death by sin; and so death passed upon all men, for that all have sinned." By "the world" the apostle, of course, means in this place the whole human race.

The state of misery to which Adam's sin reduced mankind, and the restoration effected through the mercy of God.

Thus, then, matters stood. The whole mass of the human race was under condemnation, was lying steeped and wallowing in misery, and was being tossed from one form of evil to another, and, having joined the faction of the fallen angels, was paying the well-merited penalty of that impious rebellion. For whatever the wicked freely do through blind and unbridled lust, and whatever they suffer against their will

"The Enchiridion," in *The Works of Aurelius Augustine,* ed. M. Dods, Vol. IX (Edinburgh: T. & T. Clark, 1892), pp. 194–95, 197–200, 206–7, 219, 242–45, 253–55. Courtesy of T. & T. Clark.

in the way of open punishment, this all evidently pertains to the just wrath of God. But the goodness of the Creator never fails either to supply life and vital power to the wicked angels (without which their existence would soon come to an end); or, in the case of mankind, who spring from a condemned and corrupt stock, to impart form and life to their seed, to fashion their members, and through the various seasons of their life, and in the different parts of the earth, to quicken their senses, and bestow upon them the nourishment they need. For He judged it better to bring good out of evil, than not to permit any evil to exist. And if He had determined that in the case of men, as in the case of the fallen angels, there should be no restoration to happiness, would it not have been quite just, that the being who rebelled against God, who in the abuse of his freedom spurned and transgressed the command of his Creator when he could so easily have kept it, who defaced in himself the image of his Creator by stubbornly turning away from His light, who by an evil use of his free-will broke away from his wholesome bondage to the Creator's laws,—would it not have been just that such a being should have been wholly and to all eternity deserted by God, and left to suffer the everlasting punishment he had so richly earned? Certainly so God would have done, had He been only just and not also merciful, and had He not designed that His unmerited mercy should shine forth the more brightly in contrast with the unworthiness of its objects.

· · ·

Men are not saved by good works, nor by the free determination of their own will, but by the grace of God through faith.

But this part of the human race to which God has promised pardon and a share in His eternal kingdom, can they be restored through the merit of their own works? God forbid. For what good work can a lost man perform, except so far as he has been delivered from perdition? Can they do anything by the free determination of their own will? Again I say, God forbid. For it was by the evil use of his free-will that man destroyed both it and himself. For, as a man who kills himself must, of course, be alive when he kills himself, but after he has killed himself ceases to live, and cannot restore himself to life; so, when man by his own free-will sinned, then sin being victorious over him, the freedom of his will was lost. "For of whom a man is overcome, of the same is he brought in bondage." This is the judgment of the Apostle Peter. And as it is certainly true, what kind of liberty, I ask, can the bond-slave possess, except when it pleases him to sin? For he is freely in bondage who does with pleasure the will of his master. Accordingly, he who is the servant of sin is free to sin. And hence he will not be free to do right, until, being freed from sin, he shall begin to be the servant of righteousness. And this is true liberty, for he has pleasure in the righteous deed; and it is at the same time a holy bondage, for he is obedient to the will of God. But whence comes this liberty to do right to the man who is in bondage and sold under sin, except he be redeemed by Him who has said, "If the Son shall make you free, ye shall be free indeed"? And before this redemption is wrought in a man, when he is not yet free to do what is right, how can he talk of the freedom of his will and his good works, except he be inflated by that foolish pride of boasting which the apostle restrains when he says, "By grace are ye saved, through faith."

Faith itself is the gift of God; and good works will not be wanting in those who believe.

And lest men should arrogate to themselves the merit of their own faith at least, not understanding that this too is the gift of God, this same apostle, who says in another place that he had "obtained mercy of the Lord to be faithful," here also adds: "and that not of yourselves; it is the gift of God: not of works, lest any man should boast." And lest it should be thought that good works will be wanting in those who believe, he adds further: "For we are His workmanship, created in Christ Jesus unto good works, which God hath before ordained that we should walk in them." We shall be made truly free, then, when God fashions us, that is, forms and creates us anew, not as men—for He has done that already—but as good men, which His grace is now doing, that we may be a new creation in Christ Jesus, according as it is said: "Create in me a clean heart, O God." For God had already created his heart, so far as the physical structure of the human

heart is concerned; but the psalmist prays for the renewal of the life which is still lingering in his heart.

The freedom of the will is also the gift of God, for God worketh in us both to will and to do.

And further, should any one be inclined to boast, not indeed of his works, but of the freedom of his will, as if the first merit belong to him, this very liberty of good action being given to him as a reward he had earned, let him listen to this same preacher of grace, when he says: "For it is God which worketh in you, both to will and to do of His own good pleasure"; and in another place: "So, then, it is not of him that willeth, nor of him that runneth, but of God that showeth mercy." Now as, undoubtedly, if a man is of the age to use his reason, he cannot believe, hope, love, unless he will to do so, nor obtain the prize of the high calling of God unless he voluntarily run for it; in what sense is it "not of him that willeth, nor of him that runneth, but of God that showeth mercy," except that, as it is written, "The preparation of the heart is from the Lord"? Otherwise, if it is said, "It is not of him that willeth, nor of him that runneth, but of God that showeth mercy," because it is of both, that is, both of the will of man and of the mercy of God, so that we are to understand the saying, "It is not of him that willeth, nor of him that runneth, but of God that showeth mercy," as if it meant the will of man alone is not sufficient, if the mercy of God go not with it—then it will follow that the mercy of God alone is not sufficient, if the will of man go not with it; and therefore, if we may rightly say, "it is not of man that willeth, but of God that showeth mercy," because the will of man by itself is not enough, why may we not also rightly put it in the converse way: "It is not of God that showeth mercy, but of man that willeth," because the mercy of God by itself does not suffice? Surely, if no Christian will dare to say this, "It is not of God that showeth mercy, but of man that willeth," lest he should openly contradict the apostle, it follows that the true interpretation of the saying, "It is not of him that willeth, nor of him that runneth, but of God that showeth mercy," is that the whole work belongs to God, who both makes the will of man righteous, and thus prepares it for assistance, and assists it when it is prepared. For the man's righteousness of will precedes many of God's gifts, but not all and it must itself be included among those which it does not precede. We read in Holy Scripture, both that God's mercy "shall prevent me," and that His mercy "shall follow me." It prevents the unwilling to make him willing; it follows the willing to make his will effectual. Why are we taught to pray for our enemies, who are plainly unwilling to lead a holy life, unless that God may work willingness in them? And why are we ourselves taught to ask that we may receive, unless that He who has created in us the wish, may Himself satisfy the wish? We pray, then, for our enemies, that the mercy of God may prevent them, as it has prevented us: we pray for ourselves that His mercy may follow us.

Men, being by nature the children of wrath, needed a Mediator. In what sense God is said to be angry.

And so the human race was lying under a just condemnation, and all men were the children of wrath. Of which wrath it is written: "All our days are passed away in Thy wrath; we spend our years as a tale that is told." Of which wrath also Job says: "Man that is born of a woman is of few days, and full of trouble." Of which wrath also the Lord Jesus says: "He that believeth on the Son hath everlasting life: and he that believeth not the Son shall not see life; but the wrath of God abideth on him." He does not say it will come, but it "abideth on him." For every man is born with it; wherefore the apostle says: "We were by nature the children of wrath, even as others." Now, as men were lying under this wrath by reason of their original sin, and as this original sin was the more heavy and deadly in proportion to the number and magnitude of the actual sins which were added to it, there was need for a Mediator, that is, for a reconciler, who, by the offering of one sacrifice, of which all the sacrifices of the law and the prophets were types, should take away this wrath. Wherefore the apostle says: "For if, when we were enemies, we were reconciled to God by the death of His Son, much more, being reconciled, we shall be saved by His life." Now when God is said to be angry, we do not attribute to Him such a disturbed feeling as exists in the mind of an angry man; but we call His just displeasure against sin by the name "anger," a word transferred by analogy from human emotions. But our being reconciled to God through a Mediator, and receiving the Holy Spirit, so that we who were enemies are made sons ("For as many as are led by the Spirit of God, they are the sons of God"): this is the grace of God through Jesus Christ our Lord.

.   .   .

Christ, who was Himself free from sin, was made sin for us, that we might be reconciled to God.

Begotten and conceived, then, without any indulgence of carnal lust, and therefore bringing with Him no original sin, and by the grace of God joined and united in a wonderful and unspeakable way in one person with the Word, the Only-begotten of the Father, a son by nature, not by grace, and therefore having no sin of His own; nevertheless, on account of the likeness of sinful flesh in which He came, He was called sin, that He might be sacrificed to wash away sin. For, under the Old Covenant, sacrifices for sin were called sins. And He, of whom all these sacrifices were types and shadows, was Himself truly made sin. Hence the apostle, after saying, "We pray you in Christ's stead, be ye reconciled to God," forthwith adds: "for He hath made Him to be sin for us who knew no sin; that we might be made the righteousness of God in Him." He does not say, as some incorrect copies read, "He who knew no sin did sin for us," as if Christ had Himself sinned for our sakes; but he says, "Him who knew no sin," that is, Christ, God, to whom we are to be reconciled, "hath made to be sin

for us," that is, hath made Him a sacrifice for our sins, by which we might be reconciled to God. He, then, being made sin, just as we are made righteousness (our righteousness being not our own, but God's, not in ourselves, but in Him); He being made sin, not His own, but ours, not in Himself, but in us, showed, by the likeness of sinful flesh in which He was crucified, that though sin was not in Him, yet that in a certain sense He died to sin, by dying in the flesh which was the likeness of sin; and that although He himself had never lived the old life of sin, yet by His resurrection He typified our new life springing up out of the old death in sin.

.   .   .

By the sacrifice of Christ all things are restored, and peace is made between earth and heaven.

And, of course, the holy angels, taught by God, in the eternal contemplation of whose truth their happiness consists, know how great a number of the human race are to supplement their ranks, and fill up the full tale of their citizenship. Wherefore the apostle says, that "all things are gathered together in one in Christ, both which are in heaven and which are on earth." The things which are in heaven are gathered together when what was lost therefrom in the fall of the angels is restored from among men; and the things which are on earth are gathered together, when those who are predestined to eternal life are redeemed from their old corruption. And thus, through that single sacrifice in which the Mediator was offered up, the one sacrifice of which the many victims under the law were types, heavenly things are brought into peace with earthly things, and earthly things with heavenly. Wherefore, as the same apostle says: "For it pleased the Father that in Him should all fulness dwell: and, having made peace through the blood of His cross, by Him to reconcile all things to Himself: by Him, I say, whether they be things in earth or things in heaven."

· · ·

Predestination to eternal life is wholly of God's free grace.

And, moreover, who will be so foolish and blasphemous as to say that God cannot change the evil wills of men, whichever, whenever and wheresoever He chooses, and direct them to what is good? But when He does this, He does it of mercy; when He does it not, it is of justice that He does it not; for "He hath mercy on whom He will have mercy, and whom He will He hardeneth." And when the apostle said this, he was illustrating the grace of God, in connection with which he had just spoken of the twins in the womb of Rebecca, "who being not yet born, neither having done any good or evil, that the purpose of God according to election might stand, not of works, but of Him that calleth, it was said unto her, The elder shall serve the younger." And in reference to this matter he quotes another prophetic testimony: "Jacob have I loved, but Esau have I hated." But perceiving how what he had said might affect those who could not penetrate by their understanding the depth of this grace:

"What shall we say then?" he says: "Is there unrighteousness with God? God forbid." For it seems unjust that, in the absence of any merit or demerit from good or evil works, God should love the one and hate the other. Now, if the apostle had wished us to understand that there were future good works of the one, and evil works of the other, which of course God foreknew, he would never have said, "not of works," but, "of future works," and in that way would have solved the difficulty, or rather there would then have been no difficulty to solve. As it is, however, after answering, "God forbid"; that is, God forbid that there should be unrighteousness with God; he goes on to prove that there is no unrighteousness in God's doing this, and says: "For he saith to Moses, I will have mercy on whom I will have mercy, and I will have compassion on whom I will have compassion." Now who but a fool would think that God was unrighteous, either in inflicting penal justice on those who had earned it, or in extending mercy to the unworthy? Then he draws his conclusion: "So then it is not of him that willeth, nor of him that runneth, but of God that showeth mercy." Thus both the twins were born children of wrath, not on account of any works of their own, but because they were bound in the fetters of that original condemnation which came through Adam. But He who said, "I will have mercy on whom I will have mercy," loved Jacob of His undeserved grace, and hated Esau of His deserved judgment. And as this judgment was due to both, the former learnt from the case of the latter that the fact of the same punishment not falling upon himself gave him no room to glory in any merit of his own, but only in the riches of the divine grace; because "it is not of him that willeth, nor of him that runneth, but of God that showeth mercy." And indeed the whole face, and, if I may use the expression, every lineament of the countenance of Scripture conveys by a very profound analogy this wholesome warning to every one who looks carefully into it, that he who glories should glory in the Lord.

As God's mercy is free, so His judgments are just, and cannot be gainsaid.

Now after commending the mercy of God, saying, "So it is not of him that willeth, nor of him that runneth, but of God that showeth mercy," that he might commend His Justice also (for the man who does not obtain mercy finds, not iniquity, but justice, there being no iniquity with God), he immediately adds: "For the scripture saith unto Pharaoh, Even for this same purpose have I raised thee up, that I might show my power in thee, and that my name might be declared throughout all the earth." And then he draws a conclusion that applies to both, that is, both to His mercy and His justice: "Therefore hath He mercy on whom He will have mercy, and whom He will He hardeneth." "He hath mercy" of His great goodness, "He hardeneth" without any injustice; so that neither can he that is pardoned glory in any merit of his own, nor he that is condemned complain of anything but his own demerit. For it is grace alone that separates the

redeemed from the lost, all having been involved in one common perdition through their common origin. Now if any one, on hearing this, should say, "Why doth He yet find fault? for who hath resisted His will?" as if a man ought not to be blamed for being bad, because God hath mercy on whom He will have mercy, and whom He will He hardeneth, God forbid that we should be ashamed to answer as we see the apostle answered: "Nay, but, O man, who are thou that repliest against God? Shall the thing formed say to Him that formed it, Why hast Thou made me thus? Hath not the potter power over the clay, of the same lump to make one vessel unto honour, and another unto dishonour?" Now some foolish people think that in this place the apostle had no answer to give; and for want of a reason to render, rebuked the presumption of his interrogator. But there is great weight in this saying: "Nay, but, O man, who art thou?" and in such a matter as this it suggests to a man in a single word the limits of his capacity, and at the same time does in reality convey an important reason. For if a man does not understand these matters, who is he that he should reply against God? And if he does understand them, he finds no further room for reply. For then he perceives that the whole human race was condemned in its rebellious head by a divine judgment so just, that if not a single member of the race had been redeemed, no one could justly have questioned the justice of God; and that it was right that those who are redeemed should be redeemed in such a way as to show, by the greater number who are unredeemed and left in their just condemnation, what the whole race deserved, and whither the deserved judgment of God would lead even the redeemed, did not His undeserved mercy interpose, so that every mouth might be stopped of those who wish to glory in their own merits, and that he that glorieth might glory in the Lord.

· · ·

There is no ground in Scripture for the opinion of those who deny the eternity of future punishments.

It is in vain, then, that some, indeed very many, make moan over the eternal punishment, and perpetual, unintermitted torments of the lost, and say they do not believe it shall be so; not, indeed, that they directly oppose themselves to Holy Scripture, but, at the suggestion of their own feelings, they soften down everything that seems hard, and give a milder turn to statements which they think are rather designed to terrify than to be received as literally true. For "Hath God," they say, "forgotten to be gracious? hath He in anger shut up His tender mercies?" Now, they read this in one of the holy psalms. But without doubt we are to understand it as spoken of those who are elsewhere called "vessels of mercy," because even they are freed from misery not on account of any merit of their own, but solely through the pity of God. Or, if the men we speak of insist that this passage applies to all mankind, there is no reason why they should therefore suppose that there will be an end to the punishment of those of whom it is said, "These shall go away into everlast-

ing punishment"; for this shall end in the same manner and at the same time as the happiness of those of whom it is said, "but the righteous unto life eternal." But let them suppose, if the thought gives them pleasure, that the pains of the damned are, at certain intervals, in some degree assuaged. For even in this case the wrath of God, that is, their condemnation (for it is this, and not any disturbed feeling in the mind of God that is called His wrath), abideth upon them; that is, His wrath, though it still remains, does not shut up His tender mercies; though His tender mercies are exhibited, not in putting an end to their eternal punishment, but in mitigating, or in granting them a respite from, their torments; for the psalm does not say, "to put an end to His anger," or, "when His anger is passed by," but "in His anger." Now, if this anger stood alone, or if it existed in the smallest conceivable degree, yet to be lost out of the kingdom of God, to be an exile from the city of God, to be alienated from the life of God, to have no share in that great goodness which God hath laid up for them that fear Him, and hath wrought out for them that trust in Him, would be a punishment so great, that, supposing it to be eternal, no torments that we know of, continued through as many ages as man's imagination can conceive, could be compared with it.

The death of the wicked shall be eternal in the same sense as the life of the saints.

This perpetual death of the wicked, then, that is, their alienation from the life of God, shall abide for ever, and shall be common to them all, whatever men, prompted by their human affections, may conjecture as to a variety of punishments, or as to a mitigation or intermission of their woes; just as the eternal life of the saints shall abide for ever, and shall be common to them all, whatever grades of rank and honour there may be among those who shine with an harmonious effulgence.

Gregory of Tours

The History of the Franks, perhaps the most significant writing in a generally unlettered society, was the work of the sainted bishop of Tours, Gregory. This manuscript has become the most widely known and used source for the history of the Gallo-Roman society of the sixth century. Besides portraying both the violence and the piety of the age, it gives an account of the affairs of kings and armies plus an insight into the customs, beliefs, and manners that then prevailed.

The character of the author undoubtedly contributed mightily to the vigor and the value of the work. Gregory (529–594) was the son of an old, aristocratic Gallo-Roman family of senatorial rank, which had supplied virtually all the bishops of Tours, a fact from which Gregory himself derived much pleasure (and ran the risk of falling into the first of the seven mortal sins). On both sides of his family there was a lengthy tradition of high ecclesiastical office; Gregory was both the great grandson and grandson of bishops and the cousin of the bishop's immediate predecessor. (This was before the principle of sacerdotal celibacy achieved full vigor in the doctrines of the Catholic Church.) He distinguished himself not only by his many courageous defenses of the place and privileges of the Church and by his untiring efforts on behalf of his diocesan flock, but also by his important role as adviser to the Merovingian kings of France. Despite these many and varied duties, Gregory still found time to produce a very large body of literary works which, while of indifferent stylistic merit, are invaluable to the student of the early Middle Ages.

The following selections from *The History of the Franks* are four: the first from the Preface, the second from Book II describing the conversion of Clovis to Christianity, the third from Book VIII conveying some impressions of the violence of life in the sixth century, and the fourth containing Gregory's conclusions from Book X.

The History of the Franks

PREFACE

In these times when the practice of letters declines, nay, rather perishes in the cities of Gaul, there has been found no scholar trained in the art of ordered composition to present in prose or verse a picture of the things that have befallen. Yet there have been done good things many, and evil many; the peoples savagely raged; the fury of kings grew sharp; churches were assailed by heretics and protected by catholics; the faith of Christ that glowed in many hearts was luke-warm in not a few; the faithful enriched the churches while the unbelievers stripped them bare. Wherefore the voice of lament was ofttimes raised, and men said: "Alas! for these our days! The study of letters is perished from us, nor is any found among our peoples able to set forth in a book the events of this present time."

Now when I heard these and like complaints ever repeated, I was moved, with however rude an utterance, to hand down the memory of the past to future generations, in no wise leaving untold the conflicts of the wicked and those who lived in righteousness. I was the more encouraged because I often heard with surprise our people say that while the accomplished writer is understood by few, it is the man of plain speech who has the general ear.

Further, it seemed good to me for the better computation of the years, that in this first book, of which the chapters follow, I should begin from the foundation of the world.

BOOK II
• • •

After this, Childeric died, and Clovis his son reigned in his stead. In the fifth year of his reign, Syagrius, king of the Romans, son of Aegidius, had his residence in the city of Soissons, which had before been the home of the above-mentioned Aegidius. Clovis marched against him, with his relation Ragnachar, himself also a king, and called upon him to fix a field of battle. Syagrius did not seek delay nor did he fear to stand his ground. And so when the battle was joined between them, Syagrius, seeing his army crushed, turned to flight and escaped as fast as he could to Alaric at Toulouse. But Clovis sent to Alaric calling upon him to surrender the fugitive, else he must look to be himself invaded for giving him refuge. Then Alaric, lest he should incur the wrath of the Franks for his sake, was afraid, after the craven habit of the Goths, and handed him over to the messengers in bonds.

Gregory of Tours, *The History of the Franks,* trans. O. M. Dalton (Oxford: The Clarendon Press, 1927), pp. 2, 65–75, 81, 342–46, 348–52, 476–78. Reprinted by permission of the Oxford University Press, Oxford.

When Clovis received his prisoner, he ordered him to be imprisoned; had him put to the sword in secret, while he took possession of his kingdom.

At this time many churches were plundered by the troops of Clovis, because he was yet fast held in pagan errors. Thus it happened that a ewer of great size and beauty had been taken, with other ornaments used in the service of the church. But the bishop of that church sent messengers to the king, asking that if no other of the sacred vessels might be restored, his church might at least receive back this ewer. When the king heard this he said to the envoy: "Follow us to Soissons, for there all the booty is to be divided, and if the lot gives me the vessel, I will fulfil the desire of the bishop." When they were at Soissons and all the spoil was laid out in open view, the king said: "I ask you, most valiant warriors, not to refuse to cede me that vessel" (he meant the ewer of which I have spoken) "over and above my share." After this speech all the men of sense replied: "All that is before our eyes, most glorious king, is thine; we ourselves are submitted to thy power. Do now that which seemeth good to thee, for none is so strong as to say thee nay." At these words a soldier of a vain, jealous, and unstable temper raised his axe and smote the ewer, crying with a loud voice: "Naught shalt thou receive of this but that which thine own lot giveth thee." While all stood astounded at this act, the king suppressed his resentment at the wrong under a show of patient mildness; he then took the ewer and restored it to the bishop's envoy. But the wound remained hidden in his heart. After a lapse of a year, he commanded the whole army to assemble with full equipment, and to exhibit their arms in their brightness on the field of March. The king went round inspecting them all; but when he came to the man who struck the ewer he said: "None hath appeared with his arms so ill kept as thou; neither thy lance, nor thy sword, nor thy axe is fit for use." He then seized the axe, and threw it on the ground. As the man bent down a little to take it up, the king swung his own axe high and cleft his skull, saying as he did it, "Thus didst thou treat the ewer at Soissons." The man lying dead, he dismissed the rest, having put great fear of him into their hearts by his act. Clovis waged many wars and won many victories. For in the tenth year of his reign he invaded the Thuringians, and subjected them to his rule.

At that time the king of the Burgundians was Gundioc, of the race of the royal persecutor Athanaric whom I have before mentioned. He had four sons, Gundobad, Godigisel, Chilperic, and Gundomar. Gundobad put his brother Chilperic to the sword, and drowned his wife by tying a stone to her neck. Her two daughters he condemned to exile, the elder of whom, Chrona, had adopted the habit of a nun, while the younger was called Clotild. It happened that Clovis used often to send envoys into Burgundy, and they discovered the young Clotild. Observing her grace and understanding, and learning that she was of the blood royal, they spoke of these things to King Clovis, who straightway sent an embassy to Gundobad, asking her in marriage. Gundobad was afraid to refuse, and handed her over to the men, who received her, and with all speed brought her before the king. At sight of her he greatly rejoiced and was united to her in wedlock, having already by a concubine one son named Theuderic.

Of Queen Clotild the king had a first-born son whom the mother wished to be baptized; she therefore persistently urged Clovis to permit it, saying: "The gods whom ye worship are naught; they cannot aid either themselves or others, seeing that they are images carved of wood, or stone, or metal. Moreover the names which ye have given them are the names of men and not of gods. Saturn was a man, fabled to have escaped by flight from his son to avoid being thrust from his kingdom; Jupiter also, the lewdest practiser of all debaucheries and of unnatural vice, the abuser of the women of his own family, who could not even abstain from intercourse with his own sister, as she herself admitted in the words 'sister and spouse of Jove.' What power had Mars and Mercury? They may have been endowed with magical arts; they never had the power of the divine name. But ye should rather serve Him who at His word created out of nothing the heaven and earth, the sea and all therein; who made the sun to shine and adorned the heaven with stars; who filled the waters with fish, the earth with animals, the air with birds; at whose nod the lands are made fair with fruits, the trees with apples, the vine with grapes; by whose largess every creature was made to render homage and service to the man whom he created." Though the queen ever

argued thus, the king's mind was nowise moved toward belief, but he replied: "It is by command of our gods that all things are created and come forth; it is manifest that thy god availeth in nothing; nay more, he is not even proven to belong to the race of gods." But the queen, true to her faith, presented her son for baptism; she ordered the church to be adorned with hangings and curtains, that the king, whom no preaching could influence, might by this ceremony be persuaded to belief. The boy was baptized and named Ingomer, but died while yet clothed in the white raiment of his regeneration. Thereupon the king was moved to bitter wrath, nor was he slow to reproach the queen, saying: "If the child had been dedicated in the name of my gods, surely he would have survived, but now baptized in the name of thy God, he could not live a day." The queen replied: "I render thanks to Almighty God, Creator of all things, who hath not judged me all unworthy, and deigneth to take into His kingdom this child born of my womb. My mind is untouched by grief at this event, since I know that they which he called from this world in the white robes of baptism shall be nurtured in the sight of God." Afterwards she bore another son, who was baptized with the name of Chlodomer. When he too began to ail, the king said: "It cannot but befall that this infant like his brother shall straightway die, being baptized in the name of thy Christ." But the mother prayed, and God ordained that the child should recover.

Now the queen without ceasing urged the king to confess the true God, and forsake his idols; but in no wise could she move him to this belief, until at length he made war upon a time against the Alamanni, when he was driven of necessity to confess what of his free will he had denied. It befell that when the two hosts joined battle there was grievous slaughter, and the army of Clovis was being swept to utter ruin. When the king saw this he lifted up his eyes to heaven, and knew compunction in his heart, and, moved to tears, cried aloud: "Jesus Christ, Thou are proclaimed by Clotild Son of the living God, Thou that are said to give aid to those in stress, and to grant victory to those that hope in Thee, I entreat from a devout heart the glory of Thy succour. If Thou grant me victory over these enemies, and experience confirm that power which the people dedicated to Thy name claimeth to have proved, then will I also believe on Thee and be baptized in Thy name. I have called upon mine own gods, but here is proof that they have withdrawn themselves from helping me; wherefore I believe that they have no power, since they come not to the succour of their servants. Thee do I now invoke, on Thee am I fain to believe, if but I may be plucked out of the hands of mine adversaries." And as he said this, lo, the Alamanni turned their backs and began to flee. And when they saw that their king was slain, they yielded themselves to Clovis, saying: "No longer, we entreat thee, let the people perish; we are now thy men." Then the king put an end to the war, and having admonished the people, returned in peace, relating to the queen how he had called upon the name of Christ and had been found worthy to obtain the victory. This

happened in the fifteenth year of his reign.

Then the queen commanded the holy Remigius, bishop of Reims, to be summoned secretly, entreating him to impart the word of salvation to the king. The bishop, calling the king to him in privity, began to instil into him faith in the true God, Maker of heaven and earth, and urged him to forsake his idols, which were unable to help either himself or others. But Clovis replied: "I myself, most holy father, will glady hearken to thee; but one thing yet remaineth. The people that followeth me will not suffer it that I forsake their gods; yet will I go, and reason with them according to thy word." But when he came before the assembled people, or ever he opened his mouth, the divine power had gone forth from him, and all the people cried with one voice: "O gracious king, we drive forth our gods that perish, and are ready to follow that immortal God whom Remigius preacheth." News of this was brought to the bishop, who was filled with great joy, and commanded the font to be prepared. The streets were overshadowed with coloured hangings, the churches adorned with white hangings, the baptistry was set in order, smoke of incense spread in clouds, perfumed tapers gleamed, the whole church about the place of baptism was filled with the divine fragrance. And now the king first demanded to be baptized by the bishop. Like a new Constantine, he moved forward to the water; to blot out the former leprosy, to wash away in this new stream the foul stains borne from old days. As he entered to be baptized the saint of God spoke these words with eloquent lips: "Meekly bow thy proud head, Sicamber; adore that which thou hast burned, burn that which thou hast adored." For the holy Remigius, the bishop, was of excellent learning, and above all skilled in the art of rhetoric, and so exemplary in holiness that his miracles were equal to those of the holy Silvester; there is preserved to us a book of his life, in which it is related how he raised a man from the dead. The king therefore, confessing Almighty God, three in one, was baptized in the name of the Father, the Son, and the Holy Ghost, and anointed with holy chrism, with the sign of the Cross of Christ. Of his army were baptized more than three thousand; and his sister Albofled, who not long after was taken to the Lord, was likewise baptized. And when the king was sorrowing for her death, the holy Remigius sent him a letter of consolation, beginning after this fashion: "The cause of thy sadness doth afflict me with a great affliction, for that thy sister of fair memory hath passed away. But this shall console us, that she hath in such wise left the world as that we should rather lift up our eyes to her than mourn her." And another of his sisters was converted, by name Iahthechild, who had fallen into the heresy of the Arians; she also received the holy chrism, having confessed the Son and the Holy Ghost equal to the Father.

At this time two brothers, Gundobad and Godigisel, possessed their kingdom about the Rhone and Saone with the territory of Marseilles. They and their people were in the thraldom of the Arian sect. And as the brothers were on terms of hostility, Godigisel, who had heard of the vic-

tories won by King Clovis, sent envoys to him by stealth, saying: "If thou afford me aid to pursue my brother, so that I may either slay him in battle, or drive him from the kingdom, I will pay thee every year such tribute as thou mayest thyself impose." This offer Clovis received gladly, and promised him aid whenever his necessity should demand it. At a time appointed between them he marched an army against Gundobad, who, ignorant of his brother's guile, sent to him upon this news, saying: "Come thou to my deliverance, for the Franks have risen against us, and are come up against our territory to take it. Let us therefore be of one mind against a people that hateth us, for if we hold apart we shall undergo the fate suffered by other peoples." Godigisel made answer: "I will come with my army, and will bring thee succour." So all three kings set their forces in movement together, Clovis marching against Gundobad and Godigisel; they came to Dijon with all the armaments of war. But when they joined battle on the Ouche, Godigisel joined Clovis, and their united armies crushed the force of Gundobad. But he, perceiving the treachery of his brother which till that hour he never suspected, turned his back and fled along the Rhone, until he entered the city of Avignon. After his victory thus gained, Godigisel promised Clovis a part of his kingdom, and went home in peace, entering Vienne in triumph, as though he were master of the entire kingdom. But Clovis reinforced his troops, and followed Gundobad with intent to take him from Avignon and slay him. When Gundobad heard this, he was grievously afraid, dread-ing to be over-taken by a sudden death. Now he had with him Aridius, a man of rank, who was both strenuous and astute. Him he summoned and thus addressed: "I am hemmed in by straits upon every side, and know not what to do, for these barbarians are fallen upon me with intent to slay us and lay waste all the land." Aridius answered: "Thou hadst best assuage the savagery of this man, and so preserve thy life. Now therefore, if it be pleasing in thy sight, I will feign to forsake thee and desert to him; once with him I will bring it about that he neither ruin thee nor yet this country. Do thou only have a care to satisfy all the demands which by my advice he shall make of thee, till the Lord of His goodness deign to make thy cause triumph." Gundobad made answer: "I will do all that thou shalt adjoin." Thereupon Aridius bade him farewell and departed, and came to King Clovis, to whom he said: "Behold in me, most pious king, thy humble slave, who hath forsaken the miserable Gundobad to serve thy mightiness. If now thy piety deign to look on me, thou and thy posterity shall find in me an honest and faithful follower." Clovis forthwith took him to himself, and kept him near his person; for he could tell lively tales, was active in counsel, just in judgment, and faithful in every trust. Clovis then continuing to invest the city with his army, Aridius said: "O King, if in the majesty of thy high estate thou deign to hear from me a few words of humble advice, though indeed thou hast small need of counsel, I will offer them in all loyalty; and it shall be useful to thee and to the cities through which it is thy intent to pass. Wherefore dost thou

keep afoot this army, when thy foe abideth in an impregnable place? Thou layest waste the fields and devourest the meadows, thou cuttest the vines, thou hewest down the olives, all the fruits of this region thou dost utterly destroy, and yet thou availest not to do him hurt. Send rather envoys to him and impose a yearly tribute, that this region be saved from ruin, and thou be always lord over thy vassal. If he should refuse, then do according to thy pleasure." The king harkened to this counsel, and bade his army return home. And he sent an embassy to Gundobad, commanding him yearly to pay the tribute now to be laid upon him. And he paid it forthwith, and pledged himself to pay it hereafter.

But later, when he had recovered strength, he disdained to pay the promised tribute to King Clovis, and marched an army against Godigisel his brother, besieging him in the city of Vienne. As soon as provisions began to run short among the common people, Godigisel feared the famine might extend even to him, and ordered them to be driven outside the city. It was done; but among the rest was expelled the artificer who had charge of the aqueduct. This man, indignant at his expulsion with the others, went in a fury to Gundobad, and showed him he might break into the city and take vengeance on his brother. Under his guidance armed men were led along the aqueduct, preceded by men with iron crowbars. For there was an outlet covered by a great stone, which was moved away by the crowbars under the direction of the artificer, and so they entered the city, taking in the rear the garrison who were discharging their arrows from the walls. Then at a signal given by a trumpet from the centre of the city, the besiegers seized the gates, threw them open, and crowded in. The inhabitants were caught between two forces and cut to pieces, but Godigisel took refuge in a church of the heretics, and was there put to death with the Arian bishop. The Franks who were with him held together in a tower; Gundobad commanded that none of them should be harmed, and when they were taken, sent them into banishment to King Alaric at Toulouse; but the Gallo-Romans of senatorial family and the Burgundians who had taken part with Godigisel he slew. He restored to his dominion the whole region now known as Burgundy, and instituted milder laws among the Burgundians that there should be no undue oppression of the Romans.

Gundobad, perceiving the doctrines of the heretics to be worthless, confessed that Christ, the Son of God, and the Holy Ghost are both equal to the Father and asked secret baptism of the holy bishop of Vienne. But the bishop replied: "If thou verily believest, it is thy duty to follow the teaching of our Lord Himself, when He said: 'If any man will confess Me before men, him will I also confess before My Father which is in heaven; but whosoever shall deny Me before men, Him will I also deny before my Father which is in heaven.' This also did our Lord urge even upon His holy and beloved, the blessed apostles, when He said: 'But beware of men; for they will deliver you up to councils, and in their synagogues they will scourge you; yea, and before governors and kings shall ye be brought for my

sake, for a testimony to them and to the Gentiles.' But thou that art a king, and needest not to fear that any shall lay hands on thee, see how thou dreadest revolt among the people, not daring to confess in public the Creator of all men. Forsake this foolishness, and that which thou professest to believe in thy heart declare with thy lips before the people. For according to the word of the blessed apostle: 'With the heart man believeth unto righteousness, and with the mouth confession is made unto salvation.' Likewise also the prophet saith: 'I will give Thee thanks in the great congregation, I will praise Thee among much people.' And again: 'I will give thanks unto Thee, O Lord, among the peoples; I will sing praises unto Thee among the nations.' Thou fearest the people, O king; but perceivest thou not that it is more meet for the people to follow thy belief, than for thee to indulge their weakness? For thou art the head of the people; the people is not thy head. If thou goest at warfare, it is thou that goest before the troops of thy host, which follow whither thou leadest. Wherefore it is better that thou shouldst lead them to the knowledge of the truth than that thou shouldst perish and leave them in their error. 'Fod God is not mocked,' nor doth He love the man who for an earthly kingdom refuseth to confess Him before the world." Though troubled by these arguments, Gundobad persisted to his dying day in this madness, nor ever would publicly confess that the three persons of the Trinity are equal. The blessed Avitus was at this time of great eloquence; for heresy springing up in Constantinople, both that taught by Eutyches and that of Sabellius, to the effect that our Lord Jesus Christ had in Him nothing of the divine nature, at the request of King Gundobad he wrote against them. There are today extant among us his admirable letters, which, as they once quelled heresy, so now they edify the Church of God. He wrote a book of Homilies, six metrical books on the creation of the world and on various other subjects, and nine books of Letters including those just mentioned. In a homily composed on the Rogations, he relates that these solemnities which we celebrate before the triumph of our Lord's Ascension were instituted by Mamertus, bishop of Vienne (his own see when he wrote), at a time when the city was alarmed by many portents. For it was frequently shaken by earthquakes, and wild creatures, stags and wolves, entered the gates, wandering without fear through the whole city. These things befell through the circle of the year, till at the approach of the Easter festival the whole people looked devoutly for the mercy of God, that at last this day of great solemnity might set a term to all their terror. But on the very vigil of that glorious night, while the holy rite of the Mass was being celebrated, on a sudden the royal palace within the walls was set ablaze by fire from heaven. All the congregation, stricken with fear, rushed from the church, believing that the whole city would be consumed in this fire, or that the earth would open and swallow it up. The holy bishop, prostrate before the altar, with groans and tears implored the mercy of God. What need for me to say

more? The prayer of the illustrious bishop penetrated to the height of heaven; the river of his flowing tears extinguished the burning palace. When, after these events, the day of the Lord's Ascension drew near, he imposed a fast upon the people, instituted the form of prayer, the order of their repasts, and the manner of their joyful alms-giving to the poor. Thereupon all these terrors ceased; the fame of this deed spread through all the provinces, putting all the bishops in mind to follow the example of his faith. And down to our day these rites are celebrated in all churches in Christ's name, in compunction of the heart and a contrite spirit.

Now when Alaric, king of the Goths, beheld the manner in which King Clovis kept steadily subduing his neighbours in war, he sent envoys to him with this message: "If it please thee, O my brother, I am minded that we two meet by God's grace." Clovis did not refuse, but came to him. They met on an island in the Loire near the village of Amboise in the territory of the city of Tours. There they conversed, ate and drank together, swore mutual friendship, and parted in peace. Many people in Gaul at this time ardently desired to live under the dominion of the Franks.

• • •

After these events [mostly wars] Clovis died at Paris, and was buried in the church of the Holy Apostles which he had himself built, with Clotild his queen. It was the fifth year after the battle of Vouillé that he passed away. And all the days of his reign were thirty years, and of his own age forty-five. From the passing of the holy Martin to the passing of Clovis, which was in the eleventh year of the episcopate of Licinius, bishop of Tours, there are counted one hundred and twelve years. After the death of her lord, Queen Clotild came to Tours, and, save for rare visits to Paris, here she remained all the days of her life, distinguished for her great modesty and kindliness.

BOOK VIII

. . .

During our sojourn in this place, we beheld for two nights signs in the heaven, namely rays in the north so clear and splendid, that none such were ever seen before; on both sides, east and west, were blood-red clouds. On the third night about the second hour, these rays appeared again; and while we gazed in wonder at them, lo! from the four quarters of the earth there rose others like them, and we saw them covering the whole sky. In the middle of the heavens was a gleaming cloud to which these rays gathered themselves as it were into a pavilion, the stripes of which, beginning broad at the bottom, narrow as they rise, and meet as it were in a hood at the top. In the midst of the rays were other clouds, flashing vividly as lightning. This was a great sign, and filled us with fear. For we looked that some disaster should be sent upon us out of heaven.

King Childebert, pressed by imperial envoys to surrender the gold given him the preceding year, sent an army into Italy. It was also rumoured that his sister Ingund had been removed to Constantinople. But the commanders quarrelled among themselves, and returned without winning any advantage. Duke Wintrio was driven out by the people of his district, and lost his dukedom; he would have likewise lost his life, had he not saved himself by flight. Later, when the people were appeased, he recovered the dukedom. Nicetius, who was replaced as count of Clermont by the dispatch thither of Eulalius, asked a dukedom of the king, offering immense presents to obtain it. In this manner he was appointed duke of Clermont, Rodez, and Uzes. Though young in years, he was a man of acute insight, and established peace in Auvergne and in the other places under his administration.

Childeric the Saxon, who had fallen into disgrace with King Guntram for a reason which had caused the flight of others, as I have above related, sought the church of the holy Martin, leaving his wife in Guntram's dominions. The king had adjured her not to presume to see her husband until such time as he should be restored to his royal favour; but at length, after dispatch of many messengers on Childeric's behalf, I obtained permission for her to join him, and for both to dwell south of the Loire on the understanding that he should not venture to go over to King Childebert. This notwithstanding, after he had got back his wife, he did pass over privily to that king; and receiving from him the appointment of duke over his cities beyond the Garonne, he betook himself thither.

King Guntram, desiring to govern on his own account the kingdom of his nephew Lothar, son of Chilperic, appointed Theodulf count of Angers. He entered the city, but was ignominiously driven out by the citizens, Domigisel taking a leading part. Upon this, he hastened back to the king, received a second mandate, and after being inducted by Duke Sigulf, exercised his authority as count. Gundovald, named count of Meaux in place of Werpin, made his entry, and commenced the business of his jurisdiction. But later, while on his official progress through the territory of the city, he was slain by Werpin on a certain estate. His kinsmen assembled and fell upon the murderer, whom they shut up in the bath chamber of his house. Thus did both of them lose the countship by sudden death.

The abbot Dagulf had been many times convicted of crimes, for he committed frequent robberies and murders, and in his adulteries knew no bounds. He once lusted after the wife of a neighbour, and had commerce with her; he then sought various occasions to kill the husband, who lived on land belonging to the monastery. At last the husband swore that if he came near his wife he should rue it. One day he left his dwelling, and at night Dagulf, attended by a single cleric, came to the woman's house. They drank long till they were drunken, and lay down in a single bed. But while they slept, the husband returned, lit a fire of straw, and slew them both with strokes of his axe. Let this example be a lesson to all clergy to avoid the company of strange women, since the canon law and all the holy scriptures forbid them that of any women save those on whose account they cannot be reproached.

Meanwhile the day of the council came round, and by command of King Guntram the bishops assembled in the city of Macon. Faustianus, who had been consecrated bishop of Dax by order of Gundovald, was deprived of his see on the condition that Bertram, Orestes, and Palladius, who had given him the benediction, should in turn support him, paying him a hundred pieces of gold a year. But Nicetius, who, though a layman, had induced King Chilperic to give him his diploma, now took possession of his bishopric in the city. Ursicinus, bishop of Cahors, was excommunicated because he openly confessed to having received Gundovald. Sentence was passed that he should do penance for three years, leave head and beard unshorn, and abstain from flesh and wine. Further, he must never presume to celebrate Mass, or ordain clergy, bless churches and the holy chrism, or present consecrated bread. He might, however, manage the external business of the Church in the usual manner.

At this council there was a certain bishop who defended the opinion that women could not be included under the general description "man"; but he accepted the reasoning of his brethren, and said no more. Their arguments were as follows: The holy book of the Old Testament teaches that in the beginning, when God created man, He created them male and female, and called their name Adam, which, being interpreted, means earthly man; even so He called the woman Eve; of both He used the word "man." And the Lord Jesus Christ is therefore called Son of man, because He was the Virgin's son, which is to say, the son of a woman. To her He said, when He was about to change the water into wine: "Woman, what have I to do with thee?" and that which follows. They brought other convincing testimony, and there this matter rested. Praetextatus, bishop of Rouen, recited before his brethren some prayers which he had written when in exile. Some approved of them; but others criticized, on the ground that he had too little observed the rules of art. The style, however, was in places appropriate and worthy of a true son of the Church.

There was at this time a great brawl between the servants of Bishop Priscus and those of Duke Leudegisel, and Bishop Priscus offered a large sum to buy his peace. In these days also, King Guntram fell into so sore a sickness that some believed he could never recover. To my thinking, this was an act of God's providence; for the king had it in his mind to drive a number of bishops into banishment. Bishop Theodore returned to his see, and was received with the goodwill of the whole people and with their acclamations.

While this council was being held, King Childebert met the chief men of his kingdom at his domain of Beslingen, which lies in the midst of the forest of the Ardennes. There Queen Brunhild made plaint to all the notables on behalf of Ingund her daughter, who was still detained in Africa; but scant sympathy did she receive. Then they considered a case against Guntram Boso. A few days before, a female relative of his wife died without issue, and was buried in a church at Metz with jewels of great size and much gold. This was a few days before the festival of the blessed Remigius,

which is celebrated on the first of October. Many inhabitants went out of the city with the bishop, and especially the chief personages, with the duke. The servants of Guntram Boso now came to the church where this lady was buried, and went in. They fastened the doors behind them, and opened the tomb, stripping off and removing all the jewels which they could find upon the body. The monks attached to the church heard them, and came to the doors, but were not allowed to enter. Finding their efforts vain, they sent messages to the bishop and the duke. Meanwhile the servants had taken the things, mounted their horses, and actually begun their flight. But a fear came on them that they might be caught on the road and subjected to divers punishments. They therefore returned to the church and laid the stolen jewels on the altar, but they did not dare leave the building, and kept crying out: "We were sent by Guntram Boso." When Childebert and his nobles met at the assembly convoked at the aforesaid domain, Guntram was questioned on this matter, but he could make no reply; later, he fled away by stealth. All the property which he had held in Auvergne by gift from the domain was afterwards taken from him. He had to leave behind him, in his hurry, many things which he had unjustly taken from divers persons.

• • •

Ennodius was made duke of Tours and Poitiers. Berulf, who had previously been set over these cities, together with his associate Arnegisel, was regarded with suspicion for having secretly conveyed away the treasures of King Sigibert. On his way to take up his dukedom over these two cities, he was taken by a stratagem of Duke Rauching and set in bonds, together with his accomplice. Men were at once sent to their houses, who dragged forth the whole contents; they found much property of his own, but also some of the aforesaid treasures; all of it was taken to King Childebert. The two prisoners were on the point of being put to the sword, when the bishop intervened, obtained grace for their lives, and won them their release. But they got nothing back of all that had been taken from them.

The duke Desiderius, taking with him certain bishops, the abbot Aredius, and Antestius, made haste to King Guntram. The king was scarce minded to receive him, but was conquered by the entreaties of the bishops and took him into favour. Eulalius was also there, with intent to bring forward a plaint on account of his wife, who had scorned him for Desiderius, to whom she had flown; but he was shamed and laughed down, so that he held his peace.

Ingund, as I have written above, had been left by her consort with the imperial army. While she was being conducted to the emperor with her little son, she died in Africa, and was there buried. Her lord Hermangild was slain by his father Leuvigild. King Guntram, enraged by these events, proposed to send an army into Spain; it was first to subject to his dominion Septimania, which lies within Gaulish territory, and having done that, to advance farther. While this army was being levied, a letter of instruction was found in the possession of certain unknown countrymen. It was sent for perusal to King Guntram, as purporting to be written by Leuvigild to Fredegund, enjoining her, by any trick she could, to prevent the army from marching to Spain. It ran thus: "Be thou quick to slay our enemies, which is to say, Childebert and his mother; and make peace with King Guntram; buy it at any price you will. If perchance money be lacking to thee, we will send it thee in secret; do only that which we ask. But when once we are avenged upon our enemies, then recompense Bishop Amelius and the lady Leuba, by whose good offices the way of approach hath been opened to thy presence." Now Leuba was mother-in-law of Duke Bladast.

Notwithstanding that this message had been taken to King Guntram, and by him brought to the notice of his nephew Childebert, yet Fredegund bade make two knives of iron to be cut with deep channels and smeared with poison, that even if not deadly the thrust should sever the vital nerves, the infection of the poison would as swiftly wrest the life away. These knives she entrusted to two clerics with the following orders: "Take these blades and hie you with all speed to King Childebert, feigning to be beggars. Cast yourselves at his feet, as if ye asked an alms, then pierce him from both sides, that so at last Brunhild, whose arrogance is fed through his power, may be brought down with his fall and set beneath my feet. But if the boy be so well guarded that ye may not reach his person, then slay her, that woman whom I hate. If ye die about this business, your kin shall be rewarded at my hands; I will enrich them with gifts and make them the first in my kingdom. Do ye therefore put from you all fear; let there be no dread of death in your breasts, for ye know that death is the common fate of man. Arm your hearts with manhood, and remember that ofttimes before have brave men fallen in war, but that their families are thereby ennobled; they rise above the rest by their great riches, and have precedence of all." When this woman spoke thus, the clerics began to tremble, for they deemed her bidding right hard in the fulfilment. But when she saw them doubting, she drugged them with a draught, and sent them forth whither she would have them go. Straightway their hearts grew stout, and they swore to carry out all her behest. But she told them to take with them a small vessel filled with the same potion, and said: "On the day when ye work my will, drink this draught in the morning before ye begin the work, and ye shall have great constancy to carry all through to the end." With these instructions she dismissed them. They set out, and came to Soissons. But there they were taken prisoners by Duke Rauching, and under examination revealed everything; whereupon they were bound and cast into prison. After a few days, Fredegund, uncertain whether or not her behest had been fulfilled, sent a servant to find out if there were any rumour abroad, or haply to hear from some man's lips that Childebert was killed. After leaving her presence, the servant went to Soissons. There he heard that the clerics were in the prison, and came to the gate; but when he began talking with the warders at the gate, he was himself seized and placed under guard. All the three

were then together sent to King Childebert, and questioned. They revealed the truth, admitting that they had been dispatched by Fredegund to murder him, and adding: "We were ordered by the queen to disguise ourselves as beggars; we were to throw ourselves at thy feet asking an alms, and then to pierce thee with these blades. And if the thrust were not hard enough, the poison smeared upon the blades would soon reach the source of thy life." Upon this declaration they were subjected to diverse tortures: their hands, ears, and noses were cut off, and they were put to different kinds of death.

Now King Guntram ordered his army to march against Spain, and said: "Subdue first the province of Septimania to our dominion, as lying so near to Gaul; for it is shameful that the territory of the horrible Goth should extend into Gaul." Thereupon the whole armed force of his kingdom was levied and sent thither. The peoples dwelling beyond the Saone, Rhone, and Seine joined the Burgundians and ravaged the banks of the Saone and Rhone, destroying the produce and the herds. In King Guntram's own territory they were guilty on all sides of murder, arson, and rapine; they even stripped the churches, slaying the clergy, with the bishops, as well as the lay people, even before the altars consecrated to God; in such wise did they advance to Nimes. The men of Bourges, Saintes, Perigueux, and Angouleme, with the people of other cities then under Guntram's dominion, wrought the like wrongs, pushing forward to Carcassone. Reaching that city, they found the gates opened for them by the inhabitants, and entered without resistance. But a quarrel arising between them and the people, they left the town. Terentiolus, former count of Limoges, was struck by a stone thrown from the walls, and killed: the enemy revenged themselves upon him by cutting off his head, and taking it within the city. Thereupon the whole army was stricken with panic, and intent on returning home; they left everything behind them, not only all that they had seized on the expedition, but all that they had originally brought with them. The Goths despoiled and slew many of them by taking them in ambush. The rest fell into the hands of the people of Toulouse, to whom they had done much injury during their advance; they were now robbed and so roughly handled that they hardly reached their homes. Those who had attacked Nimes devastated the whole country, setting houses and crops afire, felling olive groves, and cutting down vines, but were unable to harm the citizens, who shut themselves within their walls; they therefore marched on to other towns. These also were strongly fortified, and well stored with provisions and all other necessaries; so they ravaged the surrounding territory, but failed to make their way into the towns themselves. Duke Nicetius, who had started on this expedition with the people of Auvergne, beleaguered the cities with the other leaders. But seeing that he won no advantage, he came to a certain walled town and gave his word that no harm should be done; the people believed him, opened the gates of their free will, and received him and his men as if they came in peace. But when once they were let in, they disregarded their oath, plundered all the stores, and made the people prisoners. They then took counsel together, and returned home, committing on the way so many crimes, murdering, pillaging, and destroying even in their own king's country, that it were too long a task to recount them. But the result of their aforesaid burning of the crops throughout Provence was that they themselves now perished of hunger and want, and their dead were left behind along the roads; some of them were drowned in the rivers, many slain in uprisings of the people. It was related that more than five thousand perished in these disasters. But their fate did not restrain those that remained. The churches in Auvergne which were near the roads were stripped of their plate, and there was no end of these ill deeds until the last man of them had reached home. On their return great bitterness of heart possessed King Guntram, and the leaders of the aforesaid army took refuge in the church of the holy martyr Symphorian.

• • •

BOOK X

• • •

The nineteenth bishop was myself, Gregory, the unworthy. At the time when I succeeded to the cathedral church of Tours, in which the blessed Martin and the other bishops of the Lord were consecrated to the episcopal office, it was all ruined and destroyed by the fire. I rebuilt it greater in size and height than before, and dedicated it in the seventeenth year after my consecration. I learned from priests far advanced in years that the relics of the martyrs of Agaun had been placed in the church by the men of old time. In the treasure of the Church of the holy Martin I discovered the reliquary; the relics had fallen into great decay; they had been translated to this place on account of their miraculous power. While vigils were being celebrated in their honour, the fancy took me to visit them once more by the light of a taper. I was narrowly examining them, when the custodian of the church said to me: "There is here a hollowed stone covered by a lid, but what it may contain I know not at all; I learned that my predecessors in this office were in like manner ignorant. I will bring it, that thou mayst carefully investigate its contents." He brought it, and I of course opened it, when I found within a silver casket containing not only relics of the witnesses of the sacred legion, but also others of divers saints, both martyrs and confessors. We also found other stones hollowed in the same way, in which were relics of the holy apostles and other martyrs. Marvelling at this gift, divinely granted, and rendering thanks to God, after vigils celebrated and masses said, I placed all in the cathedral church. In the cell of the holy Martin close to the cathedral church I placed relics of the martyrs Cosmas and Damian. I found the walls of the holy basilica burned with fire, and ordered them to be painted and decorated by the skill of our craftsmen with a richness equal to that which they had known before. I caused a baptistery

to be erected close to the basilica, in which I placed relics of Saint John and of Sergius the martyr; in the earlier baptistery I placed those of Benignus the martyr. In many places within the territory of Tours I dedicated churches and oratories which I enriched with relics of the saints; but it were overlong to recount them in their order.

I have written ten books of History, seven of Miracles, and one on the Lives of the Fathers. I have composed one book of commentaries on the Psalms; I have also written one book on the Offices of the Church. These works may be written in an unpolished style, but I adjure all of you, bishops of the Lord, who after me in this my lowliness shall govern the church of Tours, by the coming of our Lord Jesus Christ and by the day of Judgment terrible to all sinners, if ye would not depart confounded from the Judgment, to be condemned with the Evil One, never to let these books be destroyed or rewritten, by choosing out some parts and omitting others, but to leave them all complete and intact in your time just as I myself have left them. But whoever thou art, O priest of God, if our Martianus hath instructed thee in the seven arts, which is to say, if by grammar he hath taught thee to read, by dialectic to discuss propositions for argument, by rhetoric to know the different metres, by geometry to reckon the measurements of surfaces and lines, by astronomy to observe the courses of the stars, by arithmetic to compute the parts of numbers, by music to bring into one harmony songs of sweet accent and modulations of sound; if in all these things thou shalt be so skilled as to hold my style inelegant, even so, I pray thee, remove naught of that which I have written. If aught therein please thee, I refuse thee not permission to translate it into verse; but leave my work complete. I completed the writing of these books in the twenty-first year after my consecration. Although in what has gone before I have set down the list of the bishops of Tours, with the years of their tenure of office, I have not computed the total number as in a chronicle, because I have not been able exactly to discover the intervals between the several consecrations.

The following, then, is the whole sum of the years of the world:

From the beginning to the Deluge, MMCCXLII years.

From the Deluge to the passage of the Red Sea by the children of Israel, MCCCCIV years.

From the passage of the Red Sea to the Resurrection of our Lord, MDXXXVIII years.

From the Resurrection of our Lord to the passing of the holy Martin, CCCCXII years.

From the passing of the holy Martin to the above-mentioned year, I mean the twenty-first of my consecration, which is the fifth of Gregory, pope of Rome, the thirty-first of King Guntram, and the nineteenth of Childebert the young, CXCVII years. The sum of all which years is MMMMMDCCXCII.

Einhard

Rarely do we complain that a biography is too short, that it tantalizes the reader without satisfying his desire to learn more. But this complaint is valid in the case of Einhard's *Life of the Emperor Charles.* This brief work, one of our major sources of information about ninth century Europe and about Charlemagne and his court, is reproduced here in its entirety.

Einhard (occasionally called Eginhard) was remarkably well qualified for the task he set himself. Born in 770 of a wealthy landholding family in the eastern part of Charlemagne's territories, he was destined for a career in the Church. At an early age he received his formal education at the monastery of Fulda (in central Germany), which had been heavily endowed by his family, and about 790 he became a member of the court of Charlemagne. Thus began the long association between the emperor and the monk.

Charlemagne loved his circle of intimates—a circle composed of many of the most highly educated and stimulating minds of the times, including the English theologian and teacher, Alcuin of York. Einhard's presence in this company enabled him to observe Charlemagne at short range and to develop the firsthand knowledge of his subject that gives the biography its authenticity. Einhard survived Charlemagne by about twenty-nine years, occupying himself with church building, acquiring holy relics, taking part in public affairs, and writing. The death of his wife and the political disintegration that set in after Charlemagne's death led Einhard finally to withdraw from public life. He died in 844.

Life of the Emperor Charles

PREFACE

Since I have taken upon myself to narrate the public and private life, and no small part of the deeds of my lord and foster-father, the most excellent and most justly renowned King Charles, I have condensed the matter into as brief a form as possible. I have been careful not to omit any facts that could come to my knowledge, but at the same time not to offend by a prolix style those minds that despise every-

Einhard, *Life of Charlemagne,* trans. S. E. Turner (New York, 1880).

thing modern, if one can possibly avoid offending by a new work men who seem to despise also the masterpieces of antiquity, the works of most learned and luminous writers. Very many of them, I have no doubt, are men devoted to a life of literary leisure, who feel that the affairs of the present generation ought not to be passed by, and who do not consider everything done to-day as unworthy of mention and deserving to be given over to silence and oblivion, but are nevertheless seduced by lust of immortality to celebrate the glorious deeds of other times by some sort of composition rather than to deprive posterity of the mention of their own names by not writing at all.

Be that as it may, I see no reason why I should refrain from entering upon a task of this kind, since no man can write with more accuracy than I of events that took place about me, and of facts concerning which I had personal knowledge, ocular demonstration, as the saying goes, and I have no means of ascertaining whether or not any one else has the subject in hand.

In any event, I would rather commit my story in writing, and hand it down to posterity in partnership with others, so to speak, than to suffer the most glorious life of this most excellent king, the greatest of all the princes of his day, and his illustrious deeds, hard for men of later times to imitate, to be wrapt in the darkness of oblivion.

But there are still other reasons, neither unwarrantable nor insufficient, in my opinion, that urge me to write on this subject, namely, the care that King Charles bestowed upon me in my childhood, and my constant friendship with himself and his children after I began to take up my abode at court. In this way he strongly endeared me to himself, and made me greatly his debtor as well in death as in life; so that were I unmindful of the benefits conferred upon me to keep silence concerning the most glorious and illustrious deeds of a man who claims so much at my hands, and suffer his life to lack due eulogy and written memorial, as if he had never lived, I should deservedly appear ungrateful, and be so considered, albeit my powers are feeble, scanty, next to nothing indeed, and not at all adapted to write and set forth a life that would tax the eloquence of a Tully.

I submit the book. It contains the history of a very great and distinguished man; but there is nothing in it to wonder at besides his deeds, except the fact that I, who am a barbarian, and very little versed in the Roman language, seem to suppose myself capable of writing gracefully and respectably in Latin, and to carry my presumption so far as to disdain the sentiment that Cicero is said in the first book of the "Tusculan Disputations" to have expressed when speaking of the Latin authors. His words are: "It is an outrageous abuse both of time and literature for a man to commit his thoughts to writing without having the ability either to arrange them or elucidate them, or attract readers by some charm of style." This dictum of the famous orator might have deterred me from writing if I had not made up my mind that it was better to risk the opinions of the world, and put my little talents for composition to the test, than to slight the memory of so great a man for the sake of sparing myself.

I. The Merovingian family, from which the Franks used to choose their kings, is commonly said to have lasted until the time of Childeric, who was deposed, shaved, and thrust into the cloister by command of the Roman Pontiff Stephen. But although, to all outward appearance, it ended with him, it had long since been devoid of vital strength and conspicuous only from bearing the empty epithet Royal; the real power and authority in the kingdom lay in the hands of the chief officer of the court, the so-called Mayor of the Palace, and he was at the head of affairs. There was nothing left the King to do but to be content with his name of King, his flowing hair, and long beard; to sit on his throne and play the ruler; to give ear to the ambassadors that came from all quarters, and to dismiss them, as if on his own responsibility, in words that were, in fact, suggested to him, or even imposed upon him. He had nothing that he could call his own beyond this vain title of King, and the precarious support allowed by the Mayor of the Palace in his discretion, except a single country-seat, that brought him but a very small income. There was a dwelling-house upon this, and a small number of servants attached to it, sufficient to perform the necessary offices. When he had to go abroad, he used to ride in a cart, drawn by a yoke of oxen, driven, peasant-fashion by a ploughman; he rode in this way to the palace and to the general assembly of the people, that met once a year for the welfare of the kingdom, and he returned home in like manner. The Mayor of the Palace took charge of the government, and of everything that had to be planned or executed at home or abroad.

II. At the time of Childeric's deposition, Pepin, the father of King Charles, held this office of Mayor of the Palace, one might almost say, by hereditary right; for Pepin's father, Charles, had received it at the hands of his father, Pepin, and filled it with distinction. It was this Charles that crushed the tyrants who claimed to rule the whole Frank land as their own, and that utterly routed the Saracens, when they attempted the conquest of Gaul, in two great battles—one in Aquitania, near the town of Poitiers, and the other on the River Berre, near Narbonne—and compelled them to return to Spain. This honour was usually conferred by the people only upon men eminent from their illustrious birth and ample wealth. For some years, ostensibly under King Childeric, Pepin, the father of King Charles, shared the duties inherited from his father and grandfather most amicably with his brother, Carloman. The latter, then, for reasons unknown, renounced the heavy cares of an earthly crown and retired to Rome. Here he exchanged his worldly garb for a cowl, and built a monastery on Mt. Oreste, near the Church of St. Sylvester, where he enjoyed for several years the seclusion that he desired, in company with certain others who had the same object in view. But so many distinguished Franks made the pilgrimage to Rome to fulfil their vows, and insisted upon paying their respects to him, as their former lord, on the way, that the repose which he so much loved was broken by these frequent visits, and he was driven to change his abode. Accordingly, when he found that his plans were frustrated by his many visitors, he abandoned the mountain, and withdrew to the Monastery of St. Benedict, on Mount Cassino, in the province of Samnium, and passed the rest of his days there in the exercises of religion.

III. Pepin, however, was raised, by decree of the Roman Pontiff, from the rank of Mayor of the Palace to that of King, and ruled alone over the Franks for fifteen years or more. He died of dropsy, in Paris, at the close of the Aquitanian war, which he had waged with William, Duke of Aquitania, for nine successive years, and left two sons, Charles and Carloman, upon whom, by the grace of God, the succession devolved.

The Franks, in a general assembly of the people, made them both kings, on condition that they should divide the whole kingdom equally between them, Charles to take and rule the part that had belonged to their father, Pepin, and Carloman the part which their uncle, Carloman, had governed. The conditions were accepted, and each entered into possession of the share of the kingdom that fell to him by this arrangement; but peace was only maintained between them with the greatest difficulty, because many of Carloman's party kept trying to disturb their good understanding, and there were some even who plotted to involve them in a war with each other. The event, however, showed the danger to have been rather imaginary than real, for at Carloman's

death his widow fled to Italy with her sons and her principal adherents, and without reason, despite her husband's brother, put herself and her children under the protection of Desiderius, King of the Lombards. Carloman had succumbed to disease after ruling two years in common with his brother, and at his death Charles was unanimously elected King of the Franks.

IV. It would be folly, I think, to write a word concerning Charles's birth, and infancy, or even his boyhood, for nothing has ever been written on the subject, and there is no one alive now who can give information of it. Accordingly, I have determined to pass that by as unknown, and to proceed at once to treat of his character, his deeds, and such other facts of his life as are worth telling and setting forth, and shall first give an account of his deeds at home and abroad, then of his character and pursuits, and lastly of his administration and death, omitting nothing worth knowing or necessary to know.

V. His first undertaking in a military way was the Aquitanian war, begun by his father, but not brought to a close; and because he thought that it could be readily carried through, he took it up while his brother was yet alive, calling upon him to render aid. The campaign once opened, he conducted it with the greatest vigour, notwithstanding his brother withheld the assistance that he had promised, and did not desist or shrink from his self-imposed task until, by his patience and firmness, he had completely gained his ends. He compelled Hunold, who had attempted to seize Aquitania after Warifar's death, and renew the war then almost concluded, to abandon Aquitania and flee to Gascony. Even here he gave him no rest, but crossed the River Garonne, built the Castle of Fronsac, and sent ambassadors to Lupus, Duke of Gascony, to demand the surrender of the fugitive, threatening to take him by force unless he were promptly given up to him. Thereupon, Lupus chose the wiser course, and not only gave Hunold up, but submitted himself, with the province which he ruled, to the King.

VI. After bringing this war to an end and settling matters in Aquitania (his associate in authority had meantime departed this life), he was induced, by the prayers and entreaties of Hadrian, Bishop of the city of Rome, to wage war on the Lombards. His father before him had undertaken this task at the request of Pope Stephen, but under great difficulties; for certain leading Franks, of whom he usually took counsel, had so vehemently opposed his design as to declare openly that they would leave the King and go home. Nevertheless, the war against the Lombard king, Astolf, had been taken up and very quickly concluded. Now, although Charles seems to have had similar, or rather just the same grounds for declaring war that his father had, the war itself differed from the preceding one alike in its difficulties and its issue. Pepin, to be sure, after besieging King Astolf a few days in Pavia, had compelled him to give hostages, to restore to the Romans the cities and castles that he had taken, and to make oath that he would not attempt to seize them again: but Charles did not cease, after declaring war, until he had exhausted King Desiderius by a long siege, and forced him to surrender at discretion; driven his son Adalgis, the last hope of the Lombards, not only from his kingdom, but from all Italy; restored to the Romans all that they had lost; subdued Hurodgaus, Duke of Friuli, who was plotting revolution; reduced all Italy to his power, and set his son Pepin as king over it.

At this point I should describe Charles's difficult passage over the Alps into Italy, and the hardships that the Franks endured in climbing the trackless mountain-ridges, the heaven-aspiring cliffs and ragged peaks, if it were not my purpose in this work to record the manner of his life rather than the incidents of the wars that he waged. Suffice it to say this war ended with the subjection of Italy, the banishment of King Desiderius for life, the expulsion of his son Adalgis from Italy, and the restoration of the conquests of the Lombard kings to Hadrian, the head of the Roman Church.

VII. At the conclusion of this struggle, the Saxon war, that seems to have been only laid aside for the time, was taken up again. No war ever undertaken by the Frank nation was carried on with such persistence and bitterness, or cost so much labour, because the Saxons, like almost all the tribes of Germany, were a fierce people, given to the worship of devils, and hostile to our religion, and did not consider it dishonourable to transgress and violate all law, human and divine. Then there were peculiar circumstances that tended to cause a breach of peace every day. Except in a few places, where large forests or mountain-ridges intervened and made the bounds certain, the line between ourselves and the Saxons passed almost in its whole extent through an open country, so that there was no end to the murders, thefts, and arsons on both sides. In this way the Franks became so embittered that they at last resolved to make reprisals no longer, but to come to open war with the Saxons. Accordingly war was begun against them, and was waged for thirty-three successive years with great fury; more, however, to the disadvantage of the Saxons than of the Franks. It could doubtless have been brought to an end sooner, had it not been for the faithlessness of the Saxons. It is hard to say how often they were conquered, and humbly submitted to the King, promised to do what was enjoined upon them, gave without hesitation the required hostages, and received the officers sent them from the King. They were sometimes so much weakened and reduced that they promised to renounce the worship of devils, and to adopt Christianity; but they were no less ready to violate these terms than prompt to accept them, so that it is impossible to tell which came easier to them to do; scarcely a year passed from the beginning of the war without such changes on their part. But the King did not suffer his high purpose and steadfastness—firm alike in good and evil fortune—to be wearied by any fickleness on their part, or to be turned from the task that he had undertaken; on the contrary, he never allowed their faithless behaviour to go unpunished, but either took the field against them in person, or sent his counts with an army to wreak vengeance and exact righteous satis-

faction. At last, after conquering and subduing all who had offered resistance, he took ten thousand of those that lived on the banks of the Elbe, and settled them, with their wives and children, in many different bodies here and there in Gaul and Germany. The war that had lasted so many years was at length ended by their acceding to the terms offered by the King, which were renunciation of their national religious customs and the worship of devils, acceptance of the sacraments of the Christian faith and religion, and union with the Franks to form one people.

VIII. Charles himself fought but two pitched battles in this war, although it was long protracted—one on Mount Osning, at the place called Detmold, and again on the bank of the river Hase, both in the space of little more than a month. The enemy were so routed and overthrown in these two battles that they never afterwards ventured to take the offensive or to resist the attacks of the King, unless they were protected by a strong position. A great many of the Frank as well as the Saxon nobility, men occupying the highest posts of honour, perished in this war, which only came to an end after the lapse of thirty-two years. So many and grievous were the wars that were declared against the Franks in the meantime, and skillfully conducted by the King, that one may reasonably question whether his fortitude or his good fortune is to be more admired. The Saxon war began two years before the Italian war; but although it went on without interruption, business elsewhere was not neglected, nor was there any shrinking from other equally arduous contests. The King, who excelled all the princes of his time in wisdom and greatness of soul, did not suffer difficulty to deter him or danger to daunt him from anything that had to be taken up or carried through, for he had trained himself to bear and endure whatever came, without yielding in adversity, or trusting to the deceitful favours of fortune in prosperity.

IX. In the midst of this vigorous and almost uninterrupted struggle with the Saxons, he covered the frontier by garrisons at the proper points, and marched over the Pyrenees into Spain at the head of all the forces that he could muster. All the towns and castles that he attacked surrendered, and up to the time of his homeward march he sustained no loss whatever; but on his return through the Pyrenees he had cause to rue the treachery of the Gascons. That region is well adapted for ambuscades by reason of the thick forests that cover it; and as the army was advancing in the long line of march necessitated by the narrowness of the road, the Gascons, who lay in ambush on the top of a very high mountain, attacked the rear of the baggage-train and the rear-guard in charge of it, and hurled them down to the very bottom of the valley. In the struggle that ensued, they cut them off to a man; they then plundered the baggage, and dispersed with all speed in every direction under cover of approaching night. The lightness of their armour and the nature of the battleground stood the Gascons in good stead on this occasion, whereas the Franks fought at a disadvantage in every respect, because of the weight of their armour and the unevenness of the ground. Eggihard, the King's steward; Anselm, Count Palatine; and Roland, Governor of the March of Brittany, with very many others, fell in this engagement. This ill turn could not be avenged for the nonce, because the enemy scattered so widely after carrying out their plan that not the least clew could be had to their whereabouts.

X. Charles also subdued the Bretons, who live on the sea-coast, in the extreme western part of Gaul. When they refused to obey him, he sent an army against them, and compelled them to give hostages, and to promise to do his bidding. He afterwards entered Italy in person with his army, and passed through Rome to Capua, a city in Campania, where he pitched his camp and threatened the Beneventans with hostilities unless they should submit themselves to him. Their duke, Aragis, escaped the danger by sending his two sons, Rumold and Grimold, with a great sum of money to meet the King, begging him to accept them as hostages, and promising for himself and his people compliance with all the King's commands, on the single condition that his personal attendance should not be required. The King took the welfare of the people into account rather than the stubborn disposition of the Duke, accepted the proffered hostages, and released him from the obligation to appear before him in consideration of his handsome gift. He retained the younger son only as hostage, and sent the elder back to his father, and returned to Rome, leaving commissioners with Aragis to exact the oath of allegiance, and administer it to the Beneventans. He stayed in Rome several days in order to pay his devotions at the holy places, and then came back to Gaul.

XI. At this time, on a sudden, the Bavarian war broke out, but came to a speedy end. It was due to the arrogance and folly of Duke Tassilo. His wife, a daughter of King Desiderius, was desirous of avenging her father's banishment through the agency of her husband, and accordingly induced him to make a treaty with the Huns, the neighbours of the Bavarians on the east, and not only to leave the King's commands unfulfilled, but to challenge him to war. Charles's high spirits could not brook Tassilo's insubordination, for it seemed to him to pass all bounds; accordingly he straightway summoned his troops from all sides for a campaign against Bavaria, and appeared in person with a great army on the river Lech, which forms the boundary between the Bavarians and the Alemanni. After pitching his camp upon its banks, he determined to put the Duke's disposition to the test by an embassy before entering the province. Tassilo did not think that it was for his own or his people's good to persist, so he surrendered himself to the King, gave the hostages demanded, among them his own son Theodo, and promised by oath not to give ear to any one who should attempt to turn him from his allegiance; so this war, which bade fair to be very grievous, came very quickly to an end. Tassilo, however, was afterwards summoned to the King's presence, and not suffered to depart, and the government of the province that he had

had in charge was no longer intrusted to a duke, but to counts.

XII. After these uprisings had been thus quelled, war was declared against the Slaves who are commonly known among us as Wilzi, but properly, that is to say in their own tongue, are called Welatabians. The Saxons served in this campaign as auxiliaries among the tribes that followed the King's standard at his summons, but their obedience lacked sincerity and devotion. War was declared because the Slaves kept harassing the Abodrite, old allies of the Franks, by continual raids, in spite of all commands to the contrary. A gulf of unknown length, but nowhere more than a hundred miles wide, and in many parts narrower, stretches off towards the east from the Western Ocean. Many tribes have settlements on its shores; and Danes and Swedes, whom we call Northmen, on the northern shore and all the adjacent islands; but the southern shore is inhabited by the Slaves and Aisti, and various other tribes. The Welatabians, against whom the King now made war, were the chief of these; but in a single campaign, which he conducted in person, he so crushed and subdued them that they did not think it advisable thereafter to refuse obedience to his commands.

XIII. The war against the Avars, or Huns, followed, and, except the Saxon war, was the greatest that he waged; he took it up with more spirit than any of his other wars, and made far greater preparations for it. He conducted one campaign in person in Pannonia, of which the Huns then had possession. He intrusted all subsequent operations to his son, Pepin, and governors of the provinces, to counts even, and lieutenants. Although they most vigorously prosecuted the war, it only came to a conclusion after a seven years' struggle. The utter depopulation of Pannonia, and the site of the Khan's palace, now a desert, where not a trace of human habitation is visible, bear witness how many battles were fought in those years, and how much blood was shed. The entire body of the Hun nobility perished in this contest, and all its glory with it. All the money and treasure that had been years amassing was seized, and no war in which the Franks ever engaged within the memory of man brought them such riches and such booty. Up to that time the Huns had passed for a poor people, but so much gold and silver was found in the Khan's palace, and so much valuable spoil taken in battle, that one may well think that the Franks took justly from the Huns what the Huns had formerly taken unjustly from other nations. Only two of the chief men of the Franks fell in this war—Eric, Duke of Friuli, who was killed in Tarsatch, a town on the coast of Liburnia, by the treachery of the inhabitants; and Gerold, Governor of Bavaria, who met his death in Pannonia, slain, with two men that were accompanying him, by an unknown hand while he was marshalling his forces for battle against the Huns, and riding up and down the line encouraging his men. This war was otherwise almost a bloodless one so far as the Franks were concerned, and ended most satisfactorily, although by reason of its magnitude it was long protracted.

XIV. The Saxon war next came to an end as successful as the struggle had been long. The Bohemian and Linonian wars that next broke out could not last long; both were quickly carried through under the leadership of the younger Charles. The last of these wars was the one declared against the Northmen called Danes. They began their career as pirates, but afterwards took to laying waste the coasts of Gaul and Germany with their large fleet. Their King, Godfred, was so puffed with vain aspirations that he counted on gaining empire over all Germany, and looked upon Saxony and Frisia as his provinces. He had already subdued his neighbours the Abodriti, and made them tributary, and boasted that he would shortly appear with a great army before Aix-la-Chapelle, where the King held his court. Some faith was put in his words, empty as they sound, and it is supposed that he would have attempted something of the sort if he had not been prevented by a premature death. He was murdered by one of his own bodyguard, and so ended at once his life and the war that he had begun.

XV. Such are the wars, most skilfully planned and successfully fought, which this most powerful king waged during the forty-seven years of his reign. He so largely increased the Frank kingdom, which was already great and strong when he received it at his father's hands, that more than double its former territory was added to it. The authority of the Franks was formerly confined to that part of Gaul included between the Rhine and the Loire, the Ocean and the Balearic Sea; to that part of

Germany which is inhabited by the so-called Eastern Franks, and is bounded by Saxony and the Danube, the Rhine and the Saale—this stream separates the Thuringians from the Sorabians; and to the country of the Alemanni and Bavarians. By the wars above mentioned he first made tributary Aquitania, Gascony, and the whole of the region of the Pyrenees as far as the River Ebro, which rises in the land of the Navarrese, flows through the most fertile districts of Spain, and empties into the Balearic Sea, beneath the walls of the city of Tortosa. He next reduced and made tributary all Italy from Aosta to Lower Calabria, where the boundary-line runs between the Beneventans and the Greeks, a territory more than a thousand miles long; then Saxony, which constitutes no small part of Germany, and is reckoned to be twice as wide as the country inhabited by the Franks, while about equal to it in length; in addition, both Pannonias, Dacia beyond the Danube, and Istria, Liburnia, and Dalmatia, except the cities on the coast, which he left to the Greek Emperor for friendship's sake, and because of the treaty that he had made with him. In fine, he vanquished and made tributary all the wild and barbarous tribes dwelling in Germany between the Rhine and the Vistula, the Ocean and the Danube, all of which speak very much the same language, but differ widely from one another in customs and dress. The chief among them are the Welatabians, the Sorabians, the Abodriti, and the Bohemians, and he had to make war upon these, but the rest, by far the larger number,

submitted to him of their own accord.

XVI. He added to the glory of his reign by gaining the good-will of several kings and nations; so close, indeed, was the alliance that he contracted with Alphonso, King of Galicia and Asturias, that the latter, when sending letters or ambassadors to Charles, invariably styled himself his man. His munificence won the kings of the Scots also to pay such deference to his wishes that they never gave him any other title than lord, or themselves than subjects and slaves: there are letters from them extant in which these feelings in this regard are expressed. His relations with Aaron, King of the Persians, who ruled over almost the whole of the East, India excepted, were so friendly that this prince preferred his favour to that of all the kings and potentates of the earth, and considered that to him alone marks of honour and munificence were due. Accordingly, when the ambassadors sent by Charles to visit the most holy sepulchre and place of resurrection of our Lord and Saviour presented themselves before him with gifts, and made known their master's wishes, he not only granted what was asked, but gave possession of that holy and blessed spot. When they returned, he despatched his ambassadors with them, and sent magnificent gifts, besides stuffs, perfumes, and other rich products of the Eastern lands. A few years before this, Charles had asked him for an elephant, and he sent the only one that he had. The Emperors of Constantinople, Nicephorus, Michael, and Leo, made advances to Charles, and sought friendship and alliance with him by several embassies; and even when the Greeks suspected him of designing to wrest the empire from them, because of his assumption of the title of Emperor, they made a close alliance with him, that he might have no cause of offence. In fact, the power of the Franks was always viewed by the Greeks and Romans with a jealous eye, whence the Greek proverb "Have the Frank for your friend, but not for your neighbour."

XVII. This King, who showed himself so great in extending his empire and subduing foreign nations, and was constantly occupied with plans to that end, undertook also very many works calculated to adorn and benefit his kingdom, and brought several of them to completion. Among these, the most deserving of mention are the basilica of the Holy Mother of God at Aix-la-Chapelle, built in the most admirable manner, and a bridge over the Rhine at Mayence, half a mile long, the breadth of the river at this point. The bridge was destroyed by fire the year before Charles died, but, owing to his death so soon after, could not be repaired, although he had intended to rebuild it in stone. He began two places of beautiful workmanship—one near his manor called Ingelheim, not far from Mayence; the other at Nimeguen, on the Waal, the stream that washes the south side of the island of the Batavians. But, above all, sacred edifices were the object of his care throughout his whole kingdom; and whenever he found them falling to ruin from age, he commanded the priests and fathers who had charge of them to repair them, and make sure by commissioners that his instructions were obeyed. He also fitted out a fleet for the war with the Northmen; the vessels required for this purpose were built on the rivers that flow from Gaul and Germany into the Northern Ocean. Moreover, since the Northmen continually overran and laid waste the Gallic and German coasts, he caused watch and ward to be kept in all the harbours, and at the mouths of rivers large enough to admit the entrance of vessels, to prevent the enemy from disembarking; and in the South, in Narbonensis and Septimania, and along the whole coast of Italy as far as Rome, he took the same precautions against the Moors, who had recently begun their piratical practices. Hence, Italy suffered no great harm in his time at the hands of the Moors, nor Gaul and Germany from the Northmen, save that the Moors got possession of the Etruscan town of Civita Vecchia by treachery, and sacked it, and the Northmen harried some of the islands in Frisia off the German Coast.

XVIII. Thus did Charles defend and increase as well as beautify his kingdom, as is well known; and here let me express my admiration of his great qualities and his extraordinary constancy alike in good and evil fortune. I will now forthwith proceed to give the details of his private and family life.

After his father's death, while sharing the kingdom with his brother, he bore his unfriendliness and jealousy most patiently, and, to the wonder of all, could not be provoked to be angry with him. Later he married a daughter of Desiderius, King of the Lombards, at the insistance of his mother; but he repudiated her at the end of a year for some reason unknown, and married Hildegard, a woman of high birth, of Suabian origin. He had three sons by her—Charles, Pepin, and Lewis—and as many daughters—Hruodrud, Bertha, and Gisela. He had three other daughters besides these—Theoderada, Hiltrude, and Ruodhaid—two by his third wife, Fastrada, a woman of East Frankish (that is to say, of German) origin, and the third by a concubine, whose name for the moment escapes me. At the death of Fastrada, he married Liutgard, an Alemannic woman, who bore him no children. After her death he had three concubines—Gersuinda, a Saxon, by whom he had Adaltrud; Regina, who was the mother of Drogo and Hugh; and Ethelind, by whom he had Theodoric. Charles's mother, Berthrada, passed her old age with him in great honour; he entertained the greatest veneration for her; and there was never any disagreement between them except when he divorced the daughter of King Desiderius, whom he had married to please her. She died soon after Hildegard, after living to see three grandsons and as many granddaughters in her son's house, and he buried her with great pomp in the Basilica of St. Denis, where his father lay. He had an only sister, Gisela, who had consecrated herself to a religious life from girlhood, and he cherished as much affection for her as for his mother. She also died a few years before him in the nunnery where she had passed her life.

XIX. The plan that he adopted for his children's education was, first of all, to have both boys and girls instructed in the liberal arts, to which he also turned his own attention. As soon as their years admitted, in accordance with the custom of the Franks, the boys had to learn horsemanship, and to practice war and the chase, and the girls to familiarize themselves with clothmaking, and to handle distaff and spindle, that they might not grow indolent through idleness, and he fostered in them every virtuous sentiment. He only lost three of all his children before his death, two sons and one daughter, Charles, who was the eldest, Pepin, whom he had made King of Italy, and Hruodrud, his oldest daughter, whom he had betrothed to Constantine, Emperor of the Greeks. Pepin left one son, named Bernard, and five daughters, Adelaide, Atula, Guntrada, Berthaid, and Theoderada. The King gave a striking proof of his fatherly affection at the time of Pepin's death; he appointed the grandson to succeed Pepin, and had the granddaughters brought up with his own daughters. When his sons and his daughter died, he was not so calm as might have been expected from his remarkably strong mind, for his affections were no less strong, and moved him to tears. Again, when he was told of the death of Hadrian, the Roman Pontiff, whom he had loved most of all his friends, he wept as much as if he had lost a brother, or a very dear son. He was by nature most ready to contract friendships, and not only made friends easily, but clung to them persistently, and cherished most fondly those with whom he had formed such ties. He was so careful of the training of his sons and daughters that he never took his meals without them when he was at home, and never made a journey without them; his sons would ride at his side, and his daughters follow him, while a number of his bodyguard, detailed for their protection, brought up the rear. Strange to say, although they were very handsome women, and he loved them very dearly, he was never willing to marry any of them to a man of their own nation or to a foreigner, but kept them all at home until his death, saying that he could not dispense with their society. Hence, though otherwise happy, he experienced the malignity of fortune as far as they were concerned; yet he concealed his knowledge of the rumours current in regard to them, and of the suspicions entertained of their honour.

XX. By one of his concubines he had a son, handsome in face, but hunchbacked, named Pepin, whom I omitted to mention in the list of his children. When Charles was at war with the Huns, and was wintering in Bavaria, this Pepin shammed sickness, and plotted against his father in company with some of the leading Franks, who seduced him with vain promises of the royal authority. When his deceit was discovered, and the conspirators were punished, his head was shaved, and he was suffered, in accordance with his wishes, to devote himself to a religious life in the monastery of Prum. A formidable conspiracy against Charles had previously been set on foot in Germany, but all the traitors were banished, some of them without mutilation, others after their eyes had been put out. Three of them only lost their lives; they drew their swords and resisted arrest, and,

after killing several men, were cut down, because they could not be otherwise overpowered. It is supposed that the cruelty of Queen Fastrada was the primary cause of these plots, and they were both due to Charles's apparent acquiescence in his wife's cruel conduct, and deviation from the usual kindness and gentleness of his disposition. All the rest of his life he was regarded by every one with the utmost love and affection, so much so that not the least accusation of unjust rigour was ever made against him.

XXI. He liked foreigners, and was at great pains to take them under his protection. There were often so many of them, both in the palace and the kingdom, that they might reasonably have been considered a nuisance; but he, with his broad humanity, was very little disturbed by such annoyances, because he felt himself compensated for these great inconveniences by the praises of his generosity and the reward of high renown.

XXII. Charles was large and strong, and of lofty stature, though not disproportionately tall (his height is well known to have been seven times the length of his foot); the upper part of his head was round, his eyes very large and animated, nose a little long, hair fair, and face laughing and merry. Thus his appearance was always stately and dignified, whether he was standing or sitting; although his neck was thick and somewhat short, and his belly rather prominent; but the symmetry of the rest of his body concealed these defects. His gait was firm, his whole carriage manly, and his voice clear, but not so strong as his size led one to expect. His health was excellent, except during the four years preceding his death, when he was subject to frequent fevers; at the last he even limped a little with one foot. Even in those years he consulted rather his own inclinations than the advice of physicians, who were almost hateful to him, because they wanted him to give up roasts, to which he was accustomed, and to eat boiled meat instead. In accordance with the national custom, he took frequent exercise on horseback and in the chase, accomplishments in which scarcely any people in the world can equal the Franks. He enjoyed the exhalations from natural warm springs, and often practised swimming, in which he was such an adept that none could surpass him; and hence it was that he built his palace at Aix-la-Chapelle, and lived there constantly during his latter years until his death. He used not only to invite his sons to his bath, but his nobles and friends, and now and then a troop of his retinue or bodyguard, so that a hundred or more persons sometimes bathed with him.

XXIII. He used to wear the national, that is to say, the Frank, dress—next his skin a linen shirt and linen breeches, and above these a tunic fringed with silk; while hose fastened by bands covered his lower limbs, and shoes his feet, and he protected his shoulders and chest in winter by a close-fitting coat of otter or marten skins. Over all he flung a blue cloak, and he always had a sword girt about him, usually one with a gold or silver hilt and belt; he sometimes carried a jewelled sword, but only on great feast-days or at the reception of ambassadors from foreign nations. He despised foreign costumes, however handsome, and never allowed himself to be robed in them, except twice in Rome, when he donned the Roman tunic, chlamys, and shoes; the first time at the request of Pope Hadrian, the second to gratify Leo, Hadrian's successor. On great feast-days he made use of embroidered clothes, and shoes bedecked with precious stones; his cloak was fastened by a golden buckle, and he appeared crowned with a diadem of gold and gems, but on other days his dress varied little from the common dress of the people.

XXIV. Charles was temperate in eating, and particularly so in drinking, for he abominated drunkenness in anybody, much more in himself and those of his household; but he could not easily abstain from food, and often complained that fasts injured his health. He very rarely gave entertainments, only on great feast-days, and then to large numbers of people. His meals ordinarily consisted of four courses, not counting the roasts, which his huntsmen used to bring in on the spit; he was more fond of this than of any other dish. While at table, he listened to reading or music. The subjects of the readings were the stories and deeds of olden time: he was fond, too, of St. Augustine's books, and especially of the one entitled "The City of God." He was so moderate in the use of wine and all sorts of drink that he rarely allowed himself more than three cups in the course of a meal. In summer, after the midday meal, he would eat some fruit, drain a single cup, put off his clothes and shoes, just as he did for the night, and rest for two or three hours. He was in the habit of awaking and rising from bed four or five times during the night. While he was dressing and putting on his shoes, he not only gave audience to his friends, but if the Count of the Palace told him of any suit in which his judgment was necessary, he had the parties brought before him forthwith, took cognizance of the case, and gave his decision, just as if he were sitting on the judgment-seat. This was not the only business that he transacted at this time, but he performed any duty of the day whatever, whether he had to attend to the matter himself, or to give commands concerning it to his officers.

XXV. Charles had the gift of ready and fluent speech, and could express whatever he had to say with the utmost clearness. He was not satisfied with command of his native language merely, but gave attention to the study of foreign ones, and in particular was such a master of Latin that he could speak it as well as his native tongue; but he could understand Greek better than he could speak it. He was so eloquent, indeed, that he might have passed for a teacher of eloquence. He most zealously cultivated the liberal arts, held those who taught them in great esteem, and conferred great honours upon them. He took lessons in grammar of the deacon Peter of Pisa, at that time an aged man. Another deacon, Albin of Britain, surnamed Alcuin, a man of Saxon extraction, who was the greatest scholar of the day, was his teacher in other branches of learning. The King spent much time and labour with him studying rhetoric, dialectics, and especially astronomy; he learned to reckon, and used to investigate the motions of the heavenly bodies

most curiously, with an intelligent scrutiny. He also tried to write and used to keep tablets and blanks in bed under his pillow, that at leisure hours he might accustom his hand to form the letters; however, as he did not begin his efforts in due season, but late in life, they met with ill success.

XXVI. He cherished with the greatest fervour and devotion the principles of the Christian religion, which had been instilled into him from infancy. Hence it was that he built the beautiful basilica at Aix-la-Chapelle, which he adorned with gold and silver and lamps, and with rails and doors of solid brass. He had the columns and marbles for this structure brought from Rome and Ravenna, for he could not find such as were suitable elsewhere. He was a constant worshipper at this church as long as his health permitted, going morning and evening, even after nightfall, besides attending mass; and he took care that all the services there conducted should be administered with the utmost possible propriety, very often warning the sextons not to let any improper or unclean thing be brought into the building, or remain in it. He provided it with a great number of sacred vessels of gold and silver, and with such a quantity of clerical robes that not even the doorkeepers, who fill the humblest office in the church, were obliged to wear their every-day clothes when in the exercise of their duties. He was at great pains to improve the church reading and psalmody, for he was well skilled in both, although he neither read in public nor sang, except in a low tone and with others.

XXVII. He was very forward in

succouring the poor, and in that gratuitous generosity which the Greeks call alms, so much so that he not only made a point of giving in his own country and his own kingdom, but when he discovered that there were Christians living in poverty in Syria, Egypt, and Africa, at Jerusalem, Alexandria, and Carthage, he had compassion on their wants, and used to send money over the seas to them. The reason that he zealously strove to make friends with the kings beyond seas was that he might get help and relief to the Christians living under their rule. He cherished the Church of St. Peter the Apostle in Rome above all other holy and sacred places, and heaped its treasury with a vast wealth of gold, silver, and precious stones. He sent great and countless gifts to the popes; and throughout his whole reign the wish that he had nearest at heart was to reestablish the ancient authority of the city of Rome under his care and by his influence, and to defend and protect the Church of St. Peter, and to beautify and enrich it out of his own store above all other churches. Although he held it in such veneration, he only repaired to Rome to pay his vows and make his supplications four times during the whole forty-seven years that he reigned.

XXVIII. When he made his last journey thither, he had also other ends in view. The Romans had inflicted many injuries upon the Pontiff Leo, tearing out his eyes and cutting out his tongue, so that he had been compelled to call upon the King for help. Charles accordingly went to Rome, to set in order the affairs of the Church, which were in great confusion, and passed the whole winter there. It was then that he received the titles of Emperor and Augustus, to which he at first had such an aversion that he declared that he would not have set foot in the Church the day that they were conferred, although it was a great feast-day, if he could have forseen the design of the Pope. He bore very patiently with the jealousy which the Roman emperors showed upon his assuming these titles, for they took this step very ill; and by dint of frequent embassies and letters, in which he addressed them as brothers, he made their haughtiness yield to his magnanimity, a quality in which he was unquestionably much their superior.

XXIX. It was after he had received the imperial name that, finding the laws of his people very defective (the Franks have two sets of laws, very differing in many particulars), he determined to add what was wanting, to reconcile the discrepancies, and to correct what was vicious and wrongly cited in them. However, he went no further in this matter than to supplement the laws by a few capitularies, and those imperfect ones; but he caused the unwritten laws of all the tribes that came under his rule to be compiled and reduced to writing. He also had the old rude songs that celebrate the deeds and wars of the ancient kings written out for transmission to posterity. He began a grammar of his native language. He gave the months names in his own tongue, in place of the Latin and barbarous names by which they were formerly known among the Franks. He likewise designated the winds by twelve appropriate names; there were hardly more than four distinctive ones in use before. He called January Wintarmanoth; February, Hornung; March, Lentzinmanoth; April, Ostarmanoth; May, Winnemanoth; June, Brachmanoth; July, Heuvimanoth; August, Aranmanoth; September, Witumanoth; October, Windumemanoth; November, Herbistmanoth; December, Heilagmanoth. He styled the winds as follows: Subsolanus, Ostroniwint; Eurus, Ostsundroni; Duroauster, Sundostroni; Auster, Sundroni; Austro-Africus, Sundwestroni; Africus, Westsundroni; Zephyrus, Westroni; Caurus, Westnordroni; Circius, Nordwestroni; Septentrio, Nordroni; Aquilo, Nordostroni; Vulturnus, Ostnordroni.

XXX. Towards the close of his life, when he was broken by illhealth and old age, he summoned Lewis, King of Aquitania, his only surviving son by Hildegard, and gathered together all the chief men of the whole kingdom of the Franks in a solemn assembly. He appointed Lewis, with their unanimous consent, to rule with himself over the whole kingdom, and constituted him heir to the imperial name; then, placing the diadem upon his son's head, he bade him be proclaimed Emperor and Augustus. This step was hailed by all present with great favour, for it really seemed as if God had prompted him to it for the kingdom's good; it increased the King's dignity, and struck no little terror into foreign nations. After sending his son back to Aquitania, although weak from age he set out to hunt, as usual, near his palace at Aix-la-Chapelle, and passed the rest of the autumn in the chase, returning thither about the first of November. While wintering there,

he was seized, in the month of January, with a high fever, and took to his bed. As soon as he was taken sick, he prescribed for himself abstinence from food, as he always used to do in case of fever, thinking that the disease could be driven off, or at least mitigated, by fasting. Besides the fever, he suffered from a pain in the side, which the Greeks call pleurisy; but he still persisted in fasting, and in keeping up his strength only by draughts taken at very long intervals. He died January twenty-eighth, the seventh day from the time that he took to his bed, at nine o'clock in the morning, after partaking of the holy communion, in the 72nd year of his age and the 47th of his reign.

XXXI. His body was washed and cared for in the usual manner, and was then carried to the church, and interred amid the greatest lamentations of all the people. There was some question at first where to lay him, because in his lifetime he had given no directions as to his burial; but at length all agreed that he could nowhere be more honourably entombed than in the very basilica that he had built in the town at his own expense, for love of God and our Lord Jesus Christ, and in honour of the Holy and Eternal Virgin, His Mother. He was buried there the same day that he died, and a gilded arch was erected above his tomb with his image and an inscription. The words of the inscription were as follows: "In this tomb lies the body of Charles, the Great and Orthodox Emperor, who gloriously extended the kingdom of the Franks, and reigned prosperously for fortyseven years. He died at the age of seventy-two, in the year of our Lord

814, the 7th Indiction, on the 28th day of January."

XXXII. Very many omens had portended his approaching end, a fact that he had recognized as well as others. Eclipses both of the sun and moon were very frequent during the last three years of his life, and a black spot was visible on the sun for the space of seven days. The gallery between the basilica and the palace, which he had built at great pains and labour, fell in sudden ruin to the ground on the day of the Ascension of our Lord. The wooden bridge over the Rhine at Mayence, which he had caused to be constructed with admirable skill, at the cost of ten years' hard work, so that it seemed as if it might last forever, was so completely consumed in three hours by an accidental fire that not a single splinter of it was left, except what was under water. Moreover, one day in his last campaign into Saxony against Godfred, King of the Danes, Charles himself saw a ball of fire fall suddenly from the heavens with a great light, just as he was leaving camp before sunrise to set out on the march. It rushed across the clear sky from right to left, and everybody was wondering what was the meaning of the sign, when the horse which he was riding gave a sudden plunge, head foremost, and fell, and threw him to the ground so heavily that his cloak-buckle was broken and his sword-belt shattered; and after his servants had hastened to him and relieved him of his arms, he could not rise without their assistance. He happened to have a javelin in his hand when he was thrown, and this was struck from his grasp with such force that it was found lying at a distance of twenty feet or more from the spot. Again, the palace at Aix-la-Chapelle frequently trembled, the roofs of whatever buildings he tarried in kept up a continual crackling noise, the basilica in which he was afterward buried was struck by lightning, and the gilded ball that adorned the pinnacle of the roof was shattered by the thunder-bolt and hurled upon the bishop's house adjoining. In this same basilica, on the margin of the cornice that ran around the interior, between the upper and lower tiers of arches, a legend was inscribed in red letters, stating who was the builder of the temple, the last words of which were *Karolus Princeps.* The year that he died it was remarked by some, a few months before his decease, that the letters of the word *Princeps* were so effaced as to be no longer decipherable. But Charles despised, or affected to despise, all these omens, as having no reference whatever to him.

XXXIII. It had been his intention to make a will, that he might give some share in the inheritance to his daughters and the children of his concubines; but it was begun too late and could not be finished. Three years before his death, however, he made a division of his treasures, money, clothes, and other movable goods in the presence of his friends and servants, and called them to witness it, that their voices might insure the ratification of the disposition thus made. He had a summary drawn up of his wishes regarding this distribution of his property, the terms and text of which are as follows:

"In the name of the Lord God,

the Almighty Father, Son, and the Holy Ghost. This is the inventory and division dictated by the most glorious and most pious Lord Charles, Emperor Augustus, in the 811th year of the Incarnation of our Lord Jesus Christ, in the 43rd year of his reign in France and 37th in Italy, the 11th of his empire, and the 4th Indiction, which considerations of piety and prudence have determined him, and the favour of God enabled him, to make of his treasures and money ascertained this day to be in his treasure-chamber. In this division he is especially desirous to provide not only that the largess of alms which Christians usually make of their possessions shall be made for himself in due course and order out of his wealth, but also that his heirs shall be free from all doubt, and know clearly what belongs to them, and be able to share their property by suitable partition without litigation or strife. With this intention and to this end he has first divided all his substance and movable goods ascertained to be in his treasure-chamber on the day aforesaid in gold, silver, precious stones, and royal ornaments into three lots, and has subdivided and set off two of the said lots into twenty-one parts, keeping the third entire. The first two lots have been thus subdivided into twenty-one parts because there are in his kingdom twenty-one recognized metropolitan cities, and in order that each archbishopric may receive by way of alms, at the hands of his heirs and friends, one of the said parts, and that the archbishop who shall then administer its affairs shall take the part given to it, and share the same with his suffragans in such

manner that one-third shall go to the Church, and the remaining two-thirds be divided among the suffragans. The twenty-one parts into which the first two lots are to be distributed, according to the number of recognized metropolitan cities, have been set apart one from another, and each has been put aside by itself in a box labelled with the name of the city for which it is destined. The names of the cities to which this alms or largess is to be sent are as follows: Rome, Ravenna, Milan, Friuli, Grado, Cologne, Mayence, Salzburg, Treves, Sens, Besancon, Lyons, Rouen, Rheims, Arles, Vienne, Moutiers-en-Tarantaise, Embrun, Bordeaux, Tours, and Bourges. The third lot, which he wishes to be kept entire, is to bestowed as follows: While the first two lots are to be divided into the parts aforesaid, and set aside under seal, the third lot shall be employed for the owner's daily needs, as property which he shall be under no obligation to part with in order to the fulfillment of any vow, and this as long as he shall be in the flesh, or consider it necessary for his use. But upon his death, or voluntary renunciation of the affairs of this world, this said lot shall be divided into four parts, and one thereof shall be added to the aforesaid twenty-one parts; the second shall be assigned to his sons and daughters, and to the sons and daughters of his sons, to be distributed among them in just and equal partition; the third, in accordance with the custom common among Christians, shall be devoted to the poor; and the fourth shall go to the support of the men-servants and maid-servants on duty in the palace. It is his wish that to this said third lot of the whole amount, which consists, as well as the rest, of gold and silver, shall be added all the vessels and utensils of brass, iron, and other metals, together with the arms, clothing, and other movable goods, costly and cheap, adapted to divers uses, as hangings, coverlets, carpets, woolen stuffs, leathern articles, pack-saddles, and whatsoever shall be found in his treasure-chamber and wardrobe at that time, in order that thus the parts of the said lot may be augmented, and the alms distributed reach more persons. He ordains that his chapel—that is to say, its church property, as well that which he has provided and collected as that which came to him by inheritance from his father—shall remain entire, and not be dissevered by any partition whatever. If, however, any vessels, books, or other articles be found therein which are certainly known not to have been given by him to the said chapel, whoever wants them shall have them on paying their value at a fair estimation. He likewise commands that the books which he has collected in his library in great numbers shall be sold for fair prices to such as want them, and the money received therefrom given to the poor. It is well known that among his other property and treasures are three silver tables, and one very large and massive golden one. He directs and commands that the square silver table, upon which

there is a representation of the city of Constantinople, shall be sent to the Basilica of St. Peter the Apostle at Rome, with the other gifts destined therefor; that the round one, adorned with a delineation of the city of Rome, shall be given to the Episcopal Church at Ravenna; that the third, which far surpasses the other two in weight and in beauty of workmanship, and is made in three circles, showing the plan of the whole universe, drawn with skill and delicacy, shall go, together with the golden table, fourthly above mentioned, to increase that lot which is to be devoted to his heirs and to alms.

This deed, and the dispositions thereof he has made and appointed in the presence of the bishops, abbots, and counts able to be present, whose names are hereto subscribed: Bishops—Hildebald, Ricolf, Arno, Wolfar, Bernoin, Laidrad, John, Theodulf, Jesse, Heito, Waltgaud. Abbots—Fredugis, Adalung, Angilbert, Irmino. Counts—Walacho, Meginher, Otulf, Stephen, Unruoch, Burchard, Meginhard, Hatto, Rihwin, Edo, Ercangar, Gerold, Bero, Hildiger, Rocculf."

Charles's son Lewis, who by the grace of God succeeded him, after examining this summary, took pains to fulfill all its conditions most religiously as soon as possible after his father's death.

Life in Country and Town

The preceding selections have given us some idea of the life of the clerics and the nobles during the Middle Ages. But we can have no genuine understanding of a society without knowing something about the ways in which the vast majority of the people made their living and about the obligations they had toward the political groups that dominated them. For example, our understanding of the ancient world would be vastly enriched if we had reliable accounts of the slave society of Athens or the small landholders of Sparta, or if we knew more of the causes of the Spartacus revolt under the Roman Republic, or if we had detailed information on the organization of the *latifundia* in the days of the Empire. Happily, our information about the daily life of everyman during the Middle Ages is somewhat more abundant, though still far from plentiful.

Generally, the social and economic historian gleans facts from hundreds of wills, deeds, transaction records, court cases, and the like. From these minuscule and fragmentary records he draws his generalizations. But we must remember that the people who lived during the Middle Ages were not quantitatively and economically oriented, as we in the modern world are. Consequently, we dare not put too much faith in their recorded statistics. The medieval chronicler might, for example, refer to an army of sixty thousand men, but the modern historian would be unwise to accept this figure at face value. Chances are the chronicler picked the number at random to dramatize the notion of a "very large" army. Moreover, general statements and observations on economic matters during the Middle Ages are rare, reflecting perhaps a lack of interest in that realm of human activity.

The first two documents that follow give us a glimpse into rural life in the Middle Ages, as it was lived by the common people. The first, *Rights and Ranks of People,* is an Anglo-Saxon account, probably dating from the early eleventh century. The second, *Surveys of Certain Manors Belonging to the Abbey of Peterborough,* is an Anglo-Norman document of the early twelfth century. The final selection, *Charter of the Liberties of Lorris,* reveals some facets of life in the towns. The charter was granted by Louis VII to the small north-central French town of Lorris in 1155. Historically it is important because it served as a model for numerous town charters in the years that followed.

Rights and Ranks of People

Thegn's law. The law of the thegn is that he be entitled to his book-right,[1] and that he shall contribute three things in respect to his land: armed service, and the repairing of fortresses and work on bridges.[2] Also in respect of many estates, further service arises on the king's order such as service connected with the deer fence at the king's residence, and equipping a guardship, and guarding the coast, and guarding the lord, and military watch, almsgiving and church dues and many other various things.

Geneat's right.[3] The geneat's right is various according to what is fixed in respect of the estate: in some he must pay rent and contribute a pasturage swine a year, ride and perform carrying service and furnish means of carriage, work and entertain his lord, reap and mow, cut deer hedges and keep up places from which deer may be shot, build and fence the lord's house, bring strangers to the village, pay church dues and alms money, act as guard to his lord, take care of the horses, and carry messages far and near wheresoever he is directed.

Cottar's right.[4] The cottar's right is according to the custom of the estate: in some he must work for his lord each Monday throughout the year, or 3 days each week at harvest-time. . . . He does not make land payment.[5] He should have 5 acres: more if it be the custom of the estate; and it is too little if it ever be less; because his work must be frequent. Let him give his hearth-penny[6] on Ascension Day even as each freeman ought to do. Let him also perform services on his lord's demesne-land[7] if he is ordered, by keeping watch on the sea-coast and working at the king's

---

[1] Land protected by charter.

[2] The ancient *trinoda necessitas.*

[3] *Geneat:* the original meaning of the word is courtier or companion. By the middle of the eleventh century some kind of service was implied. *Geneat* is translated in the Latin version as *villanus,* but his position does not correspond with that occupied by the typical villein of later surveys. Here he appears as primarily a riding servant, acting perhaps as a bailiff on a large estate. He was a man of some standing. His agricultural work is limited and is confined to boon-works at harvest-time, etc.

[4] The cottar's holding of approximately 5 acres was to be characteristic of the later manorial economy. Sometimes these men were later described as *lundinarii,* "Monday-men."

[5] *Landgafol.*

[6] Peter's Pence.

[7] "Inland."

"Rights and Ranks of People," trans. S. I. Tucker, *English Historical Documents 1042–1189,* eds. D. C. Douglas and G. W. Greenaway (London: Eyre & Spottiswoode; New York: Oxford University Press, Inc., 1953), pp. 813–16. Courtesy of Miss S. I. Tucker, Eyre & Spottiswoode, Ltd., and Oxford University Press, Inc. The footnotes are the translator's.

deer fence and such things according to his condition. Let him pay his church dues at Martinmas.

Boor's right. The boor's [8] duties are various, in some places heavy and in others light. On some estates the custom is that he must perform week-work for 2 days in each week of the year [9] as he is directed, and 3 days from the Feast of the Purification to Easter. If he perform carrying service he need not work while his horse is out. At Michaelmas he must pay 10 pence for *gafol*,[10] and at Martinmas 23 sesters of barley, and 2 hens, and at Easter a young sheep or 2 pence. And he must lie from Martinmas to Easter at his lord's fold as often as it falls to his lot; and from the time when ploughing is first done until Martinmas he must each week plough 1 acre, and himself present the seed in the lord's barn. Also [he must plough] 3 acres as boon-work,[11] and 2 for pasturage. If he needs more grass, let him earn it as he may be permitted. Let him plough 3 acres as his tribute land [12] and sow it from his own barn, and pay his hearth-penny.[13] And every pair of boors must maintain 1 hunting dog, and each boor

must give 6 loaves to the herdsman of the lord's swine when he drives his herd to the mast-pasture. On the same land to which the customs apply a farmer ought to be given for his occupation of the land 2 oxen, 1 cow, 6 sheep and 7 acres sown on his rood of land. After [14] that year let him perform all the dues that fall to him, and let him be given tools for his work and utensils for his house. When death befalls him let the lord take charge of what he leaves.

The estate-law is fixed on each estate: at some places, as I have said, it is heavier, at some places, also, lighter, because not all customs about estates are alike. On some estates a boor must pay tribute in honey, on some in food, on some in ale. Let him who has the shire [15] always know what are the ancient arrangements about the estate and what is the custom of the district.

About the bee-keeper. A bee-keeper if he holds a swarm which is subject to payment must pay what is appointed on that estate. Amongst us it is appointed that he should give 5 sesters of honey as tax: in some estates a greater tax is due. Also at certain times he must be ready for many sorts of work at his lord's pleasure besides boon-work and the cutting of corn when ordered and the mowing of meadows. And if he will be provided with land he must be provided with a horse so as to give it to supply his lord

---

[8] *Gebur.* Compare his service with those of the later villein.

[9] One of the chief characteristics of villein tenure: so many days' work each week for the benefit of the lord.

[10] Perhaps "rent" or "tribute" would be a suitable translation.

[11] Special services at special times of the year.

[12] Probably the lord's land scattered in the strips of the open fields to be cultivated by the peasant for the lord's benefit.

[13] By contrast to the above a characteristic of freedom.

[14] Or "during."

[15] Possibly the sheriff, but not necessarily so. The steward of a great lord might be so described.

with a beast of burden or to go with his horse himself, whichever he is directed. And many things must a man of such condition do: I cannot recount them all now. When death befalls him let his lord take charge of what he leaves unless there should be anything free.

A swine-herd at pay [16] ought to pay for his animals that are to be slaughtered according to the amount fixed on the estate. On many estates it is fixed that he pay every year 15 swine for killing, 10 old and 5 young. Let him have himself whatever he raises beyond that. On many estates a more severe due is incumbent on the swine-herd. Let each swine-herd take care that after the slaughter of his swine he prepare them properly and singe them: then he will be well entitled to the perquisites. Also he must be—as I said before about the bee-keeper—always ready for every sort of work, and provided with a horse at the lord's need.

A slave swine-herd and a slave bee-keeper after death are liable to one and the same law.

A herdsman slave belonging to his lord who keeps the demesne herd ought to have a young pig kept in a sty, and his perquisites when he has prepared the bacon, and also the dues that belong to a slave.

About men's provisioning. Every slave ought to have as provisions 12 pounds of good corn and 2 carcasses of sheep and 1 good cow for food [17]

and the right of cutting wood according to the custom of the estate.

About women's provisioning. For a female slave 8 pounds of corn for food, 1 sheep or 3 pence for winter food, 1 sester of beans for lenten food, whey in summer or 1 penny.

All slaves belonging to the estate ought to have food at Christmas and Easter, a strip of land for ploughing and a "harvest-handful" besides their dues.

About retainers. A retainer [18] ought to have the use of 2 acres, 1 sown and 1 not sown. Let him sow the latter himself. And he is entitled to his food and shoes and gloves.

About the sower. A sower ought to have a seedlip full of every kind of seed when he has properly sown every seed throughout the space of a year.

About the ox-herd. The ox-herd must pasture 2 oxen or more with the lord's herd on the common pasture with the cognizance of the overseer. Let him earn thereby shoes and gloves for himself. And his cow for food must go with the lord's oxen.

About the cow-herd. A cow-herd ought to have an old cow's milk for a week after she has newly calved, and the beestings of a young cow for a fortnight. His cow for food is to go with the lord's cow [?oxen].

---

[16] *Gafolswane.*

[17] Note that it is only the food of the slave that is indicated. His obligations are probably regarded as unlimited subject only to the custom of the estate.

[18] Clearly a privileged person on the estate.

About the shepherd. A shepherd's due is that he should have 12 nights' dung at Christmas, and 1 lamb from the year's young ones, 1 bell-wether's fleece, and the milk of his flock for a week after the equinox, and a bowl-full of whey or buttermilk all summer.

About the goat-herd. A goat-herd ought to have the milk of his herd after Martinmas, and before that his portion of whey, and 1 kid a year old, if he looks after his herd properly.

About the cheese-maker. 100 cheeses pertain to the cheese-maker, and it behooves her to make butter for the lord's table out of the whey pressed out from the cheese, and let her have all the buttermilk except the shepherd's portion.[19]

About the keeper of the granary. The granary-keeper ought to have the corn spilt at the barn door at harvest-time if his overseer grant it to him, and if he deserves it.

About the beadle. The beadle ought to be more free from work because of his office, since he is bound to be always ready. Also he ought to have some bit of land for his labour.

About the woodward. Every tree blown down by the wind ought to go to the woodward.

It[20] is proper that the hayward should be rewarded for his labour in those parts which lie near the pasture; because if he has neglected his work he can expect . . . (if) he has been granted such a piece of land it must be nearest the pasture by custom; because, if out of laziness he neglects his lord's land his own will not be protected if it is provided in this way. If he makes properly secure what he has to guard he will be well entitled to his reward.

The customs of estates are various, as I have said before. Nor do we apply these regulations we have described to all districts. But we declare what the custom is where it is known to us. If we learn better, we will eagerly delight in what we learn and maintain it according to the custom of the district in which we then live.

Wherefore one must delight among the people to learn laws if one does not oneself wish to lose honor on the estate.

There are many common rights: in some districts are due winter provisions, Easter provisions, a harvest feast for reaping the corn, a drinking feast for ploughing, reward for haymaking, food for making the rick, at wood-carrying a log from each load, at corn-carrying food on completion of the rick, and many things which I cannot recount.

This, however, is a memorandum of people's provisions. And all these I have enumerated before.

---

[19] This entry presents certain difficulties. The process of butter-making here described seems impossible. The cheese-maker is definitely a woman.

[20] This entry is defective and obscure. The meaning seems to be that the land of the hayward should be so situated as to suffer first from straying beasts if he has neglected his duties.

Surveys of Certain Manors Belonging
to the Abbey of Peterborough (1125–1128)

This is the description of the manors of the abbey of Peterborough as Walter the archdeacon received them and possessed them in the hand of the king.

In Kettering are 10 hides [1] for the king's geld. And of these 10 hides 40 villeins hold 40 virgates.[1] And these men plough in the spring from each virgate 4 acres for the work of the lord. And besides this they provide ploughs for the work of the lord four times in the winter, and three times in the spring and once in the summer. And these men have 22 ploughs with which they work. And all these men work for the lord 3 days in each week. And besides this they render each year from each virgate by custom 2 shillings and 3 halfpence. And all the men render 50 hens and 640 eggs. And besides this, Ailric holds 13 acres with 2 acres of meadow, and pays for them 16 pence. And there is a mill with a miller and it pays 20 shillings. And 8 cottars each of whom has 5 acres and they work (for the lord) 1 day each week, and twice a year they make malt. And each one of them gives 1 penny for a he-goat (if he has one) and 1 half-

penny for a nanny-goat. And there is a shepherd and a swine-herd who holds 8 acres. And in the court of the demesne there are 4 ploughs with 32 oxen, and 12 cows with 10 calves, 2 beasts for food, 3 draught horses, 300 sheep, 50 pigs, and 16 shillings' worth of the surplus hay from the meadow. The church of Kettering belongs to the altar of the abbey of Peterborough. And for the love of St. Peter it renders 4 rams and 2 cows or 5 shillings. . . .

In Pilsgate there are 3 hides for the king's geld. And 3 villeins hold 1 hide and 1 virgate. And these have 2 ploughs with which they plough for the lord 8 acres for the winter sowing and 8 acres for the spring sowing; and they work 3 days each week for the lord. And there is 1 bordar and 2 ox-herds holding land by service. And there is 1 shepherd. And there are 44 sokemen. And all these together with the villeins pay 44 shillings a year. And all these sokemen have 8 ploughs and with them they plough for the lord three times a year. And each one of them reaps in August half an acre of the lord's corn, and they give boon-work twice in August. And each one harrows 1 day in spring. And there is a mill which pays 4 shillings.

---

[1] [A measure of land.—*Ed.*]

"Surveys of Certain Manors Belonging to the Abbey of Peterborough," in *English Historical Documents 1042–1189*, eds. D. C. Douglas and G. W. Greenaway (London: Eyre & Spottiswoode; New York: Oxford University Press, Inc., 1953), pp. 829–30. Courtesy of Eyre & Spottiswoode (Publishers) Ltd. and Oxford University Press.

And in the court of the demesne there is 1 plough with 8 oxen, and 1 boar and 2 calves and 1 horse for harrowing and 2 foals. And 180 sheep and 20 pigs. On the Feast of St. Peter [is paid] 6 sheep or 1 cow and 5 ells of cloth.

In Thorpe Achurch are 2 hides and 1 virgate for the king's geld. And there are 12 full villeins and each of them holds 11 acres and works (for the lord) 3 days each week. And 6 half-villeins who perform the same in proportion to their holdings. And all of these make a customary payment of 10 shillings. And besides this they pay for love of St. Peter 5 "multones," and 10 ells of cloth, and 10 baskets and 200 loaves. And all these men plough 16½ acres for the lord's work. And there are 6 bordars who pay 7 shillings. And all these pay each year 22 skepfuls of oats in return for dead wood and 22 loaves and 64 hens and 160 eggs. And one sokeman is there who performs service with a horse. And William, son of Ansered, holds a fourth part of 3 yardlands by knight-service. And William, son of Odard the cook, holds a fourth part of 3 yardlands by service in the abbot's kitchen. And the men of this William perform work for the court, that is to say, they provide their ploughs for the lord twice a year. And on the land of this William there are 4 full villeins who reap half an acre in August. And Godric holds a fourth part of 3 yardlands, and for that he and his horse do the abbot's service, providing their own food. And this Godric has 3 villeins and each one of them reaps half an acre for the abbot in August, and with their ploughs they perform two boonworks. In the court of the demesne there are 2 ploughs with 16 oxen, and 3 cows and 8 beasts for food and 1 draught horse and 8 pigs.

In Collingham there are 4 carucates and 1 bovate less a fifth part of 1 bovate for the king's geld. And there are 20 villeins who hold 1½ carucates. Each one of these works for the lord throughout the year 1 day in each week. And in August he performs his boon-works. And all these men bring 60 cartloads of wood to the lord's court, and they also dig and provide 20 cartloads of turves, or 20 cartloads of thatch. And they must harrow throughout the winter. And each year they pay 4 pounds of rent. And there are 50 sokemen who hold 2½ carucates of land. And each one of these must work by custom each year for 6 days at the deer hedge. And in August each shall work 3 days. And all these have 14 ploughs and with them they shall work for the lord four times in Lent. And they plough 48 acres, and harrow, and reap in August. And the aforesaid sokemen pay 12 pounds each year. And in the court of the demesne are 2 ploughs with 16 oxen, and 4 cows and calves and 1 beast for food and 160 sheep and 12 pigs. . . .

Charter of the Liberties of Lorris

1. Let whoever shall have a house in the parish of Lorris pay a quit-rent of six deniers only for his house, and each acre of land which he shall have in this parish; and if he make such an acquisition, let that be the quit-rent of his house.

2. Let no inhabitant of the parish of Lorris pay a duty of entry nor any tax for his food, and let him not pay any duty of measurement for the corn which his labor, or that of the animals which he may have shall procure him, and let him pay no duty for the wine which he shall get from his vines.

3. Let none of them go on a [military] expedition on foot or horseback, whence he cannot return home the same day if he desire to do so.

4. Let none of them pay toll to Étampes, to Orleans, or to Milly, which is in Gâtinais, or to Melun.

5. Let no one who has property in the parish of Lorris lose any of it for any misdeed whatsoever, unless the said misdeed be committed against us or any of our guests.

6. Let no one going to the fairs or markets of Lorris, or in returning, be stopped or inconvenienced unless he shall have committed some misdeed that same day; and let no one on a fair or market day at Lorris, seize the bail given by his security; unless the bail be given the same day.

7. Let forfeitures of sixty sous be reduced to five, that of five sous to twelve deniers, and the provost's fee in cases of plaint, to four deniers.

8. Let no man of Lorris be forced to go out of it to plead before the lord king.

9. Let no one, neither us nor any other, take any tax, offering, or exaction from the men of Lorris.

10. Let no one sell wine at Lorris with public notice, except the king, who shall sell his wine in his cellar with that notice.

11. We will have at Lorris, for our service and that of the queen, a credit of a full fortnight, in the articles of provisions; and if any inhabitant have received a gage from the lord king, he shall not be bound to keep it more than eight days, unless he please.

12. If any have had a quarrel with another, but without breaking a closed house, and if it be accommodated without plaint brought before the provost, no fine shall be due, on this account, to us or to our provost; and if there has been a plaint they can still come to an agreement when they shall have paid the fine. And if any one bear plaint against another, and there has been no fine awarded against either one to the other, they shall not, on that account, owe anything to us or our provost.

13. If any one owe an oath to another, let the latter have permission to remit it.

Carta Franchesie Lorriaci, trans. W. Hazlitt.

14. If any men of Lorris have rashly given their pledge of a duel, and if with the consent of the provost they accommodate it before the pledges have been given, let each pay two sous and a half; and if the pledges have been given, let each pay seven sous and a half; and if the duel has been between men having the right of fighting in the lists, then let the hostages of the conquered pay one hundred and twelve sous.

15. Let no man of Lorris do forced work for us, unless it be twice a year to take our wine to Orleans, and nowhere else; and those only shall do this who shall have horses and carts, and they shall be informed of it beforehand; and they shall receive no lodging from us. The laborers also shall bring wood for our kitchen.

16. No one shall be detained in prison if he can furnish bail for his appearance in court.

17. Whoever desires to sell his property may do so; and having received the price, he may leave the town, free and unmolested, if he please so to do, unless he has committed any misdeed in the town.

18. Whoever shall have remained a year and a day in the parish of Lorris without any claim having pursued him thither, and without the right having been interdicted him, whether by us or our provost, he shall remain there free and tranquil.

19. No one shall plead against another unless it be to recover, and ensure the observance of, what is his due.

20. When the men of Lorris shall go to Orleans with merchandise, they shall pay, upon leaving the town, one denier for their cart, when they go not for sake of the fair; and when they go for the sake of the fair and the market, they shall pay, upon leaving Orleans, four deniers for each cart; and on entering, two deniers.

21. At marriages in Lorris, the public cryer shall have no fee, nor he who keeps watch.

22. No cultivator of the parish of Lorris, cultivating his land with the plow, shall give, in the time of harvest, more than one hermine [six bushels] of rye to all the serjeants of Lorris.

23. If any knight or serjeant find, in our forests, horses or other animals belonging to the men of Lorris, he must not take them to any other than to the provost of Lorris; and if any animal of the parish of Lorris, put to flight by bulls, or assailed by flies, have entered our forest, or leaped our banks, the owner of the animal shall owe no fine to the provost, if he can swear that the animal has entered in spite of his keeper. But if the animal entered with the knowledge of his keeper, the owner shall pay twelve deniers, and as much for each animal, if there be more than one.

24. There shall be at Lorris no duty paid for using the oven.

25. There shall be at Lorris no watch rate.

26. All men of Lorris who shall take salt or wine to Orleans, shall pay only one denier for each cart.

27. No men of Lorris shall owe any fine to the provost of Étampes, nor to the provost of Pithiviers nor to any in Gâtinais.

28. None among them shall pay the entry dues in Ferrières, nor in

Château-Landon, nor in Puiseaux, nor in Nibelle.

29. Let the men of Lorris take the dead wood in the forest for their own use.

30. Whosoever, in the market of Lorris, shall have bought or sold anything, and shall have forgotten to pay the duty, may pay it within eight days without being troubled, if he can swear that he did not withhold the right wittingly.

31. No man of Lorris having a house or a vineyard, or a meadow, or a field, or any buildings in the domain of St. Benedict, shall be under the jurisdiction of the abbot of St. Benedict or his serjeant, unless it be with regard to the quitrent in kind, to which he is bound; and, in that case, he shall not go out of Lorris to be judged.

32. If any of the men of Lorris be accused of anything, and the accuser cannot prove it by witness, he shall clear himself by a single oath from the assertion of his accuser.

33. No man of this parish shall pay any duty because of what he shall buy or sell for his use on the territory of the precincts, nor for what he shall buy on Wednesday at the market.

34. These customs are granted to the men of Lorris, and they are common to the men who inhabit Courpalais, Chanteloup, and the bailiwick of Harpard.

35. We order that whenever the provost shall be changed in the town, he shall swear faithfully to observe these customs; and the same shall be done by new serjeants when they shall be instituted.

Given at Orleans in the year of our Lord 1155.

Magna Carta

It is conventional to cite Magna Carta as one of the great charters of liberty in the Anglo-Saxon legal heritage. And yet, if we examine the document with due regard for the time and place of its signing, we may find that the fictions which have grown up around it have obscured its real significance. For example, when English parliamentarians during the civil war of the seventeenth century sought precedents for their invasion of royal prerogatives, they cited the famous Chapter 39 of the Great Charter. According to this section the Crown was to guarantee that "no freeman shall be taken or imprisoned . . . except by the lawful judgment of his peers or by the law of the land." Superficially, this passage may be taken as a guarantee of trial by jury and freedom from arbitrary arrest, and a statement of the subservience of all (including the king) to the law of the land. Thus, Magna Carta becomes a milestone on the high road to democracy.

This fiction is certainly attractive, but it remains only a fiction. In 1215 Magna Carta was imposed upon King John by a group of Anglo-Norman barons who insisted that John live within the framework of the feudal contract. The Charter was a solemn agreement—of debatable legal validity, however, since it was extracted from the king by force—that both king and baron would respect their mutual duties and obligations, as defined in the feudal ceremonies of homage, fealty, and investiture.

Here, of course, lies the real significance of Magna Carta. The document is a clear expression of feudal institutions and ideas, from which we can derive an accurate picture of the most highly developed feudal society of Western Europe. The feudalism that the Normans under William the Conqueror brought to England in 1066 reached its clearest expression when it was laid over the indigenous Anglo-Saxon society.

Magna Carta

John, by the grace of God, king of England, lord of Ireland, duke of Normandy and Aquitaine, count of Anjou, to the archbishops, bishops, abbots, earls, barons, justiciars, foresters, sheriffs, reeves, servants, and all bailiffs and his faithful people greeting. Know that by the suggestion of God and for the good of our soul and those of all our predecessors and of our heirs, to the honor of God and the exaltation of holy church, and the improvement of our kingdom, by the advice of our venerable fathers Stephen, archbishop of Canterbury, primate of all England and Cardinal of the Holy Roman Church, Henry, archbishop of Dublin, William of London, Peter of Winchester, Joscelyn of Bath and Glastonbury, Hugh of Lincoln, Walter of Worcester, William of Coventry, and Benedict of Rochester, bishops; of Master Pandulf, subdeacon and member of the household of the lord Pope, of Brother Aymeric, master of the Knights of the Temple in England; and of the noblemen William Marshall, earl of Pembroke, William, earl of Salisbury, William, earl of Warren, William, earl of Arundel, Alan of Galloway, constable of Scotland, Warren Fitz-Gerald, Peter Fitz-Herbert, Hubert de Burgh, seneschal of Poitou, Hugh de Nevil, Matthew Fitz-Herbert, Thomas Bassett, Alan Bassett, Philip d'Albini, Robert de Ropesle, John Marshall, John Fitz-Hugh, and others of our faithful.

1. In the first place we have granted to God, and by this our present charter confirmed, for us and our heirs forever, that the English church shall be free, and shall hold its rights entire and its liberties uninjured; and we will that it thus be observed; which is shown by this, that the freedom of elections, which is considered to be most important and especially necessary to the English church, we, of our pure and spontaneous will, granted, and by our charter confirmed, before the contest between us and our barons had arisen; and obtained a confirmation of it by the lord Pope Innocent III; which we will observe and which we will shall be observed in good faith by our heirs forever.

We have granted moreover to all free men of our kingdom for us and our heirs forever all the liberties written below, to be had and holden by themselves and their heirs from us and our heirs.

2. If any of our earls or barons, or others holding from us in chief by military service shall have died, and when he has died his heir shall be of full age and owe relief, he shall have his inheritance by the ancient relief; that is to say, the heir or heirs of an earl for the whole barony of an earl a hundred pounds; the heir or heirs of a baron for a

"Magna Carta," *Select Documents of English Constitutional History,* eds. G. B. Adams and H. M. Stephens (New York, 1901).

whole barony a hundred pounds; the heir or heirs of a knight, for a whole knight's fee, a hundred shillings at most; and who owes less let him give less according to the ancient custom of fiefs.

3. If moreover the heir of any one of such shall be under age, and shall be in wardship, when he comes of age he shall have his inheritance without relief and without a fine.

4. The custodian of the land of such a minor heir shall not take from the land of the heir any except reasonable products, reasonable customary payments, and reasonable services, and this without destruction or waste of men or of property; and if we shall have committed the custody of the land of any such a one to the sheriff or to any other who is to be responsible to us for its proceeds, and that man shall have caused destruction or waste from his custody we will recover damages from him, and the land shall be committed to two legal and discreet men of that fief, who shall be responsible for its proceeds to us or to him to whom we have assigned them; and if we shall have given or sold to anyone the custody of any such land, and he has caused destruction or waste there, he shall lose that custody, and it shall be handed over to two legal and discreet men of that fief who shall be in like manner responsible to us as is said above.

5. The custodian moreover, so long as he shall have the custody of the land, must keep up the houses, parks, warrens, fish ponds, mills, and other things pertaining to the land, from the proceeds of the land itself; and he must return to the heir, when he has come to full age, all his land, furnished with ploughs and implements of husbandry according as the time of wainage requires and as the proceeds of the land are able reasonably to sustain.

6. Heirs shall be married without disparity, so nevertheless that before the marriage is contracted, it shall be announced to the relatives by blood of the heir himself.

7. A widow, after the death of her husband, shall have her marriage portion and her inheritance immediately and without obstruction, nor shall she give anything for her dowry or for her marriage portion, or for her inheritance which inheritance her husband and she held on the day of the death of her husband; and she may remain in the house of her husband for forty days after his death, within which time her dowry shall be assigned to her.

8. No widow shall be compelled to marry so long as she prefers to live without a husband, provided she gives security that she will not marry without our consent, if she holds from us, or without the consent of her lord from whom she holds, if she holds from another.

9. Neither we nor our bailiffs will seize any land or rent, for any debt, so long as the chattels of the debtor are sufficient for the payment of the debt; nor shall the pledges of a debtor be distrained so long as the principal debtor himself has enough for the payment of the debt; and if the principal debtor fails in the payment of the debt, not having the wherewithal to pay it, the pledges shall be responsible for the debt; and if they wish, they shall have the lands and the rents of the debtor until they shall have been

satisfied for the debt which they have before paid for him, unless the principal debtor shall have shown himself to be quit in that respect towards those pledges.

. . .

12. No scutage or aid shall be imposed in our kingdom except by the common council of our kingdom, except for the ransoming of our body, for the making of our oldest son a knight, and for once marrying our oldest daughter, and for these purposes it shall be only a reasonable aid; in the same way it shall be done concerning the aids of the city of London.

13. And the city of London shall have all its ancient liberties and free customs, as well by land as by water. Moreover, we will and grant that all other cities and boroughs and villages and ports shall have all their liberties and free customs.

14. And for holding a common council of the kingdom concerning the assessment of an aid otherwise than in the three cases mentioned above, or concerning the assessment of a scutage we shall cause to be summoned the archbishops, bishops, abbots, earls, and greater barons by our letters individually; and besides we shall cause to be summoned generally, by our sheriffs and bailiffs all those who hold from us in chief, for a certain day, that is at the end of forty days at least, and for a certain place; and in all the letters of that summons, we will express the cause of the summons, and when the summons has thus been given the business shall proceed on the appointed day, on the advice of those who shall be present, even if not all of those who were summoned have come.

15. We will not grant to any one moreover, that he shall take an aid from his free men, except for ransoming his body, for making his oldest son a knight, and for once marrying his oldest daughter; and for these purposes only a reasonable aid shall be taken.

16. No one shall be compelled to perform any greater service for a knight's fee, or for any other free tenement than is owed from it.

17. The common pleas shall not follow our court, but shall be held in some certain place.

. . .

20. A free man shall not be fined for a small offence, except in proportion to the measure of the offence; and for a great offence he shall be fined in proportion to the magnitude of the offence, saving his freehold; and a merchant in the same way, saving his merchandise; and the villain shall be fined in the same way, saving his wainage, if he shall be at our mercy; and none of the above fines shall be imposed except by the oaths of honest men of the neighborhood.

21. Earls and barons shall only be fined by their peers, and only in proportion to their offence.

22. A clergyman shall be fined, like those before mentioned, only in proportion to his lay holding, and not according to the extent of his ecclesiastical benefice.

. . .

26. If any person holding a lay fief from us shall die, and our sheriff or bailiff shall show our letters-patent of our summons concerning a debt which the deceased owed to us, it shall be lawful for our sheriff or bailiff to attach and levy on the chattels of the deceased found on

his lay fief, to the value of that debt, in the view of legal men, so nevertheless that nothing be removed thence until the clear debt to us shall be paid; and the remainder shall be left to the executors for the fulfilment of the will of the deceased; and if nothing is owed to us by him, all the chattels shall go to the deceased, saving to his wife and children their reasonable shares.

27. If any free man dies intestate, his chattels shall be distributed by the hands of his near relatives and friends, under the oversight of the church, saving to each one the debts which the deceased owed to him.

28. No constable or other bailiff of ours shall take any one's grain or other chattels, without immediately paying for them in money, unless he is able to obtain a postponement at the goodwill of the seller.

· · ·

32. We will not hold the lands of those convicted of a felony for more than a year and a day, after which the lands shall be returned to the lords of the fiefs.

· · ·

35. There shall be one measure of wine throughout our whole kingdom, and one measure of ale, and one measure of grain, that is the London quarter, and one width of dyed cloth and of russets and of halbergets, that is two ells within the selvages; of weights, moreover it shall be as of measures.

36. Nothing shall henceforth be given or taken for a writ of inquisition concerning life or limbs, but it shall be given freely and not denied.

· · ·

38. No bailiff for the future shall put any one to his law on his simple affirmation, without credible witnesses brought for this purpose.

39. No free man shall be taken or imprisoned or dispossessed, or outlawed, or banished, or in any way destroyed, nor will we go upon him, nor send upon him, except by the legal judgment of his peers or by the law of the land.

40. To no one will we sell, to no one will we deny, or delay right or justice.

41. All merchants shall be safe and secure in going out from England and coming into England and in remaining and going through England, as well by land as by water, for buying and selling, free from all evil tolls, by the ancient and rightful customs, except in time of war, and if they are of a land at war with us; and if such are found in our land at the beginning of war, they shall be attached without injury to their bodies or goods, until it shall be known from us or from our principal justiciar in what way the merchants of our land are treated who shall be then found in the country which is at war with us; and if ours are safe there, the others shall be safe in our land.

42. It is allowed henceforth to any one to go out from our kingdom, and to return, safely and securely, by land and by water, saving their fidelity to us, except in time of war for some short time, for the common good of the kingdom; excepting persons imprisoned and outlawed according to the law of the realm, and people of a land at war with us, and merchants, of whom it shall be done as is before said.

43. If any one holds from any escheat, as from the honor of Wal-

lingford, or Nottingham, or Boulogne, or Lancaster, or from other escheats which are in our hands and are baronies, and he dies, his heir shall not give any other relief, nor do to us any other service than he would do to the baron, if that barony was in the hands of the baron; and we will hold it in the same way as the baron held it.

. . .

45. We will not make justiciars, constables, sheriffs or bailiffs except of such as know the law of the realm and are well inclined to observe it.

46. All barons who have founded abbeys for which they have charters of kings of England, or ancient tenure, shall have their custody when they have become vacant, as they ought to have.

. . .

49. We will give back immediately all hostages and charters which have been liberated to us by Englishmen as security for peace or for faithful service.

. . .

51. And immediately after the reestablishment of peace we will remove from the kingdom all foreign-born soldiers, crossbow men, serjeants, and mercenaries who have come with horses and arms for the injury of the realm.

52. If any one shall have been dispossessed or removed by us without legal judgment of his peers, from his lands, castles, franchises, or his right we will restore them to him immediately; and if contention arises about this, then it shall be done according to the judgment of the twenty-five barons, of whom mention is made below concerning the security of the peace. Concerning all those things, however, from which any one has been removed or of which he has been deprived without legal judgment of his peers by King Henry our father, or by King Richard our brother, which we have in our hand, or which others hold, and which it is our duty to guarantee, we shall have respite till the usual term of crusaders; excepting those things about which the suit has been begun or the inquisition made by our writ before our assumption of the cross; when, however, we shall return from our journey or if by chance we desist from the journey, we will immediately show full justice in regard to them.

. . .

54. No one shall be seized nor imprisoned on the appeal of a woman concerning the death of any one except her husband.

55. All fines which have been imposed unjustly and against the law of the land, and all penalties imposed unjustly and against the law of the land are altogether excused, or will be on the judgment of the twenty-five barons of whom mention is made below in connection with the security of the peace, or on the judgment of the majority of them, along with the aforesaid Stephen, archbishop of Canterbury, if he is able to be present, and others whom he may wish to call for this purpose along with him. And if he should not be able to be present, nevertheless the business shall go on without him, provided that if any one or more of the aforesaid twenty-five barons are in a similar suit they should be removed as far as this particular judgment goes, and others who shall be chosen and put upon oath, by the remainder of the

twenty-five shall be substituted for them for this purpose.

. . .

60. Moreover, all those customs and franchises mentioned above which we have conceded in our kingdom, and which are to be fulfilled, as far as pertains to us, in respect to our men; all men of our kingdom as well clergy as laymen, shall observe as far as pertains to them, in respect to their men.

61. Since, moreover, for the sake of God, and for the improvement of our kingdom, and for the better quieting of the hostility sprung up lately between us and our barons, we have made all these concessions; wishing them to enjoy these in a complete and firm stability forever, we make and concede to them the security described below; that is to say, that they shall elect twenty-five barons of the kingdom, whom they will, who ought with all their power to observe, hold, and cause to be observed, the peace and liberties which we have conceded to them, and by this our present charter confirmed to them; in this manner, that if we or our justiciar, or our bailiffs, or any one of our servants shall have done wrong in any way toward any one, or shall have transgressed any of the articles of peace or security; and the wrong shall have been shown to four barons of the aforesaid twenty-five barons, let those four barons come to us or to our justiciar, if we are out of the kingdom, laying before us the transgression, and let them ask that we cause that transgression to be corrected without delay. And if we shall not have corrected the transgression or, if we shall be out of the kingdom if our justiciar shall not have cor-

rected it within a period of forty days, counting from the time in which it has been shown to us or to our justiciar, if we are out of the kingdom; the aforesaid four barons shall refer the matter to the remainder of the twenty-five barons, and let these twenty-five barons with the whole community of the country distress and injure us in every way they can; that is to say by the seizure of our castles, lands, possessions, and in such other ways as they can until it shall have been corrected according to their judgment, saving our person and that of our queen, and those of our children; and when the correction has been made, let them devote themselves to us as they did before. And let whoever in the country wishes take an oath that in all the above-mentioned measures he will obey the orders of the aforesaid twenty-five barons, and that he will injure us as far as he is able with them, and we give permission to swear publicly and freely to each one who wishes to swear, and no one will we ever forbid to swear. All those, moreover, in the country who of themselves and their own will are unwilling to take an oath to the twenty-five barons as to distressing and injuring us along with them, we will compel to take the oath by our mandate, as before said. And if any of the twenty-five barons shall have died or departed from the land or shall in any other way be prevented from taking the above-mentioned action, let the remainder of the aforesaid twenty-five barons choose another in his place, according to their judgment, who shall take an oath in the same way as the others. In all those things, moreover, which are committed to those five and twenty barons to carry out, if perhaps the twenty-five are present, and some disagreement arises among them about something, or if any of them when they have been summoned are not willing or are not able to be present, let that be considered valid and firm which the greater part of those who are present arrange or command, just as if the whole twenty-five had agreed in this; and let the aforesaid twenty-five swear that they will observe faithfully all the things which are said above, and with all their ability cause them to be observed. And we will obtain nothing from any one, either by ourselves or by another by which any of these concessions and liberties shall be revoked or diminished; and if any such thing shall have been obtained, let it be invalid and void, and we will never use it by ourselves or by another.

62. And all ill-will, grudges, and anger sprung up between us and our men, clergy and laymen, from the time of the dispute, we have fully renounced and pardoned to all. Moreover, all transgressions committed on account of this dispute, from Easter in the sixteenth year of our reign till the restoration of peace, we have fully remitted to all, clergy and laymen, and as far as pertains to us, fully pardoned. And moreover we have caused to be made for them testimonial letters-patent of lord Stephen, archbishop of Canterbury, lord Henry, archbishop of Dublin, and of the aforesaid bishops and of Master Pandulf, in respect to that security and the concessions named above.

63. Wherefore we will and firmly command that the Church of England shall be free, and that the men in our kingdom shall have and hold all the aforesaid liberties, rights and concessions, well and peacefully, freely and quietly, fully and completely, for themselves and their heirs, from us and our heirs, in all things and places, forever, as before said. It has been sworn, moreover, as well on our part as on the part of the barons, that all these things spoken of above shall be observed in good faith and without any evil intent. Witness the above named and many others. Given by our hand in the meadow which is called Runnymede, between Windsor and Staines, on the fifteenth day of June, in the seventeenth year of our reign.

Church and State

Throughout the Middle Ages, the Church and the temporal rulers of Europe waged a running battle for political supremacy. For a time the Church seemed assured of victory. It reached the height of its power during the pontificate of Innocent III (1198–1216), who succeeded in forcing King John to surrender England to him, to be held by John in the future as a fief from the papacy. The final victory, however, went to the secular powers, who gradually effected a separation between political authority and spiritual authority, reserving the former for themselves and permitting the Church to exercise the latter.

The documents that follow illustrate two different phases of this long struggle. The first, which is concerned with a financial dispute between Pope Gregory VII and William the Conqueror, consists of an exchange of correspondence between them in the year 1080. Of particular note is the distinction William makes in his letter, first acknowledging allegiance to the pope but then going on to insist that he will not send money to Rome.

The second document, the papal bull *Unam Sanctam,* was written over two hundred years later (1302), during a controversy between Pope Boniface VIII and King Philip the Fair of France. Philip replied to the bull, which flatly asserts the political supremacy of the Church, by having the pope seized. Although Boniface was soon released, he died almost immediately afterward. Philip again took the initiative and managed to convert the papacy into an adjunct of the French throne. This episode marked the turning point in the political fortunes of the Church, for the popes were never able to regain the ascendancy over the secular monarchs that the papacy had enjoyed under Pope Innocent III.

Correspondence:
Gregory VII and William the Conqueror

Pope Gregory VII to William I
[1080]

Gregory, the bishop, servant of the servants of God, to William, king of the English, greeting and apostolic benediction. We believe it is not hidden from your wisdom that the apostolic and royal dignities excel all others in this world, and that Almighty God has apportioned his governance between them. For as he has appointed the sun and moon as lights greater than all others to show forth the beauty of the world to human eyes at diverse seasons, so, lest the creature whom his beneficence created for this world in his own image should be drawn into error and mortal peril, he has provided that he should be governed by the apostolic and royal powers through their diverse offices. Yet, according to the difference between the greater and the less, the Christian religion has so disposed that after God the royal power shall be governed by the care and authority of the apostolic see. Although, dearest son, you are not ignorant of this, yet in order that it may be ineradicably implanted in your mind for your salvation, Holy Scripture bears witness that the apostolic and pontifical authority must represent all kings, Christian and others, before the judgment seat of God and render an account to him for their sins. If then I am to represent you in the great judgment day before the righteous Judge, the Creater of all creation, in whom is no deceit, do you prudently and carefully consider whether I should not or cannot take diligent pains for your salvation, and whether you should not or cannot without delay render obedience to me, in order to possess the land of the living. Take care therefore to stand fast, to love God and place his honour before your own; serve God with a pure mind and love him with all your strength and in fullness of heart. Believe me, if you love God with a pure mind, as you now hear and as Holy Scripture commands; if you place God's honour before your own in everything, he who knows no love that is counterfeit, who is powerful also to set you up, will both here and hereafter embrace you and extend to you his kingdom with his own Almighty arm. Given at Rome, 8 May, in the third Indiction.

The King to the Pope
[later in 1080]

To Gregory, most excellent shepherd of holy Church, William, king

English Historical Documents, 1042–1189, eds. D. C. Douglas and G. W. Greenaway (London: Eyre & Spottiswoode, 1953), pp. 646–47. Courtesy of Eyre & Spottiswoode, (Publishers) Ltd.

of the English and duke of the Normans, greetings and friendship. Your legate, Hubert, most holy father, coming to me on your behalf, has admonished me to profess allegiance to you and your successors, and to think better regarding the money which my predecessors were wont to send to the Church of Rome. I have consented to the one but not to the other. I have not consented to pay fealty, nor will I now, because I never promised it, nor do I find that my predecessors ever paid it to your predecessors. The money has been negligently collected during the past three years when I was in France; but now that I have returned by God's mercy to my kingdom, I send you by the hands of the aforesaid legate what has already been collected, and the remainder shall be forwarded by the envoys of our trusty Archbishop Lanfranc when the opportunity for so doing shall occur. Pray for us and for the state of our realms, for we always loved your predecessors and it is our earnest desire above all things to love you most sincerely, and to hear you most obediently.

The Bull *Unam Sanctam* of Boniface VIII

That there is one Holy Catholic and Apostolic Church we are impelled by our faith to believe and to hold —this we do firmly believe and openly confess—and outside of this there is neither salvation or remission of sins, as the bridegroom proclaims in Canticles, "My dove, my undefiled is but one; she is the only one of her mother; she is the choice one of her that bare her." The Church represents one mystic body and of this body Christ is the head; of Christ, indeed, God is the head. In it is one Lord, and one faith, and one baptism. In the time of the flood, there was one ark of Noah, prefiguring the one Church, finished in one cubit, having one Noah as steersman and commander. Outside of this, all things upon the face of the earth were, as we read, destroyed. This Church we venerate and this alone, the Lord saying through his prophets, "Deliver my soul, O God, from the sword; my darling from the power of the dog." He prays thus for the soul, that is for Himself, as head, and also for the body which He calls one, namely, the Church on account of the unity of the bridegroom, of the faith, of the sacraments, and of the charity of the Church. It is that seamless coat of the Lord, which was not rent, but fell by lot. Therefore, in this one and only Church, there is one body and one head,— not two heads as if it were a monster—namely, Christ and Christ's Vicar, Peter and Peter's successor, for the Lord said to Peter himself,

"The Bull *Unam Sanctam* of Boniface VIII," in *Translations an from the Original Sources of European History,* Vol. III, No. 6 (Ph The Department of History of the University of Pennsylvania, 191' 23. Courtesy of the Department of History of the University of P

"Feed my sheep": *my* sheep, he said, using a general term and not designating these or those sheep, so that we must believe that all the sheep were committed to him. If, then, the Greeks, or others, shall say that they were not entrusted to Peter and his successors, they must perforce admit that they are not of Christ's sheep, as the Lord says in John, "there is one fold, and one shepherd."

In this Church and in its power are two swords, to wit, a spiritual and a temporal, and this we are taught by the words of the Gospel, for when the Apostles said, "Behold, here are two swords" (in the Church, namely, since the Apostles were speaking), the Lord did not reply that it was too many, but enough. And surely he who claims that the temporal sword is not in the power of Peter has but ill understood the word of our Lord when he said, "Put up thy sword in its scabbard." Both, therefore, the spiritual and material swords, are in the power of the Church, the latter indeed to be used for the Church, the former by the Church, the one by the priest, the other by the hand of kings and soldiers, but by the will and sufferance of the priest. It is fitting, moreover, that one sword should be under the other, and the temporal authority subject to the spiritual power. For when the Apostle said, "there is no power but of God and the powers that are of God are ordained," they would not be ordained unless one sword were under the other, and one, as inferior, was brought back by the other to the highest place. For, according to the Holy Dionysius, the law of divinity is to lead the lowest through the intermediate to the highest. Therefore, according to the law of the universe, things are not reduced to order directly, and upon the same footing, but the lowest through the intermediate and the inferior through the superior. It behooves us, therefore, the more freely to confess that the spiritual power excels in dignity and nobility any form whatsoever of earthly power, as spiritual interests exceed the temporal in importance. All this we see fairly from the giving of tithes, from the benediction and sanctification, from the recognition of this power and the control of these same things. For the truth bearing witness, it is for the spiritual power to establish the earthly power and judge it, if it be not good. Thus, in the case of the Church and the power of the Church, the prophecy of Jeremiah is fulfilled: "See, I have this day set thee over the nations and over the kingdoms"—and so forth. Therefore, if the earthly power shall err, it shall be judged by the spiritual power: if the lesser spiritual power err, it shall be judged by the higher. But if the supreme power err, it can be judged by God alone and not by man, the apostles bearing witness saying, the spiritual man judges all things but he himself is judged by no one. Hence this power, although given to man and exercised by man, is not human, but rather a divine power, given by the divine lips to Peter, and founded on a rock for Him and his successors in Him whom he confessed, the Lord saying to Peter himself, "Whatsoever thou shalt bind," etc. Whoever, therefore, shall resist this power, ordained by God, resists the ordination of God, unless there should be two beginnings, as the Manichaean imagines. But this we judge to be false and heretical, since, by the testimony of Moses, not in the *beginnings,* but in the *beginning,* God created the heaven and the earth. We, moreover, proclaim, declare, and pronounce that it is altogether necessary to salvation for every human being to be subject to the Roman Pontiff.

Given at the Lateran the twelfth day before the Kalends of December, in our eighth year, as a perpetual memorial of this matter.

St. Thomas Aquinas

St. Thomas Aquinas (1225–1274), the leading philosopher and theologian of medieval scholasticism, was one of the greatest synthesizers the West has ever produced. The task he undertook was to reconcile the philosophy of Aristotle, rediscovered by European scholars through their contacts with the Moslems in Spain and elsewhere, with Christian theology. During a relatively short lifetime, he succeeded in combining these two disparate elements into a single comprehensive system of thought capable in principle of explaining everything in the universe that people could know. Questions have been raised about the logical consistency of the Thomistic synthesis, but, whether fully successful or not, it still stands as a landmark in the intellectual career of the West.

Beyond their general historical importance, the writings of Thomas have a special significance in the history of Catholicism. Although Thomas was opposed during his lifetime by various religious leaders because of his heavy reliance on the pagan Aristotle, and although his writings were even condemned at several theological centers in the years immediately after his death, within a century his system was generally accepted as the basis for orthodox Catholic philosophy. The authoritativeness of the Thomistic doctrine was formally recognized by the Church in 1879 in the encyclical *Aeterni Patris* of Pope Leo XIII, which ordered all Catholic schools to teach Thomas's position as the true philosophy. Leo's order was reiterated in 1923 by Pius X, who wrote: "The following canon of the Church's code should be held as a sacred command: In the study of rational philosophy and theology and in the instruction of students the professor should follow entirely the method, doctrine and principles of the Angelic Doctor [Thomas], and hold them religiously."

The selection that follows illustrates Thomas's attempt to establish the consonance between the philosophers' quest for truth based on reason and the Christians' acceptance of divine truth based on revelation.

Summa Contra Gentiles

CHAPTER III

In what way it is possible to make known the divine truth

Since, however, not every truth is to be made known in the same way, *and it is the part of an educated man to seek for conviction in each subject, only so far as the nature of the subject allows,* as the Philosopher most rightly observes as quoted by Boethius, it is necessary to show first of all in what way it is possible to make known the aforesaid truth.

Now in those things which we hold about God there is truth in two ways. For certain things that are true about God wholly surpass the capability of human reason, for instance that God is three and one: while there are certain things to which even natural reason can attain, for instance that God is, that God is one, and others like these, which even the philosophers proved demonstratively of God, being guided by the light of natural reason.

That certain divine truths wholly surpass the capability of human reason, is most clearly evident. For since the principle of all the knowledge which the reason acquires about a thing, is the understanding of that thing's essence, because according to the Philosopher's teaching the principle of a demonstration is *what a thing is,* it follows that our knowledge about a thing will be in proportion to our understanding of its essence. Wherefore, if the human intellect comprehends the essence of a particular thing, for instance a stone or a triangle, no truth about that thing will surpass the capability of human reason. But this does not happen to us in relation to God, because the human intellect is incapable by its natural power of attaining to the comprehension of His essence: since our intellect's knowledge, according to the mode of the present life, originates from the senses: so that things which are not objects of sense cannot be comprehended by the human intellect, except in so far as knowledge of them is gathered from sensibles. Now sensibles cannot lead our intellect to see in them what God is, because they are effects unequal to the power of their cause. And yet our intellect is led by sensibles to the divine knowledge so as to know about God that He is, and other such truths, which need to be ascribed to the first principle. Accordingly some divine truths are attainable by human reason, while others altogether surpass the power of human reason.

Again. The same is easy to see

The "Summa Contra Gentiles" of St. Thomas Aquinas, trans. Fath̶ English Dominican Province (London: Burns & Oates, Ltd.; New Y̶ ziger Brothers, Inc., 1924), I, 4–15. Courtesy of Benziger Brothers̶ Burns & Oates, Ltd.

from the degrees of intellects. For if one of two men perceives a thing with his intellect with greater subtlety, the one whose intellect is of a higher degree understands many things which the other is altogether unable to grasp; as instanced in a yokel who is utterly incapable of grasping the subtleties of philosophy. Now the angelic intellect surpasses the human intellect more than the intellect of the cleverest philosopher surpasses that of the most uncultured. For an angel knows God through a more excellent effect than does man, for as much as the angel's essence, through which he is led to know God by natural knowledge, is more excellent than sensible things, even than the soul itself, by which the human intellect mounts to the knowledge of God. And the divine intellect surpasses the angelic intellect much more than the angelic surpasses the human. For the divine intellect by its capacity equals the divine essence, wherefore God perfectly understands of Himself what He is, and He knows all things that can be understood about Him: whereas the angel knows not what God is by his natural knowledge, because the angel's essence, by which he is led to the knowledge of God, is an effect unequal to the power of its cause. Consequently an angel is unable by his natural knowledge to grasp all that God understands about Himself: nor again is human reason capable of grasping all that an angel understands by his natural power. Accordingly just as a man would show himself to be a most insane fool if he declared the assertions of a philosopher to be false because he was unable to understand them, so, and much more, ‘ man would be exceedingly foolish,

were he to suspect of falsehood the things revealed by God through the ministry of His angels, because they cannot be the object of reason's investigations.

Furthermore. The same is made abundantly clear by the deficiency which every day we experience in our knowledge of things. For we are ignorant of many of the properties of sensible things, and in many cases we are unable to discover the nature of those properties which we perceive by our senses. Much less therefore is human reason capable of investigating all the truths about that most sublime essence.

With this the saying of the Philosopher is in accord where he says that *our intellect in relation to those primary things which are most evident in nature is like the eye of a bat in relation to the sun.*

To this truth Holy Writ also bears witness. For it is written (Job xi. 7): *Peradventure thou wilt comprehend the steps of God and wilt find out the Almighty perfectly?* and (xxxvi. 26): *Behold God is great, exceeding our knowledge,* and (I Cor. xiii. 9): *We know in part.*

Therefore all that is said about God, though it cannot be investigated by reason, must not be forthwith rejected as false, as the Manicheans and many unbelievers have thought.

CHAPTER IV

That the truth about divine things which is attainable by reason is fittingly proposed to man as an object of belief

While then the truth of the intelligible things of God is twofold, one to which the inquiry of reason can attain, the other which surpasses the whole range of human reason, both are fittingly proposed by God to man as an object of belief. We must first show this with regard to that truth which is attainable by the inquiry of reason, lest it appears to some, that since it can be attained by reason, it was useless to make it an object of faith by supernatural inspiration. Now three disadvantages would result if this truth were left solely to the inquiry of reason. One is that few men would have knowledge of God: because very many are hindered from gathering the fruit of diligent inquiry, which is the discovery of truth, for three reasons. Some indeed on account of an indisposition of temperament, by reason of which many are naturally indisposed to knowledge: so that no efforts of theirs would enable them to reach to the attainment of the highest degree of human knowledge, which consists in knowing God. Some are hindered by the needs of household affairs. For there must needs be among men some that devote themselves to the conduct of temporal affairs, who would be unable to devote so much time to the leisure of contemplative research as to reach the summit of human inquiry, namely the knowledge of God. And some are hindered by laziness. For in order to acquire the knowledge of God in those things which reason is able to investigate, it is necessary to have a previous knowledge of many things: since almost the entire consideration of philosophy is directed to the knowledge of God: for which reason metaphysics, which is about divine things, is the last of the parts of philosophy to be studied. Where-

fore it is not possible to arrive at the inquiry about the aforesaid truth except after a most laborious study: and few are willing to take upon themselves this labour for the love of a knowledge, the natural desire for which has nevertheless been instilled into the mind of man by God.

The second disadvantage is that those who would arrive at the discovery of the aforesaid truth would scarcely succeed in doing so after a long time. First, because this truth is so profound, that it is only after long practice that the human intellect is enabled to grasp it by means of reason. Secondly, because many things are required beforehand, as stated above. Thirdly, because at the time of youth, the mind, when tossed about by the various movements of the passions, is not fit for the knowledge of so sublime a truth, whereas *calm gives prudence and knowledge,* as stated in 7 *Phys.* Hence mankind would remain in the deepest darkness of ignorance, if the path of reason were the only available way to the knowledge of God: because the knowledge of God which especially makes men perfect and good, would be acquired only by the few, and by these only after a long time.

The third disadvantage is that much falsehood is mingled with the investigations of human reason, on account of the weakness of our intellect in forming its judgments, and by reason of the admixture of phantasms. Consequently many would remain in doubt about those things even which are most truly demonstrated, through ignoring the of the demonstration: when they perceive that things are taught by the va who are called wise.

among the many demonstrated truths, there is sometimes a mixture of falsehood that is not demonstrated, but assumed for some probable or sophistical reason which at times is mistaken for a demonstration. Therefore it was necessary that definite certainty and pure truth about divine things should be offered to man by the way of faith.

Accordingly the divine clemency has made this salutary commandment, that even some things which reason is able to investigate must be held by faith: so that all may share in the knowledge of God easily, and without doubt or error.

Hence it is written (Eph. iv. 17, 18): That *henceforward you walk not as also the Gentiles walk in the vanity of their mind, having their understanding darkened:* and (Isa. liv. 13): *All thy children shall be taught of the Lord.*

CHAPTER V

That those things which cannot be investigated by reason are fittingly proposed to man as an object of faith

It may appear to some that those things which cannot be investigated by reason ought not to be proposed to man as an object of faith: because divine wisdom provides for each thing according to the mode of its nature. We must therefore prove that it is necessary also for those things which surpass reason to be proposed by God to man as an object of faith.

For no man tends to do a thing by his desire and endeavour unless it be previously known to him. Wherefore since man is directed by

divine providence to a higher good than human frailty can attain in the present life, as we shall show in the sequel, it was necessary for his mind to be bidden to something higher than those things to which our reason can reach in the present life, so that he might learn to aspire, and by his endeavours to tend to something surpassing the whole state of the present life. And this is especially competent to the Christian religion, which alone promises goods spiritual and eternal: for which reason it proposes many things surpassing the thought of man: whereas the old law which contained promises of temporal things, proposed few things that are above human inquiry. It was with this motive that the philosophers, in order to wean men from sensible pleasures to virtue, took care to show that there are other goods of greater account than those which appeal to the senses, the taste of which things affords much greater delight to those who devote themselves to active or contemplative virtues.

Again it is necessary for this truth to be proposed to man as an object of faith in order that he may have truer knowledge of God. For then alone do we know God truly, when we believe that He is far above all that man can possibly think of God, because the divine essence surpasses man's natural knowledge, as stated above. Hence by the fact that certain things about God are proposed to man, which surpass his reason, he is strengthened in his opinion that God is far above what he is able to think.

There results also another advantage from this, namely, the checking of presumption which is the mother of error. For some there are who presume so far on their wits that they think themselves capable of measuring the whole nature of things by their intellect, in that they esteem all things true which they see, and false which they see not. Accordingly, in order that man's mind might be freed from this presumption, and seek the truth humbly, it was necessary that certain things far surpassing his intellect should be proposed to man by God.

Yet another advantage is made apparent by the words of the Philosopher (10 *Ethic.*). For when a certain Simonides maintained that man should neglect the knowledge of God, and apply his mind to human affairs, and declared that *a man ought to relish human things, and a mortal, mortal things:* the Philosopher contradicted him, saying that *a man ought to devote himself to immortal and divine things as much as he can.* Hence he says (11 *De Anima.*) that though it is but little that we perceive of higher substances, yet that little is more loved and desired than all the knowledge we have of lower substances. He says also (2 *De Coelo et Mundo*) that when questions about the heavenly bodies can be answered by a short and probable solution, it happens that the hearer is very much rejoiced. All this shows that however imperfect the knowledge of the highest things may be, it bestows very great perfection on the soul: and consequently, although human reason is unable to grasp fully things that are above reason, it nevertheless acquires much perfection, if at least it hold things, in any way whatever, by faith.

Wherefore it is written (Eccles. iii. 25): *Many things are shown to thee above the understanding of men,* and (I Cor. ii. 10, 11): *The things . . . that are of God no man knoweth, but the Spirit of God: but to us God hath revealed them by His Spirit.*

CHAPTER VI

That it is not a mark of levity to assent to the things that are of faith, although they are above reason

Now those who believe this truth, *of which reason affords a proof,* believe not lightly, as though *following foolish fables* (2 Pet. i. 16). For divine Wisdom Himself, Who knows all things most fully, designed to reveal to man *the secrets of God's wisdom:* and by suitable arguments proves His presence, and the truth of His doctrine and inspiration, by performing works surpassing the capability of the whole of nature, namely, the wondrous healing of the sick, the raising of the dead to life, a marvellous control over the heavenly bodies, and what excites yet more wonder, the inspiration of human minds, so that unlettered and simple persons are filled with the Holy Ghost, and in one instant are endowed with the most sublime wisdom and eloquence. And after considering these arguments, convinced by the strength of the proof, and not by the force of arms, nor by the promise of delights, but—and this is the greatest marvel of all— amidst the tyranny of persecutions, a countless crowd of not only simple but also of the wisest men, embraced the Christian faith, which inculcates things surpassing all human understanding, curbs the pleasures of the flesh, and teaches contempt of all worldly things. That the minds of mortal beings should assent to such things, is both the greatest of miracles, and the evident work of divine inspiration, seeing that they despise visible things and desire only those that are invisible. And that this happened not suddenly nor by chance, but by the disposition of God, is shown by the fact that God foretold that He would do so by the manifold oracles of the prophets, whose books we hold in veneration as bearing witness to our faith. This particular kind of proof is alluded to in the words of Heb. ii. 3, 4: *Which,* namely the salvation of mankind, *having begun to be declared by the Lord, was confirmed with us by them that heard Him, God also bearing witness by signs and wonders, and divers . . . distributions of the Holy Ghost.*

Now such a wondrous conversion of the world to the Christian faith is a most indubitable proof that such signs did take place, so that there is no need to repeat them, seeing that there is evidence of them in their result. For it would be the most wondrous sign of all if without any wondrous signs the world were persuaded by simple and lowly men to believe things so arduous, to accomplish things so difficult, and to hope for things so sublime. Although God ceases not even in our time to work miracles through His saints in confirmation of the faith.

On the other hand those who introduced the errors of the sects proceeded in contrary fashion, as instanced by Mohammed, who enticed peoples with the promise of carnal pleasures, to the desire of which the concupiscence of the flesh instigates. He also delivered commandments in keeping with his promises, by giving the reins to carnal pleasure, wherein it is easy for carnal men to obey: and the lessons of truth which he inculcated were only such as can be easily known to any man of average wisdom by his natural powers: yea rather the truths which he taught were mingled by him with many fables and most false doctrines. Nor did he add any signs of supernatural agency, which alone are a fitting witness to divine inspiration, since a visible work that can be from God alone, proves the teacher of truth to be invisibly inspired: but he asserted that he was sent in the power of arms, a sign that is not lacking even to robbers and tyrants. Again, those who believed in him from the outset were not wise men practised in things divine and human, but beastlike men who dwelt in the wilds, utterly ignorant of all divine teaching; and it was by a multitude of such men and the force of arms that he impelled others to submit to his law.

Lastly, no divine oracles or prophets in a previous age bore witness to him; rather did he corrupt almost all the teaching of the Old and New Testaments by a narrative replete with fables, as one may see by a perusal of his law. Hence by a cunning device, he did not commit the reading of the Old and New Testament Books to his followers, lest he should thereby be convicted of falsehood. Thus it is evident that those who believe his words believe lightly.

CHAPTER VII

That the truth of reason is not in opposition to the truth of the Christian faith

Now though the aforesaid truth of the Christian faith surpasses the ability of human reason, nevertheless those things which are naturally instilled in human reason cannot be opposed to this truth. For it is clear that those things which are implanted in reason by nature, are most true, so much so that it is impossible to think them to be false. Nor is it lawful to deem false that which is held by faith, since it is so evidently confirmed by God. Seeing then that the false alone is opposed to the true, as evidently appears if we examine their definitions, it is impossible for the aforesaid truth of faith to be contrary to those principles which reason knows naturally.

Again. The same thing which the disciple's mind receives from its teacher is contained in the knowledge of the teacher, unless he teach insincerely, which it were wicked to say of God. Now the knowledge of naturally known principles is instilled into us by God, since God Himself is the author of our nature. Therefore the divine Wisdom also contains these principles. Consequently whatever is contrary to these principles, is contrary to the divine Wisdom; wherefore it cannot be from God. Therefore those things which are received by faith from divine revelation cannot be contrary to our natural knowledge.

Moreover. Our intellect is stayed by contrary arguments, so that it cannot advance to the knowledge of truth. Wherefore if conflicting knowledges were instilled into us by God, our intellect would thereby be hindered from knowing the truth. And this cannot be ascribed to God.

Furthermore. Things that are natural are unchangeable so long as nature remains. Now contrary opinions cannot be together in the same subject. Therefore God does not instil into man any opinion or belief contrary to natural knowledge.

Hence the Apostle says (Rom. x. 8): *The word is nigh thee even in thy heart and in thy mouth. This is the word of faith which we preach.* Yet because it surpasses reason some look upon it as though it were contrary thereto; which is impossible.

This is confirmed also by the authority of Augustine who says *That which truth shall make known can nowise be in opposition to the holy books whether of the Old or of the New Testament.*

From this we may evidently conclude that whatever arguments are alleged against the teachings of faith, they do not rightly proceed from the first self-evident principles instilled by nature. Wherefore they lack the force of demonstration, and are either probable or sophistical arguments, and consequently it is possible to solve them.

Medieval Secular Poetry

The medieval period in Western history is often referred to as the "Age of Faith." The characterization is apt—as long as it is not taken too literally. However, if one assumes that thought and action during these centuries were wholly dominated by the Church and by visions of life in the hereafter to the consequent denigration of this life and its interests, the result will be a one-sided view of an age that in truth was remarkably varied. The poems in this selection should provide a counterbalance to such a distortion by suggesting some of the secular interests that concerned at least certain groups within medieval society (and even within the Church itself).

Secular poetry, of the type illustrated by the poems included here, developed concurrently, but far from coincidentally, with the beginnings of European universities in the twelfth century. It flourished for over a century but gradually disappeared, largely as a result of ecclesiastical suppression, around the beginning of the fourteenth century. Much of this poetry was the work of a group of writers who became known as the Goliard poets, or the tribe of Golias. The origin of the name is obscure, but it could have been derived from the Old Testament Goliath, who was a Philistine giant sent to wage war against the children of Israel. The poets themselves were wandering scholars, young men who had usually taken some work in one or more of the universities but who found themselves unwilling to endure the rigors of sustained intellectual endeavor so dropped out to join the ranks of academic flotsam drifting about the environs of the major medieval centers of learning. Rebels against the established clerical order, they wrote verses that were almost invariably irreverent and sometimes blatantly blasphemous. Yet the poems have a positive side as well, although their attitude is pagan rather than Christian. Almost always we find in them a glorification of nature, of life, of pleasures (particularly those of table and bed), and of the flesh in general.

The selection includes four poems, chosen to reveal different facets of the writers' interests and attitudes. None of the authors is known; however the first piece is generally ascribed to a man who flourished in the mid-twelfth century and referred to himself, with becoming modesty, as the archpoet of Cologne. All have been translated into English from their original Latin. They were written to be enjoyed.

The Confession of Golias

Boiling in my spirit's veins
  With fierce indignation,
From my bitterness of soul
  Springs self-revelation:
Framed am I of flimsy stuff,
  Fit for levitation,
Like a thin leaf which the wind
  Scatters from its station.

While it is the wise man's part
  With deliberation
On a rock to base his heart's
  Permanent foundation,
With a running river I
  Find my just equation,
Which beneath the self-same sky
  Hath no habitation.

Carried am I like a ship
  Left without a sailor,
Like a bird that through the air
  Flies where tempests hale her;
Chains and fetters hold me not,
  Naught avails a jailer;
Still I find my fellows out
  Toper, gamester, railer.

To my mind all gravity
  Is a grave subjection;
Sweeter far than honey are
  Jokes and free affection.
All that Venus bids me do,
  Do I with erection,
For she ne'er in heart of man
  Dwelt with dull dejection.

Down the broad road do I run,
  As the way of youth is;
Snare myself in sin, and ne'er
  Think where faith and truth is,
Eager far for pleasure more
  Than soul's health, the sooth is,
For this flesh of mine I care,
  Seek not ruth where ruth is.

Prelate, most discreet of priests,
  Grant me absolution!
Dear's the death whereof I die,
  Sweet my dissolution;
For my heart is wounded by
  Beauty's soft suffusion;
All the girls I come not nigh,
  Mine are in illusion.

'Tis most arduous to make
  Nature's self surrender;
Seeing girls, to blush and be
  Purity's defender!
We young men our longings ne'er
  Shall to stern law render,
Or preserve our fancies from
  Bodies smooth and tender.

Who, when into fire he falls,
  Keeps himself from burning?
Who within Pavia's walls
  Fame of chaste is earning?
Venus with her finger calls
  Youth at every turning,
Snares them with her eyes, and thralls
  With her amorous yearning.

If you brought Hippolitus
  To Pavia Sunday,
He'd not be Hippolitus
  On the following Monday;
Venus there keeps holiday
  Every day as one day;
'Mid these towers in no tower dwells
  Venus Verecunda.

In the second place I own
  To the vice of gaming:
Cold indeed outside I seem,
  Yet my soul is flaming:
But when once the dice-box hath
  Stripped me to my shaming,
Make I songs and verses fit
  For the world's acclaiming.

Trans. John Addington Symonds.

In the third place, I will speak
　Of the tavern's pleasure;
For I never found nor find
　There the least displeasure;
Nor shall find it till I greet
　Angels without measure,
Singing requiems for the souls
　In eternal leisure.

In the public-house to die
　Is my resolution;
Let wine to my lips be nigh
　At life's dissolution:
That will make the angels cry,
　With glad elocution,
"Grant this toper, God on high,
　Grace and absolution!"

With the cup the soul lights up,
　Inspirations flicker;
Nectar lifts the soul on high
　With its heavenly ichor:
To my lips a sounder taste
　Hath the tavern's liquor
Than the wine a village clerk
　Waters for the vicar.

Nature gives to every man
　Some gift serviceable;
Write I never could nor can
　Hungry at the table;
Fasting, any stripling to
　Vanquish me is able;
Hunger, thirst, I liken to
　Death that ends the fable.

Nature gives to every man
　Gifts as she is willing;
I compose my verses when
　Good wine I am swilling,
Wine the best for jolly guest
　Jolly hosts are filling;
From such wine rare fancies fine
　Flow like dews distilling.

Such my verse is wont to be
　As the wine I swallow;
No ripe thoughts enliven me
　While my stomach's hollow;

Hungry wits on hungry lips
　Like a shadow follow,
But when once I'm in my cups,
　I can beat Apollo.

Never to my spirit yet
　Flew poetic vision
Until first my belly had
　Plentiful provision;
Let but Bacchus in the brain
　Take a strong position,
Then comes Phoebus flowing in
　With a fine precision.

There are poets, worthy men,
　Shrink from public places,
And in lurking-hole or den
　Hide their pallid faces;
There they study, sweat, and woo
　Pallas and the Graces,
But bring nothing forth to view
　Worth the girls' embraces.

Fasting, thirsting, toil the bards,
　Swift years flying o'er them;
Shun the strife of open life,
　Tumults of the forum;
They, to sing some deathless thing,
　Lest the world ignore them,
Die the death, expend their breath,
　Drowned in dull decorum.

Lo! my frailties I've betrayed,
　Shown you every token,
Told you what your servitors
　Have against me spoken;
But of those men each and all
　Leave their sins unspoken,
Though they play, enjoy to-day:
　Scorn their pledges broken.

Now within the audience-room
　Of this blessed prelate,
Sent to hunt out vice, and from
　Hearts of men expel it;
Let him rise, nor spare the bard,
　Cast at him a pellet:
He whose heart knows not crime's
　　smart,
　Show my sin and tell it!

I have uttered openly
    All I knew that shamed me,
And have spued the poison forth
    That so long defamed me;
Of my old ways I repent,
    New life hath reclaimed me;
God beholds the heart—'twas man
    Viewed the face and blamed me.

Goodness now hath won my love,
    I am wroth with vices;
Made a new man in my mind,
    Lo, my soul arises!
Like a babe new milk I drink—
    Milk for me suffices,
Lest my heart should longer be
    Filled with vain devices.

Thou Elect of fair Cologne,
    Listen to my pleading!
Spurn not thou the penitent;
    See, his heart is bleeding!
Give me penance! what is due
    For my faults exceeding
I will bear with willing cheer,
    All thy precepts heeding.

Lo, the lion, king of beasts,
    Spares the meek and lowly;
Toward submissive creatures he
    Tames his anger wholly.
Do the like, ye powers of earth,
    Temporal and holy!
Bitterness is more than's right
    When 'tis bitter solely.

Let's Away with Study

Let's away with study,
    Folly's sweet.
Treasure all the pleasure
    Of our youth:
Time enough for age
    To think on Truth.
So short a day,
And life so quickly hasting,
And in study wasting
    Youth that would be gay!

'Tis our spring that slipping,
    Winter draweth near,
    Life itself we're losing,
    And this sorry cheer
Dries the blood and chills the heart,
    Shrivels all delight.
Age and all its crowd of ills
    Terrifies our sight.
So short a day,
And life so quickly hasting,
And in study wasting
    Youth that would be gay!

Let us as the gods do,
    'Tis the wiser part:
Leisure and love's pleasure
    Seek the young in heart
Follow the old fashion,
    Down into the street!
Down among the maidens,
    And the dancing feet!
So short a day,
And life so quickly hasting,
And in study wasting
    Youth that would be gay!

There for the seeing
    Is all loveliness,
White limbs moving
    Light in wantonness.
Gay go the dancers,
    I stand and see,
Gaze, till their glances
    Steal myself from me.
So short a day,
And life so quickly hasting,
And in study wasting
    Youth that would be gay!

Helen Waddell, *Mediaeval Latin Lyrics*, 5th ed. (London: Constable and Company, Ltd., 1948), p. 221. Courtesy of Constable and Company, Ltd.

Flora

Rudely blows the winter blast,
  Withered leaves are falling fast,
Cold hath hushed the birds at last.
    While the heavens were warm and
      glowing,
      Nature's offspring loved in May;
But man's heart no debt is owing
    To such change of month or day
    As the dumb brute-beasts obey.
Oh, the joys of this possessing!
How unspeakable the blessing
    That my Flora yields to-day!

Labour long I did not rue,
Ere I won my wages due,
And the prize I played for drew.
    Flora with her brows of laughter,
      Gazing on me, breathing bliss,
    Draws my yearning spirit after,
      Sucks my soul forth in a kiss:
    Where's the pastime matched
      with this:
Oh, the joys of this possessing!
How unspeakable the blessing
    Of my Flora's loveliness!

Truly mine is no harsh doom,
While in this secluded room
Venus lights for me the gloom!
    Flora faultless as a blossom
      Bares her smooth limbs for mine
        eyes;

Softly shines her virgin bosom,
    And the breasts that gently rise
    Like the hills of Paradise.
Oh, the joys of this possessing!
How unspeakable the blessing
    When my Flora is the prize!

From her tender breasts decline,
In a gradual curving line,
Flanks like swansdown white and fine.
    On her skin the touch discerneth
      Naught of rough; 'tis soft as
        snow:
    'Neath the waist her belly turneth
      Unto fulness, where below
      In Love's garden lilies blow.
Oh, the joys of this possessing!
How unspeakable the blessing!
    Sweetest sweets from Flora flow.

Ah, should Jove but find my fair,
He would fall in love, I swear,
And to his old tricks repair:
    In a cloud of gold descending
      As on Danae's brazen tower,
    Or the sturdy bull's back bending,
    Or would veil his godhood's
      power
    In a swan's form for one hour.
Oh, the joys of this possessing!
How unspeakable the blessing!
    How divine my Flora's flower!

Trans. John Addington Symonds.

Gaudeamus Igitur

Let us live, then, and be glad
    While young life's before us!
      After youthful pastime had,
      After old age hard and sad,
    Earth will slumber o'er us.

Where are they who in this world,
    Ere we kept, were keeping?
      Go ye to the gods above;
      Go to hell; inquire thereof:
    They are not; they're sleeping.

Trans. John Addington Symonds.

Brief is life, and brevity
  Briefly shall be ended:
    Death comes like a whirlwind
      strong,
    Bears us with his blast along;
  None shall be defended.

Live this university,
  Men that learning nourish;
    Live each member of the same,
    Long live all that bear its name;
  Let them ever flourish!

Live the commonwealth also,
  And the men that guide it!
    Live our town in strength and
      health,

Founders, patrons, by whose
  wealth
We are here provided!

Live all girls! A health to you,
  Melting maids and beauteous!
    Live the wives and women too,
    Gentle, loving, tender, true,
  Good, industrious, duteous!

Perish cares that pule and pine!
  Perish envious blamers!
    Die the Devil, thine and mine!
    Die the starch-necked Philistine!
  Scoffers and defamers!

Jean, Sire de Joinville

The *Memoirs,* or *History and Chronicle of the Very Christian King Saint Louis* by Jean, Sire de Joinville, one of the great contemporary accounts of the Crusades, provides a most valuable portrayal of French feudalism at its height. It is, as well, a very human document, for in it the author writes of his fear in battle (hardly a knightly virtue), his love of wine (preferably undiluted with water), and his doubts about his Christian faith, revealing his essential humanity. Despite his fears and misgivings, however, Joinville was a capable and brave knight, deeply dedicated to his religious beliefs.

Joinville (1224–1319) accompanied King Louis IX of France on the Crusade that sailed from southern France in 1248 bound for Cyprus. Louis, a profoundly religious man, had earlier conceived the Crusade and had decided that the way to free the Holy Land from the grip of the Saracens was by the conquest of Egypt. Such a stratagem, he believed, would severely truncate Moslem power and thus lead to reestablishment of Christian control over Jerusalem. After a nine-month delay at Cyprus waiting for a great number of French knights to join him—and incidentally giving the Moslems that much more time to prepare a warm reception for the Crusaders—Louis finally crossed the Mediterranean to the mouths of the Nile. At Damietta the royal army forced its way ashore but failed to follow up this success, with disastrous results. When Louis did push across and up the Nile toward Cairo, he was utterly defeated and his army destroyed. The king himself was captured and later ransomed. Louis and Joinville spent about four more years in Syria, returning to France in 1254.

The *Memoirs* of Joinville were written nearly sixty years (circa 1300–1309) after the events he describes. They are thus the reminiscences of an old man and as such tend to be garrulous, repetitious, and vaguely petulant. But withal they accurately depict both the grandeur and the frailty of the feudal Christian ideology.

Memoirs

• • •

Joinville leaves his castle

After these things I returned to our county, and we agreed, the Count of Sarebruck and I, that we should send our baggage in carts to Ausonne, thence to be borne on the river Saône, and to Arles by the Saône and the Rhône.

The day that I left Joinville I sent for the Abbot of Cheminon, who was held to be one of the most worthy of the order of the white monks (Cistercians). (I heard this witness regarding him given at Clairvaux on the festival of our Lady, when the saintly king was present, by a monk, who showed the abbot to me, and asked if I knew who he was; and I inquired why he asked me this, and he answered, "because I think he is the worthiest monk in all the white order. For listen," said he, "what I heard tell by a worthy man who slept in the same dormitory as the Abbot of Cheminon. The abbot had bared his breast because of the great heat; and this did the worthy man see who lay in the same dormitory: he saw the Mother of God go to the abbot's bed, and draw his garment over his breast, so that the wind might do him no hurt.")

This Abbot of Cheminon gave me my scarf and staff of pilgrimage; and then I departed from Joinville on foot, barefoot, in my shirt—not to re-enter the castle till my return; and thus I went to Blécourt, and Saint-Urbain, and to other places thereabouts where there are holy relics. And never while I went to Blécourt and Saint-Urbain would I turn my eyes towards Joinville for fear my heart should melt within me at thought of the fair castle I was leaving behind, and my two children.

I and my companions ate that day at Fontaine-l'Archevêque before Donjeux; and the Abbot Adam of Saint-Urbain—whom God have in His grace!—gave a great quantity of fair jewels to myself and the nine knights I had with me. Thence we went to Auxonne, and thence again, with the baggage, which we had placed in boats, from Auxonne to Lyons down the river Saône; and along by the side of the boats were led the great war-horses.

At Lyons we embarked on the Rhône to go to Arles the White; and on the Rhône we found a castle called Roche-de-Glun, which the king had caused to be destroyed, because Roger, the lord of the castle, was accused of robbing pilgrims and merchants.

From *Memoirs of the Crusades* by Villehardouin and de Joinville, translated by Sir Frank T. Marzials. An Everyman's Library Edition. Published in the United States by E. P. Dutton & Co., Inc., and reprinted with their permission and the permission of J. M. Dent & Sons, Ltd.

The Crusaders embark, August 1248

In the month of August we entered into our ship at the Roche-de-Marseille. On the day that we entered into our ship, they opened the door of the ship and put therein all the horses we were to take overseas; and then they reclosed the door, and caulked it well, as when a cask is sunk in water, because, when the ship is on the high seas, all the said door is under water.

When the horses were in the ship, our master mariner called to his seamen, who stood at the prow, and said: "Are you ready?" and they answered, "Aye, sir—let the clerks and priests come forward!" As soon as these had come forward, he called to them, "Sing, for God's sake!" and they all, with one voice, chanted: *"Veni Creator Spiritus."*

Then he cried to his seamen "Unfurl the sails, for God's sake!" and they did so.

In a short space the wind filled our sails and had borne us out of sight of land, so that we saw naught save sky and water, and every day the wind carried us further from the land where we were born. And these things I tell you, that you may understand how foolhardy is that man who dares, having other's chattels in his possession, or being in mortal sin, to place himself in such peril, seeing that, when you lie down to sleep at night on shipboard, you lie down not knowing whether, in the morning, you may find yourself at the bottom of the sea.

At sea a singular marvel befell us; for we came across a mountain, quite round, before the coast of Barbary. We came across it about the hour of vespers, and sailed all night, and thought to have gone about fifty leagues: and, on the morrow, we found ourselves before the same mountain; and this same thing happened to us some two or three times. When the sailors saw this, they were all amazed, and told us we were in very great peril; for we were nigh unto the land of the Saracens of Barbary.

Then spake a certain right worthy priest, who was called the Dean of Maurupt; and he told us that never had any mischance occurred in his parish—whether lack of water, or overplus of rain, or any other mischance—but so soon as he had made three processions, on three Saturdays, God and His mother sent them deliverance. It was then a Saturday. We made the first procession round the two masts of the ship. I had myself carried in men's arms, because I was grievously sick. Never again did we see the mountain, and on the third Saturday we came to Cyprus.

Sojourn in Cyprus— embassage from the Tartars— Joinville takes service with the king

When we came to Cyprus, the king was already there, and we found great quantities of the king's supplies, that is to say, the cellarage of the king, and his treasure, and his granaries. The king's cellarage was set in the middle of the fields, on the shore by the sea. There his people had stacked great barrels of wine, which they had been buying for two years before the king's arrival; and the barrels were stacked one upon the other in such sort that when you looked at them in front, the stacks seemed as if they were barns.

The wheat and the barley they had set in heaps in the midst of the fields, and when you looked at them, it seemed as if they were mountains, for the rain, which had long been beating on the grain, had caused it to sprout, so that the outside looked like green grass. Now it happened that when they wished to take the grain into Egypt, they took away the upper crust with the green grass, and found the wheat and barley within as fresh as if newly threshed.

The king himself, as I heard tell in Syria, would very willingly have gone on to Egypt, without stopping, had it not been for his barons, who advised him to wait for such of his people as had not yet arrived.

While the king was sojourning in Cyprus, the great king of the Tartars sent envoys to him, with many good and gracious words. Among other things, he signified that he was ready to help the king to conquer the Holy Land, and to deliver Jerusalem from the hands of the Saracens.

The king received the envoys in very friendly fashion, and sent other envoys in return, who remained away two years. And the king, by his envoys, sent to the King of the Tartars a tent made like a chapel, very costly, for it was all of fair, fine scarlet cloth. The king, moreover, to see if he could draw the Tartars to our faith, caused images to be graven in the said chapel, representing the Annunciation of our Lady, and all the other points of the faith. And these things he sent by two brothers of the order of Preachers, who knew the Saracen language, and could show and teach the Tartars what they ought to believe.

The two brothers came back to the king at the time when the king's brothers were returning to France; and they found the king, who had left Acre, where his brothers had parted from him, and had come to Cæsarea, which he was fortifying; nor was there at that time any truce or peace with the Saracens. How the king's envoys were received will I tell you, as they themselves told it to the king; and in what they reported you may hear much that is strange and marvellous; but I will not tell you of it now, because, in order to do so, I should have to interrupt matters already begun;— so to proceed.

I, who had not a thousand *livres* yearly in land, had undertaken, when I went oversea, to bear, beside my own charges, the charges of nine knights, and two knights-banneret; and so it happened, when I arrived in Cyprus, that I had no more left, my ship being paid for, than twelve score *livres tournois;* wherefore some of my knights apprised me that if I did not provide myself with moneys, they would leave me. But God, who never failed me yet, provided for me in such fashion that the king, who was at Nicosia, sent for me, and took me into his service, and placed eight hundred livres in my coffers; and thus I had more moneys than I required.

• • •

The host leaves Cyprus—1249

As soon as we entered into the month of March, by the king's command the king, the barons, and the other pilgrims ordered that the ships should be re-laden with wine and provisions, so as to be ready to move when the king directed. And when the king saw that all had been duly ordered, the king and queen embarked on their ships on the Friday before Pentecost (21st May 1249), and the king told his barons to follow in their ships straight to Egypt. On the Saturday the king set sail and all the others besides, which was a fair thing to look upon, for it seemed as if all the sea, so far as the eye could reach, were covered with the canvas of the ships' sails; and the number of the ships, great and small, was reckoned at eighteen hundred.

The king anchored at the head of a hillock which is called the Point of Limassol, and all the other vessels anchored round about him. The king landed on the day of Pentecost. After we had heard mass a fierce and powerful wind, coming from the Egyptian side, arose in such sort that out of two thousand eight hundred knights, whom the king was taking into Egypt, there remained no more than seven hundred whom the wind had not separated from the king's company and carried away to Acre and other strange lands; nor did they afterwards return to the king for a long while.

The day after Pentecost the wind had fallen. The king and such of us as had, according to God's will, remained with him, set sail forthwith, and met the Prince of Morea, and the Duke of Burgundy, who had been sojourning in Morea. On the Thursday after Pentecost the king arrived before Damietta, and we found there, arrayed on the seashore, all the power of the soldan— a host fair to look upon, for the soldan's arms are of gold, and when the sun struck upon them they were resplendent. The noise they made with their cymbals and horns was fearful to listen to.

The king summoned his barons to take counsel what they should do. Many advised that he should wait till his people returned, seeing that no more than a third part had remained with him; but to this he would by no means agree. The reason he gave was, that to delay would put the foe in good heart, and, particularly, he said that there was no port before Damietta in which he could wait for his people, and that, therefore, any strong wind arising might drive the ships to other lands, like as the ships had been driven on the day of Pentecost.

Preparation for disembarkation in Egypt

It was settled that the king should land on the Friday before Trinity and do battle with the Saracens, unless they refused to stand. The king ordered my Lord John of Beaumont to assign a galley to my Lord Everard of Brienne and to myself, so as that we might land, we and our knights, because the great ships could not get close up to the shore.

As God so willed, when I returned to my ship, I found a little ship that my Lady of Beyrout, who was cousin-german to my Lord of Montbéliard and to myself, had given me, and that carried eight of my horses.

When the Friday came I and my

Lord Everard went, fully armed, to the king and asked for the galley; whereupon my Lord John of Beaumont told us that we should not have it. When our people saw that they would get no galley, they let themselves drop from the great ship into the ship's boat, pell-mell, and as best they could, so that the boat began to sink. The sailors saw that the boat was sinking, little by little, and they escaped into the big ship and left my knights in the boat. I asked the master how many more people there were in the boat than the boat could hold. He told me twenty men-at-arms; and I asked him whether he could take our people to land if I relieved him of so many, and he said, "Yes." So I relieved him in such sort that in three journeys he took them to the ship that had carried my horses.

While I was conducting these people a knight belonging to my Lord Everard of Brienne, and whose name was Plonquet, thought to go down from the great ship into the boat; but the boat moved away, and he fell into the sea and was drowned.

When I came back to my ship I put into my little boat a squire whom I made a knight, and whose name was my Lord Hugh of Vaucouleurs, and two very valiant bachelors—of whom the one had the name my Lord Villain of Versey, and the other my Lord William of Dammartin—who were at bitter enmity the one against the other. Nor could any one make peace between them, because they had seized each other by the hair in Morea. And I made them forgive their grievances and embrace, for I swore to them on holy relics that we should not land in company of their enmity.

Then we set ourselves to get to land, and came alongside of the barge belonging to the king's great ship, there where the king himself was. And his people began to cry out to us, because we were going more quickly than they, that I should land by the ensign of St. Denis, which was being borne in another vessel before the king. But I heeded them not, and caused my people to land in front of a great body of Turks, at a place where there were full six thousand men on horseback.

So soon as these saw us land, they came toward us, hotly spurring. We, when we saw them coming, fixed the points of our shields into the sand and the handles of our lances in the sand with the points set towards them. But when they were so near that they saw the lances about to enter into their bellies, they turned about and fled.

The Crusaders disembark in front of the Saracens

My Lord Baldwin of Rheims, a right good man, who had come to land, requested me, by his squire, to wait for him; and I let him know I should do so willingly, for that a right good man such as he ought surely to be waited for in like case of need,—whereby I had his favour all the time that he lived. With him came to us a thousand knights; and you may be assured that, when I landed, I had neither squire, nor knight, nor varlet that I had brought with me from my own country, and yet God never left me without such as I needed.

At our left hand landed the

Count of Jaffa, who was cousin-german to the Count of Montbél-iard, and of the lineage of Joinville. It was he who landed in greatest pride, for his galley came all painted, within and without, with escutcheons of his arms, which arms are *or* with a cross of gules *patée*. He had at least three hundred row-ers in his galley, and for each rower there was a targe with the count's arms thereon, and to each targe was a pennon attached with his arms wrought in gold.

While he was coming it seemed as if his galley flew, so did the row-ers urge it forward with their sweeps; and it seemed as if the light-ning were falling from the skies at the sound that the pennants made, and the cymbals, and the drums, and the Saracenic horns that were in his galley. So soon as the galley had been driven into the sand as far up as they could drive it, both he and his knights leapt from the gal-ley, well armed and well equipped, and came and arrayed themselves beside us.

I had forgotten to tell you that when the Count of Jaffa landed he immediately caused his tents and pavilions to be pitched; and so soon as the Saracens saw them pitched, they all came and gathered before us, and then came on again, spur-ring hotly, as if to run in upon us. But when they saw that we should not fly, they shortly turned and went back again.

On our right hand, at about a long-crossbow-shot's distance, landed the galley that bore the en-sign of St. Denis. And there was a Saracen who, when they had landed, came and charged in among them,

either because he could not hold in his horse, or because he thought the other Saracens would follow him; but he was hacked in pieces.

St. Louis takes possession of Damietta

When the king heard tell that the ensign of St. Denis was on shore he went across his ship with large steps; and maugre the legate who was with him he would not leave from following the ensign, but leapt into the sea, which was up to his armpits. So he went, with his shield hung to his neck, and his helmet on his head, and his lance in his hand, till he came to his people who were on the shore. When he reached the land, and looked upon the Saracens, he asked what people they were, and they told him they were Sara-cens; and he put his lance to his shoulder, and his shield before him, and would have run in upon the Saracens if the right worthy men who were about him would have suffered it.

The Saracens sent thrice to the soldan, by carrier-pigeons, to say that the king had landed, but never received any message in return, be-cause the soldan's sickness was upon him. Wherefore they thought that the soldan was dead, and aban-doned Damietta. The king sent a knight forward to know if it was sooth that Damietta was so aban-doned. The knight returned to the king and said it was sooth and that he had been into the houses of the soldan. Then the king sent for the legate and all the prelates of the host, and all chanted with a loud voice *Te Deum laudamus*. Afterwards the king mounted his horse, and we all likewise, and we went and encamped before Damietta.

Very unadvisedly did the Turks leave Damietta, in that they did not cut the bridge of boats, for that would have been a great hindrance to us; but they wrought us very much hurt in setting fire to the bazaar, where all the merchandise is collected, and everything that is sold by weight. The damage that followed from this was as great as if—which God forbid!—some one were, tomorrow, to set fire to the Petit-Pont in Paris.

Now let us declare that God Almighty was very gracious to us when He preserved us from death and peril on our disembarkation, seeing that we landed on foot and affronted our enemies who were mounted. Great grace did our Lord also show us when He delivered Damietta into our hands, for otherwise we could only have taken it by famine, and of this we may be fully assured, for it was by famine that King John had taken it in the days of our fathers (in 1219).

Mistake of St. Louis— disorder among the Crusaders

Our Lord can say of us, as He said of the children of Israel—*et pro nihilo habuerunt terram desiderabilem*.[1] And what does He say afterwards? He says that they forgot God their Saviour. And so did we forget Him as I will shortly tell you.

---

[1] "They despised the pleasant land."

But first I will tell you of the king who summoned his barons, the clerks, and the laymen, and asked them to help him to decide how the booty taken in the city should be divided. The patriarch was the first to speak, and he spoke thus: "Sire, methinks it were well that you should keep the wheat, and the barley, and the rice, and whatever is needed to sustain life, so as to provision the city; and that you should have it cried throughout the host that all other goods are to be brought to the legate's quarters, under pain of excommunication." To this advice all the other barons assented. Now, as it fell out, all the goods brought to the legate's quarters did not amount in value to more than six thousand livres.

When this had been done, the king and the barons summoned John of Valery, the right worthy man, and spoke to him thus: "Sir of Valery," said the king, "we are agreed that the legate should hand over to you the six thousand livres, so that you may divide them as may seem best to you." "Sire," replied the right worthy man, "you do me much honour, and great thanks be yours! But, please God! that honour can I not accept, nor can I carry out your wish, for by so doing I should make null the good customs of the Holy Land, whereby, when the cities of the enemy are captured, the king takes a third of the goods found therein, and the pilgrims take two thirds. And this custom was well observed by King John when he took Damietta, and as old folks tell us, the same custom was observed by the kings of Jerusalem, who were before King John. If then it pleases you to hand over to me the two parts of the wheat, and the barley, and the rice, and the other provisions, then shall I willingly undertake to make division among the pilgrims."

The king did not decide to do this; so matters remained as they were; and many were ill-pleased that the king should set aside the good old customs.

The king's people, who ought, by liberal dealing, to have retained the merchants, made them pay, so it was said, the highest rents they could exact for the shops in which to sell their goods; and the rumour of this got abroad to foreign lands, so that many merchants forbore to come and bring supplies to the host.

The barons, who ought to have kept what was theirs so as to spend it in fitting time and place, took to giving great feasts, and an outrageous excess of meats. The common people took to consorting with lewd women; whereby it happened, after we returned from captivity, that the king discharged a great many of his people. And when I asked him why he had done this, he told me that he had found, of a certainty, that those whom he had discharged held their ill places of assemblage at a short stone's-throw from his pavilion, and that at a time when the host was in greatest distress and misery.

The Saracens attack the camp— death of Walter of Autrèche

Now let us go back to the matter in hand, and tell how, shortly after we had taken Damietta, all the horse-men of the soldan came before the camp, and attacked it from the land side. The king and all the horsemen armed themselves. I, being in full armour, went to speak to the king, and found him fully armed, sitting on a settle, and round him were the right worthy knights belonging to his own division, all in full armour. I asked if he desired that I and my people should issue from the camp, so that the Saracens should not fall upon our tents. When my Lord John of Beaumont heard my question, he cried to me in a very loud voice, and commanded me, in the king's name, not to leave my quarters till the king so ordered.

I have told you of the right worthy knights who were of the king's special following, for there were eight of them, all good knights who had won prizes for arms on the further or hither side of the seas, and such knights it was customary to call good knights. These are the names of the knights about the king: —my Lord Geoffry of Sargines, my Lord Matthew of Marly, my Lord Philip of Nanteuil, and my Lord Imbert of Beaujeu, Constable of France; but the last was not then present, he was outside the camp— he and the master of the crossbow-men, with most of the king's ser-geants-at-arms—to guard the camp so that the Turks might not do any mischief thereto.

Now it happened that my Lord Walter Autrèche got himself armed at all points in his pavilion; and when he was mounted upon his horse, with his shield at his neck and his helmet on his head, he caused the flaps of his pavilion to be lifted, and struck spurs into his horse to ride against the Turks; and as he left his pavilion, all alone, all his men shouted with a loud voice, "Chatillon." But so it chanced that or ever he came up to the Turks he fell, and his horse flew over his body; and the horse went on, covered with his arms, to our enemies, because the Saracens were, for the most part, mounted on mares, for which reason the horse drew to the side of the Saracens.

And those who looked on told us that four Turks came by Lord Walter, who lay upon the ground, and as they went by, gave him great blows with their maces there where he lay. Then did the Constable of France and several of the king's sergeants deliver him, and they brought him back in their arms to his pavilion. When he came there he was speechless. Several of the surgeons and physicians of the host went to him, and because it did not seem to them that he was in danger of death, they had him blooded in both arms.

That night, very late, my Lord Aubert of Narcy proposed that we should go and see him, for as yet we had not seen him, and he was a man of great name and of great valour. We entered into his pavilion, and the chamberlain came to meet us, and asked us to move quietly, so as not to wake his master. We found him lying on coverlets of miniver, and went to him very softly, and found him dead. When this was told to the king, he replied that he would not willingly have a thousand such men acting contrary to his orders as this man had done.

Renewed attacks on the part of the Saracens—the king decides to await the arrival of the Count of Poitiers

The Saracens entered every night into the camp on foot and killed our people there where they found them sleeping, whereby it chanced that they killed the sentinel of the lord of Courtenay, and left him lying on a table, and cut off his head, and took it away with them. And this they did because the soldan gave a besant of gold for every Christian man's head.

And we were at this disadvantage because the battalions guarded the camp, each one its night, on horseback; and when the Saracens wished to enter into the camp, they waited till the noise of the horses and of the battalions had passed, and then crept into the camp behind the horses, making their way out before it was day. So the king ordered that the battalion which had been used to keep guard on horseback should keep guard on foot, whereby all the camp was in safety, because of our men who kept guard, and were spread out in such wise that one man touched the other.

After this was done, the king decided not to leave Damietta till his brother, the Count of Poitiers, had arrived with the remaining forces of France. And so that the Saracens might not charge on their horses into the midst of the camp, the king caused all the camp to be enclosed with great earthworks, and on the earthworks were set crossbowmen to watch every night, and sergeants; and such were set also at the entrance to the camp.

Benvenuto Cellini at work. (*Culver Pictures, Inc.*)

Renaissance and Reformation

The Renaissance was a cultural and intellectual revival that began in the city-states of northern Italy during the fourteenth and fifteenth centuries. The gradual change from the medieval outlook was probably caused by several factors: the great economic prosperity of these city-states, their contacts through trade with other cultures, the reduction of the papacy to the role of an Italian principality, and the Church's loss of emotional prestige. These elements combined to produce the highly secular outlook that is the essence of the Renaissance.

This secular outlook is commonly referred to as "humanism," a term that may be defined in two ways. According to the narrower definition, humanism was a rebirth, or renaissance, of interest in classical antiquity. People turned to a rereading of the great (and not so great) works of Greek and Roman literature, a reexamination and preservation of classical architecture and sculpture, and a restudy of the classical languages themselves. This very interest in the glories of Greece and Rome, however, exacted its price, for Renaissance literature and some of its art tended to be imitative, to rely too heavily on the models of a bygone day. The conviction that it was impossible to surpass or even to equal the achievements of the ancients tended to inhibit the mind and imagination of the people of the Renaissance.

The broader definition of humanism states the typically Renaissance notion that people and their activities are the most important and interesting elements of the universe. Thus, mankind, rather than God, is the proper subject of contemplation and examination. This secular, humanistic outlook posed many interesting problems. If humankind and human life on this earth are the most important concern, how may the "good" person or the "good" life be determined? Castiglione, in his manual on conduct, *The Book of the Courtier,* claimed that virtue is its own reward, that one does not do good out of hope for reward or fear of punishment in an afterlife, but only because it is good to be good. Some of the same secular ethic is implied in the political theories of Machiavelli, whose ideal prince was not concerned with or troubled by an angry or beneficent God but only with the problems of acquiring and maintaining power to ensure a stable political order in which the citizenry could live in peace and plenty.

During the fifteenth and sixteenth centuries the Renaissance spread from Italy to France, England, Spain, the Lowlands, and throughout Germany and Poland. Italian manners and customs were widely adopted; it became fashionable to build "in the Italian fashion" and to dress "in the Italian mode." More important, however, than the adoption of these cultural superficialities was the ready acceptance by scholars in northern Europe of the critical methods developed by Pico, Valla, and others of reading and analyzing documents, literature, and writings of all kinds. Moreover, the scientific attitude and the widespread curiosity about the physical world led many Europeans to inquire, to study, to dissect, to experiment, and to seek a fuller understanding of the nature of the universe and their place in it.

Among the leaders of the New Learning in the North was Sir Thomas More of England, who looked closely at his society and found it mean and corrupt. This conclusion he elaborated in his brilliant and immensely popular satire, *Utopia,* which was published in 1516 in Latin and subsequently translated into English, French, Spanish, German, and Italian. More's close friend, Erasmus of Rotterdam, was also deeply influenced by the skeptical, critical thought of the Renaissance. Erasmus translated the New Testament from Greek into Latin, wrote various *Colloquies* containing observations and commentaries on the contemporary world, and, more lasting perhaps, published his penetrating analysis of people and affairs under the title *The Praise of Folly.*

Not everyone, however, received the New Learning with the same enthusiasm. A German monk, Martin Luther, though he accepted the typically humanistic ideas regarding the critical examination of texts, could not accept the Renaissance notion that this world and its affairs were of primary importance. He was unwilling to divorce himself from the crucial problem of the salvation of people's souls. Most of the people of the Renaissance simply shelved the problem of salvation—for them, life was for the living, to be enjoyed and possibly to be remembered without remorse or regret. Benvenuto Cellini, an Italian goldsmith, was a perfect example of this attitude. But for Luther (a contemporary of Cellini) life on this earth was merely a transient aspect of the eternal life of the soul. In this one sense, Luther represented a reversion to the medieval outlook. But at the same time he shared in the new intellectual movements, being convinced that everyone was competent to read and understand the holy writings and to find salvation through faith.

Justification by faith lay at the heart of the Lutheran break with the Catholic Church. Originally, Luther sought only the reform of church practice, not of doctrine. But the indifference of the church leaders, together with what seemed to him an almost institutionalized acceptance of abuses, made Luther's outcries go unheard. The Church finally became seriously enough concerned over Luther's protests to excommunicate him, thereby laying the ground for the Protestant movement. Launched by Luther, Protestantism quickly gained adherents in many parts of Europe. The most influential of these was a Frenchman transplanted to Geneva, John Calvin, who supplied the movement with a theology. Anything but an innovator, Calvin returned to the writings of St. Paul and St. Augustine and the doctrine of original sin, which he reiterated with a rare combination of legalistic precision and evangelical fervor.

For centuries, the Catholic Church had been flexible enough in its thinking and its practices to adjust to reform movements from within—for example, the Cluniac movement of the eleventh century, the Cistercian of the twelfth, and the Franciscan of the thirteenth. But by the end of the fifteenth century the Church was no longer able to provide the spiritual comfort required to sustain a great number of loyal and devoted followers. During the fifteenth century a group of mystics, who dedicated their lives to poverty and the education of the young, had appeared in Germany: the Brotherhood of the Common Life. This relatively obscure group felt that the conventional Catholic Church was somehow failing in its purposes, and sought to restore a measure of fervor to the traditional faith. Even Erasmus was concerned about the abuses in church practice and the indifference of church leadership to the needs of the people. He presented his solutions to these problems in what he called "the philosophy of Christ."

One of the outcomes of the conflict between the Protestant movement and the Catholic Church was a revitalization of the Catholic faith. Led mostly by the militant order of the Society of Jesus, founded in 1540 by St. Ignatius of Loyola, the Catholics reconverted Poland, Bohemia, and large areas of France and Germany. Of course, this revitalization was not accomplished without bitterness, heroism, and conflict from both Protestant and Catholic. The Peasants Revolt in Germany in the early sixteenth century, the religious wars in France in the late sixteenth century, and the Thirty Years' War in the early seventeenth century were only outstanding examples of the hatred, fear, and bloodshed provoked by conflicting religious opinions.

During the Renaissance, then, Europe was expanding intellectually and culturally through scientific investigation and literary and artistic innovation, and was attempting to find some solution to religious controversy. Europe was expanding geographically as well, for the time of the Renaissance and Reformation was also the age of exploration and commercial revolution. To the west new continents were discovered, new colonies planted, and new empires created. The discovery of a sea route around Africa immensely stimulated traffic between western Europe and the Orient, leading finally to a relative decline in the economic status of the great Italian cities and the emergence of Portugal, Spain, the Dutch Republic, and finally France and England as world powers with great fleets and vast overseas holdings. The influx of wealth (both in goods and precious metals) from East and West created severe economic dislocations and upheavals in Europe, adding another source of strife and discontent to a culture already troubled by the ferment of Renaissance skepticism and Reformation religious enthusiasm. It was from this matrix that the modern world emerged; many of the problems posed then remain today.

Pico della Mirandola

Giovanni Pico, the Count of Mirandola (1463–1494), epitomized both in his life and in his writings the Renaissance ideal of manhood. Nobly born, wealthy, handsome, and brilliant, he was well embarked on a distinguished intellectual career which would certainly have made him the undisputed leader of the humanistic movement when he unfortunately fell victim to fever at the age of thirty.

Unwilling to limit himself, as many other humanists did, to translating and imitating the literature of classical Greece and Rome, Pico undertook the task of assimilating all the great writings of the past, searching out the elements of truth contained in each of them, and assembling these truths into a new philosophical synthesis of his own. The *Oration on the Dignity of Man* is a part of this ambitious project. After seven years of study in various European universities, Pico arrived in Rome at the age of twenty-three and announced that he was prepared to defend in public debate against anyone in Europe a list of nine hundred theses representing the conclusions that he had derived from his studies. (He even offered to pay the travel expenses of scholars coming long distances.) The debate, scheduled for January 1487, never took place. Pope Innocent VIII, suspicious that Pico was straying from orthodoxy, appointed a commission to examine the list of theses. When the commission confirmed the pope's suspicions by labeling a number of them heretical, Innocent forced the debate to be canceled.

The nature of the *Oration,* which Pico had intended as an introductory address for the debate, is evident from its title. Apart from the intrinsic interest of the discussion itself, including the many references which Pico makes to the most diverse literary sources, the significance of the *Oration* lies in its eloquent summation of the Renaissance interest in humans and the belief in the dignity of human life. The selection that follows includes the first seven sections of the *Oration.*

On the Dignity of Man

Most reverend fathers: I have read in the writings of the Arabs that Azdallah the Saracen, when asked what thing on this worldly stage appeared most marvelous to him, replied that he perceived nothing more wonderful than Man. This opinion is concurred in by that famous statement of Hermes Trismegistus:

Man, Asclepius, is a great miracle.

As I pondered the sense of these sayings, I became dissatisfied with those arguments which are brought forth in profusion by many people to establish the excellence of Humanity: namely, that Man is the intermediary of all created things, slave to those above him, king to those below; that Man is the interpreter of nature, by virtue of the sharpness of his senses, the searching of his reason, and the light of his understanding; that Man is the interval between time and eternity, the copula of the universe (as the Persians say), or even its wedding, a little lower, on David's authority, than the angels. These are great things, certainly, but not of prime importance; not so great that they lay just claim to the highest admiration. For, under these conditions, why should we not give even greater admiration to the angels themselves, and to the blessed choir of Heaven? At length, I felt that I had come to understand both why Man is the most fortunate of creatures, and thus worthy of all admiration, and what, finally, this situation is which he has received in the scheme of the universe—a position to be envied, not only by the beasts, but by the stars, by the spirits beyond the world. The answer is marvelous and incredible. How could it be otherwise? For it is on this account that Man is rightly said and believed to be a great miracle, truly a being to be admired.

Hear now, Fathers, what this solution is, and, in your courtesy, grant my discourse a friendly audience.

The Supreme Father, God the Creator, had already fashioned this worldly residence which we see about us, the majestic temple of His Godhood, after the laws of His secret wisdom. He had adorned the zone beyond the heavens with intellects; He had quickened the ethereal spheres into life with eternal souls; He had filled the foul and filthy regions of the lower world with a multitude of animals of every sort. But, His work completed, the Demiurge desired that there be someone to contemplate the reason of such a great work, to love its beauty, to wonder at its vastness. Thus, when everything had been finished (as Moses and Timaeus bear witness), He turned His thoughts last of all to bringing forth Man. But there remained no archetype on which to

Giovanni Pico Della Mirandola, *De Hominis Dignitate,* trans Douglass S. Parker of the University of Texas.

pattern the new creature, no treasure to bestow on the new son as an inheritance, no place in all the new world where that contemplator of the universe might sit. By this time, all things were full; all things had been distributed in the highest, middle, and lowest orders. But it was not the nature of the Father's power to fail, as though exhausted, in the last act of creation; nor of His wisdom, to waver in a necessary deed through lack of a plan; nor of His beneficent love, to compel the very being who was to praise the divine generosity in other things to impugn that generosity in himself. At length the Greatest Craftsman decided that this being, to whom He could give nothing of its own, should share in everything which he had assigned to each of the other beings. Thus he received Man as a work of undefined pattern, and, placing him in the center of the world, addressed him as follows:

I have given you, O Adam, neither a fixed location, nor an especial appearance, nor any gift peculiarly your own; therefore, you may attain and possess, as you wish and as you will, whatever location, whatever appearance, whatever gifts you yourself desire. The nature of all other things is limited and confined within laws which I have laid down. You, confined by no limits, will determine your nature for yourself by your judgment, into whose power I have consigned you. I have placed you in the middle of the world, whence you may survey the more conveniently everything which is in the world. I have made you neither heavenly nor earthly, neither mortal nor immortal; thus, as a free and sovereign craftsman, you may mold yourself whatever form you choose. You will be able to degenerate into those lower creatures, which are brutes; you will be able, by the determination of your mind, to be reborn into those higher creatures, which are divine.

How great is the generosity of God the Father! How great and admirable is the happiness of Man, whose gift it is to have that which he wishes! Upon their birth, beasts bring with them from their mother's bag (as Lucilius says) all that they will ever possess. From the beginning of time, or soon after, the supreme spirits have been that which they will be throughout all eternity. But as Man is born, the Father has planted in him seeds of every sort, shoots of every life; those which each man cultivates will grow, and bear their fruits in him. If these are vegetable, he will become a plant; if sensual, a brute; if rational, a heavenly being; if intellectual, an angel and son of God. But if Man, not contented with any creature's lot, betakes himself into the center of his oneness, then, made one with God, in the solitary darkness of the Father he who was created above all things will excell all things.

Who would not admire this chameleon of ours? Or, rather, who would admire anything else more greatly? Asclepius of Athens does no wrong when he says of man that, in accordance with his changing aspect and his self-transforming nature, he was symbolized in the mysteries by Proteus. Hence those metamorphoses celebrated among the Hebrews and the Pythagoreans: indeed, the most secret Hebrew theology makes transformations, now of holy Enoch into an angel of the divinity, now of other men into other divine spirits; the Pythagoreans transform evildoers into beasts, and even (if we may believe Empedocles) into plants. Imitating this, Mohammed would often say, "He who departs from the divine law becomes a beast," and rightly so. For not the bark, but the dull and insensible nature makes the plants; not the hide, but the brutish and sensual soul the beast; not the circular body, but correct reason the heavens; not separation from the body, but spiritual intelligence the angel. For should you see a man given up to his belly and creeping on the ground, you see a plant, not a man; should you see someone blinded by the empty illusions of an apparition like Calypso, enticed by titillating allurements, a slave to his senses, you see a beast, not a man; should you see a philosopher perceiving all by his correct reasoning, you would revere him—he is a being of heaven, not of earth; should you see a pure contemplator, unconscious of his body, completely withdrawn into the sanctuary of his mind, this is no earthly, no celestial being:—this is a most majestic spirit dressed in human flesh.

Is there anyone, then, who would not admire man? Not wrongly, in both the Mosaic and the Christian scriptures, is he called now by the name of "all flesh," now by the name of "every creature," since he molds, fashions, and transforms himself after the appearance of all flesh and after the nature of every creature.

Therefore Evanthes the Persian, in his account of the Chaldean theology, writes that Man possesses no innate form of his own, but many extraneous and foreign ones, whence that saying of the Chaldeans that man is an animal of varied and manifold and unstable nature.

But to what end do I record this? So that, after we have been born in this condition—that of being what we wish—we shall understand that we must take especial care that it not be said against us, that we were in honor and knew it not, and became as brutes and foolish beasts. Rather, may the words of the prophet Asaph apply—"Ye are gods, and all of you are children of the most High,"—lest we, abusing the Father's most indulgent generosity, render that unfettered choice which He gave us harmful rather than beneficial. May some holy aspiration enter our hearts, so that we are not content with middling things, but pant for the highest and strain to achieve them, since we can if we will.

Let us scorn the earthly, despise the heavenly, and thus, disdaining everything which is of the world, fly to that assembly beyond the world which is nearest God, who towers over all. There, as the holy mysteries tell, Seraphim, Cherubim, and Thrones occupy the first place; let us strive to equal their dignity and glory. And, if we wish it, we shall be in no wise lower than they.

Niccolò Machiavelli

A reading of *The Prince* by Machiavelli (1469–1527) makes it easy to understand the evil connotations that have come to surround the term "Machiavellian." Written as a handbook for political leaders, *The Prince* is most famous as the source of the doctrine that, in politics, the end always justifies the means. With Machiavelli, this doctrine was no theoretical assumption; it was a conclusion derived from acute observation and analysis of the political practices of the day. As a diplomat in the service of his native city of Florence, Machiavelli was able to observe the tactics of the men who were struggling for control of the Italian peninsula in the early sixteenth century. The most colorful of these power-hungry men was the notorious Caesar Borgia, son of Pope Alexander VI, whom Machiavelli met on numerous occasions during his diplomatic career. For Borgia, power clearly was an end in itself.

Although, in *The Prince,* Machiavelli praises Borgia and advocates the pursuit of power without regard to the methods employed, to be fair we must realize that Machiavelli himself was not an unqualified Machiavellian. In the final chapter of *The Prince,* he urges Lorenzo de' Medici to exert his princely power to unify Italy and drive out foreign oppressors, an end that Machiavelli valued more highly than the mere pursuit of power for its own sake. And in his *Discourses* he concludes that the best-governed state is a state ruled, not by a Machiavellian prince, but by the people themselves. Despite these qualifications, however, Machiavelli's reputation in history is that of the champion of power politics.

To capture something of the flavor and diversity of the Italian Renaissance, we have only to realize that Machiavelli and Pico della Mirandola were contemporaries living in the city of Florence. Yet, while Pico was writing on the dignity of man, Machiavelli was observing, "For it may be truly affirmed of mankind in general, that they are ungrateful, fickle, timid, dissembling, and self-interested. . . ."

The Prince

**Niccolò Machiavelli,
citizen and secretary of Florence,
to the most magnificent
Lorenzo de' Medici**

Those who court the favour of princes generally present them with whatever they possess that is most rare, curious, or valuable; as horses, armour, embroidered cloths, precious stones, &c., according to the dignity of the personage they seek to propitiate. For my part, my anxiety to present myself to the notice of your highness, with the best proof of my devotion, has not enabled me to discover, amongst all I possess, anything that I esteem more, or account so valuable, as a knowledge of the actions of celebrated men; a knowledge acquired by a long experience of modern times, and a diligent perusal of the ancients. The observations which I have made with all the accuracy, reflection, and care of which I am capable, are contained in the small volume now addressed to you. And although I have not the vanity to deem it worthy of your acceptance, yet I am persuaded that your goodness will not refuse the offering, since it is impossible to present you with anything more valuable than a work which will place before you, in a small compass, all the experience I have acquired during many years of continual meditation and suffering in the school of adversity.

You will find in this fragment neither a glowing and lofty style, nor any of those meretricious ornaments with which authors seek to embellish their works. Its interest must depend upon the importance of the subject, the solidity of the reflections, and the truth of the facts recorded.

It will, perhaps, appear presumptuous in me, a man of humble birth, to propose rules of conduct to those who govern; but as the painter when about to sketch a mountainous country places himself in the plain, and in order to draw the scenery of a vale, ascends an eminence, even so, I conceive, that a person must be a prince to discover the nature and character of a people, and one of the people to judge properly of a prince.

I am therefore bold enough to hope that you will accept this feeble tribute in reference to the intention with which it is offered; and if you condescend to read it with attention, you will have evidence of my ardent desire to see you fill with glory those high destinies, to which fortune and your splendid talents have called you.

If from your elevated position you should condescend to look down on a person in my lowly station, you will see how long and how unworthily I have been persecuted by the extreme and unrelenting malevolence of fortune.

Niccolò Machiavelli

Niccolò Machiavelli, "The Prince," from *The History of Florence and the Affairs of Italy* (London, 1854).

• • •

CHAPTER XIV

Of the duties of a prince relative to his military force

Princes ought . . . to make the art of war their sole study and occupation, for it is peculiarly the science of those who govern. War, and the several sorts of discipline and institutions relative to it, should be his only study, the only profession he should follow, and the object he ought always to have in view. By this means princes can maintain possession of their dominions; and private individuals are sometimes raised thereby to supreme authority; whilst, on the other hand, we frequently see princes shamefully reduced to nothing, by suffering themselves to be enfeebled by slothful inactivity. I repeat, therefore, that by a neglect of this art it is that states are lost, and by cultivating it they are acquired.

Francis Sforza, from a private station, attained the rank of duke of Milan, by having an army always at his disposal; and by a deviation from this rule his children, who succeeded to the dukedom, were reduced to the station of private individuals. And this is not surprising: for, in the first place, nothing is so likely to impair our esteem for the character of a prince as to see him destitute of a military force; and, as I shall endeavour to prove hereafter, that a prince should most particularly beware of falling into general contempt.

We cannot establish a comparison between men who are armed, and those who are not so; and it would be equally absurd to suppose that the disarmed should command, and the others obey. A prince who is ignorant of the art of war can never enjoy repose or safety amongst armed subjects; he will always be to them an object of contempt, as they to him will justly be subjects of suspicion; how is it possible then that they should act in concert? In short, a prince who does not understand the art of war can never be esteemed by his troops, nor can he ever confide in them.

It is necessary therefore that princes should pay their whole attention to the art of war, which includes mental labour and study as well as the military exercise. To begin with the latter, the prince should take the utmost care that his troops be well disciplined and regularly exercised. The chase is well adapted to inure the body to fatigue, and to all the intemperances of weather. This exercise will also teach him to observe the sources and situations, as well as the nature of rivers and marshes; to measure the extent of plains, and the declivity of mountains. By these means he will acquire a knowledge of the topography of a country which he has to defend, and will easily habituate himself to select the places where war may be best carried on. For the plain and valleys of Tuscany resemble more or less those of other countries; so that a perfect knowledge of one will enable them to form a tolerably accurate judgment of the other.

This study is particularly useful to commanders. A general who neglects it will never know where to look for an enemy, nor how to conduct his troops, nor to encamp, nor the proper time to attack. The Greek and Roman historians deservedly praised Philopomenes, prince of Achaia, for his application to the study of war in time of peace. He was accustomed in his travels to stop and ask his friends, which of two armies would have the advantage, if one posted on such or such a hill, and the other in such a particular place? In what manner this, if commanded by himself, should join and give battle to the other? What steps he ought to take in order to secure a retreat, or pursue the enemy, in case he should retire? He thus proposed to them in every case which might happen in war, listened attentively to their opinion, and then gave his own, together with the reasons on which it was founded. By these means he was always prepared to meet unforeseen events.

As to that part of military science which is learned in the closet, a prince ought to read history, and to pay particular attention to the achievements of great generals, and the cause of their victories and defeats; but above all he should follow the example of those great men who, when they select a model, resolve to follow in his steps. It was thus that Alexander the Great immortalized himself by following the example of Achilles, Caesar by imitating Alexander, and Scipio by copying Cyrus. If we take the trouble to compare the life of the latter Roman with that of Cyrus, we shall see how nearly Scipio copied the modesty, affability, humanity, liberality, and the other virtues with which Xenophon adorns his hero.

It is thus a wise prince should conduct himself, and so employ his time during peace, that if fortune should change, he may be prepared equally for her frowns or her favours.

CHAPTER XV

What deserves praise or blame in men, and above all in princes

It now remains to show in what manner a prince should behave to his subjects and friends. This matter having been already discussed by others, it may seem arrogant in me to pursue it farther, especially if I should differ in opinion from them; but as I write only for those who possess sound judgment, I thought it better to treat this subject as it really is, in fact, than to amuse the imagination with visionary models of republics and governments which have never existed. For the manner in which men now live is so different from the manner in which they ought to live, that he who deviates from the common course of practice, and endeavours to act as duty dictates, necessarily ensures his own destruction. Thus, a good man, and one who wishes to prove himself so in all respects, must be undone in a contest with so many who are evilly disposed. A prince who wishes to maintain his power ought therefore to learn that he should not be always good, and must use that knowledge as circumstances and the exigencies of his own affairs may seem to require.

Laying aside, then, the false ideas which have been formed as to princes, and adhering only to those which are true, I say, that all men, and especially princes, are marked and distinguished by some quality or other which entails either reputation or dishonour. For instance, men are liberal or parsimonious, honourable or dishonourable, effeminate or pusillanimous, courageous or enterprising, humane or cruel, affable or haughty, wise or debauched, honest or dishonest, good tempered or surly, sedate or inconsiderate, religious or impious, and so forth.

It would, doubtless, be happy for a prince to unite in himself every species of good quality; but as our nature does not allow so great a perfection, a prince should have prudence enough to avoid those defects and vices which may occasion his ruin; and as to those which can only compromise his safety and the possession of his dominions, he ought, if possible, to guard against them; but if he cannot succeed in this, he need not embarrass himself in escaping the scandal of those vices, but should devote his whole energies to avoid those which may cause his ruin. He should not shrink from encountering some blame on account of vices which are important to the support of his states; for everything well considered, there are some things having the appearance of virtues, which would prove the ruin of a prince, should he put them in practice, and others, upon which, though seemingly bad and vicious, his actual welfare and security entirely depend.

CHAPTER XVI

Of liberality and economy

To begin with the first qualities of the above-mentioned, I must observe that it is for the interest of a prince to be accounted liberal, but dangerous so to exercise his liberality, that he is thereby neither feared nor respected. I will explain myself. If a prince be only liberal, as far as it suits his purposes, that is to say, within certain bounds, he will please but few, and will be called selfish. A prince who wishes to gain the reputation of being liberal, should be regardless of expense; but then to support this reputation, he will often be reduced to the necessity of levying taxes on his subjects, and adopting every species of fiscal resource which cannot fail to make him odious. Besides exhausting the public treasure by his prodigality, his credit will be destroyed, and he will run the risk of losing his dominions on the first reverse of fortune, his liberality, as it always happens, having ensured him more enemies than friends. And which is worse, he cannot retrace his steps and replenish his finances, without being charged with avarice.

A prince, therefore, who cannot be liberal without prejudicing his state, should not trouble himself much about the imputation of being covetous; for he will be esteemed liberal in time, when people see that by parsimony he has improved his revenue, become able to defend his dominions, and even to undertake useful enterprises without the aid of new taxes; then the many from whom he takes nothing will deem him sufficiently liberal, and the few only, whose expectations he has failed to realize, will accuse him of avarice. In our own times we have seen no great exploits performed, except by those who have been accounted avaricious; all the others have failed. Julius II attained the pontifical chair by means of his bounty; but he judged rightly in supposing, that in order to enable him to prosecute the war against France, it would do him injury to preserve his reputation for liberality. By his parsimony he was able to support the expense of all his wars without the imposition of new taxes. The present king of Spain could never have accomplished all his great enterprises, if he had felt any ambition to be thought liberal.

A prince, then, who would avoid poverty, and always be in a condition to defend his dominions without imposing new taxes on his subjects, should care little for being charged with avarice, since the imputed vice may be the very means of incurring the prosperity and stability of his government.

It may however be alleged that Caesar would never have attained the empire but by his liberality, and that many others have arrived at the highest honours by the same means. I answer, you are either in possession of dominion already, or you are not. In the first place, liberality would be prejudicial; in the second, the reputation of it is serviceable and necessary. Caesar endeavoured to appear liberal whilst he aspired to the empire of Rome. But if he had lived longer, he would have lost that reputation for liberality which had paved him the way to empire, or he would have lost himself in the attempt to preserve it.

There have been, however, some princes who have performed splendid actions, and who have distinguished themselves by their liberality; but then their prodigality did not come from the public purse. Such were Cyrus, Alexander, and Caesar. A prince ought to be very sparing of his own and his subjects' property; but he should be equally lavish of that which he takes from the enemy, if he desires to be popular with his troops; for that will not diminish his reputation, but rather add to it. He who is too liberal cannot long continue so; he will become poor and contemptible unless he grinds his subjects with new taxes—which cannot fail to render him odious to them. Now there is nothing a prince ought to dread so much as his subjects' hatred; unless, indeed, it be their contempt. And both these evils may be occasioned by over liberality. If he must choose between extremes, it is better to submit to the imputation of parsimony than to make a show of liberality; since the first, though it may not be productive of honour, never gives birth to hatred and contempt.

CHAPTER XVII

On cruelty and clemency, and whether it is better to be loved than feared

To proceed to other qualities which are requisite in those who govern. A prince ought unquestionably to be merciful, but should take care how he executes his clemency. Caesar Borgia was accounted cruel; but it was to that cruelty that he was indebted for the advantage of uniting Romagna to his other dominions, and of establishing in that province peace and tranquillity, of which it had been so long deprived.

And, every thing well considered, it must be allowed that this prince showed greater clemency than the people of Florence, who, to avoid the reproach of cruelty, suffered Pistoia to be destroyed. When it is necessary for a prince to restrain his subjects within the bounds of duty, he should not regard the imputation of cruelty, because by making a few examples, he will find that he really showed more humanity in the end, than he, who by too great indulgence, suffers disorders to arise, which commonly terminate in rapine and murder. For such disorders disturb a whole community, whilst punishments inflicted by the prince affect only a few individuals.

This is particularly true with respect to a new prince, who can scarcely avoid the reproach of cruelty, every new government being replete with dangers. Thus Virgil makes Dido excuse her severity, by the necessity to which she was reduced of maintaining the interests of a throne which she did not inherit from her ancestors:—

Res dura et regni novitas me talia cogunt
Moliri, et late fines custode tueri.

A prince, however, should not be afraid of phantoms of his own raising; neither should he lend too ready an ear to terrifying tales which may be told him, but should temper his mercy with prudence, in such a manner, that too much confidence may not put him off his guard, nor causeless jealousies make him insupportable. There is a medium between a foolish security and an unreasonable distrust.

It has been sometimes asked, whether it is better to be loved than feared; to which I answer, that one should wish to be both. But as that is a hard matter to accomplish, I think, if it is necessary to make a selection, that it is safer to be feared than be loved. For it may be truly affirmed of mankind in general, that they are ungrateful, fickle, timid, dissembling, and self-interested; so long as you can serve them, they are entirely devoted to you; their wealth, their blood, their lives, and even their offspring are at your disposal, when you have no occasion for them; but in the day of need, they turn their back upon you. The prince who relies on professions, courts his own destruction, because the friends whom he acquires by means of money alone, and whose attachment does not spring from a regard for personal merit, are seldom proof against reverse of fortune, but abandon their benefactor when he most requires their services. Men are generally more inclined to submit to him who makes himself dreaded, than to one who merely strives to be beloved; and the reason is obvious, for friendship of this kind, being a mere moral tie, a species of duty resulting from a benefit, cannot endure against the calculations of interest: whereas fear carries with it the dread of punishment, which never loses its influence. A prince, however, ought to make himself feared, in such a manner, that if he cannot gain the love, he may at least avoid the hatred, of his subjects; and he may attain this object by respecting his subjects' property and the honour of their wives. If he finds it absolutely necessary to inflict the punishment of death, he should avow the reason for it, and above all things, he should abstain from touching the property of the condemned party. For certain it is that men sooner forget the death of their relations than the loss of their patrimony. Besides, when he once begins to live by means of rapine, many occasions offer for seizing the wealth of his subjects; but there will be little or no necessity for shedding blood.

But when a prince is at the head of his army, and has under his command a multitude of soldiers, he should make little account of being esteemed cruel; such a character will be useful to him, by keeping his troops in obedience, and preventing every species of faction.

Hannibal, among many other admirable talents, possessed in a high degree that of making himself feared by his troops; insomuch, that having led a very large army, composed of all kinds of people, into a foreign country, he never had occasion, either in prosperity or adversity, to punish the least disorder or the slightest want of discipline: and this can only be attributed to his extreme severity, and such other qualities as caused him to be feared and respected by his soldiers, and without which his extraordinary talents and courage would have been unavailing.

There have been writers notwithstanding, but, in my opinion, very injudicious ones who, whilst they render every degree of justice to his talents and his splendid achievements, still condemn the principle on which he acted. But nothing can in this respect more fully justify him than the example of Scipio, one of the greatest generals mentioned in history. His extreme indulgence towards the troops he commanded in Spain occasioned disorders, and at length a revolt, which drew on him from Fabius Maximus, in full senate, the reproach of having destroyed the Roman soldiery. This general having suffered the barbarous conduct of one of his lieutenants toward the Locrians to go unpunished, a senator, in his justification, observed that there were some men who knew better how to avoid doing ill themselves than to punish it in others. This excess of indulgence would in time have tarnished the glory and reputation of Scipio, if he had been a prince; but as he lived under a republican government, it was not only connived at, but redounded to his glory.

I conclude, then, with regard to the question, whether it is better to be loved than feared,—that it depends on the inclinations of the subjects themselves, whether they will love their prince or not; but the prince has it in his own power to make them fear him, and if he is wise, he will rather rely on his own resources than on the caprice of others, remembering that he should at the same time so conduct himself as to avoid being hated.

CHAPTER XVIII

Whether princes ought to be faithful to their engagements

It is unquestionably very praiseworthy in princes to be faithful to their engagements; but among those of the present day, who have been distinguished for great exploits, few indeed have been remarkable for this virtue, or have scrupled to deceive others who may have relied on their good faith.

It should therefore be known, that there are two ways of deciding any contest: the one by laws, the other by force. The first is peculiar to men, the second to beasts; but when laws are not sufficiently powerful, it is necessary to recur to force: a prince ought therefore to understand how to use both these descriptions of arms. This doctrine is admirably illustrated to us by the ancient poets in the allegorical history of the education of Achilles, and many other princes of antiquity, by the centaur Chiron, who, under the double form of man and beast, taught those who were destined to govern, that it was their duty to use by turns the arms adapted to both these natures, seeing that one without the other cannot be of any durable advantage. Now, as a prince must learn how to act the part of a beast sometimes, he should make the fox and the lion his patterns. The first can but feebly defend himself against the wolf, and the latter readily falls into such snares as are laid for him. From the fox, therefore, a prince will learn dexterity in avoiding snares; and from the lion, how to employ his strength to keep the wolves in awe. But they who entirely rely upon the lion's strength, will not always meet with success: in other words, a prudent prince cannot and ought not to keep his word, except when he can do it without injury to himself, or when the circumstances under which he contracted the engagement still exist.

I should be cautious in inculcating such a precept if all men were good;

but as the generality of mankind are wicked, and ever ready to break their words, a prince should not pique himself in keeping his more scrupulously, especially as it is always easy to justify a breach of faith on his part. I could give numerous proofs of this, and show numberless engagements and treaties which have been violated by the treachery of princes, and that those who enacted the part of the fox, have always succeeded best in their affairs. It is necessary, however, to disguise the appearance of craft, and thoroughly to understand the art of feigning and dissembling; for men are generally so simple and so weak, that he who wishes to deceive easily finds dupes.

One example, taken from the history of our own times, will be sufficient. Pope Alexander VI played during his whole life a game of deception; and notwithstanding his faithless conduct was extremely well known, his artifices always proved successful. Oaths and protestations cost him nothing; never did a prince so often break his word or pay less regard to his engagements. This was because he so well understood this chapter in the art of government.

It is not necessary, however, for a prince to possess all the good qualities I have enumerated, but it is indispensable that he should appear to have them. I will even venture to affirm, that it is sometimes dangerous to use, though it is always useful to seem to possess them. A prince should earnestly endeavour to gain the reputation of kindness, clemency, piety, justice, and fidelity to his engagements. He ought to possess all these good qualities, but still retain such power over himself as to display their opposites whenever it may be expedient. I maintain, that a prince, and especially a new prince, cannot with impunity exercise all the virtues, because his own self-preservation will often compel him to violate the laws of charity, religion, and humanity. He should habituate himself to bend easily to the various circumstances which may from time to time surround him. In a word, it will be as useful to him to persevere in the path of rectitude, while he feels no inconvenience in doing so, as to know how to deviate from it when circumstances dictate such a course. He should make it a rule above all things, never to utter anything which does not breathe of kindness, justice, good faith, and piety: this last quality it is most important for him to appear to possess, as men in general judge more from appearances than from reality. All men have eyes, but few have the gift of penetration. Every one sees your exterior, but few can discern what you have in your heart; and those few dare not oppose the voice of the multitude, who have the majesty of their prince on their side. Now, in forming a judgment of the minds of men, and more especially of princes, as we cannot recur to any tribunal, we must attend only to results. Let it then be the prince's chief care to maintain his authority; the means he employs, be what they may, will, for this purpose, always appear honourable and meet applause; for the vulgar are ever caught by appearances, and judge only by the event. And as the world is chiefly composed of such as are called the vulgar, the voice of the few is seldom or never heard or regarded.

There is a prince now alive (whose name it may not be proper to mention) who ever preaches the doctrines of peace and good faith; but if he had observed either the one or the other, he would long ago have lost both his reputation and dominions [*Ferdinand of Spain*].

·　·　·

CHAPTER XXV

How far fortune influences the things of this world, and how far she may be resisted

I know that several have thought, and many still are of opinion, that all sublunary events are governed either by Divine Providence or by chance, in such a manner that human wisdom has no share in their direction; and hence they infer that man should abstain from interfering with their course, and leave everything to its natural tendency.

The revolutions which in our times are of such frequent recurrence, seem to support this doctrine, and I own, that I, myself, am almost inclined to favour such opinions, particularly when I consider how far those events surpass all human conjecture; yet, as we confessedly possess a free will, it must, I think, be allowed, that chance does not so far govern the world as to leave no province for the exercise of human prudence.

For my own part, I cannot help comparing the blind power of chance to a rapid river, which, having overflowed its banks, inundates the plains, uproots trees, carries away houses and lands, and sweeps all before it in its destructive progress;

everybody flies possessing neither resolution nor power to oppose its fury. But this should not discourage us, when the river has returned within its natural limits, from constructing dykes and banks to prevent a recurrence of similar disasters. It is the same with fortune; she exercises her power when we oppose no barrier to her progress.

If we cast our eyes on Italy, which has been the theatre of these revolutions, and consider the causes by which they have been provoked, we shall find it to be a defenceless country. If she had been properly fortified like Germany, Spain, or France, such inundations of foreigners would never have happened, or at least their irruptions would have been attended with less devastation.

Let this suffice in general concerning the necessity of opposing fortune. But to descend to particulars. It is no uncommon thing to see a prince fall from prosperity to adversity, without our being able to attribute his fate to any change in conduct or character; for, as I have already shown at large, he who relies solely on fortune must be ruined inevitably whenever she abandons him.

Those princes who adapt their conduct to circumstances are rarely unfortunate. Fortune is only changeable to those who cannot conform themselves to the varying exigencies of the times; for we see different men take different courses to obtain the end they have in view; for instance, in pursuit of riches or glory, one prosecutes his object at random, the other with caution and prudence: one employs art, the other force; one is impetuosity itself, the

other all patience; means by which each may severally succeed. It also happens that of two who follow the same route, one may arrive at his destination, and the other fail; and that if two other persons, whose dispositions are diametrically opposite, pursue the same object by wholly different means, yet both shall equally prosper; which is entirely owing to the temper of the times, which always prove favourable or adverse, according as men conform to them.

Circumstances also frequently decide whether a prince conducts himself well or ill on any particular occasion. There are times when an extraordinary degree of prudence is necessary; there are others when the prince should know how to trust some things to chance; but there is nothing more difficult than suddenly to change his conduct and character; sometimes from inability to resist his old habits and inclinations, at others, from want of resolution to quit a course in which he had always been successful.

Julius II, who was of a fiery and violent disposition, succeeded in all his enterprises; doubtless, because a prince of such a character was best adapted to the circumstances under which the church was then governed by this pontiff. Witness his first invasion of the territory of Bologna, in the life of John Bentivoglio, which gave great umbrage to the Venetians and the kings of France and Spain, but none of them dared to interfere. The first, because they did not feel themselves strong enough to cope with a pontiff of his character; Spain, because she was engaged in the conquest of Naples: and France, besides having an interest in keeping fair with Julius, wished still to humble the Venetians; so that she, without hesitation, granted the pope all the assistance he required.

Julius II, therefore, by a precipitate mode of proceeding, succeeded in an enterprise which could not have been accomplished by cool and deliberate measures. He would unquestionably have failed had he given Spain and the Venetians time to reflect on his designs, and if he had allowed France the opportunity of amusing him by excuses and delays.

Julius II displayed in all his enterprises the same character of violence; and his successes have in that respect fully justified him; but he did not perhaps live long enough to experience the inconstancy of fortune; for had an occasion unexpectedly occurred in which it would have been necessary to act with prudence and circumspection, he would infallibly have been ruined, in consequence of that impetuosity and inflexibility of character which wholly governed him.

From all these circumstances we may conclude, that those who cannot change their system when occasion requires it, will no doubt continue prosperous as long as they glide with the stream of fortune; but when that turns against them, they are ruined, from not being able to follow that blind goddess through all her variations.

Besides, I think that it is better to be bold than too circumspect; because fortune is of a sex that likes not a tardy wooer, and repulses all who are not ardent, she declares also, more frequently, in favour of those who are young, because they are bold and enterprising.

CHAPTER XXVI

Exhortation to deliver Italy from foreign powers

When I take a review of the subject matter treated of in this book, and examine whether the circumstances in which we are now placed would be favourable to the establishment of a new government, honourable alike to its founder and advantageous to Italy, it appears to me that there never was, nor ever will be, a period more appropriate for the execution of so glorious an undertaking.

If it was necessary that the people of Israel should be slaves to Egypt, in order to elicit the rare talents of Moses; that the Persians should groan under the oppression of the Medes, in order to prove the courage and magnanimity of Cyrus; and that the Athenians should be scattered and dispersed, in order to make manifest the rare virtues of Theseus, it will be likewise necessary, for the glory of some Italian hero, that his country should be reduced to its present miserable condition, that they should be greater slaves than the Israelites, more oppressed than the Persians, and still more dispersed than the Athenians; in a word, that they should be without laws and without chiefs, pillaged, torn to pieces, and enslaved by foreign powers.

And though it has sometimes unquestionably happened that men have risen, who appeared to be sent by Heaven to achieve our deliverance; yet jealous fortune has ever abandoned them in the midst of their career; so that our unfortunate country still groans and pines away in the expectation of a deliverer, who may put an end to the devastations in Lombardy, Tuscany, and the kingdom of Naples. She supplicates Heaven to raise up a prince who may free her from the odious and humiliating yoke of foreigners, who may close the numberless wounds with which she has been so long afflicted, and under whose standard she may march against her cruel oppressors.

But on whom can Italy cast her eyes except upon your illustrious house, which, visibly favoured by Heaven and the church, the government of which is confided to its care, possesses also the wisdom and the power necessary to undertake so glorious an enterprise? and I cannot think that the execution of this project will seem difficult if you reflect on the actions and conduct of the heroes whose examples I have above adduced. Though their exploits were indeed wonderful, they were still but men; and although their merit raised them above others, yet none of them certainly were placed in a situation so favourable as that in which you now stand. You have justice on your side; their cause was not more lawful than yours, and the blessing of God will attend you no less than them. Every war that is necessary is just; and it is humanity to take up arms for the defence of a people to whom no other resource is left.

All circumstances concur to facilitate the execution of so noble a project, for the accomplishment of which it will only be necessary to tread in the steps of those great men whom I have had an opportunity of mentioning in the course of this work. For though some of them, it is true, were conducted by the hand of God in a wonderful manner, though the sea divided to let them pass, a cloud directed their course, a rock streamed with water to assuage their thirst, the manna fell from heaven to appease their hunger, yet there is no occasion for such miracles at present, as you possess in yourself sufficient power to execute a plan you ought by no means to neglect. God will not do everything for us; much is left to ourselves, and the free exercise of our will, that so our own actions may not be wholly destitute of merit.

If none of our princes have hitherto been able to effect what is now expected from your illustrious house, and if Italy has continually been unfortunate in her wars, the evil has arisen from the defects in military discipline, which no person has possessed the ability to reform.

Nothing reflects so much honour on a new prince as the new laws and institutions established under his direction, especially when they are good, and bear the character of grandeur. Now it must be acknowledged that Italy soon accommodates herself to new forms. Her inhabitants are by no means deficient in courage, but they are destitute of proper chiefs; the proof of this is in the duels and other individual combats in which the Italians have always evinced consummate ability, whilst their valour in battles has appeared well-nigh extinguished. This can only be attributed to the weakness of the officers, who are unable to ensure obedience from those who know, or think they know, the art of war. Thus we have seen the greatest generals of the present day, whose orders were never executed with exactness and celerity. These are the reasons why, in the wars in which we have been for the last twenty years engaged, the armies raised in Italy have been almost always beaten. Witness Tarus, Alexandria, Capua, Genoa, Vaila, Bologna, and Mestri.

If therefore your illustrious house is willing to regulate its conduct by the example of our ancestors, who have delivered their country from the rule of foreigners, it is necessary, above all things, as the only true foundation of every enterprise, to set on foot a national army; you cannot have better or more faithful soldiers, and though every one of them may be a good man, yet they will become still better when they are all united, and see themselves honoured, caressed, and rewarded by a prince of their own.

It is therefore absolutely necessary to have troops raised in our own country, if we wish to protect it from the invasion of foreign powers. The Swiss as well as the Spanish infantry are highly esteemed, but both have defects which may be avoided in the formation of our troops, which would render them superior to both of those powers. The Spaniards cannot support the shock of cavalry, and the Swiss cannot maintain their ground against infantry that is equally resolute with themselves.

Experience has fully shown that the Spanish battalions cannot resist the French cavalry, and that the Swiss have been beaten by the in-fantry of Spain. And though there has not been any thorough trial with regard to the Swiss on this point, yet there was a sort of specimen at the battle of Ravenna, where the Spanish infantry came in contact with the German troops, who fought in the same order as the Swiss. Upon that occasion, the Spaniards, having with their accustomed vivacity, and under the protection of their bucklers, thrown themselves across the pikes of the Germans, the latter were obliged to give way, and would have been entirely defeated, if their cavalry had not come to their relief.

It is necessary therefore to institute a military force possessing neither the defects of the Swiss nor the Spanish infantry, and that may be able to maintain its ground against the French cavalry, and this is to be effected, not by changing their arms, but by altering their discipline. Nothing is more likely to make a new prince esteemed, and to render his reign illustrious.

Such an opportunity ought eagerly to be embraced, that Italy, after her long sufferings, may at last behold her deliverer appear. With what demonstrations of joy and gratitude, with what affection, with what impatience for revenge, would he not be received by those unfortunate provinces, who have so long groaned under such odious oppression. What city would shut her gates against him, and what people would be so blind as to refuse him obedience? What rivals would he have to dread? Is there one Italian who would not hasten to pay him homage? All are weary of the tyranny of these barbarians. May your illustrious house, strong in all the hopes which justice gives our cause, deign to undertake this noble enterprise, that so, under your banners, our nation may resume its ancient splendour, and, under your auspices, behold the prophecy of Petrarch at last fulfilled.

> When virtue takes the field,
>   Short will the conflict be,
>   Barbarian rage shall yield
>   The palm to Italy:
> For patriot blood still warms Italian veins,
> Though low the fire, a spark at least remains.

Benvenuto Cellini

The term "Renaissance man" has come to suggest one who has an almost universal genius, an ability to do all things well. It also implies a confidence in the human potential, a conviction that someone with reason and taste can do anything if he merely applies his human resources to the task at hand. Leonardo da Vinci once wrote a letter to Lodovico Sforza, who afterward became the Duke of Milan, applying for a job. In cataloging his abilities, Leonardo exudes self-confidence. He claims that he can ". . . construct very light bridges, easy to transport from one place to another . . . [in case of siege] remove the water from the ditches, and make an infinite variety of scaling-ladders . . . [make] a kind of cannon that is easy and convenient to carry, and that will throw out inflammable matters, causing great affright and damage to the enemy . . . make cannon, mortars, and field pieces of beautiful and useful shape, and different from those in common use . . . equal all others in architecture, in designing both public and private edifices, and in conducting water from one place to another . . . undertake in sculpture works in marble, bronze, or terra-cotta; likewise in painting can do what can be done equal to any other, whoever he may be. . . ." The letter closes with this assurance: "And if any of the above-mentioned things seem to any impossible and impracticable, I offer to make trial of them in your park, or in any other place that may please your Excellency, to whom I commend myself with all possible humility." And the remarkable thing is that Leonardo could actually do what he said he could.

Another Renaissance figure with the same kind of brash assurance was Benvenuto Cellini (1500–1571), who, though a lesser artist than Leonardo, was his equal in confidence and probably his superior in the ability to live life to its fullest. Actually, Cellini was a semi-frustrated sculptor who is best known for his work as a goldsmith. Although little of his work has survived, Cellini's great masterpiece, the gold salt-cellar made for Francis I of France, is preserved at the Kunsthistorisches Museum in Vienna.

Cellini's *Autobiography,* from which the following selections are taken, was written between 1558 and 1562, but was not published until the early eighteenth century. It enjoyed enormous popularity as a highly revealing personal document and as an intimate portrait of the sixteenth century—nor has it lost its fascination for modern readers.

The Life of Benvenuto Cellini

BOOK FIRST

I

All men of whatsoever quality they be, who have done anything of excellence, or which may properly resemble excellence, ought, if they are persons of truth and honesty, to describe their life with their own hand; but they ought not to attempt so fine an enterprise till they have passed the age of forty. This duty occurs to my own mind, now that I am travelling beyond the term of fifty-eight years, and am in Florence, the city of my birth. Many untoward things can I remember, such as happen to all who live upon our earth; and from those adversities I am now more free than at any previous period of my career—nay, it seems to me that I enjoy greater content of soul and health of body than ever I did in bygone years. I can also bring to mind some pleasant goods and some inestimable evils, which, when I turn my thoughts backward, strike terror in me, and astonishment that I should have reached this age of fifty-eight, wherein, thanks be to God, I am still travelling prosperously forward.

II

It is true that men who have laboured with some show of excel-lence, have already given knowledge of themselves to the world; and this alone ought to suffice them; I mean the fact that they have proved their manhood and achieved renown. Yet one must needs live like others; and so in a work like this there will always be found occasion for natural bragging, which is of divers kinds, and the first is that a man should let others know he draws his lineage from persons of worth and most ancient origin.

I am called Benvenuto Cellini, son of Maestro Giovanni, son of Andrea, son of Cristofano Cellini; my mother was Madonna Elisabetta, daughter to Stefano Granacci; both parents citizens of Florence. It is found written in chronicles made by our ancestors of Florence, men of old time and of credibility, even as Giovanni Villani writes, that the city of Florence was evidently built in imitation of the fair city of Rome; and certain remnants of the Colosseum and the Baths can yet be traced. These things are near Santa Croce. The capitol was where is now the Old Market. The Rotonda is entire, which was made for the temple of Mars, and is now dedicated to our Saint John. That thus it was, can very well be seen, and cannot be denied; but the said buildings are much smaller than those of Rome. He who caused them to be built, they say, was Julius Caesar, in concert with some noble Romans,

The Life of Benvenuto Cellini, 4th ed. [autobiography], trans. J. A. Symonds (New York, 1896).

who, when Fiesole had been stormed and taken, raised a city in this place, and each of them took in hand to erect one of these notable edifices.

• • •

Thus then we find; and thus we believe that we are descended from a man of worth. Furthermore, we find that there are Cellinis of our stock in Ravenna, that most ancient town of Italy, where too are plenty of gentle folk. In Pisa also there are some, and I have discovered them in many parts of Christendom; and in this state also the breed exists, men devoted to the profession of arms; for not many years ago a young man, called Luca Cellini, a beardless youth, fought with a soldier of experience and a most valorous man, named Francesco da Vicorati, who had frequently fought before in single combat. This Luca, by his own valour, with sword in hand, overcame and slew him, with such bravery and stoutness that he moved the folk to wonder, who were expecting quite the contrary issue; so that I glory in tracing my descent from men of valour.

As for the trifling honours which I have gained for my house, under the well-known conditions of our present ways of living, and by means of my art, albeit the same are matters of no great moment, I will relate these in their proper time and place, taking much more pride in having been born humble and having laid some honourable foundation for my family, than if I had been born of great lineage and had stained or so overclouded that by my base qualities. So then I will make a beginning by saying how it pleased God I should be born.

• • •

When I reached the age of fifteen, I put myself, against my father's will, to the goldsmith's trade with a man called Antonio, son of Sandro, known commonly as Marcone the goldsmith. He was a most excellent craftsman and a very good fellow to boot, high-spirited and frank in all his ways. My father would not let him give me wages like the other apprentices; for having taken up the study of this art to please myself, he wished me to indulge my whim for drawing to the full. I did so willingly enough; and that honest master of mine took marvellous delight in my performances. He had an only son, a bastard, to whom he often gave his orders, in order to spare me. My liking for the art was so great, or, I may truly say, my natural bias, both one and the other, that in a few months I caught up the good, nay, the best young craftsmen in our business, and began to reap the fruits of my labours. I did not, however, neglect to gratify my good father from time to time by playing on the flute or cornet. Each time he heard me, I used to make his tears fall accompanied with deep-drawn sighs of satisfaction. My filial piety often made me give him that contentment, and induced me to pretend that I enjoyed the music too.

• • •

XII

When I had recovered my health, I returned to my old friend Marcone, the worthy goldsmith, who put me in the way of earning money, with which I helped my father and our household. About that time there came to Florence a sculptor named Piero Torrigiani; he arrived from England, where he had resided many years; and being intimate with my master, he daily visited his house; and when he saw my drawings and the things which I was making, he said: "I have come to Florence to enlist as many young men as I can; for I have undertaken to execute a great work for my king, and want some of my own Florentines to help me. Now your method of working and your designs are worthy rather of a sculptor than a goldsmith; and since I have to turn out a great piece of bronze, I will at the same time turn you into a rich and able artist." This man had a splendid person and a most arrogant spirit, with the air of a great soldier more than of a sculptor, especially in regard to his vehement gestures and his resonant voice, together with a habit he had of knitting his brows, enough to frighten any man of courage. He kept talking every day about his gallant feats among these beasts of Englishmen.

In course of conversation he happened to mention Michel Agnolo Buonarroti, led thereto by a drawing I had made from a cartoon of that divinest painter. This cartoon was the first masterpiece which Michel Agnolo exhibited, in proof of his stupendous talents. He produced it in competition with another painter, Lionardo da Vinci, who also made a cartoon; and both were intended for the council-hall in the palace of the Signory. They represented the taking of Pisa by the Florentines; and our admirable Lionardo had chosen to depict a battle of horses, with the capture of some standards, in as divine a style as could pos-

sibly be imagined. Michel Agnolo in his cartoon portrayed a number of foot-soldiers, who, the season being summer, had gone to bathe in Arno. He drew them at the very moment the alarm is sounded, and the men all naked run to arms; so splendid in their action that nothing survives of ancient or of modern art which touches the same lofty point of excellence; and as I have already said, the design of the great Lionardo was itself most admirably beautiful. These two cartoons stood, one in the palace of the Medici, the other in the hall of the Pope. So long as they remained intact, they were the school of the world. Though the divine Michel Agnolo in later life finished that great chapel of Pope Julius, he never rose halfway to the same pitch of power; his genius never afterwards attained to the force of those first studies.

XIII

Now let us return to Piero Torrigiani, who, with my drawing in his hand, spoke as follows: "This Buonarroti and I used, when we were boys, to go into the Church of the Carmine, to learn drawing from the chapel of Masaccio. It was Buonarroti's habit to banter all who were drawing there; and one day, among others, when he was annoying me, I got more angry than usual, and clenching my fist, gave him such a blow on the nose, that I felt bone and cartilage go down like biscuit beneath my knuckles; and this mark of mine he will carry with him to the grave." These words begat in me such hatred of the man, since I was always gazing at the masterpieces of the divine Michel Agnolo, that although I felt a wish to go with him to England, I now could never bear the sight of him.

All the while I was at Florence, I studied the noble manner of Michel Agnolo, and from this I have never deviated. About that time I contracted a close and familiar friendship with an amiable lad of my own age, who was also in the goldsmith's trade. He was called Francesco, son of Filippo, and grandson of Fra Lippo Lippi, that most excellent painter. Through intercourse together, such love grew up between us that, day or night, we never stayed apart. The house where he lived was still full of the fine studies which his father had made, bound up in several books of drawings by his hand, and taken from the best antiquities of Rome. The sight of these things filled me with passionate enthusiasm; and for two years or thereabouts we lived in intimacy. At that time I fashioned a silver bas-relief of the size of a little child's hand. It was intended for the clasp to a man's belt; for they were then worn as large as that. I carved on it a knot of leaves in the antique style, with figures of children and other masks of great beauty. This piece I made in the workshop of one Francesco Salimbene; and on its being exhibited to the trade, the goldsmiths praised me as the best young craftsman of their art.

There was one Giovan Battista, surnamed Il Tasso, a woodcarver, precisely of my own age, who one day said to me that if I was willing to go to Rome, he should be glad to join me. Now we had this conversation together immediately after dinner; and I being angry with my father for the same old reason of the music, said to Tasso: "You are a fellow of words, not deeds." He answered: "I too have come to anger with my mother; and if I had cash enough to take me to Rome, I would not turn back to lock the door of that wretched little workshop I call mine." To these words I replied that if that was all that kept him in Florence I had money enough in my pockets to bring us both to Rome. Talking thus and walking onwards, we found ourselves at the gate San Piero Gattolini without noticing that we had got there; whereupon I said: "Friend Tasso, this is God's doing that we have reached this gate without either you or me noticing that we were there; and now that I am here, it seems to me that I have finished half the journey." And so, being of one accord, we pursued our way together, saying "Oh, what will our old folks say this evening?" We then made an agreement not to think more about them till we reached Rome. So we tied our aprons behind our backs, and trudged almost in silence to Siena. When we arrived at Siena, Tasso said (for he had hurt his feet) that he would not go farther, and asked me to lend him money to get back. I made answer: "I should not have enough left to go forward; you ought indeed to have thought of this on leaving Florence; and if it is because of your feet that you shirk the journey, we will find a return horse for Rome, which will deprive you of the excuse." Accordingly I hired a horse; and seeing that he did not answer, I took my way toward the gate of Rome. When he knew that I was

firmly resolved to go, muttering between his teeth, and limping as well
as he could, he came on behind me
very slowly and at a great distance.
On reaching the gate, I felt pity for
my comrade, and waited for him,
and took him on the crupper, saying: "What would our friends speak
of us to-morrow, if, having left for
Rome, we had not pluck to get beyond Siena?" Then the good Tasso
said I spoke the truth; and as he was
a pleasant fellow, he began to laugh
and sing; and in this way, always
singing and laughing, we travelled
the whole way to Rome. I had just
nineteen years then, and so had the
century.

When we reached Rome, I put
myself under a master who was
known as Il Firenzuola. His name
was Giovanni, and he came from
Firenzuola in Lombardy, a most
able craftsman in large vases and
big plate of that kind. I showed him
part of the model for the clasp which
I had made in Florence at Salimbene's. It pleased him exceedingly;
and turning to one of his journeymen, a Florentine called Giannotto
Giannotti, who had been several
years with him, he spoke as follows:
"This fellow is one of the Florentines who know something, and you
are one of those who know nothing." Then I recognised the man,
and turned to speak with him; for
before he went to Rome, we often
went to draw together, and had been
very intimate comrades. He was so
put out by the words his master
flung at him, that he said he did not
recognise me or know who I was;
whereupon I got angry, and cried
out: "O Giannotto, you who were
once my friend—for have we not
been together in such and such

places, and drawn, and ate, and
drunk, and slept in company at your
house in the country? I don't want
you to bear witness on my behalf
to this worthy man, your master,
because I hope my hands are such
that without aid from you they will
declare what sort of a fellow I am."

XIV

When I had thus spoken, Firenzuola, who was a man of hot spirit
and brave, turned to Giannotto, and
said to him: "You vile rascal, aren't
you ashamed to treat a man who
has been so intimate a comrade with
you in this way?" And with the same
movement of quick feeling, he faced
round and said to me: "Welcome to
my workshop; and do as you have
promised; let your hands declare
what man you are."

He gave me a very fine piece of
silver plate to work on for a cardinal. It was a little oblong box,
copied from the porphyry sarco-
phagus before the door of the Rotonda. Beside what I copied, I enriched it with so many elegant masks
of my invention, that my master
went about showing it through the
art, and boasting that so good a
piece of work had been turned out
from his shop. It was about half a
cubit in size, and was so constructed
as to serve for a salt-cellar at table.
This was the first earning that I
touched at Rome, and part of it I
sent to assist my good father; the
rest I kept for my own use, living
upon it while I went about studying
the antiquities of Rome, until my
money failed, and I had to return
to the shop for work. Battista del
Tasso, my comrade, did not stay

long in Rome, but went back to Florence.

After undertaking some new commissions, I took it into my head, as soon as I had finished them, to change my master; I had indeed been worried into doing so by a certain Milanese, called Pagolo Arsago. My first master, Firenzuola, had a great quarrel about this with Arsago, and abused him in my presence; whereupon I took up speech in defence of my new master. I said that I was born free, and free I meant to live, and that there was no reason to complain of him, far less of me, since some few crowns of wages were still due to me; also that I chose to go, like a free journeyman, where it pleased me, knowing I did wrong to no man. My new master then put in with his excuses, saying that he had not asked me to come, and that I should gratify him by returning with Firenzuola. To this I replied that I was not aware of wronging the latter in any way, and as I had completed his commissions, I chose to be my own master and not the man of others, and that he who wanted me must beg me of myself. Firenzuola cried: "I don't intend to beg you of yourself; I have done with you; don't show yourself again upon my premises." I reminded him of the money he owed me. He laughed me in the face; on which I said that if I knew how to use my tools in handicraft as well as he had seen, I could be quite as clever with my sword in claiming the just payment of my labour. While we were exchanging these words, an old man happened to come up, called Maestro Antonio, of San Marino. He was the chief among the Roman goldsmiths, and

had been Firenzuola's master. Hearing what I had to say, which I took good care that he should understand, he immediately espoused my cause, and bade Firenzuola pay me. The dispute waxed warm, because Firenzuola was an admirable swordsman, far better than he was a goldsmith. Yet reason made itself heard; and I backed my cause with the same spirit, till I got myself paid. In course of time Firenzuola and I became friends, and at his request I stood godfather to one of his children.

XV

I went on working with Pagolo Arsago, and earned a good deal of money, the greater part of which I always sent to my good father. At the end of two years, upon my father's entreaty, I returned to Florence, and put myself once more under Francesco Salimbene, with whom I earned a great deal, and took continual pains to improve in my art. I renewed my intimacy with Francesco di Filippo; and though I was too much given to pleasure, owing to that accursed music, I never neglected to devote some hours of the day or night to study. At that time I fashioned a silver heart's-key (*chiavaquore*), as it was then called. This was a girdle three inches broad, which used to be made for brides and was executed in half relief with some small figures in the round. It was a commission from a man called Raffaello Lapaccini. I was very badly paid; but the honour which it brought me was worth far more than the gain I might have justly made by it. Having at this time worked with many different persons in Florence, I had come to know some worthy men among the goldsmiths, as, for instance, Marcone, my first master; but I also met with others reputed honest, who did all they could to ruin me, and robbed me grossly. When I perceived this, I left their company, and held them for thieves and blackguards. One of the goldsmiths, called Giovanbattista Sogliani, kindly accommodated me with part of his shop, which stood at the side of the New Market near the Landi's bank. There I finished several pretty pieces, and made good gains, and was able to give my family much help. This roused the jealousy of the bad men among my former masters, who were called Salvadore and Michele Guasconti. In the guild of the goldsmiths they had three big shops, and drove a thriving trade. On becoming aware of their evil will against me, I complained to certain worthy fellows, and remarked that they ought to have been satisfied with the thieveries they practised on me under the cloak of hypocritical kindness. This coming to their ears, they threatened to make me sorely repent of such words; but I, who knew not what the colour of fear was, paid them little or no heed.

. . .

XIX

At Siena I waited for the mail to Rome, which I afterwards joined; and when we passed the Paglia, we met a courier carrying news of the new Pope Clement VII. Upon my arrival in Rome, I went to work in the shop of the master-goldsmith Santi. He was dead; but a son of his carried on the business. He did not work himself, but entrusted all his commissions to a young man named Lucagnolo from Iesi, a country fellow, who while yet a child had come into Santi's service. This man was short but well proportioned, and was a more skilful craftsman than any one whom I had met with up to that time; remarkable for facility and excellent in design. He executed large plate only; that is to say, vases of the utmost beauty, basins, and such pieces. Having put myself to work there, I began to make some candelabra for the Bishop of Salamanca, a Spaniard. They were richly chased, so far as that sort of work admits. A pupil of Raffaello da Urbino called Gian Francesco, and commonly known as Il Fattore, was a painter of great ability; and being on terms of friendship with the Bishop, he introduced me to his favour, so that I obtained many commissions from that prelate, and earned considerable sums of money.

During that time I went to draw sometimes in Michel Agnolo's chapel, and sometimes in the house of Agostino Chigi of Siena, which contained many incomparable paintings by the hand of that great master Raffaello. This I did on feast-days, because the house was then inhabited by Messer Gismondo, Agostino's brother. They plumed themselves exceedingly when they saw young men of my sort coming to study in their palaces. Gismondo's wife, noticing my frequent presence in that house—she was a lady as courteous as could be, and of surpassing beauty—came up to me one day, looked at my drawings, and asked me if I was a sculptor or a painter; to whom I said I was a goldsmith. She remarked that I drew too well for a goldsmith; and having made one of her waiting-maids bring a lily of the finest diamonds set in gold, she showed it to me, and bade me value it. I valued it at 800 crowns. Then she said that I had very nearly hit the mark, and asked me whether I felt capable of setting the stones really well. I said that I should much like to do so, and began before her eyes to make a little sketch for it, working all the better because of the pleasure I took in conversing with so lovely and agreeable a gentlewoman. When the sketch was finished, another Roman lady of great beauty joined us; she had been above, and now descending to the ground-floor, asked Madonna Porzia what she was doing there. She answered with a smile: "I am amusing myself by watching this worthy young man at his drawing; he is as good as he is handsome." I had by this time acquired a trifle of assurance, mixed, however, with some honest bashfulness; so I blushed and said: "Such as I am, lady, I shall ever be most ready to serve you." The gentlewoman, also slightly blushing, said: "You know well that I want you to serve me"; and reaching me the lily, told me to take it away; and gave me besides twenty golden crowns which she had in her bag, and added: "Set me the jewel after the fashion you have sketched, and keep for me the old gold in which it is now set." On this the Roman lady observed: "If I were in that young man's body, I should go off without asking leave." Madonna Porzia replied that virtues

rarely are at home with vices, and that if I did such a thing, I should strongly belie my good looks of an honest man. Then turning round, she took the Roman lady's hand, and with a pleasant smile said: "Farewell, Benvenuto." I stayed on a short while at the drawing I was making, which was a copy of a Jove by Raffaello. When I had finished it and left the house, I set myself to making a little model of wax, in order to show how the jewel would look when it was completed. This I took to Madonna Porzia, whom I found with the same Roman lady. Both of them were highly satisfied with my work, and treated me so kindly that, being somewhat emboldened, I promised the jewel should be twice as good as the model. Accordingly I set hand to it, and in twelve days I finished it in the form af a fleur-de-lys, as I have said above, ornamenting it with little masks, children, and animals, exquisitely enamelled, whereby the diamonds which formed the lily were more than doubled in effect.

XX

While I was working at this piece, Lucagnolo, of whose ability I have before spoken, showed considerable discontent, telling me over and over again that I might acquire far more profit and honour by helping him to execute large plate, as I had done at first. I made him answer that, whenever I chose, I should always be capable of working at great silver pieces; but that things like that on which I was now engaged were not commissioned every day; and beside their bringing no less honour than large silver plate, there was also more profit to be made by them. He laughed me in the face, and said: "Wait and see Benvenuto; for by the time that you have finished that work of yours, I will make haste to have finished this vase, which I took in hand when you did the jewel; and then experience shall teach you what profit I shall get from my vase, and what you will get from your ornament." I answered that I was very glad indeed to enter into such a competition with so good a craftsman as he was, because the end would show which of us was mistaken. Accordingly both the one and the other of us, with a scornful smile upon our lips, bent our heads in grim earnest to the work, which both were now desirous of accomplishing; so that after about ten days, each had finished his undertaking with great delicacy and artistic skill.

Lucagnolo's was a huge silver piece, used at the table of Pope Clement, into which he flung away bits of bone and the rind of divers fruits, while eating; an object of ostentation rather than necessity. The vase was adorned with two fine handles, together with many masks, both small and great, and masses of lovely foliage, in as exquisite a style of elegance as could be imagined; and seeing which I said it was the most beautiful vase that ever I set eyes on. Thinking he had convinced me, Lucagnolo replied: "Your work seems to me no less beautiful, but we shall soon perceive the difference between the two." So he took his vase and carried it to the Pope, who was very well pleased with it, and ordered at once that he should be

paid at the ordinary rate of such large plate. Meanwhile I carried mine to Madonna Porzia, who looked at it with astonishment, and told me I had far surpassed my promise. Then she bade me ask for my reward whatever I liked; for it seemed to her my desert was so great that if I craved a castle she could hardly recompense me; but since that was not in her hands to bestow, she added laughing that I must beg what lay within her power. I answered that the greatest reward I could desire for my labour was to have satisfied her ladyship. Then, smiling in my turn, and bowing to her, I took my leave, saying I wanted no reward but that. She turned to the Roman lady and said: "You see that the qualities we discerned in him are companied by virtues, and not vices." They both expressed their admiration, and then Madonna Porzia continued: "Friend Benvenuto, have you never heard it said that when the poor give to the rich, the devil laughs?" I replied: "Quite true! and yet, in the midst of all his troubles, I should like this time to see him laugh"; and as I took my leave, she said that this time she had no will to bestow on him that favour.

When I came back to the shop, Lucagnolo had the money for his vase in a paper packet; and on my arrival he cried out: "Come and compare the price of your jewel with the price of my plate." I said that he must leave things as they were till the next day, because I hoped that even as my work in its kind was not less excellent than his, so I should be able to show him quite an equal price for it.

XXI

On the day following, Madonna Porzia sent a major-domo of hers to my shop, who called me out, and putting into my hands a paper packet full of money from his lady, told me that she did not choose the devil should have his whole laugh out; by which she hinted that the money sent me was not the entire payment merited by my industry, and other messages were added worthy of so courteous a lady. Lucagnolo, who was burning to compare his packet with mine, burst into the shop; then in the presence of twelve journeymen and some neighbours, eager to behold the result of this competition, he seized his packet, scornfully exclaiming "Ou! ou!" three or four times, while he poured his money on the counter with a great noise. They were twenty-five crowns in giulios; and he fancied that mine would be four or five crowns *di moneta*. I for my part, stunned and stifled by his cries, and by the looks and smiles of the bystanders, first peeped into my packet; then, after seeing that it contained nothing but gold, I retired to one end of the counter, and, keeping my eyes lowered and making no noise at all, I lifted it with both hands suddenly above my head, and emptied it like a mill hopper. My coin was twice as much as his; which caused the onlookers, who had fixed their eyes on me with some derision, to turn round suddenly to him and say: "Lucagnolo, Benvenuto's pieces, being all of gold and twice as many as yours, make a far finer effect." I thought for certain that, what with jealousy and what with shame, Lucagnolo would have fallen dead upon the spot; and though he took the third part of my gain, since I was a journeyman (for such is the custom of the trade, two-thirds fall to the workman and one-third to the masters of the shop), yet inconsiderate envy had more power in him than avarice: it ought indeed to have worked quite the other way, he being a peasant's son from Iesi. He cursed his art and those who taught it him, vowing that thenceforth he would never work at large plate, but give his whole attention to those whoreson gewgaws, since they were so well paid. Equally enraged on my side, I answered that every bird sang its own note; that he talked after the fashion of the hovels he came from; but that I dared swear that I should succeed with ease in making his lubberly lumber, while he would never be successful in my whoreson gewgaws. Thus I flung off in a passion, telling him that I would soon show him that I spoke truth. The bystanders openly declared against him, holding him for a lout, as indeed he was, and me for a man, as I had proved myself.

XXII

Next day, I went to thank Madonna Porzia, and told her that her ladyship had done the opposite of what she said she would; for that while I wanted to make the devil laugh, she had made him once more deny God. We both laughed pleasantly at this, and she gave me other commissions for fine and substantial work.

Meanwhile, I contrived, by means of a pupil of Raffaello da Urbino, to get an order from the Bishop of Salamanca for one of those great water-vessels called *acquereccia,* which are used for ornaments to place on sideboards. He wanted a pair made of equal size; and one of them he intrusted to Lucagnolo, the other to me. Giovan Francesco, the painter I have mentioned, gave us the design. Accordingly I set hand with marvellous good-will to this piece of plate, and was accommodated with a part of his workshop by a Milanese named Maestro Giovan Piero della Tacca. Having made my preparations, I calculated how much money I should need for certain affairs of my own, and sent all the rest to assist my poor father.

It so happened that just when this was being paid to him in Florence, he stumbled upon one of those Radicals who were in the Eight at the time when I got into that little trouble there. It was the very man who had abused him so rudely, and who swore that I should certainly be sent into the country with the lances. Now this fellow had some sons of very bad morals and repute; wherefore my father said to him: "Misfortunes can happen to anybody, especially to men of choleric humour when they are in the right, even as it happened to my son; but let the rest of his life bear witness how virtuously I have brought him up. Would God, for your well-being, that your sons may act neither worse nor better towards you than mine do to me. God rendered me able to bring them up as I have done; and where my own power could not reach, 'twas He who rescued them, against your ex-

pectation, out of your violent hands." On leaving the man, he wrote me all this story, begging me for God's sake to practise music at times, in order that I might not lose the fine accomplishment which he had taught me with such trouble. The letter so overflowed with expressions of the tenderest fatherly affection, that I was moved to tears of filial piety, resolving before he died, to gratify him amply with regard to music. Thus God grants us those lawful blessings which we ask in prayer, nothing doubting.

XXIII

While I was pushing forward Salamanca's vase, I had only one little boy as help, whom I had taken at the entreaty of friends, and half against my own will, to be my workman. He was about fourteen years of age, bore the name of Paulino, and was son to a Roman burgess, who lived upon the income of his property. Paulino was the best-mannered, the most honest, and the most beautiful boy I ever saw in my whole life. His modest ways and actions, together with his superlative beauty and his devotion to myself, bred in me as great an affection for him as a man's breast can hold. This passionate love led me oftentimes to delight the lad with music; for I observed that his marvellous features, which by complexion wore a tone of modest melancholy, brightened up, and when I took my cornet, broke into a smile so lovely and sweet, that I do not marvel at the silly stories which the Greeks have written about the deities of heaven. Indeed, if my boy had lived in those times, he would probably have turned their heads still more. He had a sister, named Faustina, more beautiful, I verily believe, than that Faustina about whom the old books gossip so. Sometimes he took me to their vineyard, and, so far as I could judge, it struck me that Paulino's good father would have welcomed me as a son-in-law. This affair led me to play more than I was used to do.

It happened at that time that one Giangiacomo of Cesena, a musician in the Pope's band, and a very excellent performer, sent word through Lorenzo, the trumpeter of Lucca, who is now in our Duke's service, to inquire whether I was inclined to help them at the Pope's Ferragosto, playing soprano with my cornet in some motets of great beauty selected by them for that occasion. Although I had the greatest desire to finish the vase I had begun, yet, since music has a wondrous charm of its own, and also because I wished to please my old father, I consented to join them. During eight days before the festival we practised two hours a day together; then on the first of August we went to the Belvedere, and while Pope Clement was at table, we played those carefully studied motets so well that his Holiness protested he had never heard music more sweetly executed or with better harmony of parts. He sent for Giangiacomo, and asked him where and how he had procured so excellent a cornet for soprano, and inquired particularly who I was. Giangiacomo told him my name in full. Whereupon the Pope said: "So, then, he is the son of Maestro Giovanni?" On being assured I was, the Pope expressed his wish to have me

in his service with the other bandsmen. Giangiacomo replied: "Most blessed Father, I cannot pretend for certain that you will get him, for his profession, to which he devotes himself assiduously, is that of a goldsmith, and he works in it miraculously well, and earns by it far more than he could do by playing." To this the Pope added: "I am the better inclined to him now that I find him possessor of a talent more than I expected. See that he obtains the same salary as the rest of you; and tell him from me to join my service, and that I will find work enough by the day for him to do at his other trade." Then stretching out his hand, he gave him a hundred golden crowns of the Camera in a handkerchief, and said: "Divide these so that he may take his share."

When Giangiacomo left the Pope, he came to us, and related in detail all that the Pope had said, and after dividing the money between the eight of us, and giving me my share, he said to me: "Now I am going to have you inscribed among our company." I replied: "Let the day pass; to-morrow I will give my answer." When I left them, I went meditating whether I ought to accept the invitation, inasmuch as I could not but suffer if I abandoned the noble studies of my art. The following night my father appeared to me in dream, and begged me with tears of tenderest affection, for God's love and his, to enter upon this engagement. Methought I answered that nothing would induce me to do so. In an instant he assumed so horrible an aspect as to frighten me out of my wits, and cried: "If you do not, you will have a father's curse; but if you do, may you be ever blessed by me!" When I awoke, I ran, for very fright, to have myself inscribed. Then I wrote to my old father, telling him the news, which so affected him with extreme joy that a sudden fit of illness took him, and wellnigh brought him to death's door. In his answer to my letter, he told me that he too had dreamed nearly the same as I had.

XXIV

Knowing now that I had gratified my father's honest wish, I began to think that everything would prosper with me to a glorious and honourable end. Accordingly, I set myself with indefatigable industry to the completion of the vase I had begun for Salamanca. That prelate was a very extraordinary man, extremely rich, but difficult to please. He sent daily to learn what I was doing; and when his messenger did not find me at home, he broke into fury, saying that he would take the work out of my hands and give it to others to finish. This came of my slavery to that accursed music. Still I laboured diligently night and day, until, when I had brought my work to a point when it could be exhibited, I submitted it to the inspection of the Bishop. This so increased his desire to see it finished, that I was sorry I had shown it. At the end of three months I had it ready, with little animals and foliage and masks, so beautiful as one could hope to see. No sooner was it done than I sent it by the hand of my workman, Paulino, to show that able artist Lucagnolo, of whom I have spoken above. Paulino, with the grace and beauty which belonged to him,

spoke as follows: "Messer Lucagnolo, Benvenuto bids me say that he has sent to show you his promises and your lumber, expecting in return to see from you his gewgaws." This message given, Lucagnolo took up the vase, and carefully examined it; then he said to Paulino: "Fair boy, tell your master that he is a great and able artist, and that I beg him to be willing to have me for a friend, and not to engage in aught else." The mission of that virtuous and marvellous lad caused me the greatest joy; and then the vase was carried to Salamanca, who ordered it to be valued. Lucagnolo took part in the valuation, estimating and praising it far above my own opinion. Salamanca, lifting up the vase, cried like a true Spaniard: "I swear by God that I will take as long in paying him as he has lagged in making it." When I heard this, I was exceedingly put out, and fell to cursing all Spain and every one who wished well to it.

Amongst other beautiful ornaments, this vase had a handle, made all of one piece, with most delicate mechanism, which, when a spring was touched, stood upright above the mouth of it. While the prelate was one day ostentatiously exhibiting my vase to certain Spanish gentlemen of his suite, it chanced that one of them, upon Monsignor's quitting the room, began roughly to work the handle, and as the gentle spring which moved it could not bear his loutish violence, it broke in his hand. Aware what mischief he had done, he begged the butler who had charge of the Bishop's plate to take it to the master who had made it, for him to mend, and promised to pay what price he asked, provided it was set to rights at once. So the vase came once more into my hands, and I promised to put it forthwith in order, which indeed I did. It was brought to me before dinner; and at twenty-two o'clock the man who brought it returned, all in a sweat, for he had run the whole way, Monsignor having again asked for it to show to certain other gentlemen. The butler, then, without giving me time to utter a word, cried: "Quick, quick, bring me the vase." I, who wanted to act at leisure and not to give it up to him, said that I did not mean to be so quick. The serving-man got into such a rage that he made as though he would put one hand to his sword, while with the other he threatened to break the shop open. To this I put a stop at once with my own weapon, using therewith spirited language, and saying: "I am not going to give it to you! Go and tell Monsignor, your master, that I want the money for my work before I let it leave this shop." When the fellow saw he could not obtain it by swaggering, he fell to praying me, as one prays to the Cross, declaring that if I would only give it up, he would take care I should be paid. These words did not make me swerve from my purpose; but I kept on saying the same thing. At last, despairing of success, he swore to come with Spaniards enough to cut me in pieces. Then he took to his heels; while I, who inclined to believe partly in their murderous attack, resolved that I would defend myself with courage. So I got an admirable little gun ready, which I used for shooting game, and muttered to myself: "He who robs me of my property and labour may take my life, too, and welcome." While I was carrying on this debate in my own mind, a crowd of Spaniards arrived, led by their major-domo, who, with the headstrong rashness of his race, bade them go in and take the vase and give me a good beating. Hearing these words, I showed them the muzzle of my gun, and prepared to fire, and cried in a loud voice: "Renegade Jews, traitors, is it thus that one breaks into houses and shops in our city of Rome? Come as many of you thieves as like, an inch nearer to this wicket, and I'll blow all their brains out with my gun." Then I turned the muzzle toward their major-domo, and making as though I would discharge it, called out: "And you big thief, who are egging them on, I mean to kill you first." He clapped spurs to the jennet he was riding, and took flight headlong. The commotion we were making stirred up all the neighbours, who came crowding round, together with some Roman gentlemen who chanced to pass and cried: "Do but kill the renegades, and we will stand by you." These words had the effect of frightening the Spaniards in good earnest. They withdrew, and were compelled by the circumstances to relate the whole affair to Monsignor. Being a man of inordinate haughtiness, he rated the members of his household, both because they had engaged in such an act of violence, and also because, having begun, they had not gone through with it. At this juncture the painter, who had been concerned in the whole matter, came in, and the Bishop bade him go and tell me that if I did not bring the vase at once, he would make mincemeat of me; but if I brought it, he would pay its price down. These threats were so far from terrifying me, that I sent him word I was going immediately to lay my case before the Pope.

In the meantime, his anger and my fear subsided; whereupon, being guaranteed by some Roman gentlemen of high degree that the prelate would not harm me, and having assurance that I should be paid, I armed myself with a large poniard and my good coat of mail, and betook myself to his palace, where he had drawn up all his household. I entered, and Paulino followed with the silver vase. It was just like passing through the Zodiac, neither more nor less; for one of them had the face of the lion, another of the scorpion, a third of the crab. However, we passed onward to the presence of the rascally priest, who spouted out a torrent of such language as only priests and Spaniards have at their command. In return I never raised my eyes to look at him, nor answered word for word. That seemed to augment the fury of his anger; and causing paper to be put before me, he commanded me to write an acknowledgement to the effect that I had been amply satisfied and paid in full. Then I raised my head and said I should be very glad to do so when I had received the money. The Bishop's rage continued to rise; threats and recriminations were flung about; but at last the money was paid, and I wrote the receipt. Then I departed, glad at heart and in high spirits.

Martin Luther

The theory that all events are interrelated receives dramatic confirmation in the relationship between the Renaissance and the Reformation. To raise money to build St. Peter's Cathedral in Rome, the greatest monument of Renaissance art, Pope Leo X authorized the granting of papal indulgences in return for suitable donations to the Church. In 1517, one of the papal agents, a Dominican friar named John Tetzel, appeared in Central Germany, to grant these indulgences. Martin Luther (1483–1546), a professor at the University of Wittenberg, responded by posting on the door of the Castle Church a list of Ninety-Five Theses, in which he attacked the entire theory and practice of indulgences. Luther's act, in turn, set in motion a series of events that resulted finally in the Protestant Reformation.

Although Tetzel's activities had set him off, Luther based his opposition to the Church on grounds far deeper than the problem of indulgences. Basically, the question centered on the salvation of people's souls. From his studies of St. Paul and St. Augustine, Luther became convinced that, since all people are utterly condemned and lost as a result of original sin, it is impossible for them to achieve salvation by any works of their own. Rather, salvation is the free gift of God's grace through faith. This doctrine of justification by faith rather than by works undercut the position of the Catholic Church, which maintained that, since the works necessary to salvation (e.g., the sacraments) could be performed only with the aid of the priesthood, the Church provided the sole means to salvation. In place of the priestly hierarchy, Luther substituted the notion of "the priesthood of all believers."

An Open Letter to the Christian Nobility of the German Nation Concerning the Reform of the Christian Estate, 1520

To his most illustrious and mighty Imperial Majesty, and to the Christian nobility of the German nation,

DOCTOR MARTIN LUTHER

Grace and power from God, Most illustrious Majesty, and most gracious and dear Lords.

It is not out of sheer forwardness or rashness that I, a single, poor man, have undertaken to address your worships. The distress and oppression which weigh down all the Estates of Christendom, especially of Germany, and which move not me alone, but everyone to cry out time and again, and to pray for help, have forced me even now to cry aloud that God many inspire some one with His Spirit to lend this suffering nation a helping hand. Ofttimes the councils have made some pretence at reformation, but their attempts have been cleverly hindered by the guile of certain men and things have gone from bad to worse. I now intend, by the help of God, to throw some light upon the wiles and wickedness of these men, to the end that when they are known, they may not henceforth be so hurtful and so great a hindrance. God has given us a noble youth to be our head and thereby has awakened great hopes of good in many hearts; wherefore it is meet that we should do our part and profitably use this time of grace.

In this whole matter the first and most important thing is that we take earnest heed not to enter on it trusting in great might or in human reason, even though all power in the world were ours; for God cannot and will not suffer a good work to be begun with trust in our own power or reason. Such works He crushes ruthlessly to earth, as it is written in the xxxiii Psalm, "There is no king saved by the multitude of an host: a mighty man is not delivered by much strength." On this account, I fear, it came to pass of old that the good Emperors Frederick I and II, and many other German emperors were shamefully oppressed and trodden under foot by the popes, although all the world feared them. It may be that they relied on their own might more than on God, and therefore they had to fall. In our own times, too, what was it that raised the bloodthirsty

"An Open Letter to the Christian Nobility of the German Nation Concerning the Reform of the Christian Estate," trans. C. M. Jacobs, in *Works of Martin Luther* (Philadelphia: Muhlenberg Press, 1915), II, 63–84. Courtesy of the Fortress Press.

Julius II to such heights? Nothing else, I fear, except that France, the Germans, and Venice relied upon themselves. The children of Benjamin slew forty-two thousand Israelites because the latter relied on their own strength.

That it may not so fare with us and our noble young Emperor Charles, we must be sure that in this matter we are dealing not with men, but with the princes of hell, who can fill the world with war and bloodshed, but whom war and bloodshed do not overcome. We must go at this work despairing of physical force and humbly trusting God; we must seek God's help with earnest prayer, and fix our minds on nothing else than the misery and distress of suffering Christendom, without regard to the deserts of evil men. Otherwise we may start the game with great prospect of success, but when we get well into it the evil spirits will stir up such confusion that the whole world will swim in blood, and yet nothing will come of it. Let us act wisely, therefore, and in the fear of God. The more force we use, the greater our disaster if we do not act humbly and in God's fear. The popes and the Romans have hitherto been able, by the devil's help, to set kings at odds with one another, and they may well be able to do it again, if we proceed by our own might and cunning, without God's help.

I. The three walls of the Romanists

The Romanists, with great adroitness, have built three walls about them, behind which they have hitherto defended themselves in such wise that no one has been able to reform them; and this has been the cause of terrible corruption throughout all Christendom.

First, when pressed by the temporal power, they have made decrees and said that the temporal power has no jurisdiction over them, but, on the other hand, that the spiritual is above the temporal power. Second, when the attempt is made to reprove them out of the Scriptures, they raise the objection that the interpretation of the Scriptures belongs to no one except the pope. Third, if threatened with a council, they answer with the fable that no one can call a council but the pope.

In this wise they have slyly stolen from us our three rods, that they may go unpunished, and have ensconced themselves within the safe stronghold of these three walls, that they may practise all the knavery and wickedness which we now see. Even when they have been compelled to hold a council they have weakened its power in advance by previously binding the princes with an oath to let them remain as they are. Moreover, they have given the pope full authority over all the decisions of the council, so that it is all one whether there are many councils or no councils,—except that they deceive us with puppet-shows and sham-battles. So terribly do they fear for their skin in a really free council! And they have intimidated kings and princes by making them believe it would be an offence against God not to obey them in all these knavish, crafty deceptions.

Now God help us, and give us one of the trumpets with which the walls of Jericho were overthrown, that we may blow down these walls of straw and paper, and may set free the Christian rods for the punishment of sin, bringing to light the craft and deceit of the devil, to the end that through punishment we may reform ourselves, and once more attain God's favor.

Against the first wall we will direct our first attack.

It is pure invention that pope, bishops, priests and monks are to be called the "spiritual estate"; princes, lords, artisans, and farmers the "temporal estate." That is indeed a fine bit of lying and hypocrisy. Yet no one should be frightened by it; and for this reason— *viz.,* that all Christians are truly of the "spiritual estate," and there is among them no difference at all but that of office, as Paul says in I Corinthians xii, We are all one body, yet every member has its own work, whereby it serves every other, all because we have one baptism, one Gospel, one faith, and are all alike Christians; for baptism, Gospel and faith alone make us "spiritual" and a Christian people.

But that a pope or a bishop anoints, confers, tonsures, ordains, consecrates, or prescribes dress unlike that of the laity,—this may make hypocrites and graven images, but it never makes a Christian or "spiritual" man. Through baptism all of us are consecrated to the priesthood, as St. Peter says in I Peter ii, "Ye are a royal priesthood, a priestly kingdom," and the book of Revelation says, "Thou hast made us by Thy blood to be priests and kings." For if we had no higher consecration than pope or bishop gives, the consecration by pope or bishop would never make a priest, nor might anyone either say mass or preach a sermon or give absolution. Therefore when the bishop consecrates it is the same thing as if he, in the place and stead of the whole congregation, all of whom have like power, were to take one out of their number and charge him to use this power for the others; just as though ten brothers, all king's sons and equal heirs, were to choose one of themselves to rule the inheritance for them all,—they would all be kings and equal in power, though one of them would be charged with the duty of ruling.

To make it still clearer. If a little group of pious Christian laymen were taken captive and set down in a wilderness, and had among them no priest consecrated by a bishop, and if there in the wilderness they were to agree in choosing one of themselves, married or unmarried, and were to charge him with the office of baptising, saying mass, absolving and preaching, such a man would be as truly a priest as though all bishops and popes had consecrated him. That is why in cases of necessity any one can baptise and give absolution, which would be impossible unless we were all priests. This great grace and power of baptism and of the Christian Estate they have well-nigh destroyed and caused us to forget through the canon law. It was in the manner aforesaid that Christians in olden days chose from their number bishops and priests, who were afterwards confirmed by other bishops, without all the show which now obtains. It was thus that Sts. Augustine, Ambrose, and Cyprian became bishops.

Since, then, the temporal authorities are baptised with the same baptism and have the same faith and Gospel as we, we must grant that they are priests and bishops, and count their office one which has a proper and a useful place in the Christian community. For whoever comes out of the water of baptism can boast that he is already consecrated priest, bishop, and pope, though it is not seemly that every one should exercise the office. Nay, just because we are all in like manner priests, no one must put himself forward and undertake, without our consent and election, to do what is in the power of all of us. For what is common to all, no one dare take upon himself without the will and the command of the community; and should it happen that one chosen for such an office were deposed for malfeasance, he would then be just what he was before he held office. Therefore a priest in Christendom is nothing else than an officeholder. While he is in office, he has precedence; when deposed, he is a peasant or a townsman like the rest. Beyond all doubt, then, a priest is no longer a priest when he is deposed. But now they have invented *characteres indelebiles,* and prate that a deposed priest is nevertheless something different from a mere layman. They even dream that a priest can never become a layman, or be anything else than a priest. All this is mere talk and man-made law.

From all this it follows that there is really no difference between laymen and priests, princes and bishops, "spirituals" and "temporals," as they call them, except that of office and work, but not of "estate"; for they are all of the same estate,—true priests, bishops, and popes,—though they are not all engaged in the same work, just as all priests and monks have not the same work. This is the teaching of St. Paul in Romans xii and I Corinthians xii, and of St. Peter in I Peter ii, as I have said above, *viz.,* that we are all one body of Christ, the Head, all members one of another. Christ has not two different bodies, one "temporal," the other "spiritual." He is one Head, and He has one body.

Therefore, just as those who are now called "spiritual"—priests, bishops or popes—are neither different from other Christians nor superior to them, except that they are charged with the administration of the Word of God and the sacraments, which is their work and office, so it is with the temporal authorities,—they bear sword and rod with which to punish the evil and to protect the good. A cobbler, a smith, a farmer, each has the work and office of his trade, and yet they are all alike consecrated priests and bishops, and every one by means of his own work or office must benefit and serve every other, that in this way many kinds of work may be done for the bodily and spiritual welfare of the community, even as all the members of the body serve one another.

See, now, how Christian is the decree which says that the temporal power is not above the "spiritual estate" and may not punish it. That is as much as to say that the hand shall lend no aid when the eye is suffering. Is it not unnatural, not to say unchristian, that one member should not help another and prevent its destruction? Verily, the more honorable the member, the more should the others help. I say then, since the temporal power is ordained of God to punish evil-doers and to protect them that do well, it should therefore be left free to perform its office without hindrance through the whole body of Christendom without respect of persons, whether it affect pope, bishops, priests, monks, nuns or anybody else. For if the mere fact that the temporal power has a smaller place among the Christian offices than has the office of preachers or confessors, or of the clergy, then the tailors, cobblers, masons, carpenters, pot-boys, tapsters, farmers, and all the secular tradesmen, should also be prevented from providing pope, bishops, priests and monks with shoes, clothing, houses, meat and drink, and from paying them tribute. But if these laymen are allowed to do their work unhindered, what do the Roman scribes mean by their laws, with which they withdraw themselves from the jurisdiction of the temporal Christian power, only so that they may be free to do evil and to fulfill what St. Peter has said: "There shall be false teachers among you, and through covetousness shall they with feigned words make merchandise of you."

On this account the Christian temporal power should exercise its office without let or hindrance, regardless whether it be pope, bishop, or priest whom it affects; whoever is guilty, let him suffer. All that the canon law has said to the contrary is sheer invention of Roman presumption. For thus saith St. Paul to all Christians: "Let every soul (I take that to mean the pope's soul also) be subject unto the higher powers; for they bear not the sword in vain, but are the ministers of God for the punishment of evil-doers, and for the praise of them that do well." St. Peter also says: "Submit yourselves unto every ordinance of man for the Lord's sake, for so is the will of God." He has also prophesied that such men shall come as will despise the temporal authorities, and this has come to pass through the canon law.

So then, I think this first paper-wall is overthrown, since the temporal power has become a member of the body of Christendom, and is of the "spiritual estate," though its work is of a temporal nature. Therefore its work should extend freely and without hindrance to all the members of the whole body; it should punish and use force whenever guilt deserves or necessity demands, without regard to pope, bishops, and priests,—let them hurl threats and bans as much as they will.

This is why guilty priests, if they are surrendered to the temporal law, are first deprived of their priestly dignities, which would not be right unless the temporal sword had previously had authority over them by divine right.

Again, it is intolerable that in the canon law so much importance is attached to the freedom, life and property of the clergy, as though the laity were not also as spiritual and as good Christians as they, or did not belong to the Church. Why are your life and limb, your property and honor so free, and mine not? We are all alike Christians, and have baptism, faith, Spirit, and all things alike. If a priest is killed, the land is laid under interdict,—why not when a peasant is killed? Whence comes this great distinction between those who are equally Christians? Only from human laws and inventions!

Moreover, it can be no good spirit who has invented such exceptions and granted to sin such license and impunity. For if we are bound to strive against the works and words of the evil spirit, and to drive him out in whatever way we can, as Christ commands and His Apostles, ought we, then, to suffer it in silence when the pope or his satellites are bent on devilish words and works? Ought we for the sake of men to allow the suppression of divine commandments and truths which we have sworn in baptism to support with life and limb? Of a truth we should then have to answer for all the souls that would thereby be abandoned and led astray.

It must therefore have been the very prince of devils who said what is written in the canon law: "If the pope were so scandalously bad as to lead souls in crowds to the devil, yet he could not be deposed." On this accursed and devilish foundation they build at Rome, and think that we should let all the world go to the devil, rather than resist their knavery. If the fact that one man is set over others were sufficient reason why he should escape punishment, then no Christian could punish another, since Christ commands the lowliest and the least.

Where sin is, there is no escape from punishment; as St. Gregory also writes that we are indeed all equal, but guilt puts us in subjection one to another. Now we see how they whom God and the Apostles have made subject to the temporal sword deal with Christendom, depriving it of its liberty by their own wickedness, without warrant of Scripture. It is to be feared that this is a game of Antichrist or a sign that he is close at hand.

The second wall is still more flimsy and worthless. They wish to be the only Masters of the Holy Scriptures, even though in all their lives they learn nothing from them. They assume for themselves sole authority, and with insolent juggling of words they would persuade us that the pope, whether he be a bad man or a good man, cannot err in matters of faith; and yet they cannot prove a single letter of it. Hence it comes that so many heretical and unchristian, nay, even unnatural ordinances have a place in the canon law, of which, however, there is no present need to speak. For since they think that the Holy Spirit never leaves them, be they ever so unlearned and wicked, they make bold to decree whatever they will. And if it were true, where would be the need or use of the Holy Scriptures? Let us burn them, and be satisfied with the unlearned lords at Rome, who are possessed of the Holy Spirit,—although He can possess only pious hearts! Unless I had read it myself, I could not have believed that the devil would make such clumsy pretensions at Rome, and find a following.

But, not to fight them with mere words, we will quote the Scriptures. St. Paul says in I Corinthians xiv: "If to anyone something better is revealed, though he be sitting and listening to another in God's Word, then the first, who is speaking, shall hold his peace and give place." What would be the use of this commandment, if we were only to believe him who does the talking or who has the highest seat? Christ also says in John vi, that all Christians shall be taught of God. Thus it may well happen that the pope and his followers are wicked men, and no true Christians, not taught of God, not having true understanding. On the other hand, an ordinary man may have true understanding; why then should we not follow him? Has not the pope erred many times? Who would help Christendom when the pope errs, if we were not to believe another, who had the Scriptures on his side, more than the pope?

Therefore it is a wickedly invented fable, and they cannot produce a letter in defence of it, that the interpretation of Scripture or the confirmation of its interpretation belongs to the pope alone. They have themselves usurped this power; and although they allege that this power was given to Peter when the keys were given to him, it is plain enough that the keys were not given to Peter alone, but to the whole community. Moreover, the keys were not ordained for doctrine or government, but only for the binding and loosing of sin, and whatever further power of the keys they arrogate to themselves is mere invention. But Christ's word to Peter, "I have prayed for thee that thy faith fail not," cannot be applied to the pope, since the majority of the popes have been without faith, as they must themselves confess. Besides, it is not only for Peter that Christ prayed, but also for all Apostles and Christians, as he says in John xvii: "Father, I pray for those whom Thou hast given Me, and not for these only,

but for all who believe on Me through their word." Is not this clear enough?

Only think of it yourself! They must confess that there are pious Christians among us, who have the true faith, Spirit, understanding, word and mind of Christ. Why, then, should we reject their word and understanding and follow the pope, who has neither faith nor Spirit? That would be to deny the whole faith and the Christian Church. Moreover, it is not the pope alone who is always in the right, if the article of the Creed is correct: "I believe in one holy Christian Church"; otherwise the prayer must run: "I believe in the pope at Rome," and so reduce the Christian Church to one man,—which would be nothing else than a devilish and hellish error.

Besides, if we are all priests, as was said above, and all have one faith, one Gospel, one sacrament, why should we not also have the power to test and judge what is correct or incorrect in matters of faith? What becomes of the words of Paul in I Corinthians ii: "He that is spiritual judgeth all things, yet he himself is judged of no man," and II Corinthians iv: "We have all the same Spirit of faith"? Why, then, should not we perceive what squares with faith and what does not, as well as does an unbelieving pope?

All these and many other texts should make us bold and free, and we should not allow the Spirit of liberty, as Paul calls Him, to be frightened off by the fabrications of the popes, but we ought to go boldly forward to test all that they do or leave undone, according to our interpretation of the Scriptures, which rests on faith, and compel them to follow not their own interpretation, but the one that is better. In the olden days Abraham had to listen to his Sarah, although she was in more complete subjection to him than we are to anyone on earth. Balaam's ass, also, was wiser than the prophet himself. If God then spoke by an ass against a prophet, why should He not be able even now to speak by a righteous man against the pope? In like manner St. Paul rebukes St. Peter as a man in error. Therefore it behooves every Christian to espouse the cause of the faith, to understand and defend it, and to rebuke all errors.

The third wall falls of itself when the first two are down. For when the pope acts contrary to the Scriptures, it is our duty to stand by the Scriptures, to reprove him, and to constrain him, according to the word of Christ in Matthew xviii: "If thy brother sin against thee, go and tell it him between thee and him alone; if he hear thee not, then take with thee one or two more; if he hear them not, tell it to the Church; if he hear not the Church, consider him a heathen." Here every member is commanded to care for every other. How much rather should we do this when the member that does evil is a ruling member, and by his evil-doing is the cause of much harm and offence to the rest! But if I am to accuse him before the Church, I must bring the Church together.

They have no basis in Scripture for their contention that it belongs to the pope alone to call a council or confirm its actions; for this is based merely upon their own laws, which are valid only in so far as they are not injurious to Christen-dom or contrary to the laws of God. When the Pope deserves punishment, such laws go out of force, since it is injurious to Christendom not to punish him by means of a council.

Thus we read in Acts xv that it was not St. Peter who called the Apostolic Council, but the Apostles and elders. If, then, that right had belonged to St. Peter alone, the council would not have been a Christian council, but an heretical *conciliabulum*. Even the Council of Nicaea—the most famous of all— was neither called nor confirmed by the Bishop of Rome, but by the Emperor Constantine, and many other emperors after him did the like, yet these councils were the most Christian of all. But if the pope alone had the right to call councils, then all these councils must have been heretical. Moreover, if I consider the councils which the pope has created, I find that they have done nothing of special importance.

Therefore, when necessity demands, and the pope is an offence to Christendom, the first man who is able should, as a faithful member of the whole body, do what he can to bring about a truly free council. No one can do this so well as the temporal authorities, especially since now they also are fellow-Christians, fellow-priests, "fellow-spirituals," fellow-lords over all things, and whenever it is needful or profitable, they should give free course to the office and work in which God has put them above every man. Would it not be an unnatural thing, if a fire broke out in a city, and every body were to stand by and let it burn on and on and consume everything that could burn, for the sole reason that nobody had the authority of the burgomaster, or because, perhaps, the fire broke out in the burgomaster's house? In such case is it not the duty of every citizen to arouse and call the rest? How much more should this be done in the spiritual city of Christ, if a fire of offence breaks out, whether in the papal government, or anywhere else? In the same way, if the enemy attacks a city, he who first rouses the others deserves honour and thanks; why then should he not deserve honour who makes known the presence of the enemy from hell, and awakens the Christians, and calls them together?

But all their boasts of an authority which dare not be opposed amount to nothing after all. No one in Christendom has authority to do injury, or to forbid the resisting of injury. There is no authority in the Church save for edification. Therefore, if the pope were to use his authority to prevent the calling of a free council, and thus became a hindrance to the edification of the Church, we should have regard neither for him nor for his authority; and if he were to hurl his bans and thunderbolts, we should despise his conduct as that of a madman, and relying on God, hurl back the ban on him, and coerce him as best we could. For this presumptuous authority of his is nothing; he has no such authority, and he is quickly overthrown by a text of Scripture; for Paul says to the Corinthians, "God has given us authority not for the destruction, but for the edification of Christendom." Who is ready to overleap this text? It is only the power of the devil and of Antichrist which resists the things that serve for the edification of Christendom; it is, therefore, in no wise to be obeyed, but is to be opposed with life and goods and all our strength.

Even though a miracle were to be done in the pope's behalf against the temporal powers, or though someone were to be stricken with a plague—which they boast has sometimes happened—it should be considered only the work of the devil, because of the weakness of our faith in God. Christ Himself prophesied in Matthew xxiv: "There shall come in My Name false Christs and false prophets, and do signs and wonders, so as to deceive even the elect," and Paul says in II Thessalonians ii, that Antichrist shall, through the power of Satan, be mighty in lying wonders.

Let us, therefore, hold fast to this: No Christian authority can do anything against Christ; as St. Paul says, "We can do nothing against Christ, but for Christ." Whatever does aught against Christ is the power of Antichrist and of the devil, even though it were to rain and hail wonders and plagues. Wonders and plagues prove nothing, especially in these evil times, for which all the Scriptures prophesy false wonders. Therefore we must cling with firm faith to the words of God, and then the devil will cease from wonders.

Thus I hope that the false, lying terror with which the Romans have this long time made our conscience timid and stupid, has been allayed. They, like all of us, are subject to the temporal sword; they have no power to interpret the Scriptures by mere authority, without learning; they have no authority to prevent a council or, in sheer wantonness, to pledge it, bind it, or take away its liberty; but if they do this, they are in truth in the communion of Antichrist and of the devil, and have nothing at all of Christ except the name.

II. Abuses to be discussed in councils

We shall now look at the matters which should be discussed in the councils, and with which popes, cardinals, bishops, and all the scholars ought properly to be occupied day and night if they love Christ and His Church. But if they neglect this duty, then let the laity and the temporal authorities see to it, regardless of bans and thunders; for an unjust ban is better than ten just releases, and an unjust release worse than ten just bans. Let us, therefore, awake, dear Germans, and fear God rather than men, that we may not share the fate of all the poor souls who are so lamentably lost through the shameful and devilish rule of the Romans, in which the devil daily takes a larger and larger place—if indeed, it were possible that such a hellish rule could grow worse, a thing I can neither conceive nor believe.

1. It is a horrible and frightful thing that the ruler of Christendom, who boasts himself vicar of Christ and successor of St. Peter, lives in such worldly splendor that in this regard no king nor emperor can equal or approach him, and that he who claims the title of "most holy" and "most spiritual" is more worldly than the world itself. He wears a triple crown, when the greatest kings wear but a single crown; if that is like the poverty of Christ and of St. Peter, then it is a new kind of likeness. When a word is said against it, they cry out "Heresy!" but that is because they do not wish to hear how unchristian and ungodly such a practice is. I think, however, that if the pope were with tears to pray to God he would have to lay aside these crowns, for our God can suffer no pride, and his office is nothing else than this,—daily to weep and pray for Christendom, and to set an example of all humility.

However that may be, this splendour of his is an offence, and the pope is bound on his soul's salvation to lay it aside, because St. Paul says, "Abstain from all outward shows, which give offence," and in Rom. xii, "We should provide good, not only in the sight of God, but also in the sight of all men." An ordinary bishop's crown would be enough for the pope; he should be greater than others in wisdom and holiness, and leave the crown of pride to Antichrist, as did his predecessors several centuries ago. They say he is a lord of the world; that is a lie; for Christ, Whose vicar and officer he boasts himself to be, said before Pilate, "My kingdom is not of this world," and no vicar's rule can go beyond his lord's. Moreover, he is not the vicar of the glorified, but of the crucified Christ, as Paul says, "I was willing to know nothing among you save Christ, and Him only as the Crucified"; and in Philippians ii, "So think of yourselves as ye see in Christ, Who emptied Himself and took upon Him the appearance of a servant"; and again in I Corinthians i, "We preach Christ, the Crucified." Now they make the pope a vicar of the glorified Christ in heaven, and some of them have allowed the devil to rule them so completely that they have maintained that the pope is above the angels in heaven and has authority over them. These are indeed the very works of the very Antichrist.

2. What is the use in Christendom of those people who are called the cardinals? I shall tell you. Italy and Germany have many rich monasteries, foundations, benefices, and livings. No better way has been discovered to bring all these to Rome than by creating cardinals and giving them the bishoprics, monasteries, and prelacies, and so overthrowing the worship of God. For this reason we now see Italy a very wilderness—monasteries in ruins, bishoprics devoured, the prelacies and the revenues of all the churches drawn to Rome, cities decayed, land and people laid waste, because there is no more worship or preaching. Why? The cardinals must have the income. No Turk could have so devastated Italy and suppressed the worship of God.

Now that Italy is sucked dry, they come into Germany, and begin oh so gently. But let us beware, or Germany will soon become like Italy. Already we have some cardinals: what the Romans seek by that the "drunken Germans" are not to understand until we have not a bishopric, a monastery, a living, a benefice, a *heller* or a *pfennig* left. Antichrist must take the treasures of the earth, as it was prophesied. So it goes on. They skim the cream off the bishoprics, monasteries, and benefices, and because they do not yet venture to turn them all to shameful use, as they have done in Italy, they only practise for the pres-

ent the sacred trickery of coupling together ten or twenty prelacies and taking a yearly portion from each of them, so as to make a tidy sum after all. The priory of Würzburg yields a thousand *gulden;* that of Bamberg, something; Mainz, Trier and the others, something more; and so from one to ten thousand *gulden* might be got together, in order that a cardinal might live at Rome like a rich king.

"After they are used to this, we will create thirty or forty cardinals in a day, and give to one Mount St. Michael at Bamberg and the bishopric of Würzburg to boot, hang on to these a few rich livings, until churches and cities are waste, and after that we will say, 'We are Christ's vicars and shepherds of Christ's sheep; the mad, drunken Germans must put up with it.' "

I advise, however, that the number of the cardinals be reduced, or that the pope be made to keep them at his own expense. Twelve of them would be more than enough, and each of them might have an income of a thousand *gulden* a year. How comes it that we Germans must put up with such robbery and such extortion of our property, at the hands of the pope? If the Kingdom of France has prevented it, why do we Germans let them make such fools and apes of us? It would all be more bearable if in this way they only stole our property; but they lay waste the churches and rob Christ's sheep of their pious shepherds, and destroy the worship and the Word of God. Even if there were not a single cardinal, the Church would not go under. As it is they do nothing for the good of Christendom; they only wrangle about the incomes of bishoprics and prelacies, and that any robber could do.

3. If ninety-nine parts of the papal court were done away and only the hundredth part allowed to remain, it would still be large enough to give decisions in matters of faith. Now, however, there is such a swarm of vermin yonder in Rome, all boasting that they are "papal," that there was nothing like it in Babylon. There are more than three thousand papal secretaries alone; who will count the other offices, when they are so many that they scarcely can be counted? And they all lie in wait for the prebends and benefices of Germany as wolves lie in wait for the sheep. I believe that Germany now gives much more to the pope at Rome than it gave in former times to the emperors. Indeed, some estimate that every year more than three hundred thousand *gulden* find their way from Germany to Rome, quite uselessly and fruitlessly; we get nothing for it but scorn and contempt. And yet we wonder that princes, nobles, cities, endowments, land, and people are impoverished! We should rather wonder that we still have anything to eat!

John Calvin

The success of Protestantism as an international reform movement was due largely to the work of a younger contemporary of Luther, the Frenchman John Calvin. Born Jean Cauvin in Picardy in 1509, Calvin went to Paris in 1523 to study first for a clerical and later for a legal career. During his student days he became acquainted with the writings of Luther, which were beginning to circulate through France at the time. His growing sympathy for the German "heresies" brought him to the attention of the authorities and he was forced to flee from the country. After some wandering he established himself permanently in the small city of Geneva, Switzerland. Thus began one of the most remarkable social and political experiments of modern times. Under Calvin's leadership Geneva was organized as a theocratic state. The clergy assumed control not only of the political affairs of the city but of the moral life of its citizens as well. In his attempts to realize a society of saints, Calvin systematically set about to banish gaiety, frivolity, and sin from the city. Although he was unusually successful, and Geneva became a city of piety and sobriety, Calvin was never fully satisfied. Sin, he discovered, could not be eradicated completely but would periodically rear its ugly head in the midst of his saintly society.

From Geneva, which came to be known as the Protestant Rome, Calvinism spread throughout most of Europe, into Germany, Poland, Bohemia, Hungary, and the Low Countries. The French Huguenots were Calvinists as were the Scottish Presbyterians and the English Puritans, who brought both the religious doctrines and the theocratic social organization of Calvin across the Atlantic to the colony of Massachusetts.

Calvin was not only a religious and social reformer but also one of the greatest of all Christian theologians. In his *Institutes of the Christian Religion,* which he first published at the age of twenty-seven, he reiterated and defended the Augustinian doctrine of original sin, with its implied notions of election, faith, and grace. On the subject of predestination, about which most theologians had spoken in muted tones, Calvin was particularly vehement. God in his omnipotence has decreed from all eternity the ultimate destiny of every individual soul. We, guilty sinners, can do nothing to alter this divine decree; all that rests with us is to praise God's infinite grace if he has elected us for salvation or to accept his just condemnation if he has damned us to hell.

The selection from the *Institutes* that follows outlines the main features of Calvin's theology.

Institutes of the Christian Religion

**Discussion of human nature
as created, of the faculties
of the soul, of the image of God,
of free will, and of the original
integrity of man's nature**

We must now speak of the creation of man: not only because among all God's works here is the noblest and most remarkable example of his justice, wisdom, and goodness; but because, as we said at the beginning, we cannot have a clear and complete knowledge of God unless it is accompanied by a corresponding knowledge of ourselves. This knowledge of ourselves is twofold: namely, to know what we were like when we were first created and what our condition became after the fall of Adam. While it would be of little benefit to understand our creation unless we recognized in this sad ruin what our nature in its corruption and deformity is like, we shall nevertheless be content for the moment with the description of our originally upright nature. And to be sure, before we come to the miserable condition of man to which he is now subjected, it is worth-while to know what he was like when first created. Now we must guard against singling out only those natural evils of man, lest we seem to attribute them to the Author of nature. For in this excuse, impiety thinks it has suffi-

cient defense, if it is able to claim that whatever defects it possesses have in some way proceeded from God. It does not hesitate, if it is reproved, to contend with God himself, and to impute to him the fault of which it is deservedly accused. And those who wish to seem to speak more reverently of the Godhead still willingly blame their depravity on nature, not realizing that they also, although more obscurely, insult God. For if any defect were proved to inhere in nature, this would bring reproach upon him.

Since, then, we see the flesh panting for every subterfuge by which it thinks that the blame for its own evils may in any way be diverted from itself to another, we must diligently oppose this evil intent. Therefore we must so deal with the calamity of mankind that we may cut off every shift, and may vindicate God's justice from every accusation. Afterward, in the proper place, we shall see how far away men are from the purity that was bestowed upon Adam. . . .

In this integrity man by free will had the power, if he so willed, to attain eternal life. Here it would be out of place to raise the question of God's secret predestination because our present subject is not what can happen or not, but what man's nature was like. Therefore Adam could

From *Calvin: Institutes of the Christian Religion,* LCC, Vols. XX and XXI, ed. John T. McNeill and trans. Ford Lewis Battles. Published simultaneously in the U.S.A. by The Westminster Press and in Great Britain by S.C.M. Press, Ltd., London. Copyright © 1960, by W. L. Jenkins. Used by permission.

have stood if he wished, seeing that he fell solely by his own will. But it was because his will was capable of being bent to one side or the other, and was not given the constancy to persevere, that he fell so easily. Yet his choice of good and evil was free, and not that alone, but the highest rectitude was in his mind and will, and all the organic parts were rightly composed to obedience, until in destroying himself he corrupted his own blessings.

Hence the great obscurity faced by the philosophers, for they were seeking in a ruin for a building, and in scattered fragments for a well-knit structure. They held this principle, that man would not be a rational animal unless he possessed free choice of good and evil; also it entered their minds that the distinction between virtues and vices would be obliterated if man did not order his life by his own planning. Well reasoned so far—if there had been no change in man. But since this was hidden from them, it is no wonder they mix up heaven and earth! They, as professed disciples of Christ, are obviously playing the fool when, by compromising between the opinions of the philosophers and heavenly doctrine, so that these touch neither heaven nor earth, in man—who is lost and sunk down into spiritual destruction—they still seek after free choice. But these matters will be better dealt with in their proper place. Now we need bear only this in mind: man was far different at the first creation from his whole posterity, who, deriving their origin from him in his corrupted state, have contracted from him a hereditary taint. For, the individual parts of his soul were formed to upright-

ness, the soundness of his mind stood firm, and his will was free to choose the good. If anyone objects that his will was placed in an insecure position because its power was weak, his status should have availed to remove any excuse; nor was it reasonable for God to be constrained by the necessity of making a man who either could not or would not sin at all. Such a nature would, indeed, have been more excellent. But to quarrel with God on this precise point, as if he ought to have conferred this upon man, is more than iniquitous, inasmuch as it was in his own choice to give whatever he pleased. But the reason he did not sustain man by the virtue of perseverance lies hidden in his plan; sobriety is for us the part of wisdom. Man, indeed, received the ability provided he exercised the will; but he did not have the will to use his ability, for this exercising of the will would have been followed by perseverance. Yet he is not excusable, for he received so much that he voluntarily brought about his own destruction; indeed, no necessity was imposed upon God of giving man other than a mediocre and even transitory will, that from man's Fall he might gather occasion for his own glory.

God by His power nourishes and maintains the world created by Him, and rules its several parts by His providence

Moreover, to make God a momentary Creator, who once for all finished his work, would be cold and barren, and we must differ from profane men especially in that we see the presence of divine power shining as much in the continuing state of the universe as in its inception. For even though the minds of the impious too are compelled by merely looking upon earth and heaven to rise up to the Creator, yet faith has its own peculiar way of assigning the whole credit for Creation to God. To this pertains that saying of the apostle's to which we have referred before, that only "by faith we understand that the universe was created by the word of God." For unless we pass on to his providence—however, we may seem both to comprehend with the mind and to confess with the tongue— we do not yet properly grasp what it means to say: "God is Creator." Carnal sense, once confronted with the power of God in the very Creation, stops there, and at most weighs and contemplates only the wisdom, power and goodness of the author in accomplishing such handiwork. (These matters are self-evident, and even force themselves upon the unwilling.) It contemplates, moreover, some general preserving and governing activity, from which the force of motion derives. In short, carnal sense thinks there is an energy divinely bestowed from the beginning, sufficient to sustain all things.

But faith ought to penetrate more deeply, namely, having found him Creator of all, forthwith to conclude he is also everlasting Governor and Preserver—not only in that he drives the celestial frame as well as its several parts by a universal motion, but also in that he sustains, nourishes, and cares for everything he has made, even to the least sparrow. Thus David, having briefly stated that the universe was created by God, immediately descends to the uninterrupted course of His providence, "By the word of Jehovah the heavens were made, and all their host by the breath of his mouth." Soon thereafter he adds, "Jehovah has looked down upon the sons of men," and what follows is in the same vein. For although all men do not reason so clearly, yet, because it would not be believable that human affairs are cared for by God unless he were the Maker of the universe, and nobody seriously believes the universe was made by God without being persuaded that he takes care of his works, David not inappropriately leads us in the best order from the one to the other. In general, philosophers teach and human minds conceive that all parts of the universe are quickened by God's secret inspiration. . . .

But because we know that the universe was established especially for the sake of mankind, we ought to look for this purpose in his governance also. The prophet Jeremiah exclaims, "I know, O Lord, that the way of man is not his own, nor is it given to man to direct his own steps." Moreover, Solomon says, "Man's steps are from the Lord and how may man dispose his way?" Let them now say that man is moved by God according to the inclination of his nature, but that he himself turns that motion whither he pleases. Nay, if that were truly said, the free choice of his ways would be in man's control. Perhaps they will deny this because he can do nothing without God's power. Yet they cannot really get by with that, since it is clear that the prophet and Solomon ascribe to God not only might but also choice and determination. Elsewhere Solomon elegantly rebukes this rashness of men, who set up for themselves a goal without regard to God, as if they were not led by his hand. "The disposition of the heart is man's, but the preparation of the tongue is the Lord's." It is an absurd folly that miserable men take it upon themselves to act without God, when they cannot even speak except as he wills!

Indeed, Scripture, to express more plainly that nothing at all in the world is undertaken without his determination, shows that things seemingly most fortuitous are subject to him. For what can you attribute more to chance than when a branch breaking off from a tree kills a passing traveler? But the Lord speaks far differently, acknowledging that he has delivered him to the hand of the slayer. Likewise, who does not attribute lots to the blindness of fortune? But the Lord does not allow this, claiming for himself the determining of them. He teaches that it is not by their own power that pebbles are cast into the lap and drawn out, but the one thing that could have been attributed to chance he testifies to come from himself. In the same vein is that saying of Solomon, "The poor man and the usurer meet together; God illumines the eyes of both." He points out that, even though the rich are mingled with the poor in the world, while to each his condition is divinely assigned, God, who lights all men, is not at all blind. And so he urges the poor to patience; because those who are not content with their own lot try to shake off the burden laid upon them by God. Thus, also, another prophet rebukes the impious who ascribe to men's toil, or to fortune, the fact that some lie in squalor and others rise up to honors. "For not from the east, nor from the west, nor from the wilderness comes lifting up; because God is judge, he humbles one and lifts up another." Because God cannot put off the office of judge, hence he reasons that it is by His secret plan that some distinguish themselves, while others remain contemptible. . . .

How we may apply this doctrine to our greatest benefit

. . . All who will compose themselves to this moderation will not murmur against God on account of their adversities in time past, nor lay the blame for their own wickedness upon him as did the Homeric Agamemnon, saying: "I am not the cause, but Zeus and fate." And they will not, as if carried off by the fates, out of desperation cast themselves to destruction like that youth of Plautus: "Unstable is the lot of things, the fates drive men according to their own pleasure. I will betake myself to the precipice, that there I may lose my goods with my life." And they will not follow the example of another, and cover up their own evil deeds with the name "God." For thus Lyconides says in another comedy: "God was the instigator; I believe the gods willed it. For I know if they had not so willed, it would not have happened." But rather let them inquire and learn from Scripture what is pleasing to God so that they may strive toward this under the Spirit's guidance. At the same time, being ready to follow God wherever he calls, they will show in very truth that nothing is more profitable than the knowledge of this doctrine.

Profane men with their absurdities foolishly raise an uproar, so that they almost, as the saying is, mingle heaven and earth. If the Lord has indicated the point of our death, they say, we cannot escape it. Therefore it is vain for anyone to busy himself in taking precautions. One man does not dare take a road that he hears is dangerous, lest he be murdered by thieves; another summons physicians, and wears himself out with medicines to keep himself alive; another is afraid of living in tumble-down houses. In short, all devise ways and forge them with great purpose of mind, to attain what they desire. Now either all these remedies which attempt to correct God's will are vain; or else there is no fixed decree of God that determines life and death, health and disease, peace and war, and other things that men, as they desire or hate them, so earnestly try by their own toil either to obtain or to avoid. Also they conclude that believers' prayers, by which the Lord is asked to provide for things that he has already decreed from eternity, are perverse, not to say superfluous. To sum up, they cancel all those plans which have to do with the future, as militating against God's providence, which, without their being consulted, has decreed what he would have happen. Then whatever does happen now, they so impute to God's providence that they close their eyes to the man who clearly has done it. Does an assassin murder an upright citizen? He has carried out, they say, God's plan. Has someone stolen,

or committed adultery? Because he has done what was foreseen and ordained by the Lord, he is the minister of God's providence. Has a son, neglecting remedies, with never a care awaited the death of a parent? He could not resist God, who had so appointed from eternity. Thus all crimes, because subject to God's ordinance, they call virtues. . . .

The same men wrongly and rashly lay the happenings of past time to the naked providence of God. For since on it depends everything that happens, therefore, say they, neither thefts, nor adulteries, nor murders take place without God's will intervening. Why therefore, they ask, should a thief be punished, who has plundered someone whom the Lord would punish with poverty? Why shall a murderer be punished, who has killed one whose life the Lord had ended? If all such men are serving God's will, why shall they be punished? On the contrary, I deny that they are serving God's will. For we shall not say that one who is motivated by an evil inclination, by only obeying his own wicked desire, renders service to God, at His bidding. A man, having learned of His will, obeys God in striving toward the goal to which he is called by that same will. From what source do we learn but from his Word? In such fashion we must in our deeds search out God's will which he declares through his Word. God requires of us only what he commands. If we contrive anything against his commandment, it is not obedience but obstinacy and transgression. Yet, unless he willed it, we would not do it. I agree. But do we do evil things to the end that we may serve him? Yet he by no means commands us to do them; rather we rush head-long, without thinking what he requires, but so raging in our unbridled lust that we deliberately strive against him. And in this way we serve his just ordinance by doing evil, for so great and boundless is his wisdom that he knows right well how to use evil instruments to do good. And see how absurd their argument is: they would have transgressors go unpunished, on the ground that their misdeeds are committed solely by God's dispensation.

I grant more: thieves and murderers and other evildoers are the instruments of divine providence, and the Lord himself uses these to carry out the judgments that he has determined with himself. Yet I deny that they can derive from this any excuse for their evil deeds. Why? Will they either involve God in the same iniquity with themselves, or will they cloak their own depravity with his justice? They can do neither.

· · ·

By the fall and revolt of Adam the whole human race was delivered to the curse, and degenerated from its original condition; the doctrine of original sin

With good reason the ancient proverb strongly recommended knowledge of self to man. For if it is considered disgraceful for us not to know all that pertains to the business of human life, even more detestable is our ignorance of ourselves, by which, when making decisions in necessary matters, we

miserably deceive and even blind ourselves!

But since this precept is so valuable, we ought more diligently to avoid applying it perversely. This, we observe, has happened to certain philosophers, who, while urging man to know himself, propose the goal of recognizing his own worth and excellence. And they would have him contemplate in himself nothing but what swells him with empty assurance and puffs him up with pride.

But knowledge of ourselves lies first in considering what we were given at creation and how generously God continues his favour toward us, in order to know how great our natural excellence would be if only it had remained unblemished; yet at the same time to bear in mind that there is in us nothing of our own, but that we hold on sufferance whatever God has bestowed upon us. Hence we are ever dependent on him. Secondly, to call to mind our miserable condition after Adam's fall; the awareness of which, when all our boasting and self-assurance are laid low, should truly humble us and overwhelm us with shame. In the beginning God fashioned us after his image that he might arouse our minds both to zeal for virtue and to meditation upon eternal life. Thus, in order that the great nobility of our race (which distinguishes us from brute beasts) may not be buried beneath our own dullness of wit, it behooves us to recognize that we have been endowed with reason and understanding so that, by leading a holy and upright life, we may press on to the appointed goal of blessed immortality.

But that primal worthiness cannot come to mind without the sorry spectacle of our foulness and dishonour presenting itself by way of contrast, since in the person of the first man we have fallen from our original condition. From this source arise abhorrence and displeasure with ourselves, as well as true humility; and thence is kindled a new zeal to seek God, in whom each of us may recover those good things which we have utterly and completely lost. . . .

Because what God so severely punished must have been no light sin but a detestable crime, we must consider what kind of sin there was in Adam's desertion that enkindled God's fearful vengeance against the whole of mankind. To regard Adam's sin as gluttonous intemperance (a common notion) is childish. As if the sum and head of all virtues lay in abstaining solely from one fruit, when all sorts of desirable delights abounded everywhere; and not only abundance but also magnificent variety was at hand in that blessed fruitfulness of earth!

We ought therefore to look more deeply. Adam was denied the tree of the knowledge of good and evil to test his obedience and prove that he was willingly under God's command. The very name of the tree shows the sole purpose of the precept was to keep him content with his lot and to prevent him from becoming puffed up with wicked lust. But the promise by which he was bidden to hope for eternal life so long as he ate from the tree of life, and conversely, the terrible threat of death once he tasted of the tree of knowledge of good and evil, served to prove and exercise his

faith. Hence it is not hard to deduce by what means Adam provoked God's wrath upon himself. Indeed, Augustine speaks rightly when he declares that pride was the beginning of all evils. For if ambition had not raised man higher than was meet and right, he could have remained in his original state.

But we must take a fuller definition from the nature of the temptation which Moses describes. Since the woman through unfaithfulness was led away from God's Word by the serpent's deceit, it is already clear that disobedience was the beginning of the Fall. This Paul also confirms, teaching that all were lost through the disobedience of one man. Yet it is at the same time to be noted that the first man revolted from God's authority, not only because he was seized by Satan's blandishments, but also because, contemptuous of truth, he turned aside to falsehood. And surely, once we hold God's Word in contempt, we shake off all reverence for him. For, unless we listen attentively to him, his majesty will not dwell among us, nor his worship remain perfect. Unfaithfulness, then, was the root of the Fall. But thereafter ambition and pride, together with ungratefulness, arose, because Adam by seeking more than was granted him shamefully spurned God's great bounty, which had been lavished upon him. To have been made in the likeness of God seemed a small matter to a son of earth unless he also attained equality with God—a monstrous wickedness! If apostasy, by which man withdraws from the authority of his Maker—indeed insolently shakes off his yoke—is a foul and detestable offense, it is vain to extenuate Adam's sin. Yet it was not simple apostasy, but was joined with vile reproaches against God. These assented to Satan's slanders, which accused God of falsehood and envy and ill will. Lastly, faithlessness opened the door to ambition, and ambition was indeed the mother of obstinate disobedience; as a result, men, having cast off the fear of God, threw themselves wherever lust carried them. Hence Bernard rightly teaches that the door of salvation is opened to us when we receive the gospel today with our ears, even as death was then admitted by those same windows when they were opened to Satan. For Adam would never have dared oppose God's authority unless he had disbelieved in God's Word. Here, indeed, was the best bridle to control all passions: the thought that nothing is better than to practice righteousness by obeying God's commandments; then, that the ultimate goal of the happy life is to be loved by him. Therefore Adam, carried away by the devil's blasphemies, as far as he was able extinguished the whole glory of God.

As it was the spiritual life of Adam to remain united and bound to his Maker, so estrangement from him was the death of his soul. Nor is it any wonder that he consigned his race to ruin by his rebellion when he perverted the whole order of nature in heaven and on earth. "All creatures," says Paul, "are groaning," "subject to corruption, not of their own will." If the cause is sought, there is no doubt that they are bearing part of the punishment deserved by man, for whose use they were created. Since, there-

fore, the curse, which goes about through all the regions of the world, flowed hither and yon from Adam's guilt, it is not unreasonable if it is spread to all his offspring. Therefore, after the heavenly image was obliterated in him, he was not the only one to suffer this punishment— that, in place of wisdom, virtue, holiness, truth, and justice, with which adornments he had been clad, there came forth the most filthy plagues, blindness, impotence, impurity, vanity, and injustice—but he also entangled and immersed his offspring in the same miseries.

This is the inherited corruption, which the church fathers termed "original sin," meaning by the word "sin" the depravation of a nature previously good and pure. There was much contention over this matter, inasmuch as nothing is farther from the usual view than for all to be made guilty by the guilt of one, and thus for sin to be made common. This seems to be the reason why the most ancient doctors of the church touched upon this subject so obscurely. At least they explained it less clearly than was fitting. Yet this timidity could not prevent Pelagius from rising up with the profane fiction that Adam sinned only to his own loss without harming his posterity. Through this subtlety Satan attempted to cover up the disease and thus to render it incurable. But when it was shown by the clear testimony of Scripture that sin was transmitted from the first man to all his posterity, Pelagius quibbled that it was transmitted through imitation, not propagation. Therefore, good men (and Augustine above the rest) labored to show us that we are corrupted not by derived wickedness, but that we bear inborn defect from our mother's womb. . . .

So that these remarks may not be made concerning an uncertain and unknown matter, let us define original sin. It is not my intention to investigate the several definitions proposed by various writers, but simply to bring forward the one that appears to me most in accordance with truth. Original sin, therefore, seems to be a hereditary depravity and corruption of our nature, diffused into all parts of the soul, which first makes us liable to God's wrath, then also brings forth in us those works which Scripture calls "works of the flesh." And that is properly what Paul often calls sin. The works that come forth from it—such as adulteries, fornications, thefts, hatreds, murders, carousings —he accordingly calls "fruits of sin," although they are also commonly called "sins" in Scripture, and even by Paul himself. ·

We must, therefore, distinctly note these two things. First, we are so vitiated and perverted in every part of our nature that by this great corruption we stand justly condemned and convicted before God, to whom nothing is acceptable but righteousness, innocence, and purity. And this is not liability for another's transgression. For, since it is said that we became subject to God's judgment through Adam's sin, we are to understand it not as if we, guiltless and undeserving, bore the guilt of his offense but in the sense that, since we through his transgression have become entangled in the curse, he is said to have made us guilty. Yet not only has punishment

fallen upon us from Adam, but a contagion imparted by him resides in us, which justly deserves punishment. For this reason, Augustine, though he often calls sin "another's" to show more clearly that it is distributed among us through propagation, nevertheless declares at the same time that it is peculiar to each. And the apostle himself most eloquently testifies that "death has spread to all because all have sinned." That is, they have been enveloped in original sin and defiled by its stains. For that reason, even infants themselves, while they carry their condemnation along with them from the mother's womb, are guilty not of another's fault but of their own. For, even though the fruits of their iniquity have not yet come forth, they have the seed enclosed within them. Indeed, their whole nature is a seed of sin; hence it can be only hateful and abhorrent to God. From this it follows that it is rightly considered sin in God's sight, for without guilt there would be no accusation.

Then comes the second consideration: that this perversity never ceases in us, but continually bears new fruits—the works of the flesh that we have already described—just as a burning furnace gives forth flame and sparks, or water ceaselessly bubbles up from a spring. Thus those who have defined original sin as "the lack of the original righteousness, which ought to reside in us," although they comprehend in this definition the whole meaning of the term, have still not expressed effectively enough its power and energy. For our nature is not only destitute and empty of good, but so fertile and fruitful of every evil that it cannot be idle. . . .

Man has now been deprived of freedom of choice and bound over to miserable servitude

We have now seen that the domination of sin, from the time it held the first man bound to itself, not only ranges among all mankind, but also completely occupies individual souls. It remains for us to investigate more closely whether we have been deprived of all freedom since we have been reduced to this servitude; and, if any particle of it still survives, how far its power extends. But in order that the truth of this question may be more readily apparent to us, I shall presently set a goal to which the whole argument should be directed. The best way to avoid error will be to consider the perils that threaten man on both sides. (1) When man is denied all uprightness, he immediately takes occasion for complacency from that fact; and, because he is said to have no ability to pursue righteousness on his own, he holds all such pursuit to be of no consequence, as if it did not pertain to him at all. (2) Nothing, however slight, can be credited to man without depriving God of his honour, and without man himself falling into ruin through brazen confidence. Augustine points out both these precipices.

Here, then, is the course that we must follow if we are to avoid crashing upon these rocks: when man has been taught that no good thing remains in his power, and that he is hedged about on all sides by most miserable necessity, in spite of this

he should nevertheless be instructed to aspire to a good of which he is empty, to a freedom of which he has been deprived. In fact, he may thus be more sharply aroused from inactivity than if it were supposed that he was endowed with the highest virtues. Everyone sees how necessary this second point is. I observe that too many persons have doubts about the first point. For since this is an undoubted fact, that nothing of his own ought to be taken away from man, it ought to be clearly evident how important it is for him to be barred from false boasting. At the time when man was distinguished with the noblest marks of honor through God's beneficence, not even then was he permitted to boast about himself. How much more ought he now to humble himself, cast down as he has been—due to his own ungratefulness—from the loftiest glory into extreme disgrace! At that time, I say, when he had been advanced to the highest degree or honor, Scripture attributed nothing else to him than that he had been created in the image of God, thus suggesting that man was blessed, not because of his own good actions, but by participation in God. What, therefore, now remains for man, bare and destitute of all glory, but to recognize God for whose beneficence he could not be grateful when he abounded with the riches of this grace; and at least, by confessing his own poverty, to glorify him in whom he did not previously glory in recognition of his own blessings?

Also, it is no less to our advantage than pertinent to God's glory that we be deprived of all credit for our wisdom and virtue. Thus those who bestow upon us anything beyond the truth add sacrilege to our ruin. When we are taught to wage our own war, we are but borne aloft on a reed stick, only to fall as soon as it breaks! Yet we flatter our strength unduly when we compare it even to a reed stick! For whatever vain men devise and babble concerning these matters is but smoke. . . .

If this be admitted, it will be indisputable that free will is not sufficient to enable man to do good works, unless he be helped by grace, indeed by special grace, which only the elect receive through regeneration. For I do not tarry over those fanatics who babble that grace is equally and indiscriminately distributed. But it has not yet been demonstrated whether man has been wholly deprived of all power to do good, or still has some power, though meager and weak; a power, indeed, that can do nothing of itself, but with the help of grace also does its part. The Master of the Sentences meant to settle this point when he taught: "We need two kinds of grace to render us capable of good works." He calls the first kind "operating," which ensures that we effectively will to do good. The second he calls "co-operating," which follows the good will as a help. The thing that displeases me about this division is that, while he attributes the effective desire for good to the grace of God, yet he hints that man by his very own nature somehow seeks after the good—though ineffectively. Thus Bernard declares the good will is God's work, yet concedes to man that of his own impulse he seeks this sort of good will. But this is far from Augustine's thought, from whom Peter Lombard pretended to have taken this distinction. The ambiguity in the second part offends me, for it has given rise to a perverted interpretation. They thought we co-operate with the assisting grace of God, because it is our right either to render it ineffectual by spurning the first grace, or to confirm it by obediently following it. This the author of the work *The Calling of the Gentiles* expresses as follows: "Those who employ the judgment of reason are free to forsake grace, so that not to have forsaken it is a meritorious act; and what could not be done without the co-operation of the Spirit is counted meritorious for those whose own will could not have accomplished it." I chose to note these two points in passing that you, my reader, may see how far I disagree with the sounder Schoolmen. I differ with the more recent Sophists to an even greater extent, as they are farther removed from antiquity. However, we at least understand from this division in what way they grant free will to man. For Lombard finally declares that we have free will, not in that we are equally capable of doing or thinking good and evil, but merely that we are freed from compulsion. According to Lombard, this freedom is not hindered, even if we be wicked and slaves of sin, and can do nothing but sin.

Man will then be spoken of as having this sort of free decision, not because he has free choice equally of good and evil, but because he acts wickedly by will, not by compulsion. Well put, indeed, but what purpose is served by labeling with a proud name such a slight thing? A noble freedom, indeed— for man not to be forced to serve sin, yet to be such a willing slave that his will is bound by the fetters of sin!

. . .

Eternal election, by which God has predestined some to salvation, others to destruction

In actual fact, the covenant of life is not preached equally among all men, and among those to whom it is preached, it does not gain the same acceptance either constantly or in equal degree. In this diversity the wonderful depth of God's judgment is made known. For there is no doubt that this variety also serves the decision of God's eternal election. If it is plain that it comes to pass by God's bidding that salvation is freely offered to some while others are barred from access to it, at once great and difficult questions spring up, explicable only when reverent minds regard as settled what they may suitably hold concerning election and predestination. A baffling question this seems to many. For they think nothing more inconsistent than that out of the common multitude of men some should be predestined to salvation, others to destruction. But how mistakenly they entangle themselves will become clear in the following discussion. Besides, in the very darkness that frightens them not only is the usefulness of this doctrine made known but also its very sweet fruit. We shall never be clearly persuaded, as we ought to be, that our salvation flows from the wellspring of God's free mercy until we come to know his eternal election, which illuminates God's grace by this contrast: that he does not indiscriminately adopt all into the hope of salvation but gives to some what he denies to others.

How much the ignorance of this principle detracts from God's glory, how much it takes away from true humility, is well known. Yet Paul denies that this which needs so much to be known can be known unless God, utterly disregarding works, chooses those whom he has decreed within himself. "At the present time," he says, "a remnant has been saved according to the election of grace. But if it is by grace, it is no more of works; otherwise grace would no more be grace. But if it is of works, it is no more of grace; otherwise work would not be work." If—to make it clear that our salvation comes about solely from God's mere generosity—we must be called back to the course of election, those who wish to get rid of all this are obscuring as maliciously as they can what ought to have been gloriously and vociferously proclaimed, and they tear humility up by the very roots. Paul clearly testifies that, when the salvation of a remnant of the people is ascribed to the election of grace, then only is it acknowledged that God of his mere good pleasure preserves whom he will, and moreover that he pays no reward, since he can owe none.

They who shut the gates that no one may dare seek a taste of this doctrine wrong men no less than God. For neither will anything else suffice to make us humble as we ought to be nor shall we otherwise sincerely feel how much we are obliged to God. And as Christ teaches, here is our only ground for firmness and confidence: in order to free us of all fear and render us victorious amid so many dangers, snares, and mortal struggles, he promises that whatever the Father has entrusted into his keeping will be safe. From this we infer that all those who do not know that they are God's own will be miserable through constant fear. Hence, those who by being blind to the three benefits we have noted would wish the foundation of our salvation to be removed from our midst, very badly serve the interests of themselves and of all other believers. How is it that the church becomes manifest to us from this, when, as Bernard rightly teaches, "it could not otherwise be found or recognized among creatures, since it lies marvelously hidden . . . both within the bosom of a blessed predestination and within the mass of a miserable condemnation?"

But before I enter into the matter itself, I need to mention by way of preface two kinds of men.

Human curiosity renders the discussion of predestination, already somewhat difficult of itself, very confusing and even dangerous. No restraints can hold it back from wandering in forbidden bypaths and thrusting upward to the heights. If allowed, it will leave no secret to God that it will not search out and unravel. Since we see so many on all sides rushing into this audacity and impudence, among them certain men not otherwise bad, they should in due season be reminded of the measure of their duty in this regard. First, then, let them remember that when they inquire into predestination they are penetrating the sacred precincts of divine wisdom. If anyone with carefree assurance

breaks into this place, he will not succeed in satisfying his curiosity and he will enter a labyrinth from which he can find no exit. For it is not right for man unrestrainedly to search out things that the Lord has willed to be hid in himself, and to unfold from eternity itself the sublimest wisdom, which he would have us revere but not understand that through this also he should fill us with wonder. He has set forth by his Word the secrets of his will that he has decided to reveal to us. These he decided to reveal in so far as he foresaw that they would concern us and benefit us. . . .

Profane men, I admit, in the matter of predestination abruptly seize upon something to carp, rail, bark, or scoff at. But if their shamelessness deters us, we shall have to keep secret the chief doctrines of the faith, almost none of which they or their like leave untouched by blasphemy. An obstinate person would be no less insolently puffed up on hearing that within the essence of God there are three Persons than if he were told that God foresaw what would happen to man when he created him. And they will not refrain from guffaws when they are informed that but little more than five thousand years have passed since the creation of the universe, for they ask why God's power was idle and asleep for so long. Nothing, in short, can be brought forth that they do not assail with their mockery. Should we, to silence these blasphemies, forbear to speak of the deity of Son and Spirit? Must we pass over in silence the creation of the universe? No! God's truth is so powerful, both in this respect and in every other, that it has nothing to fear from the evil-speaking of wicked men.

So Augustine stoutly maintains in his little treatise *The Gift of Perseverance.* For we see that the false apostles could not make Paul ashamed by defaming and accusing his true doctrine. They say that this whole discussion is dangerous for godly minds—because it hinders exhortations, because it shakes faith, because it disturbs and terrifies the heart itself—but this is nonsense! Augustine admits that for these reasons he was frequently charged with preaching predestination too freely, but, as it was easy for him, he overwhelmingly refuted the charge. We, moreover, because many and various absurdities are obtruded at this point, have preferred to dispose of each in its own place. I desire only to have them generally admit that we should not investigate what the Lord has left hidden in secret, that we should not neglect what he has brought into the open, so that we may not be convicted of excessive curiosity on the one hand, or of excessive ingratitude on the other. For Augustine also skillfully expressed this idea: we can safely follow Scripture, which proceeds at the pace of a mother stooping to her child, so to speak, so as not to leave us behind in our weakness. But for those who are so cautious or fearful that they desire to bury predestination in order not to disturb weak souls—with what color will they cloak their arrogance when they accuse God indirectly of stupid thoughtlessness, as if he had not foreseen the peril that they feel they have wisely met? Whoever, then, heaps odium upon the doctrine of predestination openly reproaches God, as if he had unadvisedly let slip something hurtful to the church.

No one who wishes to be thought religious dares simply deny predestination, by which God adopts some to hope of life, and sentences others to eternal death. But our opponents, especially those who make foreknowledge its cause, envelop it in numerous petty objections. We, indeed, place both doctrines in God, but we say that subjecting one to the other is absurd.

When we attribute foreknowledge to God, we mean that all things always were, and perpetually remain, under his eyes, so that to his knowledge there is nothing future or past, but all things are present. And they are present in such a way that he not only conceives them through ideas, as we have before us those things which our minds remember, but he truly looks upon them and discerns them as things placed before him. And this foreknowledge is extended throughout the universe to every creature. We call predestination God's eternal decree, by which he determined with himself what he willed to become of each man. For all are not created in equal condition; rather, eternal life is foreordained for some, eternal damnation for others. Therefore, as any man has been created to one or the other of these ends, we speak of him as predestined to life or to death. . . .

As Scripture, then, clearly shows, we say that God once established by his eternal and unchangeable plan those whom he long before determined once for all to receive into salvation, and those whom, on the other hand, he would devote to destruction. We assert that, with respect to the elect, this plan was founded upon his freely given mercy, without regard to human worth; but by his just and irreprehensible but incomprehensible judgment he has barred the door of life to those whom he has given over to damnation. Now among the elect we regard the call as a testimony of election. Then we hold justification another sign of its manifestation, until they come into the glory in which the fulfillment of that election lies. But as the Lord seals his elect by call and justification, so, by shutting off the reprobate from knowledge of his name or from the sanctification of his Spirit, he, as it were, reveals by these marks what sort of judgment awaits them. Here I shall pass over many fictions that stupid men have invented to overthrow predestination. They need no refutation, for as soon as they are brought forth they abundantly prove their own falsity.

The Counter Reformation

The Counter Reformation of the Catholic Church expressed itself in three major institutions: the Society of Jesus (usually called the Jesuits), the Inquisition (or Holy Office), and the Council of Trent. The Company or Society of Jesus was founded by St. Ignatius of Loyola (1491–1556), an unlettered Spanish soldier who, as the result of a religious experience he underwent after being wounded in battle, resolved to become a "soldier of Christ." Once he had recovered, he set about educating himself, starting with elementary school and countinuing through the University of Paris, where he began organizing the Jesuit order. Loyola's new Society was established along military lines; and iron discipline demanded that each member show complete obedience to his immediate superiors and ultimately to his supreme commander, the pope. During the religious conflicts of the sixteenth and seventeenth centuries, the Jesuits were always to be found on the side of the papal forces, in opposition primarily to the Protestants but to Catholic liberals as well.

The Inquisition was an old organization, which had been developed by the Dominican order in the thirteenth century primarily to combat the Albigensian heresy in southern France. It gained its greatest strength, however, in Spain, where it was used as the prime agent of persecution against the Moors and Jews, particularly under the leadership of the notorious Torquemada. After the Reformation the Inquisition joined forces with the Jesuits to combat the "Protestant heresy."

The Council of Trent, called originally by Pope Paul III in 1545, met at irregular intervals over a period of nearly twenty years under three different popes in the capital of the Italian Tyrol. The Council responded to the Protestant movement by reaffirming the basic doctrines of the Catholic Church while at the same time calling for a reform of abuses within the Church. The selection that follows includes some of the more important decrees, concerning both doctrine and practice, as adopted by the Council.

The Canons and Decrees of the Council of Trent

Decree touching the opening of the Council

Doth it please you,—unto the praise and glory of the holy and undivided Trinity, Father, and Son, and Holy Ghost; for the increase and exaltation of the Christian faith and religion; for the extirpation of heresies; for the peace and union of the Church; for the reformation of the Clergy and Christian people; for the depression and extinction of the enemies of the Christian name,—to decree and declare that the sacred and general council of Trent do begin, and hath begun?

They answered: It pleaseth us.

Decree concerning the canonical scriptures

The sacred and holy, oecumenical, and general Synod of Trent,—lawfully assembled in the Holy Ghost, the same three legates of the Apostolic See presiding therein,—keeping this always in view, that, errors being removed, the purity itself of the Gospel be preserved in the Church; which (Gospel), before promised through the prophets in the holy Scriptures, our Lord Jesus Christ, the Son of God, first promulgated with His own mouth, and then commanded to be preached by His Apostles to every creature, as the fountain of all, both saving truth, and moral discipline; and seeing clearly that this truth and books, and the unwritten traditions which, received by the Apostles from the mouth of Christ himself, or from the Apostles themselves, the Holy Ghost dictating, have come down even unto us, transmitted as it were from hand to hand; (the Synod) following the examples of the orthodox Fathers, receives and venerates with an equal affection of piety, and reverence, all the books both of the Old and the New Testament—seeing that one God is the author of both—as also the said traditions, as well those appertaining to faith as to morals, as having been dictated, either by Christ's own word of mouth, or by the Holy Ghost, and preserved in the Catholic Church by a continuous succession.

Decree concerning the edition, and the use, of the sacred books

Moreover, the same sacred and holy Synod,—considering that no small utility may accrue to the Church of God, if it be made known which out of all the Latin editions, now in circulation, of the sacred books, is to be held as authentic,—ordains and declares, that the said old and vulgate edition, which, by the lengthened usage of so many ages, has

The Canons and Decrees of the Sacred and Oecumenical Council of Trent, trans. J. Waterworth (London, 1848).

been approved of in the Church, be, in public lectures, disputations, sermons and expositions, held as authentic; and that no one is to dare, or presume to reject it under any pretext whatever.

Furthermore, in order to restrain petulant spirits, It decrees, that no one, relying on his own skill, shall, —in matters of faith, and of morals pertaining to the edification of Christian doctrine,—wresting the sacred Scripture to his own senses, presume to interpret the said sacred Scripture contrary to that sense which holy mother Church,—whose it is to judge of the true sense and interpretation of the holy Scriptures, —hath held and doth hold;—or even contrary to the unanimous consent of the Fathers; even though such interpretations were never (intended) to be at any time published. . . .

Decree concerning original sin

That our Catholic *faith, without which it is impossible to please God,* may, errors being purged away, continue in its own perfect and spotless integrity, and that the Christian people may not *be carried about with every wind of doctrine;* whereas that old serpent, the perpetual enemy of mankind, amongst the very many evils with which the Church of God is in these our times troubled, has also stirred up not only new, but even old, dissensions touching original sin, and the remedy thereof; the sacred and holy, oecumenical and general Synod of Trent,—lawfully assembled in the Holy See presiding therein,—wishing now to come to the reclaiming of the erring, and the

confirming of the wavering—following the testimonies of the sacred Scriptures, of the holy Fathers, or the most approved councils, and the judgment and consent of the Church itself, ordains, confesses, and declares these things touching the said original sin:

1. If any one does not confess that the first man, Adam, when he had transgressed the commandment of God in Paradise, immediately lost the holiness and justice wherein he had been constituted; and that he incurred, through the offence of that prevarication, the wrath and indignation of God, and consequently death, with which God had previously threatened him, and, together with death, captivity under his power who thenceforth *had the empire of death, that is to say, the devil,* and that the entire Adam, through that offence of prevarication, was changed, in body and soul, for the worse; let him be anathema.

2. If any one asserts, that the prevarication of Adam injured himself alone, and not his posterity; and that the holiness and justice, received of God, which he lost, he lost for himself alone, and not for us also; or that he, being defiled by the sin of disobedience, has only transfused death, and pains of the body, into the whole human race, but not sin also, which is the death of the soul; let him be anathema:— whereas he contradicts the apostle who says; *By one man sin entered into the world, and by sin death, and so death passed upon all men, in whom all have sinned.*

3. If any one asserts, that this sin of Adam,—which in its origin is one, and being transfused into all by propagation, not by imitation, is

in each one as his own,—is taken away either by the powers of human nature, or by any other remedy than the merit of the *one mediator, our Lord Jesus Christ, who hath reconciled us to God in his own blood, made unto us justice, sanctification, and redemption;* or if he denies that the said merit of Jesus Christ is applied, both to adults and to infants, by the sacrament of baptism rightly administered in the form of the Church; let him be anathema: *For there is no other name under heaven given to men, whereby we must be saved.* Whence that voice; *Behold the lamb of God, behold him who taketh away the sins of the world;* and that other; *As many as have been baptized, have put on Christ.*

· · ·

That a rash presumptuousness in the matter of predestination is to be avoided

No one, moreover, so long as he is in this mortal life, ought so far to presume as regards the secret mystery of divine predestination, as to determine for certain that he is assuredly in the number of the predestinate; as if it were true, that he that is justified, either cannot sin any more, or, if he do sin, that he ought to promise himself an assured repentance; for except by special revelation, it cannot be known whom God hath chosen unto Himself.

· · ·

On the sacraments in general

Canon I. If any one saith, that the sacraments of the New Law were not all instituted by Jesus Christ, our Lord; or, that they are more, or less, than seven, to wit, Baptism, Confirmation, the Eucharist, Penance, Extreme Unction, Order, and Matrimony; or even that any one of these seven is not truly and properly a sacrament; let him be anathema.

Canon II. If any one saith, that these said sacraments of the New Law do not differ from the sacraments of the Old Law, save that the ceremonies are different, and different the outward rites; let him be anathema.

Canon III. If any one saith, that these seven sacraments are in such wise equal to each other, as that one is not in any way more worthy than another; let him be anathema.

Canon IV. If any one saith, that the sacraments of the New Law are not necessary unto salvation, but superfluous; and that, without them, or without the desire thereof, men obtain of God, through faith alone, the grace of justification;—though all (the sacraments) are not indeed necessary for every individual; let him be anathema.

Canon V. If any one saith, that these sacraments were instituted for the sake of nourishing faith alone; let him be anathema.

Canon VI. If any one saith, that the sacraments of the New Law do not contain the grace which they signify; or, that they do not confer that grace on those who do not place an obstacle thereunto; as though they were merely outward signs of grace or justice received through faith, and certain marks of the Christian profession, whereby believers are distinguished amongst men from unbelievers; let him be anathema.

Canon VII. If any one saith, that grace, as far as God's part is concerned, is not given through the said sacraments, always, and to all men, even though they receive them rightly, but (only) sometimes, and to some persons; let him be anathema.

Canon VIII. If any one saith, that by the said sacraments of the New Law grace is not conferred through the act performed, but that faith alone in the divine promise suffices for the obtaining of grace; let him be anathema.

Canon IX. If any one saith, that, in the three sacraments, Baptism, to wit, Confirmation, and Order, there is not imprinted in the soul a character, that is, a certain spiritual and indelible sign, on account of which they cannot be repeated; let him be anathema.

Canon X. If any one saith, that all Christians have power to administer the word, and all the sacraments; let him be anathema.

Canon XI. If any one saith, that, in ministers, when they effect, and confer the sacraments, there is not required the intention at least of doing what the Church does; let him be anathema.

Canon XII. If any one saith, that

a minister, being in mortal sin,— if so be that he observe all the essentials which belong to the effecting, or conferring of, the sacrament, —neither effects, nor confers the sacrament; let him be anathema.

Canon XIII. If any one saith, that the received and approved rites of the Catholic Church, wont to be used in the solemn administration of the sacraments, may be condemned, or without sin be omitted at pleasure by the ministers, or be changed, by every pastor of the churches, into other new ones; let him be anathema.

· · ·

**On the real presence
of our Lord Jesus Christ
in the most holy sacrament
of the Eucharist**

In the first place, the holy Synod teaches, and openly and simply professes, that, in the august sacrament of the holy Eucharist, after the consecration of the bread and wine, our Lord Jesus Christ, true God and man, is truly, really, and substantially contained under the species of those sensible things. For neither are these things mutually repugnant,— that our Saviour Himself always sitteth at the right hand of the Father in heaven, according to the natural mode of existing, and that, nevertheless, He be, in many other places, sacramentally present to us in his own substance, by a manner of existing, which, though we can scarcely express it in words, yet can we, by the understanding illuminated by faith, conceive, and we ought most firmly to believe, to be possible unto God: for thus all our forefathers, as many as were in the true Church of Christ, who have treated of this most holy Sacrament have most openly professed, that our Redeemer instituted this so admirable a sacrament at the last supper, when, after the blessing of the bread and wine, He testified, in express and clear words, that He gave them His own very Body, and His own Blood; words which,—recorded by the holy Evangelists, and afterwards repeated by Saint Paul, whereas they carry with them that proper and most manifest meaning in which they were understood by the Fathers,—it is indeed a crime the most unworthy that they should be wrested, by certain contentious and wicked men, to fictitious and imaginary tropes, whereby the verity of the flesh and blood of Christ is denied, contrary to the universal sense of the Church, which, as *the pillar and ground of truth,* has detested, as satanical, these inventions devised by impious men; she recognising, with a mind ever grateful and unforgetting, this most excellent benefit of Christ.

· · ·

On the most holy sacrament of the Eucharist

Canon I. If any one denieth, that, in the sacrament of the most holy Eucharist, are contained truly, really, and substantially, the body and blood together with the soul and divinity of our Lord Jesus Christ, and consequently the whole Christ; but saith that He is only therein as in a sign, or in figure, or virtue; let him be anathema.

Canon II. If any one saith, that, in the sacred and holy sacrament of the Eucharist, the substance of the bread and wine remains conjointly with the body and blood of our Lord Jesus Christ, and denieth that wonderful and singular conversion of the whole substance of the bread into the Body, and of the whole substance of the wine into the Blood— the species only of the bread and wine remaining—which conversion indeed the Catholic Church most aptly calls Transubstantiation; let him be anathema.

· · ·

Canon IX. If any one denieth, that all and each of Christ's faithful of both sexes are bound, when they have attained to years of discretion, to communicate every year, at least at Easter, in accordance with the precept of the holy Mother Church; let him be anathema.

· · ·

Canon XI. If any one saith, that faith alone is a sufficient preparation for receiving the sacrament of the most holy Eucharist; let him be anathema. And for fear lest so great a sacrament may be received unworthily, and so unto death and condemnation, this holy Synod ordains and declares, that sacramental confession, when a confessor may be had, is of necessity to be made beforehand, by those whose conscience is burthened with mortal sin, how contrite even soever they may think themselves. But if any one shall presume to teach, preach, or obstinately to assert, or even in public disputation to defend the contrary, he shall be thereupon excommunicated.

.   .   .

On the ecclesiastical hierarchy, and on ordination

But, forasmuch as in the sacrament of Order, as also in Baptism and Confirmation, a character is imprinted, which can neither be effaced nor taken away; the holy Synod with reason condemns the opinion of those, who assert that the priests of the New Testament have only a temporary power; and that those who have once been rightly ordained, can again become laymen, if they do not exercise the ministry of the word of God. And if any one affirm, that all Christians indiscriminately are priests of the New Testament, or that they are all mutually endowed with an equal spiritual power, he clearly does nothing but confound the ecclesiastical hierarchy, which is *as an army set in array;* as if, contrary to the doctrine of blessed Paul, *all* were *apostles, all prophets, all evangelists, all pastors, all doctors.* Wherefore, the holy Synod declares that, besides the other ecclesiastical degrees, bishops, who have succeeded to the place of the apostles, principally belong to this hierarchical order; that they are *placed,* as the same apostle says, *by the Holy Ghost, to rule the Church of God;* that they are superior to priests; administer the sacrament of Confirmation; ordain the ministers of the Church; and that they can perform very many other things;

over which functions others of an inferior order have no power. Furthermore, the sacred and holy Synod teaches, that, in the ordination of bishops, priests, and of the other orders, neither the consent, nor vocation, nor authority, whether of the people, or of any civil power or magistrate whatsover, is required in such wise as that, without this, the ordination is invalid: yea rather doth It decree, that all those who, being only called and instituted by the people, or by the civil power and magistrate, ascend to the exercise of these ministrations, and those who of their own rashness assume them to themselves, are not ministers of the Church, but are to be looked upon as *thieves and robbers, who have not entered by the door.* These are the things which it hath seemed good to the sacred Synod to teach the faithful of Christ, in general terms, touching the sacrament of Order.

.   .   .

.

On the sacrament of matrimony

.   .   .

Canon IX. If anyone saith, that clerics constituted in sacred orders or Regulars, who have solemnly professed chastity, are able to contract marriage, and that being contracted it is valid, notwithstanding the ecclesiastical law, or vow; and that the contrary is nothing else than to condemn marriage; and, that all who do not feel that they have the gift of chastity, even though they have made a vow thereof, may contract marriage; let him be anathema: seeing that God refuses not that gift to those who ask for it rightly, neither does *He suffer us to be tempted above that which we are able.*

Canon X. If any one saith, that the marriage state is to be placed above the state of virginity, or of celibacy, and that it is not better and more blessed to remain in virginity, or in celibacy, than to be united in matrimony; let him be anathema.

· · ·

On the invocation, veneration, and relics, of saints, and on sacred images

The holy Synod enjoins on all bishops, and others who sustain the office and charge of teaching, that, agreeably to the usage of the Catholic and Apostolic Church, received from the primitive times of the Christian religion, and agreeably to the consent of the holy Fathers, and to the decrees of sacred Councils, they especially instruct the faithful diligently concerning the intercession and invocation of saints; the honour (paid) to relics; and the legitimate use of images: teaching them, that the saints, who reign together with Christ, offer up their own prayers to God for men; that it is good and useful suppliantly to invoke them, and to have recourse to their prayers, aid, (and) help for obtaining benefits from God, through His Son, Jesus Christ our Lord, who is our alone Redeemer and Saviour; but that they think impiously, who deny that the saints, who enjoy eternal happiness in heaven, are to be invocated; or who assert either that they do not pray for men; or, that the invocation of them to pray

for each of us even in particular, is idolatry: or, that it is repugnant to the word of God; and is opposed to the honour of the *one mediator of God and men, Christ Jesus;* or, that it is foolish to supplicate, vocally, or mentally, those who reign in heaven. Also, that the holy bodies of holy martyrs, and of others now living with Christ—which bodies were the living members of Christ, and *the temple of the Holy Ghost,* and which are by Him to be raised unto eternal life, and to be glorified —are to be venerated by the faithful; through which (bodies) many benefits are bestowed by God on men; so that they who affirm that veneration and honour are not due to the relics of saints; or, that these, and other sacred monuments, are uselessly honoured by the faithful; and that the places dedicated to the memories of the saints are in vain visited with the view of obtaining their aid; are wholly to be condemned, as the Church has already long since condemned, and now also condemns them.

Moreover, that the images of Christ, of the Virgin Mother of God, and of the other saints, are to be had and retained particularly in temples, and that due honour and veneration are to be given them; not that any divinity, or virtue, is believed to be in them, on account of which they are to be worshipped; or that anything is to be asked of them; or, that trust is to be reposed in images, as was of old done by the Gentiles who placed their hope in idols; but because the honour which is shown them is referred to the prototypes which those images represent; in such wise that by the images which we kiss, and before which we uncover the head, and prostrate ourselves, we adore Christ; and we venerate the saints, whose similitude they bear: as by the decrees of Councils, and especially of the second Synod of Nicaea, has been defined against the opponents of images.

· · ·

Cardinals and all prelates of the churches shall be content with modest furniture and a frugal table: they shall not enrich their relatives or domestics out of the property of the Church

It is to be wished, that those who undertake the office of a bishop should understand what their portion is; and comprehend that they are called, not to their own convenience, not to riches or luxury, but to labours and cares for the glory of God. For it is not to be doubted, that the rest of the faithful also will be more easily excited to religion and innocence, if they shall see those who are set over them, not fixing their thoughts on the things of this world, but on the salvation of souls, and on their heavenly country. Wherefore the holy Synod, being minded that these things are of the greatest importance toward restoring ecclesiastical discipline, admonishes all bishops, that, often meditating thereon, they show themselves conformable to their office, by their actual deeds, and the actions of their lives; which is a kind of perpetual sermon; but above all that they so order their whole conversation, as that others may thence be able to derive examples

of frugality, modesty, continency, and of that holy humility which so much recommends us to God.

Wherefore, after the example of our fathers in the Council of Carthage, it not only orders that bishops be content with modest furniture, and a frugal table and diet, but that they also give heed that in the rest of their manner of living, and in their whole house, there be nothing seen that is alien from this holy institution, and which does not manifest simplicity, zeal toward God, and a contempt of vanities. Also, it wholly forbids them to strive to enrich their own kindred or domestics out of the revenues of the Church: seeing that even the canons of the Apostles forbid them to give to their kindred the property of the church, which belongs to God: but if their kindred be poor, let them distribute to them thereof as poor, but not misapply, or waste, it for their sakes: yea, the holy Synod with the utmost earnestness, admonishes them completely to lay aside all this human and carnal affection toward brothers, nephews and kindred, which is the seed-plot of many evils in the Church. And what has been said of bishops, the same is not only to be observed by all who hold ecclesiastical benefices, whether Secular or Regular, each according to the nature of his rank, but the Synod decrees that it also regards the cardinals of the holy Roman Church; for whereas, upon their advice to the most holy Roman Pontiff, the administration of the universal Church depends, it would seem to be a shame, if they did not at the same time shine so pre-eminent in virtue and in the discipline of their lives, as deservedly to draw upon themselves the eyes of all men.

· · ·

Decree concerning Indulgences

Whereas the power of conferring Indulgences was granted by Christ to the Church; and she has, even in the most ancient times, used the said power, delivered unto her of God; the sacred holy Synod teaches, and enjoins, that the use of Indulgences, for the Christian people most salutary, and approved of by the authority of sacred Councils, is to be retained in the Church; and It condemns with anathema those who either assert, that they are useless; or who deny that there is in the Church the power of granting them. In granting them, however, It desires that, in accordance with the ancient and approved custom in the Church, moderation be observed; lest, by excessive facility, ecclesiastical discipline be enervated. And being desirous that the abuses which have crept therein, and by occasion of which this honourable name of Indulgences is blasphemed by heretics, be amended and corrected, It ordains generally by this decree, that all evil gains for the obtaining thereof,—whence a most prolific cause of abuses amongst the Christian people has been derived,—be wholly abolished. But as regards the other abuses which have proceeded from superstition, ignorance, irreverence, or from whatsoever other source, since, by reason of the manifold corruptions in the places and provinces where the said abuses are committed, they cannot conveniently be specially prohibited; It commands all bishops, diligently to collect, each in his own church, all abuses of this nature, and to report them in the first provincial Synod; that, after having been reviewed by the opinions of the other bishops also, they may forthwith be referred to the Sovereign Roman Pontiff, by whose authority and prudence that which may be expedient for the universal Church will be ordained; that thus the gift of holy Indulgences may be dispensed to all the faithful, piously, holily, and incorruptly.